MW01145785

A Study *of the* Ancestry *and* Posterity *of*
John Goode *of* Whitby

A VIRGINIA COLONIST OF THE SEVENTEENTH CENTURY

WITH NOTES UPON RELATED FAMILIES, A KEY TO SOUTHERN
GENEALOGY AND A HISTORY OF THE ENGLISH SURNAME
GODE, GOAD, GOODE, OR GOOD

FROM 1148 TO 1887

BY *G. Brown Goode*

WITH A PREFACE BY *R. A. Brock*
Secretary of the Virginia and Southern Historical Societies

HERITAGE BOOKS
2008

VIRGINIA COUSINS.

"And there would be no telling when the conversation would end—not until you had ascertained the degree of your relationship—if it took three hours, *for all the great grandparents of Virginians were second cousins at the very least.*" VIRGINIANS IN TEXAS.

BRITONS, you stay too long;
Quickly aboard bestow you,
   And with a merry gale
   Swell your stretch'd sail
With vows as strong
As the winds that blow you.

And cheerfully at sea
Success you still entice
   To get the pearl and gold,
   And ours to hold
VIRGINIA,
Earth's only paradise.

And in regions far
Such heroes bring ye forth
   As those from whom we came,
   And plant our name
Under that star
Not known unto the North.

MICHAEL DRAYTON, *The Virginian Voyage*, 1605.

VIRGINIA, which is the most ancient and loyal, the most plentiful and flourishing, the most extensive and beneficial colony belonging to the Crown of Great Britain, upon which it is most dependent. . . . Virginia is esteemed one of the most valuable Gems·in the Crown of Great Britain, . . . the happy retreat of true Britons and true churchmen for the most part.

HUGH JONES, *Present State of Virginia*, 1724, p. 47-8.

PATRIOTISM with a Virginian is a noun personal. He loves Virginia *per se* and *propter se*. He loves to talk about her. It makes no odds where he goes he takes Virginia with him. He never gets acclimated elsewhere. He never loses citizenship in the old home. He may breathe in Alabama, but he lives in Virginia.

There is nothing presumptuously forward in the Virginian. He does not reproach the poor Carolinian or Tennesseeian with the misfortune of his birthplace. No; he thinks the affliction is enough without the triumph. The franchise of having been born in Virginia is too potent of honor to be arrogantly pretended. Like a ducal title, there is no need of saying more than to name it. Eminently social and hospital, kind, humane and generous is a Virginian at home or abroad.

J. G. BALDWIN, *Flush Times of Alabama*, 1853, p. 73.

IT would have been in strict accordance with Texas usage if we had stopped him, when we had first met him and proceeded thus :
"Good morning, sir," "Good morning,.sir," he would have replied. "Moving, I reckon?" "Yes, sir." "What State are you from?" "Virginia." Then if you happened to be from Virginia too, you would instantly ask, "Ah, indeed ! What county?" And if you were from the same county or bordering counties, there would be no telling when the conversation would end—not until you had ascertained the degree of your relationship to him, if it took three hours ; for all the great-grandparents of Virginians were second cousins at the very least.

WILLIAM M. BAKER, *Virginians in Texas*, 1878, p. 1.

VIRGINIANS of to-day have continually before them the melancholy forms of decayed churches, dismantled seats, impoverished fields, the disinherited with tears bidding a final farewell to the playground of childhood, the ancestral hearth and patriarchal oak, and ancient families, scattered like autumnal leaves before the winds of·Heaven. Virginia's pilgrim sons, scattered from the Alleghanies to the banks of the Colorado, wherever destiny may cast their lot, like the fireworshippers, with pious devotion, turn their eyes back to their father-land in the East.—CHARLES CAMPBELL, 1839.

PERHAPS the descendants of these emigrants may return and hunt out the faded and perishing memorials of their forefathers, and cast their tents beside them and say, " Here will we and our posterity dwell forever in the land given to our fathers." Well would it have been for thousands and tens of thousands had they been content to dwell in this most.favored land, endowed by nature with all that should content the mind of man. In less than half a century the tide of emigration will roll backward, and the desolate shores of the Chesapeake yet blossom as the rose.

Oh ! may that day soon come when Virginians will learn to venerate more and more the land where the bones of their sires lie ; that land consecrated as the burial place of a whole generation of high-hearted patriots, where virtue and talents and worth alone were consecrated to reverence through hereditary lines of descent.

W. A. CARUTHERS, *Knights of the Horseshoe*, 1845.

THE AUTHOR AFFECTIONATELY

DEDICATES THIS VOLUME

TO THE MEMORY OF HIS FATHER,

FRANCIS COLLIER GOODE,

WHO WAS AT THE TIME OF HIS DEATH, NOV. 29, 1887,

THE SENIOR REPRESENTATIVE OF THE

DESCENDANTS OF

JOHN GOODE OF WHITBY.

BEGUN AT HIS SUGGESTION, ITS PREPARATION HAS BEEN CONTINUED FOR TWENTY-FIVE

YEARS THROUGH THE INSPIRATION OF HIS INTEREST, AND ITS FINAL PUB-

LICATION WAS IN LARGE PART DUE TO HIS SUBSTANTIAL AID.

WASHINGTON, MAY 1, 1888.

EVERY family should have a record of its own. Each has its peculiar spirit running through the whole line, and, in more or less development, preceptible in every generation. . . . Nor need our ancestors have been Scipios or Fabii to interest us in their fortunes. We do not love our kindred for their glory or their genius, but for their domestic affections and private virtues, that, unobserved by the world, expand in confidence toward ourselves. An affectionate regard to their memory is natural to the heart; it is an emotion totally distinct from pride—an ideal love, free from that consciousness of requited affection and reciprocal esteem, which constitutes so much of the satisfaction we derive from the love of the living. . . . If the virtues of strangers be so attractive to us, how infinitely more so should be those of our own kindred, and with what additional energy should the precepts of our parents influence us when we trace the transmission of their precepts from father to son through successive generations, each bearing the testimony of a virtuous, useful and honorable life to their truth and influence.

THE LIVES OF THE LINDSAYS, *London*, 1849.

THE genealogical passion is one sort of the "enthusiasm of humanity." There is a special pleasure in the study of men in their families and generations; there is scientific gain in the knowledge of their acquired and transmitted tendencies; as character rubs against character, light is struck, to fall upon the pages of history, until the past is illuminated afresh with these household fires. And when the families and generations are the student's own, when it is the lines which he himself has descended that he is exploring to their source, the pastime becomes in the deepest degree a passion, and consumes its object until almost he is turned into a victim. We know of no better literary service which a person properly qualified may undertake than the preparation of a family history. Beginning with his contemporaries, to locate these in their several environments, and then trace them back step by step to the common stock, eliciting from a thousand quarters the names, facts, dates, pictures, portraits and anecdotes which make up history, is as useful an occupation as it is fascinating. Happy the man whose patience is equal to its perfect work in such enterprise. If one has the divine spark to begin with, it burns more and more brightly by what it feeds on.—*Literary World, Jan.* 10, 1885, p. 10.

THERE is really nothing more valuable in the historical and biographical ways than genealogy. Little grains of sand make the earth; little drops of water make the ocean, and little bits of Genealogy make the History of the World.--ALEXANDER BROWN, 1886.

A complete genealogy as representing any family in this State is a conception as yet undreamed of within its limits, and for its successful achievement a degree of interest, system and familiarity and intelligent investigation would be requisite which has not hitherto been manifested by Virginians, *per se*, the most self-satisfied race upon the globe.—R. A. BROCK in the *Richmond Standard*, 1879.

PREFACE.

ONORABLE ancestry has ever been held in veneration by mankind. This is abundantly exhibited in Sacred Writ and in the ancient classics, and is now patent among every existing people. It is a just instinct that yields nothing to the animadversion of the cynic, and is naught but ennobling in its influences. It inspires self-respect, and is a potent incentive to virtue, as in a dutiful contemplation of the worthy lives of our progenitors, we can but desire to walk in their footsteps. The historian Sallust tells us that he had often heard Quintus Maximus, Publius, Scipio and other illustrious men of Rome say that whenever they regarded the effigies of their ancestors their minds were most powerfully incited to virtue: *cum majorum imagines intuerentur vehementissime sibi animum ad virtutem accendi.**

The late venerable and admirable Marshall P. Wilder, in his last penned effort—an address to be delivered before the New England Historic Genealogical Society, upon the completion of nineteen years' service as the president of that learned body, at its annual meeting in 1887, remarked : "Recall the traditions of men : each generation in its day bears testimony to the character of the preceding. He who worships the past believes we are connected not only with those that came before us, but with those who are to come after. What mean those hierogly-

---

* Appropriately cited by the Hon. William A. Maury, LL. D., in his felicitous tribute to the memory of the late Philip Phillips at a meeting of the Bar of the Supreme Court of the United States, held at Washington, D. C., February 16, 1884.

phic inscriptions on the Egyptian monuments? Says one of them:
'I speak to you who shall come a million of years after my death.'
Another says, 'Grant that my words may live for hundreds and thousands of years.' The writers were evidently thinking, not only of their
own time, but of the distant future of the human race, and hoped, themselves, never to be forgotten.''

The essential value of genealogy in establishing the heritable rights
of title and of property is obvious, and its importance as the ''hand-
maiden of truth'' is now attested by every careful historian. To its
study more than aught else of discovery is due, it is believed, the
revolution in the presentation of history, in the precision which it has
afforded in fixing actor, time and locality in event and in the exaction
of authority for statement, which has been its legitimate result.

It has been sagely remarked that the tastes of the naturalist are in
many respects akin to those of the antiquary.

In this country some of the best family histories have been prepared
by naturalists and philologists, as for instance, Prof. B. A. Gould, Dr.
W. C. Redfield, Prof. Elias Loomis, Dr. John C. Warren, Prof. Alexander Winchell, Dr. W. H. Prescott, Prof. Lyman Coleman, Chancellor Walworth and Noah Webster. Benjamin Franklin begins his
autobiography with the remark, ''I have ever had a pleasure in obtaining any little anecdotes of my ancestry,'' and gives a long account of
his genealogical researches at Ecton in Northamptonshire, the residence
of his forefathers for three centuries. Isaac Newton, in the sixty-third
year of his age, wrote out with his own hand a genealogical account of
his family, with directions that the registers of certain parishes should be
searched from the beginning to the year 1650, and ''extracts be taken
by copying out whatever may be met with about the family of the Newtons without omitting any of the words.'' De Witt Clinton, naturalist
as well as statesman, in his discourse before the New York Historical
Society, December 6, 1811, made a strong plea for the usefulness of
genealogy.

The accompanying ''study,'' as the erudite and accomplished naturalist, its author, modestly terms it, will it is confidently believed, be held
not only by those immediately interested, but by the intelligent reader
at large, in sensible esteem, in its manifold illustrative exemplifications
of the past, more particularly, politically and socially of our own country for more than two centuries.

The merit of the work in careful investigation and in conscientious statement is manifest, as is, most appealingly, its comprehensiveness in historic incident and reminiscence. I do not recall any similar work so fully freighted with interest. A correspondence of years with Prof. Goode and the privilege of perusal of the proofs of the work, as printed, have made me sensibly cognizant of its inestimable value, and of his just and admirable system of preparation. His appendix of armorial bearings of Virginia families and references to genealogical authorities, novel as they are in their presentation, will be of great value to the genealogist.

R. A. BROCK.

Richmond, Virginia, August 2, 1887.

MONUMENT OF JOHN TRENOWYTH,

(on the floor of the aisle of St. Michael Penkivel Church in Cornwall.)

John Trenowyth was born, A. D. 1426, died A. D. 1497.

He was grandfather of the grandmother of Isabell Goode of Whitley, whose
great-grandson, John Goode of Whitby, came to Virginia. (See Dunkin's
"Monumental Brasses of Cornwall," pl. xix; "Virginia Cousins," p. 452;
Maclean's "Trigg Minor," 1, p. 12.)
The effigy of "John Trenowyth, Squire," represents him in military costume.
He probably took part in the wars of the Roses, and died five years after
the discovery of America.

PROLOGUE.

In this big, greasy, great, grey, jolly, small, mouldy little pamphlet the said genealogy was found written all at length, in a chancery hand; yet so worn with the long tract of time, that hardly could three letters together be there perfectly discerned.

I, though unworthy, was sent for thither, and with much help of those spectacles whereby the art of reading dim writings is practised, did translate the book. Wicked vermin had nibbled off the beginning; the rest I have hereto subjoined, for the reverence I bear to antiquity.

RABELAIS : *The Inestimable Life of the Great Gargantua.*

Twenty-four years ago, a boy of twelve, I stood one winter evening by the fireside, between my father's knees, and questioned him about his parents and his grandparents, and the ancestors of previous generations, until he told me of the earliest of them all—that forefather who, loyal to King Charles, was driven from England and established a home in the wilderness at the falls of the James River. I still have sheets of printers' paper, upon which, in my boyish chirography, I penciled the rough pedigree, which has since expanded into the present volume. Had I then known the extent of my task, I fear I should not have had the courage to undertake it. I saw before me a single mountain which I aspired to climb; I found beyond valleys and mountains and valleys still, and now the labor is brought to an end, not because it is finished, but because other work demands all my attention.

I imagine that many students of genealogy are like myself, rather sensitive upon the subject of their favorite pursuit, and are disposed to make a family secret of the fact that they are devoted to a specialty whose utility is not generally supposed to be of the highest order. We do not feel disposed to speak without reserve of the days and weeks and months spent over our pedigree-making.

We print in prominent places on the title pages, and at the beginnings of chapters, and in the preface, quotations from Thucydides, from Taine and Gibbon, from Habakkuk, from Benjamin Franklin, and from Daniel Webster, in which they have said that it is praiseworthy to desire to know the names of our ancestors in order that we may emulate their virtues. We look with hatred upon satirists like Sydney Smith* and our humorous acquaintances who chaff us concerning our visits to those treasuries of genealogical lore which they are pleased to call "bone-orchards," and console ourselves with the moral of Æsop's best-known fable.

Genealogists have, however, a common foe, in whose presence they may boast of their toils and labors, before whose eyes they flaunt the statistics of the thousands of letters and circulars mailed, of the extent of their bills for postage stamps, including always the stamps to prepay the answer, which every wise genealogist is sure to enclose, to whom they may speak unreservedly of printers' bills, of weary midnights, endless sittings over illegible records, and tedious tasks of copying, tabulating and indexing. This personage is he who neglects to subscribe to the fund for publishing the completed memoir of his own family, and he is one of a numerous class. The philosophic genealogist, profiting by the experience of others, does not in these days expect his family to bear this expense; he does not deceive himself into the belief that he has worked solely for the good of others. He knows that he has written pedigrees solely because he could not help it; he begrudges neither the time nor the money expended, and is thankful if a few of his nearest of kin are willing to help settle the printer's bill. In early American genealogies may be found some most entertaining philippics, written by authors who have in vain expected gratitude from the families whose history they have perpetuated.

Although conscious of certain guilty feelings when I consider what might have been accomplished if my youthful energy and enthusiasm in pedigree-making had been applied to any one of a score of projects for scientific research, I am, nevertheless, not very penitent. No

---

* When Lady L——asked me about my grandfather, I told her he disappeared about the time of the assizes, and we asked no questions.—SYDNEY SMITH.

hobby is more absorbing than this, and I abandon it, not without the misgiving that I shall not soon find another so entertaining.

The study has been particularly interesting on account of its numerous side-issues, especially the studies upon certain periods of English and colonial history, not otherwise approachable, into which it has led. Delightful have been the hours in the British Museum, among old volumes of country histories, manuscripts of herald's visitations and files of musty old newspapers, and the hasty peeps into hundreds of volumes of records of every description, the existence of which I should otherwise never have known, and the acquaintance of which it is pleasant to have made. Delightful, too, the visits to ancestral homes and out-of-the-way parish churches, the little excursions to inspect and interview colonies of remotely connected kinsfolk, who look upon the stranger who bears their own surname, and who knows more about their grandparents than they themselves, as if he were a chance guest from the moon.

Even the letter-writing has had its interest—an interest more absorbing than that of any game of chance—for out of a score of letters sent out to unknown persons, one or two are sure to return bringing clues of the greatest value in the solution of the puzzle, and what is of even greater moment, curious fragments of history and tradition, facts throwing light upon the customs of early days, incidents of pioneer life and reminiscences of traits of personal character.

Every well-prepared American genealogy is a most valuable contribution to the history of America, for the history of the country is a history of its people, and the people is but an aggregation of families. As an illustration of this statement I may say that my own immigrant ancestor who died in Virginia in 1709 left thirteen children, whose descendants in the sixteenth generation may safely be estimated at six thousand, taking as a foundation the size of the families whose full record has been preserved. Of these six thousand, in the seventh generation from our English patriarch, one-half may fairly be credited to him, one-half to the progenitors of the various stocks with which his descendants intermarried. I have record of hundreds of surnames under which his descendants are known to-day, and perhaps not more than two-thirds of the actual number are known. In 1700 there were estimated to be 80,000 white people in the South—Maryland, Virginia, the Carolinas and Georgia, and 170,000 in the North. In 1880 there were living east of the Rocky Mountains, in the South, 14,000,000 white people of American birth, in the North about 28,000,000, of whom at least 4,000,000 were descended from ancestors living in southern colonies, for contrary to common belief, Ohio, Indiana and Southern Illinois owed much the larger share of their original settlers to Virginia, and not to New England and New York. Bearing in mind the fact that the interior of our continent has been peopled by westward migrations somewhat in the line of the parallels of latitude, and that the descendants of the Southern colonists are to-day for the most part resident south of Mason & Dixon's line, it is probable that most of the white people of the South to-day derive a considerable percentage of their blood from the early colonists. I am of the opinion that in my own family not ten per cent. of the marriages have been with persons whose paternal ancestors came to America later than 1725. In the South, where immigration has been comparatively small, the old colonial stocks seems to have absorbed those of more recent date so completely that there are not even traditions remaining to bear witness to the fact, and it is probable that this is true also in the North, owing to the fact that the early colonists of America were of a more vigorous type than the majority of the immigrants of later years, and that their descendants, in the midst of an harmonious environment, have gained in vigor to such a degree that the infusion of a large amount of foreign blood has not affected materially the characters of the mental and physical traits inherited from their colonial ancestors.

The time is coming when the sociologist and the historian will make an extensive use of the facts so laboriously gathered and systematically classified by genealogists, and it is probable that this can be better done in the United States than elsewhere. The thousands of pedigrees of New England families which fill the shelves in the rooms of the New England Historical Genealogical Society, and crowd the pages of the Historic-Genealogical Register, will, under skillful treatment by men trained in scientific methods, yield a harvest of new ideas concerning the constitution of the population of North America, and no more important work can be done than that which this society has undertaken, in stimulating the production of works of this class and in carrying on researches tending to connect early American families with their English kindred. The time is not very far distant when the history of the majority of representative American surnames will have been published, and our people are now so much more stable in their residences than formerly, that there is little fear of their later stages being lost to view. At the same time it is to be regretted that in the interests of science, a more thorough system of public records is not kept. Even in England, where so much attention is given to family history, the writer has found a lamentable ignorance in these matters pervading the middle classes, an ignorance quite as great as can be found in this country, and much less excusable, owing to their better systems of records. The most recent index to English printed pedigrees, Marshall's " Genealogist's Guide," printed in 1879, contains references to about fifty thousand arranged under about ten thousand surnames, excluding many hundreds which can only be found in the Peerages and the Baronetages, which are not indexed in this work. Durries' "Alphabetical Index to American Genealogies " is only an insignificant volume in comparison, but American genealogies are much more comprehensive than English ones—a single American family history often containing as many distinct pedigrees as one of the immense and sumptuously printed English parish or county histories, which would be indexed under a large number of heads in such a work as that of Marshall, and having usually the advantage of being more systematically constructed and better adapted to scientific purposes.

The work, whose results are here published, has been of greater interest from the fact that the harvest has been gleaned from a comparatively little worked field. Although hundreds of books of family history have been published in New England, and thousands almost have been more or less exhaustively discussed in the New England Historic Genealogical Record, and the histories of the various counties and townships, Virginia which has done fully as much toward populating the United States, has had comparatively little placed upon record. My friend, Mr. R. A. Brock, has done a noble work in this direction, and other genealogists of mark, like Dr. Philip Slaughter, Mr. Alexander Brown and Mr. H. E. Hayden have made important contributions to Southern genealogical history. At the same time there is a vast hoard of unrecorded genealogic lore in Virginia and the South, which will perish with the old people now living. I hope that this little book will stimulate some others to try to save a part of this invaluable material, for it will soon be too late. Even now, with the experience of twenty years, I could not possibly, starting into the work from the beginning, gather together the facts which would make a good nucleus for the pedigree of the Goode family. It would have been too late. I have been amazed at the quantities of names and facts which are stored away in the minds of the old gentlewomen of Virginia. I once sat for two hours, pencil in hand, recording the statement of a charming old lady, as she reclined upon her couch telling about the members of our family in one of its ramifications. She gave me at least two hundred names, each as a rule accompanied by a date, and I have never been able to detect an error in her memory. I have no doubt that she was equally well versed in the history of a score of other families. Time and again have I found in Virginia elderly people who knew intimately the history of numerous families for generations, and whose knowledge seemed to include at least all of the county in which they lived. This wonderful memory on the part of the patriarchs scarcely compensates, however, for the lack of written records. The absence of these is a sad trammel to the Southern genealogist, and in the case of this particular work must be my excuse for the large number of dates which are lacking or are stated approximately. Few Virginian families remained in the early days for more than ten or fifteen years in one place. Migrations were frequent, and before a community was sufficiently well established to develop a system of records, its elements were dispersed to other countries, and the younger members of the family had moved to the frontier in some adjoining State, there to repeat the experience of their parents. As a consequence of these moves the family traditions have been lost. I know a branch of the Goode family in Georgia and Alabama, wealthy and intelligent planters, the middle-aged members of which did not know the name of their grandfathers or their uncles, the family bible having been destroyed by fire. The writer's father has a number of first cousins in Virginia, Georgia and Mississippi whom he cannot find, and whose names he does not know, owing to one of those family feuds which were so common in the South and West in former days—the families having separated, and all intercourse been suspended. The records of Henrico County are fairly complete, and have been of great service to me ; the records of the various parishes of the established churches before the revolution, so many of which have been deposited by Bishop Meade and Dr. Slaughter in the archives of Alexandria Theological Seminary, are also of great moment. Incalculable loss resulted from the destruction of public and private papers, family portraits, college archives, etc., during the occupation of Virginia by the Northern army in 1861–65. Another circumstance unfavorable to the genealogist has been the Virginia custom of burial, not in cemeteries, but in private inclosures, of which each estate had one, usually without inscribed headstones. In a pioneer community, with settlements remote from each other, this was necessary, and the epitaphs to be found in Virginia are comparatively very few. All these things render it desirable that family-histories should be written. The writer cannot claim to be a son of Virginia, but as a loyal grandson he offers this volume as a contribution to the history of the State. The history of the State, I say, for the history of the State is the history of its people, and the people is nought but an aggregation of families.

With this idea in mind, I have taken especial pains to preserve every fragment of history or tradition which might throw light upon the customs of the day, reminiscences of personal traits, and incidents of pioneer life, mindful of the words of Sir Walter Scott : '' Family tradition and genealogical history are the very reverse of amber, which, itself a valuable substance, usually includes flies, straws and other trifles ; whereas these studies, being themselves very insignificant and trifling, do, nevertheless, serve to perpetuate a great deal of what is rare and valuable in ancient manners and to record many curious and minute facts which could have been preserved and conveyed in no other way.''

Scarcely less interesting than to trace the ramifications of descent from our emigrant ancestor and the manner in which the family has spread itself over the continent, has been the study of what might not inappropriately be called the lines of ascent, the various sources from which our ancestor derived his hereditary physical and mental traits. This has been particularly easy, owing to the interest and pride taken by the people of Cornwall and Devon in the family histories which is even greater than that of the old Virginians. The results have been better in the old country than here, and the records of four centuries ago in Cornwall are fuller than those of the present period in any of our Southern States. The record for the Cornish families is very complete, and I have also been able to trace ancestry in several lines connected with the governing families of early times. These I have placed upon record in the chapter on ancestral families, and I hope no one will feel disposed to accuse the writer of presumption in publishing in this private book such claims of ancestry. I have found it interesting to trace them out, and I hope my cousins may find it equally amusing to examine them.

One of the elements of satisfaction in genealogical study legitimately arises from the success of 'our attempts to establish personal relations with past ages, and to be able to people our minds with the images of our forefathers as they lived two, three, four hundred years ago. In a country which has drawn its population from so many sources, from every country in Europe, from Africa and Asia even, it is a satisfaction in the first place to know that our parents were English, or (if not English) Scotch, Irish, German or French. It is also a gratification to know that a large percentage of all the thirty-two or sixty-four individuals who preceded each one of us, seven or eight generations back, were counted among the pioneer colonists of America in the seventeenth century. Crossing the Atlantic, it is a pleasure to us all, if we love the fatherland of our ancestors, its literature, its scenery, its historical associations (and what true American does not) to know from what part of old England our forefathers came, and what their condition in life. I consider it very pardonable even in cases where exact documentary evidence cannot be obtained, that Americans should in virtue of good circumstantial evidence, such as traditionary kinship with individuals in England, identity of Christian names, or customary use of coat-armor, claim connection with families of the same name known to have lived in England at the time of the emigration; and, in spite of the savage attacks which the practice has received at the hands of certain American writers, I can see no great harm in the appropriation of the coats of arms of these families by Americans of the same name.

To any American member of the Goode family who wishes to use a coat of arms, I would say that, in my judgment, he has a perfect right to do so if he be satisfied with the arguments hereafter to be brought forward to prove that John Goode, of Virginia, was a descendant of the Goodes of Whitby and Whitstone. The evidence, not being documentary, would not be sufficient to establish in an English court rights of heirship to Whitstone barton, if that estate were now without a claimant, consequently it would be impossible to establish a right to the arms which the Heralds College would feel bound to respect. At the same time it is as good as that of many generally accepted historical statements, and there are probably not one hundred families of American colonial stock which can furnish evidence more positive. Any descendant of John Goode of the eleventh generation, who bears the patronymic of Goode may use these arms if it amuses him to do so, and they will probably afford him as much satisfaction as if he had bought a new set at the Heralds College, as he might do any day, if he were an Englishman, for the sum of $363.75.

And why should the use of these ancient insignia expose the user to the charge of family pride. Every person of English origin in America has undoubtedly had scores and hundreds of ancestors in early days in England who were entitled to use badges of this description, and but for the carelessness or illiteracy of the members of intervening generations a record of them might have been preserved. In Burke's "General Armory" are the names of at least ten thousand English families to which armorial bearings have been assigned.

Even genealogical researches are believed by many to be the offspring of a tendency to pride of family; but in my judgment, their leading is toward the humiliation rather than the exaltation of such sentiments.

A lady correspondent writes as follows :

"I have written to Georgia to get some knowledge of my great aunt. I have a strong suspicion that Aunt M's descendants are boorish rustics—what in Georgia we call 'grand crackers.' It will be odd to see such branches on the same tree that bore, —— —— and —— ——, who would be elegant gentlemen anywhere."

I cannot resist the temptation to quote the words of another correspondent, who writes somewhat in the same vein :

"I do not envy you the tedious task of poring over the prosy and oftimes vain and egotistical letters of your many and distant kinsmen. I notice in the accounts which have been sent to you a disposition on the part of some to hide facts, to magnify others, and altogether, '*to puff Daddy.*' This is natural, and not to be wondered at in the children.

"I recall a very amusing incident connected with the M. H—— mentioned in my letter. He and his wife were very aristocratic and lived in great style. He traveled in great style, too. His wife went in a coach-and-four with her servants, and H —— followed in a lighter carriage and pair with his servant. Mrs. H —— had, as a *femme de chambre*, on a visit to my mother at 'Invermay,' a very finely dressed, but raw and untutored colored girl. The family were at breakfast, when the most fearful noise and lumbering occurred in the front hall. The man servant, around the table, immediately rushed out and picked up Mrs. H's maid servant, who had fallen down a long stairway and lodged near the dining-room door, a confused mass of petticoats and calico. When asked what on earth was the matter she replied, 'I fall out dat loft.' Mrs. H —— was greatly worried at her awkwardness, and, as a child, I remember the report, among the servants, of a long lecture to the maid on her conduct, as well as grammar, by her mistress. The old man-servant said to me, 'Lor, chile! It so like iceing on ash-cake. Dat gal jis come out de cornfield.'"

In this connection I should like to suggest that the methods of the genealogist and the historian are of necessity very different. We must not take our genealogy too seriously. The genealogist must be content with traditions and reminiscences, some of which have become vague by repetition from generation to generation. He cannot insist on the verification of every statement by the testimony of public records and tombstones, because they have been destroyed if they ever existed. Indeed, in dealing with the history of individuals unknown to fame, such minute verifications are scarcely necessary. In the same way the estimates of personal character must be that of admiring neighbors and relatives. If a man was a "prominent citizen," "universally beloved and respected," "a leader in all good works," he should be so described. These words describe accurately his relation to the community in which he lived, and it is not appropriate to bring him into comparison with men of national reputation. I will go a step further, and maintain that a trained genealogist may with perfect propriety supply missing links in the pedigrees of colonial families, if he does it conscientiously and with due regard to the testimony of Christian names, and places of residence. Colonial Virginia was very small and compact, and there were social limitations which I cannot discuss here, the understanding of which is a great aid to the genealogist. A colonist coming to Virginia in the middle of the seventeenth century cannot have had more than three or four generations of adult progeny prior to the Revolution. Even at the present time a skillful investigator might trace almost any colonial family to its origin by the use of existing records.

One of the results of my studies has been to convince me that almost every one who descends from Virginia colonial ancestry may rest assured that he has among his forefathers representatives of the three classes of colonists: (1) the great colonial proprietors, who corresponded to the county families of England, and who in a very few instances were descended from the nobility of the day, though usually from English country squires or well-to-do yeomen, and often from merchants in the cities; (2) the planters, who corresponded to the yeomanry of England, from whom the most of them were descended, though others were derived from the colonial clergy and merchants; (3) the indentured servants, many of whom were political exiles, others kidnapped, and still others, unfortunate and penniless individuals of wholesome origin, who sold their services for a period of years to pay for a passage to the New World. The descendants of the better classes of these soon became planters, while the offspring of the comparatively few felons who were transported to Virginia, retreated to the mountains and pine forests and became "crackers" or "tackeys," and have spread throughout the South.

The family names of the old colonial magnates are of little prominence to-day, even in Virginia, and least prominent of all, perhaps, are those of the colonists closely allied to the titled families of England in their day—West, for instance, Lunsford, Wormeley, Bathurst, Fleming, Ludwell, Fairfax, Wyatt, Skipwith and Digges. The Lee family is of course an exception.

The yeoman blood, mingled with that of the Huguenots and the Scotch-Irish who came to Virginia in the early part of the eighteenth century, has been by far the best in Virginia and in the West and Southwest colonized by Virginians. These people have "hungered for the horizon," and their energies have been strengthened by the struggles of pioneer life. For generations some of the most robust elements of the population of the State have been pouring over its western and southern boundaries, and to Georgia and Alabama, to Texas and Kansas and Missouri, to Ohio, Kentucky, Tennessee and Indiana, we must look to-day for the Greater Virginia. The old State, the mother of pioneers, must, like her own motherland—Great Britain—live to a considerable degree in the glory of her children who have, within the past century, transferred allegiance to other States.

Though many of the leading families of colonial Virginia were descended from the "county families of England;" others quite as prominent were of the yeomanry of England, Ireland and Wales, and from the Huguenot immigrants of 1701. I have given in the closing pages of this book a list of about 170 Virginia families who claimed in colonial days the right to use coat-armor, and there were doubtless very many more whose claims are not of record, or whose republican views led them to ignore these insignia.

The conditions of life were very different in New England, and the social problems were worked out in a very different way. Writers of New England genealogical history, not being familiar with Virginia life, have in many instances misinterpreted its significance. The Puritan colonists were not in sympathy with the homeland, and rarely made any effort to preserve its traditions. The Virginians, on the other hand, as Esten Cooke has shown, were:

"Simply a society of Englishmen of the age of Shakespeare, taken out of England and set down in Virginia. There they worked out the problem of living under new conditions. But they were Englishmen still, with the vices and virtues of the original stock, and Virginia was essentially what it has been styled, a continuation of England."

As a consequence, it is not strange that a much larger number of Virginians than of New Englanders are able to carry their lineage across the Atlantic.

The sectional jealousies of the past, and particularly of the war period, are now rapidly disappearing, and the outlook for the future seems promising when the utterances of a man like John Esten Cooke, who by knowledge and sympathy is qualified to speak of the true character of the long misunderstood Virginians, are received in a kindly and indulgent spirit, as they have been since he has published his "Virginia." It is a pity that the author of the essay, "A Social Study of our Oldest Colony," recently published in Macmillan's Magazine (March and April, 1886), should have marred an otherwise judicious and valuable social study by paying so much attention to a time-worn superstition, thus disseminating a false impression throughout England. He writes:

"No part of America is quite free from a sort of insensate craving, among its educated classes, to connect their names with those of illustrious English homes, on grounds that an Englishman, similarly circumstanced and named would not dream of making himself ridiculous by so doing. The disease is common in the South, and particularly common in Virginia. * * * It is quite a common belief among the people in Virginia that they are sprung in some way from the loins of the ' British nobility,' who apparently forsook their estates and tenants at home during the seventeenth century and took to the backwoods. * * * So the cavalier and the British nobleman flourish in a hazy and picturesque fashion at the root of every Virginian's family tree."

Ridicule of this sort is too groundless to be annoying. Every intelligent Virginian knows just what the author of this statement goes on to say, prefixing it with the assertion that it is *just what Virginians forget*—that the yeomanry and common folk formed the bulk of the Royalist army, and that there were many men of birth and consideration in the other ; and every intelligent Virginian knows that the blood derived from "younger sons of English country squires," and even of the "yeomanry and common folks" is as pure and honorable as if it had come from elder sons (even though the former were unjustly deprived of their share of the paternal heritage by the laws of entail, which were cast aside over a century ago in Virginia as relics of barbarism), and perhaps more to be derived as a heritage than if it had come from the British nobility—"those old prize fighters, with iron pots on their heads, to whom," remarks Oliver Wendell Holmes, "some great people are so fond of tracing their descent through a line of small artisans and petty shop-keepers whose veins have held 'base' fluid enough to fill the Cloaca Maxima."

Educated Virginians are also well aware that yeoman blood is not necessarily a "base fluid."

> "A Spanish Don, a German Count and a French Marquis—
> A yeoman of Kent is worth them all three,"

so runs the old saying, and it is known that two centuries ago more than half the farmers of England owned their own farms, while now less than one-twentieth are occupying owners.*

It was a Virginian, Thomas Jefferson, who, though like many prominent Virginians of colonial days, was descended from a family of good repute in England, said of his maternal ancestors, "They trace their pedigrees far back in England and Scotland, to which let every one ascribe the faith and merit he choses."

Had Jefferson been in a position to indulge his well-known antiquarian tastes in the direction of a study of family history, and had he attempted to trace back his lineage for ten generations he would have been obliged to go in the direction of the "British nobility." He would undoubtedly have much preferred to carry his investigations in the line of the name of Jefferson, but three steps would have taken him to the base of Mount Snowdon, where his grandfather, whose given name is unknown, lived a quiet, rustic life, far from the track of the Herald's Visitations, and no doubt too humble to attract the attention of any Rouge Croix or Blue Mantle, who might have passed in his vicinity, though in all probability carrying in his system as large a proportion of the blood of the Kings of the Cymri as the Germans who occupy the throne of England have derived from the Kings of the

*See John Rae's "Why Have the Yeomanry Perished?" in *Contemporary Review*, October, 1883.

English race.* Failing in this direction, he must needs have carried his studies back through recorded lines of pedigrees. This is what every pedigree-hunter must do; if he cares to look into his ancestral past he must follow certain beaten tracks. He is a wise man who knows all his own great grandfathers and grandmothers by name, and he is a bold man who will say that he owes the most to those who by accident have used his own patronymic.

As for the assertion that Americans are more willing than Englishmen to connect themselves with "illustrious English houses," it is simply false.

The best evidence of this assertion is the existence not only of the massive volumes filled with pedigrees of "English Families of Royal Descent," but of hundreds of parochial and country histories, filled with pedigrees of English families, a large percentage of them beginning with personages hardly distinguishable, to my perception, from those which have been referred to as "flourishing in picturesque and hazy fashion at the root of every Virginian's family tree." In fact the writer has himself seen the grandson of a British peer, a capable, intelligent man, seeking employment as a clerk in a London public office with his printed pedigrees in his hand for credentials, a thing hardly likely to occur in America.

The English writer, to whom reference has been made, seems to be more or less aware of the existence of the "educated Virginian," but he goes on to remark : "He has probably succumbed more or less to the fetish, while Southern writers and stump-speakers, from time immemorial, have done their best to encourage these extravagant absurdities as if they were ashamed of the brown, hard-fisted pioneers that carved out those lands from the primeval forests which they now enjoy."

The writer of these words is evidently incapable of understanding things from the American standpoint. The "educated Virginian," like other educated Americans, is a democrat of the most reasonable type. He is proud of his pioneer ancestors, and proud of his pioneer cousins of the present time, whom he elevates to the highest offices,

---

* In Mr. Fargus' late novel, "A Family. Affair," one of the characters proposed the question, "Doesn't it sometimes jar. upon your pride to think that we are obliged to anoint full-blooded Germans as our kings and queens? How much English blood has the Prince in his veins? This was a very startling question." The author continues, "The Talberts immediately begun to run down the Royal family-tree. Frank took a piece of bread. 'I'll show you by illustration,' he said, 'you'll be frightened. Here is James the First,' he pointed to the bread. 'Here is his daughter Sophia,' he cut the bread in half. 'Here is George the First,' he cut the bread again. 'Here is George the Second,' cutting again. 'Here is George the Third,' cutting again. 'Here is Edward, Duke of Kent,' cutting again. 'Here is Albert Edward, Heaven preserve him!' He cut the bread for the last time, and sticking the tiny morsel that remained on a fork, gravely handed it to Beatrice.'"

from the factory, the forest, the tow-path and the sheriff's desk. At the same time he is proud of his descent from Aryan forefathers, through which alone he could have acquired those qualities which enabled him to do the pioneer work, with his own toil-worn hands, and afterwards in his own person or in that of his children, to assume a position among the educated and cultured people of the world.

The writer in Macmillan admits "that many cadets of good family found their way to Virginia ;" but remarks, "that there is no trace of any persons of title in lists of vestrymen and burgesses that marked the most influential colonists, but that nearly all these names have an ordinary, middle-class ring about them." The Virginian is aware of this, and also of the fact that a large part of our common surnames are identical with those which underlie the titles of the members of the English peerage ; Hamilton, for instance, Russell, Osborne, Churchill, Gordon, Spencer, Bruce, Kennedy, Stuart, Robinson, Townshend, Ligon, Duncan, Howard, Dawson, Stanley, Douglas, Scott, Reynolds, Ward, Edgerton, Wentworth, Graham, Grey, North, Ryder, Hill, Blundell, Trumbull, Howe, Hastings, Parker, Harris, Murray, Elliott, Nelson, Freeman, Lumley, Cooper, Talbot, Somers, Bennet, St. John, Sutton, Hood, Hardy, Shaw, Gough, Ward, Harding, Hutchinson, Lynn, Lowe, West, and so on *ad libitum*. In fact, fully 25 per cent. of the names in Bishop Meade's list of Virginia families prominent early in this century (exclusive of German names) are common surnames among the British nobility.

"The educated Virginian " also knows that many of the descendants of the De Mohuns, the Norman barons of Dunster, are now basketmakers and tinkers in the south of England under the name of Moon, and that there is living in England, or was there living not long ago, a butcher, who by admission of heraldic authorities, had the right to quarter the Royal arms of Great Britain.

Just as Virginia lost the flower of her young men through emigration, so has every family in the South lost a large percentage of its most promising scions—those who would now be in the prime of manhood—in the late war. The deadly battles around Richmond and Petersburg were on the lands where our family has lived for nearly two centuries and a half, and it was here that so many of them gave up their lives. For this reason I have taken especial care to gather the war record of the family. Although the descendants of John Goode of "Whitby" have not been prominent in the public service in days of peace, it surely cannot be said that they failed of their duty in the time of public distress.

In the Indian wars of 1754–58 there were engaged at least five of the family, Nos. 66, 70, 75, 131 and 131½, the latter a member of Braddock's expedition.

In the war of the Revolution there were at least twenty-one, two of whom, 83 and 201, were killed. In the war of 1812, a partial list includes nineteen names. In the Florida Indian war four were engaged, and in the war with Mexico and the struggle which preceded it thirteen were engaged and four lost their lives.

In the civil war of 1861–65 hundreds of members of the family were engaged, and who shall say that those of the one army were more patriotic than those who opposed them. In the South every able-bodied man and youth bore arms, and there were probably at least 500 descendants of John Goode of "Whitby" in the field, and about 75 are recorded as having lost their lives in the Southern army, while two died from service with that of the North.

As members of the great Aryan race, we may justly take pleasure in tracing back our lineage, so far as possible, in that broad stairway of ancestral derivation which is the most illustrious in the world. Whether the Aryans lived upon the table lands of Central Asia, or as is now more generally believed, in the northern and central parts of Europe— Scandinavia, Germany, France, Austria and Western Russia—it is undoubtedly true that at least 3,000 years before Christ they were a people living in fixed dwellings, well clothed, possessed of flocks and herds, tillers of the soil, and possessing the rudiments of that family and political life which is regarded at the present day as a necessity of true civilization; a race with a civilization which survived until the advent of Christianity, and already at that time far ahead of many of the present inhabitants of the earth. We are conscious as we ascend toward the source whence we all sprang, by this great genealogical staircase of fifteen or sixteen hundred steps, that before we have gone one-twentieth of its length we reach a point where the units of discussion become races rather than families, and that fifty or a hundred generations back all existing family distinctions vanish. In fact the absence of family surnames, until within a comparatively recent period of time renders it practically impossible for any family of English origin to carry back its records more than fifteen or twenty generations, save in some royal line.

Genealogical investigations are growing more reputable of late in the eyes of those sternly practical men who represent the working side of science. Francis Galton's "Hereditary Genius" and "Men of Science" have opened up a new field of investigation which no one is following up as vigorously as Mr. Galton himself in the laborious task of tracing the ancestral origin of physical and mental traits, and the manner in which they pass from the sixteen ancestors, in the fourth generation above, to the individual to whose make-up they have all contributed. The present and increasing tendency to the investigation of psychological phenomena will lead to the establishment of a school of observers who will study man in a succession of generations as Darwin and others have studied pigeons, guinea-pigs and rabbits—not only observing the transmission of physical traits, which can perhaps better be done with lower animals, but especially with reference to psychic traits which cannot be discussed in speechless beings. The use of composite photographs will also be applied by the scientific genealogist of the future.

Prof. Alexander Graham Bell's invaluable investigations into the origin of deaf-mutism have only been rendered possible by the elaborate genealogies of New England families which are in execution.

No one has written more appreciatively of the phenomena of heredity than that eminent physician and essayist, Oliver Wendell Holmes, for, says he : " The natural groups of human beings are as proper subjects of remark as those of different breeds of horses, and if horses were men, I don't think they would quarrel with us because we made a distinction between a ' Morgan ' and a ' Messenger.' "*

Holmes has drawn extensively upon the strange possibilities of heredity, in the construction of his plots, but in the " Professor at the Breakfast Table " he has touched upon a truth which I think has never elsewhere been so well expressed :

" Young folks look on a face as a unit ; children who go to school with any given little John Smith see in his name a distinctive appellation, and in his features as special and definite expression of his sole individuality as if he were the first created of his race. As soon as we are old enough to get the range of three or four generations well in hand and to take in large family histories, we never see an individual in a face of any stock we know, but a mosaic copy of a pattern with fragmentary tints from this and that ancestor. The analysis of a face

* The Poet at the Breakfast Table. Routledge Ed. London, 1883, p. 177.

into its ancestral elements requires that it should be examined in the very earliest infancy before it has lost that ancient and solemn look it brings with it out of the past eternity; and again in that brief space when Life, the mighty sculptor, has done his work, and Death, his silent servant, lifts the veil and lets us look at the marble lines he has wrought so faithfully ; and lastly, while a painter who can seize all the traits of a countenance is building it up, feature after feature, from the slight outline to the finished portrait. * * * There is one strange revelation which comes out as the artist shapes your features from his outline. It is that you resemble so many relations to whom you yourself never had noticed any particular likeness in your countenance."

"He is at work at me now, when I catch some of these resemblances, thus:

"There ! there is just the look my father used to have sometimes ; I never thought I had a sign of it. The mother's eyebrow and grayish-blue eye, those I knew I had. But there is a something which recalls a smile which faded away from my sister's lips—how many years ago ! I thought it so pleasant in her, that I love myself better for having a trace of it."

Still another consideration, of importance, perhaps, in genealogical inquiry, is the probability that in some future state of existence we may encounter those who have preceded us on the earth and from whom we have derived our being.

"To fancy we go into the other world," writes George MacDonald, "a set of spiritual moles, burrowing in the dark of a new and unknown existence is worthy only of such as have a lifeless law to their sire. We shall enter it as children with a history, as children going home to a long line of living ancestors to develop closest relations with them."

Aside from my desire to gratify certain of my kinsmen, the chief object in printing this book is to place upon record the story of a family whose growth and dispersion has kept pace very closely with that of the southern and southwestern portion of the United States, in the hope that it may not be devoid of historical importance. The Virginia families whose records have hitherto been accessible are those which have been prominent in the history of the State, and who have not been like the Goodes, always upon the frontiers ; buried in the forest, sheltered by humble roofs as a rule, but none the less rendering important service to the State.

The marvel of the growth of the United States is perhaps best appreciated by those who have studied it in connection with the units of its population.

The interval between the present and the earliest colonial days seems wonderfully short, when it can be spanned by two human lives : but this can be done in the direct line of my own descent. I have talked with my own grandmother, Rebecca Goode, No. 171, she had talked with her grandfather, Samuel Goode, No. 47, and he, with his grandfather, John Goode, No. 26, the original immigrant. Thus, reflected by only two mirrors, I have seen the light of the eyes of a man who was born in England in the reign of James the First, when the two settlements at Jamestown and Plymouth were the only strongholds of the English in America—the contemporary of Milton, Bunyan and Newton—a man whose father might have seen Shakespeare on the stage, who lived through the days of the Cavaliers and the Roundheads, and came to America within thirty or forty years of its first colonization, and has been the progenitor of at least six or eight thousand Americans.

In the three persons mentioned we may recognize three historic types of American citizens. John Goode, No. 21, was the European immigrant, the colonial frontiersman, driven from home by political and ecclesiastical wars, yet loyal to his motherland ; an Englishman, though an American, loyal to the established church, living in the midst of the virgin forest, yet still in the narrow belt along the coast to which the earliest colonists were restricted.

The second type was Samuel Goode, No. 47, the colonist of the eighteenth century, the child of the frontier, untrammeled by reverence for traditionary authority, independent, progressive, casting off the bonds of the State church, moving his family westward toward the mountains, which, until he was past the age of manhood, had never been crossed by white men. He was the man of the commonwealth, the neighbor and supporter of Patrick Henry and Thomas Jefferson, prepared to throw off the now useless connections with Great Britain, and to help in the beginning of a new nation. Although too old to be a soldier, his sons-in-law and nephews were in the ranks of the Virginia Continentals.

The third type is exemplified by Samuel and Rebecca Goode, No. 171. Born at the time of the Revolutionary struggle, not on the extreme frontier but on the site of the forest subdued by their parents and grandparents, they obtained a fair education notwithstanding the dearth of schools, to which was added a knowledge of pioneer life which fitted them to go beyond the mountains and share in the development of the new America in the Mississippi valley. These were frontiersmen like the others, but as they subdued the forest, they built not only dwellings but schools and churches. They were the pioneers of the nineteenth century civilization.

The fourth type is that exemplified by the men and women recorded in this book, the sixteenth and seventeenth generations—too complex by far to be quickly comprehended, and in many respects approximating, more closely than the other three, the characteristics of the Englishmen of to-day.

In conclusion, I wish to thank my kinsmen for their interest in this book and the hearty aid received from one and all, for I have never asked for help which has not been willingly given. I am sorry that the book is not better and more accurate. No one can understand its imperfections so well as the author. I can only give in explanation of many of its faults, that the work of printing, which it was supposed would occupy about three months has dragged along through three years, and that in this time the volume has swelled to nearly three times its intended size. The amount of research and correspondence necessitated in this extension has been very great, and the time for this work has been stolen from the leisure hours of a life overcrowded with perplexing official duties. Such as it is however, I commend the book to the charity of its readers, and hope that it may lead to the preparation of similiar contributions to Southern History, which shall be more accurate and more complete.

ARMY ROLL.

BACON'S INDIAN WAR.

John Goode ....26 |

INDIAN WARS. 1754-58.

John Goode ....66 | Mackerness Goode................75 | Richard Goode 131½
Philip Goode....................70 | Philemon Goode................131 |

BRADDOCK'S CAMPAIGN.

Richard Goode ....131½ |

REVOLUTIONARY WAR.

Col. Robert Goode.....................	Edmund Goode.....................79	Robert Goode......................138
Col. Edward Tate	Edward Goode 121	William Goode 116
Maj. Richard Goode............131½	John Goode 66	William Goode 132
Capt. Henry P. Goode .....(p. 428)	John Goode 77	Mackerness Goode...............201
Capt. Jacob Goode............(p. 428)	*John Goode 83	*Philip Goode......................101
Capt. William Goode 210	Joseph Goode...................p. 428	Benjamin Megginson............116-7
Capt. William Megginson ...116-3	Philemon Goode 131	John Andrews......................182

WAR OF 1812.

Maj. William Goode 210	Surgeon S. C. Horsley, USN..309	John Goode 638
Maj. William Goode............351½	Serg't Bennet Goode..............290	John Hawkins Goode 1033A
Capt. Benjamin Goode 217	Serg't Harry Randolph 738	Richard Goode 353
Capt. Dabney Collier 159	Alfred Goode.......................352	Col. John Tucker..................108
Lieut. John Goode...................177	Burwell Goode 176	Capt. William Magruder........644
Lieut. Robert Goode...............245	Francis Goode......................246	Capt. Benjamin Sherrod.....556-3B
Surgeon Samuel G. Dawson...441	Gaines Goode......................163	And several others.
	John Goode 315	

FLORIDA INDIAN WAR.

Major Garland Goode...... .....194 | Major Hamilton Goode ....557 | Capt. Sidney M. Goode.........295
| Lieut. S. B. Thornton............1842 |

MEXICAN WAR.

In this war two brave fellows lost their lives—Capt. S. B. Thornton of the 182nd Dragoons, U. S. A., No. 1842, killed in front of Mexico, by whom the first stroke in the war was made, and Col. Gustavus Dyson of the Tennessee Volunteers, killed at Chapultepec.

Maj. Goode Bryan, of the 1st Alabama, No. 569, Surgeon J. L. Clarke, 1868. Lieut. Alfred Iverson, of the Georgia Infantry, No. 1381, and Lieut. Lafayette Maynard, U. S. N., No. 1822, rendered excellent service, and D. A. Weisiger, 957. Samuel Goode Ward, 734. Felix Tait, 906, and W. C.

Holt, 1375, were also engaged. In the previous war between Texas and Mexico, Gen. William Fisher, No. 1825, was prominent as Secretary of War of the Texas Republic, and Frank Burt, 1318, and Whitfield Brooks, 1325, laid down their lives.

CIVIL WAR. 1861-1865.

Union Army.

Gen. W. P. Carlin U. S. A ...2902	Lieut. Siloam Goode, 5th Tennessee Reg't (M't'd)	M. M. Goode 1168½
Capt. Philip Goode, 1st Lieut. 15th Iowa Inf., Capt. 15th Iowa Inf. and 3rd Iowa Battalion......1056	*Lieut. George W. Goode, 12th Ohio Inf.......................1128	Lieut. G. H. Wilkerson, 79th Ohio Inf....................1123
Com'r Simeon P. Gillett, U. S. N 1068	Lieut. Daniel B, Goode, 27th Ky. Inf	Lieut. S. C. Botts, Scott's Five Hundred N. Y. Vol...........1859
Paymaster F. T. Gillett, U.S.N. 1067	Lieut. Edmund R. Goode, 27th Ky. Inf...................1013	Capt, Randolph Botts, O. M. O, U. S. A.....................1858
Capt. W. N. Wilkerson, 79th O. Inf........ 1121	Lieut. Daniel G. Goode, 35th Ky. Inf.	Joseph Goode, 7th Ky. Inf., 370 Thomas Goode, 7th Ky. Inf., 371
Lieut. Thos. O. Goode, 1st Md. Cavalry.	Lieut. Elbert R. Goode, 6th Tenn. Inf.	Jacob Goode ....403 R. F. Goode................1012-1
Capt. B. W. Goode, 54th Ohio Inf. Brigade Q. M. 1053	Lieut. Nathan M. Goode, 4th Tenn. Inf.	Thomas J. Goode................1015 Thomas Goode................9-63-2
Lieut. Wilson M. Goode, 12th Ohio Inf.	William H. Goode, 4th Iowa Cavalry 1059	J. W. Goode ....1016 D. B. Goode 1016
Lieut. James K. Goode, 35th Kentucky Inf ....1012?	Omer T. Gillett, 132nd Ind. Inf. 1069	Richard Goode.......... ....1017 R. A. Goode 1018
		S. V. Goode 1020

H. A. Goode ....1022 | D. M. Goode....................1023 | Thos. G. Wilkerson 1142
Burwell S. Goode..............77

Confederate Army.

Gen. Goode Bryan, Ga. Inf 569
Gen. Alfred Cumming, Ga. Inf., 1358
*Gen. A. A. Greene, Ala. Inf., 1240
Gen. Alfred Iverson, Ga. Cav. 1381
Gen. I. M. St. John, Commissary General 2326
Col. Garnett Andrews, 8th Confederate Battalion...............1234
*Col. Franklin K. Beck, 23rd Ala. Inf.........................909
Col. G. W. Brent, Chief of Staff of Gen. Bragg 807
Col. J. Lyle Clarke, "Clarke's Batt. Sharpshooters"........1905
Col. Powhatan Clarke, Chief of Ordinance Dept. of W. La and Miss 1906
Col. J. B. Cumming, Ga. Inf., 1362
Col. S. Bassett French, Aid to Gov. Letcher.................1897
Col. Charles T. Goode, 10th Confederate Cavalry..............1200
*Col. Edmund Goode, 58th Va. Inf 534
Col. Edmund J. Goode, 7th Miss. Inf. 665
Col. J. T. Goode, 34th Va. Inf., 822
Col. T. F. Goode, 2nd Va. Cav., 804
Col. Arthur Herbert, 17th Va. Inf 1920
Col. B. W. Johnson, 15th Ark. Inf 1222
Col. Wm. Rice Jones, Staff of Gen. Magruder................2056
*Col. G. P. Smoote, Tennessee Volunteers 1205
Col. Thos. Goode Tucker, North Carolina Reserves.............276
Col. W. J. Vason, 10th Confederate Cavalry..................1263
Maj. H. F. Andrews, Ga. Inf., 1232
Maj. J. F. Andrews, Miss. Inf., 1231
*Maj. Colin D. Clarke, Q. M. Dept.........................1904
*Maj. J. W. Daniel, Adj't Early's Division
*Maj. James Goode Johnson, Brig. Q. M. Trans Miss. O., 1223
Maj. G. F. Maynard, Comissary Dept.........................1824
Maj. J. C. Maynard, Q. M. Dept. 1829
Maj. J. H. Morgan, Superintendent of Conscriptions, Ga....1331
Maj. Robert Goode Mosby, 59th Va. Inf.
Maj. W. C. Sherrod, Commissary Dept.........................1315
Maj. C. W. Tait, Tex. Inf., 905
Maj. Felix Tait, 23rd Ala. Inf., 906
*Maj. G. E. Ward, Mo. Vols. 731
Maj. W. N. Ward, 55th Va. Inf., 729

Lieut. Com'r Maxwell T. Ciarke, C. S. N 1913
*Chaplain Henry Moore........2392
Surgeon J. T. Andrews, Ga. Inf. 1229
*Surgeon F. M. Bledso.........1340
*Surgeon M. A. Chivers, 1st Tex. Inf.........................3527
Surgeon R. H. Ervin, Ala. Cav. 908
*Surgeon J. J. Goode, La. Vols. 899
Surgeon R. H. Goode, N. C. Inf.........................541
*Surgeon T. C. Goode, Va. Inf. 588
Surgeon P. H. Hamilton 921
Surgeon Samuel Goode Harriss, 787
Surgeon Cicero Holt...........1379
Surgeon S. R. Lampkin, Va. Artillery.......................1099
Surgeon Edmunds Mason, Wise's Brigade.......................2045
Surgeon W. M. Mayes...........923
Surgeon R. H. Tatum, 18th Ga. Inf.........................772
Surgeon J. H. Tucker, CSN., 842
Surgeon Frederick Vaughan, 2229
Surgeon Samuel W. Vaughan, 222
Surgeon Thomas P. Shields, 2337
*Capt. W. R. Abbott, Lynchburg Artillery................1849
*Capt. W. A. Adams Va. Inf., 296
*Capt. G. T. Baskerville, 13th N. C. Inf.....................790
*Capt. Troup Butler, O. M. Ga. Vols.
*Capt. Thomas Capehart, N· C. Cav.........................840
*Capt. James Carey, Aide to Gen. Hood.....................180
Capt. Julien Cumming, Adjt. 48th Ga. Inf...................1359
Capt. Thomas W. Cumming, Adjt. 16th Ga. Inf....1360
Capt. John Goode Finley, 23rd Ala. Inf....................1345
Capt. David Mack Goode, 9th Va. Inf.....................1683
Capt. E. B. Goode, 34th Va. Inf. 823
Capt. F. M. Goode, 44th Ala. Inf. 973
Capt. F. S. Goode, Grivot Guards La 897
Capt. Giles Goode, 5th Ala. Inf. 547
Capt. James Goode, 19th Ga. Cav. 1204
Capt. J. J. Goode...............903
Capt. J. T. Goode, Q. M. Dept. 1338
Capt. John Goode, Staff of Gen. Early.......................536
Capt. Thad. Goode Holt, Va. 1369
Capt. George Hylton, Va. Inf. 455
Capt. Thomas Goode Jones, Aide to Gen. Gordon..............2030
*Capt. R. V. Kidd, 4th Ala. Inf. 2223
Capt. F. S. Mosby.............1866

*Capt. T. F. Maury, Miss. Cav 1843
Capt. Norman V. Randolph, Aide to Gen. Pegram.............4389
*Capt. Tucker S. Randolph, Staff of Gen. Pegram.............4388
Capt. E. A. Spotswood, Staff of Gen. Forrest.
Capt. John E. Rawlins, Tex. Cav.
*Capt. Albert Smith, Mo. Cav., 1518H
Capt R. J. Tucker, Mo. Cav., 1817
Capt. Paul T. Vaughan, 4th Ala. Inf.........................2230
Capt. E. G. Ward, Mo. Vols. 1814
Capt. J. T. Ward, Mo. Cav., 1816
*Capt. W. N. Ward, 47th Va. Inf.........................1801
Capt. James H. Wright, Ga, Inf., 1258
Capt. W. M. Gwin jr., Miss. Cav.........................4362
Lieut. W. H. H. Bagwell, 1st Va. Inf.........................1539
Lieut. James H. Blakeman, Magruder's Staff................2332
Lieut. D. W. Collier, 154th Confederate Inf................3245
Lieut. L. W. Dugger, Selden Battery.......................2243
Lieut. Thomas Finley, Engineer Corps.......................1347
Lieut. T. M. Green, Ga. Cadets, 1869
Lieut. E. C. Mosby, Tex. Vols., Dept.......................1867
Lieut. F. W. Mosby, Q. M. Dept.........................1867
Lieut. Richard Goode Wharton, 56th Va. Inf 2156
Midshipman R. H. Fleming, C. S. N 4385
Serg't F. R. Carrington, 13th Va. Cav.
*Serg't F. E. Dugger, Selden's Battery.......................2260
Serg't R. W. Goode, Stuart's Staff.........................1479
W. M. Andrews 3532
*Wm. Archer 1524
B. Bailey, 6th Va. Inf 661-1
E. L. Baptist, 3rd Va. Cav 793
R. E. Bradley.................2337
*Sons of Mrs. Lucy Benton...4718
W. F. Beall 1225
W. T. Brooke 1272
*H. C. Bradley 2343
William Buchanan, 1st Va. Cav., 2706
Bernard Carrington.............2302
E. W. Carrington...............2301
*Richard C. Carrington 2340
Jackson Condry, 6th Va. Inf.602-4
Julius Condry 602-5
J. W. Childrey.................
Joel M. Chivers .A.............3529
H. T. Chivers..................3528
*Charles D. Chiver............3531
Dabney C. Collier. 10th Ark. Inf.,
W. A. Collier, 7th Tenn. Cav., 3240
W. D. Collier, Scout with Price, 3248

* Died in service or killed in battle.

COLLEGE LIST.

This list is very incomplete, owing to the indefiniteness of many college catalogues, and the absence of others. The date of graduation is given when it is known, but in many instances, such as William and Mary, the date indicates the last year of attendance. A date in brackets shows *approximately* the time of attendance.

William and Mary College.

1790.	Richard Bland Goode.
1806.	William Harrison.
1811.	Cohn Clarke.
[1811]	John Chesterfield Goode.
1811.	Edw'd Carrington Mosby.
1815.	George Mason.
1817.	James Lyle.
1819.	William Osborne Goode.
1832.	Richard J. Harrison.
1832.	William J. Harrison.
1835.	John Jackson Scott.
1837.	James Lyle Clarke.
1840.	Thomas Harrison.
1840.	James Davidson Lyle.
1841.	Richard Herbert Tatum.
1842.	Edwin Burwell Jones.
1844.	Humphrey Singleton Belt.
1848.	Beverley Blair Botts.
1848.	John Todd Lyle.
1853.	Samuel Goode Harriss.
1854.	James Thomas Harriss.
1857.	Edward L Baptist.
1857.	Edmunds Mason.
1858.	Thomas W. Mason.
1860.	John H. Tucker.
1861.	George Mason.
1870.	Robert Wash Goode.

University of Virginia.

1826.	John Lyle.
1830.	Thomas Goode Tucker.
1831.	Richard Goode Wharton.
1835.	Wm. J. Harrison, M. D.
1835.	Rich. J. Harrison, M. D.
1835.	John E. Tucker.
1836	George W. Goode, B. L.
1836.	John Jackson Scott.
1836.	James Lyle Clarke.
1837.	Robert Seth Goode.
1838.	William A. Horseley.
1839.	Charles D. Wharton.
1840.	M. M. Jordan.
1842.	George W. Brent, B. L.
1854.	James Taylor Jones, B. L.
[1856]	William Waverly Dugger.
[1856]	Powhatan Clarke.
[1858]	Maxwell T. Clarke.
[1861]	William Norvell Ward.
	See Memorial Volume.
[1861]	Wm. McKendry Gwin jr.
[1861]	Henry St. John Dixon.
[1861]	Harvie Chambers.
[1861]	John Warwick Daniel.
1861.	George Mason.

1867.	Geo. Taylor Goode, M. D.
1873.	Rich. Harris Maury, B. L.
1876.	Rob't Goode Southall B. L
1878.	Richard Urquhart Goode.
	Wm. T. Brooke.
	Charles T. Baskerville.
	Stephen O. Southall jr.

Randolph-Macon College

1834.	William Hamlin Harriss.
—	William T. Price.
—	John Breckenridge Goode.

Hampden-Sidney College

[1823]	Edward Parks Goode.
[1836]	William Henry Goode.
	S. Bassett French.
	William R. Goode.
1870.	John Kercheval Mason.
1872.	Benjamin Goode.
1881.	Wm. W. Richardson B. A.
	Samuel Pride Daniel.
	Edward Chambers Goode.

Emory and Henry College

1848.	John Goode.
1870.	Jack Buchanan.

Washington and Lee University.

1811.	Nicholas Cabell Horsley.
1842.	Frederick Cabell Horsley.
1868.	Benjamin Green Maynard.
—	George E. Murrell.
—	Robert Hanson Fleming.

Virginia Military Institute.

1846.	Edmond Goode.
	John Thomas Goode.
1861.	Edward Branch Goode.
	Col. Thos. Goode Jones.
1861.	Richard Goode Wharton.
	Harvie Chambers.
1872.	Muscoe Livingston Spotswood.
	William Hart Murrell.
	Chas. Thomas Baskerville
	William O. Baskerville.
	Henry Tayloe Ward.

Richmond College.

Oscar S. Bunting.

Georgetown College.

Franklin King Beck.
Robert Goode Mosby.
Wm. Washington Mosby.
Albert De Vere Burr.

University of North Carolina.

1798.	John Goode.
1848.	George T. Baskerville.
	Flavillus Sidney Goode.

Chapel Hill College, N. C.

Cullen Capehart Tucker.
John H. Tucker.
Thomas Capehart.

University of Georgia.

1810.	James A. Tait.
1814.	Thaddeus Goode Holt.
1820.	Pulaski S. Holt.
1827.	Hines Holt.
1829.	William J. Vason.
1837.	David A. Vason.
	Samuel Watkins Goode.
	Leroy Holt.
	William Chandler Holt.
1844.	Benjamin Harvey Hill.
1855.	David Finley.
1853.	Charles Thomas Goode.
1859.	Joseph B. Cumming.
1859.	Thaddeus Goode Holt.
1868.	Edgar Thompson.
1869.	Benjamin H. Hill jr.
1872.	Charles Dougherty Hill.

Olgethorpe University, Georgia.

1846.	Hines Holt Goode.
	Alfred Iverson.

Mercer University, Ga.

1869.	Charles Lane.
	Algernon Goode Price.

Emory College, Georgia.

1897.	Iverson R. Branham D. D.
	Charles Goode Mercer.

La Grange College, Ga.

Charles Fox Sherrod

University of Alabama.

1834. Charles W. Tait.
1852. James Jefferson Goode.
    John Goode Finley.
    Franklin King Beck.
1843. Felix Tait.
1860. Frederick E. Dugger.
1885. Percy Walton Jones.

Spring Hill College, Ala.

Rhett Goode.
Garland Goode Stallworth.

Oakland College, Miss.

Flavillus Sidney Goode.
James Jefferson Goode.
Joseph Scudday Goode.

Waco University, Tex.

Richard Pavius Goode.
James W. Goode.
Robert J. Goode.
John Goode.

St. John's College, Ark.

1862. William E. Goode.

Union University, Tenn.

1863. Charles Slocumb Goode.

Vanderbilt University, Tenn.

Wm. M. Baskerville (Prof.)

Louisville University, Ky

Benj. Whitfield Johnson.
David Murrell.

Jefferson College, Ky.

Richard L. Goode.

Transylvania University, Ky.

R. H. Ervin.
Sam. Mackerness Goode.

Miami University.

1845. James Smith Goode.
1861. Burwell Goode Wilkerson.

Kenyon College.

Charles M. Poague.

Ohio Wesleyan University.

Burwell Philip Goode.
Sam. Goode McCullough.
Evans Goode.
George W. Goode.
W. H C. Goode.
[Smith Stimmel.]
M. N. Goode.

Indiana University.

Omer Tousey Gillett.
G. Brown Goode, Ph. D.

Indiana Asbury University.

Walton Pearson Goode.
Philip Goode Gillett, A. M. LL. D.
Sam. Mackerness Goode.
Wm. Henry Goode, D. D.
S. T. Gillett, D. D.

Whitewater College, Ind.

S. T. Gillett, D. D., Pres.

Hanover College, Ind.

1870. Samuel Goode Hass.
    M. C. Garber.

Illinois Wesleyan University.

William E. Barns.

William Jewell College Mo.

John E. Ward.

Drury College, Mo.

Richard L. Goode.

Middlebury College, Vt.

1822. Hamilton Goode.

Williams College, Mass.

John Ravenscroft Jones.
Samuel Goode Jones.

Harvard University.

1886. Hugh Campbell Ward,
    Samuel Goode, (Law.)

Brown University, Conn.

1863. Monroe Goode.
    Isaac Bowen.

Trinity College, Conn.

Seth Brett Thornton,

Yale College.

1842. William H. Goode, M. D.
    Franklin King Beck.
    Robert Peachy Maynard.
    Charles Henry Hall.
1872. Frank Cowan Goode.
1873. Edward Benedict Cobb.

Wesleyan University.

1856. Burwell Philip Goode
1870. George Brown Goode.

Princeton College.

Thomas Finley.
Edward H. Murrell.
Alfred Iverson.
James Taylor Jones.
Matthew B. Lowrie.

University of New York.

William Henry Goode.
Powhatan Clarke.

Columbia College.

Edward B. Cobb, (Law.)

Madison College, Pa.

Wm. Waverly Dugger.

Dickinson College, Pa.

Austin Wharton.

St. John College, Montreal,

Henry Boisseau Clarke.

U. S. Military Academy.

[West Point.]

1829. Rev. W. N. Ward.
1834. Gen. Goode Bryan.
1849. Gen. Alfred Cumming.
1850. Gen. W. P. Carlin.
1857. *Col. Wm. Rice Jones.
    * Rufus K. Harrison.
    Col. J. Thomas Goode.
    * W. M. Gwin jr.
1880. Lieut. G. W. Goode.
    Lieut. Powh'n H. Clarke.
1889. Samuel Goode Jones jr.

Appointed to Regular Army by Examination.

Lieut. John Goode.
Lieut. Robert Goode.
Capt. S. B. Thornton.
Alfred Iverson.

U. S. Naval Academy and Earlier Naval Schools.

Lieut. Lafayette Maynard.
Lieut. S. T. Gillett.
Lieut. Com'r S. P. Gillett.
Lieut. Alex. C. Maury.
Lieut. Herbert Winslow.
Surg. Samuel C. Horsley.
Surg. Richard J. Harrison

Rennsellaer Polytechnic Institute.

Edward Goode.
William E. Carlin.

Vassar College.

M. E. Poague.
Elizabeth Goode.

The Medical Schools and Colleges.

D. M. Andrews.
H. F. Andrews, Balt.
J. T. Andrews.
J. G. Baptist.
W. O. Baskerville, Va.
H. S. Belt.
F. M. Bledso, Jeff.
Isaac Brown.
J. G· Burt.

* Resigned to enter the Confederate Army.

Pearson Chapman.
M. A. Chivers.
J. L. Clarke, U. S. A.
Powhatan Clarke.
John Cruger.
C. H. Cole, Miami.
William Crump.
S. G. Dawson.
T. H. B. Dillard.
H. C. Dugger, Mobile.
R. H. Dugger. Univ. Pa.
R. H. Ervin, Trans.
John Feild, Va.
O. T. Gillett, Prs. N. Y.
B. P. Goode, Miami.
G. H. Goode, Miami.
H. J. Goode.
John Goode.
J. J. Goode.
J. W. Goode.
Mackerness Goode
Philip Goode, Mobile.
R. H. Goode, Richmond.
Rhett Goode, Mobile.
S. B. Goode, Miami.
S. M. Goode, Richmond.
S. W. Goode, N. Y.
Thos. Goode, Edinb.
Thos. C. Goode.
W. H. Goode, Yale.

Douglas Gordon, Un. N Y
Joseph Green.
Willis Green.
P. H. Hamilton.
R. J. Harrison, U. S. N.
Wm. J. Harrison.
Wesley Harrison.
S. G. Harriss, Jeff.
W. J. Hening.
Cicero Holt.
Leroy Holt.
F. C. Horsley.
S. C. Horsley, U. S. A.
W. A. Horsley.
W. N. Horsley.
D. W. Humfreville.
John Izard.
Walter Izard.
Thos. W. Jones.
M. M. Jordon, Va. Balt.
Alex. Laird.
Harvie Laird.
S. R. Lampkin.
E. S. Lemoine.
Edmunds Mason.
George Mason, Jeff.
E. C. Mayo.
W. M. Mayes.
B. C. Megginson.
J. W. Mercer.

E. H. Murrell, U. Pa.
D. G. Murrell.
W. S. Overton.
N. R. Powell.
J R. Price.
Robert Ridley.
Charles F. Saunders.
T. P. Shields.
Albert Smith.
P. F. Southall.
P. T. Southall.
Charles Spivey.
E. T. Spotswood.
R. H. Tatum, U. Pa.
Rives Tatum, Va.
J. L. Talbert, Mobile,
J. E. Tucker.
J. H. Tucker, Rich.
S. H. Tucker, Jeff.
M. E. Vason.
A. G. Vaughan.
Frank Vaughan.
S. W. Vaughan.
S. W. Vaughan.
Austin Wharton, Va.
R. G. Wharton, U. Pa.
R. G. Wharton.
R. H. Wharton, Jeff.
Luke White.

ARMS

OF

BLAND.

THE FAMILY NAME.

Fortunes are amassed and dissipated; dynasties rise and pass away, but one's name is yet safely transmitted from father to son—an inheritance of to-day from a remote, and otherwise unknown ancestry.
—BOWDITCH.

HE English surnames GOODE, GOOD and GOAD appear to me, after much study of the ancient records of Great Britain, in the British Museum and elsewhere, to be derived, not, as ordinarily supposed, from some moral excellence inherent in the characters of the first of the name [1] but through the transformation of the Anglo-Saxon personal name—GODA or GODE.[2] This name appears to have been somewhat common among the Saxons, for in *Domesday Book* are recorded the names of thirty or forty Godes and Godas holding land in various parts of England as tenants of William the Conqueror.

We find that in the reign of King Æthelred II., A. D. 988, Goda, earl or thane of Devon, a Saxon, commanded the inhabitants of the shire in a severe conflict with the Danes, in which the latter were put to flight but not without great loss and lamentation, for the earl, with another valiant warrior named Stenuwold, was there slain.[3]

Goda, brother of Edric Streone, Ealdorman of Mercia, is named in the Historical Collections of Walter de Coventry, A. D. 1007. Goda, a minister, was a witness to the charter of Draitun and Suttun, in 1000, to that of Walthaus, 1006, and that of Whitchurch, 1012. Goda, sister of Eadward the Confessor, was married to Eustace, Count of Boulogne, in 1052.

---

1. "Let us turn" writes Bardsley for instance, in his *English Surnames*, "to the varied characteristics of the human heart. If we wish to know how many good and excellent qualities there are in the world, and at the same time to deceive ourselves with the belief that the evil are few, we must look into our directories. Scan their contents and we might almost persuade ourselves that Utopia was a fact and that we were consulting its muster-roll. At every turn we meet with virtue in the guise of a 'Goode' or a 'Patient' or a 'Best' or a 'Faithful,' or infallibility in a 'Perfect' or a 'Faithless.'"

2. Lower, in *Patronymica Britannica*, p. 16, remarks: "A large number of modern surnames are identical with Anglo-Saxon personal names before the conquest."

3. Risdon, quoted in Harding's *History of Tiverton*, ii. p. 2. *Anglo-Saxon Chronicles*, p. 338.

Gode is mentioned as one of the proprietors of the land given by King Henry to the Monastery of Abingdon in Berkshire, 1100–1105.

Gode was provost (*præpositus*) of the Hundred of Backerthorp (Bagthorp), Norfolk, before the time of King John, and Asseline, daughter of Gode, gave half an acre and half a rood of land to the monks of St. Mary of Acre at the same period or very soon thereafter.[1]

The names Goda and Gode occur frequently in *Domesday Book*. Gode was a "tenant in capite," holding land in fee from William the Conqueror. Persons of this name held land in Wiltshire, Devon, Hertford, Hampshire, Nottingham and Suffolk. "Gode, homo Regis Edwardi" is mentioned in the Hertfordshire record, as are also "Gode et filius ejus"

Goda was a "liber homo" in Suffolk, and "Gode liber fœmina," in Suffolk in the time of Eadward the Confessor, and men called Goda were landed proprietors in Oxford, Cambridge, Somerset, Rutland, Sussex, Essex, Suffolk, and Devon previous to the Domesday Survey.

Judging from these indications, it would appear that there were many thousands of Godes in early England. The writer has made no attempt to ascertain the origin of the personal name, but it is not unlikely that it referred to some conspicuous virtues,—warlike, domestic or physical, in the persons to whom it was applied.

The transformation of the personal name into a surname took place during the twelfth and thirteenth centuries by a series of gradual steps, the study of which is full of interest to the student.

Walter the son of Gode (*Walter filius Gode*) is named in the early records, A. D. 1206, as a land-owner in Normandy, and in *Winterburne, terra canonicorum de Constanciæ*,[2] Goda, daughter of Brichtive and Goda, the wife of William (*Goda, fil. Brichtive et Goda uxor Wilielmi*) in 1290,[3] Lowis fil. Gode[4] in 1202 and Matilda fil. Gode[5] in 1232. In all of these instances the name of the parent is given solely as an aid to identification there being no attempt toward the use of a fixed patronymic.

At quite as early a period however, the surname seems to have been gradually creeping into use. In the old Latin cartulary of the Monastery of St. Peter, in Gloucestershire, it is recorded that in 1154 Robertus le Gode, filius Walteri le Gode, bought land in Travelone:[6] Johannes le Gode is mentioned in the same cartulary as a tenant of the Monastery, A. D. 1135–54, holding lands near "the Barton" and at Cutbrithleya.[7] John le Gode, in 1210, paid sixpence (vi. d.) to Malmesbury Abbey.

1. Blomefield : *Norfolk*, vii. p. 41.
2. *Rotulus de valores terrarum Normannorum, inceptus anno Regis Johannis Sixti.*
3. *Great Roll of the Pipe*, 1st year Richard I, p. 72.
4. *Rotulus Cancellarii*, Buckingham and Bedfordshire, 3d year of King John, 1833, p. 347.
5. *Rotuli de finibus*, 16th Henry II.
6. *Hist. et Cart. Mon. Sancti. Petri*, Gloucester ii, p. 141.
7. Ibid. i, p. 178; ii. p. 212.

Such instances enable us to see the following steps by which the surname advanced from an experimental to an assured acceptance. After the middle of the thirteenth century, there seems to have been no uncertainty in the manner in which the name was employed.

Adam God sold land 1148–79 to Simon the cellarer (*Symon de Cellário*) of Gloucester Abbey,[1] and Gervas God is mentioned in 1200, in the records of the courts of Bedfordshire.[2] Walterus Gode in 1207 signed a petition to King John, and the same name occurs in the Chronicon of the Priorate of Dunstaple in connection with certain bonds redeemed in 1263 :—*Eodem tempore redemimus a Johanne de Ellesdone et Waltero Gode liberationes in quibus eis tenebamus.*[3] Alexander and John Gode of Yaxley, Norfolk, lived in the thirteenth century.[4] Simon Gode was rector of Chenies Church, Bucks, in which position he died in 1296,[5] and in 1307 John Gode was a Burgess in Parliament from Agmondesbury :[6] these were perhaps the ancestors of the Goads of Buckinghamshire. Robert God was manucaptor for Ralph Trevysa, a Burgess of the Borough of Bodmin, in the 34th year of Edward III, (1360). The name was perhaps pronounced *Gode*, judging from the other names in the same list.[7]

Thomas Gode, escheator to King Henry IV, held inquest at Cirencester, upon Elizabeth, wife of Sir John Arundel.[8] John Gode was one of the Knights in the retinue of Lord Camoys, and William Gode in that of Sir William Phelipe, at the battle of Agincourt in 1415.[9] John Gode in 1449, gave bonds to the officers of the University of Oxford to repair Coleshill Hall. In the Account of the Proctors of the church of Yeovil, Somerset, 1457–8 is mention of a gift by John Gode for the support of the church, and also of the burial of John Gode in this church. Robert Gode, Sr., was demandant in an entry of fines levied at New Windsor.[10]

A very interesting instance of the early use of the hereditary patronymic occurs in a document filed among the Inquisitions for the 20th year of Edward I. (1294) in the Record office in London: it relates to the Monastery of St. Botolph in Lincolnshire, and the phrase runs thus:—*Johannes de*

---

1. *Hist. et Cart. Mcn. Sancti. Petri.* i., p. 187.
2. Palgrave's *Rotuli Curiæ Regis,* ii. p. 101.
3. Chronicon, p. 357.
4. Blomefield : *Norfolk.*
5. Lipscomb : *history of Bucks,* iii. p. 251.
6. Ibid. iii. p. 161.
7. Maclean : *Trigg Minor* i. p. 240.
8. Nichols : *Topographer and Genealogist* ii. 1853, p. 327.
9. Roll of the men at arms in the English army in Sir Harris Nicolas' *Battle of Agincourt,* 1832, pp. 343 and 360.
10. Ashmolean MSS. Cat. Col., p. 886, note.

Sutton et Petronilla, uxor ejus, et Petrus Gode (filius Wilielmi Gode) pro Priore et Conventu ordinis Patrum Prædicatorum de Sancto Botolpho, etc.[1] The name first assumed the form of Goode about the end of the fourteenth century. Richard Gode was presented to the rectorship of Busham St. Andrew, Norfolk, by the prior and convent of Walsingham, in 1398. Two years later, in 1400, Richard Goode was presented to the rectorship of St. Mary's, Peak Hall, Norfolk, by the prior and convent of Walsingham.[2] The two names evidently belong to the same clergyman, and the sudden evolution of the new name thus illustrated is very instructive. Richard Good, probably the same, was in 1416, rector of St. Peters, Norton Hall, and in 1416, of St. Peter's, Chiveres manor. Norfolk. A similar instance is noted in the case of Richard Goode, who in 1500 was one of the tenants of the Trinity Brethren or Corporation of Windsor, paying a rental of 3s. 4d. for 10 acres of land[3] whose name appears in a list ot jurors in the 12th year of Henry VIII, 1520–21, spelled Richard Gode.[4] Thomas Gode and Thomas Goad, are names evidently referring to one individual. In Newcomb's *Repertorium Ecclesiasticum Londinense* Ralph Goode is mentioned as a tenant of the Abbey of Winchcombe, in Kiftsgate Hundred, Gloucester, I. Henry VII. (1485) holding a tenement called "Oscomes Mead."[5]

"Walter Good or Brunscombe, Bishop of Exeter," who died in 1280, founded the college of Glaseney in Penryn, planting the same " yn a morse called Glasenith in the bottom of a park of his for a provost, twelve prebendaries," etc.[6] The next subsequent appearance of the name in this form is in the case of Nicholas Good, S. T. P., Magister in the college of St. Michael Royal, London, 1478, who died in 1479 ; he was vicar of Northall in 1476. J. Good, a priest, educated at Oxford, was a schoolmaster in Limerick, Ireland, in 1566.

The name was spelled in the various forms Goad, Good, Goode and Good, both in manuscript records and in printed documents, with very little regard for consistency, up to the beginning of the eighteenth century. In the will of John Goode, recorded in Henrico County, Virginia, 1708, some of the sons are called Good,[7] others Goode, and the same

1. Roberts *Calendarium Genealogicum*, i. p. 452.
2. Blomefield : *Norfolk*, x. p. 68.
3. *Ashmolean* MSS. 1126, fo. 10, b.
4. Ibid. 1126.
5. Fosbrooke : *Gloucester*, ii. p. 291.
6. Leland, quoted in Lysons' *Magna Britannia*.
7. In the American Journal of Science and lists for October, 1882, a journal remarkable for its accuracy, the name of Richard U. Goode, one of the staff of the Northern Pacific Railroad Survey, is given Richard Good. Mistakes or variations of this kind were much more likely to occur in the days when few people could write, and when records were less commonly accessible than now.

uncertainty prevails in the Herald's records of the names of his ancestors. The Buckinghamshire branch have retained the archaic form, or its nearest approximation in GOAD and GOODE. Those of Oxford, Cambridge, Worcester, Surrey and Hampshire, Lincoln and Dorset have adopted the form GOOD, which is also largely prevalent in the Irish branches. The Cornish wing of the family, which is the one most numerous in the United States, seems to have used the form GOODE very consistently since the year 1600. The adoption of this form is, very possibly, to be explained by the fact that in the sixteenth and seventeenth centuries, there existed in Cornwall an old and powerful family by the name of COODE, whose surname having passed through somewhat the same history of modification, had then assumed a form as similar as possible to our own.

An example of similar modification may be observed at Richmond, Virginia, where the German *Gude* has become within one generation GOODE, by reason of the familiarity of Virginians with that name, while elsewhere it has become Goody and Good.

The name has its analogues in other Teutonic races. Some of the Goods in America are descended from the German family named *Guth*, the word *guth* in German corresponding to the Saxon *god*. The name occurs in Denmark; the Danish Consul at Hull, England, in 1880, was a Mr. Good. There is a celebrated Norwegian painter named Hans Frederick Gude, born in Christiania, March 13, 1825.

A similar name appears to have existed in early days in Normandy. Alvered and Ralph Godes are mentioned among other land-owners in Normandy, living in 1188, Henry, William and Hugh Godde are mentioned in the *Rotuli Hundredorum*, as living about 1272, and Roger Godde is referred to in the *Writs of Parliament* at a very early date. Arnaldus Garsye del God was a magistrate of "Vasconia," A. D. 1294. John Godes, a monk of St. Florence, in Arigon, was in 1301 admitted as prior of St. Mary of Spirle, Norfolk; he died in 1378. Guillam Reymund de Gut signed a petition to the King at "Porcestre," September 13, 1329. The possessions of Gaillard de Goot, Lord of Roaillac in Aquitania, were confiscated by proclamation of King Henry IV, A. D. 1400.

The name has few geographical monuments. GOODE'S CREEK, in Chesterfield Co., Virginia, runs through the Whitby estate, and was a prominent land-mark during the siege of Richmond, being shown upon all the military maps. GOODE'S ROCK is a dangerous feature in the James River at Whitby. GOODE'S BRANCH is a stream in the western part of Chesterfield Co., probably the one crossed by GOODE'S BRIDGE across the Appomattox which gave name to the post-office of "GOOD'S BRIDGE," now discon-

tinued. This was upon the estate of Col. Robert Goode ; there is now a
Baptist church in the vicinity known as the Goode's Bridge Church which is
38 miles south-west from Richmond and 160 miles from Washington.
GOODE'S FERRY crosses the Roanoke river, 22¼ miles south of Boydton,
Va. GOODES or GOODE'S CROSSING is a railway station near Liberty, Bedford Co., Va., upon the estate of the late John Goode, Esq., of Bedford.
GOODE AVENUE, St. Louis, was named for the late Hon. George W. Goode
of that city and GOODE PLACE in Atlanta, Ga., named for S. W. Goode,
Esq. There is a GOOD STREET in Dallas, Texas, in Akron, O., in Chicago,
and in Philadelphia. GOODE, is a post-office in Phillips Co., Kansas.
GOODE ISLAND is a small island in Torres Straits between New Guinea
and North Australia, Lon. 142° 15' E., Lat. 10° 35': it was named doubtless for some English Naval officer.

In many parts of the United States the names GOOD and GOODE are
pronounced exactly alike. In the west of England, and in the Southern and
South-western States, where the latter form is common, the pronunciation
is invariably *goude*, as would apparently be indicated by the presence of a
terminal e.

Puns upon the name are probably regarded by all members of the family
with feelings of abhorrence, since the opportunity is so obvious, that only
the veriest tyro in the punster's art would venture to attempt what has so
evidently been attempted thousands of times before. I venture, however,
to repeat the following anecdote, not on account of the merits of the puns
as because of the eminence of their authors, who ought, to be sure, to have
known better.

"In 1835," says a correspondent of the New York *Tribune*, "John
Howard Payne, author of "Home Sweet Home," spent some time in the
South, and formed the acquaintance of a daughter of Judge Samuel Watkins
Goode, of Montgomery, Ala. An old autograph album of hers, now in the
possession of her son, contains the following lines, in Payne's handwriting
and over his signature :

> " Lady, your name, if understood,
>   Explains your nature, to a letter:
> And may you never change from *Goode*,
>   Unless, if possible, to *better*."

On the next page is a response, written by Mirabeau B. Lamar, afterwards
President of the " Lone Star Republic" of Texas. It runs as follows :

> "I am content with being *Goode*;
> To aim at *better* might be vain ;
> But if I do, 'tis understood,
> Whate'er the cause—it is not *Payne*."

THE FAMILY ARMS.

But by hir cote-armure, and hir gere,
The heraudes knew him wel.
CHAUCER: *The Knight's Tale*, v. 1029.

" ——— To be worthy of your father's name
Learn out the GOODE they did, and do the same,
For it you beare their ARMES and not their fame
Those ensigns of their worthe will be your shame."
GRAZEBROOK.

Y a study of the distribution of the Goode arms through England we have reached the conclusion that William Gode of the third generation was probably the one who was mentioned among the "men at arms" in the retinue of Sir William Phelipe at the battle of Agincourt ; though it may have been Richard Gode, his grandsire, who was the first to bear the armorial insignia, which with slight modifications, have been used by men of the name in various and widely separated parts of England. In view of the fact that these arms were used by a Suffolk family in the fifteenth century, it seems probable however that they were originally bestowed upon some warrior as soon at least as the early part of the Hundred Years' War, perhaps indeed at Cressy or Poitiers.

No record of the original grant of arms appears to be in existence, but the Herald's Visitations of the sixteenth century mention the confirmation of the chevron and rampant lions to several branches of the family. Sir Thomas Good of Worcestershire, is mentioned in the *Calendar of State Papers* as a Royalist in the service of King Charles in 1646 : this was however at least two centuries after the first use of this coat of arms by various branches of the Goads, Goods and Goodes.

In order to render this chapter intelligible to all its readers, it will doubtless be necessary to review briefly the history of heraldry.[1]
Coat armor did not become hereditary until the time of Henry III.,
(1216–73) and Edward I., (1247–1307).[2]
In the reign of Richard II. (1377–99) and even later, the nobility exercised the right of conferring arms upon their followers for faithful services
in war, and in the fourteenth century, according to Lower, and even as
late as the reign of Henry IV., it was the general practice for persons of
rank to assume whatever insignia they choose.

No attempt was made until the sixteenth century to register or control
in any way the use of arms, the matter in earlier days having been self-
regulated, since none but warriors were of sufficient social distinction, or
in any way in circumstances which would render their use of arms desirable.
When civilians began to assume importance in the community, and the
title *armiger* ceased to indicate military rank, this title was coveted by
many whose ancestors had never borne arms in battle, and it became
necessary to found the Herald's College, which was charged with the duty
of regulating the use of heraldic insignia, and of granting the privilege of
using arms under proper restrictions.   One of their earliest steps was to
organize the Herald's Visitations, by sending out officers of the college to
visit every family-seat in England, to collect evidence in the shape of pedigrees, to record the arms claimed by each family, and to confirm or disallow
questionable claims, in accordance with the evidence.   Visitations were
made to all the counties in the sixteenth and early part of the seventeenth
centuries, and the records of these expeditions, filling thousands of volumes
of manuscript are preserved in the British Museum, the Herald's College
and elsewhere, and in many instances have been printed.

A study of the Herald's Visitation records in the British Museum shows
that at the end of the sixteenth century there were several families of Goods
and Goodes, living in different parts of England who claimed arms which
were the same in all essential features.   This fact would indicate that these
families had a common origin.   The diverging point, as will be shown
subsequently, cannot well have been later than the third or fourth generation
in the system of numeration adopted in this book.   It may however have
been earlier.   The first records of the arms are in the Lincolnshire Visitation of 1504,[3] and in an old Ordinary of Arms,[4] which gives a colored

1. For fuller information see Cussan's *Handbook of Heraldry* and the article *Heraldry* in the last
edition of the *Encyclopedia Brittannica.*
2. Hallam : *Middle Ages,* chapter ii., p. 2.
3. Harleian MSS., British Museum, 1190, fo. 48.
4. Additional MSS., British Museum. 5803.

drawing of the arms of GOODE OF CORNWALL. There is, however, an indication of earlier date in the fact that the families of Tyrell and Suleyard quarter the arms of Goode.[1] Sir John Tyrell, Bart, (1809) is descendant, in the eleventh generation, and Sir John Suleyard, Knight, justice to the Queens bench in 1445, in the third generation, of Joan, daughter and heir of ——— Goode of Wilbye, Co. Suffolk, Esq., who married, about 1400–30, "William Sulyard of Eye, Suffolk, Esq."[2] This seems to show that the family of Goode bore arms as early as 1400, and confirms the judgment arrived at already from another class of data.

The arms of Good, Goode, and Goad consist of a shield, *gules* or red, upon which is a chevron, or band shaped like an inverted V (∧), between three rampant lions. The lions may be either gold (*or*) or silver (*argent*), and the same is true of the chevron : there exist other minor differences of blazon, while some of the branches of the family made use also of crests, which are, of course, various in design.

The several records are as follows :

1. GOODE OF WHITSTONE, CORNWALL. (1609–1620). Gules, on a chevron between three lions, rampant, or, as many cinquefoils of the first. (*Harleian MSS.* 1079, etc. ; *Burke's General Armory* ; *Edmonstone's Heraldry* ; *Additional MSS.*, British Museum, 5803).
2. THOMAS GOOD, D. D., Fellow of Baliol College, Oxford, (1609–78). Gules, a chevron between three lions, rampant, or. (*History of Oxfordshire*).
3. GOOD OF LINCOLNSHIRE. Gules, a chevron between three lions, rampant, or. (*Burke, Edmonstone*).
4. GOOD OF WORCESTERSHIRE. Gules, a chevron between three lioncels, rampant, double queue, argent, or or. (*Nash : History of Worcestershire*).
5. GOAD OF CRUXTON, NORFOLK. Gules, a chevron, or, between three lions, double queue, argent.
6. GOOD OF LINCOLNSHIRE, (1550). Gules, a chevron, or, between three lions, rampant, argent. (*Harleian MS.*, 1550, fo. 220).
7. "GOOCHE, GOOGE OR GOOD." (No locality). Gules, a chevron, or, between three lions, rampant, argent. (*Burke's Armory*).
8. ROGER GOAD, D. D. Gules, a chevron, or, between three lions, rampant, argent. (*Old Heraldry*).
9. GOOD OF SURREY, (1660). Gules, a chevron, argent, between three lions, rampant, or. (*Additional MSS.*, British Museum, 4963).
10. GOODE OF SUFFOLK, 1400–1420. Gules, a chevron, or, between three lions argent. (Quartered with Sulyard on tomb).
11. GOODE OF WARWICK, (1620–1654). Azure, a chevron, or, between three lions rampant, argent (Impaled by St. Nicholas on tomb in St. Mary's, Lutterworth, Leicester).
12. GOOD OF DORSET. Chevron, between three lions, rampant.

1. *Visitation of Suffolk*, 1561, p. 69.
2. Berry: *County Genealogies: Essex*, p. 14.

13. GOOD, Fellow of Baliol College (b. 1680).   Gules, a cross, engrailed, with five ermine spots.

14. GOOD OF REDMARLEY D'ABITOT, WORCESTERSHIRE. Gules, a chevron, or, between three lions, rampant, argent. [*Grazebrook*, p. 230—entered at the Visitation of 1634, and borne by Thos. Good, High Sheriff in 9th of Charles I., C. 30. *Coll. Arms.*] See No. 4, above.

15. GOOD OF WORCESTERSHIRE.? Sable, a fesse, between three dolphins, argent.— (quartered by "Buck of the Nash," Worcestershire.—*Grazebrook, Harl.* MS. 615.)

I find records of Crests as follows :

1. GOODE OF CORNWALL. Talbot's head, erased, gules, ducally crowned, or. (*Burke, Edmonstone, Fairbairn's Crests*).   See figure 1.

2. GOOD OF OXFORD. On a ducal coronet, or, an otter, passant, argent. See figure 2.

3. GOOD OF LINCOLNSHIRE. Same as above.

4. GOOD OF LINCOLNSHIRE. On a ducal coronet or, a leopard, passant, or, spotted sable.

5. GOOD OF SURREY. Same as above.

6. "GOOCHE, GOOGE OR GOOD." The mythical family of Burke. Same as above.

7. GOOD, England. On a ducal coronet, or, a leopard, or, spotted sable. (*Fairbairn's Crests.*) See figure 3.

8. GOOD. An antelope head, erased, in mouth a laurel branch. See fig. 4 (laurel branch omitted).

9. GOOD. The Holy Bible, closed.—Probably Good of Baliol, No. 2 or No. 13.

I had hoped to be able to learn something about the migrations of the family in early times through the study of the arms of the different branches. Having carefully considered the facts, I am compelled to confess that I cannot make anything out of them. They appear to me to teach nothing except that the family was widely dispersed at an early day, though probably not until after the period of the RICHARD GODE, No. 1, whose name heads the pedigree in the following pages.

REMOTE ANCESTRIES.

[From Dr. John Mason Good's Translation of Book V. of Lucretius, *De Rerum Natura*, B. C. 58.]

Yet man's first sons, as o'er the fields they trod,
Rear'd from the hardy earth, were hardier far ;
Strong built, with ampler bones, with muscles nerv'd,
Broad and substantial ; to the power of heat,
Of cold, of varying viands, and disease,
Each hour superior ; the wild lives of beasts
Leading, while many a lustre o'er them roll'd.
Nor crooked plough-share knew they, nor to drive
Deep through the soil the rich returning spade.

     ·   ·   ·

Not knew they yet the crackling blaze t' excite
Or clothe their limbs with furs or savage hides ;
But groves conceal'd them, woods and hollow hills ;
And when rude rains, and bitter blasts o'erpower'd
Low bushy shrubs their squalid members wrapp'd.

     ·   ·

Yet when at length rude huts they first devis'd
And fires, and garments, and, in union sweet,
Man wedded woman, the pure joys indulg'd
Of chaste connubial love, and children rose,
The rough barbarians soften'd.   The warm hearth
Their frames so melted they no more could bear,
As erst th' uncover'd skies ; the nuptial bed
Broke their wild vigor, and the fond caress
Of prattling children from the bosom chac'd
Their stern ferocious manners.   Neighbours now
Join'd in the bonds of friendship, and resolv'd
The softer sex to cherish ; and their babes ;
And own'd by gestures, signs and uncouth sounds
'Twas just, the weaklier to protect from harm.

     ·   ·   ·

  Then nature next the tongue's innumerous tones
Urged them to try ; and sage convenience soon
To things applied them, as the embryo speech

Of infants first the aid of gesture claims,
And pointing finger to define its sense.

．　　　　．　　　　．

Man's earliest arms were fingers, teeth and nails
And stones, and fragments from the branching woods.
Then fires and flames they joined, detected soon;
Then copper next; and last, as latest trac'd,
The tyrant iron.   .   .   .
But nature's self th' untutor'd race first taught
To sow, to graft; for acorns ripe they saw,
And purple berries, shatter'd from the trees,
Soon yield a lineage like the trees themselves.
When learn'd they, curious, through the the stem mature
To thrust the tender slip, and o'er the soil
Plant the fresh shoots that first disordered sprang.

Then, too, new cultures tried they, and, with joy,
Mark'd the boon earth, by ceaseless care caress'd,
Each barbarous fruitage sweeten and subdue.
So loftier still and loftier up the hills,
Drove they the woodlands daily, broad'ning thus
The cultur'd foreground, that the sight might trace
Meads, corn-fields, rivers, lakes, and vineyards gay,
O'er hills and mountains thrown; while thro' the dales,
The downs, the slopes, ran lavish and distinct
The purple realm of olives; as with hues
Distinct, though various still the landscape swells,
Where blooms the dulcet apple, 'mid the tufts
Of trees diverse that blend their joyous shade.

And from the liquid warblings of the birds
Learn'd they their first rude notes, e're music yet
To the rapt ear and tun'd the measur'd verse;
And Zephyr, whisp'ring through the hollow reeds,
Taught the first swains the hollow reeds to sound :
Whence woke they soon those tender trembling tones
Which the sweet pipe when by the fingers prest,
Pours o'er the hills, the vales, and woodlands wild,
Haunts of lone shepherds, and the rural gods.

Thus navigation, agriculture, arms,
Laws, buildings, highways, drapery, all esteem'd
Useful to life, or to the bosom dear,
Song, painting, sculpture—their perpetual need
And by experience fashion'd and refin'd.
So growing time points ceaseless something new,
And human skill evolves it unto day,
And art harmonious, ever aiding art,
All reach at length perfection's topmost point.

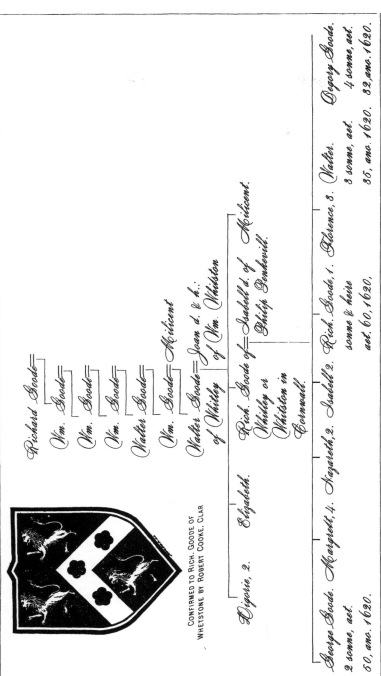

Richard Goode=

Wm. Goode=

Wm. Goode=

Wm. Goode=

Walter Goode=

Wm. Goode= Milicent.

Walter Goode= Joan d. & h.
of Whitley | of Wm. Whiston

Rich. Goode of= Isabell d. of Milicent.
Whitley or | Philip Penkevill.
Whiston in
Cornwall.

CONFIRMED TO RICH. GOODE OF
WHETSTONE BY ROBERT COOKE, CLAR.

Digorie, 2. Elizabeth.

George Goode. Margrett, 4. Auzareth, 2. Isabell 2. Rich. Goode, 1. Florence, 3. Walter. Degory Goode.
2 sonne, aet.   sonne & heire   3 sonne, aet. 4 sonne, aet.
60, ano. 1620.   aet. 60, 1620.   86, ano. 1620. 82, ano. 1620.

PEDIGREE OF GOODE OF WHITLEY.

From Harleian MSS. 1079, fo. 224 b.—(in the British Museum.)

TEN EARLY–ENGLISH GENERATIONS.

Pleust à Dieu qu'un chascun sceust aussi certainement sa généalogie, depuis l'arche de Noé jusques à cest age. Je pense que plusieurs sont au jourd'hui empereurs, rois, ducs, princes, et papes, en la terre, lesquels sont descendus de quelques porteurs de rogatons et de coustrets. Comme au rebours plusieurs sont gueux de l'hostière, souffreteux et miserables lesquels sont descendus de sang et lignes de grands rois et empereurs, attendu l'admirable transport des regnes et empires.—RABELAIS.

FIRST GENERATION.

1.

N the Harleian collection of manuscripts in the British Museum is a time-worn volume, known to few besides the antiquary, containing records of the visitations of Cornwall by officers of the Herald's College in 1573 and 1620.[1] In this book may be found the names of those members of the Goode family of Whitley and Whitstone who were living in 1620, together with a sketch of the family arms, and a pedigree extending back eight generations from RICHARD GOODE, at that time the head of the family and owner of the barton of Whitstone, and probably also of the adjoining estates now known as Upper, Lower and Middle Whitley, which had belonged to his father's family, and possibly to his father, Walter Goode, before his marriage with Joan Whitstone, heiress.

RICHARD GODE, whose name heads this pedigree, was the ancestor of the Goode family in America, the writer of this little book being his descendant in the seventeenth generation, and representatives of the nineteenth generation having already been born among his near relatives.

The same Richard is, in all probability, the ancestor of a large number of those families in England bearing the name Good, Goad and Goode,

---

1. The Visitation of the Countie of Cornewall made and taken by Henry St. George, Esq. : Richmond and Sampson Lennard, Blew-mantle, officers of arms; Marshalls and Deputies of William Camden, Esq., Clarenceux King of Armes of all the South, East and West parts of England from the River of Trent, Anno Dom. 1620, together with The Visitation made Anno Dom. 1573. *Harleian MSS.* 1079, *folio 224, b.*

if the identity in the coat-armor of the Goods of Surrey, Lincolnshire, Dorsetshire, Oxfordshire, Worcestershire ; the Goads of Buckinghamshire, and the Goodes of Cornwall, Suffolk and Warwick may be cited in evidence.

Nothing is known concerning Richard Gode except his name. His residence can only be surmised, though, as has already been stated, the name seems to have been most common in the west of England. It is the opinion of the writer that the original seat of the family was in Gloucestershire, near the borders of Worcestershire and Warwick. Although the pedigree of the heralds professes to be that of a Cornish family, it is very evident that Goode is not a Cornish name, and that the family must have migrated to Cornwall from some more eastern county. Lyson in his chapter upon the extinct families of Cornish gentry, gives this record :

"GOODE of Whitstone, traced eight generations above 1620, had been settled for only three descents at Whitstone by a match with the heiress of Whitstone, became extinct in the seventeenth century; heiress named Badcock. *Arms:* Gules, on a chevron, between three lions, rampant, or, as many cinquefoils."*

Cornish names were almost all of local origin, and the families with which the descendants of the first Richard Gode intermarried in the seventh, eighth and ninth generations can all stand the test of the Cornish shibboleth, quoted by Camden the antiquary.

"By, Tre, Ros, Pol, Lan, Caer and Pen,
    You may know most Cornish men."

There is no evidence to prove that the name of Goode was known in Cornwall prior to 1500, and I think we are justified in assuming that the first five or six generations of the heralds pedigree were brought into this shire with the other family belongings, and that the earlier names, at least, belong as well to other English divisions of the family, as has already been suggested, and as will be explained in the discussion of the fifth generation.

Richard Gode the first then may be supposed to have lived in some county other than Cornwall, though somewhere in the west of England.

We must next endeavor to ascertain the period of his lifetime. This may be done with sufficient accuracy in either of two ways. We know the date of the birth of Richard Goode of the ninth generation to have been 1560. Allowing twenty-four years to each generation, the year of birth of Richard, the first, would be 1360 : allowing thirty it would be 1320 : allowing thirty three, 1296. The latter date is perhaps a little too early, the first undoubtedly much too late, the ordinary allowance being three generations to the century.

Another method of getting at the fact is to ascertain the periods at which

---

* Lyson : *Magna Britannia*, Cornwall, part I., p. cxxxv.

lived the maternal ancestors in the same degree of Richard Goode, the third, as he might be called for distinction's sake. This is practicable in only a few instances. John Penkevil, his grandfather four times removed, according to an old pedigree recorded at the Herald's Visitation of Cornwall in 1570 [1] was lord of the manor or Barton of Penkevil St. Michael in 1342. Sir Reginald Mohun, an ancestor in the same degree, was a little later, his father the last Lord Mohun of Dunster having died in 1331 ; Benedict and Jordan Rayneward of Penmayne flourished between 1296 and 1348, Raphe Trenouth, was born before 1377, and died in 1427, Sir Christopher Fleming about the same time and Ricardo Tregarrack, of Tregarrack was alive in 1327. From these data we may safely conclude that Richard Goode of the first generation flourished about the middle of the fourteenth century.

SECOND GENERATION.

2.

WILLIAM GODE, the son of Richard Gode, lived at the close of the fourteenth century, a subject of Kings Richard the Second and Henry the Fourth. His contemporary Chaucer has left us in the *Canterbury Tales*, a delineation of the men and women of that day, their customs, language and modes of thought, by the aid of which we may transport ourselves back to the period of this ancestor :—

" We see the ' verray perfight gentil knight ' in cassock and coat of mail, with his curly headed squire beside him, and behind them the brown faced yeoman, in his coat and hood of green, with the good bow in his hand. A group of ecclesiastics lights up for us the mediæval church—the brawny, hunt-loving monk, whose bridle jingles as loud and clear as the chapel bell—the wanton friar, first among the beggars and harpers of the country-side,—the poor parson, threadbare, learned and devout, the summoner with his fiery face,—the pardoner with his wallet ' bret full of pardons, come from Rome all hot'—the lively princess with her courtly French lisp, her soft little red mouth, and ' *Amor vincit omnia* ' graven on her brooch. Learning there is in the homely person of the doctor of law,—the hollow-cheeked clerk of Oxford, with his love of books. Around them crowd types of English industry ; the merchant ; the franklin, in whose house it snowed of meat and drink ; the sailor fresh from frays in the channel ; the buxom wife of Bath ; the broad shoul-dered miller ; the haberdasher, carpenter, weaver, dyer, tapestry maker, each in the new livery of his craft ; and last the honest plowman who would dike and delve for the poor without price.''[*]

Nearly every one of these types is unquestionably represented many times over among the progenitors, over one hundred thousand in number, who were our representatives and fore-runners *Anno Domini* 1400.

---

1. *Herald's College, MS.* H. 16, fo. 117.
* *Green :* Short History of England.

THIRD GENERATION.

3.

WILLIAM GODE, son of William, No. 2, lived in the early part of the fourteenth century.   It was, very probably, he who was a man-at-arms in the retinue of Sir William Phelipe at the battle of Agincourt in 1415, and John Gode, who was in the train of Lord Camoys upon the same occasion,[1] may have been his brother.

He had one son, WILLIAM GODE, No. 4, whose name appears in the Whitstone pedigree, and doubtless one of many others, one of whom may have been the "——Goode of Wilbye, County Suffolk " whose daughter Joan married, 1420–30, "William Sulyard of Eye, Suffolk, Esq," and from whom were descended Sir John Tyrell, created baronet, 1809, and Sir John Suleyard, Knight, Justice of the Queens Bench in 1485.   (See chapter on THE FAMILY ARMS.)

FOURTH GENERATION.

4.

WILLIAM GODE, lived in the days described by Bulwer in *The Last of the Barons*, the days of establishment of the first printing press in England, when Savonarola and Luther were moving Europe to a new religious life and Raphael, Da Vinci and Michael Angelo were creating a fresh world of art.   Little did he know of such matters, a stalwart man-at-arms, or a yeoman, or mayhap a plain country squire, in the quiet West of England. He had a son WILLIAM GODE, No. 5, and no one now knows how many more, and there is little reason to doubt that he has hundreds of thousands of descendants living to-day, only one of whom, the present writer, is, at the time when these lines are penned, aware that he ever existed.   As to his own ancestors, in various lines, they were like those of Miller Loveday, in Thomas Hardy's novel *The Trumpet Major*.

"Miller Loveday," writes Hardy, "was the representative of an ancient family whose history is lost in the mists of antiquity.   His ancestral line was contemporaneous with that of De Ros, Howard and De la Zouche ; but owing to some trifling deficiency in the possessions of the house of Loveday the individual names and intermarriages were not recorded during the Middle Ages, and thus their private lives in any given century were uncertain.   It was ascertained that Mr. Loveday's great-grandparents had been eight in number, and his great-great-grandparents, sixteen, every one of whom reached years of discretion : at every stage backwards his sires and gammers thus doubled till they became a vast body of Gothic ladies and gentlemen of the rank known as ceorls or villeins, full of importance to the country at large, and ramifying throughout the unwritten history of England."

---

1. Roll of the Men-at-Arms in the English army in Sir Harris Nicolas' *Battle of Agincourt*, 1832, pp. 343–360.

FIFTH GENERATION.

5.

WALTER GODE.—Warrior, squire or yeoman, Walter Gode, son of the third William, lived, doubtless, in the beautiful southwest of England at the end of the fifteenth and beginning of the sixteenth centuries. He was a member of the only church existing in England, the reformation not having yet taken place. He, perhaps, heard read the new English bible of Tyndale and saw the suppression of the abbeys in his vicinity. He had a son William, and doubtless many other sons and daughters, and from him, his father and his grandfather, are descended the numerous branches of Goods, Goodes and Goads in various counties in England.

As has already been suggested, the first three or four generations of the Cornwall pedigree are probably common to all the branches of the family which use the same armorial badge. The divergence of these several branches must have occurred as early as the fifteenth century, however, for nine or more distinct families were established in as many different counties at the beginning of the seventeenth century, were all owners of landed estates, and claimed pedigrees three or four generations long, which in no two instances coalesce in their earlier steps. The Herald's Visitations embrace, as a rule, the heads of the families in the ninth or tenth generations, with their fathers and grandfathers, and in one or two cases their great-grandfathers—the records, in fact, such as would be likely to be held in the memories of the middle-aged members of each family. No record except that of Cornwall goes back beyond the fourth generation. It is evident that three or four generations would be sufficient for the dispersal of the family to all quarters of England, and that the several related families may readily be descended from William Gode, No. 1, or William, No. 2. There are numerous families named Good, Goad and Goode in all parts of Britain : their ancestors may or may not have sprung from the same stock as that under consideration. When there are no arms there is no means of identification. I will however briefly review, county by county, the notes which I have gathered. A study of·the distribution of the family in the early centuries of its history, A. D. 1300 to A. D. 1700, fails to bring to light any very important facts. It appears to me, however, from the relative abundance of families of the name now and in the past, that the family probably originated in one or more of the four counties of central England, Gloucester, Worcester, Oxford or Buckingham ; sending out, early in the fifteenth century, branches into Cornwall, Suffolk, Dorset and Lincoln. The Worcester-Oxford branch soon overflowed into the neighboring counties of Warwick, Leicester and

Shropshire, that of Bucks into Cambridge and Surrey, and thence to Hampshire, while a current from all the counties set to London as early as the beginning of the seventeenth century. The Norfolk branch is, by the the spelling of its name, more closely assimilated to those of Bucks and Cambridge.

In Bucks, Cambridge and Norfolk, the spelling *Goad* prevailed ; in Oxford, Worcester, Surrey, Hampshire, Dorset and Lincoln, *Good;* in Gloucester, Cornwall, Warwick and Leicester, *Goode*, though uniformity was apparently never thought of until the eighteenth century.

The following distinct branches are recognized :—

1. THE CORNWALL BRANCH.—Located in that county as early as 1550. See below the record of Walter, No. 7, the ancestor of the Virginia Goodes.

2. THE WORCESTERSHIRE AND OXFORDSHIRE BRANCH.—Established here as early as the sixteenth century if not before, and owning a considerable estate at Redmarley d'Abitot (where, in the parish church, are many tombs) and at Aston Court. The Rev.Thomas Good, D.D., b. 1609, Rev. John Good, S. T. B., b. 1621, fellows of Baliol College, Oxford. Rev. Richard Good, rector of Neen Savage, and Richard Good, mayor of Oxford, b. 1609, were among the most prominent men in this branch.

3. THE WARWICKSHIRE BRANCH.—Basil Goode, gent., of Stretton under Fosse, Warwick, living 1550–1650, connected with the families of St. Nicholas and Appulderfield, and Thomas Good, living about 1600, were the earliest representatives in this county, where the name is still well known.

4. THE LEICESTERSHIRE BRANCH.—Established as early as the seventeenth century.

5. THE LINCOLNSHIRE BRANCH.—Established as early as the beginning of the sixteenth century at Girsby and Ownby, a few miles north of Lincoln. The Herald's Visitations of 1504 have the record of six generations.

6. THE GLOUCESTERSHIRE BRANCH.—The name occurs in this county as early A. D. 1154, and has been frequently noted in subsequent years, especially from the twelfth to the fifteenth century. The only landed estate connected with the family name was at Newent, in the hands of William Goode, Esq., in the latter part of the last century.

7. THE DORSETSHIRE BRANCH.—The Dorset Herald's Visitations record five generations of Goods at Mayden-Newton prior to 1630. The Manor of East Axnolles passed out of the hands of John Good, gent. after 1630.

8. THE BUCKS, BURKS and CAMBRIDGE BRANCHES.—The names Goad and Gode were somewhat common in these counties from 1307 down to the last century, Dr. Roger Goad and Dr. Thomas Goade being the most prominent men.

9. THE SURREY BRANCH.—Good and Goode were rather numerous in this shire as early as the middle of the sixteenth century. One or two families were for some generations located at Malden, where monuments still remain in the parish church.

10. THE HAMPSHIRE BRANCH.—Located at Romsey as early as the sixteenth century, and prominent and successful proprietary manufacturers of shalloons. Dr. John Mason Good was of this branch; his grandson Peter Peyto Good lives in New Jersey and has made numerous contributions to literature, and another grandson, the Rev. John Mason Neale, was the author of our beautiful translation of the Latin hymn "Jerusalem, the Golden."

11. THE NORFOLK BRANCH.—A family of Goads was located at Croxton in the sixteenth century, and another owned the manor of Abergavelly.

12. THE SUFFOLK BRANCH.—Established in the fourteenth century.

13. THE IRISH BRANCH.—Several Goods and Goodes moved in the seventeenth and eighteenth centuries to Ireland, where their descendants are numerous, many having emigrated to the United States.

14. THE SCOTCH BRANCH.—The name Good or Gude occurred in Ayrshire as early as 1535; a wealthy family of Goodes are engaged in shawl manufacturing at Paisley, some having emigrated to America. They are probably of the same stock.

A full discussion of these various branches will be given in the Appendix, if the printing of this book is ever carried to that limit.

SIXTH GENERATION.

6

WILLIAM GOOD OR GODE, No. 6, was the son of Walter Gode No. 7, was born 1470 to 1520, and was married to a dame named Milicent. It is not unlikely that he was the first of the name in Cornwall. His son Walter it was, who, about 1530 or 1540, married Joan Whitston. This William Good was probably the possessor of Whitley or Whetley—manors or farms, adjoining Whitstone in the north of Cornwall, now the property of the Duke of Bedford. There is a "Whitley" in Worcestershire, near Redmarley d'Abitot, the seat of one branch of the Goods.

SEVENTH GENERATION.

7.

WALTER GOOD OR GOODE of Whitley, son of William Good, born 1500-1510, married as early as 1540, Joan Whitston, daughter and heir of William Whitston, and by this match came into the possession of the manor or barton of Whitston, in the north of Cornwall, which remained the homestead of the family in that county, until the name became extinct about 1660, by the emigration of the younger branches to America or to other parts of England, and the marriage of the heiress of the last male representative of the name.

He had four children :—

8. RICHARD GOODE.	10. MILICENT.
9. DIGORIE.	11. ELIZABETH.

EIGHTH GENERATION.

8.

RICHARD GOODE, son of Walter Goode, (designated in the Herald's Visitation already quoted, as "Richard Goode of Whitley or Whitston in Cornwall," also mentioned in Vivian and Drake's Visitation as "Richard Goode of Whitston in Cornwall, living 1620," and in the pedigree of Penkevill, in Macleans *Trigg Minor*, as "Rich. Good" and "Richard Goode of Whytley") married Isabell, daughter of Philip Penkevill of Penkevill and Rosorrow, 1558-9, and had eight children :—

12. RICHARD GOODE, b. 1560, "sonne and heire, aet. 60" in 1620.	15. DIGORIE, b. 1585, "4 sonne, aet. 32."
13. GEORGE, b. 1570, "2 sonne, aet. 50."	16. ISABELL.
14. WALTER, b. 1585, "3 sonne, aet. 35," married Alice, daughter of Richard de la More, or Moringe, of Little Torrington, Devonshire* whose other daughter, Jane, m. Richard Lanion, Esq. of Cornwall.	17. NAZARETH.
	18. FLORENCE.
	19. MARGRETT.

The date of Richard Goode's marriage is fixed not only by the age of his eldest son, but by the statement of Sir John Maclean that "Goode" and "Penkevill" are among the earliest names mentioned in the Parish Register of St. Minver, which begins in the year 1558.†

Isabell, wife of Richard Goode, was descended in the eighth generation from John, "Lord of Penkevill," *anno*. 16, *Edward II.*, (A. D. 1322). Her father was Philip Penkevill of Penkevill and Rosorrow ‡ who died in 1622, leaving his estate greatly impoverished.

The family was prominent in Cornwall from the fourteenth to the seventeenth century. Richard Penkevill, of Rosorrow, in Cornwall, received license to discover the passage to China, Cathay, the Moluccas, and other regions of the East Indies, by the N., N. E., or N. W. for seven years, and to form a company to be

---

* *Visitation of Devon*. (Harleian Soc. Publication,) p. 694.

† Maclean: *History of the Rural Deanery of Trigg Minor*, p. 33.

‡ "Penkevill of Penkevill, in St. Michaels Penkevill, traced to the reign of Edward II, married the heiress of Trevilla. A younger branch of the family, which in the reign of Queen Elizabeth was settled at Roserrow in St. Minver, and had married co-heiresses of Mohun, Tregarrick, Raynewarne and Hernance, succeeded to Penkevill on the failure of the elder branch, and became extinct by the death of Benjamin Penkevill in 1699." Lyson: *Magna Britannia*, iii., p. cxlv.

ARMS OF PENKEVILL.

ARGENT, THREE CHEVRONELS, AND IN CHIEF A LION, PASSANT, GULES.

CREST :—Upon a Mount, vert, a Lion, couchant, purpure.

called "The Collegues of the Fellowship for the Discoverie of the North Passage," January 19, 1667.

Thomas, Peter, and John Penkevill, three brothers, were implicated in the first conspiracy against James I. (*Dodd's Church History, IV*). Philip Penkevill, born prior to 1530, was a proprietor of some importance in the northwest of Cornwall, his son and heir Francis, brother of our ancestress, having had in his possession in 1578 "divers great bartons, &c., amounting to one-fourth of the whole area of the parish [of St. Minver]."

St. Minver is adjacent to Padstow and Wadebridge, and is beautifully situated in the midst of the most romantic scenery of the west of Cornwall, and a few miles south of Trevena and Tintagel, the ruined castle, around which cluster most of the mediæval romances relating to King Arthur. This region is of great interest to us, since here lived not only the Penkevills, but also the Raynewards, one of whose seats, Penmayne, still remains, in name at least, on the other side of the river Camel, the Tregarricks, the Hernances, and other ancestral families described hereafter, as well as many ancestral branches whose names we shall never know. The spire of St. Minver is prominent in the beautiful prospect which delights the eye of the tourist from St. Columb to Camelford and Boscastle or Launceston. The characteristics of this region are described somewhat vaguely in James Payn's novel, *Carlyon's Year*, the scene of which is apparently laid in the parish of St. Minver.

St. Minver is distant only twenty miles or so from Whitston and Whitley, where Richard Goode was born, and the daughters of the Penkevill family appear, in several instances, to have found husbands among the youth of northern Cornwall and the adjoining northwestern portion of Devon, the Mohuns, Goodes, Arscotts, Kempes and Arundells.

It would be interesting if we could know something of the social life of these rural families in the reigns of Mary and Elizabeth, and how the young suitors journeyed across the bleak Cornish moors, to seek their brides at Rosorrow. Francis Penkevill, the brother of Isabell Goode, married an heiress of the ancient family of Roscarrock, the remains of whose seat, *Roscarrock House*, still exist about eight miles from St. Minver, on the road to Bodmin, "a ponderous building, castellated and loop-holed, and entered through a heavy arch of granite." Her sister, Winifred, married in 1572, John Kempe or Kympe, and from her have descended many prominent men, as well as the late Mrs. Anna Eliza Kempe Stothard Bray, (b. 1790, d. 1883), who has written several books, illustrating the history of Cornwall and Devon. The name of Penkevill appears to have died in 1699 with Benjamin Penkevill, of Pensiquillis, in the parish of St. Ewe.*

The name, slightly modified, is, however, perpetuated in that of the parish of St. Michael Penkivil, whose church, founded in 1319, is at the gates of "Tregothnan," the seat of Viscount Falmouth.

The name is now pronounced *Pen-kiv'-el*, and was, doubtless, formerly *Pen-kev'-il*. "Pen" is old Cornish or Cymric for "the head of a hill," and the whole is said to signify "the headland of the horse."

I have dwelt thus at length upon the Penkevill family, because, although we do

---

* Pensiquillis is now attached to the estate of Sir Christopher Hawkins, "Trewithen," not far from the hamlet of Probus.

not inherit her name, we inherit from our ancestress, Isabell Penkevill, as many physical traits as from her husband, Richard Goode, and because through her we can claim descent from many old Cornish families, while the maternal ancestral lines of her husband are untraceable. It is evident that our emigrant-ancestor was endowed with fifteen, if not thirty-one, parts of Celtic blood, derived from a Cornish ancestry to the one of Saxon origin, which he inherited with his surname.

NINTH GENERATION.

12.

RICHARD GOODE, of Whitstone, son of Richard and *Isabell Penke-vill* Goode, No. 8, was born at Whitstone, 1560, and died after 1620. Married Joan, daughter of John Downe, of "Pilton," in Devon. Children:

> 20, JOHN GOODE. 21, RICHARD. 22, DOROTHY, m. *Rev. John Badcock.* 23, ISABELL, d. 1670. 24, ROBERT, tenant of Trelightres in the manor of Tregvide, Cornwall, in 1656.

WHITSTONE, the seat of the Goodes from about 1540 to 1669, was the principal estate in the parish of Whitstone, in the north of Cornwall. Whitstone was the "Whitestan," of *Domesday Book*, and in the time of Eadward the Confessor, was held by one "Aluuold." The manor was given by William the Conquerer to his half-brother, Robert, Earl of Moriton, by whom it was granted to one of his knights called Carminow, who undertook, as a fee, to supply to the Earl's castle of Dunheved, at Launceston, ten miles away, a certain number of men, skilled in arms, whenever he might be called upon. The manor, according to one authority, continued in the Carminow family until 1400, when it passed to the Arundells of Lanherne and Wardour; according to another, it became the seat of the Cobham family. How it passed to the Whitstons, no one knows. William Whitston must have owned it in the early part of the sixteenth century, for he died before 1560.

It is quite possible that the name of the estate may have been assumed by some member of the Cobham or Arundell families. However this may be, the family, doubtless, originated in the very spot where we now find it. Tonkin states that the names of most of the Cornish gentry were of local origin, and, that indeed there were scarcely any exceptions but those of familes which had removed from other counties into Cornwall.

A late "Parochial History" of the county remarks:

"Whitestone house and its demesne lands were formerly the property of the family of Goode. Johanna, daughter, and sole heir of John Goode of *Whitstone in Parochia de Sancti Nicholæ de Whitestone*, carried the estate in marriage to Henry Badcock, merchant of Penzance, and was sold by the Badcocks to Thomas I'Ans, Esq., of Bideford."

The old manor house was remodeled about 1780, by Wrey I'Ans, Esq., and then took its present form; a portion of the old walls still remain. It is now the property of Edward Mucklow, Esq., of "Castlehead Grange," Lancashire.

In the center of the parish, stands the trunk of a very ancient oak, beneath the spreading arms of which, in the ancient days, it is said that the young and old folks of the village were wont to congregate, the former to play and dance, and the latter to hold grave debate.

The parish church, situated under the hill which is the site of "Whitstone House," was built about 1400, on the site of a more ancient structure.

"Now it forms a charming picture, situated as it is, in the midst of its tree-encircled God's acre, on the sunny side of gently sloping ground, from which a lovely and extensive view of a valley, stretching down towards Week St. Mary and the sea coast is obtained."

In September, 1883, the writer visited the old home of the family, and through the courtesy of the Rev. William Kingdon, rector of the parish, was permitted to examine the old parish records, in which appeared the names of most of the Goodes mentioned in this connection, and also, to inspect the beautiful old parish church. This has been recently restored, in a most judicious manner.

Concerning The Downe Family, the following records are quoted:

DOWNE OF PILTON AND EAST-DOWNE. In the *Harleian MSS.*, (1080, fo. 221 and 1091, fo. 103,) is the following pedigree:

ARMS OF DOWNE,
Gu., a buck's head, caboshed, ermine attired, or.

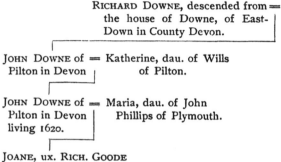

RICHARD DOWNE, descended from = the house of Downe, of East-Down in County Devon.

JOHN DOWNE of = Katherine, dau. of Wills
Pilton in Devon   of Pilton.

JOHN DOWNE of = Maria, dau. of John
Pilton in Devon   Phillips of Plymouth.
living 1620.

JOANE, ux. RICH. GOODE
of Plymouth.

TENTH GENERATION.
20.

JOHN GOODE, Esquire, M. P., of Whitstone, son of Richard and *Joan Downe* Goode, was born 1580–90, and in 1604 represented the neighboring borough of Camelford in Parliament. Children:

25, JOHN GOODE, b. 1610–20, married June 20, 1648, Dorothy Penkevill, of "St. Kew," his second cousin. He is described in the parish register as "John Goode, Gent. of Whitstone." He was the last male representative of the Goodes at Whitstone, and probably died about 1650. He had two daughters. 30, DOROTHY GOODE, b. 1649, d. unm., and 31, JOHANNA, b. 1649–50, d. 1677, married in 1669 *Henry Badcock*, her cousin No. 28.

21

RICHARD GOODE, son of Richard and *Joan Downe* Goode, No. 12, was born 1580–1600, died 1620–1650. He is supposed to have lived at

Whitley, or elsewhere in the vicinity of Whitstone, and to have been the father of the two brothers who were emigrants to America.

26, JOHN GOODE, born 1620–40, died at "Whitby" or "Whitley," in Virginia, 1709. 27, RICHARD, born 1630–40, died in old Rappahannock County, Virginia, 1719.

22

REV. JOHN BADCOCK, Rector of Whitstone, Cornwall, was born 1600–1620, and died at Whitstone, January 13, 1684. Married Mar. 4, 1656, DOROTHY GOODE, daughter of Richard Goode, Esq., No. 12, who was born 1630–40, died Jan. 29, 1676. Children :

28, HENRY BADCOCK, (probably son by prior marriage), married JOHANNA GOODE, No. 31, daughter of John Goode, of Whitstone, No. 25, and heiress to the Whitstone estate. He had a son *Henry*, b. 1677, and grandchildren : 1, *Joan*, b. 1703. 2, *Parthopia*, b. 1706. 3, *Henry*, b. 1707. 4, *Mary*, b. 1709. 5, *Johanna*, b. 1709, and 6, *John*. Robert Leigh Badcock, Esq., living 1883, at St. Stephens, by Launceston, appears to be a descendant of Henry Badcock.

29, HONNER, married *John Gayer* Gent, and died 1690, leaving four children.

Her epitaph in Whitestone Church runs as follows :

> " Whilst here among us she did live,
> To God due honour she did give,
> True love unto her neighbours show'd
> And on the poor reliefe bestow'd
> Four hopeful branches shee hath left behind,
> Shee proved to them a mother kind.
> If you'll so much lamented be,
> Then learn to live as well as shee.
> Reader, y'n guess ye rest by this,
> Shee was a soul made fit for bliss."

SONG OF EMIGRATION.

There was heard a song on the chiming sea,
A mingled breathing of grief and glee;
Man's voice, unbroken by sighs was there,
Filling with triumph the sunny air;
Of fresh green lands, and of pastures new,
It sang, while the bark through the surges flew.

   But ever and anon
    A murmur of farewell
   Told, by its plaintive tone,
    That from woman's lip it fell.

"Away, away o'er the foaming main!"
—This was the free and the joyous strain—
"There are clearer skies than ours, afar,
We will shape our course by a brighter star;
There are plains whose verdure no foot hath pressed,
And whose wealth is all for the first brave guest."

   "But alas! that we should go"
    —Sang the farewell voices then—
   "From the homesteads, warm and low,
    By the brook and in the glen!"

"We will rear new homes under trees that glow,
As if gems were the fruitage of every bough;
O'er our white walls we will train the vine,
And sit in its shadow at day's decline;
And watch our herds, as they range at will
Through the green savannas, all bright and still."

   "But wo for that sweet shade
    Of the flowering orchard-trees,
   Where first our children played
    'Midst the birds and honey bees!"

"All, all our own shall the forests be,
As to the bound of the roebuck free !
None shall say, 'Hither, no further pass !'
We will track each step through the wavy grass ;
We will chase the elk in his speed and might,
And bring proud spoils to the hearth at night."

"But, oh ! the gray church-tower,
And the sound of Sabbath-bell,
And the sheltered garden-bower,—
We have bid them all farewell ! "

"We will give the names of our fearless race.
To each bright river whose course we trace ;
We will leave our memory with mounts and floods,
And the path of our daring in boundless woods !
And our works unto many a lake's green shore,
Where the Indian's graves lay, alone, before."

"But who shall teach the flowers,
Which our children loved, to dwell
In a soil that is not ours ?
Home, home and friends, farewell ! "

FELICIA HEMANS.

THE VIRGINIA GOODES.

ELEVENTH OR FIRST AMERICAN GENERATION.

Tis opportune to look back upon old times and contemplate our forefathers. Great examples grow thin and to be fetched from the passed world. Simplicity flies away and iniquity comes at long strides upon us. We have enough to do to make up our places from present and passed times, and the whole stage of things scarce serveth for our instruction. A compleat piece of virtue must be made up from the Cento's of all ages, as all the beauties of *Greece* could make but one handsome *Venus*.

SIR THOMAS BROWN, *Hydriotaphia*, 1649.

JOHN GOODE, THE IMMIGRANT.

26.

Y far the larger number of the Goodes in America are descendants of JOHN GOODE, son of Richard Goode, of Cornwall, No. 21, who was born in England, probably either at Whitstone or Whitley, in the north of Cornwall, 1620–1630, and removed to Barbados, one of the Caribbee Islands, 1643–1650, and to Virginia prior to 1660. He settled at a place on the colonial frontier, four miles from the present site of Richmond, which he named Whitby[1] (Whitley) in memory of his English home, and where he died in 1709, the proprietor of a considerable plantation. He married in Barbados, 1650–1660, a lady named Mackarness, who accompanied him to Virginia, where she soon died leaving ~~one~~ two sons Samuel ;

[1.] It is not difficult to understand how the name of a large and famous town like *Whitby* should have come to replace that of an obscure little hamlet, such as is *Whitley*. It would have required little argument to convince the owners of the plantation on the James that their ancestor had been in error in his spelling of the name, and that there was no such place as Whitley in England. Careless writing, as well as imperfect tradition, may have caused the change. The word at the head of this note is fairly within my own average hand, and I defy any one to say whether it spells *Whitley* or *Whitby*. Little attention was given to accuracy in such trifling matters as topographical nomenclature. In Lyson's *Magna Britannia*, a scholarly work printed with great care at the close of the last century, the name of the Cornish locality is printed variously in different places as " *Whiston*," " *Whitston*," " *Whetstone*," and " *Whiley*" or " *Whyston*," while " *Witston*," " *Whytston*," " *Whetley*," and " *Whytley*" occur in contemporary records. In another place in Lyson we find Fentongollan and Fenton Goran used interchangeably. The name of another ancestral manor is variously spelled in contemporary and recent records as " Polslinch," " Poslinch," " Postlynch," " Postlinch," " Polyslinche," " Puswithe," and " Polslithe," the last two spellings occurring in adjacent lines in Maclean's scholarly *Trigg Minor*. Bearing in mind the fact that there never were any Goodes in the north of England and in the vicinity of Whitby, the case seems very plain.

subsequently he married Anne Bennet, who died prior to 1708. He had thirteen children :—

>   32, SAMUEL GOODE, born in Barbados before 1660. 33, ROBERT, born in Virginia. 34, JOHN. 35, KATHARINE, married *Mr. Roberts* before 1708. 36, ELIZABETH, married *Mr. Blackman* before 1708. 37, SUSANNA. 38, ANNE. 39, THOMAS, born after 1687. 40, JOSEPH. 41, FRANCES. 42, MARY. 43, MARTHA. 44, URSULA.

The date of John Goode's arrival in Virginia is not definitely fixed, but it was prior to 1661, at which time he was the owner of Whitby plantation. In the records of Henrico county occurs the following entry :—

"January 2, 1684, Thomas Howlett presented before grand jury John Goode, who had been sixteen years in ye parish, and never at church."[*]

We cannot, however, be certain that this irreverent person was our ancestor. There was one John Goad who came to Virginia, aged nineteen, in 1635, in the ship "Assurance,"[†] who was probably not of our family.

John Goode and his brother Richard were by no means the first of the name to come to America. One Thomas Goode, probably from Devon or Cornwall, and perhaps a kinsman, was one of the companions of Sir Francis Drake in the "Golden Hind" in 1577, and therefore a member of the first party of Englishmen who landed on the shores of America and the first to circumnavigate the globe. He was prominent in the trial of Thomas Doughty, a mutineer, who was condemned, executed, and buried on a small island in the harbor of Port St. Julian, on the coast of Brazil.[‡]

Traditions concerning John Goode are vague and few. The Hon. Garnett Andrews, of Georgia, has preserved the reminiscence that he was "an old, fox-hunting English squire," and in several branches of the family, the story has been handed down that he was a cavalier, loyal to King Charles, and driven from home a political exile, after the death of his sovereign. This tradition also has it that after the restoration of the Stewarts his loyalty was rewarded by large grants of land to him and to his descendants in Virginia, but no evidence of such good fortune is to be found either in the colonial records or in the history of the family. It is further related that upon the voyage from Barbados to Virginia, John Goode was accompanied by his wife (born *Mackarness*), an infant son (Samuel), and a serving-maid, and that his name was entered upon the passenger list, as it was also in his will, under the style of "John Goode, gentleman."[§]

---

[*] By statute of 1661 the penalty for non-attendance at church upon every Sunday and the four holidays, was fifty pounds of tobacco.

[†] Savage : *Genealogical Dictionary*, p. 271.

[‡] New England Historic Genealogical Register, I, p. 130.

[§] The use of the term "gentleman" by the early colonists of Virginia has been made a subject of ridicule by a certain class of writers, who thereby have simply demonstrated their own lack of information. The use of this title by an Englishman in those days, as at the present time, did not imply any assumption of superiority, for it was simply a customary and proper designation of his state in society. "This term," remarks Robson, "originally comprehended all above the rank of yeoman. All who were entitled to coat-armor or whose ancestors had been freemen were included in the word '*gentleman*.' But it was more particularly applied to the lowest rank of these, because, not having any title of honor, for want of a specific term it was necessary to employ the general one to distinguish them from the ignoble or plebeian."

John Goode did not proceed at once from England to Virginia, but went first to the island of Barbados in the West Indies, where there was in the time of Cromwell an extensive colony of loyalists. It is not known how long he remained there, but it is probable that it was for a considerable period of time, since it was there that he became acquainted with and married Miss Mackarness.*

Our emigrant ancestor came to Barbados somewhere between 1645 and 1650, during which period, according to Ligon, the inhabitants of the island increased so rapidly in number that the population, twenty years before amounting to 1,900 or 2,000, was then estimated at 50,000, while the island could muster for its defence 10,000 foot soldiers and 1,000 horsemen. Our ancestor did not, however, remain in Barbados. Coming as he did from a poor parish in the by no means wealthy region of North Cornwall, he cannot well have had the capital to enter into competition with the wealthier men who were establishing themselves in the island as sugar planters. Ligon estimated at this period that less than 14,000 pounds sterling would not be sufficient to establish a planter in sugar work "in a plantation of 500 acres of land, with a proportional stock of servants, (30) slaves, (50 men and 50 women), horses, camels, cattle, assinegoes, &c." There is no record that our ancestor was wealthy, and every reason to believe that he was

---

* MACKARNESS.—This is one of the most unusual of surnames. No one of the name, so far as I can learn, has ever come to America. It does not occur among the million or more of surnames in the London Directory, nor have I been able to find it in any of the county post office directories of England.

In Lower's *Patronymica Britannica* it is given only as one ot seven hundred names with the prefix "Mac." In one of Blackmore's novels Sarah Mackarness is the name of a minor character. Mrs. M. A. Mackarness, formerly Miss Planche, is the author of "Sunbeam Stories," and a number of other novels popular in England. The late Very Rev. George Mackarness was Lord Bishop of Oxford and his brother, the Very Rev. Henry Mackarness, Bishop of Argyle and the Isles.

To the latter I am indebted for the following information, conveyed in a letter dated Bishopton, Lochgilphead, N. B., April 22, 1878:—"So far as I can gather from a somewhat diligent research the family of Mackarness came from Scotland about the end of the seventeenth century. They are then found located in Oxfordshire and several parts of the Midland counties of England. In the church of Chipping Norton there are many monuments to them, and my great grandfather has this highly eulogistic epitaph : JOHANNI MACKARNESS. DELICIÆ PAGI, QUI VIRTUTEM IPSAM VIRTUTE ORNAVIT. I find that he was in the first form at Rugby school in 1699 or 1701. From that time the family continued to reside at Chipping Norton. Several of my ancestors were well known medical practitioner in those parts, but they seem, as a rule, to have had small families, and for the last three generations the succession has been through an only son. I cannot tell you about any emigration to America. One went out as a judge to Australia at the beginning of this century, and his memory is still respected in Oxford, where my brother now resides as Lord Bishop of Oxford."

According to Hotten's "Lists of Emigrants to America" Jacob Mackerness and his wife, with two servants and four slaves, and William Mackerness, with one child, three servants, and two slaves, were living in 1680 near the town of St. Michaels, Barbadoes. They were doubtless near kinsmen of the wife of John Goode.

The name of Macarness is also connected with the early history of America through the following eulogistic verses printed in the introductory pages to "The True Travels of Capt. John Smith," in 1629.

THOMAS MACARNESSE TO HIS WORTHY FRIEND AND COUNTRYMAN
CAPTAINE JOHN SMITH.

Who *loves* to *live* at home, yet *looke* abroad,
And know both *passen* and *unpassen* road,
The prime Plantation of an unknown shore,
The *men*, the *manners*, *fruitfulnesse*, and store :
Read but this little Booke, and then Confesse
The *lesse* thou *lik'st* and *lov'st*, thou *liv'st* the lesse.

He writ it with great labour, for thy good,
Twice over, now in *paper*, 'fore in blood.
It cost him deare, both paynes, without an ayme
Of *private* profit, for the *publicke* gaine,
That thou might'st *read* and know and safely *see*
What he by *practice*, thou by *Theoree*.

Commend him for his loyall loving heart,
Or else *come mend* him and take thou his part.

not. He was, therefore, soon speeding his way to the Virginia colony, where land was more abundant, and where there were better outlets for the activity of a man of small means.

Before his departure, he perhaps witnessed the great pestilence of 1647, when "the inhabitants of the islands and the shipping, too, were so grievously visited with the plague that before a month had expired, after our arrival, the living were hardly able to bury the dead."* Many thousands of the Barbadians, especially those newly arrived who dwelt in the town of Bridgetown, were carried away by this pestilence, among them possibly many comrades and kinsmen of our ancestor.

At this time Ligon describes the bay as a scene of great activity. He found "riding at anchor twenty-two good ships, with boats plying to and fro with sails and oars, so quick, strong and numerous as I have seen it below the bridge at London." A merchant fleet plied between Barbados and Virginia, giving occasional opportunities of a change of location. Our ancestor remained here for some years, and here he married Miss Mackarness, and here it is supposed his son Samuel was born. If he was still here in 1649 he was a witness of the punishment of the eighteen negro slaves, ring-leaders in the conspiracy to massacre all the white inhabitants of the island. It is not impossible either that he was one of the army of 3,000 under Lord Willoughby, who resisted the invasion by a Cromwellian army, under Sir George Ayscue, in 1652, and were the last of all the adherents of King Charles to capitulate. He may even have belonged to the army of 3,500 Barbados volunteers, who in 1655, in conjunction with the English force, under command of Admiral William Penn, effected the conquest of Jamaica.

In those days the colony was more prosperous, its people more active and merry than ever since. The old song, "Barbadoes Bells," is supposed to reflect the spirit of this period long gone by. It runs :—

> "Come let us dance and sing
> While Barbadoes bells do ring ;
> Quashi scrapes the fiddle string,
> And Venus plays on the lute."

"During the government of Mr. Bell, (1641-50)," wrote H. Frere in his *Short History of Barbadoes*: "Barbadoes was settled and a constitutional system established. . . . Then it was that the calamities of England served to people Barbadoes. Then it was that this infant colony afforded a retreat to the inhabitants of her mother country, where many families, antient and opulent, having expended their patrimony in support of monarchy, or having been plundered of their wealth by usurpers, sought in this distant isle the re-establishment of that fortune they had been robbed of, and the enjoyment of that peace they had been denied in their native land. An old author tells us that Barbadoes was soonest peopled of all our colonies, and was settled by gentlemen of good families and moderate fortunes. To prove this assertion, we could here mention many of the first settlers, who were tempted to migrate hither, and make this colony their asylum ; whose ancestors were seated with a comfortable affluence in different parts of England, and particularly in the counties of Cornwall, Devonshire, Stafford, Worcester, Hereford, Essex, Suffolk, and Kent ; but mankind are all of a race equally antient, and the business of writers is not to follow

---

* A True and Exact history of the Island of Barbadoes by Richard Ligon, Gent.   London, 1673, p. 20.

the whimsical genealogist, but to present objects and relate facts worthy to employ the attention of reasonable beings." (p. 31.)

This statement is confirmed by Schomburgk :—

"The fame of the fertility of the island, and the civil war caused many English to emigrate to Barbadoes. The emigrants consisted mostly of persons of a peaceable disposition, and when the King's affairs seemed irretrievable, many individuals of rank followed their example. This circumstance gave a certain tone and character to the colonists, which is more evident in their general bearing and manners than in other colonies.*

Among the Virginia families resident in Barbados at this time, may be mentioned among others, the Carringtons, the Codringtons, the Mayos, the Washingtons, and some of the Tuckers.

Many New England families also made their way over the Atlantic by way of this bridge, for the emigrations were almost as numerous as the immigrations. In 1667, it was remarked that 12,000 good men had gone away, 1,200 to New England, 600 to Trinidad and Tobago, in the years 1643 to 1647; and between 1646 and 1658, when the current of emigration turned in another direction, 2,400 to Virginia and Surinam, etc., etc.*

John Goode, after his arrival in Virginia, soon settled down into the occupation of a tobacco planter, and after the death of his Barbadian wife married Anne Bennet, a recent arrival from Holland, who bore him twelve children, some of whom, including his two sons, Thomas and Joseph, were minors in 1708 when his will was drawn up, and were consequently born after 1687.

The date of his birth is not known, but it was probably somewhere from 1610 to 1620. He must have been a grown man at the time of the Cornwellian revolt, and according to traditions already mentioned was advanced in years when he married Anne Bennet. This was probably about 1668 to 1670, at which period, according to my theory of the date of his birth, he would have been from fifty to sixty years of age.

Samuel Goode was his son by the first marriage. He must have been several years old when the second marriage took place, for we are told that he was a mischievous youth who delighted to play practical jokes upon his old father's young wife. Be this as it may, Mistress Anne Goode was estranged from her too demonstrative stepson, and the property of her husband was inherited chiefly by her own children. Mr. Sam's posterity, of whom the writer is one, have heard from our grandparents that the stepmother gained influence over her husband in his old age, and was instrumental in the disinheritance of his first-born, but we may well imagine that the old gentleman might have had cause for just wrath, and if we of the seventh and eighth generations have inherited our temperaments from these forefathers, we know that the young Samuel was too independent to make many concessions.

Estrangements necessarily followed the disinheritance of the elder son, and the two branches of the family soon lost sight of each other. Of the sons of Samuel Goode, some of them appear to have remained in the vicinity of Rich-

---

* History of Barbadoes, 1847, p. 80.

† *Calendar of State Papers. Colonial. America and West Indies,* 1661–68, which see for much additional information of interest.

mond, others, or their descendants, moved to the western part of the state, and some of them ultimately to the unsettled regions further west. The accumulations of John Goode, the first, went mainly to his younger sons Robert and John, and their descendants, who for generations, have owned extensive estates in southern Virginia, and have intermarried with many of the prominent lowland families, such as the Blands, the Randolphs, the Spotswoods, the Clarkes, the Burwells and the Bollings, Tuckers, Wards and Harrisons.

The elder son, Samuel, inherited one article which still exists; this is a "hone" or oil-stone, brought from England by his father, which is now in the possession of the writer, having passed down through the hands of the following persons:

1, JOHN GOODE; 2, SAMUEL GOODE; 3, SAMUEL GOODE; 4, SAMUEL GOODE; 5, GAINES GOODE; 6, SAMUEL MACKARNESS GOODE; 7, REV. WILLIAM HENRY GOODE; 8, G. BROWN GOODE.

It shall be delivered by me to my successor as the historiographer of the family.

The history of the family for the first half century centers around Whitby on the James River, where John Goode seems to have become established soon after his arrival in America. Having landed at Jamestown he soon made his way to the frontier, where he bought about 500 acres of land from Captain Matthew Gough. Brock, in his historical notes upon Richmond, states that "Whitby" was settled as early as 1620. Captain Gough was one of the burgesses for Henrico County, in 1642, and doubtless resided upon this spot of ground. The old house at Whitby, torn down in 1878, was said by local tradition to have been the first house built on the James River, near the present site of Richmond. Whitby lies nearly opposite "Powhatan," the seat of the Mayo family, the very place where Captain John Smith had his first interview with the great Indian werowance, whose descendants have in several instances intermarried with those of John Goode. The following memoranda furnished me by my friend, Mr. R. A. Brock, gives the substance of the Virginia land records concerning this tract of land. It may be remarked that Stony Creek is the rivulet now known as Goode's Creek, and that the Byrd mentioned in these transactions, was the father of the famous William Byrd of "Westover," who subsequently became possessed of all the land within several miles of Richmond, with the exception of "Whitby," and perhaps a few other small plantations, and who was the founder of the city of Richmond.

Captain Matthew Gough or Goff dying without heirs, seized of 500 acres of land in Henrico Co., Thomas Styge, the uncle of Wm. Byrd, the first of the name in Virginia, obtained about 1661, a patent for it.

The same Captain Matthew Gough had also granted about 500 acres to John Goode, which he called by the name of Whitby. Of this, the said Goode conveyed 200 acres, (whereof 150 lay above Stoney Creek, and joined the land of Henry Ayscough), to John Stowers and Wm. Giles by deed dated August 29, 1681, as follows: Consideration, 6000 lbs. of good merchantable tobacco and cask. Witnesses, Wm. Tolley and Thomas Buck. The above conveyed the same land to Wm. Byrd, February 17, 1682. Witnesses, John Goode, Thomas Osbourne.

Samuel Goode conveys to Wm. Byrd 100 acres of land upon the river, a mile below Stoney Creek, which was granted him by his father, John Goode, October 1, 1698, and also 428 acres of land lying high upon Stoney Creek, a part of a patent for 888 acres, dated April 29, 1694, to said Samuel Goode—the 528 acres in consideration of £100, January 5, 1711. Witnesses, Henry Randolph, John Pleasants.

The Will of John Goode, A. D. 1709.

In the name of God, Amen! the twenty-ninth day of November, in the year of our Lord God, seventeen-hundred-and-eight, I, John Goode of the County and Parish of Henrico, in Virginia, Gent., being sick and weak of body, but of sound and perfect mind and memory, thanks be to God for it, do make, ordain, constitute and appoint this to be my last will and testament, in manner following:—

Imprimis, I resign my soul into the hands of God who gave it, trusting through the merits of Jesus Christ my blessed Lord and Savior to obtain free pardon and forgiveness of all my sins; and my body to the earth, to be decently interred, at the discretion of my Executor, hereafter named.

Item, That my debts and funeral charges be first paid.

Item, I give, bequeath and devise to my son Robert Goode, one hundred acres of my land, lying next, and adjoining to the river, and north by the lands of William Byrd, Esq., to him the said Robert and his heirs forever.

Item, I give, bequeath and devise to my son John Goode, one hundred acres of my land lying next James River, and adjoining the land of my son, Samuel Goode, to him the said John and his heirs forever.

Item, I give, bequeath and devise to my sons Thomas Goode, and Joseph Goode, my tract of land lying in the woods on the north side of Stony Creek, and at the heads of the aforementioned lands, estimated to be four hundred acres, more or less, to be equally divided between them when they shall come to lawful age: and my will is, that if either the said Thomas or Joseph shall decease in their nonage, the survivor of them shall have, hold, occupy, possess and enjoy the aforesaid tract of land, containing four hundred acres, to him and his heirs forever. But if my two sons shall arrive to lawful age, then my will is, that Thomas enjoy two hundred acres of the aforementioned land, to him and his heirs forever, and that Joseph enjoy the other two hundred acres, to him the said Joseph and his heirs forever.

Item, I give and bequeath to my daughter Katherine Roberts. two thousand pounds of tobacco.

Item, I give and bequeath to my daughter Elizabeth Blackman, two thousand pounds of tobacco.

Item, I give and bequeath to my daughter Susanna Goode, two thousand pounds of tobacco to be paid when she comes to age or is married.

Item, I give and bequeath to my daughter Anna Goode, two thousand pounds of tobacco, to be paid when she come to age or are married.

Item, I give and bequeath to my son Thomas Goode, two thousand pounds of tobacco when he comes to lawful age.

Item, I give and bequeath to my son Joseph Goode, two thousand pounds of tobacco to be paid when he comes of lawful age.

Item, I give and bequeath to my son Robert, two negroes, by name, Jupiter and Moll, and to his heirs forever.

Item, I give and bequeath to my son John, two negroes, by name George and Sabrina, and to his heirs forever.

Item, I give and bequeath to my son Thomas, two negroes, Abraham and Ned, and to his heirs forever.

Item, I give and bequeath to my son Joseph, one negro woman, by name Rose, with her increase, and to his heirs forever.

Item, I give and bequeath to my daughter Katherine Roberts, besides the two thousand pounds of tobacco already given, one thousand pounds of tobacco more, to be paid four years after my decease.

Item, I give to my son Samuel, ten shillings, and a way for cart and horse on the outside of the low-grounds by long swamp, during the term of his natural life.

Item, I give to my daughter Frances, one shilling.

Item, I give to my daughter Mary, one shilling.

Item, I give to my daughter Martha, one shilling.

Item, I give to my daughter Ursula, one shilling.

All the rest of my goods and chattels I give and bequeath to my two sons Robert and John, and do make my said two sons Robert and John whole and sole Executors of this my last will and testament, hereby revoking all former wills by me made and done.

In testimony whereof, I hereunto set my hand and seal, this the day and year first written. *Item,* my will is, that if Thomas and Joseph should die before they come to lawful age, their estate to be equally divided between their own brothers.

Signed, sealed, delivered and acknowl- }
edged as his last will and testament }
in presence of us, }

JOHN GOODE. [seal.]

Thomas Byrd, Giles Webb, All.
Clerke, Mary Forest.

Henrico County, *April 1st, Ano.* 1709.

The aforegoing will was this day proved in open Court by the oaths of the subscribed witnesses.

Teste.: James Cocke, Cl. Cur.

Matthew Gough, sailed from London for Virginia, embarking in the ship "Safety" Aug. 10, 1635. On the 25th of July, 1869, he received from the Crown a grant of 350 acres (Land Register, Vol. I., p. 658,) and " Whitby " thus came into the hands of a colonist.

The site of " Whitby" was first seen by white men May 23, 1607, when Capt. Christopher Newport, with twenty-three men, made his exploration of the James. "We came," he wrote, " to the second ilet discovered in the river, over against which, on Popham syde,† is the habitatyon of the great Kyng, Pawatah, which I call Pawatah's Tower. It is scituat upon a highe hill by the water syde; a playne between it and the water, twelve score over, whereon he grows his wheat, bran, peaze, tobacco, pompions, gowrds, hemp, flaxe, &c., and were any art used to the naturall state of this place, it would be a goodly habitatyon. * * * But now rowing some three myle in shold water, we came to an overfall, impassable for boats any further. Here the water falls down through great mayne rocks, from ledges of rock above, two fadoms highe, in which fall it maketh divers little iletts."

On the islet, between ;'Powhatan " and " Whitby," there lived at this time six or seven families of Indians.

Next below "Whitby " is "Ampthill," once the seat of Archibald Cary— " Old Ironsides "—here Thomas Jefferson was temporarily resident in 1782, when he received notice of his appointment by Congress as Minister Plenipotentiary to Europe, to be associated with Dr. Franklin and Mr. Adams in negotiating peace.‡ A little farther down the James, and adjoining "Ampthill," lies " Warwick," the seat of Henry Randolph, who married one of the daughters of " Whitby." Still below was " Sheffield," the seat of the Wards, who also found a bride at " Whitby." Across the river first " Powhatan," then "Tree Hill," the seat of the Seldens, then "Wilton" and " Chatsworth," belonging to two well-known branches of the Randolph family, while far above upon the hills of Richmond, in early colonial days, the " Nathaniel Bacon, the rebel," had a plantation. Bacon was, indeed, one of the nearest neighbors of our ancestor, and it is not at all strange that John Goode should have been associated with the impetuous young soldier in his early expeditions. It appears, however, that he was too old a warrior and too loyal an Englishman to follow him in his later rebellious schemes.

I am glad to be able to present a document which has not to my knowledge ever been printed; which, indeed, I have not seen alluded to in any publication save Doyle's " English Colonies in America, vol. I, p. 250. It cannot fail to interest all readers of this book, for it is the only thing which remains to show what manner of man he was by whom the name of Goode was brought across the Atlantic. I refer to a letter written to Sir William Berkeley by John Goode, which gives in dialogue form the "full substance of a discourse" between himself and Nathaniel Bacon, early in Sept., 1676, and which seems to indicate that Bacon was from the beginning of his career in Virginia a

---

*See Archeologia Americana, p. 44.
†" Popham side " was the term used by Newport to designate the north bank of the James, "Salisbury side " its south bank.
‡ S. N. Randolph's " Domestic Life of Thomas Jefferson," p. 67.

seditious personage, and that his rebellion was not as Bacon's admirers have sometimes argued, the direct result of Berkeley's failure to support the colonists in their efforts to repel the incursions of the Indians, but was premeditated.

Bacon was a young man, "not yet arrived to 30 years," and was, from all accounts, impetuous, turbulent and dissipated. He had been only a few months in the colony, and " fame did lay to his charge, he having run out his patrimony in England, except what he brought to Virginia, and for that the most part to be exhausted, which together, made him suspecting of casting an eye to search for retrievement in the troubled waters of popular discontents, watting patience to wait the death of his opulent cousin, old Col. Bacon, whose estate he expected to inherit."*

Goode, on the other hand, was a man of sixty or more, a veteran colonist, frontiersman, and Indian fighter. Doyle characterizes him as "a leading colonist apparently a man of moderate views and a personal friend of Bacon." If Lawrence—"thoughtfull Mr. Lawrence "—and " Mr. Drummond, the sober Scotch gentleman," who were also advanced in years and also in Bacon's confidence, had been equally prudent and sagacious in discriminating between a rebellion against Berkeley and a rebellion against the Crown, the impetuous young leader might have been spared his untimely death.

Goode was, without doubt, one of the little band of planters at the head of the James, who rose to resist the incursions of the Indians in May, 1676, and placing Bacon at their head, marched into the wilderness. Unterrified by Berkeley's proclamations, he remained with Bacon until he began to talk of rebellion against the King's authority, instead of simple Indian warfare. He was doubtless one of the band of fifty-seven horsemen who fought the battle of Bloody Run, and perhaps also one of the six hundred who marched with Bacon to Jamestown and obtained from the Governor and Council a commission for him as general and commander-in-chief against the Indians. He was with Bacon at Middle Plantation, and it was probably here that the conversation took place.

It is recorded in the Colonial Entry Book, Vol. LXXI, pp. 232–240. My attention was first called to it by Dr. Edward Eggleston, who has been carrying on an extensive study of Bacon, the results of which, it is hoped, he may soon make public. Commenting upon Goode's letters, Dr. Eggleston writes: " The paper is far from being a cringing one; it is indeed dignified, if one considers the reign of terror under which it is written."

A DIALOGUE BETWEEN THE REBEL BACON AND ONE GOODE
   AS IT WAS PRESENTED TO THE RIGHT HONORABLE SIR
   WM. BERKELEY, GOVERNOR OF VIRGINIA :

HON'D SR.—

In obedient submission to your honours command directed to me by Capt. Wm. Bird I have written the full substance of a discourse Nath: Bacon,

---

*T. M. (=Thomas Matthews.)

deceased, propos'd to me on or about the 2d day of September last, both in order and words as followeth :

B.—There is a report Sir Wm. Berkeley hath sent to the King for 2,000 Red Coates, and I doe beleive it may be true, tell me your opinion, may not 500 Virginians beat them, wee having the same advantages against them the Indians have against us.

G.—I rather conceive 500 Red Coates may either Subject or ruine Virginia.

B.—You talk strangely, are not wee acquainted with the Country, can lay Ambussadoes, and take Trees and putt them by, the use of their discipline, and are doubtlesse as good or better shott then they.

G.—But they can accomplish what I have sayd without hazard or coming into such disadvantages, by taking Opportunities of Landing where there shall bee noe opposition, firing our houses and Fences, destroying our Stocks and preventing all Trade and supplyes to the Country.

B.—There may bee such prevention that they shall not bee able to make any great Progresse in such Mischeifes, and the Country or Clime not agreeing with their Constitutions, great mortality will happen amongst them, in their Seasoning which will weare and weary them out.

G.—You see Sir that in a manner all the principall Men in the Countrey dislike your manner of proceedings, they, you my bee sure will joine with the Red Coates.

B.—But there shall none of them bee.

G.—Sir, you speake as though you design'd a totall defection from Majestie, and our native Country.

B.—Why (smiling) haue not many Princes lost their Dominions soe.

G.—They haue been such people as haue been able to subsist without their Prince. The poverty of Virginia is such, that the Major part of the Inhabitants can scarce supply their wants from hand to mouth, and many there are besides can hardly shift, without Supply one yeare, and you may bee sure that this people which soe fondly follow you, when they come to feele the miserable wants of food and rayment, will bee in greater heate to leave you, then they were to come after you, besides here are many people in Virginia that receive considerable benefitts, comforts, and advantages by Parents, Friends and Correspondents in England, and many which expect patrimonyes and Inheritances which they will by no meanes decline.

B.—For supply I know nothing: the Country will be able to provide it selfe withall, in a little time, saue Amunition and Iron, and I believe the King of France or States of Holland would either of them entertaine a Trade with us.

G.—Sir, our King is a great Prince, and his Amity is infinitely more valuable to them, then any advantage they can reape by Virginia, they will not therefore provoke his displeasure by supporting his Rebells here; besides I conceive that your followers do not think themselves ingaged against the King's Authority, but against the Indians.

B.—But I think otherwise, and am confident of it, that it is the mind of this country, and of Mary Land, and Carolina also, to cast off their Governor and the Governors of Carolina haue taken no notice of the People, nor the People of them, a long time; and the people are resolv'd to own their Governour further; And if wee cannot prevaile by Armes to make our Conditions for Peace, or obtaine the Priviledge to elect our own Governour, we may retire to Roanoke, and here hee fell into a discourse of seating a Plantation in a great Island in the River, as a fitt place to retire to for Refuge.

G.—Sir, the prosecuting what you haue discoursed will unavoidably produce utter ruine and destruction to the people and Countrey, & I dread the thoughts of putting my hand to the promoting a designe of such miserable consequence, therefore hope you will not expect from me.

B.—I am glad I know your mind, but this proceeds from meere Cowardlynesse.

G.—And I desire you should know my mind, for I desire to harbour noe such thoughts, which I should fear to impart to any man.

B.—Then what should a Gentleman engaged as I am, doe, you doe as good as tell me, I must fly or hang for it.

G.—I conceive a seasonable Submission to the Authority yow haue your Commission from, acknowledging such Errors and Excesse, as are yett past, there may bee hope of remission. I perceived his cogitations were much on this discourse, hee nominated, Carolina, for the watch word.

Three days after I asked his leaue to goe home, hee sullenly Answered, you may goe, and since that time, I thank God, I never saw or heard from him. Here I most humbly begg your Honours pardon for my breaches and neglects of duty, and that your Honour will favourably consider in this particular, I neither knew any man Amongst us, that had any means by which I might give intelligence to you honour hereof, and the necessity thereof, I say by your honors, prudence, foresight, and Industry may bee prevented. So praying God to bless and prosper all your Councells and Actions I conclude.

Your Honors dutifull servant,

JOHN GOODE.

JANUARY YE 30th,
   1676.

[This paper is followed by " Bacon's Letter."]

Before the second month had elapsed Bacon was dead, and a number of his followers had been hanged by the revengeful Berkeley.

One century later, in 1776, Colonel Robert Goode, of "Whitby," greatgrandson of Bacon's adviser, was an active participant in a revolt which proved successful, as were also a dozen or more of his kinsmen, at least two of whom were killed in the struggle.

"WHITBY" IN 1860.

In October, 1880, the writer visited "Whitby" in company with Mr. Francis C. Goode and Mr. R. A. Brock. It is a beautiful spot, about four miles below Richmond, the house occupying a commanding view of the river and the whole city. Between the house and the river is a large area of bottom land, upon which was growing a luxuriant crop of corn. The higher land, south of the house and away from the river, is poor, and apparently exhausted by tobacco-culture. It is overgrown with alders, persimmons and sweet gum trees. Along the main road at the outer gate is a series of deserted fortifications. Although the old house had been taken away, the quaint old stone barn still stood, and in the farm-yard were feeding a flock of black pigs, perhaps lineal descendants of those owned by our English ancestor, nearly two centuries ago, and it may be of the famous swine brought from Bermuda by Admiral Somers. In the bottom-land, an eighth of a mile from the house, is the family burying ground, marked by a clump of sycamore, butternut and sassafras trees. There are no formal monuments, but I found six rude head-stones.

In the river, in front of the plantation, is a rock, dangerous to navigation, familiar to the James River pilots as "Goode's Rock," while through the middle of the plantation, ripples a brook known as "Goode's Creek," well known as a military landmark during the late war.*

Whitby remained in the family until 1876, when it was purchased by Mr. A. D. Williams, of Richmond, from Col. S. Bassett French of Manchester, Va., by whose wife, Helen Lyle it had been inherited.

It is unquestionable that our ancestor John Goode, is the "John Good" to whom, October 3, 1690, in connection with John Stowers, were granted 888 acres in Henrico Co., Va. At the close of the century then the family held, at least, 2270 acres of land, in what is now Chesterfield Co.

The traditions of the family of the first wife is to the effect that John Goode, the first, settled on the James River, not very far from old Jamestown. The distance from Jamestown to Whitby was about 115 miles.

The characteristics of the country to which our ancestors came, has been thus naively described :—

"The genial climate and transparent atmosphere delighted those who had come from the denser air of England Every object in nature was new and wonderful. The hospitality of the Virginians became proverbial, labor was valuable, land was cheap. There was no need of a scramble ; abundance gushed from the earth for all. The morasses were alive with waterfowl ; the forests were nimble with game ; the woods rustled with covies of quails and wild turkies, while they sang with the merry notes of the singing birds ; and hogs, swarming like vermin, ran at large in troops." (*Howe's Virginia.*)

The readers of this book are earnestly urged to study with care the Virginia known to their immigrant ancestors, as it is depicted in the early chapters of John Esten Cooke's *Virginia*, a little volume recently published in the American Commonwealth Series, which every American ought to own.

---

* Goode's Creek was laid down upon all the war maps of the vicinity of Richmond. It may be found on Johnson's war map, No. 36.

† Virginia Land Register, Book iii., p. 124.

RICHARD GOODE, No. 27, son of Richard Goode of Cornwall, No. 21, was an immigrant from England like his brother John. Family tradition states that there were two brothers, who settled first upon the " eastern shore," and afterwards came to the James river. Whether or not John and Richard Goode were for a time residents of Accomac, we shall, probably never know; nor is it known that Richard Goode accompanied his brother to Barbados. It is possible that he may rather have come to Virginia by way of New England. One Richard Goode was juryman at a court in Massachusetts in 1646,[1] who may have been the same, since there are no subsequent traces of him in the more northern colony. In 1670, Richard Goode received a grant of 250 acres of land in Virginia, "between the Chickahominy River and the Great Swamp." This would appear from the land register, to have been in the old Rappahannock county, abolished in 1690, and now included in part in Essex, Richmond, Caroline and Spottsylvania counties. The records of this region, were in great part destroyed during the civil war, but a portion of them is still preserved at Tappahannock, and has enabled us to connect Richard Goode, the emigrant, with some, at least, of his descendants. He died about 1719, at which time, July 19, his will is recorded. He would appear, therefore, to have been younger than his brother John.

45, RICHARD GOODE, b. bef. 1680. 46, EDWARD, d. about 1744.

---

1. *Massachusetts Historical Collections.*

TWELFTH GENERATION.

'Among many other blessings,' said their statute-book : 'God Almighty hath vouchsafed increase of children to this colony, who are now multiplied to a considerable number;' and the huts of the wilderness were as full as the birds' nests of the woods.—HOWE : *Virginia.*

THE WHITBY GOODES.

32.

SAMUEL GOODE, the Barbadian, son of John and *Frances (?) Mackarness Goode*, No. 26, p. 27, was born in the island of Barbados, 1655-8, came to Virginia with his parents, and died after 1734 ; married MARTHA JONES. Children :—

> 47, SAMUEL GOODE, b. about 1700, d. 1797. 48, WILLIAM. 49, PHILIP. 50, MACKARNESS. 51, EDWARD. 52, JOHN. 53, FRANCES. 54, MARTHA. 55, MARGARET.

Samuel Goode accompanied his parents from Barbados to Virginia, there being, at that time, and for more than a century later, a considerable fleet of small vessels plying to and fro between the Old Dominion and the islands in the Caribbean Sea,—vessels of twenty to fifty tons, usually carrying a number of cannon, and under the convoy, frequently, of larger vessels.

He lost his mother at an early age. The mischievous pranks by which the little West Indian made miserable his young step-mother, fresh from Holland, have been matters of tradition in the past, but their memory is now lost. Rev. Dr. Goode of Indiana, writes:— "Some amusing incidents were related of the ill-treatment of young Sam. by his pseudo-mother, and his rather savage revenges ; finally, her influence over the father, in old age, was so great, that she induced him to leave all his (considerable) estate to her own children." Dr. Henry J. Goode, of Ohio, wrote :— "My brother Gaines was well acquainted with the other branch of the Goodes. In his social talk with them, they would laugh at the advantage their mother, through her influence with the old gentlemen had gained for them by persuading him to give the whole of his estate to her children, which made them wealthy. These, I think, Brother Gaines claimed as second cousins."*

These traditions agree with the testimony of the Henrico county records. We have seen that John Goode, although he had given land in 1698 to his son Samuel, ignored him in his will, except to mention him in defining the boundaries of the tracts left to his younger brothers.

---

* This was an error ; they were third cousins.—G. B. G.

Samuel Goode received, April 20, 1694, a grant of 888 acres of land in Henrico County.* In 1734, when his will was made, he devised 1900 acres to his several children, and gave to his wife and two daughters the remainder of his estate. It would appear from this, that it must have been this same Samuel who, in 1730, received an additional grant of 2200 acres in Henrico county.‡ Another grant was made on the same day, Sept. 28, to Samuel Good, probably the eldest son, No. 47.

The land grants to Samuel Goode were probably on the north side of the James.

There is no way of distinguishing father and son, but it is certain that before 1731, nearly 4000 acres of land in Henrico had been granted to one, two or three persons named Samuel Goode. It is also certain, that at the beginning of the present century, large tracts of land were owned by members of the family to the southeast of Richmond, in the neighborhood of localities known as the "White Oak Swamp" and "Four Mile Creek," and including the hamlet now known as Derbytown. The battle-field of "Seven Pines" was upon, or in the immediate neighborhood of this estate.

Land in this region is now of small agricultural value, what little fertility it once had having been exhausted by tobacco culture. In earlier days, with slave labor, its owners doubtless acquired wealth. The old homestead of Benjamin Goode, grandson of Samuel Goode, and probably of his father John Goode, was pulled down in 1875. It was a large plantation house, in old Virginia style, and bore evidence of having been the home of enterprising and prosperous men. Traditions of the meets of the fox hunters and of the feasts they enjoyed here, still linger about the place. Its glories have long since departed, and those of the descendants who have lingered in the vicinity, lead quiet, unambitious farmers' lives. Most of the members of the sixth and seventh generations have emigrated or drifted into the cities.

"Samuel—he of the second generation," wrote the Rev. Dr. Goode "married a Miss Jones.* An incident told me by my mother, illustrates the rudeness of the times in which they lived. Indians were numerous, and frequently annoyed them.† Samuel Goode, our progenitor, was fearless and decided, keeping them in awe, and when occasion required, driving them away from his home. Old Mr. Jones, his father-in-law, was timid and yielding, and this led them to trouble his family the more. At length, in the absence of all but a grown son and daughter, an attack was made by several Indians, which culminated in a hand-to-hand fight in the house, between young Jones and an Indian man. Jones was wounded and fainting with loss of blood. Still, he mastered the Indian, and seizing his long hair and winding it around a bed post, he held him fast until his sister despatched him with a tomahawk. This done, he said: 'I have done what I can for you,' and expired."

---

* Virginia Land Register, Book iii., p. 380.

† Ibid, Book xiii., p. 517.

*Jones.—The only clew we have to the family of *Martha Jones* Goode is a rather vague tradition which seems to indicate that her parents came from Wales, settling first on the Eastern Shore of Virginia. They afterwards settled in the vicinity of Richmond, perhaps at "Jones' Neck." The name was not very common in Virginia in early days. One family, that to which Mark Catesby, the naturalist, and Gen. Roger Jones, U. S. A., belonged, was not related, as their records show. Gen. Samuel Jones, C. S. A., Gen. John M. Jones, C. S. A., Judge William G. Jones of Mobile, and John W. Jones, Speaker

Will of Samuel Goode, 1734.

IN THE NAME OF GOD, AMEN! I, Samuel Goode, of the County of Henrico, being very sick and weak in body, but in perfect mind and memory, thanks be to Almighty God for the same, do hereby make my last will and testament in the manner and form as followeth : First and principally I give my soul into the hands of Almighty God that gave it in full and certain hope of a joyful reserection at the last Day of our Lord Jesus Christ and my body to the earth to be decently buryed at the discretion of my executors hereafter named, and as for what worldly estates it hath pleased God to endow me with I give and bequeath as followeth :

Item, I give and bequeath to my son, Mackerness Goode, the uppermost part of my land at Middle Creek, containing three hundred acres, bounding as followeth, to him and his heirs forever. * * *

Item, I give and bequeath to my son, Samuel Good, three hundred acres of land joining to his brother, Mackerness, to him and his heirs forever.

Item, I give and bequeath to my son, William Goode, three hundred acres of land joining to his brother, Samuel Goode, to him and his heirs forever.

Item, I give and bequeath to my son, Philip Good, three hundred acres of land joining to his brother, Will Good, to him and his heirs forever.

Item, I give and bequeath to my son, John Good, three hundred acres of land joining to his brother, Philip Good, to him and his heirs forever.

Item, I give and bequeath to my daughter, Frances Goode, the plantation at Winepeck, containing a hundred acres, to her and her heirs forever ; also, it is my will and desire that three hundred acres of the lower part of my land joining to John Goode, may be sold to pay my debts at the discretion of my executors.

Ipris, I give and bequeath to my beloved wife, Martha Goode, and my two daughters, Martha and Margaret Good, all the residue of my estate and negroes, to be equally divided when my said daughters shall be of age, twenty-one, or at the day of marriage, nominating and appointing my wife to be my executrix of this my last will and testament.

In witness whereof, I have hereunto set my seal the 10 day of December, 1734.

Signed, sealed and delivered in presence of us, Thos. Jones, John Tillotson, Elizabeth + Tillotson.
    mark.

SAMUEL GOODE. SEAL.

At a court held for Henrico the seventh day of April, Anno Dom. 1735, this will was presented by Martha Goode upon oath, and proved by the oaths of the witnesses hereto whereupon it was admited to record.

Test : BOWLER COCKE, Ct. Cur.

33.

ROBERT GOODE of Whitby, son of John and *Anne Bennet* Goode, his second wife, No. 26, p. 27, was born on the old plantation on the James, and died 1711–50. He married, 1710, Elizabeth Curd* who died at Whitby, Nov. 30, 1766. Children :—

56, ROBERT GOODE, b. July 19, 1711, d. March 6, 1765.

The eldest son of John Goode's second wife, in accordance with an arbitrary entail, came into possession of the paternal estate, or at any rate that portion upon which the home was built, and by the removal of his brothers, would appear to have become owner of nearly, if not quite all, of the plantation. He was a planter of considerable wealth, though living almost upon the frontier.

34.

JOHN GOODE, of "Falls Plantation," Chesterfield Co., Va., son of John Goode, No. 26, p. 27, was born at Whitby, 1670–80, and was killed by Indians, 1720–30. Children :—

57, JOHN GOODE. 58, THOMAS. 59, BENNET. 60, A daughter, who m.
Mr. Megginson, who lived near Bent Creek, Buckingham Co. : descendants in Tennessee.

He left three sons and a daughter, who removed with their widowed mother to the south-western boundary of the colony, where they bought land and settled on the banks of the Roanoke River. The date of this removal is not known, but it was probably in 1738, or soon after, at which period colonization upon the Roanoke was strongly encouraged by the colonial government, the region "being for the most part unseated and uncultivated," (See Hening's "Statutes,") and settlers were exempted for five years from all taxes and tithes; though required to perform a share of the work of exterminating the wolves. Traces of the pitfalls dug for the wolves by the early settlers are visible to this day in Mecklenburg County.

39.

THOMAS GOODE, son of John Goode, No. 26, p. 27, was born at Whitby, 1687–1700. He was a minor when his father made his will in

---

of the U. S. House of Representatives, 1843-45, were born in the vicinity of Richmond, and are, perchance, of the same family with Martha Jones Goode.

The City of Petersburg was named after Peter Jones. Col. Byrd, in his Journal of a trip to the Roanoke in 1753, wrote : " When we got home, we laid the foundation of two cities,—one at Shoccos, to be called Richmond, and the other at the point of Appomattox River, to be called Petersburg. Thus, we do not only build castles in the air, but cities also."

There is a curious circumstance connected with the name, narrated in the following paragraph in the *Richmond Examiner*, August 23, 1859 :

" Garibaldi, is said in the Petersburg *Express*, to be a descendant of Mr. John Johnston Jones, who died in Blandford about 1767. It is a fact that a beautiful daughter of Mr. Jones eloped from Petersburg about the year 1753, with an Italian tight-rope dancer named Garibaldi, who, having amassed an immense fortune in this country, returned to Italy, where a large family blessed the union between himself and his Blandford bride. Mrs. Garibaldi corresponded with her father until the day of the latter's death ; the letters subsequently sent over by the children of Mrs. G. leave but little doubt of the fact that the warrior Garibaldi is a direct descendant of the Jones family, so well known in Blandford during the first half of the past century."

*CURD.—This is a very unusual name. Curdsville is a small hamlet in Buckingham Co. The name occurs in the vestry records of St. James Parish, Goochland Co., 1734.

1709, by the terms of which he was to receive on coming of age, 200 or 400 acres of land, and two negro slaves. His sons were, probably :—

    61, THOMAS GOODE. 62, RICHARD. 63, EDWARD.

40.

JOSEPH GOODE, son of John Goode, No. 26, p. 27, was born at Whitby, 1688–1700. He was a minor in 1709, and had the same provision as his brother Thomas in his father's will. Son :—

    64, JOHN OR DANIEL GOODE.

Mr. Alexander Brown, of Norwood, informs me that Joseph and Thomas Goode are mentioned among the early settlers of old Albermarle Co., about the middle of the last century. These were, without much doubt, Joseph Goode, No. 40, and his elder brother.

THE RAPPAHANNOCK GOODES.

45.

RICHARD GOODE, of Essex Co., Va., son of Richard Goode, No. 27, p. 34, was born in old Rappahannock Co., Va., before 1683. He had children, among whom are supposed to have been the following :—

    65, RICHARD GOODE. 66, JOHN.

46.

EDWARD GOODE, of Essex Co., Va., son of Richard Goode, No. 27, was born in old Rappahannock Co., 1670–1700, died after 1744, as is shown by his will, recorded March 19 of that year. (Will Book, Essex Co., No. 23, p. 263.) Son, probably :—

    68, WILLIAM GOODE.

There can be little doubt that the Rappahannock Goodes were more numerous than our record shows, but tradition has failed to preserve their history and connections.

THIRTEENTH GENERATION.

A lively desire of knowing and recording our ancestors so generally prevails, that it must depend on the influence of some common principle in the minds of men. We seem to have lived in the persons of our forefathers. . . . The satirist may laugh, the philosopher may preach; but reason itself will respect the prejudices and habits which have been consecrated by the experience of mankind.
EDWARD GIBBON : *Autobiography.*

THE PRINCE EDWARD GOODES.

47.

SAMUEL GOODE, of Prince Edward Co., Va., son of Samuel and *Martha Jones* Goode, No. 32, p. 35, was born in Henrico Co., about 1700, died in Prince Edward Co., 1797. A pioneer and a planter. His wife is believed to have been a Miss Burwell. Children :—

> 69, ROBERT GOODE. 70, PHILIP. 71, PRUDENCE, m. *Andrew Moorman.* 72, ANN, m. *William Pride Daniel.* 73, SARAH, m. *Mr. Barksdale.* 74, A daughter, m. *Mr. Pollard,* (perhaps *Benjamin*). 75, MACKARNESS. 76, SAMUEL, b. March 30, 1749, d. 1792. •

Samuel Goode received 300 acres in 1734, by his father's will. It was, probably, he also, who in 1730, had a grant of 400 acres in Henrico Co., and July 15, 1760, a grant of 400 acres in Prince Edward (Virginia Land Register, Book xxiv., p. 573), 302 in Brunswick, 1746 (Ibid xxv., p. 233), and 400 in Lunenburg, 1758, (Ibid, xxxiii., p. 467). In considering these frequent changes, it should be remembered that in those days removals were very frequent, owing to the peculiar kind of agriculture in vogue. "Within the tobacco belt," says Shaler, "agriculture was a much more profitable occupation than it ever became within the northern colonies during the colonial times. This and the other crops produced by slave labor, were won by a careless tillage, that rapidly reduced the fertility of the land, and made it desirable to seek new fields for the devastating ploughs. It would not be possible to contrive a more perfect means of rapidly exhausting the soil than the method of tillage commonly in use in the old days in this Virginian country. The 'tilth' or depth of the ploughing, rarely exceeded six inches, and oftener was less; ploughs were run year after year at the same depth, until there was a hard pan formed by the action of the plough heel which shut the roots of the crops out of the sub-soil. Manuring was never undertaken. When the exhaustion of this abused soil was so complete that it could no longer be profitably cultivated, the place was 'turned out,' the healing forest again possessed it, while the proprietor went over 'the divide,' and set about his devastating work on another farm."*

The early part of Samuel Goode's life was probably passed in the vicinity of the present site of Richmond, where the present city was founded by his neighbor, William Byrd, in 1737. He watched the beginning and early development of the young city, and of its rival, Manchester, on the opposite side of the James River, and was, probably, among the first to ship tobacco from the Richmond wharves to England. He lived to know of the Revolutionary struggle, though he was too old to take part in it. He did not remove to Prince Edward County until late in life, and appears at one time to have lived in Charlotte Co.

The soil in Prince Edward Co., is said to be good, and especially for the culture of tobacco. The 400-acre tract owned by Samuel Goode in his old age, appears to have been in the northwestern angle of the county, near Jamestown, or perhaps including its site, and adjoining the counties of Amelia and Cumberland.

In a letter received eight years ago, Samuel Mackerness Goode wrote:

"In 1857, I was at the tomb of Samuel Goode, where once stood his house. I looked upon these spots of earth with great interest. The old stone-walled spring was in a state of preservation, and from it I took a drink. No vestige of a house was to be seen, but only the ground indicated a residence had been there. This is some mile or two from the line of the Richmond and Danville Railroad, and not far from a small stream called Later Creek, which empties into Appomatox River, a few miles distant."

Traditions, as well as the evidence of family names, indicate that his wife was a member of the Burwell family, (see sketch of THE BURWELL FAMILY, below) but her first name has been forgotten, and the only record of her existence, has been the tradition and the frequent use of BURWELL as a christian name by her descendants.

THE LUNENBURG GOODES.

48.

WILLIAM GOODE, son of Samuel Goode, No. 32, was born in Henrico Co., about 1700, died 1760-1800. Married Pheby Goode. Children, (provisional list) :—

77. JOHN GOODE. 78. WILLIAM. 79. EDMUND.

William Goode received 300 acres from his father in Henrico Co., subsequent to 1754. Ten or twelve years later, we note that William Goode and Pheby, his wife, of Lunenburg Co., sold land to William Maury, of Henrico, from which we infer that they had in the interim removed to Lunenburg, and were disposing of the patrimonial estate.† In 1751, William Goode received a grant of 2075 acres in Lunenburg Co.,‡ which was probably in the section in 1764, cut off from this county to make Charlotte Co., for in 1769, we find the record that William Goode, Gent., was one of the justices of Charlotte.§

---

* Kentucky, p. 56.
† Deed Book of Henrico Co., 1744-48, p. 365.
‡ Virginia Land Register, Book xxxi, p. 365.
§ Virginia State Papers, i. p. 261.

THE EDGEFIELD GOODES.

49.

PHILIP GOODE, son of No. 32, was born 1700–20. There being no record of his presence in Virginia, it seems reasonable to identify him with Philip Goode, who settled in South Carolina at an early day, 1760–70, and who lived in Edgefield District, S. C. Tradition seems to indicate that he lived for a time in Mecklenburg Co., probably near his brother, Mackarness. Children :—

80, PHILIP GOODE, b. 1760–85. 81, SAMUEL. 82, MACKERNESS.

THE CHARLOTTE GOODES.

50.

MACKARNESS GOODE, of Charlotte Co., Va., son of No. 32, was born in Henrico Co., 1690–1709, and died 1747–70. Children :—

83, SAMUEL GOODE. 84, MACKARNESS, d. about 1815.

He inherited 300 acres in Henrico Co., from his father, and June 25, 1747 took up 1030 acres in Brunswick Co.* It was, probably, he who was granted, June 27, 1764, 3241 acres in Lunenburg Co.† His estates seem to have been located in the southeastern part of Charlotte Co., adjoining Mecklenburg. These grants of land were made at a time when many new counties were being laid out within the boundaries of the original shires into which the state was divided in 1634, and it is not impossible that the original Brunswick grant may have been located within the borders of Charlotte Co., as now defined, and that by subsequent grants the estate was extended over the boundary into Mecklenburg. Martin's *Gazetteer of Virginia*, printed in 1835, speaks of "Mack Goode's Plantation" as being situated upon the ridge separating the waters of the Meherrin River, from a branch of the Bluestone—somewhere, perhaps, in the vicinity of the present Wiliesburg.

THE WEST-CHESTERFIELD GOODES.

51.

EDWARD GOODE is not mentioned among the children of Samuel Goode, No. 32, but is included in the list, because a place must be found somewhere for the ancestors of the Goodes of Skinquarter who would appear from the occurrence of the name Mack(erness) among them, to be descendants of the first wife of John Goode, No. 26.

The father of Rev. John Goode lived in 1738, in the southeastern part of Henrico Co., a place where the children of No. 32, were at that time chiefly located. The traditions of the West-Chesterfield Goodes do not go back of the Rev. John Goode, but there is a vague tradition of an an-

---

* Virginia Land Register, Book xxviii., p. 109.
† Ibid, Book xxxv., p. 497.

cestor Edward, and since the Henrico Goodes claim the "old Goodes" of West-Chesterfield as second cousins, Edward Goode is provisionally placed here,—he cannot be far out of his proper position at the farthest Son :—

85, REV. JOHN GOODE, b. 1738, d. 1790.

THE HENRICO GOODES.

52

JOHN GOODE, of Henrico Co., Va., son of No. 32, was born 1690–1700, died 1740–1800. Sons :—

86, JOHN. 87, BENJAMIN.

He received after 1734, 300 acres from his father. John Goode, living in Richmond, 1881, claimed to be great grandson to John Goode, son to Samuel Goode—old Samuel—the first of the race in these parts. He was, undoubtedly right, save in the omission of one generation. He claimed, also, that his father was second cousin to "the old Goodes," of Chesterfield, and on the strength of this tradition, I admit, as one of the sons of this progenitor, Edward, father of the Rev. John Goode, who would otherwise be unlocated.

THE WHITBY GOODES.

56.

ROBERT GOODE, No. 2, of Whitby, son of Robert and *Elizabeth Curd* Goode, No. 33, p. 37, was born July 19, 1711, died October 29, 1760. Married, 1737, Mary Turpin, born September 6, 1720, d. March 6, 1765. Both are buried at Whitby. Children :—

88, ELIZABETH GOODE, b. Mar. 2, 1738. 89, MARY, b. Apr. 6, 1741, m. *Seth Ward.* 90, ROBERT, b. Feb. 8, 1743, d. Apr., 1809. 91, FRANCIS, b. Dec. 20, 1744, d. Apr. 23, 1795. 92, OBEDIENCE, b. Apr. 12, 1747, d. unm. 1800. 93, MARTHA, b. Aug. 10, 1749, d. Sept. 30, 1751. 94. MARTHA, 2d, b. Oct. 24, 1751, d. Dec. 15, 1752. 95, THOMAS, b. Dec. 31, 1753, m. *Eliz. Prosser,* who died Apr. 6, 1813. 96, SAMUEL, b. Mar. 21, 1756, d. Nov. 14, 1822. 97. MARTHA, 3d, b. June 13, 1760, d. March 29, 1774.

Robert Goode received a grant of 480 acres in Goochland County, July 30, 1742.* This was, doubtless, the man now under consideration, who at the time of his marriage, took up land and formed a home for himself, Whitby probably not having come into his possession until some years later.

During the later years of his life, he must have taken great interest in watching the growth of the new town of Richmond, as it spread its boundaries over the hills on the opposite side of the river. He was a man of ample means, a planter of the old school, and his sons were family educated, married into the best of the neighboring families, and occupied positions of prominence.

Mary Turpin, his wife, was daughter of Thomas and Obedience Turpin, of

*Virginia Land Register, Book xx., p. 400.

Powhatan Co. Thomas Turpin, his uncle, married Mary Jefferson, aunt of Thomas Jefferson, and sister-in-law of Bennet Goode, No. 58.

THE ROANOKE GOODES.
57.

JOHN GOODE, of "Cox's Creek," son of No. 34, was born in Chesterfield Co., Va., 1700–30, and died after 1783. Children :

98, "SANDY" GOODE, M. D. 99, JOHN TWIGG, b. 1783, d. Aug. 26, 1874. 100, BENNET, d. 1879. 101, JINNY, m. *Jack Bolling.* 102, LUCY, m. *Abner Adams.* 103, A daughter, m. *Mr. Yancey,* of North Carolina.

He sold out his estate on the Roanoke, and bought a large and valuable tract of land on Cox's Creek, Mecklenburg Co. He had the largest negro estate in the county. "He was remarkably fond of his farm, and of fine horses, for the possession of which he was noted. He owned the celebrated quarter race-horses 'Twigg' and 'Paddy Whack.'"

A peculiar form of the amusement known as "quarter-racing" was in favor in this part of Virginia in the last century. This is described by Anburey in his *Travels through America*:—"It is a match between two horses, to run a quarter of a mile in a straight direction, and near most of the ordinaries, there is a piece of ground cleared in the woods where there are two paths about six or eight yards asunder which the horses run in. They have a breed of horses to perform it with astonishing velocity, beating every other, for that distance, with the greatest ease. I think I can assert that even the famous Eclipse could not excel them in speed, for our horses (in England), are some time before they are able to get into full speed, and these are trained to set out in that manner the moment of starting. It is the most ridiculous amusement imaginable, for if you happen to be looking another way the race is terminated before you can turn your head; notwithstanding which, very considerable sums are betted on these matches."

58.

THOMAS GOODE, of Chesterfield Co, Va., son of No. 34, was born 1700–30. He died after 1780. Married Agnes Osborne, of "Osbornes,'' Chesterfield Co. Children :—

104, THOMAS GOODE, d. unm. yg. 105, JOHN CHESTERFIELD, b. 1750–70, d. 1830–40. 106, MARTHA, m. *William B. Hamlin.* 107. ELIZABETH, d. unm. 108, AGNES EPPES, b. May 15, 1781, d. Dec. 25, 1814, m. *Col. John Tucker.*

"Thomas Goode removed with his mother to southwest Virginia, where he lived and acquired an estate on the Roanoke River. He returned to Chesterfield Co., where he possessed land, still retaining his lands in Mecklenburg Co., which his son, John C. Goode, inherited. He was a planter, and amassed a very large property. Like his elder brother, he was remarkably fond of fine horses; he owned the famous 'Diomede,' and 'Imported Archduke,' 'Imported Precipitate,' and 'Imported Sir Robin' partly belonged to him, or were in some manner in his service."

THE POWHATAN GOODES.
59.

BENNET GOODE, of "Fine Creek," Powhatan Co., Va., son of No.

34, was born in Chesterfield Co., 1700–20, removed with his mother to Mecklenburg Co., and subsequently settled in Powhatan, where he was a prosperous planter. Married about 1740, Martha Jefferson, of "Osbornes," aunt of Thomas Jefferson, President of the United States. Children:—

109, JOHN GOODE, b. 1743, d. 1834. 110, BENNET, b. 1744–6, d. 1812–16. 111, A daughter, m. *Mr. Henderson* and moved to Kentucky. 112, A daughter, m. *Mr. Saunders* of Lynchburg, d. s. p. 113. A daughter m. *Mr. Baskerville*, of Dinwiddie Co. 114, A daughter, m. *Mr. Royster*, and removed to Dinwiddie Co. 115, MARTHA, m. *Charles Povall.* 116, WILLIAM, b. 1765.

Bennet Goode settled first at a place in Powhatan Co., near the mouth of Genito Creek, doubtless the spot referred to in the Colonial Statutes of 1842, establishing a ferry "from the land of Bennett Goode, across the James River to the land of Col. John Flemming, in Goochland Co." This he sold in 1758–9, to a man named Jude, and it has since been known as "Jude's Ferry." He then removed to a place on "Fine Creek," about five miles distant, which was inherited by his son John. Sept. 5, 1768, 369 acres in Goochland Co., were granted to Bennet Goode.* Goochland at that time included what became, in 1777, Powhatan Co.

Like his elder brother, Bennet Goode found his bride at "Osbornes," a hamlet on the James River, fifteen miles below Whitby, where his boyhood was passed. The JEFFERSON FAMILY of Virginia, were from Wales. Their ancestor emigrated from near Mount Snowdon, and was a representative of Flower de Hundred in the Colonial Assembly, convened July 30, 1619, in the choir of the church at Jamestown. His grandson lived at "Osbornes," and had five children: 1, THOMAS, d. yg. 2, FIELD, who emigrated to a place on the Roanoke, near the Carolina line. 3. COL. PETER, b. Feb. 29, 1708, m. 1738, *Jane Randolph*; began life as a surveyor, settled in "Shadwell," an estate including the present site of "Monticello. (An estimate of his character is given in Randall's *Life of Thomas Jefferson*, p. 13). 4, MARTHA, m. *Bennet Goode*, and 5, MARY m. Wm. Turpin, great grandfather of Gen. Edward Johnson, C. S. A., uncle of Mary Turpin Goode, No. 34. Col. Peter Jefferson's daughter Mary was grandmother of the wife of Col. Francis Goode, No. 91.

61.

THOMAS GOODE is a hypothetical personage placed here to fill a hiatus between Thomas Goode, No. 35, and THOMAS GOODE, No. 117, supposed to be his grandson,—certainly great grandson to John Goode, No. 32, and who has no other place as yet in this arrangement.

62.

RICHARD GOODE, of Henrico Co., grandson of No. 26, is placed here provisionally. He was born 1720–50, and is supposed to have lived and died in the vicinity of Richmond. Children:—

118, JOHN GOODE, lived in valley of Va.(?) 119, WILLIAM. 120. ROBERT.

* Virginia Land Register, Book ccccxxvi., p. 875.

THE NORTH CAROLINA GOODES.
63.

EDWARD GOODE, of Virginia, son of Thomas Goode, No. 39, p. 37, was probably born in Henrico Co., and died in Mecklenburg Co., Va. Sons:—

121, EDWARD GOODE, b. 1740–60, d. 1808–10. 122, RICHARD, lived and died in Rutherford Co., N. C. 123, JOSEPH. 124, ABRAHAM, b. in Mecklenburg Co., Va., lived and died in Rutherford Co., N. C. Son or grandson *James Goode*, Rutherford Co., N. C., 1881. 125, THOMAS.

THE CULPEPER GOODES.
64.

JOHN OR DANIEL GOODE, son of Joseph Goode, No. 40, p. 38, was born in Virginia 1715–20, and lived at different times in Culpeper, Amherst and Bedford Counties. Married Miss Campbell. Sons:—

126, WILLIAM GOODE, b. 1743, in Culpeper Co., Va., d. 1815. 127, CAMPBELL. 128, BENJAMIN, b. 1745–60 in Amherst Co., Va. 129, JOSEPH, b. 1750–60 in Bedford Co., Va. 130, JOHN, b. 1750–60, moved West, probably the Rev. John Geode, Baptist preacher in Columbia, S. C., 1813.

The personality of this man is retained in the memories of his great-grandchildren, but they are not exactly sure of his name. Mrs. Mary Goode Carlin wavers between John and Daniel. John Goode of Taylorsville, Ill., thinks it was John. Both recall that his wife was Miss Campbell.

THE RAPPAHANNOCK GOODES.
66.

JOHN GOODE, a Kentucky pioneer, son of Richard Goode, No. 45, p. 38, was born on the James River, early in the 18th century. Was probably a soldier in the Continental Army, and perhaps previously in the Indian wars of Braddock, if traditions are to be trusted. Removed to Kentucky at an early day, and died about 1800 in Lincoln Co. Sons:—

131, PHILEMON GOODE, b. 1745, d. 1850. A soldier in the war of 1812.

Lieutenant Anburey, of the British army, a prisoner of war in Virginia, in 1779, thus describes in his "Travels," the removal of a family westward, which is here quoted as an illustration of a feature in the lives of hundreds of the family in the westward. migrations which will be freqnently recorded in the history of the following generations.

I think nothing more fully evinces the real distresses of the inhabitants in general throughout America, and how great the spirit of persecution and oppression reigns throughout all the provinces, as the amazing emigrations to a new settlement, at a place called Kentucky, where the soil is extremely fruitful, and where there are abundance of buffaloes; the country around, for a great number of miles, is an extensive plain, with very few trees growing on it.   New discoveries are continually making, as to the vast extent of the continent of America, and in some future day it may be learnt, what the boundaries are to the westward. This new settlement is near a thousand miles from this place, nevertheless, those travelling to it, though to so great distance, and perhaps have left houses and plantations, which have been the labor of their whole lives to clear and bring to perfection, appear cheerful and happy, pleased with the idea that they will be free from the tyranny and oppression of the Congress, and its upstart dependents. Their mode of traveling greatly resembles that of the patriarchs of old, for they take with them their horses, oxen, sheep, and other cattle; as likewise all kinds of poultry.   On my journey, I saw a family setting off for this new settlement, leaving behind them a neat habitation, which appeared surrounded with every requisite to make it at once the mansion of content and happiness.   As to the manner of quitting it, the favorite poet, Doctor Goldsmith, has most charmingly described it in the following lines:

> "Good Heavens! What sorrows gloom'd that parting day,
> That called them from their native walks away ;
> When the poor exiles, every pleasure past,
> Hung 'round the bow'rs and fondly look'd their last."

Nor can I more forcibly describe the family's setting out on their journey than he has done, where he says:

> "The good old sire, the first prepared to go,
> To new-found-worlds, and wept for others woe ;
> But for himself in conscious virtue brave,
> He only wished for worlds beyond the grave ;
> His lovely daughter, lovelier in her tears,
> The fond companion of his helpless years ;
> Silent went next, neglected of her charms,
> And left a lover's for a fathers arms ;
> With tender plaints, the mother spoke her woes,
> And blest the cot where ev'ry pleasure 'rose,
> And kist her thoughtless babes with many a tear ;
> And claspt them close in sorrow doubly dear,
> Whilst her fond husband strove to lend relief
> In all the silent manliness of grief."

68.

WILLIAM GOODE, of Essex Co., Va., son of Edward Goode, No. 46, p. 38, was born 1720–60.   The following are supposed to have been his children :—

132, WILLIAM GOODE.   133, CLARA, m. *Joseph Tucker*, 1787.   134, ELEANORA, m. *John Gayle*, 1792.   135, BETSY, m. *Bevin Abbott*, 1798. 136, EWEN, a soldier in the war of 1812.

The family were apparently Baptists,—the names are taken from old marriage records still preserved in Essex Co.

FOURTEENTH GENERATION.

From the moment that (to use the words of Homer) "an infant first falls on the knees of a woman," he possesses, at least in germ, faculties and instincts of a certain kind, and to a certain degree; he is a compound of his father, of his mother, and in general of his race; furthermore, inherited qualities, transmitted through the blood, take in him dimensions and proportions by which he is distinguished from his compatriots and from his relatives.—TAINE: *On the Ideal in Art.*

Both justice and decency require that we should bestow on our forefathers an honorable remembrance.
—THUCYDIDES.

THE PRINCE EDWARD GOODES.

69.

ROBERT GOODE, of Prince Edward Co., Va., son of Samuel Goode, No. 47, p. 39, was born 1720–30, died after 1804. Eldest son an executor of his father's will, 1798. Children:—

137, JOHN COLLIER GOODE, b. 1750–60. 138, ROBERT. 139, SUSANNAH, m. *John H. Osborne.* 140, POLLY, m. *Mr. Brown.* 141, LUCY, m. *Mr. Hatton.* 142, SARAH. 143, FRANCES. 144, ANNE. 145, ELIZABETH. 146, JOSEPH. 147, THOMAS, b. 1780, d. 1865. 148, SAMUEL. 149, WILLIAM.

The will of Robert Goode is recorded at Prince Edward Court House, dated April 8, 1804. Judge F. N. Watkins writes:—

"His will shows great piety, and is a rare paper. He makes provisions for emancipating his slaves thereafter born. It was an almost unheard of thing in those days for a Virginian to favor abolition."

WILL OF ROBERT GOODE.

IN THE NAME OF GOD, AMEN, I, Robert Goode, of Prince Edward County, being, thro the abundant mercy and goodness of God, tho weak in body, yet of a sound and perfect understanding and memory, do constitute this my last will and testament, and desire it to be received by all as such.

Imprimis, I most humbly bequeath my soul to God, my maker, beseeching his most gracious acceptance of it thro the all-sufficient merits and mediation of my most compassionate Redeemer, Jesus Christ, who gave himself to be an atonement for my sins, and is able to save to the uttermost all that come unto God by him, seeing he ever liveth to make intercession for them, and who I trust, will not reject me, a returning, penitent sinner, when I come to him for mercy. In this hope and confidence, I render up my soul with comfort, humbly beseeching the most Blessed and Glorious Trinity, one God, most holy, merciful and gracious, to prepare me for this time of my dissolution, and to take me to himself, unto that peace and rest, and incomparable felicity which he has prepared for those that love and fear his holy name, Amen, blessed be God.

Imprimis, I give my body to the earth from whence it was taken, in full assurance of its resurrection from thence at the last day. As far as my burial, I desire it may be decent, without pomp or state, at the discretion of my dear wife and my executors hereafter named, who I doubt not will manage it with all requisite prudence. As to my worldly estate, I will and positively order that all my just debts be paid.

Item, I give and bequeath to my son Robert Goode, all my tract of land lying in the state of Kentucky, upon Green River, containing five hundred acres, be the same more or less, which land I give to him and his heirs forever.

(Here follow certain special bequests of slaves and money to the children).

Item, my positive will and desire is that after the death of my wife, Sally Goode, that the whole of my negroes, together with those that are or may be lent to any of my children (except all that shall be born of any of my negroes after this date) with eighty pounds, cash, from my daughters Polly Brown, and forty pounds, do., from my daughter Susana Osborne be deposited into one general stock, all of which negroes (to wit.: Gloster, Pheby, Grace, Isabel, Sancho, Ephraim, Bird, Kit, Isham, Nat, Hannah, Jack, Patrick, Nathan, Martin, Judy, Nancy, Dilsey, Caty, and old Dilsey, Effy and Dinah,) and sums of money, I give to be equally divide between my sons and daughters—Susana Osborne, Polly Brown, Lucy Hatten, Sarah, Frances, Anne, Elizabeth G., Joseph and Thomas Goode, all of which I give to them and their heirs forever; also after the decease of my wife, my will and desire is that the whole of my estate, both real and perishable (not before given or accepted) be sold at the discretion of my executors hereafter named, and the money arising from such sale, after paying to John C., Samuel and William Goode the several sums I have before given them, I give, to be equally divided between my sons and daughters, Susana Osborne, Polly Brown, Lucy Hatten, Sarah, Frances, Anne, Elizabeth G., Joseph and Thomas Goode, which legacy I give to them and their heirs forever.

Item, my positive will and desire is that all the unborn negroes that may or shall be born of any of my negroes after this date, be born free, though to be held in servitude by those legatees to whom they may fall till they arrive to the age of twenty-five years, provided those legatees to whom they may fall learn them to read and write, and in case any should refuse to educate them as much as that, my will is they be free at the age of twenty-one years, and I do hereby constitute my sons Joseph and William Goode executors, with my wife, Sallie Goode, executrix of this my last will and testament.

In witness whereof, I have hereunto set my hand and seal, this eighth day of April, in the year of our Lord, eighteen hundred and four.

Signed, sealed and acknowledged:

JOHN H. OSBORNE, THOMAS GOODE, FRANCES GOODE, SUSANA OSBORNE, PHILIP GOODE, REBEKAH GOODE, ANN GOODE.

ROBERT GOODE, SEAL.

70.

PHILIP GOODE, of Amelia Co., Va., son of No. 47, was born in Henrico Co., 1725–35, died in Amelia Co., probably after 1788. Children:—

150, THOMAS GOODE, b. 1750–60. 151, JOHN, b. 1760, d. 1853–60.

The youth of Philip Goode and his brother was passed upon their father's frontier clearing, in Lunenburg Co. He and his brother Mackerness were soldiers in the Indian war of 1758.*

* Hening's Statutes, vii., p. 323.

71.

ANDREW MOORMAN, of Waynesville, Ohio, was born 1730–63, and moved 1800–10 to Warren Co., Ohio. Married PRUDENCE GOODE, daughter of No. 47. Children :—

152, SAMUEL MOORMAN, b. May 16, 1792, d. Aug. 20, 1875. 153, PEYTON.
154, SARAH, m. *Joseph Barker*, had children; all dead, family extinct. 155, KITTY JONES, m. *David Hemmick*, four sons and three daughters; all dead except *Madison* (Iowa, 1885), *Washington*, (Columbia City, Ind.), *David B.*, (Indiana). 156, SUSAN, m. *James L. Johnson*, lived at Jamestown, Ohio. Children :—1, *Clark Johnson; 2, Patsy; 3, Calvin; 4, Jennings; 5, Caroline; 6, Isabel Anna; 7, Nancy Ann; 8, Elizabeth; 9, Susan.*

72.

WILLIAM PRIDE DANIEL, son of William and *Patsy Allen* Daniel, married ANN GOODE, daughter of Samuel Goode, No. 47. Children :—

156-1, SAMUEL DANIEL. 156-2, JOHN. 156-3, WILLIAM PRIDE. 156-4, MARY, m. MR. GOODE (perhaps Thomas Goode, No. 117, who was probably identical with 82½ and son of 49. 156-5, daughter, m. Major Fuqua, of Cumberland Co. 156-6, HEZEKIAH GOODE, b. 1798, d. Dec. 20, 1859.

The Daniel family came to Virginia early in the seventeenth century, and settled in old Rappahannock Co., and its roll bears many distinguished names. The genealogy now being prepared by Rev. Horace E. Hayden will be one of the most important of such works relating to the South. William Pride Daniel was ·uncle of Judge William Daniel, Sr., the grandfather of Hon. John W. Daniel, of Lynchburg, who married a great-granddaughter of No. 73.

73.

THOMAS CLAIBORNE BARKSDALE, of Amelia Co. Va., married, about 1769, SARAH GOODE, daughter of No. 47, and (2), Mrs. Jane Carter (born Morton). Children :—

157, LUCY BARKSDALE, b. Dec. 6, 1766, m. *Col. Edward Tate.* 158, SUSANNAH, b. July 22, 1768, m. *Mr. Crenshaw.* 159, SARAH, b. Oct. 17, 1769, m. *Capt. Dabney Collier.* 160, WILLIAM, b. March 6, 1771, d. unmarried. 161, GRIEF, b. Dec. 25, 1772.
162, AGNES MORTON BARKSDALE, m. *A. W. Whitlock*, has dau. *Sallie N. Barksdale*, of Whitlock P. O., Halifax Co., who has given valuable information. 163, CLAIBORNE, m. *Sallie Read*, dau. *Rev. Clement Read*, and aunt of Martha Goode Read, who m. Dr. Thomas C. Goode, No. 588 (see note on the Read family, page 395). Sons : *Col. Clement R. Barksdale*, C. S. A., Richmond ; *Isaac Barksdale*, Richmond, State Treasurer of Virginia; *T. E. Barksdale*, of Halifax Co. 164, MARY, m. THOMAS GOODE, No. 266.

75.

MACKERNESS GOODE, of Amelia Co., Va., son of No. 47, was born in Henrico Co., 1737–40, and died 1780–1810. A soldier in the Indian wars, 1754–8. Married Mrs. Anderson. Children : —

> 165, ELIZABETH GOODE, m. *Thomas Steger.* 166, NANCY ANN, b. 1774, d. 1841, m. *Gaines Goode.* 167, POLLY, m. *Churchwell Anderson,* of King and Queen Counties, and had many children. 168, GARLAND, d. unmarried. 169, WILDIN, d. unmarried. 170, MACKERNESS, d. unmarried.

76.

SAMUEL GOODE, of Charlotte Co., Va., son of No. 47, was born in Brunswick or Lunenburg Co., March 30, 1749. Married, 1770, Mary Collier, daughter of John and *Elizabeth Meredith* Collier, born Feb. 8, 1756, died in Charlotte Co. about 1804. She was married at the age of 14, and had eleven children : —

> 171, PHILIP GOODE, b. Mar. 15, 1771, d. Sept. 24, 1824. 172, SARAH, b. Feb. 12, 1773, d.y. unmarried. 173, LUCY, b. Feb. 5, 1775, m. *Nelson Dawson.* 174, GAINES, b. Dec. 12, 1776, d. June 13, 1837. 175, SAMUEL, b. Mar. 20, 1779, d. April 28, 1863. 176, NANCY, b. Aug. 17, 1771, m. *Martin Parks.* 177, BURWELL, b. Jan. 30, 1784, d. Dec. 21, 1851. 178, JOHN, b. 1786. 179, ELIZABETH, b. Feb. 19, 1789, d. 1840, m. *Charles Wingfield.* 180, SUSANNA, b. July 30, 1791, d. May, 1841, m. *Jacob Haas.* 181, HENRY JONES, b. April 6, 1799, d. July 10, 1879.

Samuel Goode settled first in Mecklenburg Co., afterwards in Prince Edward Co., whence he moved in 1789 or 1790 to Charlotte Co., and settled upon a small stream called Cub Creek, not far from the noted meeting-house called Rough Creek Church.

He was a planter, owning a few slaves, and an active man, fond of horses and of field sports, especially fox hunting. His wife was a woman of good intellect, and of a very positive, self-reliant nature. She was probably born at " Porto Bello " or in King and Queen Co.

Samuel Goode and his wife were people of sterling character, and were among the earliest in Virginia, and indeed in America, to become identified with the Methodist Church, which was established on this side of the Atlantic soon after their marriage. *

EXCURSUS.—THE COLLIER FAMILY OF VIRGINIA.

The first of the name in America was SAMUEL COLLIER, who came from England in 1607 with the first company of colonists, and who, being a youth,

---

* Methodism was established in Virginia in 1772 by Rev. Robert Williams. A great revival took place in 1776, and in a single year 1993 members were added in this State to the membership of the church in the United States. The number added in other States was 54 The total membership in the United States was 4379 south of the Potomac and 2987 north, with 36 preachers, 18 of whom were sent to Virginia. In 1777, there were 498 members in Mecklenburg Co., 620 in Amelia, and 186 in Charlotte; so it will be seen that Virginia was the stronghold of American Methodism in its early days.—See BENNETT'S *Memorials of Methodism in Virginia,* Richmond, 1871.

Will of Samuel Goode, 1796.

(FROM ORIGINAL IN HIS OWN HANDWRITING IN POSSESSION OF THE AUTHOR.)

In the name of God, Amen! I, Samuel Goode, of the County of Prince Edward, being at this time of sound mind and memory, and recollecting the mortality of my body, do make, ordain and constitute my last will and testament in manner and form following :

Imprimis, I give to my son, Robert Goode, a negro boy named Isham and a negro girl named Lucy, which negroes, them and their increase, I give to him and his heirs forever.

Item, My will and desire is to give to my son, Philip Goode, my negroes, Frank, Rachel and Hezekiah, provided he will pay one hundred pounds in gold or silver, which money I desire to be equally divided among my grandchildren, the sons and daughters of Mackerness Goode, dec'd ; but in case the said Philip Goode should refuse to pay one hundred pounds, that Frank, Rachel and Hezekiah should all be sold together in my family, and the money arising from such sale be equally divided among my grandchildren, the sons and daughters of Mackerness Goode, dec'd, as before mentioned.

Item, I give to my son, Philip Goode, all the negroes which he had of me, being now in his possession ; them and their increase I give to him and his heirs forever.

Item, I lend to my daughter, Prudence Moorman, a negro woman named Lydda and a negro girl named Lydda during her natural life, and after her death to be equally divided between my two granddaughters, Susanna Moorman and Kitty Jones Moorman, which negroes, and what they hereafter increase I give to them and their heirs forever.

Item, I lend to my granddaughter, Susanna Crenshaw, daughter of Sarah Barksdale, dec'd, four negroes, namely, a negro woman named Hannah, a negro woman named Lueisa, a negro boy named Spencer, and a negro boy Jack during her natural life, and after her decease to leave the said negroes to be equally divided among all her children as they arrive to the age of twenty-one or marry ; but if they should die before they arrive to that age or marry, I give and bequeath the said negroes and their increase to be equally divided between my grandchildren, the sons and daughters of Sarah Barksdale, dec'd, namely, Lucy Tate, Sarah Barksdale, William Barksdale and Grief Barksdale, to them and their heirs forever.

Item, I give and bequeath to my great granddaughter, Sally Mackerness Tate, daughter of my granddaughter, Lucy Tate, a negro girl named Polly, and whatsoever increase she may hereafter have, to her and her heirs forever.

Item, My will and desire is that my grandson John C. Goode, son of Robert Goode, should have the use and benefit of the houses, land and plantation whereon I now live until the expiration of the year 1797.

Item, I give and bequeath to my son-in-law, William P. Daniel, the plantation whereon I now live, and all my land adjoining thereto, except half an acre reserved for a burying place, to him and his heirs forever, reserving to my grandson, John C. Goode, the use and benefit of the houses, land and plantation till the expiration of the year 1797.

Item, I lend to my daughter, Ann Daniel, the following negroes during her natural life, namely, a negro man named Isaac, a negro woman named Dilsy, a negro woman named Phillis, and what they have already increased, or shall hereafter increase, and after his death I leave them to be equally divided among all her children, which negroes are in possession of Wm. P. Daniel, them and their increase I give to them and their heirs forever. I also lend to my daughter, Ann Daniel, a negro woman named Nancy, and her child Franky, during her life, and after her death I leave them and their increase to be equally divided amongst all her children, which I give to them and their heirs forever.

Item, I give and bequeath to my grandson, John C. Goode, son of Robert Goode, a negro man named Jesse, to him and his heirs forever.

The remaining part of my estate, after my just debts are paid, I leave to be equally divided between my son, Robert Goode, my daughter, Prudence Moorman, and my granddaughter, Nancy Goode, daughter of Samuel Goode, dec'd

I do hereby appoint my son, Robert Goode, executor of this my last will and testament, revoking and disannulling all other wills by me heretofore made, acknowledging this and no other to be my last will and testament. In confirmation of the whole and every part of it I have hereto set my hand and seal this 19 day of August, 1796.

Signed, sealed and acknowledged in the presence of John Crute, John Arms.

SAMUEL GOODE.

acted as "page" to Capt. John Smith, whom he accompanied in his exploring excursions into the unknown parts of Virginia.*

In 1609, he was left among the Indians at Warraskoyack to learn their language, and in 1622 we read that : "Quartering about Kecoughtan, after the watch was set, *Samuel Collyer*, one of the most ancientest planters and very well acquainted with their language and habitation (that of the salvages), humors and conditions, and Governor of a Town, when the watch was set, going the round, unfortunately by a centinell that discharged his piece, was slaine."†

Samuel Collier, of course, left no children. The next record of the name is in the case of DANIEL COLLIER, aged 30, who sailed July 6, 1635, "in the Paule of London, bound to Virginia."‡ HENRY COLLIER, probably a recent arrival, received Aug. 28, 1657, a grant of 50 acres in New Kent Co.§ Rev. Mr. Collier, of Hunger's‖ Parish, who about 1703 married the Widow Kendall, was possibly the *propositus* of the Virginia Colliers. The children of Cornelius Collier, No. 3, were told by their parents that they were related to Sir George Ralph Collier (b. 1773), which is an indication that their ancestor left England after 1650, for otherwise the connection would have been too remote to be remembered. Capt. Ralph Collier, of "Eton Court," Oxfordshire (b. 1670–90, d. 1759), was grandfather of Sir George, may have been brother or own cousin of John Collier, the *propositus* of the Virginia family, in which case the children of Cornelius Collier would have been second or third cousins of the conqueror of St. Sebastian.

The arms of the Oxfordshire Colliers are identical with those of the Colliers of "Darliston," in Staffordshire, viz : *or, a cross patchee, fitchee, gules*, and

there can be little doubt that the following deduction, given in the Staffordshire Visitation of 1663 belongs in the early generations to the *Colliers of Virginia.*

John Dodington=
Sir John Dodington=
Ralph Collier=Isabel Dodington, d. and h.
a Frenchman,   James Collier=d. of—Levenson.
came to Eng-   Robert Collier=Agnes, dau. of Sir
land last years   Thomas Venable.
of Henry VI.,   James Collier=Jane Needham, of
sojourned at   "Shenstone."
"Darliston."   Francis Collier=Ann, dau. of Wm.
         Crumpton.
Robert Collier=Margaret, dau. of Edw. Aston.
Jane Collier=Oct. 28, 1663.

FIRST GENERATION.

"JOHN COLLIER, of Little York, Va.," was born 1670-1685, and was, it is believed, either a native of England or the son of an Englishman. He lived

---

* See Records of the Virginia Company and Smith's writings.
† Smith's General Historie, IV., p. 158.
‡ Hotten's Lists of Emigrants.
§ Virginia Land Register, IV., 147.
‖ Spelled Hungars usually.

on the York River, not far above Yorktown, and his estate was named " Porto Bello." This name was given to it after the return of his two sons, who were, according to family tradition and record, officers in one of the Virginia regiments accompanying Admiral Vernon in the Carthagena expedition in 1740–42, and in honor of the famous fortress of "Porto Bello" on the Spanish Main. Lawrence Washington was a Captain in the same regiment, and at about the same time gave his plantation on the Potomac the name "Mount Vernon." Porto Bello appears to have passed out of the family about the middle of the last century,* perhaps when the sons or grandsons joined Braddock's Expedition.

John Collier married (1) Miss Ballard, (?) of Virginia, no issue; (2) Miss Gaines, and had one son; (3) Nancy Eppes or Eyes; issue: 2, JOHN; 3, CORNELIUS; 4, WILLIAM; 5, JAMES; 6, BENJAMIN; 7, MARY; 8, FRANCIS; 9, JUDITH (dau. or niece) m. *James Hicks;* 10, THOMAS (son or nephew).

SECOND GENERATION.

2. JOHN COLLIER, of "Porto Bello," was born 1707–17. He probably inherited the paternal estate, and was one of the sons who accompanied Admiral Vernon to Carthagena, for most of his brothers would have been too young. It seems probable that before his father's death he engaged in planting on the right bank of the James, for we find that John Collier took up 50 acres in Isle of Wight Co. July 20, 1738; in 1745 John and Thomas (perhaps No. 10) Collier were extensive planters of tobacco in Surry. Married 1730–40 Elizabeth (?) Meredith,† probably of New Kent or King William. Issue :—

    11, THOMAS. 12, JOHN. 13, JOSEPH. 14, MARY, b. 1756, m. *Samuel Goode.* 15, *Mrs. Hutchinson*, of Mecklenburg Co. 16, SALLY, m. *Robert Goode.* 17, MRS. INGRAM. 18, *Mrs. Turner.*.

3. CORNELIUS COLLIER, of Abbeville District, S. C., son of No. 1 by third wife, was born at Porto Bello 1720–30, and removed about the middle of the century to a place on the Meherrin River, where he owned large tracts, probably in Lunenburg Co., and in or near what is now Charlotte Co. His plantation houses were occupied by Tarleton during his raid in 1776. After the Revolution in 1802 he removed with his family to South Carolina. Married Elizabeth, dau. of John W. Wyatt, of Gloucester Co., who was grandson either of Sir Francis Wyatt, Governor of Virginia, or more probably of Rev. Hawte Wyatt, his brother. Issue :—

    20, JOHN. 21, JAMES. 22, WYATT. 23, WILLIAM. 24, EDWARD. 25, NANCY WYATT, m. *Joshua Hill.*

4. WILLIAM COLLIER, probably of Surry Co., was perhaps the William Collier who took up 500 acres in Surry in 1731. Married Miss Carter (probably niece of "King Carter"). Issue :

    26, CARTER COLLIER. 27, MRS. TOWNLEY. 28, MRS. MANN. 29, MRS. MILLER. 30, MRS. WEBLEY.

5. JAMES COLLIER, Sr., who probably lived on "The Peninsula. Issue :

---

* "Porto Bello" was the country residence of Lord Dunmore, last Colonial Governor of Virginia, and it was thither that his household retired from Williamsburg at the outbreak of the Revolution. It now belongs to Col. Timberlake.

† For notice of MEREDITH FAMILY see page 290.

31, JAMES. 32, THOMAS, perhaps the ancestor of the Colliers of Elizabeth City Co.

6. BENJAMIN COLLIER lived on "The Peninsula," married Miss Cox. Issue:—
34, THOMAS. 35, MRS. IRONMONGER. 36, MRS. JACOB MCGEEHEE.

7. MARY COLLIER m. ROBERT CARTER, brother of wife No. 4. Issue :
38, JOHN CARTER. 39, JAMES. 40, WILLIAM. 41, MRS. WHITE. 42, MRS. MERREDY (Meredith ?). 43, MRS. PHILLIPS, of New Castle, Va.

8. FRANCIS COLLIER m. CAPT. JAMES SCOTT. Issue : —
44, THOMAS SCOTT. 45, JAMES. 46, GEN. JOHN. 47, NANCY, m. *Micajah McGeehee.* 48, POLLY. 49, MILLY. 50, FRANCIS. 51, LUCY, d. unmarried.

9. JUDITH COLLIER m. JAMES HICKS, of Brunswick Co., Va., and had two daughters and five sons, four of whom were officers in the Continental Army, and two of whom were captured by the British at the battle of Brier Creek, Ga. Probably lived at Hicksford, in that part of the county subsequently set aside as Greensville Co. Issue :—
52, CAPT. CHARLES HICKS, revolutionary patriot. 53, ISAAC. 54, GEORGE, d. in Georgia. 55, JOHN, d. near Bruce's Church, Brunswick Co. 56, JAMES, d. near Jericho, Brunswick Co. 57, VINES, moved to Tennessee. 58, SARAH, b. 1762, m. *Robert Hardaway.* 59, ANN VINES, b. 1766, m. *Dr. William G. Walker.*

10. THOMAS COLLIER, of "Wyanoke," Charles City Co., Va., took up June 16, 1738, 225 acres of land at a place called Wyanoak (Land Register XVII, 8). Issue :—(Provisional).
60, Daughter, m. *Mr. Harrison.* 61, Daughter, m. *Mr. Minge.*

THIRD AND LATER GENERATIONS.

11, CAPT. THOMAS COLLIER, of Charlotte Co., Va., a soldier in Braddock's campaign and the Revolution, took up 282 acres in Brunswick Co. in 1763, and for public services was granted 3,000 acres in Mason Co., Ky., to which his descendants removed. Married Miss Dabney, of Hanover Co. Children: 101, BENJAMIN COLLIER, of Early Co., Ga., who had issue : 1, *Elizabeth*, m. John Bacon, of Charlotte Co., and was ancestor of the Bacons, Steptoes and Picketts, of Mason Co., Ky. 2, *Robert*, of Barnesville, Ga., m. Martha Booker; descendants live in Georgia and Alabama. 3, *Benjamin*. 4, *Mrs. Hardeman*, whose son, Hon. Thomas Hardeman, of Macon, Ga., was member of Congress, C. S. A. and U. S. A. 102, MARTHA, m. Daniel Osborne, of Mason Co., Ky. 103, ANNE, m. *Frank Gaines*, of Charlotte Co. 104, *Elizab.th*, m. John Ingram, of Nottoway, son moved to Missouri. 106, DABNEY (see No. 159 of the Goode Pedigree.) 107, FRANCES, m. *D. D. Morgan*, of Charlotte Co. Issue: 1, *Frances Collier*, m. Col. Henry Bacon, of Charlotte Co. 2, *Martha Dabney*, m. Capt. Thomas Jones, of Nottoway. 3, *Thomas*. 4, *Angelina*, m. W. W. Bouldin. 5, *William E.*, m. Sallie Puryear, of Mecklenburg Co.

12, MAJ. JOHN COLLIER, of Madison Co., Ky.; a soldier of the Revolution, and had a wooden leg, m. Miss Cary(?). Issue: 108, JAMES, of Madison Co., Ky.; had son Lewis, b. 1802, d. 1881, who went to Howard Co., Mo., in 1824, and had son, Luther T. Collier, of Chillicothe, Mo., and others.   109, JOHN, of Indiana.   110, LUCY, m. *Joseph Henderson*, of Mo.; also, probably 110, CAPT. NATHANIEL, of Dinwiddie Co., an officer in the war of 1812, who died in service at Norfolk in 1814.   Married Sally Williamson, of S. C., (related to the Goodwyns and Boisseaus) and had son, Hon. ROBERT RUFFIN COLLIER, of Petersburg, Va., a prominent public man, b. Oct. 16, 1804, d. March 3, 1870, m. Mary Ann, daughter of Samuel and Francis (Tinsley) Davis, and had *Hon. Chas. Fenton Collier*, Mayor of Petersburg, member of Confederate Congress, President Petersburg and Weldon R. R.   *James E., Nathaniel Macon, Robert Williamson*, member of the Petersburg City Council, *Fannie* and *Stirling Kennon*.   Col. James Collier, of Steubenville, Ohio, born in 1792, died in 1873, soldier in the war of 1812, member of the Ohio and Virginia Boundary Commission and pioneer settler of California, was grandson of No. 12 or 13.

13, JOSEPH COLLIER, of South Carolina; had, it is believed, 112–13, MEREDITH and MERRILL COLLIER, twins, who went to Georgia in 1800; former had son, HENRY GAINES COLLIER, whose son, W. E. Collier, lives at Fort Valley, Ga.; other descendants named Talbert in Yalabusha Co., Miss.

20, JOHN COLLIER, of Columbia Co., Ga., a soldier in the Revolution, m. (1) Peggy Tyler, (2) Lucinda Glover.   Issue: 151, DR. WILLIAM COLLIER, m. Sarah German; descendants in Georgia named Elliott, Hart, Miller and Sibley.   152, EDWARD WYATT, of Augusta, Ga., m. Lucy Key; descendants in Edgefield, S. C.

21, JAMES COLLIER, of Madison Co., Ala., born 1757, died 1832; Revolutionary soldier, m. Elizabeth Bouldin, daughter of James and *Sally Watkins* Bouldin, granddaughter of Col. Thomas and *Nancy Clark* Bouldin, of Charlotte Co.; moved in 1802 to South Carolina, and in 1818 to Alabama.   Issue: 153, BOULDIN COLLIER, planter of Morgan Co., Ala., m. Sarah Slaughter. 154, WYATT, of Florence, Ala., m. James Walker, aunt of Gen. William Walker, of Nicaragua.   Issue in Alabama and Tennessee named Simpson, Colyer and Estes; his daughter Mary m. Col. Arthur S. Colyer, of Nashville. 155, MARTHA WATKINS, m. *William A. Slaughter;* descendants lived in Alabama and Mississippi.   156, DR. JAMES BOULDIN, descendants in South and West.   157, ELIZA WYATT, m. *W. H. Blackwell*, cousin of President Tyler; children in Alabama and Arkansas named Blackwell, Pickett, Wiggs, &c. 158, WILLIAM E., of Alabama; descendants in Alabama and Arkansas named Pickett, Handy, Ferrill.   159, HENRY WATKINS, b. Jan. 17, 1801, d. Aug. 28, 1855, an eminent jurist and Governor of Alabama.   (See Brewer's Alabama, Garrett's Public Men of Alabama, and the Encyclopædias), m. 1826, Mary Williams Battle.   Among his children were: 1, Mary W., m. Prof. G. W. Benagh, of the University of Alabama; 2, Evelyn H., m. Capt. W. T. King, C. S. A., killed at Manassas ; 3, Sally B., m. Battle Fort, of Columbus, Miss. 160, THOMAS B.   161, CHARLES E., of Triana, Ala.

22, WYATT COLLIER, a soldier of the Revolution; killed in the battle of

Eutaw Springs. 23, WILLIAM COLLIER, of Alabama, a soldier of the Revolution; no living descendant. 24, EDWARD COLLIER, of Augusta, Ga.; no descendants.

25, JOSHUA HILL, of Virginia, b. 1763, left descendants, in Alabama, Georgia and Mississippi named Foster, Jones, Buchanan, Bruce, Daniel. His son, Judge Edward Y. Hill, of La Grange, Ga., was a prominent lawyer and politician, and his son, Hon. Joshua Hill, of Madison, has represented his State in Congress in House and Senate.

31, JAMES COLLIER had 181, COL. JAMES COLLIER, of Xenia, Ohio. 182, Moses, of Green Co., Ohio. 183, MRS. AGNES PARKS, of Garrett Co., Ky.

53, ISAAC HICKS, of Brunswick Co., Va., a Captain in the Continental army; had issue: 201, REBECCA, m. *Gilliam Booth*, of Nottoway; their son, Edward Gilliam Booth lived in Philadelphia, and built the Virginia House at the Centennial. (See his Life by H. E. Dwight.) His son, Dr. E. G. Booth, owns "Carter's Grove." 202, REUBEN BOOTH, a weathy planter; had daughter-Louisa, who married Maj. Gen. William E. Starke, C. S. A., killed at Sharpsburg. 203, THOMAS, of Brunswick Co. 204, SALLY, m. *Benj. Booth*, of Amelia. 205, BET'SY, m. *Robert C. Booth*, of Dinwiddie. 206, MINERVA, m. *Dr. Cabaniss*, of Petersburg, and left issue.

58, ROBERT HARDAWAY, has grandson, Prof. R. A. Hardaway, of the University of Alabama.

60, MRS. ELIZABETH HARRISON, has son, COLLIER HARRISON, of Charles City Co., whose daughter, Elizabeth Collier, m. Benj. Carter Harrison, whose daughter Mary, m. George Minge, of Alabama. 61, MRS. MINGE, of " Wyanoke," had son, JOHN, of " Wyanoke," who m. Sarah Harrison, sister of President Harrison, and had issue, who are named in the " Carter Tree : " among them were John Minge, who graduated at William and Mary in 1870. Sally m. Gen. George E. Pickett, C. S. A., Collier Harrison Minge, of Mobile, Eliza m. Hugh Nelson, of Petersburg, and Margaret, who m. Dr. Reuben H. Dugger, No. 1259 of the *Goode Genealogy*—others named Wilkins, Dixie, Adams, Carter, Routh, Harris, Gwathmey, Otey.

(Fuller records of the Collier family are in the possession of Mrs. Mary Collier Benagh, of Birmingham, Ala., and of the writer. Copies will be given to the Virginia Historical and the N. E. Historic Genealogical Societies.)

THE LUNENBURG GOODES.

77.

JOHN GOODE, of Wilkes Co., Ga., son of William Goode, No. 48, p. 40, was born in Virginia in 1720–50, and married Francis Hunter. Children : —

> 181, JOHN GOODE. 182, ANN or NANCY, b. Sept. 16, 1770, m. *John Andrews.* 183, SARAH, m. *John Wright.* 184, MARTHA, m. *Mr. Morgan.* 185, RICHARD. 186, WILLIAM. 187, a son, supposed to have lived in Western Georgia or Alabama. 187½, MARY, m. *William Vason.*

John Goode is supposed to have been one of the early settlers in Georgia before or immediately after the Revolution, since all his children were there at an early age, probably one of the considerable colony who settled at the time of the Revolutionary War, or a little before, in Wilkes County.

THE BEDFORD GOODES.

79.

EDMUND GOODE, of Bedford Co., Va., son of No. 48, born 1730-50, died 1800-30. Married Miss Branch, his cousin, daughter of No. 88, p. 42. Elizabeth Goode, who married Mr. Branch. Children :—

188, JOHN.GOODE, b. 1796, d. 1876. 189, SUSAN, m. *Samuel Hobson*, of Bedford Co. No issue. (See note on Povall Family.)

Edmund Goode lived for a time in Bowling Green, Caroline Co., whence he removed to Bedford Co. It was probably he to whom, Aug. 27, 1770, was granted 1630 acres of land in Bedford Co. He was a soldier in the war of the Revolution, and either before or immediately after the war removed to the beautiful region near the base of the Peaks of Otter.

THE EDGEFIELD GOODES.

80.

PHILIP GOODE, of Edgefield District, S. C., son of Philip Goode, No. 49, p. 41, was born in South Carolina, 1769-85, died 1808. Married Caroline Williams. Children :—

190, PHILIP GOODE, d. y. 191, SAMUEL d.y. 192, THOMAS, removed to Mississippi; had sons. 1, *Thomas Goode*, (see No. 313, P, 70, p. 132). 2, *Richard*, (No. 314, p. 70.) 193, MACKERNESS. 194, GARLAND, b. 1811. 195, DUKE, d. in Mobile, 1830-50. 195½, LLWELLYN, d. y.

81.

SAMUEL GOODE, of Edgefield District, S. C., son of No 49, is a person of whom we know little. The hazy recollections of 149 would seem to indicate that he or one of his brothers was a man of prominence— member of the legislature of South Carolina or Virginia. Son :—

196, JOHN GOODE, of Abbeville District, S. C., b. 1760-80, m. Ann Freeman, had issue as enumerated upon p. 186.

THE LUNENBURG GOODES.

83.

JOHN or SAMUEL GOODE, of Mecklenburg Co., Va., son of Mackerness Goode, No. 50, p. 41. Children :—

197, SAMUEL WATKINS GOODE, b. 1768. 198, ANN, m. *Joseph Bryan*. 199, MARTHA, m. *Thaddeus Holt*. 200, MACKERNESS. 201, JOHN. 202, PHILIP ?. 203, a son, settled in Ky. or Tenn.

No. 83 appears to have been a soldier in the Revolution ; he undoubtedly met his death either in war or at the hands of the Tories. The family appears to have been driven from its home near Richmond to the lower part of Virginia by the persecutions of the Tories. The wife of No. 83 was probably a Miss Watkins, who after his death seems to have married Mr. Lancaster about 1780.

THE CHARLOTTE GOODES.

84.

MACKERNESS GOODE, of Charlotte Co., Va., son of Mackerness Goode, No. 50, p. 41, was born 1710–40, and died about 1815. Married Miss Moseley.   Children :—

204, EDWARD GOODE, b. 1760–70, d. 1803, m. Joyce Holmes, and had issue. 581, *Martha Mackerness Goode*, b. 1799, m. 1818 William Rawlins. Issue: 1, *James M. Rawlins*, of Rockingham, N. C.; 2, *Samuel*, of Tennessee; 3, *Martha Ann*, m. Samuel Ferguson, and had two daughters, Bettie and Mackerness, who live in Union Level, Va. 582, *Elizabeth Ann*, b. 1801, m. John E. Rawlins, hand issue : 1, *Walter M.*, m. Miss Hugarths, and has several children; 2, *Minerva*, m. Branch Cheatham, of Lunenburg Co., Va., and had issue : Thomas, John, Conrad, Walter, and Annie, who m. John P. Finch; 3, *John E.*, m. (1) Harriet Price, and has son Cabell Price, of Prince Edward Co., m. (2) a lady in Texas and died in Fanning Co., Texas, while raising a company for the Confederacy; 4, *Harriet J.*, m. John Ingram, of Fanning Co., Texas; 5, *Robert S.;* 6, *Ann Eliza;* 7, *Conrad;* 8, *Marcellus;* 9, *Lavinia*, m. Mr. Cheatham, of Manchester, Va., has daughter Ruth, said to be very beautiful. 583, *Harriette Edward*, b. Feb. 23, 1803, d. April 21, 1826, m. James McCargo, issue : 1, *Thomas Edward McCargo;* 2, *James David;* 3, *Harriette M.*, m. Samuel W. Simmons, children :—James Edward and Richard Green ; 4, *Jeannette W.*, m. Samuel W. Simmons (her brother-in-law), issue: Orlando Lee, Samuel Wilkins, Redford McCargo, Thomas Goode, Lolo Otilia, (Mrs. William Gill) Angelina Jeannette; 5, *Maria L.* m. J. H. Warren. Issue: Miller Walker, Harriett Rebecca, Joseph H., Mary E., Samuel McCargo. 6, *Ann Eliza*, m. J. E. Gregory, of Five Forks, Va. Issue: Bettie, m. Lawson Jones, of Charlotte Co.; Irene, m. J. Lawson Jones, of Granville, N. C.; 7, *Joyce H.*, m. C. C. Smithson, had daughter Ellen, (Mrs. W. W. Warren,) who has several children; 8, Martha F., m. P. H. Hubbard, of Cuscowilla, Va., has adopted Thomas Goode Simmons, son of her sister, No. 4.

205. JOHN, m. Mary Jones. Issue: 1384, *Mackerness Hillery Goode*. 1385, *Edward Jones*. 1386, Mary E., m. Asa Breckinridge, (see p. 330). 1387, *Nathaniel Bacon*. 1387-1, *John*. 1387-2, *Langston T.* 1387-3, *Frances*, m. T. J. North. 1387-4, *Agnes*, m. John Gregory. 1387-5, *Virginia*, m. Stephen May. 1387-6, *Margaret*, m. William Billups. (For issue see pages 329, 330.)

206. THOMAS. (Descendants given on page 99.)

207. WILLIAM, m. Mary Tabb. (For issue see pages 195, 196.)

208. HILLERY, (Descendants given on page 99.)

209. MACKERNESS, m. Ann Elizabeth Hayes; had five daughters, one of

whom, Mrs. Martha Green Hatcher, lived in 1886 in Winfield, Conley Co., Kan.; her daughter Eloise married No. 817, p. 240.

209–A. SALLY, m. *John McCue* (or McQuoy,) Mecklenburg Co.

209–B. MARY, m. *James Jones*, of Mecklenburg Co.

209–C. ELIZABETH, m. *Robert Jones*, of Mecklenburg Co.

Mackerness Goode was apparently a man of some prominence in his county in his day. Mr. Brock sends the following extract from the *Journal of the House of Delegates* of Virginia, June 6, 1777 :

"*Resolved*, That Paul Carrington, William Hubard, William Booker, John Morton, James Speed and Mackerness Goode, gentlemen, or any three of them, be appointed commissioners to inquire into the state of the arms lodged in the public magazine, built during the last war in the county of Lunenburg, under the direction of Col. Clement Read, deceased, and make report to the next session of assembly; and they are to have power to send for persons, papers and records for their information."

THE WEST–CHESTERFIELD GOODES.

85.

REV. JOHN GOODE, of Goode's Bridge, Va., son of Edward Goode, No. 51, p. 41, was born near Four-Mile Creek, Henrico Co., Va., March, 1738, died June 12, 1790. Married Sarah Brown, of Chesterfield Co., b. Feb. 13, 1745, d. 1812. Children :—

210, WILLIAM GOODE, b. Oct. 25, 1761. d. Sept. 27, 1845. 211, JOHN, b. Jan. 22, 1766. 212, ROBERT, b. Jan. 22, 1766. ANNE, b. Feb. 16, 1764, d. Sept. 18, 1830, m. *David Ford.* Issue : 1, *Reuben Ford;* 2, *John;* 3, *Enoch;* 4, *David;* 5, *Polly;* 6, *Nancy;* 7, *Betsy;* 8, *Caty.* Descendants numerous in Chesterfield and Augusta counties. 215, POLLY, b. Jan. 10, 1782, m. *Towns Binns,* went to Kentucky, names of children not known. 216, SUSANNA, b. Dec. 1, 1784, m. *Benjamin Farmer;* went to Kentucky; children unknown. 217, BENJAMIN, b. March 3, 1771, d. July 10, 1830. 218, JOSEPH, b. April 4, 1776. 219, MACK, b. March 9, 1779. 220, REV. EDMOND, b. Feb. 27, 1780. 221, ELIZABETH, b. June 9, 1778, d. Aug. 20, 1821, m. *Williamson H. Pitman.* Issue: 1, *Jefferson;* 2, *Silas;* 3, *John;* 4, *Edmund.* 222, MARGARET, b. July 12, 1770, m. *Jesse Butler.* Issue: 1, *Archer;* 2, *William;* 3, *Harriet.* 223, SARAH, b. Sept. 30, 1786, m. *Rev. Boswell Traylor,* of Cumberland Co. Issue: 1, *Archer;* 2, *Joseph;* 3, *James* (soldier C. S. A.); 4, *Sally;* 5, *Martha;* 6, *Geo. W.* (soldier C. S. A., killed in war.) 224, TARPLEY, b. May 12, 1780, d. Jan. 21, 1814.

John Goode removed in 1759 from Henrico to Chesterfield Co. In 1778 he was converted under the ministry of Elder William Hickman, with whom he accompanied in an early missionary exploration of Kentucky. He soon engaged in preaching, and was ordained June 18, 1780. He was pastor of Skinquarter Church till 1790. His biography is printed in Taylor's *Lives of*

Virginia Baptist Ministers, Richmond, 1838, (2d ed.), a work full of interest to students of the history of early religious movements in Virginia.

The children of John Goode were all residents of Chesterfield Co., except three of the sisters who moved to Kentucky. They seem to have been men and women of great force of character, who made a strong impression upon the community in which they lived. All the brothers, except Tapley, lived to an advanced age, the average being, I think, somewhere near sixty-eight years. They are spoken of to this day by every one in that region as the "old Goodes." All, except two, Benjamin and Tapley, were members of the Baptist church. They were remarkable for their strict integrity. It is said that they would never sell anything for a cent less than they considered it worth, and that if one of them had a horse to sell and was offered more than what he considered to be its value, he would refuse to receive it.

The eight brothers had 68 sons and daughters. The total number of their grand-children in 1870, was 229, and of great grand-children, 271. The latter number, in 1880, probably exceeds 400, while the total number of descendants, of Rev. John Goode in the third and fourth generation, cannot be estimated at less than 1000. As may be imagined, the whole of the western part of Chesterfield County in which the brothers lived, is peopled with their posterity. I visited this region in 1880, and found scarcely any one who did not claim to inherit a share of Goode blood.

Miss Anna Lewis Goode, grand-daughter of John Goode, one of the brothers, No. 211, contributes the following reminiscence :

"All the old Goodes were Baptists, and the most of them very pious. When I was very small, my parents used to take me to Skinquarter Baptist Church, of which Elder John Goode was once pastor ; at the time I speak of, Elder Goode was dead, but he had four or five sons who appeared to me to be real 'Patriarchs,' so venerable looking they were, and I think that all of his sons, and the most of his grand-sons were noted for their integrity and uprightness in every respect ; none of them were very wealthy (save Col. Bob), but the most of them were in comfortable circumstances, some quite independent. Their characteristic features were a good, rather broad forehead, heavy brows, large mouth, nose, and hair inclined to light color, though some of them have very black hair and eyes, while others have blue and hazel eyes.

"My father's brother William was called the handsomest man in his county, and his sister Lavinia, was one of the prettiest women I have ever seen. In size, they were rather above the medium, as a general thing."

THE HENRICO GOODES.

86.

JOHN GOODE of Darbytown, son of No. 52, p. 42, born in Henrico Co., 1730–50, died at his home near the present site of Darbytown, a suburb of Richmond, 1780–1820. Married twice ; three sons by first marriage, one by last.

225, DANIEL GOODE, b. about 1760, d. at Deep Run, 1800–30. 226, CHARLES, b. 1750–1800, d. at Four Mile Creek, about 1840. 227, JOHN, b. 1780–90, d. 1824–40, m. *Polly Goode*. 228, THOMAS.

87.

BENJAMIN GOODE, of the White Oaks, son of No. 52, p. 42, was born 1730–50, died 1780–1810, in Henrico Co., Va.

229, SAMUEL GOODE, b. 1750–80, d. before 1822. 230, BENJAMIN. 231, JOSEPH. 232, THOMAS. A farmer in the White Oak Swamp.

Benjamin Goode owned large estates in Henrico County, in the White Oak Swamp district, inheriting the old homestead of his father, and perhaps of his grandfather. The house was torn down in 1875.

Previous to 1822, the family is said to have been prosperous, owning many slaves who were hired out in Richmond, the house being a favorite meeting-place for the fox hunts in that neighborhood.

Concerning the decay of the well-to-do Virginia families, Bishop Meade writing of a parish in tide-water Virginia, remarks:

"Formerly this was one of the most flourishing parishes in Virginia. In my early youth I remember to have heard my parents speak of it as having what is called the best society in Virginia. The families were interesting, hospitable, given to visiting and social pleasures. The social glass, the rich feast, the card-table, the dance and the horse-race were all freely indulged in throughout the county, and what has been the result ? I passed through the length and breadth of this parish more than twenty years ago, (about 1835), in company with my friend, David Meade Walke, son of the old minister of the parish, who was well acquainted with its past history and present condition, and able to inform me where were once the estates through which we passed; who could point me to the ruins of family seats which had been consumed by fire; could tell me what were the causes of bankruptcy and ruin, and untimely death of those who once formed the gay society of the county. Cards, the bottle, the horse-race, the continual feasts,—these were the destroyers."

A graphic description of an old-time Virginia fox-hunt may be found in John Esten Cooke's romance, *The Virginia Comedians*, Vol. II., p. 100.

THE WHITBY GOODES.

89.

SETH WARD, of Powhatan Co., Va., son of Thomas Ward, was born at "Sheffield," 1720–30. Married MARY GOODE, daughter of Robert Goode, No. 56, p. 42. Children :—

233, SETH WARD, b. 1760–70. 234, MARY, m. (1), *Mr. Hylton*, (2), *Dr. Cringan* of Richmond. 235, LUCY, m. *Henry Randolph* of Warwick.

90.

COL. ROBERT GOODE, of Whitby, son of Robert and *Mary Turpin* Goode, No. 56, p. 42, was born at Whitby, Feb. 8, 1743, d. April 20, 1809. A wealthy planter, an officer in the Continental Army, member of the Council for Virginia, 1790–97. Married, June 18, 1768, Sally Bland,* of "Jordans," Prince George Co., b. Sept. 30, 1750, died May 13, 1807. Children :—

---

*THE BLAND FAMILY is of ancient origin (see Carlisle's *History of the Bland Family*, London, 1826; *The Bland Papers*, ed. by C. Campbell, Petersburg, 1840; Slaughter's *History of Bristol Parish*, etc.)

236, SALLY BLAND GOODE, b. Sept. 30, 1750, d. y. 237, ROBERT, b. Mar. 9, 1769, d. Nov. 22, 1788. 238, RICHARD BLAND, b. Dec. 7, 1770, m. Dec. 10, 1796, *Sally H. Woodson*, of Chesterfield Co., graduated William and Mary College, 1794, d. July 28, 1812, s. p. 239, FRANCIS, b. May 5, 1773, d. April 7, 1814. 240, THEODORICK BLAND, b. Dec. 12, 1774, d. May 3, 1800, unm. 241, MARY, b. July 25, 1776, d. July 21, 1847, m. *John Spotswood.* 242, SALLY BLAND, b. Aug. 5, 1779, d. Jan. 19, 1816, m. (1) *James Lyle*, (2) *Tarlton Saunders.* 243, MARTHA CURRIE, b. Feb. 22, 1787, d. May 1, 1814, m. *James Scott.* 244, THOMAS, b. Jan. 4, 1789, d. May 3, 1810, unm.

Col. Robert Goode, of Whitby, was more prominent than any other member of the family in the social and political life of old Virginia,—a man of wealth and influence, the possessor, by entail, of the ancestral estate and its belongings, and a member of the wealthier class of planters, whose characteristics have been so well depicted by John Esten Cooke, in his novel, *The Virginia Comedians*, and his other writings, and by Thackeray in *The Virginians.*

Mrs. Lemoine, now living in St. Louis at an advanced age, remembers her grandfather—"an officer of the Revolutionary war, as a genial, open-hearted, hospitable gentleman, who entertained largely at his seat, Whitby, the elite of Richmond, and of all tide-water Virginia."

and of purely English extraction. They derive their name from "Bland" or "Bland's Gill," in the parish of Sedburg, Yorkshire. The Blands of Virginia are descended from the branch seated since 1337 at "Orton" in Westmoreland, England, now owned by Miss Fanny Bland.

The following line of descent is based upon memoranda handed down by Sally Bland, wife of Robert Goode of Whitby :—

I. ROGER BLAND of "Orton," was descended from a second brother of the house of Gybard.

II. ADAM BLAND of London, Sergeant to Queen Elizabeth, &c., m. 1549, Jane Atkyns, had several children.

III. JOHN BLAND, tenth son of Adam, b. 1573, was of Lyth Lane, parish of St. Antholm's, London, and of Plaistow in Essex, free of the "Grocer's and Merchant's Adventurer's Company," died leaving a great personal estate, and nine sons and seven daughters. His second son John, was father of Giles Bland, "a man of good parts, of courage and resolution, who came to Virginia in the time of Sir William Berkeley's government, and having a personal quarrel with the governor, sided with Bacon in his rebellion, and after Bacon's death surrendering himself upon a proclamation of a general pardon, he was hanged under pretence of being the ringleader." Another son was *Edward*, a Spanish merchant, afterwards of "Kimages," Charles City Co., Va., who d. 1653, leaving descendants named *New* and *Horton.*

V. THEODORICK BLAND, ninth son of John, sometime merchant of St. Luca, Spain, came to Virginia 1654, and settled at "Westover," where he d. 1671,—"one of the Kings council for Virginia, and was both in fortune and in understanding, inferior to no person of his time in the country." He m. 1652, Ann dau. of Col. Richard Bennett of "Wyanock" and "Ricaton," sometime governor of the colony. He had two sons who lived in Yorkshire, and

VI. RICHARD BLAND of "Jordans," b. 1665, d. 1720. His second wife, Elizabeth, dau. of Col. William Randolph of "Turkey Island," the founder of the Randolph Family in America, bore him five children, among whom were *Mary*, who m. Col. Henry Lee of Westmoreland, whose grandson, Gen. "Light Horse Harry Lee," of Revolutionary fame was father of GEN. ROBERT E. LEE, C. S. A.; Theodorick of "Cawsons," who m. Frances Bolling and was mother of Col. Theodorick Bland, Jr., a famous officer of cavalry in the Revolution, and of Frances Bland, wife of John Randolph, and St. George Tucker, grandfather of JOHN RANDOLPH OF ROANOKE, and of several eminent Tuckers, and

VII. RICHARD BLAND of "Jordans," the "Virginia Antiquary," called the Cato of the Revolution, b. 1710 d. 1776. Richard Bland, according to printed accounts currently received, m. Anne, dau. of Peter Poythress, but the traditions of Whitby establish the fact that he had a second wife, Elizabeth Harrison of "Brandon," (probably dau. of Nathaniel, son of Nathaniel, son of Hon. Benj. Harrison of Surrey, the first of the name in Virginia) whom he must have married before 1750, and who was the mother of SALLY BLAND GOODE. I will leave it to others to divide up the children between the two wives; it is quite possible that the Randolph genealogy is entirely in error in the statement that this Richard Bland married Miss Poythress, since there were so many marriages of Blands, Randolphs and Bollings, with the female members of the Poythress line at about this period. One of the daughters of Richard Bland married Jabob Rubsamen, a prominent contractor for arms for the Continental army, another, Mr. Atkinson of Petersburg, another Mr. Mayo, and another was

VIII. SALLY BLAND, who m. COL. ROBERT GOODE of "Whitby."

ARMS.—Argent, on a bend sable, three pheons of the field.

CREST.—Out of ducal coronet, or, a lions head, ppr.

MOTTO.—*Sperate et virite forte.*

In a volume of travels, published by Lieut. Anburey, a British officer, captured at Saratoga by the Continental Army, and confined on parole in Virginia, I find this note:—

"Many gentlemen around Richmond, though strongly attached to the American cause, have shown the liberality and hospitality so peculiar to this province, in their civilities to our officers, who are quartered here and in the adjacent country; among those who are most distinguished in this line, are Col. Randolph, of Tuckahoe, Col. Goode, of Chesterfield, Col. Cary, of Warwick, etc. The illiberal part of their countrymen charge them with being partial to Great Britain; but these are gentlemen of fixed principles, of affluence and authority, and therefore despise all popular clamor." *

Smyth, in his *Travels in Virginia*, also refers to the liberal hospitality afforded him at Whitby.

A very interesting circumstance connected with the early life of John Wickham, the great Virginia lawyer, may perhaps, be recounted here without impropriety. It is given in the words of our kinsman, Prof. Powhatan Clarke.

Some thirty or more years ago, my mother, on her return from the White Sulphur Springs, told my father (I being by), that Mr. McClurg Wickham renewed an acquaintance of their childhood, and said that but for her grand-father, Col. Robert Goode, of Whitby, the Wickham family would never have existed in Virginia; that in the time of the Revolution, his grand-father, John Wickham, then a mere youth, was making his way on foot from New York to Charleston, to join an uncle, an officer in the English army, who promised to send him to England to be educated. He was captured near Hicksford in Virginia, tried and condemned as a spy, because of papers found on his person, of whose purport he claimed to be ignorant. Col. Goode, who presided over the Court Martial, was so impressed by the character and bearing of the youth, that he urged and obtained a respite, pledging himself for his good conduct. He sent him to Williamsburg, where he remained till the war closed. In the mean time he studied law, and when the capital was removed to Richmond, he followed the Government and soon attained the prominence of which his descendants are so justly proud.

I also print another version of the same story, kindly written out for this book by an eminent Virginian living in Baltimore, whose name I am not at liberty to mention:

John Wickham, the great lawyer, and loved and honored citizen, was a conspicuous specimen of the learned, pure-minded, and cultivated men, who contributed to the formation of public and private character in his day and generation, on which Virginians look back with pride and complacency.

Mr. Wickham devoted himself to the practice of law during a long life in the city of Richmond, Virginia, and was a recognized leader in his profession, measured by the standard of Chief-Justice Marshall, and others of like eminence. He never held office, but on the contrary, shunned political discussion in public and private. This was noted by his friends and associates with more or less interest, inasmuch as it was well-known, that his qualities of mind and equipment were so large and complete, that he could have easily won the highest distinction in matters of State.

Tradition has left some explanation of the characteristics mentioned. It has been brought down to these times, that the early life of this eminent man was surrounded by circumstances peculiarly trying, and especially so, when the sensibilities of a refined nature were confronted by the temper of the people when these circumstances transpired.

The story as I have heard it, is substantially, as follows:

---

* ANBUREY: Travels, London, 1791, ii, pp. 307-8.

The father of John Wickham was a clergyman of the Church of England, and was such a strong adherent of the cause of the mother country, against the United colonies, in their struggle for independence that he became obnoxious to the constituted authorities, and was put on his parole, and confined to the limits of Williamsburg in Virginia, and that immediate section. During this period, it was deemed important, on some account connected with the family affairs, that his son John should get out of the country. It was arranged that he proceed to Charleston, S. C., then in possession of the British, where friends would meet him and provide for his departure. The youth was used to take dispatches from New York to the British commandant in Charleston, but on some suspicion being excited, he was arrested and detained at Hicksford,—a crossing of the Meherrin River, in Greensville Co., Va., near the North Carolina border, and not far from the Roanoke. On examination and search, the youthful traveler was found with the important papers alluded to. The affair was the subject of proper investigation, and the extreme youth of Wickham, and the interest of influential citizens, growing out of mitigating circumstances, were entirely sufficient to relieve him of the consequences ordinarily attending a discovery of this kind.* In the long years after, it is stated that Mr. Wickham never forgot the persons who concerned themselves for his comfort and relief ; and it is remembered that some good people who gave him aid and protection when in alarming extremity at the point of arrest, were substantially cared for as long as they lived.

It has been supposed that these circumstances had much to do with Mr. Wickham's absolute disconnection with political life and affairs, as highly as he was qualified to take front rank, and as much as it was the fashion of his day, with the men of his character and ability. He seemed to have no desire to go beyond the duties of his profession, to meet with the people at large in public concerns ; and the nearest that his duties ever brought him to political associations, was as senior counsel for Aaron Burr, in his trial for treason.

In 1780, Robert Goode was member of a commision to which also belonged Thomas Jefferson, Edmund Randolph, James Buchanan, Archibald Cary, and others, appointed to locate the public squares in Richmond, and to propose plans for the enlargement of the city.

Robert Goode and his brother Francis, were, in 1786, patrons of the Academy of Arts and Sciences of the United States of America, a scientific society which was projected by *M. Quesnay de Beaurepaire,* under the patronage of the French Academy of Sciences.† The projectors of this society, which was based upon the most comprehensive ideas, was at least a century ahead of the times, for no similar organization, has up to this day been developed in the South, unless we compare with it the group of scientific societies now existing in Washington. The Richmond Academy never got beyond the erection of a fine building, in which in later years was held the convention to ratify the Constitution of the United States. (See Mordecai's *Richmond in Bygone Days.*)

Another interesting circumstance is that Col. Goode had built at Whitby one of the very first ice-houses in the United States.

It is related that the idea was suggested by the discovery by one of the plantation-hands of a mass of ice on the bank of the James, where the earth had fallen over it and kept it till midsummer. It seemed such a luxury that an ice-house was immediately built near the house at Whitby. It was in the shape of an egg,

---

* *Sabine's Loyalists* ii., p. 427, says that he entered the Queen's Rangers as ensign and was promoted to captain, etc. I have heard that when he was arrested in Virginia, he had in his pocket a commission in the British army. He plead that he had not accepted it. It had been sent him by his uncle, Col. Edmund Fanning.—R. A. Brock.

† A copy of his pamphlet proposals, etc., is in our State Library.—R. A. B.

with the small end embedded in the soil, and the large end forming a half globe-shaped structure above. It was built of masonry, and the lower part is still in existence, about thirty feet deep, and twenty feet wide, and holds about one hundred four-horse loads of ice. It was built about the year 1780.

Robert Goode and his heirs were involved in a long and wasteful lawsuit, growing out of his appointment as executor to the estate of William Black, owner of Falls Plantation. The case is recorded in *Leigh's Reports*, vii., p. 452. The case was a peculiar one, and since it involved so many of the family it may be interesting to review it briefly.

The will of Wm. Black, proved April 5, 1782, bequeathed to John Blair, Esq. and Peter Lyons, Esq., the Great Falls Plantation, in trust for his grandson, William Black, son of William Black, provided that this grandson should have two sons who should reach the age of twenty-one. Robert Goode, with his brother Samuel, as surety, was one of the executors, giving bond in the penalty of fifty thousand pounds, and Turner Southall was the other executor, Francis Goode, another brother of Robert, being one of the sureties. The will was contested from 1782 on by Mrs. Frances Black, widow of the testator, after her death, by her daughters, Anne Dent Black, subsequently Mrs. Hardeman, and Mrs. James Hayes, and Frances T. Black, subsequently Mrs. John Garland.* Decisions were rendered against Robert Goode, in 1793, in 1797, in April 1809, against his executors, Richard Bland Goode and Francis Goode in 1812, after the death of the latter in 1715, against Tarlton Saunders, his brother-in-law, as as executor of the estate of Robert Goode. The matter was finally adjusted in 1836, after running for fifty-four years, by the decision that the contestants of the will were wrong. Several other members of the family, his son Francis Goode, Col. Samuel Goode, Thomas Goode, (son of Robert), Dr. Thomas Goode and his brother-in-law, Dr. Thomas W. Jones, Col. Francis Goode of Powhatan Co., Mrs. Alice Goode, his wife, as his executor, and Thomas Harris, probably her brother and the executor of her husband's estate in 1818, were involved in this vexatious affair.

91.

COL. FRANCIS GOODE, of "Seven Oaks," son of Robert Goode, No. 51, was born at Whitby, 1750–60, died April 23, 1795, at sea, off the Capes of Virginia. Married 1775–80, Alice Harris, of Powhatan Co., daughter of Thomas Harris, died 1824.

> 245, ROBERT GOODE, b. 1780. 246, FRANCIS, d. unm. He was familiarly known as "Whisker Frank," to distinguish him from his cousin of the same name. He was a dissipated man; he served in the war of 1812 as a member of "Capt. Benjamin Goode's Company," in the 23d Regiment, Virginia Militia. 247, POLLY, m. *Henry Tatum*, of Amelia Co. 248, LOUISA, m. *Mr. Harrison*, of Brunswick Co. one son, two daughters, one m. *Mr. Mason*, principal of a school in

---

*I have not consulted Leigh but Wm. Black married Anne Dent, of a noted Maryland Family. He accompanied in 1744 the Commissioners from Virginia who made the treaty with the Indians at Lancaster, Pa. This journal, edited by me, has been printed in the Pennsylvania Magazine of *History and Biography*. A daughter of James and Anne (Dent Black) Hayes married Herbert A. Claiborne of Richmond, a descendant of the "rebel," Col. Wm. Claiborne.—R. A. B.

Brunswick Co., one m. *Thomas Goode* of Mecklenburg. 249, BETSY, m. *William James* of Cumberland Co.

Col. Francis Goode owned a fine estate in Chesterfield Co., known as "Seven Oaks." The house was destroyed by fire about the time of his death and the property was afterwards owned by Walthall C. Goode, son of 211. His wife is buried on the estate.

In 1795, he went to Philadelphia to be treated for cancer, and died on the vessel on the return voyage. The ship was blown out to sea when off Norfolk and remained sixty days out of sight of land, and he was buried at sea. He was accompanied at this time by his nephew, Francis Goode.

Miss M. A. L. Goode writes,—"I have heard my father say that Madam Goode (for no one called her 'Mistress,') was one of the sweetest gentlewomen he ever met, and I know his impression was that she was very aristocratic in her feelings. The habits of the household were those of English country gentry, and until the handsome residence was destroyed by fire, everything was kept in elegant style. The surroundings made a lasting impression on my then childish mind as I played through the groves and gardens."

95.

THOMAS GOODE, of Manchester, Va., son of Robert Goode, No. 51, was born at Whitby, lived in Manchester, where he died April 6, 1813, married 1777, Elizabeth Prosser of "Bloomfield," Henrico Co., who died in 1839.

Col. Thomas H. Prosser, the father of Mrs. Thomas Goode, was the owner of Gabriel, the ring-leader in the insurrection of 1800, and since this insurrection took place in the heart of the Goode community, I find it appropriate to quote, briefly, Marion Harland's account of this affair in her recent novel, "Judith; a chronicle of old Virginia," which is indeed recommended to all readers of this little book, who want to know more of the ways of their Virginia kinsmen at the beginning of the century.

"Gabriel was an unusually intelligent negro. His master had petted him from his childhood and his mistress taught him to read. He showed what a dangerous thing a little learning is by plotting a general massacre of the white people, sparing only some young women, who were to be the maids of the leaders' colored wives, and half a dozen who were to marry the principal men. They meant to fire the city in three places at once; then a trumpet, 'blown long and loud,' would let the conspirators know that the hour had come, and be the signal of attack upon the armory. The small company of soldiers there would be killed, the arms secured, and the building held as a fort by a certain number, while the rest went from house to house, slaughtering young and old. A chosen band was to make sure of the ladies already selected, and guard them to the armory. 'Every thing else that wears a white skin must die,' was one of Gabriel's general orders. A paper containing the list was found in his pocket, and a rough sketch of the government he hoped to establish. He was known among his followers as 'General Gabriel.' When the white folks were all dead, he was to be crowned 'King of Virginia.' Richmond was chosen as his capital, and Mrs. Randolph, a beautiful widow, for his queen.

"The next in office were to be presidents. Then came princes and governors and counsellors," went on the narrator. Each of these officers, as I have said, was to have a white wife to add dignity to his position. The plot had been working for a year. It will never be known in this world how many knew of it or would have joined in the bloody work. There were a thousand at Gabriel's back when he halted his horse on the bank of a branch of the Chickahominy River, that lay between them and the city. It was a shallow creek they could have crossed on foot at sundown that day; but the heavy rain had swelled it into a deep, rushing stream they dared not try to ford. Gabriel called a council of war in the storm. They knew, of course, that Colonel Prosser and his man had escaped, but they were not sure that they had gone to Richmond. While they argued and disputed among themselves, a negro boy, about twenty years old, named Pharaoh, belonging to Mr. William Mosby, stole down the creek in the darkness, plunged in, and swam to the other side. That shows what might have been done by many had not the Lord, in mercy to us, withheld them from the attempt. Pharaoh started to Richmond, and met the white troops about a mile outside of the city. From him they had full information as to the state of affairs, and marched directly to the creek. The negroes were still on the other side when the troops got to the bank nearest town. Five or six of the braves, urged by Gabriel and Jack Bowler, his right-hand man, had tried to swim over, and been drowned. The stream was boiling like a pot and rising every minute, and they were sucked right under in the sight of the rest. After that nobody would risk the crossing.

"Gabriel was preaching to them when the troops arrived. The constant glare of lightning lit up both parties. The white men had heard Gabriel before they saw him standing on the edge of the water, and close by him Jack Bowler, who was a perfect giant, almost six and a half feet high, and as strong as four or five ordinary men. He had persuaded the negroes that the Lord had made him on purpose to deliver them, as He did Samson to deliver the Israelites. His hair was long and thick, and had never been cut. He wore it generally in a cue, like a gentleman's, but this night he let it hang loose on his shoulders to remind his men of Samson's hair, 'wherein his great strength lay.' Both of these men were under thirty, and could read and write. They were armed to the teeth, and Gabriel had put on Colonel Prosser's regimental suit. Around and behind them was a crowd that looked like tens of thousands, heaving and murmuring. Walter Blair said the sound reminded him of the pushing and grunting of a herd of hogs. It bristled with all sorts of weapons. Some had guns, some axes, some hatchets, and many had side-blades (scythes) fastened to the ends of poles. The lightning flashed on hundreds of these, ground sharp and rubbed bright.

"The white men fired directly into the body of the crowd, for the creek was not, even in the freshet, twenty yards wide. A few shots were fired back, but most of the poor, foolish things had never thought of keeping guns and powder dry. The leaders hallooed to them to 'stand and see the salvation of the Lord,' but it was of no use. They scattered in all directions, like scared sheep."

"Gabriel, and I think, three others of the ring-leaders, were taken in different hiding-places and brought to Richmond jail. They had a fair trial, and were condemned to death. They were hanged in October of the same year—1800."

"But the thousands of followers?" questioned Mr. Bradley. "Surely they were not suffered to go unpunished?"

"Why not, poor things?" Aunt Betsey's merciful eyes put the query more emphatically than did her tongue. "If they had not been deceived and tempted and led on by designing men, they would never have thought of lifting a finger against us. The day after the rising, they were all back in their homes, doing housework, hoeing corn, picking of tobacco-worms—whatever was the business set for them, just as if nothing had happened. Their owners asked no questions. They didn't want to know which of them had meant to butcher them in their beds not twelve hours before."

An additional account of the same affair has been kindly communicated by Mr. Brock. It is based upon an article upon James Monroe in *Hardisty's Encyclopedia*, a work not generally accessible.

The period of the first service of James Monroe as Governor of Virginia was marked by an event tragical in its sequence, which though frequently referred to as "Gabriel's Insurrection," but few of the present generation have any definite knowledge of, as there has been no circumstantial account of it published, since that which contemporaneously appeared in the newspapers, of which but few files have been preserved, and they are practically inaccessible to the public. Some notice of it, therefore, in these pages, can not but prove interesting.

In a message of Governor Monroe to the General Assembly of Virginia, dated December 5, 1800, he states that on the 30th of August preceding, about two o'clock in the afternoon, Mr. Mosby Shepherd, a reputable citizen of Henrico Co., who resides about three miles north of the city of Richmond, beyond a small stream known as the Brook, called upon him and informed him that he had just received advice from two of his slaves that the negroes in the neighborhood mentioned intended to rise that night, kill their masters and their families, and proceed to Richmond, where they would be joined by the negroes there, and would seize all the public arms and ammunition, murder the white inhabitants and take possession of the city. Thereupon Governor Monroe took immediate measures to avert the threatened fell design by stationing guards at the state penitentiary, where the public arms were deposited ; at the magazine, and at the state capitol, and by disposing the city troop of cavalry (commanded by Captain Moses Austin, then conducting a shot tower in the city of Richmond, and who was subsequently noted as a Texan pioneer) in detachments to patrol the several routes leading to the city from the suspected neighborhood. "The close of the day, however, was marked by one of the most extraordinary falls of rain ever known in our country. Every animal sought shelter from it." The brook was so swollen in its volume as to be impassable, thus interposing a bar to the execution of the plan of the negroes. Nothing occurred during the night of the alarming character suspected, to disturb the tranquility of the city, and the only unusual circumstance reported by the patrolling troopers in the morning following, was, that all negroes passed on the road, in the interval of the storm, were going from the city, whereas it was their usual custom to visit it on that night of the week (Saturday), which circumstance was not unimportant, as it had been reported that the first rendezvous of the negroes was to be in the country. The same precautions being again observed the succeeding night without developments of the alleged design, Governor Monroe was on the point of concluding that the alarm was groundless, when from further information from Major William Mosby and other gentlemen, residents of the suspected neighborhood, he was fully satisfied that the insurrection had been planned by the negroes, and that they still intended to carry it into effect. He therefore convened the Executive Council of the State on Monday, September 1, who took such measures that in the afternoon of the same day twenty of the negro conspirators were apprehended on the estate of Colonel Thomas H. Prosser, a prominent and influential gentlemen, and from those of others in the suspected neighborhood, and brought to Richmond. "As the jail could not contain them, they were lodged in the penitentiary." The ringleaders, or chiefs, had fled and were not then to be found.

Every day now threw light on the diabolical plot and gave it additional importance. In the progress of the trials of the conspirators, it was satisfactorily demonstrated that a general insurrection of the slaves in the State was contemplated by the originators of the plot. A species of organization had taken place among them, and at a meeting held for the purpose, they had elected a commander, one Gabriel, the slave of Col. Prosser, and to whom they had given the title of General. They had also appointed subordinate officers, captains, sergeants, etc. They contemplated a force of cavalry as well as of infantry, and had formed a plan of attack on the city, which was to commence by setting fire to the wooden buildings in the lower portion of it, called Rocketts, with the expectation of attracting the inhabitants thither whilst they assailed the penitentiary, magazine and capitol ; intending, after capturing these and getting possession of arms and ammunition, to meet the people on their return and slaughter them. The accounts varied as to the number who were to inaugurate the movement. According to the testimony adduced in the trials of the conspiring wretches, it was variously stated it was from five hundred to ten thousand. It was manifest, however, that it embraced a majority of the slaves in the city of Richmond and its neighborhood, and that the combination extended to the adjacent counties of Hanover, Caroline, Louisa, Chesterfield, and to the neighborhood of Point of Fork in Fluvanna County, and there was good cause to believe that the knowledge of the project pervaded other portions, if not the whole of the State. It was suspected "that the design was prompted by others who were invisible, but whose agency might be powerful." To meet such contingency, Governor Monroe called into service the 9th, 29th, and 23d, and a portion of the 33d regiments of the State Militia, which were chiefly stationed in Richmond and the adjacent town of Manchester. The military force was gradually diminished, until, on the 18th of October following, the residue was discharged.

The judicial disposition of the ring-leaders of the plot was summary, five of them were executed on the 22th of September, and five more on the 15th thereafter. "General" Gabriel, the sable chief, was apprehended on the 27th of the same month, in the city of Norfolk, and suffered death in January following. The savage disposition of Gabriel, according to the records of Henrico County Court, had, a year previous to his final heinous conception, subjected him to punishment and lengthy imprisonment for biting off the ear of a fellow slave. In the testimony given by the witnesses (who were all negroes), in the trials of the conspirators, there were some curious as well as characteristic communications made. The whole plot was stupidly conceived, with a provision ludicrously trifling. The entire armament captured consisted of twelve rude swords which had been manufactured from scythe blades by one of the conspirators, Solomon, the brother of "General" Gabriel, a blacksmith, and the slave, also, of Colonel Prosser. A broken pistol was owned by one of the conspirators, and it was stated by some of the witnesses at the trial, that "General" Gabriel had provided also six guns, ten pounds of gunpowder, and five hundred bullets, which he had molded. It was evidently the expectancy of the bloody-minded wretches to secure primarily, arms from the residences of their masters, whose households were to be the unsuspecting victims of midnight assassination. As in the case of Nat. Turner, the leader in the subsequent and more serious insurrection which occurred in Southampton County, in August, 1831, religious fanaticism seems also to have been a factor in Gabriel's insurrection, as it was urged by Martin, one of the prime instigators, that God had said in the Bible, "If we will worship him, we should have peace in all our land, five of you shall conquer an hundred, and a hundred, a thousand of our enemies." A piece of silk for a flag was to be provided, with the motto "Death or Liberty" inscribed upon it. "None of the whites were to be spared except Quakers, Methodists and French people, unless they agreed to the freedom of the blacks, in which case they would at least cut off one of their arms." It was also designed to send a messenger to the nation of the Catawba Indians in North Carolina, and to request their co-operation. The immunity, stated as having been designed, the Quakers might have been actuated by a conciousness of the active philanthropy of that society towards the negroes, but why Methodists should be spared is less satisfactorily comprehended. Perhaps there were many followers of that church among the negroes. The coincidence of mercy to the French, and the proposed mission to the Catawba Indians is strikingly curious, and affords grounds for the supposition that a tradition had lingered in the minds of the benighted negroes of the dread French and Indian War of some fifty years previous. The Indians of North Carolina, it may be added, had given the colonists much trouble some forty years earlier, even in the administration of Governor Spotswood. The matter is one to engage interest and speculative thought.

96.

COL. SAMUEL GOODE, M. C., of Mecklenburg Co., Va., son of Robert

Goode, No. 56, was born at Whitby, March 21, 1756, died in Mecklenburg Co., Nov. 14, 1822. Married Oct. 5, 1786, Mary Armistead Burwell, (who died March 20, 1829) daughter of Col. Lewis Burwell, of "Stoneland."*

250, ALICE GOODE, m. *James Harriss*, of Nottoway Co. 251, LUCY, m. *Col. Charles Baskerville* of "Lombardy Grove." 252, MARTHA, m. *Judge Thomas T. Bouldin*. 253, SALLY, m. *Hon. R. H. Baptist*. 254, MARY ARMISTEAD, m. *Thomas W. Jones, M. D.*, of Brunswick Co. 255, THOMAS, b. Oct. 31, 1787, d. April 2, 1858. 256, SAMUEL HOPKINS, b. 1805, d. 1855. 257, FRANCIS, d. yg. 257½, LEWIS ROBERT, d. yg.

Col. Samuel Goode doubtless served in the Continental Army. He was member of Congress from 1799–1801, attending its sessions in Philadelphia. A portrait painted by Charles Wilson Peale, is in the possession of his grandson, Dr. Samuel Goode Harriss of Boydton.

THE ROANOKE GOODES.

99.

JOHN TWIGG GOODE, of Roanoke Co., Va., son of John Goode, No. 57, p. 43, was born, 1783, died August 26, 1874.

At the age of eighty-seven, he wrote an article on the Goode family, which was published in the "Tobacco Plant" of Petersburg, in which were preserved many of the facts concerning the Mecklenburg branch of the family, which would

---

* THE BURWELL FAMILY has been discussed at considerable length by Mr. Brock in the *Richmond Standard*, vol. ii., 1881, Nos. 42-45, and has received much attention from the Virginia genealogists, all of whom admit that its records are in an exceedingly confused condition.

The family is said to be of very ancient date upon the borders of England and Scotland. The Burwells were settled at Berwick-upon-Tweed as early as 1250. Robert Walpole and Horatio, Lord Nelson, were descendents of the Burwells in female lines.

The ancestor of the family in Virginia was Major Lewis Burwell, (b. 1623, d. 1658) who settled about 1640 at "Fairfield," Gloucester Co., and who in 1646, was member of a delegation sent to invite Charles II. to come to Virginia. He married Lucy Higginson, daughter of "the valiant Capt. Robert Higginson, one of the first commanders who subdued the country of Virginia from the power of the heathen." Besides his son Major Lewis Burwell of "Queen's Creek," York County, he had other sons, ancestors of the Burwells of Canada and of Connecticut: a granddaughter of a younger son of Lewis Burwell and Lucy Higginson was undoubtedly the Miss Burwell who married SAMUEL GOODE, No. 47, and was ancestor of THE PRINCE EDWARD GOODES.

The wife of Col. Samuel Goode was of the sixth generation,—the line being as follows :—

I. Major Lewis Burwell m. Lucy Higginson. II. Major Lewis Burwell of Queen's Creek, and Abigail Smith, (b. 1632, d. 1672), own cousin of "Nathaniel Bacon, the rebel." III. Lewis Burwell, (b. 1684, d. 1744) and Miss Armistead. IV. Armistead Burwell (b. 1718, d 1754) and Christian, dau. of Hon. John Blair. V. Col. Lewis Burwell of "Stoneland" and Anne, granddaughter of Gov. Alexander Spotswood.

The wife of Samuel Gaines Dawson, M. D., grandson of Samuel Goode, No. 76, was a descendant in the same degree from Lewis Burwell of "Queen's Creek."

Burwell has been a favorite christian name in the Prince Edward branch of the Goode family,—reference to the index will show that it has been borne by eight or ten individuals at least.

"Carter's Creek, the old seat of the Burwells," says Campbell's *History of Virginia*, "is situated in Gloucester, on a creek of that name, and not far back from York River. The stacks of antique diamond-shaped chimneys, and the old fashioned paneling of the interior remind the visitor that Virginia is truly 'The Ancient Dominion.' There is the family grave-yard, shaded with locusts, and overrun with parasites and grape-vines. The family arms are carved on some of the tomb-stones, and hogs show that the Bacon arms are quartered upon those of the Burwells."

At the "Burwell Family Picnic," held at "Burwell Farm," Milford Conn., Aug. 18, 1870, there was exhibited an old quilt, an heirloom owned by Mrs. Armistead Burwell of Vicksburg, Miss., which was said to contain pieces of dresses once owned by Ladies Dunmore, Dinwiddie, De la War, Spotswood, Fairfax and Skipwith and by Mesdames Randolph, Blair, Page, Nelson, Harrison, Bolling, Powell, McCandlish, Maitland, Barron, Pendleton, Boyd, Meade, GOODE, Mason, Wythe, and others.

otherwise have been lost. Unmarried. A prominent lawyer, and an eccentric character, familiarly known as "Twigg Goode."

101.

JOHN BOLLING, of Dinwiddie Co., Va., was born 1760–90. Married JINNY GOODE, daughter of John Goode, No. 57. Children:—

    258, EMILY BOLLING, m. *Mr. Hineston*, a lawyer of Halifax Co. Children: 1, Mary Jane, m. *Girard Huiscull* of Dinwiddie Co.; 2, Ellen, m. *William C. Tucker*, grandson of No. 108. 259, RICHARD, d. unm. 260, LUCY, d. yg. unm.

The Bollings were one of the best known of the old families of Virginia. Many of the most distinguished Virginians trace their descent through the Bollings and Rolfes to the Indian Princess POCAHONTAS, whose romantic story forms one of the most charming episodes in the early history of America, and which is fortunately so enveloped in mystery, and withal so deeply impressed upon the minds of the people, that the iconoclastic efforts of too enthusiastic critics are powerless to destroy it. (See "My Lady Pocahontas," by J. E. Cooke.—Address of William Wirt Henry before Virginia Historical Society, Feb. 24, 1882, etc., etc.) The story is so dear to Virginians, that it seems appropriate here to notice the Bollings at some length, particularly since very many of the descendants of John Goode are also descendants of Pocahontas, and several of of them bear the name of lordly old Powhatan, her father. A full account of the early generations, with eighteen photographic portraits is found in the Memoirs of the Bolling family, published by T. H. Wynne, Richmond, 1868, of which only fifty copies were printed,—the rarest of American genealogies.

Through the courtesy of Mr. Wynne, I was allowed to examine, some years ago, a MS. in the hand of the gifted John Randolph of Roanoke, whose pedigree, as recorded by himself, began as follows:

Powhatan

Pocahontas . . . . . *married to John Rolfe.*[*]

Thos. Rolfe . . *married to a* . . *Miss Poyers.*

Jane Rolfe . *married to Robert Bolling of London.*

Col. Robert Bolling, the first of the name in Virginia, son of John and Mary Bolling of Barking Parish, London, and descended from the Bollings of "Bolling Hall," near Bradford in Yorkshire, was born Dec. 16, 1646. He came to Vir-

---

[*] John Rolfe, curiously enough in connection with this tradition, married three times. His first wife died in Bermuda, his second was Pocahontas, his third wife Jane Pyers, Poyers, Pearse or Peirce.—R. A. B.

ginia in 1660, and settled at "Kippax" or "Farmingdale," Prince George Co. and married in 1675, Jane Rolfe, who bore him one son, Major John Bolling, b. 1676. He married again in 1681, Anne Stith, who bore him eight children, ancestors of the "Petersburg Bollings," the "Prince George Bollings, the Hics, the Beverlys, the Meriwethers, etc." (See Slaughter's *Bristol Parish*.)

Major John Bolling married Mary Kennon, and had 1, Col. John Bolling of "Cobbs," Chesterfield Co., born in 1700. 2, Jane, m. Col. Richard Randolph of "Curles." (See note on Bland Family, p. 55). 3, Mary, m. Col. John Fleming. 4, Elizabeth, m. Dr. William Gay. 5, Martha, m. Dr. Thomas Eldridge. 6, Anne, m. James Murray. From these children, especially Mrs. Randolph, are descended numerous distinguished families who rightly claim descent from Pocahontas, a list of whom is, I believe, in preparation by Hon. Wyndham Robertson, of Abingdon, Va. (See also Browning's *Americans of Royal Descent*). Some of them will be referred to under names Randolph, Thornton, Abbott, Hall, Adams, Botts, Watkins, Harrison, etc., further on in this volume.

Of the "Petersburg Bollings," was Alexander Bolling of Mitchells, Prince George Co., (grandson of Col. Robert Bolling), who married Martha Bolling, (grandaughter of same, dau. of Robert and *Ann Cocke* Bolling) and had four sons, born in the last century, Samuel, Alexander, Jack and Richard, all of whom lived and died in Dinwiddie Co., except the last, a physician who removed to the vicinity of Vicksburg, Miss. Jack was the husband of JINNY GOODE, No. 101. Samuel, married Miss Elliott of Brunswick Co., and had two sons, Dick, a bachelor, John, the father of several children, both of whom, with the entire Elliott family, removed to the vicinity of Vicksburg; also a daughter who married Dr. John Feild, and had children, Dr. Hume Feild, Col. Feild, C. S. A., of Petersburg, a distinguished officer, and Dr. John Feild, who married Maria, daughter of Col. E. B. Tucker, No. 279.

102.

ABNER ADAMS, of Dinwiddie Co., Va., married LUCY GOODE, daughter of John Goode, No. 57, p. 43, Children : Several,—one a dashing officer in the Confederate army, killed in the war.

105.

CAPT. JOHN CHESTERFIELD GOODE, of "Inglewood," Mecklenburg Co., Va., son of Thomas Goode, No. 58, p. 43, was born 1750–70, and died 1830–40 at the paternal estate, upon the Roanoke River. Was educated at William and Mary College, served as a captain in active service at Norfolk, Va., in the war of 1812. Was a wealthy planter. Married (1) Lucy Claiborne,* who died about 1800, leaving one son, (2) Miss Nuttall of Granville Co., N. C. Children :—

271, WILLIAM OSBORNE GOODE, M. C., b. Sept. 16, 1798, d. July 3, 1859.

272, AGNES EPPES, m. *James Williamson*, inherited a fine farm on the Roanoke River, and removed 1848 to Fayette Co., Tennessee.

273, ELIZABETH, m. *Thomas Baily*, and emigrated with her sister to to Tennessee.

---

*THE CLAYBORNE FAMILY.—Conspicuous among the picturesque characters with which the history of the Old Dominion abounds is William Clayborne, the rebel, "among the tall figures of the epoch in which he lived, one of the tallest and haughtiest,"—he who for twenty years was the leading spirit in the conflict between Virginia and the younger sister colony of Maryland. (See Campbell's *History of Virginia*, pp. 188, 324, (genealogy); Cooke's *Virginia*, pp. 178-216; Carpenter's novel, *Clayborne, the Rebel*, 1846; also for genealogy, Slaughter's *Bristol Parish*, pp. 164-71; Neill's *Founders of Maryland*, pp. 38-9, 177-8.)

Col. William Clayborne, son of Edward and *Grace Bellingham* Cliborne of Westmoreland, England,

"John C. Goode," writes a contemporary, "was finely educated and was licensed to practice the law. He did not however attend to the profession. He turned his attention to politics, he spoke finely in the hustings, he represented the county of Mecklenburg in the House of Delegates of Virginia." Another writes: "To my boyish eyes he was the impersonation of grace and dignity, and was eminently handsome."

See "My Life as a Slave," in *Harper's Monthly Magazine*, October, 1884,— the narrative of Charles Stewart, an aged negro, celebrated in the annals of Virginia Jockeydom.

"In dem times, New Market was 'bout de head place in de Nu-united States fur horse racin', and all de genlem fum far an' near used to come. Nobody dat was anybody staid away, an' it was a fine sight when de spring an' autumn races come I tell you. Dem was de grandest times dat eber lived. King of Heaven! it was a sight to see my ole marster, an' yothers like him a struttin' up an' down wid deir shirts all frilled an' ruffled doun de front. Why, den you could build a ball-room as long as fum here to de stable, an' fill it wid folks—an' ebery one of 'em de real stuff. But now-a-days, what's it like? Name o' Heaven! blue trash, red trash, green trash, speckled trash,—dars plenty ob ebery qualinfication, but nary one dat washes in lye soap, an' dries on de grass widout fadin'. Why, dar was Otway Hare, Parker Hare, JOHN C. GOODE, Colonel Peter Mason, John Drummond and Allen Drummond, all belong to de New Market Jockey Club. How I did love dem horses! It 'peared like dey loved me too, an' when dey turned deir rainbow necks, all slick an' shinin' aroun' sarchin' for me to cum an' give 'em deir gallops, whewe-e! how we did spin along dat ole New Market course."

For an excellent account of a Virginia horse race in the olden days, see *The Virginia Comedians*, II, xxi., "How the whole colony of Virginia went to the Jamestown races."

106.

WILLIAM B. HAMLIN, of Amelia Co., Va., married about 1800, MARTHA GOODE, daughter of Thomes Goode, No. 58. Child:—

274, MARY ANN HAMLIN, m. *Samuel Pryor*.

108.

COL. JOHN TUCKER, of Brunswick Co., Va., was born Nov. 8, 1780, and died Mar. 5, 1843. He was a prosperous planter, all his life a magistrate, and in early life a public man, representing his district in the Virginia Senate; a whig and an elector upon the Clay ticket. In the war

was born about 1600 and came to Virginia in 1621, and was Secretary of State for the Colony in 1628. He settled at "Romancock," King William Co., and married Mrs. Buller. He had two sons, Col. William Clayborne, Jr. and Lieut.-Col. Thomas Clayborne. The latter had a son, Col. Thomas Clayborne, who is said to have married three times, and to have been the father of twenty-seven children, including Col. Augustine Claiborne, and another, William Claiborne, b. 1753, who m. Miss Leigh, and had among other children, Hon. William Charles Cole Claiborne, Governor of Mississippi, 1801-5, whose daughter m. John H. B. Latrobe, Esq. of Baltimore, Gen. Ferdinand Leigh Claiborne of Mississippi, who assisted Gen. Jackson in planning the battle of New Orleans, and Lucy Claiborne who m. CAPT. JOHN C. GOODE.

ARMS.—Argent, three chevronels, braced in base, sable. A chief and border of the last. CREST, A dove and olive branch. MOTTO, *Pax et copia.*

of 1812 he commanded a regiment in active service at Norfolk, Va. He married, May 18, 1803, AGNES EPPES GOODE, dau. of Thomas Goode, No. 58, who was born at "Inglewood" May 15, 1781, d. Dec. 25, 1814. Children :—

> 275, LUCY TUCKER, b. Dec. 8, 1805, d. May 20, 1854, m. *Judge Edward R. Chambers.* 276, THOMAS GOODE, b. April 7, 1807. 277, STERLING H., b. Jan. 22, 1809, d. Mar. 5, 1852. 278, HARTWELL, b. Aug. 21, 1810, d. April 12, 1811. 279, EDWARD BENNETT, b. April 4, 1812, d. Mar. 22, 1855. 280, JOHN EPPES, b. Dec. 1814, d. Jan. 30, 1885.

The TUCKER FAMILY has been prominent in Virginian, and indeed in American History. Col. John Tucker was son of WRIGHT, son of DAVID, son of. COL. JOSEPH TUCKER, who came from Bermuda to Virginia, whose wife was Patsy Colson, a Portuguese lady.

THE POWHATAN GOODES.

109.

JOHN GOODE, of "Fine Creek," Powhatan Co., Va., son of Bennet and *Martha Jefferson* Goode, No. 59, p. 43, was born at Jude's Creek, 1743, died at "Fine Creek" 1834. Married about 1790 Mrs. Martha Simmons, (born Embry) of Powhatan Co. Children :—

> 281, WILLIAM EMBRY GOODE, b. 1794, d. 1824. 282, JOHN, d. yg. 283, THOMAS, b. about 1800, d. unm. A physician, and insane. 284, LUCY, b. 1787, d. 1818, m. *Dr. Austin Wharton.* 285, EMILY, m. *Thomas Taurman.* 286, ELIZABETH, m. *Mr. Underwood* of Hanover Co., (uncle of U. S. Senator J. R. Underwood of Kentucky). No issue.

110.

BENNET GOODE, of Mecklenburg Co., Va., son of Bennet Goode No. 59, was born, 1744–6, died 1812–16, leaving a widow and four children. He was a wealthy planter, represented his county in the Virginia House of Burgesses, and in the Conventions of Delegates at Richmond and Williamsburg, 1775, as well as in the Convention which formed the first constitution of Virginia. He married, about 1770, Miss Lewis of North Carolina. Children :—

> 287, JOHN B. 288, Daughter, d. yg. 289, ELIZABETH W., m. *Mr. Taylor* of N. C. 290, BENNET, b. 1770–80, and served through the war of 1812 as a sergeant in Captain William Goff's company, in the 23d Virginia Regiment. He married but left no son.

In 1776, Bennet Goode, Esq., of Mecklenburg Co., was appointed Commissioner to collect evidence in behalf of Virginia against persons professing to have claims for lands on the colony under deeds and purchases from the Indians. (*Virginia State Papers,* I, p. 273.)

"Bennet Goode," writes a contemporary, "had a fine estate. He quickly turned his attention to politics, he became a candidate for Mecklenburg in the House of Burgesses, opposing Col. Robert Munford of Richland in Roanoke, a gentleman of considerable estate. He had been elected for the county of Mecklenburg,—he was what they called an aristocrat. Bennet Goode defeated him in the election. Mr. Goode was a man of commanding talents, and was very happy in his address in the hustings."

115.

CHARLES POVALL, of Powhatan Co., Va., son of Robert and *Winifred Anne Miller* Povall,* was born 1763, and died 1830. He married 1785–95, MARTHA GOODE, dau. of Bennet Goode No. 59, born 1760–70, d. 1810–40. Children :—

291, WILLIAM GOODE POVALL, d. 1851–2.   292, BENNET, d. unm. 293, MARTHA, b. Nov. 1, 1784, d. Apr. 30, 1826, m. *William Carrington,* 294, CAROLINE, m. *Cullen Adams,* d. s. p.

116.

WILLIAM GOODE, of Alabama, son of Bennet Goode No. 59, was born in Powhatan Co., Virginia, 1765 ; he removed to Georgia about 1785–90, and subsequently to Clarke Co., Alabama, where he died in 1837, leaving to his children a large property and many slaves. He mar- in Columbia, S. C., about 1795, Sarah James, born near Petersburg. Va., 1770–1775, and died in Elbert Co., Georgia, 1817. Children :—

295, SIDNEY MOORE, b. 1797, d. 1846. 296, JEFFERSON, d. about 1800. 297, CAROLINE, m. *James A. Tait.* 298, SARAH ANN, m. *Benjamin Coleman.* 299, MARTHA JEFFERSON, b. 1806, d. 1870, m. *Isaac W. Nicholson.*   300, REBECCA, m. *Theophilus Nicholson.*

William Goode, Sr. was one of a committee appointed by the Alabama Legis-

---

* THE POVALL FAMILY.—The name Povall, often pronounced and written Povey is not uncommon in England, and was well known in Virginia in early days. We are indebted to our kinsmen, Peyton Rodes Carrington, Esq., of Boston Hill, near Richmond, for the following sketch of the family, which has been extended in some of the later generations by Mr. Brock.
ROBERT or ROBIN POVALL, first of the name in Virginia, was from St. Martins-in-the-Fields, London. He was indentured for six years, as a servant to Robert ("King") Carter of "Corotoman," Charles City Co.,Va. Upon the adjoining plantation of Soloman Knibbs, was employed—so runs the tradition,— a girl named Elizabeth Hooker, whom Robin knew and hoped to marry. Robin was one day in attend- ance as a servant at a dinner given by Carter to the neighboring gentry, when his master read a letter from England, in which enquiry was made concerning Elizabeth, daughter of "Lord Hooker," who had died leaving a large estate called "Malvern Hills"—this Elizabeth being his only daughter and heir. Profiting by what he had learned, Robin at once married his sweetheart, and sailed with her for England.
In the records of Henrico Co., June 2, 1679, occurs the following minute :—
"A deposition of *Elizabeth Hooker,* aged 22 years or thereabouts, That she did see in the custody of Katherine Knibbs since the death of her husband, Soloman Knibbs, a small trunk or cabinet about half full of money, which she said her husband had resolved to carry with him to England, because he would not be beholding to his friends, y likewise in her custody, a dozen of Pewter Plates, one Tankard, y a Salt Seller, y 2 Pewter porringers."
Arriving in England, the Povalls, the tradition continues, obtained possession of "Malvern Hills," having been re-married in England to satisfy legal requirements. The estate was then leased for 99 years, at the end of which period it is said it became escheated to the Crown.
Returning to America, they became possessed of an estate called "Malvern Hills," in Henrico Co., Va., where they were living in 1685. In 1686, Robert Povall was upon the jury lists of Henrico Co., and in 1687, it is recorded that a child was bound out to him.

FIRST GENERATION.

1. ROBERT POVALL, of England, born 1650, died 1728, (Record of Wills, Henrico Co., Sept. 16, 1728),

lature in 1818, to choose a site for the Court house of Clarke County. (Brewer's *Alabama*).

116-I.

SAMUEL MEGGINSON, of Buckingham Co,, Va., son of Capt. William and *Martha?* *Goode* Megginson No. 60, p. 37, was born 1730–40. A soldier in the Revolution. His arm was broken about 1760 and set by old Dr. Cabell.

I am indebted to Alexander Brown, Esq., of Norwood, for important notes upon the Megginsons. His memorandum concerning William Megginson, No. 60, being received too late to be printed in its proper place, is inserted here :—

William Megginson bought 580 acres of land on the south side of James River, (across from the present [1885] Greenway, P. O.) in 1739, of Mrs. Elizabeth Cabell, (wife of Dr. Wm. Cabell, the ancestor of the Cabells of Virginia, etc ; the Doctor was then in England).—In 1740, Mrs. Cabell wrote to her husband in England,— "Please bring a saddle-cover and furniture for Wm. Megginson's wife's side-saddle." In 1743, Capt. Wm. Megginson "laid the levies" in the upper part of St. Ann's Parish ; in 1747, he had 6 negroes among his tithables in that Parish.

---

m. Elizabeth Hooker. Issue: 2, JOHN POVALL; 3, ROBERT; 4, MARY, m. *Mr. Carter*; 5, SARAH, m. *Mr. Roach.*

SECOND GENERATION.

2. JOHN POVALL, d. bef. 1762. Issue: 6, JOHN POVALL, JR., d. bef. 1762, leaving issue: 1, ROBIN; 2, ELIZABETH.
3. ROBERT POVALL, b. about 1680, d. 1732, m. *Judith ———.* Issue: 7. ELIZ. POVALL; 8. ROBERT.

THIRD GENERATION.

7. ELIZABETH POVALL, b. Dec. 1729, m. *Peter Winston,* son of Isaac and Marianna Fontaine Winston. Issue: 9, ISAAC WINSTON; 10, MARY ANNE; 11, PETER, m. two sisters, *Misses Jones,* had son Peter, (see No. 37 below); 12, ELIZ. m. *Hezekiah Mosby*; 13, SUSANNA, m. *Mr. Grubbs*; 14, JOHN, m. *Miss Austin*; 15, WILLIAM, m. *Martha Mosby*; 16, ANN, m. *Benj. Mosby.* (See notes on Mosby Family hereafter).
8. ROBERT POVALL, m. *Winifred Anne Miller* about 1755. Issue: 17, SARAH POVALL; 18, JOHN; 19, MARY EDITH, b. July, 1761; 20, CHARLES, b. 1763. (See Goode Genealogy, No. 115).

FOURTH GENERATION.

10. MARY ANNE WINSTON, m. *Alexander Jones.* (See note on Jones Family, p. 36). Issue: 21, JOHN WINSTON JONES; 23, ELIZA, m. *John Mosby.* (See Mosby Family, hereafter). 24, GUSTAVUS, m. *Eliz. Winston,* and moved to Paducah, Ky.
17. SARAH POVALL, m. *Samuel Hobson,* of Powhatan Co. Issue: 25, SAMUEL HOBSON, m. *Eliz. Johnson* of Powhatan Co., had a son—SAMUEL, m. SUSAN GOODE, No. 189; 26, RICHARD, m. *Martha Moore* of Powhatan; 27, BENJAMIN, m. *Miss Moore* of Powhatan; 28, JOHN, m. *Miss Littlepage* of Henrico; 29, MATTHEW, m. *Mary Stagg* of Charles City; 30, WILLIAM; 31, ELIZABETH, m. *David Crenshaw* of Amelia; 32, LUCY, m. *John Worth* of Bedford Co.; 33, SUSAN, m. *William Royall.*
18. JOHN POVALL, b. about 1760, m. widow of Dr. Edward Johnston of Powhatan, (born Turpin.) Issue: 34, RICHARD, m. *Ann Bores* of N. Y., d. s. p.; 35, FRANK PRESTON, d. unm.

FIFTH GENERATION.

21. HON. JOHN WINSTON JONES, d. Jan. 29, 1848. A prominent politician. M. C. 1835–45: Speaker of the U. S. House of Representatives, 28th Congress, married *Harriet Boisseau.* Issue: 36, MARY JONES; 37, JAMES B.; 38, ALEXANDER.
33. SUSAN POVALL, m. *William Royall* of Charles City Co. Issue: 39, SAMUEL H. ROYALL, m. *Adaline Smith* of Goochland Co., Va.; 40, BENJAMIN, m. *Ann M. Emerick* of Philadelphia, d. s. p.; 41, LUCY E., m. *Wm. W. Winfree* of Chesterfield, one son; 42, WILLIAM E., b. 1824, m. *Mary S. Cofer,* of Bedford Co., Va., seven children 1882.

SIXTH GENERATION.

36. MARY JONES, m. *Hon. George W. Townes,* Governor of Georgia. Issue: 43, HARRIET WINSTON TOWNES; 44, MARGARET; 45, JOHN; 46, MARY WINSTON; 47, ANN LOU. MARTIN; 48, GEORGE W.
37. JAMES B. JONES, m. *Ann Crawley Winston,* dau. of PETER W., g.-dau. of No. 11. Issue: 49, JOHN WINSTON JONES; 50, PETER E.; 51, WM. GUSTAVUS; 52, LOUISA WINSTON; 53, AUGUSTUS DRURY. (See Slaughter's *St. Mark's Parish*).

He entered for a large body of land lying between Greenway and Bent Creek—was one of his Majesty's Justices, and died about 1762. Children :—

116—1, SAMUEL MEGGINSON. 116—2, THOMAS. 116—3, WILLIAM. 116—4, BENJAMIN, a soldier in the Revolutionary army. 116—5, MARTHA, m. *William Horsley.*

One or more of the brothers would appear to have emigrated to Tennessee at an early day.

116-3.

CAPT. WILLIAM MEGGINSON of Virginia, son of No. 60, p. 37, was born 1735–40. A soldier in the Continental army in August, 1776. Married 1769, Elizabeth Cabell,* daughter of Col. Joseph Cabell, b. 1732, d. 1798 ; granddaughter of Dr. William Cabell,† born 1700, d. 1774. Children :—

301, JOSEPH CABELL MEGGINSON, m. *Sarah*, dau. of Col.. Archibald Bolling of " Red Oak," and niece of Col. Robert Bolling of " Chellow," (see note on Bolling Family, p. 64), and had numerous descendants. 302, ELIZABETH (?) m. *Francis Moseley.* (?)

116-5.

WILLIAM HORSLEY, son of William and *Mary Cabell* Horsley, born 1745–6, died prior to 1796, married before Jan. 13, 1768, MARTHA MEGGINSON, daughter of No. 60, p. 37.‡ Children :—

303, WILLIAM HORSLEY, one of the earliest magistrates of Nelson Co., Va., m. *Sarah Christian.* 304, MARY, m. *Micajah Pendleton,* (the founder of the first temperance society in America). 305, JOSEPH, d. unm. 306, JUDITH, d. unm. 307, ROBERT, m. *Anna Hopkins.* 308, MARTHA, m. *Richard Phillips,* d. s. p. 309, SAMUEL CABELL. 310, ELIZABETH, d. unm. 311, JOHN, m. (1), *Miss P. H. Dunscombe,* (2), *Mary Mildred Cabell.* 312, NICHOLAS, m. *Miss Scott* of Kentucky, who after his death, m. U. S. Senator George M. Bibb of Kentucky.

117.

THOMAS GOODE, son of No. 61, was born in Virginia, died in Mississippi. He had at least two sons.

313, THOMAS (?) of Raymond, Miss. 314, RICHARD of South Carolina or Mississippi.

Thomas Goode who removed from Virginia to South Carolina, about 1790, and subsequently to Mississippi, is one of th few men whose names cannot be definately fixed in this genealogical system. He is provisionally assigned to a place

---

*The Hon. Geo. C. Cabell descends from her brother Joseph. Her sister Mary Hopkins Cabell m. the John C. Breckenridge, from whom the Kentucky family came. He sister Ann m. Robert Carter Harrison from whom Hon. Carter Harrison, Mayor of Chicago, etc. Her youngest sister, born about the time of her death and named for her, *Elizabeth*, m. the Hon. W. J. Lewis of " Mt. Athos " and d. s. p.

† Dr. William Cabell, a native of Warminister, England, who came to Virginia about 1723, was the ancestor of the Cabell's of Virginia, and of many distinguished Virginians of other patronymics. A brief biography was printed in the *Richmond Standard*, April 23, 1881, by Mr. Alexander Brown.

‡ Mr. Alexander Brown remarks : " the descendants of these people are so numerous that I cannot undertake to begin to give them,"—and I, myself, do not feel like undertaking the task of hunting them up at a time when the book is rapidly going through the press.

among the descendants of one of the younger sons of our emigrant ancestors, because, had he been connected with either of the three elder sons, tradition would in all likelihood have given us indications of the fact. Was this the Thomas Goode who in 1765 received 275 acres of land in Henrico Co., or was it No. 26?

THE MORRISETTE GOODES.

119.

WILLIAM GOODE, of Chesterfield Co., Va., son of Richard Goode, No. 62 was born 1740–60. Married Mlle. Marie Morrisette,* a daughter of one of the Huguenot colonists, probably of Manakin Town.   Children :—

> 315, JOHN GOODE, b. 1770–90.   316, WILLIAM.   317, ROBERT, d. in Washington Co., Va., 1834; children.   318, BENNET, d. in Louisa Co. 319, A daughter, m. *Mr. Morrisette.*   320, MARY, m. *Mr. Moore.* 321, ELIZABETH, m. *Mr. Johnson,* and removed to Lexington, Ky., where are numerous descendants.   322, PATSY, m. *Mr. Weisiger* of Richmond.   323, WINNIE, m. *Mr. Chastain.*

William Goode was high-sheriff of Chesterfield Co., and "inspector of tobacco for the French." He owned coal mines ten or twelve miles west of Richmond.

THE NORTH CAROLINA GOODES.

121.

EDWARD GOODE, son of Edward Goode No. 63 p. 45, born 1749–60, married Polly Turpin, settled in Mecklenburg Co., and subsequently in Rutherford Co., North Carolina. Died 1808–10.   Children :—

> 324, THOMAS GOODE, b. April 1, 1871, d. Sept. 27, 1861, m. *Sarah F. Elliott.* 325, JOHN, b. 1780–90 in Mecklenburg Co., Va., m. *Miss Webb,* son, Edward Goode, Rutherfordton, N. C., 1881.   326, RICHARD.   327, SARAH, m. *Mr. Watson,* d. in Georgia ; no children.   328, NANCY, m. *Mr. Jones.* Present residence unknown ; has children.   329, AGNES, m. *Mr. Watson.* Was living in 1837, in Alabama.   330, PATSY, b. 1785–95, m. *Mr. Jay.* Lives in Rutherford Co., N. C. ; children : *James, Joseph, Edward, John, Turpin, Narcissa, Polly, Nancy.*   331, PRISCILLA, m. *Mr. Christopher.* Lives in Georgia ; children : *Lewis, Polly, Sallie, etc.*

123.

JOSEPH GOODE, of Rutherford Co., N. C., son of No. 63, was born at Mecklenburg Co., Va., removed 1770–80, from Richmond to North Carolina, where he died.   Children :—

> 332, ABRAHAM GOODE.   333, NICHOLAS.   334, THOMAS.   335, A daughter, m. *Mr. Hudlow,* has son *Andrew Hudlow,* Rutherfordton, N. C., 1881.

* The name is rendered in the Registry of Manakin Town " Morriser."—R. A. B.

125.

THOMAS GOODE, of Oglethorpe Co., Ga., son of Edward Goode, No. 63, was born 1760–70 in Virginia ; emigrated at an early day to North Carolina, thence to Oglethorpe County, Georgia, where he died, 1855–6. Married Margaret ———. Children :—

> 336, JABEZ WATSON GOODE, died at the age of 62.   337, JOSEPH T., Point Peter, Oglethorpe Co., Ga.   338, A son, Talking Rock, Pickens Co., Ga.   339, MARTHA ELIZABETH, m. *Mr. Vaughan.*

THE CULPEPER GOODES.
126.

WILLIAM GOODE, of Halifax Co., Va., son of John or Daniel Goode, No. 64, p. 45, was born in Culpeper Co., 1743, lived in Greenbrier and later in Halifax Co. Died April 16, 1815. Married Miss Glidwell of Halifax Co. Children :—

> 340, DANIEL C. GOODE, went to Georgia.   341, JOHN, d. at Norfolk, 1804. 342, WILLIAM, b. 1775, d. 1844.

127.

CAMPBELL GOODE, of Kentucky, son of No. 64, was born in Virginia, 1745–60. Moved to Kentucky with his children, 1795–1810. Children :—

> 343, WILLIAM GOODE, b. 1770–90, died 1844–50.

128.

BENJAMIN GOODE, of Lincoln· Co., Ky., son of No. 64, p. 45, was born in Amherst Co., Va., 1745–60, died 1810–30. Moved to Lincoln Co., Ky., 1790–1810. Married Elizabeth ———. Children :—

> 344, JOHN GOODE.   345, JOSEPH.   346, WILLIAM.   347, DANIEL.   348, MICAJAH, b. 1790–1800.   349, ELIZABETH.   350, AMARILLA.

129.

JOSEPH GOODE, of Botetourt Co., Va., was born in Bedford Co., 1750–60. Married Betsy ———. Son :—

> 351, GEORGE GOODE, b. 1770–80.

THE RAPPAHANNOCK GOODES.
131.

PHILEMON GOODE, of Kentucky, son of John Goode, No. 66, p. 45, was born in Virginia, 1745, died in Marion Co., Ky., 1850. Said to have lived near North Fork (Norfolk ?), Va. Son :—

> 352, ALFRED GOODE, b. 1796, d. 1872, and probably others.

Philemon ("Flemon") Goode was a soldier of the Revolution, and also in the early Indian wars. Removed with his parents to Kentucky at an early day, and settled in Lincoln Co.

131½.

MAJ. RICHARD GOODE, of Kentucky, grandson of Richard Goode, No. 45, was born 1730–40, died 1802. Married twice, having by first marriage two sons, by second three :—

353, RICHARD GOODE, b. 1760–90.   354, JOEL H.   355, A son, (ROBERT)? 356–7, Sons.

Richard Goode removed from Virginia to Rockingham, Stokes Co., North Carolina, 1760–70, and afterwards settled in Kentucky with his family. He fought with distinction at Braddock's defeat: was a Major in the Continental army, serving in the battle of Guilford Court House, and in the operations about Fort Duquesne. His descendant, Richard L. Goode, writes :—

" There is now in my possession a fine silver knee-buckle which once belonged to this ancestor, worn by him in the engagement at Guilford Court House. It has since descended as an heirloom by primogeniture. Major Goode started from Stokes Co., N. C., for Kentucky in 1802, but his leg was broken on the journey, and gangrene setting in, he died at Abingdon, Va., where he is buried. His widow secured a pension from the Government."

132.

WILLIAM GOODE, of Essex Co., Va., son of William Goode, No. 68, p. 40, was born 1750–60. Probably a soldier of the Revolution, m. (1) 1785, Polly Green ; (2) Oct. 30, 1794, Polly Dennett. Son :—

358, DENNETT, b. 1795, d. 1840.

132½.

GEORGE GOODE married Ann Markham, daughter of James Markham of the Virginia Navy, died before 1784. He is of this generation but we know nothing of his antecedents or descendants. (See *Richmond Standard*, Dec. 10, 1881).

———— ◦ ————

The generation whose record is included in this chapter came into existence during the golden days of the Old Dominion—in that period so full of fascination for the student of history, which has already furnished scenes for the pages of many a skillful word-painter, and which will hereafter, no one can doubt, be perpetuated in many a poem and romance. No one has entered so well as J. Esten Cooke into the spirit of " that striking and composite society of Virginia in the last century, with its black and white servants, working on the glebe,—its wealthy land-holders rolling in their coaches, and ruling supreme on their large estates far from towns ; its parsons of the parish, prone to easy living, quarrels with their vestries and intolerance of the 'New Light' dissent, led by Wesley, Fletcher and Whitfield ; its fishermen dredging the waters of the Chesapeake; its factors driving a profitable business in the few towns, and its stalwart borderers in the mountains and the great valley, grasping their rifles and as free as the eagle sweeping above them," and the reader is again advised to become familiar with his glowing descriptions. His characterization of the planter-class to which with few exceptions the people named in this book belonged, is here given in an abridged form.

"The planter was almost always an Englishman of unmixed race. He was a descendant of the first emigrants who took root at Jamestown, or of those who afterwards sought Virginia as a place of refuge from the heavy hand of Cromwell. If they brought any means with them, they purchased rich tracts on the lowland rivers, and built fine houses. If they were poor they went further up, 'took up' tracts which they engaged to defend from the Indians, paying so many shillings rent to his Majesty annually 'at the feast of Michael the Archangel,' as the old deeds ran; and if these latter were prudent, energetic, and acquisitive of land, as almost all of their race were, they died wealthy.

"This was the origin of the planter-class. Their ancestors had been men of social position but impoverished fortunes. The descendants held the same position, but were the owners of great estates. With the family blood they inherited all the family proclivities; and as they were the controlling class from social influence, and almost from their numbers, the commonwealth received from them an impress which it has never lost. Able writers—among them Mr. Bancroft—have contested this controlling influence, but it existed in spite of other important elements. These were the brave and conscientious Huguenot element—men who had fled from bigotry and persecution in France to the free air of Virginia—and the Scotch-Irish element, chiefly encountered in the rich Valley of Virginia. The Valley was also the home of large numbers of thrifty and law-abiding Dutch and and Germans, owners of comfortable houses, huge red barns, and broad fertile acres."—(*Virginia in the Revolution*).

"Although coming from the British mother country," writes Shaler, "the origin of the Virginia blood was in many ways different from that of the people who settled the Massachusetts colonies. The settlers of Massachusetts were, in the main, from the towns of Britain; they were much more trained to the arts, and less to agriculture, than the Virginia settlers; a larger portion of them were educated men. They were by habit a more social or perhaps a more gregarious people. This is shown in their settlements, which took the shape of villages, and did not lead to the settling of the folk in isolated farm-houses, as was already the custom of the rural English. In Virginia the colonists were principally from the country districts of England. Their absorbing passion was not for religious discussions; it was for the possession of land, for the occupations and diversions of rural life. When their interests were involved they tended not to religious disputations, but to politics. This appetite for land seems never to have been a part of the New England desires; in Virginia and Kentucky it was the ruling passion.—(*Kentucky*, p. 19).

FIFTEENTH GENERATION.

Nous n'avons que faire d'aller trier des miracles et des difficultez estrangieres ; il me semble que par-my les choses que nous veoyons ordinairement, il y a des estrangetez si incomprehensibles, qu'elles sur-passent toute la difficulté des miracles. Quel monstre est ce, que cette goutte de semence, de quoy nous sommes produicts, porte en soy les impressions, non de la forme seulement, mais des pensements et des inclinations de nos peres? cette goutte d'eau, ou loge elle ce nombre infiny de formes? et comme porte elle ses ressemblances, d'un progrez si temeraire et si desreglé, que l'arriere-fils repondra a son bisayeul, le nepveu à l'oncle.—MICHEL DE MONTAIGNE, Essais, II., xxxvii.

THE PRINCE EDWARD GOODES.

137.

JOHN COLLIER GOODE, of Warren Co., Ky., son of Robert Goode, No. 69, p. 47, was born 1750–60. Removed to Kentucky, probably remaining a time in North Carolina 1790–95, and died in Warren Co., 1830–50. Married (1) Dorothea Venable.* Children :—

    368, SAMUEL VENABLE GOODE, d. 1862. 369, EBENEZER, Tompkinsville, Ky., 1885. 370, JOSEPH, Nobob, Barren Co., Ky., 1885. A soldier in the civil war, in 7th Kentucky Infantry, U. S. A. 371, THOMAS, dead, 1885. A soldier in the 7th Kentucky Infantry, U. S. A. 372, ROBERT, dead. 1885.

138.

ROBERT GOODE, of Kentucky, son of No. 69, was born 1750–60,

*THE VENABLE FAMILY.—"The luminous assemblage of names which have been engrafted on the family tree," remarks Brock "attests the estimation in which the Venable family is held, whilst the re-cords of the descendants in distinguished station, and in literature and science is most honorable." (See *The Venable (or Venables) Family* by R. A. Brock, *Richmond Standard*, Nov. 27, 1880). The Venables, Barons of Kinderton, from whom Abraham Venable, who came to Virginia in 1680, claimed descent, were descended from Richard Venable, one of the retainers of William the Conqueror. Abraham Venable m. Mrs. John Nix. His son Joseph was ancestor of the Maryland Venables; his son Abraham of Louisa Co., b. 1700, had three daughters and seven sons, fore-fathers of all the name in Virginia.

Dorothea Venable, wife of John C. Goode and Agnes Venable, wife of William Goode were daughters of Charles (son of Abraham) Venable, and Elizabeth, dau. of Robert Smith of Port Royal. Her uncle, John Venable, was commissary in the Continental Army, and the hero of the affair with the tory, John Hook, whom Patrick Henry has immortalized in his celebrated speech in defense of Venable, who had taken two of Hook's steers for the use of the troops.—"But hark! what notes of discord are there which dis-turb the general joy and silence the notes of victory—they are the notes of *John Hook* hoarsely bawling through the American camp, beef! beef! beef!" Her uncle Nathaniel, in whose store in Prince Ed-ward Co., Philip Goode, No. 171, grandfather of the writer, received his early training, was father of Col. Samuel W. Venable, and U. S. Senator Abraham B. Venable, (perished in burning of the Richmond Theatre, 18:1,) and grandfather of Abraham W. Venable, M. C. of N. C., Col. Chas. S. Venable, C.S.A., Aid-de-camp to Gen. R. E. Lee, and Prof. in Univ. of Va., Maj. R. V. Gaines, C.S.A., Maj. A. V. Ca-bell, C.S.A., etc., his granddaughter, Eliz. Gaines m. Samuel Pryor, son of 106, g. s. of Thomas Goode, 58, his gr. grandson Mr. Ligon m. MARIA F. GOODE, No. 385. Mr. Peyton R. Carrington has extensive MSS. relating to this family.

and received from his father five hundred acres on Green River, Ky. He is believed to have moved to Kentucky as early as 1790. He had, doubtless, several children, the name of one only being known. Perhaps Rebecca Goode, who was living in 1840 in Kentucky, receiving pension as the widow of a Revolutionary soldier, was his wife. Children:—

> 374, ROBERT GOODE, and others.

147.

THOMAS GOODE, of Jamestown, Va., son of Robert Goode, No. 69, was born about 1780, died 1865. Married Miss Farley. Children:—

> 381, MARY E. A. GOODE, m. *Thomas Vaughan* of Rice's Depot, Prince Edw. Co., Va. ; living 1875. 382, LOUISA, m. (1) *Rev. Mr. Blanton*; (2) *Albert Farley*, who d. bef. 1880, moved to Texas 1850–60. A widow 1880. 383, ROBERT J., moved to Texas bef. 1861, living at La Grange, 1870. 384, WESLEY, m. 1859–60; moved to North Carolina ; d. 1805; left three children. 385, MARIA F., m. *Mr. Ligon*; moved to Texas bef. 1861 ; had children. 386, HENRY L., d. 1865–70, near Prince Edw. C. H. ; m. a sister of Robert Venable Davis of Prospect, dau. of *Martha Venable* Davis, dau. of Robert Venable, (brother of the wives of Nos. 137 and 149) who m. Sarah Madison.

Prof. S. O. Southall of the University of Virginia, knew Thomas Goode in the later days of his life, and speaks of him as one of the most excellent men of his acquaintance,—a strict and enthusiastic Methodist who often rode thirty miles to a preaching,—a prosperous man who left a handsome property to be divided among his children. Mr. E. A. Edwards of Petersburg, writes: "He was a thrifty farmer, and one of the best men I ever knew,—a man of sterling worth, and high respectability and social standing." He bore the name of "Good Tom" among his kinsmen, to distinguish him from other Thomas Goodes.*

149.

WILLIAM GOODE, of Prince Edward Co., Va., son of Robert Goode, No. 69, p. 47; was born 1755–75, died before 1820. Married Mrs. Holloway, (born *Agnes Venable*). Children:—

> 387, WILLIAM GOODE. 388, PATSY, m. *Thomas Baldwin*. 389, NANCY, m. *Anderson B. Miller* of Prince Edw. Co. 390, A daughter, d. yg.

This family lived at the lower end of Prince Edward Co., near the Amelia line.

150.

THOMAS GOODE, son of Philip Goode, No. 70, p. 48, was born in Amelia Co., Va., 1760–1800. A planter in Amelia Co. Removed to Missouri in 1839. Married Miss Jones. Children:—

> 391, ROBERT S. GOODE. Graduated, Hampden Sidney College, 1839. Moved to Missouri. 392, A daughter, m. *John G. Wiley* of Missouri.

---

*At his house, Philip Goode, grandfather of the writer, passed the last night in Virginia when moving to Ohio in 1805.—G. B. G.

393, (—1024) LOUISA MARIA, m. *P. S. Smith.* 394,(—1026, A) MARY ELIZA, m. (1) *William Burwell Smith*, (2) *J. L. Minor.* 394¼, (—1026, A) SALLIE C., m. *Gen. J. L. Minor.* 392–3, (—1026, B) MARTHA M., m. *Theodore Stanley.* 392–4, (—1027) FANNIE, m. *David Humphreys.* This Thomas Goode was known among his kinsmen as "River Tom," to distinguish him from his cousin of the same name. He was a wealthy man for his time, and in 1840 removed to Cole Co., Mo., with his entire family. (See page 400.) His wife was Eliza Royall Jones. The record of 392 on page 76 is erroneous : later information enables me to give full accounts of his descendants on pages 271 and 400. Cancel No. 392.

151.

JOHN COLLIER GOODE, of Prince Edward Co., Va., son of No. 70, page 48, was born 1750–70, died 1830–40. Married Elizabeth J. Hawkins. He raised a large family of children, emigrated West early in the century, probably to North Carolina and thence to Kentucky. Children : —

395, BENJAMIN M., b. in Trigg Co., Ky., 1800. 396, WOODSON. 397, JOHN. 398, HARRY.

152.

SAMUEL MOORMAN, of Waynesville, O., son of Andrew and *Prudence Goode* Moorman, was born in Virginia, and removed with his parents to Ohio. Married March 4, 1824, Lucy W. Johnson, b. March 21, 1800, d. July 7, 1876. Children : —

400, PAMELIA W. MOORMAN, b. March 4, 1825, m. *Ezekiel Leonard*, who d. March 30, 1882 ; lives near Wilmington, O. 401, EMILY W., b. March 4, 1825, m. *David Leach*, who d. Feb. 5, 1885, lives near Wilmington, O. 402, HENRY H., b. Aug. 23, 1827, d. 1827. 403, MARY ANN GOODE, b. Nov. 25, 1830, d. Sept. 1, 1854, m. *Jacob Good*, a soldier U. S. A., died in the war. 404, JOHN J., b. June 7, 1833, d. June 14, 1881, m. Feb. 12, 1858, *Lydia H. Whinrey*, d. March 11, 1881. No issue. 405, BARNET GOODE, b. July 21, 1836, m. Dec. 9, 1869, *Annie C. Robinson*, lives near Xenia, O. Has contributed valuable information to this work. 406, SUSAN, b. June 23, 1839, m. (1), *William Fawcett*, who d. 1860, (2), *Lewis Bainbridge*, who d. 1876, (3) *Washington Hemmick*, (son of 155), lives at Columbia City, Ind. 407, WILLIAM D., b. April 3, 1845, m. Feb. 12, 1876, *Martha Starbuck*, lives near Wilmington, O.

156-1.

SAMUEL DANIEL, of "Level Green," Charlotte Co., Va., son of William Pride and *Ann Goode* Daniel, No. 72, p. 49, was born 1750–70, and died about 18 —. Married Martha Friend. Children : —

1030-1, MARTHA DANIEL, m. *Mr. Shepperson*, of "Cottage Home," Charlotte Co., Va., a well-to-do planter. Son : 1, *John Shepper-*

son, planter, of Charlotte Co., who married Miss Burton, of Petersburg. and had five children.

1030-2, SAMUEL. 1030-3, MARY, m. *Hilary G. Richardson.* 1030-4, LUCY, m. *P. Ligon.* 1030-5, JOHN W. 1030-6, SUSAN, m. *John Hutchinson.* 1030-7, Son ; moved to Mississippi, a wealthy planter.

156-2.

JOHN DANIEL, of "Hickory Grove," Charlotte Co., Va., a prosperous planter, son of No. 72, p. 49, was born 1750–70, and died before 1850. Married (1) Miss Spencer, who had four children ; (2) Francis A. Dupuy, dau. of Capt. John Dupuy.* Children : —

1031-1, WILLIAM DANIEL, m. Bettie McGeehee. Children : 1, *John Daniel* (a lawyer in West Virginia); 2, *Nathan ;* 3, *Bettie;* 4, *Sallie ;* 5, *William.* 1031-2, ROBERT, of "Level Green," m. Agnes Anderson. Children , 1, *Bettie ;* 2, *Sterling ;* 3, *Mary ;* 4, *Agnes.* 1031-3, KATE, m. *Samuel Clark.* Children : 1, *Laura,* m. Mr. Buford, of Lynchburg ; 2, *Bettie ;* 3, *Walter,* of Bedford or Campbell Co. 1031-4, JOEL W. 1031-5, JULIA, m. *Henry I. Venable.*

156-3.

WILLIAM PRIDE DANIEL, of Charlotte Co., Va., daughter of No. 72, p. 49, was born 1750–70, died 18 —. A prosperous planter. Married (1) Miss Moseley, of Halifax Co., Va.: (2) Miss Hill, of Cumberland. Children : —

1032-1, MARTHA DANIEL, m. *John Doran Hunt.* 1032-2, SUSAN, m. *J. D. Hunt.* 1032-3, JULIA, d. unmarried.

156-4.

MARY DANIEL, daughter of No. 72, p. 49, removed to Mississippi with her husband, —— GOODE who was her cousin, and who was possibly THOMAS GOODE, No. 117, who was probably identical with Thomas Goode, No. 82½, son of Philip Goode, No. 49. She had a daughter.

156-6.

HEZEKIAH GOODE DANIEL, of "Oak Grove," Pittsylvania Co., Va., son of William Pride and *Ann Goode* Daniel, No. 82, p. 49, was born 1798, died Dec. 20, 1859. Married 18 —, Mary Le Fevre Watkins, daughter of Benjamin and *Susan Dupuy* Watkins, of Pittsylvania Co., who was born 1806, died 1849. Children : —

1033-1, SUSAN DANIEL, m. *J. J. Tinsley,* of Cascade, Pittsylvania Co. Children : 1, *James W.;* 2, *Mary F.* 1033-2, BENJAMIN WATKINS,

---

* Note error in Brock's Dupuy pedigrees (p. 154), in reversing the sexes of the Dupuy and Daniel partners in this marriage. (See Watkin's Genealogy, p. 28.)

d. unmarried. 1033-3, CHRISTINA AGNES, m. *J. N. Tinsley*, of Pittsylvania Co., Va. Children : 1, *Mary Jessie*, m. T. S. Smith, planter of Pittsylvania Co. Children : 2, *Alonzo C.;* 3. *William Daniel;* 4, *Agnes Lee.* 1033-4, WILLIAM E. 1033-5, ROBERT PRIDE, d. y. 1033-6, JOHN H., of Baltimore, Md., m. Georgia Garland. Child : 1, *Garland H.* 1033-7, MARY A., m. *Dr. H. S. Belt.* 1033-8, EDWIN DUPUY, d. y. 1033-9, JENNIE C., m. *W. H. Ward*, of Tazewell C. H., son of William Ward, of Wythe Co., who d. 1881.

Hezekiah Goode Daniel was, like his brothers, a planter of extensive landed estate. He was a man of aristocratic feelings and indomitable pride, though easily approachable, kind and lovable. He was a strict Presbyterian, following the bent of his kinsfolk, the Watkinses and the Dupuys, rather than that of the Goodes, who adhered to the Established Church, and who appear to have been regarded by their Daniel descendants as somewhat too fond of the things of this world. H. G. Daniel's grandfather, who was the great-great-grandfather of the writer of this book, appears to have been a famous huntsman, especially devoted to riding across country. An old slave ("Uncle Spencer"), inherited by H. G. Daniel from his maternal grandfather, was accustomed to find reasons in the doctrine of heredity for any non-Presbyterian tendencies among the children, and to remark : "Dem Goodes was allus mighty fox-huntin' people."

The Dupuy family, with which the Goode-Daniels intermarried, trace their descent from Bartholomew and *Susanne Lavillon* Dupuy, Huguenot refugees, who came from France to Virginia in 1700, and were among the most prominent of the colonists at Manakintown on the James River. One of Mr. Brock's late contributions to Virginia family history is the "Partial List of the Decendants of Bartholomew Dupuy" in Volume V of the Collection of the Virginia Historical Society, pp. 151-82, which I am glad to be able to extend in some slight degree in this volume.

The old sword of Bartholomew Dupuy, who was an officer of the guards of King Louis XIV. is referred to in Mr. Brock's paper. This old sword, "used in fourteen pitched battles and four duels on the Continent, and always wielded in a good cause," was regarded with great veneration by the Dupuys, and was used by members of the family in the war of the Revolution, the war of 1812, the Mexican war, and was left at the house of Mr. Edmund Ruffin, Prince George Co., father-in-law of the then owner Dr. J. J. Dupuy, at the beginning of the civil war and was lost. Its romantic history has been well told by John Esten Cooke in his "Story of the Huguenot Sword."

The Dupuys who are included in the Goode pedigree are all descendants of John Bartholomew Dupuy, second son of the refugee who married Mlle. La Garronde. The eldest son, John Dupuy, Captain of Cavalry in the Revolution, married Miss Watkins, and had twelve children, one, Susan, who married Benjamin Watkins, the father of the wife of Hezekiah Goode Daniel, No. 156-6, another Frances A., who married John Daniel, No. 156-2, one Dr. Joel W., whose daughter Martha married Joel W. Daniel No. 1031-5. The second son of J. B. Dupuy, Peter Dupuy, of Richmond, was the grandfather of Peter Dupuy McKinney, who married Sarah A. Lyle, No. 1896.

157.

COL. EDWARD TATE, of Lynchburg, Va., was born about 1760, in Southwestern Virginia. Died, 1823, in Lynchburg. Married LUCY BARKSDALE, daughter of Claiborne and *Sarah Goode* Barksdale, No. 73, who was born Dec. 6, 1766.   Children :—

> 408, SALLY MACKARNESS TATE, m. *Mr. Dyson.* 409, HARRIET CLAIBORNE, m. *Col. John M. Harriss.* 410, ALICE, b. 1785, m. *David G. Murrell.* 411, CALVIN. 412, GRIEF BARKSDALE. 413, GARLAND. 414, EDMUND.

Col. Tate was one of the early settlers of Lynchburg, had a long and vexatious lawsuit with the Lynch family, and which he lost, concerning the ownership of the land upon which the city is built. He was very active in the movements which preceded the Declaration of Independence by the colonies.

He fought in many battles of the Revolution, especially at the Cowpens and Guilford Court House, and for gallant conduct he received the compliments of the commanding officers and, subsequently, the thanks of Gen. Washington.

He had two brothers, Caleb and John, early settlers of Lynchburg ; other members of his family were early settlers of Tennessee.

158.

SUSANNAH BARKSDALE, daughter of No. 73, was born July 22, 1765, and married Mr. CRENSHAW, probably son of David and *Elizabeth Povall* Crenshaw, of Amelia Co. (See note p. 69.)   Son :—

> 415, JOHN CRENSHAW, b. 1785-95.

159.

CAPT. DABNEY COLLIER, of Haywood Co., Tenn., was born about 1770, died June 14, 1844. Married (1) March 24, 1796, Patsy Pulliam, (2) June 10, 1802, SARAH BARKSDALE, daughter of Maj. Thomas Claiborne and *Sarah Goode* Barksdale, of Charlotte Co., who died Jan. 23, 1823, (3) June 3, 1824, Phœbe P. Elam.   Children :—

> I. AMELIA COLLIER, m. Mr. Jackson, of Charlotte Co.
> 416, (—1048-1) THOMAS BARKSDALE COLLIER, b. March 31, 1803, d. July 9, 1854. 417, (—1049-2) DABNEY CLAIBORNE, b. March 24, 1807, d. July 17, 1843. 418, (1050-3) AGNES HOWARD, b. Jan. 26, 1809, d. Aug. 22, 1843, m. *William Thompson Collier.*

Capt. Collier was an officer of Virginia troops in the war of 1812, a man of education and culture, and an extensive and successful planter. He lived in Mecklenburg Co., Va., until in 1838 he removed to Haywood Co., Tenn.

161.

GRIEF BARKSDALE, of Charlotte Co., Va., son of No. 73, was born

Dec. 25, 1772. A planter living near Rough Creek Church. Married Miss Elliott. Children :—

419, WILLIAM H. BARKSDALE. 420, CHARLOTTE, m. *Samuel Hannah*, lives a widow, at Aspinwall, Charlotte Co., 1885. 421, LUCY JANE, m. *Mr. Edwards* of Charlotte Co. 422., NANNIE, m. *Mr. Townes* of Mecklenburg Co. 423, A daughter, m. *Mr. Emmett* of Kanawha Co.

165.

THOMAS STEGER, of Amelia Co., Va., married ELIZABETH GOODE, daughter of Mackerness Goode No. 75, p. 49. Both were born, lived and died in Amelia Co., between the years 1770 and 1850. Children :—

424, MARY STEGER, m. *Armistead Adams* of Cumberland Co., living 1870, several children. 425, MARIA, d. bef. 1870, m. *Thomas Pride.* Son, *Thomas Pride,* soldier C. S. A., killed in war, and others. 426, JULIA, m. *John Pride,* dau. m. *Mr. Wood* of Amelia C. H., 1882. 427, HARRIET, m. *Wade Steger* of Amelia Co., d. 1840. 428, LOUISA, m. *Garland Hendricks* of Cumberland Co., liv. 1870. 429, THOMAS, liv. Amelia Co., 1870, married. 430. WADE, liv. 1857, Petersburg, Va., unm.

171.

PHILIP GOODE, of Waynesville, Ohio, eldest son of Samuel and *Mary Collier* Goode, No. 76, p. 50, was born in Prince Edward Co., Va., March 15, 1771, died at Campbell C. H., Va., Sept. 24, 1824. Married March 7, 1793, Rebekah Hayes, who was born in Amelia Co., Nov. 17, 1770, died in Sidney, Shelby Co., O., 1855. Children :—

431, SAMUEL MACKERNESS GOODE, b. Sept. 2, 1795, d. June 29, 1826. 432, PATRICK GAINES, b. May 10, 1798, d. Oct. 17, 1862. 433, PHILIP BURWELL, b. Feb. 2, 1801, d. Apr. 28, 1803. 434, MARTHA ANN, b. Mar. 24, 1805, d. Aug. 28, 1809. 435, Rev. WILLIAM HENRY, b. June 9, 1807, d. Dec. 16. 1879. 436, ELIZABETH REBEKAH, b. Nov. 5, 1809, d. Aug. 1, 1829. She was for two years teacher in the Port William Academy Carroll Co., Ky. 437, FRANCIS COLLIER, b. Aug. 28, 1811. 438, HARRIET ANN, b. Aug. 24, 1813, m. *Rev. Samuel Trumbull Gillett, D. D.*

Rev. W. H. Goode, D. D., has kindly supplied the following reminiscences of his father :—

Philip Goode was physically and intellectually a superior person. Five feet ten inches high, weighing 216 pounds, well proportioned, portly and active, he was a man of great physical force. His boyhood days were passed on a farm in Virginia. He spent a period of clerkship in the store of Mr. Nathaniel (?) Venable, whom he always greatly esteemed. Previous to coming of age, his father formed for him a partnership with Mr. Richard Bibb—father of the Hon. George M. Bibb, the celebrated Kentucky jurist and U. S. Senator.*

*See Gilmer's *Georgians*, p. 106, for THE BIBB FAMILY.

His life was mainly spent in mercantile pursuits, changing once or twice, for a time, to farming.

He opposed slavery as a great national and social evil, though I have no recollection of ever hearing him express any opinion as to the personal guilt or moral impropriety of holding slaves. He saw its demoralizing influences, and was unwilling to raise his family in a slave state. At one time he thought of removing to New England, but was at length induced, I think through the influence of John Randolph of Roanoke, to go out and take a look at the North-western Territory. He was pleased, and determined to make it his home, but did not remove till 1805, several years after the formation of a state government in Ohio. He settled near Waynesville, Warren Co., and remained there till 1814, when he moved to Xenia. He died a deeply and consistently pious man, a sound Methodist, with strong friendship for Presbyterian forms in some respects, owing probably to his long connection with the Venable family, before mentioned. He was well educated, a good business man, a great reader, and pretty well versed in elementary law, history, theology, ethics, and political economy, a vigorous and correct writer, and a ready and interesting talker,—withal a stern, decided, independent man—too much so for general popularity, though always securing respect. He died in 1824. His dying expression was—"My house is ready."[*]

He was skillful in breeding fine horses. He owned the blooded stallion "Curiosity," for which he paid one thousand dollars, an enormous price in those days, and the celebrated white mare "Cleopatra," and was instrumental in greatly improving the breed of horses of western Ohio.

Francis C. Goode, his son, gives the following account of Philip Goode :—

He probably attended some college in Virginia, but did not graduate. He was a merchant in Jamestown, Prince Edward Co., Va. At an early period of his life he entertained a desire to remove to a free state, that he might rear up his children in the habits of personal labor and industry, and save them from the corrupting influences of slavery, to which he was by principle opposed. His attention was turned to the North-western Territory to which, by the ordinance of 1787 for the government of the territory of the United States north-west of the Ohio River was secured exemption from slavery. He accordingly visited the territory twice (while yet a territory) before he removed his family. His first visit was to the north and north-east of what is now the State of Ohio. His second visit was to the southern part of the territory on the Ohio River and the Miamies. He traversed the Alleghanies by the south pass, crossed the river at the place where Cincinnati now stands, and hesitated between settling there or at Waynesville, but liking the location of the latter place best, and preferring the neighborhood of the largest town, he decided in its favor. He accordingly bought a tract of fifteen hundred acres on the east bank of the little Miami, opposite Waynesville, where the village of Corwin now stands. To this tract of land in the spring of 1805, the brothers, Gaines, Burwell, John and Henry J., moved and Philip and Samuel followed in the fall of the same year. The land was now divided, and Philip soon erected a log house with windows of paper, tightly

[*] The advanced ideas on the subject of slavery held by Philip Goode were, perhaps, in part due to his connection with Methodism. As early as 1780, in the Conference held at Baltimore, the church committed itself to the opinion that the preachers who held slaves should promise to set them free, and that slavery was "contrary to the laws of God, man and nature and hurtful to society ; contrary to the dictates of conscience and true religion, and doing that which we would not others should do to us and ours." Thus was begun the struggle which culminated sixty-four years later, in the separation of the church into two great branches North and South. Many of the southern Methodists, familiar with slavery in its milder aspects, did not agree to these doctrines. Others, among whom was Philip Goode, adopted them as a guide for personal action only.

stretched and made translucent with bear's grease, and, previous to 1811, a brick house. The house of hewn logs (see record of Gaines Goode, No. 173) into which he moved on his first arrival, was on the north side of the state road from Waynesville to Wilmington, about one-third of a mile east of Waynesville. Adjoining it on the north stood the one-story cabin erected in the spring of 1805 by the four brothers.

The following article, signed "The Antiquary," (written by George T. O'Neall, Esq.,) appeared in the *Waynesville News*, July 31, 1886:

A HOUSE WITH A HISTORY.

There is at present a house standing at "Wood-End," the suburban home of Mr. Charles F. Chapman, which, for well-authenticated age and interesting association, is without a rival in Wayne Township.

It is a hewn log-house, 29 feet wide by 38 feet long, is one story and a half high, with a six-foot fireplace, and a little opening for the greased-paper windows. But few of the logs are a foot in diameter, and the joists and rafters were small trees with one side flattened by the axe. The history of the house is that it was erected in 1805 by the Goode brothers, Philip, Gaines and Burwell; that the family arrived on the ground in the late spring of that year; that they dwelt in cloth tents until they got their corn planted, which they were unable to do until the 30th of June; and, notwithstanding this late date of planting, they gathered ninety bushels per acre from their ground.

After planting their corn, they proceeded to build their house, which continued to be the home of one of the brothers until 1828, and was still used as a residence until 1848, when it was removed a short distance from the original site: and although now in good preservation, it is used by Mr. Chapman as a shelter for his fine flock of merino sheep.

This house was a typical pioneer home. The family whose home it was, was an Old Virginia family who had left their native State to escape the stain of slavery. They were educated, intelligent and refined, and although living in a cabin in the wilderness, they wove around them a web of culture and refinement.

Mrs. Goode, the wife of Philip, the only married brother, was a woman of rare cultivation, and, contented and happy in a pioneer's cabin, she quickly made her home the social center of the neighborhood.

Reminiscences of early days and pioneer life at Waynesville are numerous. Silk gowns, with brocade petticoats stiff enough to stand alone, and imported from England before the Revolution, were strange treasures for a log cabin in a frontier settlement; but such were in the wardrobe brought from Virginia by Mrs. Goode. A black silk gown with a blue satin petticoat, and an olive silk gown with a red brocade petticoat—the latter worn in a play about seventy years ago by Miss Angelina Lorrain (sister of the Rev. Alfred M. Lorrain and great aunt of W. D. Howells, the novelist and critic), who was dressed as a shepherdess and carried a crook. The Goode family all being members of the Methodist Church, this primitive cabin became the home of all the traveling Methodist preachers, and such men as Arthur Elliot, Russell, Bigalow, John Strange, James B. Finley, were frequently at home beneath its roof. In this connection I may be pardoned for telling an anecdote: In 1809, when the venerable Bishop Francis Asbury was on one of his annual tours through the West, he stayed all night at the Goode cabin, and as a matter in course, the next day, at 10 o'clock A. M., he preached to the assembled pioneers. After the service a bountiful dinner was spread, of which all partook, and the Bishop mounted his horse and proceeded on his way, when Gaines, one of the brothers, called the scattered groups together and said: " Now, brothers, we have had a good meeting ; the good Bishop has preached us a fine sermon, we have had our dinners, and now I want you all to go and help me roll the logs on that nine-acre clearing." And it is to be supposed hat many knotty theological points were discussed and their labor lightened by many a well-applied scriptural text.

The Goode brothers were not only prominent in matters of religion, but were also to some extent politicians. At one time there had been a heated political canvass, and the result had been an almost solid Whig vote at Waynesville. A passing stranger inquired why it was so—why such a unity of political sentiment. The reply given was that the population consisted of three classes—Quakers, Methodists and Whiskymen—and that they were all controlled by three men who all happened to be Whigs : Noah Haines controlled the Quaker vote, Burwell Goode the Methodist vote, and —— controlled the whisky vote.

The old house still stands ; let the hallowed recollections of old associations still cling around the old walls, and may its present owner long care for them.

THE ANTIQUARY.

Our kinsman, Frank C. Goode, (No. 1141) at my request, visited the site of the Goode homestead, and in the following letter gives the results of his investigations. Philip Goode, No. 171, referred to in the letter, was the grandfather of the author of this volume; Burwell Goode, No. 176, the grandfather of the writer of the letter, Gaines is No. 173, Garland No. 445, Col. Clement Read, a neighbor of the Goodes of Charlotte Co., was the greatgrandfather of Mary Goode Read, wife of Dr. T. C. Goode, No. 588. Col. Clement Carrington was another neighbor and a distinguished officer of the Revolution, wounded at Eutaw Springs. He was own cousin to William Carrington, No. 296 (293), of the Goode Pedigree.

SPRINGFIELD, OHIO, May 16, 1886.

ON Tuesday last I visited Waynesville and the old· Goode farms, accompanied by my friend, Mr. George A. Warder, a young gentleman with a penchant for amateur photography. Under the guidance of Mr. George T. O'Neall we went over the land and located some of the ancient landmarks.

On Wednesday, I examined at Lebanon the county land records sufficiently to note the early transfers of the Goode lands and the division thereof between the brothers.

The title to this land is founded upon Virginia military land warrant No. 46, issued to Clement Read, eldest son and heir-at-law of Col. Isaac Read, of Charlotte Co., Va., and based upon the military service of the latter as an officer of the Virginia line on Continental establishment, and I have referred you to certain acts of the Virginia legislature awarding to her soldiers of the Revolution bounties in land, and prescribing the quantity according to the rank. The other leading legislative enactments, &c., worthy of notice in this connection are, briefly as follows :

You know, as matter of history, that at the epoch of the Revolution the sovereignty of the territory northwest of the Ohio was the subject of conflicting claims on the part of several of the old colonies, notably Virginia and Connecticut, growing out of indefinite territorial limitations under their respective royal charters. The situation was not conducive to harmony, and upon September 6, 1780, Congress, by resolution or enactment, recommended the States maintaining these claims to make liberal cession thereof to the United States for the common benefit of the Union.

Virginia had then already made some progress with her legislature upon the subject of land bounties to her revolutionary soldiers, and had no doubt looked to the appropriation for the purpose of the lands claimed by her on both sides the Ohio.

On January 2, 1781, the General Assembly of Virginia, in response to the Congressional recommendation, passed an act yielding to Congress her sovereign claims to the territory northwest of the Ohio, but imposing certain conditions to the grant, and making reservations which were apparently unacceptable to Congress, for we find the latter, September 13, 1783, in a further enactment defining the conditions upon which the proposed cession would be accepted. October 20 of the same year the Virginia legislature adopted the formal act of cession, embodying the conditions and reservations proposed by Congress, and authorizing her delegation in Congress to make conveyance by deed unto "the United States in Congress assembled" the Northwest Territory.

The most important reservation made by Virginia was the stipulation that in case the quantity of good land on the southeast side of the Ohio should prove insufficient to satify the bounties already engaged to her should be made up to such troops in good lands on the northwest side of the Ohio and between the Little Miami and Scioto Rivers.

In pursuance of their authority in the premises, Thomas Jefferson, Samuel Hardy, Arthur Lee and James Monroe, delegates in Congress from the commonwealth, formally delivered the deed of cession provided for, which was by Congress formally accepted and enrolled March 1, 1784.

The next Congressional legislation we have upon the subject is in 1788 (July 17), when a resolution was adopted calling attention to the fact that certain locations and surveys have been made of lands within the reserved district ; reciting the condition in the act and deed of cession, and declaring invalid all locations and surveys made northwest of the river until Congress shall have been officially informed of the exhaustion of available lands on the southeast side. The required notification was speedily made, and soon after Congress adopted the legislation providing for the making of title, &c., so as to carry into effect the Virginia bounty laws, and the condition reserved in the cession.

I mention this only because the Read survey was one of those located prior to the time when Congress had received official notice of the existence of a deficiency of land, authorizing the Ohio reservation to be drawn upon, and it was therefore one of the locations impeached by the resolution of 1788. However, it was subsequently acquiesced in, and the future steps taken in receiving the title from the Government were all taken after the regular order of procedure had been established by Federal legislation.

From time to time Congress extended the period in which claims for land under these old vague bounty laws might be proven and warrants obtained until long after all the territory in the Virginia military district had been taken up. After the exhaustion, in this manner, of the Ohio lands, a scrip was issued to the holders of warrants, which were finally, under the act of 1852, honored by commutation in land beyond the Mississippi. Over one million acres in the Western States were thus disposed of.

The location and entry of survey No. 399 was made by or for Clement Read, August 2, 1787 ; the land was officially surveyed as 1333⅓ acres in 1794. Clement Read sold and transferred his right to this survey unto Clement Carrington, of Charlotte Co., Va., and to Carrington, the assignee, accordingly was issued the patent to the land under date of March 11, 1797. Mr. Carrington retained the title until August 20, 1805, the date of his conveyance thereof unto "Gaines Goode, Philip Goode, Jr., and Burwell Goode" as tenants in common. The deed unfortunately omits to state the amount of consideration paid, the recital being —— pounds, Virginia currency. The execution was acknowledged in open court at Charlotte Co., and attested by Thomas Read, clerk of the court.

Apparently the Reads, Carringtons and Goodes had other similar dealings. I found on record in Warren Co. a document from which it appeared that Carrington had conveyed to the Goode brothers at least one other survey which he in turn had bought of Clement Read. This last was a tract of 1,000 acres lying in an adjoining county.

The record discloses no other changes of title until January 11, 1809, when the three brothers Goodes assuming to act as a partnership or association (and apparently not recognizing any individual property rights), by two deeds of conveyance divided the land into two parcels of 913 and 673 acres, respectively, the former of which, being the northeastern part of the survey, was granted unto Philip and the latter unto Gaines Goode.

July 10, 1800, Gaines and wife, Nancy, for the consideration expressed of $1,180, conveyed unto Burwell the east half of his moiety, viz, 337 acres. Notwithstanding the expression of a pecuniary consideration, I am convinced this deed was but one step in performance of the scheme to equally divide among the three brothers the land according to its value. Philip Goode, 913 acres at the northern part, was never broken and contained proportionately much less tillable land than the southern part, beside it was more distant from Waynesville and the other settlements already effected in the neighborhood.

In November, 1810, "Philip Goode and Rebecah," his wife, out of their moiety conveyed to Burwell, for the consideration $340, 76 acres more.

The three brothers were the proprietors then, respectively: Philip, 837 acres ; Gaines, 336 acres ; Burwell, 413 acres.

I have made a rough drawing of the survey to explain the lay of the land and the relative location of the several homesteads. You will understand my plat is only approximately correct, but I am sure it is not far wrong in essential features, and it will give a clearer idea of the situation than I could otherwise convey. On my map the line AB marks the dividing line between Philip and Gaines as established by the deed of 1808. DT is the line separating the farms of Gaines and Burwell, and the triangular parcel BEC represents the 76-acre tract conveyed by Philip to Burwell.

I believe I have omitted to state that a resurvey of the entire tract in 1808, before the division, disclosed a total of 1,586 acres.

The course of the river as indicated on my map is that described in the ancient deeds of conveyance ; at present it more nearly approaches a straight line. The more tortuous old channel is still plainly visible in the depression of the bottom.

The straightening of the couse of the river is accounted for in part by a local tradition to this effect : At a point near the upper end of the loop in the river shown at the westerly corner of my plat, some one had erected a dam to obtain the necessary supply of water for operating his mill. He omitted taking the pains to secure the assent of our Uncle Gaines, the proprietor of the eastern bank at that time, but it seems the gentleman was not interrupted during his constructive work.

Subsequently, when Uncle Gaines' family were attacked with ague, the malarial influence was attributed to the obstruction of the water by the dam.

Our uncle rose to the necessities of the occasion and proceeded to dig a ditch through his own land from a point above the obnoxious dam to another point below the curve. The tradition does not inform us the results of this engineering work upon the health of Uncle Gaines's family, nor what may have been the miller's remarks upon the occasion ; the river become beautifully straight at this point.

On the east side and about a quarter of a mile, generally speaking, from the river, the land rises from the level bottom, by abrupt incline, some 75 feet. Much the larger part of the Goode lands were upon this plateau which slopes gently northward from the southern boundary of the survey to the bluffs overlooking the valley—the vicinity of my grandfather's house being the highest.

The location was admirably chosen ; such an one as the first comers to a new country might well make. From almost every point a commanding prospect may be had, the valley as seen from the brow of the hill being one of the fairest rural landscapes in the world.

The soil was of first quality, and although portions of the survey have been badly used through exhaustive farming, there is none of it but is still highly

Map showing Philip Goode, Burwell Goode, and James Goode land tracts near Waynesville, with Wilmington Road, the Little Miami River, L.M.R.R., Samuel Goode's Cabin, Chenoweth Farm, Butterworth and O'Neall farms, Cemetery, and Present site of Corwin.

N ← → S E / W compass

S. 38° W. @ 485 poles

L.M.R.R.

Wilmington Road

Philip Goode

Burwell Goode

James Goode

Samuel Goode's Cabin

Chenoweth Farm

Little Miami River

Cemetery

Butterworth and O'Neall farms

Present site of Corwin

To Xenia 15 miles, and Dayton ... miles

To Cincinnati, 50 miles

Waynesville

N. 39° W.

along Wm. Mott's line

1. Original log-houses (1805)
2. Philip Goode's brick-house (1810)
3. Burwell Goode's dwellings (1808, 15, 25)
4. James Goode's house (or Garland's) (1830-1)

productive. The bottom lands of the Little Miami are of unsurpassed furtility.
The railroad runs just under the hills skirting the valley, and the station opposite Waynesville, called Corwin, is itself quite a village.

Referring to my map, "No. 1," the site of the original settlement is about one mile, rather more than less, from Waynesville. It is one mile and a quarter from Waynesville by the Wilmington pike to the gate in front of my grandfather's old home, from which latter point to the gate in front of No. 1 is perhaps an eighth of a mile or more.

That part of the Gaines Goode farm, including the side of the early log-houses and 104 acres of surrounding land, now belongs to Mr. Charles F. Chapman, an intelligent and courteous gentleman, who has resided thereon some fifteen years.

His residence is a handsome cottage situated in a tasteful, well-kept inclosure shaded with fine old trees, and with a grassy lawn stretching out to the road 200 yards away.

His house stands on the Pilgrim Rock of our family, for incorporated in the structure is the rough log-house built by Gaines and Burwell Goode on their first coming to Ohio. There is one room, perhaps two, of the house, included within the old log framing. I was shown into the ancient room, and a snug one it is, with a ceiling hardly more than seven feet high. Modern civilization has hidden, both externally and within the room, the logs which form the walls, but the outlines of two heavy beams supporting the ceiling attest the architecture of a former time.

The hewn log-house which was built for your grandfather no longer serves for human habitation, and has been moved from its former location to a point about 100 yards northeast of the Chapman house, where it now does modest but efficient duty as part of a sheep barn.

The log framework seems nearly intact and in good preservation. Its outside measurements are 28 by 20 feet.

Notwithstanding its present humiliation, our party of visitors entered its honorable inclosure with uncovered heads.

Fifty yards north of the Chapman house are several fine springs of water, the presence of which determined our forefathers in the choice of location of their dwelling.

The present owner has collected the water of the springs, and with a hydraulic ram forces it up a hill to his house and supplies it to a fountain upon the lawn.

In an adjoining field are some monuments of the remote proprietors, mound builders or Indians; a detached mound, and also a clearly-defined and elevated circumference surrounding a depression or shallow ditch, which in turn circumscribe an interior mound. We were told that many human bones had been found in one of the gravelly knolls close by.

The brick house built by your grandfather, in 1810, stands more than a quarter of a mile away, and a little north of east from the Chapman house. It is one of the most venerable mansions in the neighborhood, and is in an advanced state of decay. For a great many years it was the home of a couple of respectable but parsimonious Quakers, Seth and Dinah Furniss, of whom I often heard my grandmother speak, and who are both now dead.

The house seems to have been constructed with principal front to the east, but afterwards, because of changes in the location of the public roads or for other reasons, the original arrangements was reversed, and at present, as shown in the picture, it fronts westward. The brick building has no door upon that side, and the adjoining frame addition in which is now the front door was evidently a later construction.

The most interesting portion of the house internally is an old-time fireplace originally of mammoth size, as is still plainly to be seen, somewhat reduced of late years. I measured the original opening, and found it 6 feet long by 4½ feet high. The hearth is formed of rough, undressed stones, and extends out into the room nearly four feet.

The old house, with three hundred acres or more of your grandfather's farm, belongs to Mr. Davis Furniss, a grandson of the couple just mentioned. In this connection I note that your grandfather disposed of all his portion of the survey during the year 1814, and in some five or six different parcels. The aggregate amount of the consideration realized by him from the sales of his share of the land as expressed in his deeds was about $7,000.

My grandfather, Burwell, after marriage, built and successively occupied three different houses, all south of the road, the first two of logs and the third of frame. The dates of erection were about 1808, 1815 and 1825. Of the two log houses nothing remains. My father (No. 474) was born in the second of these log houses. The frame house, which was my grandfather's house from 1825, is still a comfortable dwelling, and is occupied by the family of Mr. Andrew H. Williamson, who owns the larger part of the Burwell Goode farm.

From the veranda we could see the smoke rising above Xenia, fifteen miles distant, and it is said that at night is plainly visible the illumination of electric lights at Dayton, fully twenty miles away.

The white brick house, covered with creeping vines, is the dwelling erected in 1830 or 1831 by Uncle Gaines Goode or his son Garland. The house is in excellent repair, and it stands near the road and just back from the brow of the hill. The west part of Uncle Gaines's farm, on which stands this old mansion, now belongs to a Mr. Andrew J. Thorpe, of Waynesville.

With continued good wishes for your success, I am yours very truly,

F. C. GOODE.

In addition to the three brothers referred to in the letter, three others came to Ohio. Samuel Goode (No. 174), who before he went back to Virginia lived in a cabin on land given him by Philip, on the banks of the Little Miami. Henry J. Goode, No. 180, who lived for a time in the oldest cabin on Burwell's farm, and Lieut. John Goode, who, while serving with his regiment in Ohio in the war of 1812 sometimes came to Waynesville.

A certain idea of the life in those days may be gained from W. D. Howells's sketch, "My Life in a Log Cabin," in the "Youth's Companion," July 12, 1887. This cabin was a few miles further up the Little Miami River.

The dam episode referred to on page 81C resulted in a long law-suit, in which John Satterthwaite, the dam-builder, defended by John Maclean, afterwards of the U. S. Supreme Court, was victorious.

I have a letter in verse dated May 26, 1808, written by Philip to Gaines at the time :

" WELL, SIR :—

"I finished planting my corn yesterday while you were taking a civil game at law.

> Who takes this game ought first to know his cards ;
> No doubt your adversary knew them well,
> Else he would not have ventured to the seat
> Of justice with his dark surprise."

(The seventy-one lines omitted display a profound knowledge of the laws of euchre, and also a considerable acquaintance with common law.)

" You did not expect to find this depravity in dignified characters. Did you not know that there are two kinds of dignity, one looking up and the other down? and that equity, like Joseph's coat, has divers colors. He that gets justice ought to be satisfied, and he that don't has the fun of trying, unless he misses it through chagrin, which, like the angry wind cloud, leaves devastation behind it.   Y'rs,   P. G.''

Philip Goode, about 1815, for the purpose of better educating his boys, he removed to Xenia, where he kept a store. Specie being scarce, he bought merchandise in the following manner : On his annual trips east he took with him a drove of horses, which he sold in Virginia and Carolinas, and with the money bought his goods in Philadelphia. On his last trip east he caught cold from exposure in a rain storm, and died a few days afterward at Campbell Court House, Va. It was his intention, had he lived, to remove to Illinois, where he had bought a fine tract of land on Peoria Lake, which is now occupied by the city of Peoria. It is believed that the title to the site of Peoria still stands in his name. He always dressed in a shad-bellied coat and knee breeches, and a broad-brimmed white hat, turned up behind. He was usually seen smoking. Politically, he was a firm adherent to the Republican school of Jefferson, Madison and Monroe. He was a great admirer and personal friend of Patrick Henry, after whom he named one of his sons. He way very fond of the violin in his youth, and frequently played with Mr. Henry who was a proficient performer on the flute. He was given to political discussion and a frequent correspondent of the newspapers on political questions. A short time before his death he was candidate for the State Senate. The election took place after his death, but before it was known by his family, and he was defeated by a small majority on account of rumors of his death. His house was the stopping place of all Methodist ministers in Xenia.

Concerning his mother, Mistress Rebekah Hayes Goode, Rev. William H. Goode writes :

" My mother was a sweet tempered woman. She was tenderly raised, without practice in domestic labors, as was common in the slave-holding section. Removing West she adapted herself to the changed circumstances and became, at least in our estimation, a model house-keeper. Nobody ever baked so sweet a cake as she. She was neat and tidy in person ; brisk in movement even in the feebleness of age. Converted at the age of fourteen, she was a pious and consistent member of the Methodist Church for over seventy years. She was always modest, diffident, rather timid in her expression of personal Christian experience, and I do not recollect ever to have heard her speak on the subject without tears. As she advanced in years, her Christian confidence strengthened and she passed triumphantly to rest at the age of eighty-five. She was a sweet singer and never lost the old spirit of Revolutionary patriotism. At her knee and around her chair I learned the tune and the words of ' Hail Columbia,' and at the same place and of the same voice I learned to sing—

There is a Heaven o'er yonder skies,
A Heaven where pleasure never dies—
A Heaven I sometimes hope to see,
But fear again 'tis not for me."

Mistress Rebekah was a model house-wife of the old Virginia school. The writer has seen a cotton counterpane woven from cotton grown upon her father's plantation, and spun by herself a century ago, and also a beautifully woven fabric made by her,—produced by shredding silk scraps, soaking them in boiling water, combing, carding, spinning and weaving,—a species of domestic industry in vogue in Virginia in her early days. She received as her marriage portion thirteen negro slaves, but the bulk of her father's property went to the sons.

Richard Hayes was a wealthy tobacco-planter in the county of Amelia, the owner of two hundred slaves, and a man of extensive influence. He was reared a member of the established church, but with his wife was among the earliest members of the Methodist Church, which was established in Virginia in 1772. The story of his conversion to Methodism is one of the curious bits of family tradition. He cultivated large tracts of tobacco, the product of which it was his practice to carry to Richmond for sale. Richmond, about forty miles distant, was then a village with a number of tobacco warehouses, and a large export trade with England, and the planters were in the habit of "rolling" their tobacco over the country roads; tobacco hogsheads having a block nailed to each head, were made to traverse the whole distance on their own peripheries, several oxen pulling on the up-grades, and as many negroes holding fast to ropes behind, when a down-hill grade was encountered. The journey to Richmond took part of two days, and our planter, who was supervising his gangs of tobacco-rollers, riding along with them on horseback, stopped over night at the house of another planter. His hostess invited him to accompany her to a school-house, near at hand, to listen to a traveling preacher who was introducing a new religion. From that day he was a Methodist, and his house a home for the circuit-riders. At the house of his daughter, Mrs. White, was held, in 1787, one of the earliest Conferences of the Methodist Church. (Bennett's "Memorial of Methodism in Virginia," p. 239.) His children were, however, confirmed in the established church, of which the Methodists were at first considered to be only a society. In the time of the Revolution his acknowledged patriotism enabled him to protect the preachers, who were by principle non-combatants. His sons, however, were officers in the Continental army.

Some memories of the Revolutionary war were told by Rebekah to her grandchildren. She remembered seeing the red-coated procession of Col. Tarleton's troopers as they passed by her father's door on their famous raid into Virginia. A party of these rode up to the door and ordered her father to tell them were he kept his horses. "The best of them are with the Continental army, the others are in yonder field," replied the old gentleman, whereupon the raiders helped themselves to what they wanted.

EXCURSUS.—THE HAYES FAMILY.

This family was probably of Irish extraction, and was one of the first to settle in Virginia. A family of the same name came from Donegal, Ireland, to Pennsylvania in the middle of the eighteenth century, and some of their descendants appear to have come to Virginia.

Richard Hayes, from whom we claim descent, was one of the earliest planters in Virginia, and must have been a man of means; since before 1642 he bought a plantation from John Howard instead of taking up public land. An act of the Virginia Assembly passed in March, 1642, (*Hening I*, 247) defines the boundaries of the counties of Isle of Wight and Upper Norfolk (afterwards Nansemond), and the eastern line of the first was made to coincide with that of the plantation of Richard Hayes, which was included in the Isle of Wight. The plantation was on the south side of the James and the west side of Chucatuck Creek, looking to the east over Hampton Roads, and and directly across the river from Newport News. This was a part of the Warraskoyack settlement, nearly as old as Jamestown. Robert Hayes, who was granted 1,400 acres in Lower Norfolk Co., prior to 1644, was probably a son of Robert Hayes 2d, who received, in 1648, 500 acres in the same shire,

and Joseph Hayes, gent, who recorded 300 acres in York Co. in 1651. Owen and Adam Hayes, who received 500 acres in 1664 and 660 in 1690 in Lower Norfolk Co., were probably grandsons.

The Hayes plantation in Isle of Wight Co. is mentioned in the Virginia Statutes of 1674. James Hayes, publisher of the *Virginia Gazette* in colonial days, was probably of this family; also Lieutenant John Hayes and Robert Hayes, mentioned in the *Virginia State Papers* as veterans of the Revolution.

Richard Hayes, probably great grandson of Richard Hayes, the 1st, was a wealthy planter, born 1710-20, who settled in Amelia Co. near the court house about the middle of the century. John Hayes, who was granted 604 acres in same county, 1750, was possibly his brother. The family was connected by marriage with the Venables, Pegrams, Pryors and other families of the region. ("Cousin Polly Venable" and "Cousin Betsy Pegram" were spoken of by Rebekah Hayes Goode in her old age.) The Hayes homestead was about thirty miles from Richmond. Though its owners are forgotten in Amelia Co., the family descendants remember the hospitable old plantation, with its great orchards and troops of servants. The deduction here given is derived from family tradition, confirmed by statements in the will of Mary Hayes, recorded at Amelia Court House April 23, 1789.

FIRST TO FOURTH GENERATION.

1-4. RICHARD HAYES, of Isle of Wight Co., and his son, grandson and great-grandson.

FIFTH GENERATION.

5. RICHARD HAYES, of Amelia Co., b. 1710-20: He removed to Georgia about 1790, in company with his sons, and was one of the early settlers in the southwest portion of the State. He had many children:—

6, CAPT. RICHARD HAYES; 7, WILLIAM; 8, HENRY; 9, MARTHA, m. *William White;* 10, MARY, d. 1789; 11, POLLY, m. *John Mann;* 12, A daughter, m. *Mr. Branch;* 13, BETSY, m. *Mr. Madison;* 14, REBEKAH, m. PHILIP GOODE, No. 171. (See Goode Genealogy.)

SIXTH GENERATION.

6, CAPT. RICHARD HAYES of the Virginia Line, Continental army, removed to Georgia with his father, 1790-1800. Had children:—

16, JAMES HAYES, living in the Mississippi Territory, 1826. From him was perhaps descended Gen. H. T. Hays, C. S. A.

7. WILLIAM HAYES, an officer in the Revolutionary war, had at least two sons:—

17, JAMES, went south; 18, GEORGE, b. about 1770.

8. LIEUT. HENRY HAYES, a soldier of the Revolution, wounded at "The Cowpens," m. in Virginia *Mary Clarke* (own cousin to Gen. Winfield Scott, U. S. A.) and after living for a time in North Carolina, went to Georgia, settling first in Green Co., afterwards in Habersham Co., where he died 1810-30. Children: 19, ELISHA HAYES, drowned in early manhood; 20, JOSEPH T., d. unmarried. 1875-80; 21, JUDGE JAMES HENRY; 22, MARY, m. *Mr. Bird;* 23, ELVIRA, m. *Mr. Dorsey,* of Alabama; 24, MRS. JORRALD; 25, A daughter. m. *Col. Sims,* of Talladega Co., Ala.; 26,

A daughter, m., descendants in Illinois; 27, SARAH, d. unmarried; 28, MARY, d. unmarried.

9. MARTHA HAYES, m. *William White*, children : 29, daughter who m. *Mr. Armistead*, of Rough Creek Church, and had a grandson in Hampden Sidney College, 1826 ; 30, KATHERINA.

11. POLLY HAYES, m. *John Mann*, b. 1757, d. 1826, removed to the District of Tennessee.

12. MRS. BRANCH, had children : 32, CAPT. BRANCH, of Buckingham Co.; 33, A daughter, m. *Capt. Weisiger*. (See above, p. 134.) 34, MRS. GUNN, who has descendants in Kentucky, at one time in Bloomington, Ind.

SEVENTH GENERATION.

18, GEORGE HAYES, of Early Co., Ga., was born at Amelia Court House, 1770, settled about 1800 near Athens in Clarke Co., Ga., subsequently in Early Co., where he died 1840 (White's *Statistics of Georgia* mentions the Hayes and Collier families as among the earliest settlers of Early Co.) " He was a true type of the Virginia gentleman of the old regime—hospitable, generous and chivalrous." He married about 1810, Mary Hamilton, of Clarke Co., Ga., b. 1787, d. 1870. Children :—

    35, JOHN RICHARD HAYES ; 36, ELIZABETH WHITE ; 37, JAMES THWEATT; 38, WILLIAM EVERARD ; 39, MARY ANN TABITHA ; 40, DUKE HAMILTON, b. 1819, a planter, living 1885, at Coushatta, Red River Parish, La., has eight daughters and one son ; 41, GEORGE SMITH, living 1885, in Barrier Parish, La.

21, JUDGE JAMES HENRY HAYES, of Georgia, living 1855, in Lakeland, Fla. Children :—

    42, ROBERT A. HAYES, soldier C. S. A., killed ; 43, REV. WILLIAM M., b. 1845, a soldier C. S. A., lost his arm in the service, a minister in the Georgia Conference of the Methodist Church, stationed in 1885 at Talbotton, Ga.; six children ; 44, MARY T., m. *Rev. Eppes Tucker*, of Fla.; 45, ELLA R., m. *Mr. Manus*, of Ga.; 46, MRS. A. E. EVANS, of Fla.; 47, MRS. M. G. MOORE, of Fla., d.; 48, HENRY G., Lakeland, Fla.

16, JOHN RICHARD HAYES, b. about 1812, lived at Macon till 1838, in Charleston, S. C., 1839–45, and in Thomas Co., Ga., 1845, m. *Sarah Ann Wiley*, b. 1804, (dau. of Ann Jack, own cousin of Capt. James Jack, bearer of the Mecklenburg Declaration of Independence to the Continental Congress) d. in Thomasville, Ga., 1880; had nine children, four soldiers C. S. A.; two only survivors, 1885 ; 48, J. R. HAYES, a planter, living on the Chattahoochee River, near Eufaula, Ala.; 49, SAMUEL L., a cotton broker and prominent man of Thomasville, Ga., of which he is mayor ; 50, GEORGE E., was killed in the battle before Petersburg, Va., and is buried in the old church at Blandford.

The writer inherited from his grandmother, REBEKAH HAYES, a pin-cushion made of the wedding-gowns of her sisters, Mrs. Branch and Mrs. Madison, and many of her descendants have her peculiar sparkling blue eyes.

172.

NELSON DAWSON, of Amherst Co., Va., son of Martin Dawson, an

immigrant from Scotland, was born about 1760.* A farmer and tobacco planter. Married LUCY GOODE, daughter of No. 76. Children:—

439, MARY GOODE DAWSON was born 1792, m. *John Wingfield.* 440, MATIL-
DA, m. *Mr. Burford,* of Lynchburg, Va. 441, SAMUEL GAINES, b.
1796, d. 1835. 442, ELIZABETH, m. *Mr. Ware* of Amherst Co., moved
to Missouri. 443, ANN GOODE, m. *James L. Lamkin.* 444, A daughter, m. *Mr. Holley,* moved to Missouri.

Col. John L. Eubank describes Mrs. Dawson and Mrs. Parks (whom in his youth he knew as old ladies,) as old-fashioned Methodists of the strictest type, wearing the plain dress and discarding all ornaments. Their daughters, who were all beautiful girls, were not allowed to wear rings or adornments of any sort, yet the neatness and becomingness of their dress was proverbial. Their husbands wore broad brimmed hats and shad-bellied coats, fastened at the neck with one button.

173.

GAINES GOODE, of Warren Co., O., son of Samuel Goode, No. 74, was born in Prince Edward Co., Va., Dec. 12, 1776, died in Warren Co., O. A soldier in the war of 1812. Married in 1804, NANCY ANN GOODE, No. 166, his cousin, who died March 19, 1841. Children:—

445, GARLAND, b. in Ohio, Oct. 19, 1805, d. Nov. 1843, m. *Susan McGuire,*
but had no children. 446, MARY ANN, b. July 10, 1807, in Warren
Co., O., d. Sept 5, 1875, m. *Rev. J. C. Bontecou,* a native of western
N. Y., minister of Cincinnati Conference M. E. Church, s. p. 447,
NARCISSA, b. Sept. 19, 1800, d. 1833, unm. 448, ELIZABETH PRIDE,
b. Feb. 5, 1811, d. July 11, 1841, m. *Joseph L. Lyle,* of Waynesville,
O. 449, SAMUEL MACKERNESS, b. Dec. 29, 1815, d. 1875. A Virginian of the old school, who visited much among his relatives in the
old state, and kept up always the sympathies, customs and dialect
of that region. He was a cripple, and a man of eccentric character. He was an extensive contributor to this Genealogy, and had he
lived to see its completion, no one could have taken so much interest
in it as he.

After the death of his father, Gaines being the oldest son at home, stayed with his mother and kept the family together till after her death, in 1802. They moved from Virginia in the spring of 1805, and settled on the east bank of the Little Miami River, opposite the town of Waynesville, O., Burwell, John and Henry accompanied him, and they were six weeks in making the trip. They pitched their tents of cloth in the woods, and in them they lived till they cleared a patch of ground for corn which they did not get planted till the 21st of June. After this they put up a house of unhewn logs in which they lived, then put up another of hewn logs, into which Philip and family moved on their arrival, the

---

* THE DAWSON FAMILY is descended from Martin (?) Dawson, a native of Scotland and his welsh wife, who came to Virginia about 1745. His son, MARTIN, m. Miss Carter, and had children, 1, *Nelson,* m. LUCY GOODE; 2, *Zachariah,* who m. *Lucy Rucker,* (afterwards Mrs. John McDaniel), and had sons: 1, *Benjamin,* a clergyman; 2, *Martin;* 3, *Nelson Carter* (whose daughter Lucy m. Mr. Page) 4, *Lewis;* 5, *Susan,* m. *Mr. Heiskell.*

fall of the same year; Samuel and family came at the same time. He lived in the house of hewn logs until he was quite advanced in years, when he erected a a brick house in which he died.

174.

SAMUEL GOODE, of Jasper Co., Texas, son of Samuel Goode, No. 76, was born in Charlotte or Prince Edward Co., Va., March 20, 1779, died in Jasper Co., Texas, April 28, 1863. Married, 1801, Frances W. Rowlett, of Virginia. Children:—

> 450, GIDEON J. GOODE, b. Dec. 27, 1802. 451, WILLIAM R., b. Feb. 6, 1805. 452, MATHEW MACKERNESS, b. 1807, d. 1863.

He emigrated from Halifax Co., Va., to Ohio, with his brothers in 1805, but becoming dissatisfied he returned to Virginia, then went to Tennessee where he lived for some years, and finally, in 1835, settled in eastern Texas, near the banks of the Red River, where he was one of the pioneers, and was the owner of about 30,000 acres of land.

175.

MARTIN PARKS, of Amherst Co., Va., married NANCY GOODE, daughter of Samuel Goode, No. 76, born Aug. 17, 1781. They lived and died near Pedlar's Mills. Children:—

> 453, WILLIAM HENRY PARKS, b. Oct. 27, 1802, died in Lafayette, Mo., March, 1802, leaving children. 454, SAMUEL GOODE, b. March 14, 1804, d. 1864, m. *Miss Berks* of Rockbridge Co. Issue: 1, *Charles*, (C. S. A., killed in battle), and others. 455, ELIZABETH GAINES, b. May 21, 1809, m. *Capt. Geo. Hylton*, C. S. A., of Allwood, Amherst Co. Issue: 1, *Valentine*, (Tye River, Nelson Co., Va.), 2, *Lucy* and others. 456, MARY COLLIER, b. July 4, 1805, d. Nov. 1883. 457, WILDIN BURWELL, b. March 21, 1809, m. dau. of *Kemp Davies* of Amherst, moved to Missouri, 1840, d., children. 458, JOHN MARTIN, b. March 19, 1812,, moved to Missouri, 1856, liv. 1880, Irene, Hill Co., Texas, two sons, soldiers C. S. A., one killed in war; one died from effects of exposure. 459, SARAH A. S., m. *Whiting Davies* of Pedlar's Mills, a farmer. Issue, 1, *William*, b. 1841, soldier C. S. A., d. 1862, from wounds received in battle; 2, *Roderick*, b. 1846, soldier C. S. A., 2d Va. Cav., d. 1867 from effect of wounds; 3, *Charles Parks*, 4, *Samuel*, 5, *Lizzie*, 6, *Lucie*, 7, *Mary*, 8, *Sarah*. 460, LUCY AMANDA, b. June 9, 1816, m. *Richard P. Jones* of Sandridges, Amherst Co. Children. 461, MILTON MACKERNESS, b. 1818, m. *Sarah Jane Wortham* of Amherst Co., six sons and four daughters. 462, GEORGE W., b. May 7, 1820, d. 1855, two sons and two daughters. 463, NANCY MARGARET, b. June 7, 1824, d. May 27, 1859. 464, GRANVILLE PHILIP, b. Aug. 8, 1829, d. March 12, 1882, at Big Island, Bedford Co., Va., m. *Eliza Morris*. Children: 1, *Lucie A. Goode*, b. 1854, m. *W. J. Carper*, Wytheville, Va.; 2, *Nancy;* 3, *Frank Oscar*, Balcony Falls, Rockbridge Co., Va.; 4, *Granville Beauregard*, b. 1862; 5, *Mary F.;* 6, *Willie Jones;* 7, *Georgiana*, b.

1874. 465, CAROLINE T., b. Dec. 27, 1811, liv. 1885, Big Island, Bedford Co., Va. 466, GAINES PARKS, Pedlar's Mills, 1881, m. *Miss Ogden,* of Amherst Co.

Mrs. Parks was visited by F. C. Goode in 1843. She was then living at Pedlar's Mills on Tobacco Row Mountains She had a large family of negroes. Speaking of adebt which she wished to pay, her cousins asked her why she did not sell a negro if she could not meet it in any other way. She was greatly astonished and replied that she would about as soon sell one of her own family.

The manner in which slavery was regarded by many representative people of Virginia, is well illustrated by the following words put by Mrs. Terhune (Marion Harland), into the mouth of Mrs. Summerfield, one of the characters in her novel, "Judith ":—

The inconveniences and injustice of slavery—which nobody spelled with a capital S, or thought it safest to mention under his breath—were freely admitted by serious thinkers. The divine origin of what had not then been dubbed "The Peculiar Institution," was not an article of the Virginian's creed. Many influential planters had openly expressed their intentions of manumitting their servants by will, and were shaping their financial plans to that effect. I heard my own parents commend such a course ; was familiar with the idea that by the time I was grown, "the colored folks" would all be free with comfortable homes of their own. From babyhood I was taught to be respectful to the elder servants and not to maltreat the younger. "Because," as was often impressed upon me, "it is mean to strike one who has no right to strike back." The affectionate intercourse between the white family and their negroes was a matter of course—a perfectly natural state of affairs in the estimation of all parties concerned. "The children" included those of all complections. "Mam Peggy," the cook, for forty years in the Summerfield kitchen, swept me out of her domain when she was cross or busy, as emphatically as she did her grandchildren. My grandmother and aunt sat up at night with the sick at "the Quarter," tending them as assiduously as they cared for invalids of their own blood and name. The oldest colored person on the plantation had been born there and his parents before him. "Our family" was referred to and quoted oftener by them than by their owners.

Tupper in his "Ode to the South," writes of the slaves.

"Yes, it is slander to say you oppressed them,
Does a man squander the prize of his pelf?
Was it not often that he who possessed them,
Rather was owned by his servants himself.

The fact which is crudely suggested here, is vividly illustrated in Page Thacker's "Plantation Reminiscences," a charming little book, already rare. Now that sectional jealousies are being set aside, the people of the North are beginning to understand that the patriarchal system of the South, though to the slave-holders themselves a curse, in the emancipation from which they rejoice, was an undoubted benefit to the barbaric races, thus brought under the influence of European culture—a benefit conferred upon them at a severe cost to our Republic.

Mr. Brock in modification of the statement upon page 47 of this book, calls attention to the will of Richard Randolph, the elder brother of John Randolph of Roanoke, to which Whittier referred in a letter to Mr. Brock, dated April 24, 1885, as "condemning slavery in stronger terms than I ever ventured to use in regard to it." In "Randolph of Roanoke," the Quaker poet has perpetuated in immortal verse, the sentiments of that noble Virginian, which were shared by very many of his associates in the South.

He held his slaves, yet made withal
    No false and vain pretences,
Nor paid a lying priest to seek
    For Scriptural defences.
His harshest words of proud rebuke,
    His bitterest taunt and scorning,
Fell fire-like on the Northern brow
    That bent to him in fawning.

He held his slaves; yet kept the while
    His reverence for the Human;
In the dark vassals of his will
    He saw but Man and Woman!
No hunter of God's outraged poor
    His Roanoke valley entered;
No trader in the souls of men
    Across his threshold ventured.

And when the old and wearied man
    Lay down for his last sleeping,
And at his side, a slave no more,
    His brother-man stood weeping,
His latest thought, his latest breath,
    To Freedom's duty giving,
With failing tongue and trembling hand
    The dying blest the living.

In collecting material for this little book, I have found records of at least ten men who manumitted their slaves during their own lifetimes, or by their wills, and the number of those who looked forward to their freedom, as finally to be accomplished by some generally adopted system, was large. The speech of Hon. W. O. Goode in the Virginia Senate, upon the gradual emancipation of the slaves, is spoken of as a valuable contribution to this subject. (See also the record of Judge Samuel W. Goode, No. 197.) Robert Goode, No. 69, manumitted his slaves by will, as we have seen. Philip Goode, No. 171, Gaines, 173, Samuel, 174, Burwell, 176, Susanna, 179, and Henry 180, removed to a free state, in order that their children might be reared in a different atmosphere. Tristram Capehart, mentioned further on in this book, liberated his slaves, 75 in number, provided well for them, and sent them to Liberia. Other instances are those of Dr. Bradley of Wilkes Co., Ga., (Gilmer's *Georgians*, p. 146), Gen. Samuel Blackburn of Bath Co., Va., Mr. Dinwiddie, Jonathan R. Cushing, Richard Randolph of "Bizarre," just alluded to, and John Randolph of Roanoke. Members of the Society of Friends in Virginia, quite generally freed their slaves, absolutely or at specified ages of maturity, as early as 1776. The teachings of the early Methodist preachers, which in many instances, no doubt, influenced their hearers, are too well known to need mention here.

176.

BURWELL GOODE, of Waynesville, O., son of Samuel and *Mary Collier* Goode, No. 76, was born in Prince Edward Co., Va., Jan. 30, 1784, died in Waynesville, O., Dec. 21, 1851.   Married Jan. 9, 1807, Elizabeth Smith, (see p. 164) born Jan. 29, 1787, died Oct. 7, 1863. Children :—

> 467, JAMES SMITH GOODE, b. April 2, d. Aug. 7, 1808.   468, MARTHA ANN, b. Mar. 28, 1810, m. *Charles N. Wilkerson.* 469, SAMUEL, b. May 7, 1811, d. July 27, 1813. 470, THOMAS MILTON, b. Dec. 24, 1812, d. Mar. 2, 1885. 471, JOHN COLLIER, b. Nov. 28, 1814, d. Feb. 25, 1822. 472, PHILIP GATCH, b. July 11, 1818, d. Mar. 31, 1822. 473, MARY ELIZABETH, b. April 23, 1820, m. *Robert D. Poague.*   474, JAMES SAMUEL, b. Jan. 23, 1822. 475, GEORGE HENRY, b. Aug. 4, 1824, d. Mar. 25, 1833. 476, DANIEL GAINES, b. Dec. 14, 1826, d. May 7, 1833. 477, BURWELL SMITH, b. Aug. 9, 1830, d. Mar. 21, 1864.

Burwell Goode removed at the age of 20 to Ohio, in company with his brothers, and settled with them at Waynesville, where he lived, until his death, upon a portion of the original tract already referred to. He was a soldier in the war of 1812, serving for more than thirty days, his company commander being John McLean, afterward Chief Justice of the United States. He was an active, energetic farmer, a communicant and class-leader of the Methodist Church, and for many years one of the magistrates of his county. In the records of the county still stands a minute of one of his decisions, which was as unusual as it was pertinent. Two men having traded horses, each claimed to have been defrauded ; the squire's verdict was that they should trade back.

He was six feet tall, of large frame, with complexion inclined to swarthiness, and strong, positive cast of countenance ; of a disposition passionate, though not revengeful, and easily placated. His industry was proverbial, and he loved hard work for its own sake. His religious convictions were controlling, and he was a diligent student of the Bible, of which he had minute knowledge. He was courteous and hospitable, and delighted in conversation, especially the discussion and argument of theological subjects, to which he was greatly addicted.

177.

LIEUT. JOHN GOODE, U. S. A., son of No. 76, was born in Prince Edward Co., Va., July 20, 1780. He was Lieutenant in the 19th and 20th Regiments, U. S. Infantry in the war of 1812.   Died in South America.

When last heard from John Goode was in New Orleans in 1815, having received a commission from Gen. Simon Bolivar, " the liberator," and was about to sail for South America to take part in the struggle which led to the establishment of the present governments of Venezuela and Colombia.

The secret of his voluntary exile is explained by the following incident : He served in a company commanded by Capt. Richard Talbot, afterwards of Madison, Ind. A dispute sprung up between the officers of two companies as to which should have the place of honor in one of the engagements in Northern Ohio. Capt. Talbot's company was the oldest, but the captain of the other company was his senior. In the course of the dispute Capt. Talbot was insulted by the other captain. After the battle John Goode wrote a challenge to this person and insisted that Capt. Talbot should act as his second, which he refused to do, saying that if fighting must be done he was the man to do it, so the duel took place, with Talbot as principal and Goode as second. Talbot killed his man, and John Goode was never afterwards known to smile. He was a very large, fine looking man, with a very stern face.

178.

CHARLES WINGFIELD, of Lynchburg, Va., was born in 1788, and was living in 1880, aged 92. He married ELIZABETH GOODE, daughter of No. 76, born Jan. 30, 1784, died 1840. He was brother of the husband of No. 439. No issue.

179.

JACOB HAAS, of Jefferson Co., Ind., was born in Virginia, 1780–90, died in Jefferson Co., Ind., about 1855. Married, about 1819, SUSANNA GOODE, (widow of ―― *Tinsley*) daughter of No. 76, born in Prince Edward Co., Va., July 30, 1791, died in Jefferson Co., Ind., May, 1841. The family record is lost. Children : —

> 478, ANN HAAS, b. 1815–20, m. *Eden Shotwell*, a native of New Jersey, lived in Kansas and reared many children. 479, SUSAN, b. 1820, d. 1838. 480, SAMUEL GOODE, b. 1821, d. Nov. 14, 1859. 481, VIRGINIA, m. *Jeremiah Pierce*, d. s. p., Valparaiso, Ind. 482, JULIA, m. *Joseph Pierce*, her brother-in-law, lived in Valparaiso, Ind. Children :—
> 1, *Susan;* 2, *Rebecca;* 3, *Andrew;* 4, *Virginia;* 5, *Charles;* 6, *Sarah;* 7, *Logan,* all alive in 1869.

Jacob Haas was descended from a German family, one of the first to settle in the Valley of Virginia. He lived at Dawson's Mill, about four miles from Lynchburg, Va.; was editor of the *Lynchburg Jeffersonian*, a contractor for public roads and member of the Virginia House of Delegates. In 1834 he moved to Laporte, Ind., where he entered large tracts of Government land, and grew wealthy, and was also of the firm of Brown & Haas in Michigan City. In 1837 he removed to his farm at Madison, Ind., where he died.

180.

DR. HENRY JONES GOODE, of Sidney, O., son of Samuel and *Mary Collier* Goode, No. 76, was born in Charlotte Co., Va., April 6, 1793, died in Carthage, O., July 10, 1879. When a youth he removed with his elder brothers to Warren Co., O. A soldier in the war of 1812, though less than 21 years of age, he served as 1st lieutenant in one of the Ohio regiments in campaigns around Sandusky. He was for a time a surveyor and civil engineer in Illinois, and laid out the town of Lebanon. A farmer and physician, living most of his life at Sidney O., and in its vicinity, a man highly respected and beloved in the community. Married March 25, 1824,

Margaret McKay, who was born in Frederick Co., Va., June 16, 1804, and died in Sidney, O., Jan. 19, 1864. Children :—

483, ABIGAIL ANN GOODE, b. Jan. 19, 1825, d. June 5, 1874, m. *Joseph Shambaugh.* 484, MOSES MCKAY, b. May 15, 1816. 485, SAMUEL GAINES, b. July 1, 1830, m. his cousin, No. 444. 486, MARY ELIZABETH, b. Feb. 21, 1828, d. July 3, 1860, m. *Charles W. Wells.* 487, BURWELL PHILIP, b. Feb. 25, 1833. 488, RACHEL SUSAN, b. June 17, 1835, d. April 29, 1854. 489, SARAH JANE, b. Jan. 26, 1836, d. Feb. 13, 1854, while at school in Xenia. 490, MARIA CATHERINE, b. Feb. 5, 1841, d. Nov. 15, 1872. 491, WILLIAM HENRY COLLIER, b. Dec. 3, 1843. 492, MARGARET NARCISSA, b. Nov. 4, 1846, m. *Smith Stimmel.*

EXCURSUS.—THE McKAY FAMILY.

From notes communicated by W. H. C. GOODE, Esq.

ROBERT MCKAY came from Scotland to America early in the eighteenth century. In 1732, accompanied probably by wife and children, he formed one of the little company headed by JOIST HITE, who cut their way through the virgin forest, from York, Pennsylvania to the Shenandoah Valley, crossing the "Cohongoruton" or Potomac, a mile or two above what is now Harper's Ferry, and settling near where the town of Winchester now stands.

They numbered sixteen families in all, and were the first persons to settle west of the Blue Ridge, the pioneers of that mighty wave of emigration which within a century was to lay the foundation of many new commonwealths west of the Alleghanies, the Mississipppi and the Sierra-Nevadas.

Robert McKay settled on Crooked Run, eight or nine miles S. E. of Stephensburg, in the present Frederick Co. His descendants have a quaint old instrument engrossed upon parchment, dated Williamsburg, Oct. 7, 1734, which granted to him 828 acres, "on the Western side of the Sherando River, and on both sides of Crooked Run." He was a member of the firm of Hite, McKay, Green & Duff, who obtained about this time a grant of 100,000 acres in the northern neck of Virginia. (See Kercheval's *History of the Valley,* 2d ed., p. 139.)

His descendants, of whom there are now, doubtless, at least one thousand, are, so far as we know, all thrifty farmers, business or professional men in Virginia, Ohio, Indiana, Iowa, etc. Very many of them are like their pioneer ancestors, members of the Society of Friends, others are Methodists and Baptists.

CHILDREN OF ROBERT McKAY, NO. 1.

(Second Generation, Nos. 2–6; Third, 7–13; Fourth, 14–49; Fifth, unnumbered.)

2. ANDREW MCKAY of Frederick Co., Va., b. 1728, d. 1804, m. 1755, Jane Ridgeway, (b. 1731 in New Jersey, d. 1806, in Warren Co., O., whither she removed in 1805 with No. 9, and where she married at the age of 75, Joel McCloud). Children :—
    7, JACOB MCKAY of Virginia, "Big Jacob," m. Mary Hains; issue: 14, HAINS MCKAY; 15, WASHINGTON; 16, NOAH; 17, CASSANDRA; 18, MADISON; 19, AMOS of Delaware Co., Iowa.

8, MOSES McKAY of Warren Co., O., b. 1776, d. Jan. 28, 1828, m. Mar.
3, 1793 in Frederick Co., Va., Abigail Shinn, b. 1776 d. 1828, step-
dau. of No. 12. Removed 1818 to Warren Co., O., making part of
the journey on Ohio River flat-boats. Settled on Cezar's Creek, a
mile below Harveysburg, later, on a farm on the Little Miami River,
four miles above Waynesville, where he d. Jan. 28, 1828, possessed of
about 6,000 acres, which he devised by will to his twelve children.
In 1882 there were 97 grand-children, 197 great grand-children, and
33 great, great grand-children,—in all 349 descendants, of whom 263
were living. Children:
19½, RACHEL McKAY, b. Jan. 19, 1794, d. April 16, 1850. m. 1814,
   NathanHaines; (children: Robert Haines, Francis, Amos, Jane,
   Margaret, Noah.)
20, ROBERT, b. Dec. 17, 1795, d. June 10, 1862, m. 1818–19, Virginia
   Grubbs; (children:—Wm. McKay, Henry Clay, Patrick), m. again
   Nancy McKay; (children: Betty McKay, James, Jesse, Amanda,
   Catharine, Helen, Jacob, Robert), m. again *Mr. Wells*. He lived
   and died on the old farm at Crooked Run, Virginia.
21, SARAH, b. Nov. 11, 1796, d. Oct. 22, 1832, m. March, 1823, *Jonathan
   Collett*, (children: Ann Collett, Moses, Benjamin, George, Francis,
   Martha, Aaron, William, Robert, Asahel.)
22, GEORGE, b. Mar. 11, 1800, d. June 10, 1850, m. Feb. 6, 1823, Mary
   Ferguson who d. Sept. 24, 1878; (children: Moses McKay, Samuel,
   Mildred, Jane Tilghman, Franklin, Alfred, Mary Massie, Lucinda,
   Geo. Washington.)
23, FRANCIS, b. Jan. 9, 1802, d. Mar. 26, 1871, m. Oct. 7, 1830, Mary
   Collett; (children: Rebecca McKay, Moses Collett, Jonathan, Nathan,
   Robert, Mary Elizabeth, Sarah J.)
24, MARGARET, b. Jan. 16, 1804, d. Jan. 8, 1804, m. Dr. HENRY J. GOODE,
   (children named in GOODE GENEALOGY, No. 181.)
25, VIRGINIA, b. Aug. 22, 1808, d. Jan. 15, 1826, m. *Mr. Collett* who d.
   1762, (son of Daniel M. Collett.)
26, MARIA, b. May 23, 1811, d. Aug. 15, 1882, m. No. 4, 1830, *Daniel
   H. Collett*, who died Jan. 11, 1871; (children: Thoursin Collett, Mo-
   ses, M., Rebecca, Abigail, Elizabeth, Sarah Ann, Oliver, Francis,
   Horace.)
27, JONAS TILDEN, b. May 10, 1813, d. Dec. 11, 1883, m. Nov. 13, 1832,
   Matilda Ferguson, who d. June 1, 1855; (children: Emeline McKay,
   Sarah C., Joshua, Harriet, Horace, Euseba, Lutetia A.,) m. again
   May 24, 1864; (children: Lida McKay, Belle.)
28, LEVI DUFFY, b. Feb. 29, 1816, d. Feb. 3, 1869, m. 1836, Mary A.
   Goddis, who d, 1848–49; (children: Maria McKay, Hiram, Emily,
   Francis, Rachel,) m. again Rachel Jane Goddis; (children: Sallie
   McKay, Mary, Alrisa, Jessie, Lucy.)
29, JACOB FRANKLIN, b. June 3, 1819, m. 1854, Lucy Spangler, who d.
   Nov. 29, 1883; (children: Laura V. McKay, Charles F.)
30, MARY ELIZABETH, b. July 27, 1822, d. Dec. 12, 1873, m. Dec. 14,
   1843, *Edward Bond Hackney*; (children: Daniel Hackney, Aaron,
   Ann M., Sarah, Ellen, Harriet, Oscar, Abigail Jane, Lyda Alice, Elizabeth C., Albert.)
9, PATIENCE McKAY m. *Robert Whitacre*, moved 1805, to Warren Co., O.;
   children—(all Quakers):
       31, JOHN WHITACRE; 32, ANDREW; 33, AQUILA; 34, MOSES; 35, PRIS-
       CILLA; 36, RHODA; 37, Mrs. BENJ. MUDE of Indiana. (All raised
       families.)
10, MARGARET McKAY, m. *Robert Funston* of White Post, Frederick Co.,
   Va. Children: 38, OLIVER FUNSTON; 39, DAVID; 40, FRANCIS; 41,
   EMILY; 42, Mrs. WARD of Winchester, and others.

11, ENOS MCKAY. Children: 43–6, DAVID MCKAY, b. about 1800, living 1882 at Front Royal, Va., and three others.

12, JACOB MCKAY m. Mrs. Shinn. Children: 47, JOHN MCKAY of Cedarville, Va. Had large family; 48, Hannah, m. *Joshua Wood* of Belmont Co., O., large family; 49, JACOB of Cedarville, Va., m. Eliz. Antram; (children: Nancy McKay, m. No. 20, Joshua, Jesse Y. of Ninevah, Va., William, Sarah, Thomas, Oscar.)

3. JACOB or ROBERT MCKAY of Frederick Co., Va. m. Miss Ridgway. Children:

    13, JACOB MCKAY of Va. and others.

4. —— MCKAY, who settled in N. C. where he has many descendants, among them Hon. JAMES J. MCKAY, of Goldsborough, N. C., b. 1793, d. 1853, member of Congress, 1831–49.

5 and 6. SONS who settled in Pennsylvania and higher up the Shenandoah Valley.

THE LUNENBURG GOODES.

181.

JOHN GOODE, of Georgia, son of John and *Frances Hunter* Goode, No. 77, p. 50, was born in Virginia, 1760–80, and removed to Georgia at an early day, probably with his parents. Married Elizabeth Whitfield, of Putnam Co., Ga., sister of Hon. James Whitfield of Columbus, Miss., Governor of Mississippi. Children:—

    500, THOMAS WHITFIELD GOODE, b. in Sparta, Ga., 1802, d. 1859. 501, JAMES, d. yg. 502, BENJAMIN. 503, SARAH, m. *Sanders Simms*. 504, NANCY, m. *William Spivey*. 505, MARY E., m. *Moses Johnson*. 506, FRANCES ANNE, m. *Edwin Turner* of Arkansas, d. s. p. 1870.

182.

JOHN ANDREWS, of Wilkes Co., Georgia, was born in Virginia, May 4, 1762; He emigrated to Georgia at the close of the Revolutionary war. Married March 17, 1789, ANN (NANCY) GOODE, daughter of John and *Frances Hunter* Goode, No. 77, born September 16, 1770.

    507, MARCUS AURELIUS ANDREWS, b. Oct. 9, 1790. 508, FRANCES GOODE, b. April 19, 1794, m. *James Daniel*, d. s. p. 509, JOHN GOODE, b. Nov. 4, 1796, m. *Mary Ann*, dau. of Rev. Thos. Polhill, of Burke Co., Ga. 510, GARNETT, b. Oct. 10, 1798, d. Aug. 14, 1873. 511, ELIZABETH, b. Nov. 8, 1800, d. yg. 512, SARAH MARTHA, b. Feb. 23, 1803, d. 1845, m. *Dr. Isaac Bowen*. 513, ELIZABETH, b. May 10, 1805, m. *Dr. Willis Greene*. 514, EMILY, b. July 17, 1809. 515, JAMES A., b. Feb. 20, 1812. 516, DANIEL MARSHALL, b. 1812–15. 517–19, Three others, d. yg.

John Andrews was a native of Fairfax or Essex Co., Va. His mother was probably Miss Garnett, one of the younger daughters of James Garnett, (b. 1692, d. 1765) the son of John Garnett, the emigrant and ancestor of all the Garnetts of Virginia. Although a boy, he was a soldier in the Continental army, and fought at the battle of Yorktown, soon after emigrating to Georgia, to take up lands offered by the state to veterans. He was a member of the colony of Virginians who settled up and down Broad and Little Rivers, in what was then called Wilkes

Co., among whom lived the family of Miss Nancy Goode, whom he married. One of his descendants humorously writes: "Our kinsman, Robert Toombs, always said that our ancestor 'won his land by his sword,' which is, as you know, a very high old way indeed. Nancy, his wife, was considered a woman of great intelligence. I don't mean it as a proof of that character, but she wrote verses which her contemporaries called poetry. She wrote two of the hymns in *Mercer's Cluster*, a quaint old volume of sacred songs, edited by Jesse Mercer, a famous Baptist preacher of those days." One verse runs as follows:—

> I've tried to act the prudent part,
>   In all I do or say,
> But so deceitful is my heart
>   It often leads astray.

In another hymn, lamenting the death of her husband, she says very prettily:—

> This promise hath been sent to me,
>   And doth my soul sustain,
> Thy Maker shall thy husband be,
>   The Lord of Hosts his name.

Judge D. A. Vason of Albany, Ga., furnishes the following reminiscences of this energetic old lady:—

"She was a great Baptist, one of the leaders of that denomination, very intelligent, and as popular and widely known as Jesse Mercer, the famous preacher. She traveled much in the counties of middle Georgia, and attended many of the associations and religious meetings of her church. She never preached from the pulpit, but impressed her notions, feelings, and convictions upon all the gatherings of the people, and did much to enlighten them as to the usages and traditions of the church.

I remember reading a plea signed by her, in favor of the solvency of the churches, and protesting against the action of Associations which undertook to legislate for the churches of which they were composed. She claimed that the action of such bodies was advisory rather than legislative, maintaining her position with great boldness and power. Such now is the rule and law.

I much regret that her writings were not preserved. She wrote a few songs, some of which were included in *Mercer's Cluster*, a song book now very popular among the colored Baptists of middle Georgia.

183.

JOHN WRIGHT, planter, of Wilkes Co.. Ga., married about 1790–94, SARAH GOODE, daughter of John and *Frances Hunter* Goode, No. 77.

> 520, GEORGE W. WRIGHT, d. y. 521, FRANCES, b. 1797, d. 1843, m. *William Slaton.* 522, ESTHER, m. *Charles Gresham*, d. s. p. She was a woman universally honored for her sense and character. 523, MARY, d. 1873. 524, JOHN GOODE, b. Jan. 1, 1803. 525, WILLIAM, b. 1806, d. 1882, unm.

184.

MARTHA GOODE, daughter of No. 77, married MR. MORGAN, lived and died in Hancock Co., Ga.; traces of descendants lost. (527).

186.

WILLIAM GOODE, son of No. 77, removed to Jasper Co., Ga., died of quinsy. His family are lost to sight. (528).

187.

THOMAS GOODE, son of No. 77, married Clara Burch, died young, one child. (529).

187½.

WILLIAM VASON, of Wilkes Co., Ga., planter, married 1770–80, MARY (POLLY) GOODE, daughter of John Goode, No. 77. Children:—

> 530, JOHN VASON, b. 1781, d. 1847. 531, JOSEPH, b. 1783, d. in Morgan Co., Ga., 1834, three children, all dead but *Joseph C. Vason*, Madison, Morgan Co., Ga. 532, EDNA, m. *William Merritt*, of Monroe Co. Ga., d. 1836. 533, MARY, m. *Jesse Thomas*, of Morgan Co., Ga., d. 1832.

THE BEDFORD GOODES.

188.

JOHN GOODE, of Bedford Co., Va., son of Edmund Goode, No. 79, was born in Bedford Co., Va., October, 1796, 25, died January, 1876. A farmer, and a soldier in the war of 1812. Married 1824, Ann M. Leftwich, who was born| March, 1804, died October, 1868, daughter of John and *Sally Walton* Leftwich, and grand-daughter of Gen. Joel Breckenridge Leftwich, b. 1759, d. 1846, a distinguished officer of the war of 1812. (See Johnson's Cyclopedia, p. 1712). Children:—

> 534, Col. EDMUND GOODE, b. May 4, 1825, d. Mar. 1862. 535, ROBERT, b. Feb. 21, 1827, d. Dec. 1845. 536, JOHN, b. May 27, 1829. 537, WILLIAM, b. Jan. 21, 1831. 538, SALLY, b. Nov. 9, 1832, m. *Walter Izard.* 539, SAMUEL, b. and d. Jan. 1835. 540, SUSAN, b. Oct. 8, 1836, d. Dec. 1864, unm. 541, REGINALD HEBER, b. Feb. 2, 1838. 542, VICTORIA, b. Oct. 23, 1839, m. *Thos. E. Harris* of Lynchburg, who d. 1884. Children:—1, *Fanny*, b. 1871, d. 1875; 2, *Ruth*, b. Aug. 1874; 3, *Anne*, b. 1877, d. yg.; 4, *Edward*, b. 1879, d. y.; 5, *John*, b. 1881, d. yg. 543, MARY CHANNING, b. Nov. 1, 1841. 544, G. BRECKENRIDGE, b. May 17, 1843. 545, FRANCIS C., b. Mar. 16, 1845, m. *Mr. Scott*, of Kentucky.

GOODE'S CROSSING, a station on the Atlantic, Mississippi and Ohio R. R., is on John Goode's plantation, and GOODES is the name of the recently established post office at that place.

THE EDGEFIELD GOODES.

194.

MAJ. GARLAND GOODE, of Mobile, Ala., son of Philip Goode, No. 80, p. 41, was born in Edgefield, S. C., 1811. Married (1) Mary Moore of Edgefield, S. C., son and daughter; (2) Annis Burton, of Edgefield, two sons; (3) Frances Burns of Edgefield. Children:—

> 546, MARY GOODE, m. *B. Frank Stallworth.* 547, GILES, b. June 24, 1833, d. Sept. 26, 1861.

548, Burton Goode, b. Sept. 1, 1841.   549, Philip.
550, Kate Matthis Goode, b. Aug. 8, 1848.   551, Ellen, b. Mar. 18,
  1850, m. *Dr. John L. Talbert.*   552, Barnwell Rhett, b. Dec. 5,
  1852.   553, Mackerness, b. Sept. 16, 1854.   In 1885, the owner
  of a cattle-ranch near Dolores, La Plata Co., Col. 554, Mary B.,
  b. July 24, 1856; m. *Mr. Palmes*, Mill View, Fla.   555, Hathie,
  b. Apr. 19, 1858.   556, Bettie, b. Nov. 15, 1860.

Garland Goode was a planter, was brought up in South Carolina.   He moved
to Conecuh Co., Ala., and to Mobile before 1840.   At the opening of the war
he was one of the wealthiest and most influential men in Mobile, owning several plantations, cattle-ranges, saw-mills, and a cotton-mill to supply clothes
to his slaves, of whom he had several hundreds.   At the outbreak of the
war he staked everything on the success of the South.   He provided a company
of Mobile troops with uniforms and tents at his own expense, and sent his three
sons to the front, each with a negro boy for a servant.   The northern troops
burned his mills and lumber, his slaves were liberated, and the close of the war
found him ruined.   He was too old to resist the shock, and his intellect gave
way.   He still lives in Mobile, with a portion of his family.

Major Goode was a type of the old South ; his sons, whose records appear in
the next generation, represent the enterprising thrifty spirit of the new regime.

197.

JUDGE SAMUEL WATKINS GOODE, son of Samuel Goode, No.
83, p. 51, was born in Mecklenburg Co., Va., 1768, and died in Montgomery, Ala., Aug. 1851.   He married, (1) Miss Eliza Hamilton of Athens,
Wilkes Co., Ga., (2), Miss Francis Pheason Douglas, (daughter of James
Douglas, of Middlebury, Vermont, sister of Rev. Orson Douglas, founder
of the Mariners' Home in Philadelphia, and cousin of Hon. Stephen A.
Douglas,) who died 1862.*   Children : —

  557, Hamilton Goode, b. Jan. 1, 1801, d. 1867.   558, Mackerness,
  b. 1803, d. 1842.   559, Ann Eliza, b. 1805, d. 1846–8, m. *Rev.
  Thomas Sydenham Witherspoon*, a Presbyterian divine of Greensboro, Ala., long dead, no issue.   560, Samuel Watkins, b. 1809.
  d. 1860.   561, Emily Worsham, m. *Rev. David Finley.*   562.
  Thomas, d. yg.   563, Son, d. yg.

  564, Hines Holt Goode.   565, Joseph Bryan.   566, Martha Douglas, m. *James M. Montgomery.*

Judge Goode removed when quite a lad to Edgefield District, South Carolina,
where he was educated   He settled, 1790–95, in Washington, Wilkes Co., Ga.,
and engaged in practice of law.   Here he married and brought up his elder
sons, and was at one time the wealthiest man and heaviest tax-payer in
the state, owning extensive plantations, and serving as Judge of the Circuit
Court.   In 1830 he gave up public life and removed to Montgomery, Ala., where

---

*See *Douglas Genealogy*, Providence, R. I., 1879, p. 214.

he was a prominent citizen for many years. He was a man of fine culture and elegant manners, upright and devout, and noted for his charities and good works. Forty-five years an elder in the Presbyterian Church, his plantation, 'Oakley,' was known far and near as a haven of rest for all who desired its shelter : his house was the home of the ministry, and was frequented by many of the leading public men of the South. It was in his daughter's album that John Howard Payne and Mirabeau B. Lamar inscribed the verses quoted in the chapter on THE FAMILY NAME, p. 6. Judge Goode was a man of medium size, light and florid complexion, and in his old age was said to resemble strikingly Gen. Andrew Jackson. His portrait is in the possession of his grandson, John Goode Finley of Montgomery. The family bible was destroyed by the Northern soldiers on the occasion of Wilson's raid upon Montgomery in 1864, and the records are consequently imperfect.

The following reminiscences are contributed by his daughter :—

"One of the most beautiful characteristics of my father was his justice and kindness to his slaves. He employed an overseer on his plantation, but never allowed any one to strike one of his servants. He compelled them to be kind and polite to each other, and held a prayer meeting once a week, at which he prayed with and for them. He made Saturday a day of preparation for the Sabbath, and that day was kept by all as a day unto the Lord. He believed a time would come when they would be liberated, and never desired other than their good. He was venerated and dearly loved by all of his servants, and those who still live are always eager to tell you of their dear old Master and Mistress.

"Another pleasing reminiscence is with the earlier days of my father. A negro boy, seven years younger than himself, and belonging to Col. Seaborn Jones, of Georgia, took a wonderful fancy to him and gave him no rest until he consented to purchase him. After his maiden speech and success in his first important case at law my father bought 'Lemmon' with the money obtained as his fee, to the great happiness of the boy. So perfectly did he ape my father in walk, manner and dress, that he was always called 'Judge Goode, No. 2.' · He went with my father to Alabama, and he with his wife 'Lavinia,' united with the Presbyterian church, and were well beloved and respected by all, white and black. 'Lemmon' lived fifty years at 'Oakley' without being disturbed, and died there in 1880, aged 105 years. I am sure every member of my own branch of the family will appreciate every mention of this worthy pair, who devoted their lives to the children of our family, and whose graves are in the same cemetery with those of the ones who loved and appreciated them.

"I visited in 1865, in company with Judge Garnett Andrews, 'Chantilly,' my father's old home, one mile south of Washington, Ga. Two forlorn old chimneys and three heart-broken old pear trees marked the spot. A ·monument in the pine thicket, back from the house, remained, in memory of Ann Eliza Goode, wife of Samuel W. Goode, and by its side, six little white stones to the memory of my own little brothers and sisters, whose deaths had nearly broken the heart of my mother in her early married life."

MEDICUS JONES, of Cotton Gin, Texas, was adopted by Judge Goode when a boy and reared as one of his own family.

198.

JOSEPH BRYAN, of Sparta, Ga., born at Old Milford, Conn., Dec. 1767, married about 1796, ANN GOODE, daughter of Samuel Goode, No.

83, born in Virginia, 1772–77, and died 1837, her husband dying Dec. 1861. Children :—

> 567, JUDGE JOSEPH BRYAN, b. 1796–1801, d. unm., about 1865. He spent the last twenty years of his life in Washington, and was at one time Commissioner of Indian Lands. He called himself "Joseph Bryan of Alabama," 568, JULIA ANN, b. 1803, d. 1879, m. *Judge Henry H. Cumming.* 569, GEO. GOODE, b. 1813. 570, MARIA, b. 1808, m. *Mr. Harford,* died in Florida, without issue; "a person of great literary ability, and one of the most learned women of her time." 571, SOPHIA, b. 1815, m. *Robert Y. Harriss,* of Augusta, Ga. ; children : 1, *Robert Y.* 2, *Joseph Bryan.*

Mr. Bryan was a planter and a teacher, and became a man of considerable wealth. He lived from 1796 to 1861, near Sparta, Hancock, Co., Ga.

199.

THADDEUS HOLT,* of Baldwin Co., Ga., son of Simon Holt, was born about 1770, died after 1820, married, about 1800, MARTHA GOODE,† daughter of No. 83. Children :—

> 572, HON. THADDEUS GOODE HOLT. 573, PULASKI, b. 1805. 574, LEROY. 575, MILTON, planter, Greenville Co., Ga., d. leaving issue. 576, CICERO, d. 1830. 577, FOWLER. 578, CAROLINE, d. 1830.

"Thaddeus Holt was a planter in Baldwin Co., Ga., near Milledgeville, where he died, being waylaid and killed by an enemy. A man of undaunted courage, who was wounded on 'the field of honor' more than once, and who met his death on account of his outspoken and fearless character."

200.

MACKERNESS GOODE, son of No. 83, was born in Virginia, 1760–76, and lived and died a prosperous planter near Milledgeville, Ga. Children :—

> 579, MARTHA GOODE, m. *Daniel R. Tucker,* planter of Milledgeville, Ga. Both are dead, but their children lived many years near Milledgeville. 580, Daughter, m. *Mr. —— Bivens.*

THE CHARLOTTE GOODES.

204.

EDWARD GOODE, of Amelia, or Charlotte Co., Va., son of Mackerness Goode, No. 84, was born 1760–75, married Elizabeth (Woodson)

---

*THE HOLT FAMILY.—Simon Holt, one of the earliest citizens of Georgia, had ten sons and one daughter Nancy, who m. Gov. Walter T. Colquitt, (b. Halifax Co., Va., 1799, d, 1855,) and was grandmother of Alfred H. Colquitt, General, C. S. A., and U. S. Senator. The ten brothers were all men of fine standing, and progenitors of many prominent people in Georgia. Hines Holt of Baldwin Co., Ga., had a son Hines, a leading politician and member of the Confederate Congress, 1861.

†Through inaccurate information, wrongly entered on page 52 as CAROLINE.

Martin, widow of Thomas Martin, and daughter of Richard Woodson of Poplar Hill, known as "Baron Woodson" on account of his great landed estates.*

581–7, He had no son, but several daughters; one of them apparently m. about 1770–80, *William Mann*, (whose bro., John Mann, m. a sister of Rebekah Hayes Goode, No. 171) and removed to "the district of Tennessee." A Miss Goode, probably another daughter, dying early in the century, left to Edward Mann, her nephew, son of William, "a fine estate in Dinwiddie Co.—land, negroes, horses, and stock of every description, valued at about $50,000."

206.

THOMAS GOODE, of Charlotte Co., Va., son of Mackerness Goode, No. 84, was born 1775–80, and lived and died on a plantation fifteen miles south of Charlotte Court House. He married Mary Barksdale, No. 164 of the Goode Genealogy. Children:—

588, Thomas C. Goode, M. D., b. 1819, d. 1864. 589, Mackerness, b. about 1819, accidently killed in youth. 590, Mary J., m. *Isaac Bugg*,Wyliesburg, Va.; Issue : 1, *John*, 2, *Robert Thomas*, 3, *Mary*, 4, *Sarah*, 5, *Nancy*, 6, *Anna*, 7, *Eliza*. 591, Minerva, m. *John Gaines*, whose widow, (2d marriage) lived, 1881, eight miles from Charlotte C. H.; Issue: 1, *Thomas*, 2, W. B., 3, *John C.*, 4, *Edward,* 5, *Mary*, 6, *Virginia*.

208.

HILLERY GOODE, of Charlotte Co., Va., son of Mackerness Goode, No. 84, was born Nov. 1783, died 1815. Married Sarah Bacon, (who after the death of her first husband married —— Smith, Esq., and had a son, Wm. A. Smith, Esq., of Charlotte C. H., to whom I am indebted for valuable information.) Children:—

592, Edward Parks Goode, b. 1804–11, d. 1863. 593, Martha Ann W., m. *Marshall L. Harris*. 594, Hillery Mackerness Langston, b. Oct. 15, 1816.

THE WEST CHESTERFIELD GOODES.

210.

MAJ. WILLIAM GOODE of Chesterfield Co., Va., son of Elder John Goode, No. 85, p. 52, was born Oct. 25, 1761, died Sept. 27, 1845, married Dec. 18, 1788, Phebe Bass, born Nov. 25, 1767, died Dec. 11, 1804. Children:—

---

*See Genealogy of the Woodson Family in *Richmond Standard*, II, No. 20.

600, COL. ROBERT GOODE, b. Sept. 21, 1789, d. Dec. 31, 1840. 601, JANE, b. Sept. 5, 1791, d. 1865, unm. 602, JUDAH W., b. May 23, 1794, d. Dec. 31, 1840, m. *Young Condry*, farmer ; Issue : 1, *William*, b. 1820, d. 1850–60, 2, *Robert*, Manchester, Va., d., 3, *Brown*, Powhatan Co., d., 4, *Julius*, soldier, C. S. A., Co. K, 6th Va. Inf., m. Amelia Forsee, No. 624–6, 5, *Jackson*, soldier C. S. A., 603, ELSIE, b. Aug. 23, 1796, m. *Samuel Perdie* ; issue : i, *Nora*, m. Thos. Flournoy of Powhatan ; (Issue : 1, *Samantha*, ii, *Bartholomew*, d. 1840, and others. 604, COL. JOHN B., b. June 13, 1800, d. Oct. 5, 1843. 605, SPENCER R., b. Nov. 23, 1798, d. Sept. 25,, 1817, unm. 606, PHEBE, b. Mar. 11, 1801, d. Dec. 1848, *Rev. Jos. G. Woodfin* (3d wife ; see Nos. 667 and 671.)

Major William Goode was a member of the Baptist Church, and a useful public man, holding the position of High Sheriff three times. He was a soldier in the Revolution of 1776, and on account of his gallantry, was made Captain. He was still further promoted to the rank of Major in the Virginia line in the war of 1812.

211.

JOHN GOODE, of Chesterfield Co., Va., son of No. 85, p. 52, born Jan. 22, 1766, died after 1814. A farmer and member of the Baptist Church. He was one of the companions of his brother-in-law, Rev. William Hickman, on his removal to Kentucky in 1784. He married, (1795), Martha Walthall Cheatham.* Children : —

607, WILLIAM GOODE. 608, WALTHALL CHEATHAM, b. July 8, 1798, d. June 16, 1870. 609, JOHN. 610, FRANK, d. y. 611, BENJAMIN, d. y. 612, MEECAH PRIDE, m. about 1820, *Wm. Moody*, farmer of Dinwiddie Co. ; Issue : 1, *Mary*, 2, *Martha*, m. Mr. Clark, 3. *William* 4, *Samuel*, 5, *John*, 6, *Robert*, soldier, C. S. A., disabled in the war. 7, *Benjamin*, 8, *Rebecca*, 9, *Lavinia*, 10, m. Mr. Clark of Dinwiddie, who m. (1), Martha Moody, 612–2. 613, SAMUEL PLEASANTS. 614, REBEKAH, m. (1), *Wm. W. Archer*, of Powhatan ; Issue : 1, *William*, soldier, C. S. A., killed in war ; m. (2), *James H. Bass* ; Issue : 2, *Mary*, 3, *John Goode*, 4, *James*. 615, MARTHA, m. *Alex. Simms*, (1st wife) ; Issue : 1, *Fannie*, d. unm., 2, *Sallie*, m. Matthew Ford of Richmond, soldier, C. S. A., has children, 3, *William*, 4, *Indiana*, d. y., 5, *Lucius*, dentist of Chesterfield, Co., m. *Hannah Goode*, has children ; 6, *Emmett*, d. unm., 7, *Ophelia*, m. *Caleb Goode*, No. 663–3, has children, 8, *Jennie*, 9, *Clifford*, of Skinquarter, Va., m. Miss Rudd. 616, SARAH, m. *Alex. Simms*, (2d wife). 617, LAVINIA, m. *William Bagwell*.

212.

ROBERT GOODE, of " Clover Hill," Chesterfield Co., Va., son

---

* THE CHEATHAM FAMILY were numerous in the last century in Chesterfield and the adjoining counties, and connected with the Goodes by many intermarriages. The brothers of Martha Cheatham Goode, No. 211, removed to Kentucky and Tennessee ; Gen. B. F. Cheatham, C. S. A., was her nephew.

of No. 85, p. 52, was born Jan. 22, 1766. A farmer and a member of the Baptist Church; married, (1), Ann Cheatham, (2), Miss Watkins. In 1870 there were living forty-five grandchildren and sixty-six great grandchildren. Children:—

> 619, JOHN GOODE, d. yg. 620, ROBERT, b. about 1790, d. 1852-3, m. *Eliz. Cheatham.* 621, THOMAS, d. unm. 622, ABNER, d. unm. 1863, a merchant in Richmond. 623, SARAH, m. *Mr. Wilkinson,* removed to Tennessee. 624, ELIZABETH, m. *John Forsee;* Issue: 1, *John,* 2, *Abner,* soldier, C. S. A., 6th Va. Inf., m. Esther Wilkinson, No. 629, 3, *Charles,* soldier, C. S. A., 4th Va. Cavalry, 4. *David,* 5, *Mary,* d. yg. 6, *Aurelia,* m. Julius Condry, No. 602-4, 7, *Jennie,* m. Jefferson Rudd. 625, NANCY, m. WALTHALL C. GOODE, No. 528. 626, MARIA, m. *Elijah Gresham,* of Chesterfield Co. ; Issue : 1, *Robert,* soldier, C. S. A., 2, *Edwin,* Petersburg, Va., 3, *Thos.,* d., 4, *William,* farmer in Chesterfield, 5, a daughter m. James Ivey of Petersburg, 6, *Augusta,* m. Wm. H. Bagwell, son of 537.
>
> 626, POLLY GOODE, d. unm. 628, EMELINE, m. *Samuel Wilkinson,* d. 629, MATILDA, m. *Edward P. Wilkinson,* of Chesterfield Co. ; Issue : 1, *Esther* m. Abner Forsee, No. 624-2, 2, *Victoria,* m. James Simms, three children, 3, *Samuel,* soldier, C. S. A., 6th Va. Inf., 4, *Edgar,* 5, *Willie.* 630, FRANCIS, m. *Mrs. Watkins;* Issue: 1, *Sarah,* m. Elijah H. Simpson, four children, 2, *Martha Hill,* m. Bennet Maxie, son in Tennessee.

213.

REV. WILLIAM HICKMAN, of Kentucky, one of the most famous of the pioneer Baptist ministers, was born, Feb. 4, 1767, in King and Queen Co., Va. He Visited Kentucky in 1776, and in 1784 became a resident of the State, and died in 1830, having "labored faithfully in the fields of the gospel for more than fifty years." Married about 1780, ELIZABETH GOODE, a daughter of No. 85, p. 52. Children:—

> 631, COL. PASCHAL HICKMAN, b. 1780-82, d. 1813. 632, WILLIAM, a Baptist preacher, many years pastor of South Benton Church. 633, DAVID M. 634, THOMAS, registered in Frankfort, Ky., 1797, and others.

"The Baptists were the pioneers of religion in Kentucky," says Collins in his *Historical Sketches of Kentucky.* "They came with the earliest permanent settlers. In 1776, William Hickman commenced his labors in the gospel ministry. He was the first to proclaim the unsearchable works of Christ in the valley of Kentucky."

After the close of the American Revolution, a flood of Baptists poured into Kentucky, chiefly from Virginia, and churches began to spring up everywhere in the wilderness. It was a time of great peril. Before houses of worship were erected, worshippers would assemble in the forest, each man with his gun;

sentinels would be placed to guard against surprise from the Indians, while the minister, with a log or stump for his pulpit, and the heavens for his sounding board, would dispense the word of life and salvation.

Taylor, in his *Virginia Baptist Ministers*, writes thus concerning Elder William Hickman, who was an Episcopalian by early training, entertaining great contempt for the Baptist Church, with which he afterwards identified himself: " This venerable and truly useful servant of Christ was born about the year 1746 in one of the counties south of the James River, Virginia.   He professed religion during those seasons of ecclesiastical violence, when devoted and useful ministers of the gospel were seized and immured within the walls of prisons and by various other methods most cruelly persecuted. In the county of Chesterfield, while several ministers were preaching from the windows of the jail, scores were converted to God ; of this number was William Hickman. He visited the state of Kentucky, and while there in 1776, he began to preach. Returning to Virginia he was greeted by his brothers with holy joy as a herald of the gospel, and multitudes followed to hear the word at his lips. In the southern part of Chesterfield Co., especially was his ministry successful, for here in 1778 he was instrumental in the formation of Skinquarter Church.   In 1781, the church called Tomahawk also secured his services. In 1784, he became a prominent resident of the state of Kentucky. The whole of the country was but sparsely populated, while tribes of wandering savages were continually making depredations on the property and lives of the settlers.   But he did not allow himself to remain within the narrow compass of the neighborhood in which he lived. For a number of years, at the peril of his life, he visited the frontier settlements, conveying the tidings of redemption, (attended by a guard to protect him from the Indians). The church known by the name of the " Forks of Elkhorn," selected him at that early period, and in this church alone he baptized over five hundred persons. He lived to see a very old age. In 1822 it was remarked 'that though now about seventy-six years of age he walks and stands erect as a palm tree,' being at least six feet high and of rather slender form. His whole deportment is solemn and grave, and he is much like Caleb the servant of the Lord, who at four-score years of age was as capable to render service as when young. His style of preaching is plain and solemn, and the sound of it is like thunder in the distance, but when he becomes animated it is like thunder at home."

Cathcart's *Baptist Biography* remarks: " A contemporary supposes that in his ministry he baptized more people than any other minister in Kentucky. He probably formed more churches than even the famous Lewis Craig.   He baptized over five hundred in one winter."

It should be stated that Shaler, in his *Kentucky*, erroneously refers to this old hero as the Rev. *John* Hickman.

Miss. Anna Lewis Goode of Staunton, Va., contributes the following reminiscenses :

" About the year 1784, my grandfather went with Elder Hickman, who had married his sister 'Biddy Goode,' to Kentucky. There were several families in the train. They traveled through a very dangerous place called the wilderness, which was infested by hostile Indians, bears, wolves and all kinds of dreadful 'varmints.' They traveled on pack-horses, there being no roads, only bridle paths. After traveling a hundred miles or more through this lonesome region, the party emerged upon the Kentucky side, when Aunt Biddy, who had a great deal of piety, and a rich, magnificent voice, struck up a well known hymn, and made the forest ring with her glorious tones, as she lead the emigrants in singing :

> " Thus far the Lord hath led me on,
> Thus far his pow'r prolongs my days,
> And ev'ry ev'ning shall make known,
> Some fresh memorial of his grace."

216.

BENJAMIN FARMER, of Kentucky, was born in Virginia 1760. Emigrated to Kentucky 1790–1800 ; married SUSANNA GOODE, daughter of No. 85. Children :—

> 636, JOHN FARMER. 637, BENEDICT.

217.

CAPT. BENJAMIN GOODE, of Chesterfield Co., Va., son of No. 85, was born Mar. 3, 1771, died July 10, 1830. A captain in the war of 1812. (See *Virginia Muster Rolls*, Richmond, 1851.) A farmer and prominent member of the Baptist Church : married, 1794, Mrs. Martha (Lewis) Robertson. In 1870, he had 42 grand-children and 66 great-grand-children living. Children :—

> 638, JOHN GOODE, b. 1794, d. 1839. 639, EDWARD, m. Miss Shears, moved to Hickman, Ky.; Children : 1, *Patrick Goode* and others. 640, JOSEPH, b. 1805, d. 1859. 641, RICHARD, b. Feb. 23, 1802, d. 1867. 642, REV. BENJAMIN E., grad. Hampton Sidney Coll., 1872. 643, NANCY, m. (1), *George Bailey*, of Chesterfield : (2), *John Faudray*, of Powhatan : Issue : 1, *Benjamin*, moved to Tennesse, had many children ; 2, *Abraham*, farmer, of Powhatan, many children. 3, *Ann Eliza*. 4, *Julia Faudray*, m. Benj. Jennings, of Genito, Va. ; 5, *Rebecca*, m. Wm. Childrey : her daughter, m. *Rowlett Darien*, of Powhatan ; children ; 6, *John*, d. yg. 644, ELIZABETH, m. Capt. *William Magruder*, a soldier in the war of 1812, lived in Powhatan Co. ; Children :—1, *Hardaway*, m. Miss Atkinson ; Issue:—i, Anna, b. 1856 ; ii, Olivia, m. H. H. Pollard, Richmond, Va., soldier, C. S. A.; iii. Betty, m. Jas. W. Phaup ; children : iv, Adema Frank, m. Mr. Phillips, of Louisville, Ky.; children : 2, *William ;* 3, *Martha*, m. John Phaup, of Chesterfield Co., Va.; Issue : i. Alice, b. 1858 ; ii, Betty; iii, Jack ; iv, Ella. 4, *Ann Eliz.*, m. M. Waldron, of Richmond. 645, MARTHA, m. *Benjamin Watkins Gates*, nephew of 218, of Genito, Powhatan Co., who d. 1866. Children :—1, *Thomas Gates*, b. 1830, d. 1862, m. Eliza

Cheatham.   Children, i, John, Manchester, Va.. b. 1850,
m. Julia A. Perdue, children, ii, James, Richmond, children,
iii, William, Powhatan Co., m. Miss Bailey, children, iv, Molly,
v, Alice, m. Mr. Harper, Powhatan Station, Va., vi, Edmonia,
b. 1858.

218.

Rev. JOSEPH GOODE, of Chesterfield Co., Va., son of No. 85, was
born April 4, 1776, died October 13, 1823.   Joined Skinquarter Baptist
Church, 1799, and became deacon and elder.   Married about 1796,
Judith Watkins, dau. of Rev. Benjamin Watkins of Powhatan Co., a
prominent Baptist divine, whose wife survived him.*   Children :—

646, BENJAMIN GOODE, d. yg. 647, ELIZA, m. *John S. Sims* of Chesterfield
Co., farmer.   Children :—1, *Cornelius;* 2, *Benj.*, had 5 children,
1880; 3, *David;* 4, *Wm.*, of Ashland, Va., 2 children, 1880; 5,
Catherine, m. Thos. Smith. 648, SARAH, d. unm. 649, MARY D.
m. *Mr. Perdie*.   Children :—1, *Sarah Ann*, b. 1848, m. John
Crump; 2, *Joseph D;* 3. *Wm.*, a soldier, C. S. A., has 3 children,
1880; 4, *Ann*. 650, REV. JOSEPH, m. Miss Bowles of Powhatan,
Baptist Minister and farmer in Chesterfield Co., near Genito : insane in 1880. 651, JOHN W., d. 1845, unm. 652, DAVID, b. Mar.
17, 1817, farmer near Skinquarter, m. 1850, Mary J. Graves, of
Chesterfield;   children :— 1, *Mary W. Goode*, b. Dec. 27, 1859,
d. yg.; 2, *Matilda Ann*, b. 1853; 3, *Mary Watkins;* 4, *Susan*, b. 1856;
5, *William Lonsford*, b. 1862; 6, *Henrietta*, b. 1864; 7. *Lee Ollia*. b.
1867; 8, *Sallie*, b. 1871. 653, MAHALA ANN, m. 1839, *Joseph J.
Gates*, of Chesterfield Co.,Va.; children :—1, *Victoria Henningham*,
b. 1840. m. James Mack, children; 2, *Judith Ann*, m. JAMES B.
GOODE (son of 595); 3, *Louisa Watkins*, m. Mr. Sellers of N. C.;
4, *Mary E.*, m. J. W. Ferguson of Clover Hill; 5, *Silas
Sylvanus*, d.; 6, *Cornelia Agnes*, m. Mr. Baker of N. C.; 7,
Joseph Willie; 8, *Kate Otilia;* 9, *Edwin Lee*. 654, WILLIAM,
d. unm. 655, SILAS SHELBURNE, b. 1823, d. 1881, farmer,
merchant and postmaster at Skinquarter, Va., a soldier, C. S. A.,
in Co. B, 15th Va, Inf., imprisoned at Point Lookout, 1864,
m. Virginia Graves of Amelia Co.   Children :—1, *Ollin*, b.
1859; 2, *Wickliff Taylor;* 3. *Silas S.;* 4, *Fletcher Webster;* 5,
Benjamin Watkins; 6, *Sallie Brown;* 7, *Joseph;* 8, *Virginia
Hatcher;* 9, *Robert Cecil;* 10, *Henry Hobson;* 11, *Luther Moore*, b. 1882.

Rev. Joseph Goode, whose biography is given in Taylor's *Virginia Baptist
Ministers*, pp. 446–7, was one of those simple minded devoted country preachers so numerous in our rural districts. "He had serious impressions at the
age of eight or ten years, and would often hold conversation with his brothers

---

*For Biography, see Taylor's " *Virginia Baptist Ministers*," pp. 233–7.

on the subject of religion. In 1799, a revival commenced in the bounds of Skinquarter Church. He had long been waiting at the ministration of the word without deep feeling; but at a night meeting, the spirit of the Lord reached his heart, and he was compelled to cry out with anguish. In the fall of 1799, while securing his crop, deliverance was realized. His countenance bespoke the change, and constrained his friends to believe he had passed from death to life.

"After some time he reached the conclusion that there was something required at his hands in warning his fellow beings of their dangerous situation, as sinners against God. He was considerably gifted as an experimental preacher, and at times was exceedingly forcible in the elucidation of doctrinal subjects, and pungent in his appeals to the conscience. His countenance was usually lighted up with a smile, while he dwelt on the loving character of Jesus, and recommended him as the Saviour of the lost."

219.

MACK (ERNESS) GOODE, of Chesterfield Co., son of No. 85, was born 1778–80, died, 1840–50. A member of the Baptist Church, and a useful public man—a farmer by occupation. Married about 1823, Sarah Gates of Chesterfield, and had 25 grandchildren and 27 great grandchildren living in 1870. Children:—

> 656, WILLIAM GOODE, d. unm. 657, JOSEPH, b. 1825, a farmer, and sheriff of Chesterfield Co., m. (1) Miss Adkins, 2 children, (2) Miss Cheatham, children, 1, *Josephine* m. DAVID MACK GOODE, No. 592-2, *William Richard*, b. 1850, killed in Chesterfield coal pits, 1875, m. Miss Wilkinson, 1 daughter; 3, SALLY, m. Irvin Bass of Skinquarter. 658, DANIEL BROWN, b. 1827, d. 1865. 659, CELIA m. *S. Wilkinson*, (1st wife) d. s. p. 660, MARTHA, m. *S. Wilkinson*, (2d wife,) son, 1, *Cornelius*. 661, POLLY, m. *Elijah Bailey* of Chesterfield, children, 1, *B.*, soldier, C. S. A., 6th Va. Inf., 2, *John*, Appomattox Co., Va., 3 children, 1880. 3, *Charles*, d. in California in 1878.

220.

ELDER EDMOND GOODE,* of Chesterfield Co., Va., son of No. 85, was born about 1780. A Baptist preacher, pastor of Zoar and Skinquarter churches. Married about 1800, Patience Rucks. Children:—

> 663, CYRUS GOODE, b. about 1800, d. before 1870, m. Miss Phaup, children, 1 *James Goode*, farmer, Chesterfield Co., Va., soldier, C. S. A., Co. K, 6th Va. Inf., m. Judith Ann Gates, No. 653-2, children, 1, Ellis Goode, and several more; 2, *Cyrus*, a soldier. C. S. A., Co. K, 6th Va. Inf., killed in the Crater, Petersburg; 3, *Caleb*, soldier, C. S. A., farmer, Chesterfield Co., Va., m. Ophelia Sims, No. 615-7, children, several; 4, *Margaret*, m. Wm. Woodfin,

*Wrongly printed EDWARD GOODE, p. 52.

children, several in 1880. 5, *Mary E.*, m. Michael Vaden, soldier, C. S. A., a farmer in Chesterfield Co., children, eight sons and three daughters, 1880. 664, GEORGE W., m. Miss Forsee, has 10 children, lives in Bedford Co. 665, COL. EDMOND J. 666, MARGARET, m. *Mr. Wharton*, of Campbell or Bedford Co. has children. 667, POLLY, m. *Rev. 'Joseph Woodfin*, (1st wife). 668, ELISHEBA, m. *William Wilkinson*, children, 1, *Martha*, m. Egbert Bass, 7 children; 2, *Louisa*, m. Rev. Thos. Reynolds of Cumberland Co., Baptist preacher 4 children; 3, *Dr. David*, physician, Bedford Co., Va.; 7 children. 4, *Charles*, soldier, C. S. A., 18th Va. Inf., m. Miss Hancock, 6 children; 5, *Mary*, m. John W. Pritchett, soldier, C. S. A., 18th Va. Inf., 6 children; 6, *Richard*, soldier, Co. K, 6th Va. Inf., killed in battle. 669, ROXANNA, m, Mr. Hillsman of Bedford Co., Va., 7 children. 670, SUSANNA, m. *William Phaup.* 671, ORPHA (OPIE), m. *Rev. 'J. G. Woodfin*, (2d wife), d. s. p., April 28, 1848. 672, EUNICE, m. *'John Phaup*, children, 1, *Edward Phaup*, soldier, C. S. A., in Co. K, 6thVa. Inf., killed in the Crater at Petersburg; 2, *Emma;* 3, *Bettie*, m. Mr. Capitaine of Richmond, children; 4, *Ellis*, of Skinquarter, Va.; 5, *Mattie*, m. Mr. Smith of Chesterfield Co., Va., children; 6, *'John.* 673, ASENATH AURELIA, m. Mr. Smith, d. 674, HESTER DAMARIUS, m. *Mr. Smith* of Bedford or Campbell Co., living 1870, Issue: 1, *Sallie Smith*, m. Mr. Lee of Richmond.

224.

TARPLEY GOODE, of Chesterfield Co., Va., son of No. 85, was born 1780–90, died, 1810–20, married Miss Cheatham.   Children:—

675, TARPLEY GOODE.   676, CHEATHAM.

224½.

JAMES ROBERTSON, of Henrico Co., Va., grand-son of Edward Goode, No. 51, page 41, is mentioned in will of the latter, dated Jan. 9, 1785. He is probably one of the many descendants in a line of which we have no record, and the history of which it is too late to recover.

James Robertson, was son of —— Robertson who was probably born 1700–1720, and who married a sister of Rev. John Goode No. 85. It is not at all improbable that the Robertson family of Tennessee and Kentucky are of this descent. The wife of Edward Goode was named Mary, and in addition to Rev. John Goode, 85, and Mrs. Robertson, 85–1, there were PATSY GOODE 85–2, and MARY GOODE, 85–3, who doubtless have numerous descendants living.

Mr. Brock writes, "I have met with the name Harrison Robertson of Chesterfield Co., in records of the close of the last century. David Robertson of Petersburg, Va., a lawyer of ability was Grand Master of Masons of Virginia, Dec. 15, 1807, to Dec. 11, 1810."

THE HENRICO GOODES.

225.

DANIEL GOODE, of Deep Run, Henrico Co., Va., son of John Goode, No. 86, p. 53, was born about 1760, d. 1800–1820. A farmer at Deep Run. Children:—

677, ISAAC GOODE, b. 1790, d. 1838, children, 1, *John Goode*, b. Oct. 20, 1813, manager of tobacco factory, Richmond, children, i. Ellen Virginia ; ii. Walter Cabell. 2. *Edmond F.*, b. June 30, 1816, children, i. Henry C., Switzerland, Ala. ; ii. Ida, m. Edmund Herbert, Richmond. 3, *Caleb*, b. 1818, no children living 1880. 4, *William T.*, blacksmith, Charlottesville, Va., children, i. Ella ; ii. Maggie. 5, *Mart..a*, m. James Marshall of Richmond, blacksmith, children, i. Thomas Marshall blacksmith, Richmond. ii. Julia. 678, SOPHIA, m. *Mr. Clark* of Henrico, children, 1, *Daniel ;* 2, *Willie ;* 3, *Sarah.* 679, MOLLIE, m. *Orlando Thomas*, daughter, 1, *Susan*, m. Chas. Tenser. 680, FANNIE, m. *Thos. Breeden*, children, (sons, all blacksmiths.) 1, *John*, North Carolina ; 2, *Nathaniel*, Fredericksburg, Va. ; 3, *William*, Fredericksburg ; 4, *Susan.* 681, A son, has son, 1, *Pleasant Goode*, Manchester, Va.

226

CHARLES GOODE, of Four Mile Run, Henrico Co., Va,, son of No. 86, was born 1790–1800, died before 1857, a farmer, married Sarah Ann Evans, of Henrico Co. Children:—

682, WILLIAM GOODE, b. 1814, d. 1850, provision merchant in Richmond, Va., m. Miss Minson, children, 1, *Sylvanus*, soldier, C. S. A., died in prison at Fort Delaware, 1865 ; 2, *Joseph C.*, Nance's Shop, Charles City Co., Va. ; 3, SUSAN, m. J. H. Sharp of Charles City Co., Va. ; 4, *Virginia*, m. Charles Robertson of Henrico Co., Va. 683, JOHN HENRY, b. 1816, a merchant, moved to Harrodsburg, Ky., and afterwards perhaps to Indiana, m. Sarah H. Moore, of Ky., children, 1, *Loren Cleveland*, b. 1867–70 ; 2, *Virginia Lee*, 684, DANIEL, d. unm. 685, CATHERINE, unm. 686, MARTHA, b. 1820–24, d. unm., Richmond, 1879. 687, LOUVENIA, unm. 688, CHARLES, b. 1825, d. 1860, lived in Richmond, m. Isabella Roach, children, 1, *Joshua*, b. 1848–50, a wheelwright, Baltimore, 1875 ; 2, *John*, b. 1855, d. 1870.

227

JOHN GOODE, of the White Oak Swamp, Henrico Co., Va., son of No. 86, was born 1770–80, died 1830–40, married 1820, MARY GOODE, No. 700. Children:—

689, ALBERT GOODE of Richmond, b. 1822, m. Miss Carter of Henrico Co., Va., children:— 1, *George A.*, harnessmaker, Richmond,

b. 1848; 2, *Charles Otterley*, carpenter, Richmond, b. 1852; 3, *John Washington*, clerk, Richmond, b. 1854; 4, *Albert Sherwood*, clerk, Richmond, b. 1858. 690, SAMUEL, b. 1824, unmarried 1880, and farming on the paternal estate.

John Goode was a farmer in Henrico Co., ten or twelve miles from Richmond, owning the property belonging formerly to his wife's father, Samuel Goode, No. 229, and now owned by Samuel Goode No. 690. This region was devastated during the war by the contending armies particularly during the Seven Days Battles around Richmond. The battle of Frayser's Farm was fought very near the farm of Samuel Goode. For pictures of this region see the war articles in "The Century Magazine," 1885.

228.

THOMAS GOODE, of Henrico Co., Va., was son of No, 86, Children : —

> 691, JAMES GOODE, d. unm. 692, FRANCIS, and perhaps others.

229.

SAMUEL GOODE, of the White Oak Swamp, Henrico Co., Va., son of Benjamin Goode, No. 87, p. 54, was born 1750–60, and died before 1822. He was a farmer, owning the paternal acres which had belonged to his great-grandparents, and whence a large portion of the Goode family has emanated. Children : —

> 693, THOMAS GOODE, b. 1770–75, d. unm. 1830. 694, JOHN. 695, MARY, m. JOHN GOODE, No. 227. 696, SARAH, m. *Thos. Goodman*, a farmer in the White Oak Swamp district, children, 1, *Isaac Goodman;* 2, *Jackson*. 697, ELIZABETH, m. *Joseph Goodman*, children, 1, *Emeline*, m. Mr. Higgins of Baltimore ; 2, *Lucy Ann;* 3, *Frank;* 4, *Samira Ann*, m. Mr. Powell of Richmond, Va.

230.

BENJAMIN GOODE, of Henrico Co., Va., son of Benjamin Goode No. 87, was born 1750–70, died 1805: Married Betty (Hobson?) Will recorded in Will Book of Henrico Co., Va., iii. p. 441. Children: —

> 699, THOMAS GOODE. 700, HOBSON. 701, ELIZABETH, m. Mr. Lindsay. 702, PATSY, m. *Mr. Timberlake*, children, 1, *Sarah Timberlake*, m. Mr. Alexander ; 2, *Robert*.

231.

JOSEPH GOODE, of Henrico Co., Va., son of No. 87, was born 1750–80. Children: —

> 703, JOSHUA GOODE, d. a tobacco manufacturer in Richmond, children, 1, *James*; 2, *Susan Marian* 704, JOSEPH, tobacco manufacturer Richmond, 1, daughter, married *Mr. Clark*, of Philadelphia. 705, NANCY, m. *Mr. Johnson*, son, 1, *Silas L. Johnson*, merchant of

Richmond, Va. 706, ELIZA. 707, ELIZABETH, m. *Captain Moore*, C. S. A. 708, ADELAIDE. 709, DEBORAH.

232-1 to 232-6.

THOMAS GOODE, of Henrico Co. Va., son of No. 48, 51 or 52, died in 1788, his will being dated Sept. 13, (Will book of Henrico Co., 2, 58). Married Elizabeth ———. Children:—

232–1, JUDITH GOODE, m. *Mr. Jordan*. 232–2, ELIZABETH m. *Mr. Matthews*. 232–3, FRANCES, m. *Mr. Sharpe*. 232–4, THOMAS. 232–5, JOSEPH. 232–6, SAMUEL.

No record of their descendants is in existence.

THE WHITBY GOODES.

233.

SETH WARD,* of Lynchburg, Virginia, son of Seth and *Mary Goode* Ward, No, 89, p. 54, was born at "Sheffield," Chesterfield Co., Va., April 10, 1772, died in Tennessee, about 1859. Married, Feb. 4, 1796, Martha Norvell, daughter of Hon. William Norvell of Lynchburg.† Children:—

725, SETH WARD, b. July 9, 1798, m. Miss Hendricks; Issue:— 1, *Edmund*, a wealthy citizen of St. Louis; 2, *Georgiana*. 726, MARY, b. Oct. 9, 1800, d. Nov. 10. 1802. 727, BENJAMIN, b. Oct. 5, 1802, lived near Flat Rock, Bedford Co., a farmer, m. Eliza White, dau. of Col. White of Bedford Co.; Issue ;— 1, *Seth;* 2, *James Pegram*, a soldier, C. S. A., others d. yg. 728, MARTHA, b. Mar. 29, 1805, d. May 10, 1806. 729, WILLIAM NORVELL, b. Apr. 19, 1807, d. Feb. 25, 1881. 730, LUCY E., b. May 12, 1809, m. *Fielding Williams*. 731, GEORGE EDWARD, b. April 2, 1811. 732, NANCY EDMONIA, b. June 24, 1813, m. *Mathew M. Kerr*. 733, MARY GOODE, b. Feb. 19, 1816. 734, SAMUEL GOODE, b. Aug. 27, 1818. 735, (Adopted son), JAMES W. PEGRAM.

Seth Ward was early left without a father and was placed under the guardianship of his uncle, Col. Robert Goode of "Whitby," No. 90. He was

---

*THE WARD FAMILY. This is one of the old Virginia stocks. Seth Ward was granted 350 acres in Henrico Co., Va., in 1643, (probably the nucleus of the "Sheffield" estate in what was subsequently Chesterfield), and the name of Seth Ward was handed down for five generations, as the name of the first born son in the eldest branch of the family. Tradition tells us that the English ancestor was Seth Ward, a Bishop in the English Church—perhaps Seth Ward, F. R. S., Bishop of Salisbury and Exeter, Savilian professor of Astronomy and president of Trinity College in the University of Oxford, born in Hertfordshire, 1617. Colonel Seth Ward grandson of the first of the name in America would appear to have had at least three children, viz.: SETH WARD of Sheffield who married MARY GOODE, (see Goode genealogy, No. 89.) 2, BENJAMIN WARD of "Wintopoke," Chesterfield Co., whose daughter Maria Ward was affianced to Randolph of Roanoke, and who afterward married Peyton Randolph, (for descendants, see Carter family tree), and 3, MARY WARD, b. 1749, d. 1787, who married 1, William Broadnax, and 2, Richard Gregory, (for descendants, see Richmond Standard, ii. 4, p. 4.) Martha Ward Gregory, dau. of Richard Gregory, m. Gen. John Pegram, and was ancestor of many well-known Virginians, (see Slaughter's *Bristol Parish*, pp. 205–9.)

†The signatures of William Norvell and Robert Carter Nicholas appear on many issues of the Virginia Continental paper currency. For an account of the NORVELL FAMILY see *Sketches and Recollections of Lynchburg*, by Mrs. Cabell, p. 231.

heir to a large estate, but through unfortunate endorsements of papers belonging to his friends, he lost his property and removed to Lynchburg. He was a man of sterling and beautiful character, one of the patriarchs of the Episcopal Church in Southwestern Virginia, and greatly esteemed by all who knew him. The widow of one of his sons writes, "I always found him a charming companion, usually cheerful but sometimes sad, when he reverted to his changed circumstances. Pleasant evenings we spent in the piazza at old Brecknock, my husband's home, when he told over incidents of his youth, and of his old friends John and Edmund Randolph and many others of their time. He told many interesting anecdotes of the oldest friend of his boyhood William Henry Harrison, afterwards President of the United States, whom his mother received into her household as a companion for him, and who had the same tutor.* He removed to Tennessee with two of his married daughters, and accompanied by his youngest daughter, Mary Goode Ward, to whom he gave, when I was at his house, a beautiful miniature of her mother, Mary Goode, and her diamond ring."

His mother's niece was left a widow with 12 children by the death of her husband, Gen. John Pegram, and herself died soon after. Their fourth son, James West Pegram was brought up by Mr. Ward as one of his own sons. He was subsequently General of Virginia troops and was killed by a steamboat explosion in 1844. He married Virginia, dau. of Col. Wm. Ransom Johnson—'the Napoleon of the turf.' His children were, i. MAJ. GEN. JOHN PEGRAM, C. S. A., killed in. battle; m. Hettie, dau. of Wilson Miles Cary, Esq., of Baltimore, now wife of Prof. Henry Newell Martin, of Johns Hopkins University. ii. MAJ. JAMES W. PEGRAM, C. S. A., iii. VIRGINIA, wife of Col. David G. McIntosh, C. S. A. iv. BRIG. GEN. WILLIAM R. J. PEGRAM, C. S. A., killed at the battle of Five Forks, April, 1865. v. MARY, wife of Gen. Joseph R. Anderson, of the Tredegar Iron Works, Richmond.

Maria Ward, who was the object of the romantic attachment of John Randolph of Roanoke, and whose loveliness is still a tradition in Virginia, was daughter of Benjamin Ward of "Wintopoke," uncle of Seth Ward, and after her father's death was a member of the household at ''Sheffield," where occurred the estrangement which embittered the life of the eccentric Virginia statesman. (See Garland's *Life of John Randolph*.)

234.

DANIEL L. HYLTON, of Richmond, Va., born 1735–50, married MARY WARD, daughter of No. 89. Children:—

736, LUCY E. A. HYLTON, b. 1790–1800, m. *Stith Maynard.*

Mr. Hylton was one of the first vestrymen of old St. Johns church, Richmond, 1785, in company with Edmund Randolph, Turner Southall, Jaqueline Ambler, Thomas Prosser, (see No. 95), and others.† "He was," says Mr. Brock, "a prominent contractor for supplies in Revolutionary times, and a wealthy, useful and influential citizen."

---

*PRESIDENT HARRISON was born at "Berkeley" on the James River in 1773. His parents died before he was seventeen. He was educated at Hampden Sidney 'College.
†Meades Old Churches, &c. 1. p. 541.

𝕴𝖓 𝕸𝖊𝖒𝖔𝖗𝖞 𝖔𝖋 PEGGY WARD, and of the hundreds of faithful African servants, who have considered
themselves no less members of the family than if connected with it by ties of common descent. Peggy Ward
and her children were the property of Seth and Mary
Goode Ward, No. 54, and their descendants. "Aunt
Peggy" was one of the principal contributors to the famous "Virginia Cook-Book," by Mrs. Randolph.

IN MEMORIAM.

Died at Whitehall, on the 24th of December, (1868 ?)
PEGGY WARD, aged 93 years ; a pious Christian, and
a life long servant in the Ward family.

Ninety-three years old, and faithful and true, in her
loving obedience to the end. Heaven opens wide its
gates to receive such souls.

Thus has passed away another of that true type of
the old colored family servant, now growing rarer every
day—a representative of that civilization, which time
may show to have been the best for the true happiness
of both races. "Old Aunt Peggy;"—her name has long
been a household word in many families, three generations of children has she petted and dangled upon her
knees. A sincere Christian, true to all her duties, she
embodied in her character all those fine traits so much
admired in old Virginia family servants of the olden
time.

Thirty years ago, her active labors ceased, since
then a petted pensioner in her Mistress' family—nursed
tenderly in all her ailments. For many years "Mam-
my Lou," one of her daughters, has devoted her life to
her, giving almost hourly that care which her growing
decrepitude required.

Uncle Buck when dying, asked "that he might be
buried at his dear Master's feet." Necessity requiring
the removal of his Master's family, the remains of
Uncle Buck were exhumed, and buried with Aunt
Peggy, Brother and Sister, side by side—united again
in death.

Every care and attention that her Mistress's family
could give to the burial of these old loved servants
were given·with the greatest respect.

Aunt Peggy was faithfully nursed when sick, and
her last hours soothed with soft words of Christian
comfort, and the poor weary eyes closed at last, when
all was over, by the gentle hands of the ladies of the
family. Dear "Old Aunt Peggy" rests in peace.
F.

Clarkesville (Tenn.) Newspaper.

234-A.

DR. JOHN CRINGAN, of Richmond, Va., a well-known practitioner of early days, married (1) Miss Stuart, (2) Mary Ogilvie, (3) MARY WARD, widow of Daniel L. Hylton. The latter had no issue, but brought up for him his two children.

736 *a*, ROBERT CRINGAN, father of John W. Cringan, Esq. of Richmond, and others. 736 *b*, MARY ANN, m. *John Green Williams*, and had children, 1, *Rev. Wm. Clayton Williams, D. D.*, of Georgia; 2, *Rev. Channing Moore*, Episcopal Bishop of Japan; 3,. *John G.*, lawyer, of Richmond; 4, *Robert F.*, merchant, of Richmond; 5, *Mary Ogilvie*, m. Prof. H. P. Lefebvre; 6, *Alice*, m. Maj. Carter Harrison, C. S. A., killed at the first battle of Manassas.

235.

HENRY RANDOLPH, of "Warwick," Chesterfield Co., Va., son of Brett and Mary Scott Randolph of "Chester," Powhatan Co., Va., was born at Woodmancoat, Dursley, England, Oct. 7, 1758. Married about 1780, LUCY WARD, daughter of Seth and *Mary Goode* Ward, No. 89, p. 54. Children :—

738, HENRY RANDOLPH, d. 1837. 739, MARY m. (1,) *George W. Thornton*, (2,) *James Maury.* 740, BRETT, d. yg. 741, ROBERT GOODE, d. yg. 742, CATHERINE COCHARAINE, m. *Josiah B. Abbott.* 743, LUCY, d. yg. 744, LUCY GOODE, d. yg. 745, GEORGIANA WASHINGTON, d. unm. 746, LUCY WARD, d. yg. 747, SUSAN FRANCES, m. *Alex. L. Botts.* 748, LUCY, d. yg. 749, PERCY BRETT, d. yg.

"Henry Randolph was descendant in the fifth degree from Thomas Rolfe and the Virginian Princess POCAHONTAS, (see p. 64.) Little is remembered of his life and character. " His father," says an old MS., "married Mary Scott in London on the 14th of July, 1753, of a Saturday, *embarqued* on board the ' Tryall' Captain John Hilson, August 20, following, arrived in Virginia, Oct. 20th.

" Richard their son, born on 17th of August, of a Saturday, half after six in the morning, at ' Curls' Anno. Dom. 1754. Departed this life 8th September 1775, of a Monday morning betwixt one and two, at 'Chester,' interred at 'Curls' the day following at noon.

"They again *embarqued* aboard the ' True Patriot' Capt. Wm. Randolph, and sailed March 4th 1757, arrived at Bristol, 15th April.

" Henry, son of the above Brett and Mary, born the 7th of October, of a Saturday betwixt 3 and 4 of the clock in the afternoon at Woodmancoat, Dursley, Anno. Dom. 1758. Brett Randolph departed this life the 4th of September, 1759 (was born Sept. 4, 1732) of a Tuesday, 11 minutes after 7 at night, with that fatal distemper the small pox, was interred at Dursley Church near the stone man in the aisle on the right hand. Henry and his sister Susannah we are told, "had the small pox in the natural way in 1760 and Henry the measles at Cirencester."

"Warwick"* was on the south side of the James River, bounded above by "Whitby" and "Falls Plantation" owned by the Goodes, below by "Ampthill," the seat of Archibald Cary, the old patriot who threatened to stab Patrick Henry, if he assumed the dictatorship of the colonies : on the opposite side of the James were "Powhatan" the seat of the Mayos, and next below the Randolph plantations, "Wilton" and "Chatsworth."

On Henry Randolph's plantation of Warwick, Benedict Arnold's troops once encamped during the Revolution, and here a rather sharp engagement took place.

EXCURSUS.—THE RANDOLPH FAMILY.

"The Randolphs," says Anburey (Travels, 1780), "are descended from one of the first settlers in this province and are so numerous that they are obliged, like the clans of Scotland, to be distinguished by their places of residence." This family is one of the most interesting in America and has included on its rolls more men distinguished in public life than perhaps any other. Since the boughs of the family tree of the Randolphs frequently intertwine with those of the Goodes, nearly 400 names being common to the two records, I cannot resist the temptation of giving here a brief sketch of the Randolph family in its earlier generations, especially since I have been allowed the use of several unpublished manuscripts relating to its history.

A "black letter pedigree" found among the papers of Sir John Randolph carries the line back to ROBERT RANDOLPH (b. 1650–60) who married Rosa Roberts. His son WILLIAM. (b. 1582 d. 1670), m. Eliz. Smith, and had children, THOMAS RANDOLPH the poet, and WILLIAM, m. Dorothy Law. WILLIAM RANDOLPH, son of the above, b. Nov. 27, 1623, is generally assumed to have been the emigrant to Virginia, but cannot have been WILLIAM RANDOLPH, of "Turkey Island ;" as has been pointed out by Mr. Brock, since the latter was born in 1657. There is apparently nothing to prove that William of "Turkey Island," may have been accompanied to Virginia by his father, or indeed that he may not have been born in Virginia—he is said to have come to the colony about 1674, but this date seems to have been fixed by the fact that he began to come into prominence about that time, when he received a grant of 591 acres in Henrico Co. Since he was poor, when a young man, and it was said laid the foundation of his fortune by building barns upon the colonial plantations, it is not impossible that his advent had been much earlier. Be this as it may, family tradition fixes the fact that he was the nephew of Thomas Randolph the poet, and consequently descendant in the fifth generation from Robert and Rosa Roberts Randolph.

"The Randolphs," wrote John Randolph of Roanoke, "are from the midland counties of Warwick and Northampton : the late Bishop of London and several of the heads of colleges at Oxford were of the same family." The arms on the book-plate of Sir John Randolph, 1742, were, according to Brock,

---

*The town of Warwick, prior to the Revolution, was a more important shipping port than Richmond A few scattered brick have for years alone marked its site.   R. A. BROCK.

Gules, upon a cross, or, 5 mullets of the field. I have an impression of a seal, belonging to Brett Randolph, father of No. 233, now in the possession of his great-grandson, J. W. Randolph, Esq., of Richmond, upon which these same arms are impaled upon those of Tucker.*

The old homestead on Turkey Island disappeared long ago and scattered bricks alone remain. It was in its day quite a curiosity. From its position and its dome-like top, it could be seen for a long distance up and down the river—and from the great number of birds flocking up and down in its grove it was called the "bird cage" by the navigators on the James River. It is said to have been seven years in building. Not a rod of this vast estate now belongs to any of Randolph blood. Bishop Meade in "Old Churches and Families of Virginia," praises its builder for his wisdom in living himself in a house of moderate dimensions and building, during his lifetime, good houses for his numerous children in various parts of the state.

William Randolph of Turkey Island, Henrico Co., "the patriarch," b. 1651, d. 1711, was member of the Governor's Council, charter trustee and member of the first board of visitors to William and Mary College. On his tomb is the inscription :—

Col. WILLIAM RANDOLPH,

of Warwickshire, but late of Virginia,

Gentleman,

died April 11, 1711.

He married Mary, dau. of Henry and Katharine Isham, of Bermuda Hundred, descended from the Ishams of Northamptonshire, and had issue :

1, WILLIAM RANDOLPH, OF CHATSWORTH, ancestor of the Randolphs of Chatsworth, Wilton, Green Creek, Norwood and Fauquier, M. H. B., Councillor of State, and Treas. of Va., m. Eliz. dau. of Peter Beverley of Gloucester Co. Of their children PETER R. of Chatsworth had children. 1, *William R.*, who m. Mary, dau. of Sir William Skipwith, who had a son : *Peter Skipwith R.* who m. Eliz. Southall, and had s. *William Beverley*, m. Sarah, dau. of Thomas Rutherfoord, and d. s. p., the last of the Chatsworth line. 2. *Beverly*, of Green Creek, Cumberland Co., M. H. B., and Governor of Va. 3, *Robert*, of Eastern View, Fauquier Co., Col. of Cavalry in the Revolution, left many desc. 4. *Anne*, m. William Fitzhugh of Ravenscroft, had dau. *Mary*, who m. G. W. P. Custis of "Arlington," and had daughter *Mary*, wife of Gen. Robert E. Lee. WILLIAM R, of Wilton, m. 1734, Anne Harrison of Berkeley. Of his children, *Peter* m. Mary, g. d. of Gov. Spotswood : ELIZABETH, b. 1725, m. 1745, Col. John Chiswell; her dau. Lucy, m. Col. Wm. Nelson of the Revolutionary Army, and her dau. Sarah was g. m. of W. W. Seaton, Editor of the National Intelligencer, Mayor of Washington, etc.

2. THOMAS RANDOLPH OF TUCKAHOE, ancestor of the Randolphs of Tuckahoe, Edgehill, Chellowe and Middle Quarter, had two daughters, JUDITH, who m. Rev. W. Stith, historian of Va., and LUCY, m. Rev. Wm. Keith, and had a dau. *Mary*, who m. Col. Thos.

---

*It is of interest to note that the names Randolph and Randall were used interchangeably in Colonial Virginia, as is numerously evidenced in its records. The following is an instance :

Minutes of the proceedings of the General Courts of Virginia, held at Jamestown, March 16, 1675-6. " Judith Randall, widow of Henry Randolph, seized of 1,000 or 1,200 acre of land in Henrico Co., ordered that patent be granted to Henry Randolph son of Henry Randolph dec'd.   R. A. BROCK."

Marshall of Oakhill, had son CHIEF JUSTICE JOHN MARSHALL.
WILLIAM, son of Thos. R. of Tuckahoe, b. 1712, d. 1745, m. Mary,
dau. of Mann Page of Rosewell : His dau. *Mary R.* m. Tarlton
Fleming of Rock Castle, and was ancestor of the Maynards of
the Goode pedigree : his son Col. *Thomas Mann R.* of Tuckahoe, member of the Va. Convention of 1775, had numerous
issue. His son Thos. Mann R. jr., Col. of Infantry in war of
1812, and Governor of Va., m. Maitha, dau. of Thos. Jefferson ;
his dau. Mary m. Gouverneur Morris of N. Y.; his dau. Lucy m.
Wilson J. Cary of Cary's Brook, and had son Wilson Miles Cary
of Baltimore, and a dau. Mary, who m. Dr. Orlando Fairfax, son
of Rev. Bryan Fairfax of Alexandria—*Baron Fairfax* of the British
Peerage,—whose son Randolph Fairfax, killed in battle, was the
subject of Dr. Slaughter's biography—and also a son.Archibald who
m. Monimia Fairfax, and whose dau. Constance Cary, (wife of Burton N. Harrison, private secretary of Pres. Jefferson Davis, C. S.
A.,) is well-known in the literary world. Another son, Gen.
George Wythe R., Secretary of War C. S. A., b. 1818, d. 1867, m.
grand-dau. of No. 759 of the Goode Pedigree. William R. of Chellowe, son of Thos. Mann, had a son Col. Thos. Beverley R., U.
S. A., an officer of the war of 1812 and the Mexican war ; his son
William Mayer, an eminent lawyer of New Orleans, has son *William Beverley R.* of Fla., who m. Mary C. Iverson, granddaughter
of No. 199 of the Goode Genealogy. The Randolphs of Charlottesville are desc. from John, son of Thos. Mann Randolph.

3. ISHAM RANDOLPH OF DUNGENESS, Adj. Gen. of Va., ancestor of the
   Randolphs of Dungeness and Ben Lomond, d. 1742. His dau. JANE
   b. in London, 1720, m. Col. Peter Jefferson, and had son PRESIDENT
   THOMAS JEFFERSON. His dau. ANNE m. Jonathan Pleasants and
   was m. of *Gov. Jas. Pleasants* of Va. His dau. SUSANNA, m. Carter
   H. Harrison of Clifton, and was g. m. of *Col. Randolph Harrison*,
   Virginia Commissioner of Agriculture. His son WILLIAM of Bris-
   tol, England, had son *Thos. Esten R.*, whose g. d. m. Dr. David
   Murrell, g. s. of No. 410 of the Goode Genealogy.

4. RICHARD RANDOLPH OF CURLES, M. H. B., and Treasurer of the
   Colony, ancestor of the Randolphs of Curles, Roanoke, Bizarre,
   Warwick, Chester and Fighting Creek, m. Jane Bolling, great
   granddaughter of Pocahontas. Their son, RICHARD R. of Curles,
   had 10 children,of whom *Mary R.* m. Col. Wm. Bolling of Chellowe, whose dau. Ismay m. Wm. Robertson and had sons Thos.
   Bolling Robertson, M. C. and Gov. of La., and John, Attorney
   Gen. and Chancellor of Va., also g. s. Hon. Wyndham Robertson,
   of Abingdon, Gov. of Va. *Susan R.* m. Benj. Harrison of Berk-
   eley, M. C., Signer of the Declaration of Independence and Gov.
   of Va. and had son PRESIDENT W. H. HARRISON, (who had son
   Hon. J. S. Harrison, M. C. from Ind., and grandson Gen. Benj.
   Harrison, M. C. from Indiana, and John S., whose s. Benj. m.
   Maria Goode, dau. of No. 477 of the Goode Genealogy.): *Jane
   R.* m. Archibald Bolling of Red Oak and had dau. Sarah, m. J. C.
   Megginson, No. 301 of Goode Genealogy; *Elizabeth R.* m. Col.
   Richard K. Meade of the Revolution, and had son Bishop Wm.
   Meade, author of "Old Churches and Families of Virginia".
   David Meade R. m. Mary Randolph, (dau. of Thos. Mann), author
   of the famous "Virginia Cook Book," and had s. *William B. R.*, of
   the U. S. Treasury, Washington, whose dau. m. Prof. W. W.
   Turner of the Smithsonian Institution; and whose son James R. is
   Chief Engineer of the Baltimore and Ohio R. R. (Connected
   with this branch of the family is Gen. D. H. Strother,—" Porte

Crayon,"—whose facile pen and pencil have preserved to us so much of Old Virginia life.) MARY, dau. of Richard of Curles, m. Col. Archibald Cary—old Ironsides—of Ampthill, and had numerous posterity. BRETT R. m. Miss Scott of London : his posterity are discussed in the Goode Genealogy. JOHN m. Francis Bland, his cousin and had Richard R. of Bizarre, antiquary and philanthropist, and John R. of Roanoke one of the most picturesque figures in American history.

5. SIR JOHN RANDOLPH of Williamsburg, Speaker of the House of Burgesses, Treas. and Att'y Gen. of Va., had son, PEYTON, R., Speaker H. B. and 1st President of U. S. Congress, who d. s. p., and JOHN R., Att'y Gen. of Va., a leading Royalist, whose son *Edmund*, Aide to Gen. Washington, Att'y Gen. of Va., Governor of Va., Attorney General and Sec. of State of U. S., and d. 1813, leaving issue, among whom were Peyton R., an eminent lawyer. Sir John Randolph lived in what is now "Tazewell Hall " in Williamsburg.

6. HENRY RANDOLPH OF LONGFIELD, d. unm.

7. EDWARD RANDOLPH OF BREMO, lived in England, and had a son EDWARD R., a sea captain, mentioned in note to No. 235 of the Goode Genealogy, and daughter ELIZA, m. Rev. William Yates, Pres. of William and Mary College, and MARY, m. married Rev. Robt. Yates, ancestors of most of the Yates family of Va.

8. MARY RANDOLPH, m. 1688, *Capt. John Stith* of Charles City Co., Issue : 1, REV. WILLIAM STITH, who was Pres. of William and Mary College and historian of Virginia. 2, CAPT. JOHN, ancestor of the Maynards of the Goode Genealogy, 3, MARY, m. Commissary Wm. Dawson.

9. ELIZABETH RANDOLPH, m. *Richard Bland* of Jordans Point. Their son, RICHARD, the Virginian Antiquary member of the Convention of 1775, and of the first Congress, had numerous descendants including the "Whitby Goodes" enumerated in the Goode Genealogy, the Lees. the Munfords, the Tuckers, Sinclairs, Atkinsons, Mayos and Kennons. (See note on THE BLAND FAMILY, page 54.)

239.

FRANCIS GOODE, of " Post Oak," Powhatan Co., Va., son of Col. Robert and *Sally Bland* Goode, No. 90, p. 54, was born at "Whitby," May 5, 1773, died Jan. 13, 1815; married Oct. 28th, 1795, Martha Hartwell Hughes, daughter of Robt. Hughes, the third, of " Hughes' Creek," and Mary, daughter of Littleberry and *Judith Michaux* Mosby. Children : —

750, MARY MOSBY GOODE, b. Feb. 22, 1797, d. Aug. 21, 1821, m. *B. S. Morrison*, 751, SALLY BLAND, b. 1801, m. *E. C. Mosby*. 752, ELIZ. HUGHES, b. July 4, 1803, d. Dec. 7, 1839, m. *William W. Mosby*. 753, ROBERT HUGHES, b. April 1805, d. July 18, 1807.

241.

JOHN SPOTSWOOD, of " Orange Grove," Orange Co., Va., son of John and *Sallie Rowzie* Spotswood, was born 1760–70, married Oct. 28, 1705, MARY GOODE, dau. of No. 90, born July 25, 1776, died July 21, 1847. Children : —

754, ROBERT GOODE SPOTSWOOD, b. Aug. 27, 1797, d. y.   755, JOHN ROWZIE, b. June 22, 1799, living 1885.   756, MARY BLAND, b. July 17, 1805, living 1885, m. *John E. Lemoine.*   757, RICHARD THORNTON, b. Nov. 7, 1803.   758, EDWIN, b. Nov. 14, 1805, died 1828—a young physician.   759, SALLY BLAND, b. Oct. 10, 1807, d. Sept. 1808.

While Mary Goode, afterward Mrs. Spotswood, was an infant, an incident occurred at "Whitby" which is perhaps worthy of mention. It was in war times, but her father, Col. Goode, was at home for a day. A company of British dragoons came riding over the river bottom, and surrounding the house demanded that the master should come out and surrender. Mistress Goode told them that he was not at home, which was the truth, for when, after a moment of delay, they entered the house to search it, she led them to the top of the house and told them that she would show them her husband. There he was, half way to Rocky Mount, on one of the swift horses for which he was famous. He had slipped away as the troopers approached, and pursuit was useless, although he had but a few seconds the start.

Mary Goode was a noted belle,—one of a celebrated quartette of Richmond beauties,—of which the other members were Betsy Mc. Clurg,* afterward the wife of John Wickham (see "Harper's Magazine," 1885, for her portrait); Charlotte Foushee (Mrs. Carter), and Nellie Pollard (Mrs. Howell Lewis). Mary Goode's miniature, painted by Thomas Sully, is owned by Mrs. Lemoine, of St. Louis. For a picture of the social life of those days see Mordecai's fascinating *Richmond In Bye-Gone Days.*

John Spotswood's plantation included the battlefield of the Wilderness. The house was ransacked in 1864 by Northern troops, and lt is said that the only existing portraits of Col. Robert Goode and his wife were then destroyed.

EXCURSUS.—THE SPOTSWOOD FAMILY.

Governor Alexander Spotswood, the first of the name in America, came to the colony in 1710, bringing with him to the colonists the right of habeas corpus. He was regarded as the model governor, and from having been the pioneer of iron manufacture in North America, has been styled the Tubal Cain of Virginia. He served as governor until 1752, and was deputy Postmaster General for the American Colonies from 1730 to 1739. Promoted to Major General, he was on the eve of embarking for Carthagena, when he died at Annapolis, June 7, 1740. An estimate of his character is given in the introduction to *The Spotswood Letters,* so judiciously edited and elegantly printed in behalf of the Virginia Historical Society, by its Secretary, Mr. Brock, and in an essay by John Esten Cooke in "Harper's Magazine," June, 1879. Spotswood was born in Tangier, Africa, in 1676, being grandson of Sir Robert Spottiswood, President of the Court of Sessions of Scotland, who was executed in 1646 for his loyalty to King Charles, and whose father was John, Archbishop of Glasgow, ninth in descent from Robert of Spottiswood, who was born in Berwick, Scotland, about 1240. (See Campbell's *Genealogy of the*

---

*Daughter of James Mc. Clurg, an eminent and learned physician, and member of the Conventions that ratified the Federal Constitution.—R. A. BROCK.

Spotswood Family.) Governor Spotswood was also descended, in the thirteenth generation, through the families of Plantagenet, DeBohun and Butler, from King Edward of England. His Virginia home was "Temple Farm," near Yorktown, where the old mansion still stands, and is known as "The Moore House,"—a place of great historic interest, not only from its earlier associations, but because within its walls Cornwallis signed the articles of capitulation.

Governor Spotswood has many hundreds of descendants in America, a score or two of whom, including a large percentage of those now living who bear the name of Spotswood, are included in the record of the Goode family. Dr. William A. Caruthers, in his amusing romance, *The Knights of the Horse Shoe, a Traditionary Tale of the Cocked Hat Gentry of the Old Dominion*, treats extensively of the early history of the Spotswoods, and of the famous trip across the mountains to the Valley of Virginia. He has, however, taken unwarrantable novelist's license in many particulars, in none more so than in allowing the Governor's eldest son, John Spotswood, the grandfather of John Spotswood, the husband of Mary Goode, to be murdered by the Indians, unmarried, on account of an intrigue with the Indian girl, Wirgina, a figure in Colonial history second in romantic interest only to Pocahontas, who was in fact the nurse of this same John Spotswood's son, Alexander.

Governor Spotswood married Ann Butler Brayne of Westminster, England, whose god-father was James Butler, Duke of Ormond, and who bore him four children, John, Ann Catherine, Dorothea and Robert. The latter, ROBERT, a subaltern under Washington, was killed near Fort Du Quesne in the Indian war of 1756. An elegiac poem, published in "Martin's Miscellany," London, shortly after his death, is quoted in Campbell's *History of Virginia.*

DOROTHEA, (b. 1727, d. 1773,), married, in 1747, Capt. Nathaniel West Dandridge of the Royal Navy, and had ten children, a very full list of whom is given in Browning's *Americans of Royal Descent.* Both Slaughter and Campbell are wrong in stating that her son, *John Dandridge,* married Miss Goode : his wife was Elizabeth Boothe, and his cousin, *John Spotswood,* married Miss Goode. Her daughter, *Dorothea,* was the second wife of PATRICK HENRY, the patriot and statesman. A list of their descendants is given in Slaughter's *Winston-Henry Genealogy,* in the *History of St. Mark's Parish.* Martha Clarke, of William H. Clarke and Elvira, dau. of *Patrick Henry,* jr., married COL. J. LYLE CLARKE son of No. 763 of the Goode Genealogy. Among the distinguished posterity in this line are *Maj. Alexander Spotswood Dandridge,* A. D. C., to Washington (who had a son of the same name, a prominent physician of Cincinnati, and daughters, Sarah, wife of U. S. Senator Anthony Kennedy, of Maryland, and Mary E., wife of U. S. Senator R. M. T. Hunter, of Virginia.) *Sarah Butler Henry,* who m. Robert, bro. of Thomas Campbell. the poet, *William Wirt Henry,* orator and historian, and *Rev. Wm. Spotswood Fontaine,* of North Carolina.

ANN CATHERINE SPOTSWOOD, who died 1820, married Col. Bernard Moore, sr., of "Chelsea," King William Co., Va. A full list of her descendants was given by Mr. Brock in a *Genealogy of the Moore Family,* in the "Richmond Standard," Sept.,1881, and Browning in *Americans of Royal Descent,*the *Carter Family*

Tree, the *Genealogy of the Page Family*, also give facts. Among the prominent posterity are *Charles Campbell*, historian of Virginia, the Carters of "Shirley," and Gen. Robert E. Lee and his distinguished kinsmen.

JOHN SPOTSWOOD, married 1745, Mary, dau. of Capt. William Dandridge, R. N., and Unity West, his wife, a descendant of a brother of Lord De La Warr. They had two sons, 1, *Gen. Alexander Spotswood* of "Newport" and "Nottingham," who m. Elizabeth Washington, niece of General Washington, and had 5 daughters, (one of whom, *Henrietta*, m. Judge Bushrod Washington,) and two sons, 1, *George W.* who m. his cousin, Lucy Spotswood, and had son, *Capt. C. F. M. Spotswood* of Norfolk, an officer in the U. S. Navy and subsequently in the Confederate Navy, and 2, *William L. M.*, (b. 1791, d. 1871,) of "Sedley Lodge," Orange Co. Captain William A. Spotswood, C. S. A., (Biography in Appleton's Annual Cyclopedia, 1860, p. 54,) was of this line. 2, *Capt. John Spotswood* of the Virginia Line in the Revolution, wounded at the battle of Brandywine, m. Sallie Rowzee. His son, *John*, m. Mary Goode, No. 241. I have not been able to trace the descendants of his other sons, *Robert* (m. Louisa Bolt), *Elliott* (m. Sallie Littlepage), *Dandridge*, (m. Catherine Francisco), and *Norborne Berkley* (m. Sally Markham).

The arms of the Spotswoods are *Azure, a chevron, gules, between three oak trees eradicated, vert.* Crest, *An eagle displayed, gules, looking to the sun in splendor.* Motto, *Patior ut potior.—*BROCK.

It is worthy of note here, that three at least of Gov. Spotswood's "Knights of the Golden Horseshoe," as named by Caruthers,—Theodorick Bland, Dudley Digges and Benjamin Harrison, were ancestors of certain scions of the Goode family.

242.

JAMES LYLE, Jr., of Rocky Mount, (Manchester) Va., married June 18, 1796, SALLY BLAND GOODE, daughter of No. 90, born Aug. 8, 1779. Mr. Lyle died July 30, 1806, of gout of the stomach, and was buried at "Whitby." Issue :—

> 760, SALLY LYLE, b. Jan. 29, 1797, died of smallpox May, 1797; buried at "Whitby." 761, JAMES, b. Mar. 3, 1798. 762, JANE, b. Dec. 3, 1799, d. Oct. 5, 1804. 763, MARY GOODE, b. Oct. 25, 1801, d. Dec. 22, 1884. m. *Colin Clarke.* 764, MARTHA b. Sept. 5, 1804, d. 1805. 765, JOHN, b. Sept. 27, 1806, d. Sept. 17, 1827.

James Lyle was a prominent merchant, and a man of culture and liberal tastes, as is proven by the large library which he collected. A block of houses known as "Lyle's row," was long one of the prominent features in the Richmond of former days.

James Lyle, his father, was a native of Scotland, and one of the pioneers of the young settlement. An incident connected with the opening of the Richmond and James River Canal may be worthy of mention here. This canal, the first commenced in the United States, was projected in 1784 by George Washington and completed in 1795. Samuel Mordecai, in his *Richmond In Bye-Gone Days*, writes :—" A wealthy Scotch merchant believed that if the ca-

252.

Hon. JAMES W. BOULDIN, of Virginia, son of Wood Bouldin, of Charlotte Co., and Joanna Tyler, his wife, (sister of Gov. John Tyler, aunt of President John Tyler and daughter of John Tyler, Marshal of the Colony of Virginia, by his wife, Ann, dau. of Dr. Comptesse, a Huguenot,) married (1) about 1810, MARTHA GOODE, dau. of No. 95, (2) Miss Jouett, (3) Mrs. Almira (Reed) Kennon. Children (first marriage): —

791, SAMUEL GOODE BOULDIN, d. yg.. and others.

POWHATAN BOULDIN, of Danville, Va., editor of the *Danville News* and author of *Home Life of John Randolph of Roanoke*, was a son of Judge Bouldin by a late marriage—also Louis and Edwin, and a daughter, Harriet. In Mr. Powhatan Bouldin's fascinating book, which is based chiefly upon the recollections of his father, any one interested in the history of the social characteristics of Virginia at the beginning of this century will find a mass of valuable suggestions.

WOOD BOULDIN, who m. Joanna Tyler, was fifth son of COL. THOMAS BOULDIN, who came to Virginia from Maryland in 1744. Besides James W., he had issue, *Louis C., Mary Francenia,* and *Judge Thos. Tyler Bouldin,* M. C., who died in his seat in the House of Representatives in Washington in 1834; the children of the latter by his wife, Nancy Lewis, were; 1, Judge Wood Bouldin, who m. (1) Maria Louise Barksdale; (2) Martha, dau. of Judge Wm. Daniel, Sr., and aunt of Hon. John W. Daniel, (See GOODE GENEALOGY, No. 410) and had numerous issue. 2, Martha, m. John Breckenridge Cabell, many children. 3, Thomas Tyler, Jr. 4, Joanna, m. Robert Carrington, who owned the plantation next to "Roanoke," and of whom it is said John Randolph of Roanoke was afraid. (Letter of Alexander Brown, Esq.)

253.

Hon. R. H. BAPTIST, of Mecklenburg Co., Va., descended from the Baptists of the Eastern Shore of Virginia, Member of the Virginia Assembly and County Judge, married March 27, 1878, SALLY GOODE, dau. of No. 96, who was born 1790-1800, d. 1829. Children : —

792, MARTHA BAPTIST, m. *Mr. Brame*, of Boydton, Va. 793, SAMUEL GOODE, of Brooklyn, N. Y., widow living in Brooklyn, in 1885. 794, R. H. 795, T. W. J. 796, JOHN GOODE. 799, REV. EDWARD L., Lombardy Grove, Va., 1880.

254.

THOMAS W. JONES, M. D., of Brunswick Co., Va. Born June 25, 1788, died July 21, 1824, married February 17, 1814, MARY ARMISTEAD GOODE, daughter of No 96, who was born February 17, 1795, died May 22, 1871. Children : —

798, SAMUEL GOODE, b. Sept. 20, 1815, m. (1) Nov., 1842, MARTHA W. GOODE, No. 758; (2) 1862, Aurie Elmore, Suwannee University,

Suwannee, Tenn.   799, LUCY BINNS, born March 26, 1801, m. March 2, 1836, George Mason, M. D., (bro. of the late Hon. John Y. Mason, Sec. of the U. S. Navy and Minister to France, b. 1799, d. 1859,) living 1881, near Hicksford, Greenville Co., Va. 800, JOHN RAVENSCROFT, b. Aug. 21, 1818.   801, THOMAS W., b. March 25, 1820, d. y.   802, MARY ARMISTEAD, b. February 25, 1722, d. y. 803, EDWARD BURWELL, M. D., b. October 31, 1823, m. February 17, 1846, Cornelia Campbell, living 1881, San Marina, Dinwiddie Co., Va.

255.

Dr. THOMAS GOODE, of Hot Springs, Bath Co,, Va., son of Col. Samuel Goode, No. 96, was born 1780–90, died 1858, married Mary Ann Knox.* Children :—

804, COL. THOMAS F. GOODE. 805, SAMUEL, b. 1827. 806, MARTHA. W. m. SAMUEL GOODE JONES, No. 798.   807, LUCY, m. *Col. George William Brent. C. S. A.*   808, MARGARET, m. *William P. Garland,* of Lynchburg. 809, ELLEN, m. *J. M. Friend,* of Charlotte Co., 810, SOPHIA, Boydton, 1881. 811, ISABELLA, Boydton, 1881. 812, ALICE, m. *Dr. Crump,* of Culpeper Co., Va.

Dr. Thomas Goode removed, about 1825, to Botetourt Co. (the portion now known as Roanoke Co.), near the Big Lick, and in 1833, to Bath Co., when he bought the Hot Springs, and by his wisdom and energy built up the famous sanitarium at that place, of which he was proprietor at the time of his death. He published "The Invalids' Guide to the Virginia Springs," of which editions were printed at Richmond 1831, 1846, 1857.   He was a very enthusiastic politician, and the memory of the discussions which took place at his Hot Springs sanitarium, in which he was the most prominent participant, are still traditionary in Virginia.

The writer has visited his grave, which is in the little burying-ground near the Hot Springs Hotel.

256.

SAMUEL HOPKINS GOODE, of Mecklenburg Co., son of No. 96, was born September 14, 1802, died April 19, 1855.   "A farmer and magistrate of the county and a most estimable gentleman."   Married (1) Mary E. Price, of Brunswick Co., no children.   (2), March 29, 1840, Martha Jones of Mecklenburg Co., who died 1845, no children. (3) Mary Frion of North Carolina, August 1855.   Children :—

*THE MURRAY, KNOX, AND GORDON FAMILIES.—James Murray was a native of Scotland, and of the lineage of William Murray, Lord Mansfield, the celebrated English jurist : he perpetuated the name of the ancestral seat in Scotland in that of his house, "Athol," near Petersburg.   He married ANNE BOLLING, a great grand-daughter of Pocahontas.   (See note in the Bolling Family, pages 64, 70 preceding.) His daughter, Mary, b. 1757, d. 1823, m. (1) Alexander Gordon ; (2) Col. Wm. Davies, son of Rev. Samuel Davies, "the apostle of Presbyterianism in Virginia," and Commissioner of War under Washington in the Revolution.   Alex. Gordon, a native of Kirkcudbright, Scotland.   (*Arms,* Az. a besant between three boars, heads erased, or.   *Crest.* A dexter hand issuing out of a mouth, grasping a sabre, proper. *Motto,* Dread God) and a merchant of Petersburg, had by his wife, Mary Murray, a daughter of Peggy Gordon, who m. 1 William Knox, of Philadelphia, who d. 1809 in Petersburg—had daughter, Mary Ann Knox, who married No. 255.   (For full pedigree see Slaughter's *Bristol Parish,* pp. 199–205.)

813, M. B. Goode, b. Sept. 6, 1841, m. *Mr. Morrison M. Jordan.* Samuel B., b. June 23, 1844. Lives, 1885, Meridian, Miss. 814, Robert, Goode, b. 1847, d. 1865. 819, Thomas, Tuscaloosa, Ala., 1885. 817, Frank, Winfield, Kansas, 1885. 818, Margaret, m. *J. L. Hendrick,* of Boydton, Va., about 1869, children, 1 *William,* 2 *Samuel,* 3 *Thomas,* 4 *John,* 5 *Mary* and 6 *Frank.*

291.

Capt. WILLIAM A. ADAMS, C. S. A., of "Bonneville," son of Abner Adams, of Dinwiddie Co., Va., No. 102, a gallant officer, killed in battle.

271.

Hon. WILLIAM OSBORNE GOODE, M. C., of "Inglewood," Mecklenburg Co., Va., son of John C. Goode, No. 105, p. 65, was born at "Inglewood," September 16, 1798, died July 3, 1859, married 1829, Sarah Maria, daughter of Thomas Massie, of , "Level Green," a major in the Virginia Line of the War of the Revolution, and Lucy Waller, of "Bellfield."* Children : —

819, William Osborne Goode, b. Sept. 16, 1830, d. May 8, 1863. An officer, C. S. A., killed in battle. 820, Lucy Waller, m. *Capt. George T. Baskerville,* No 789. 821, Eliza. 822, John Thomas, 823, Edward Branch. 824, Juliet Virginia, m. *Dr. Jordan.* 825, Henrietta Wise, m. *Thomas H. Boyd.* 826, Sarah.

He was graduated from William and Mary College, 1819, studied law, and commenced practice as an attorney, in 1821. He was soon elected to the Legislature and took an active part in the debates on slavery in 1832. He continued in this body many years, and was, during several sessions, Speaker of the House of Delegates, member of the State Reform Convention, 1827 and 1832. Member of the U. S. House of Representatives, 1841-3, and 1853-9. In the XXXVth Congress he was Chairman of the Committee on the District of Columbia.

John T. Goode writes, " He assuredly reached a high rank as a debater— few superior—look to his speech on the gradual emancipation question in the House of Delegates of Virginia—it may be said it immortalized him—look to all his speeches in the House of Delegates of Virginia and the Congress of the United States. They were of the highest grade of oratory."

Hambleton, in his *History of the Political Campaign of Virginia,* in 1855, (Richmond, J. W. Randolph, 1856,) speaks of him thus in the famous Knownothing struggle :—" In the fourth District, Hon. William O. Goode, a gentleman of great political experience, ripe years, and of State reputation, was the Democratic Candidate for Congress. Mr. Goode was a member of the Conventions of 1829-30 and of 1850, and was for many years a distinguished

*For an account of the Massie Family, see *Richmond Standard,* March 5, April 2, 1881.

member of the Legislature and had served in Congress two sessions with distinction. He was opposed by Mr. Tazewell, of Mecklenburg, (a Knownothing candidate) a young gentleman of great facetiousness, whose anecdotes during the canvass were exceedingly entertaining and pleasing to his auditors. The district was regularly canvassed by the candidates, and Mr. Tazewell was beaten by about 2,000 majority."

274.

SAMUEL PRYOR,* of Dinwiddie Co., Va., planter, married MARY ANN HAMLIN, daughter of William B. and *Martha Goode* Hamlin, No. 106, p. 66. Living in 1885. Children:—

> 827, SAMUEL PRYOR, m. a dau. of Richard J. Gaines,† of Charlotte Co., Va., 7 children, (796–802). 828, WILLIAM H., m. 1856, *Margaret Walker*.‡

275.

JUDGE EDWARD R. CHAMBERS, of Mecklenburg Co., Va , member of the Virginia Convention of 1854, and the Secession Convention of 1861, married 1825-30, LUCY TUCKER, daughter of Col. John and *Agnes Eppes Goode* Tucker, No. 108, born December 8, 1805, died May 20, 1857. Children:—

> 829, EDWARD ST. JOHN CHAMBERS, of Olcolona, Miss., an extensive planter, m. Maggie Waddell, of Hartford Co., N. C., now of Baltimore, s. p. 830, STERLING, d.yg. 831, HARVIE, born about 1845. Was educated at the Virginia Military Institute and the University of Virginia. Served in the latter part of the war as a member of some junior company. A lawyer living near Olcolona, Miss. "He was wild, and a dangerous man in personal difficulties, which he rather sought than declined. His health gave way early and he went to sea to revive it, and died on the return voyage. A very gifted man." 832, HENRIETTA, d. yg. 833, ELIZABETH, d. yg. 834, MARTHA, m. *Dr. Alexander Laird*, son, *Charles Laird*, m. dau. of F. M. HOLT, of Haut Rein, N. C. 835, JENNIE, m. *Dr. Harvie Laird*. 836, MOLLIE, d. yg. 837, JULIET, m. *L. M.*

---

*THE PRYOR FAMILY.—This family was settled in Virginia at an early day, and was connected with the Hayes and Goode families of Amelia and Prince Edward. Richard Pryor, of Dinwiddie Co. born 1760-70, had a daughter, who married John Atkinson. (See Atkinson Genealogy, *Bristol Parish*, p. 137. Rev. Theodorick Pryor, D. D., of Nottoway Co., who married Lucy Atkinson, brother of John Atkinson, just mentioned, and whose son is Gen. Roger Atkinson Pryor, C. S. A., and Samuel Pryor, 120–254, were brothers.

†THE GAINES FAMILY.—This family was early settled in Virginia, and some one of its members was ancestor of the wife of Samuel Goode, No. 96, as the frequent occurrence of the name *Gaines Goode* attests. Richard J. Gaines, m. Martha Venable. (*Richard N,——Nathaniel,——Abraham.*)

‡THE WALKER FAMILY.—Major Thomas Walker, who was a Burgess from Gloucester Co., Va., 1662-6, is believed by Dr. Slaughter to have been of Staffordshire extraction. His grandson, Thomas Walker, of King and Queen Co., was born about 1680-5, and had a son, Dr. Thomas Walker, of "Castlehill," Albemarle Co., born 1714, died 1794, the first white man who explored Kentucky, Commissary General of Virginian troops in Braddock's war, M. H. B., Member of the Virginia Convention of 1741. Married, 1741, Mildred, widow of Nicholas Merriwither, (b. Thornton). Among the distinguished descendants of this pair were, Col. John Walker, Senator and A. D. C. to Washington; Col. Francis Walker, M. C.; Col. R. T. Duke, C. S. A., M. C; Prof. F. W. Gilmer, of the Univ. of Va. Thos. W. Gilmer, Governor of Va.

Wilson, of Baltimore. 838, ROSA, m. COL. THOMAS F. GOODE, No. 804.

276.

THOMAS GOODE TUCKER, of "Mount Rekcut," near South Gaston, N. C., son of Col. John Tucker, No. 108, was born April 7, 1807. Moved to North Carolina in 1836, to his present residence on the Roanoke. Married (1) Elizabeth Lewis, of Brunswick Co., Va. (2) Mary Carey Capehart, daughter of Cullen Capehart, of Avoca, N. C., a descendant of the Stanleys of England, the Ogilvies of Scotland, the Razeures (who were well-known Huguenots), and the Byrds of Virginia. Children : —

> 839, BETT, b. 1835, m. *Col. Junius K. Long.* 840, AMELIA EPPES, b. 1843, m. *Capt. Thomas Capehart.* 841, CULLEN CAPEHART, b. 1855, educated at the Maryland Agricultural College and at the University of North Carolina. Lives at Avoca, Bertie Co., N. C., "an energetic, prudent and extensive planter." Others died young.

He was educated at the University of Virginia, where he was a classmate of Hon. A. H. H. Stuart, Hon. John S. Preston, Gen. Robert Toombs and Judge Wm. A. Daniel, and was the intimate friend of Edgar Allen Poe. "While there," he writes, " I often saluted ex-President Jefferson, who daily attended his 'dear pet' to superintend the operations of every class." Although a lawyer he never practiced, having large plantations and numerous negroes in Virginia, North Carolina and Mississippi.

He writes, at the age of seventy-eight : " I am and have ever been free from any description of dissipation. My health has always been good. My only sport has been fox-hunting, of which I am passionately fond. I weigh only 112 pounds, but am as active in the chase as when only twenty-five. In politics I could not be other than a Jeffersonian Republican (now Democratic), but have never engaged in them. I never aspired to any public trust, although as magistrate I acted until the whole framework of the old government was upset. During the war, which, by the bye, in a limited sphere I attempted to arrest, I was earnest in its support. Being in constant communication with the State authorities I organized a Home Guard, whose duty was to arrest deserters, give courage to the faltering and secure supplies and aid for those in the field. The latter duty was with marked success performed by me. The 'history of my side campaign would be really romantic in many of its features."

277.

DR. STERLING H. TUCKER, of Mississippi, son of Col. John Tucker, No. 108, was born June 22, 1809, died March 5, 1852, married Martha, daughter of Theophilus Feild, of Brunswick Co. Died childless.

Educated at Ebenezer Academy, Brunswick Co., Va., and at the Jefferson Medical College of Philadelphia. After a few years' residence in

Virginia, he settled in Mississippi, planting on an extensive scale, and practicing his profession. His health failing he returned to his native state, where
he died from the effects of an operation for stone in boyhood.

279.

COL. EDWARD BENNETT TUCKER, of Brunswick Co., Va., son
of Col. John Tucker, No. 108, was born April 4, 1812, died March 22,
1885. Was educated at Ebenezer Academy. A planter, owning the old
homestead of the family. Married Eliza Black Cummings, of Petersburg, Va. Children : —

> 842, JOHN H. TUCKER, b. 1841. 843, MARIA, m. *Dr. John Feild*, 844,
> WILLIAM C., b. 1852. 845, THOMAS GOODE, b. 1864.

280.

DR. JOHN EPPES TUCKER, of Olcolona, Miss., son of Col. John
Tucker, No. 108, p, 67, was born December 30, 1784, died Jan. 30,
1815. A physician and planter. Married Mary, daughter of Hon. David
Hubbard, of Alabama. Childless.

281.

WILLIAM EMBRY GOODE, of Dinwiddie Co., Va., son of John
Goode, No. 109, was born in Brunswick Co., 1794, died 1825. A
planter. Married Martha, daughter of Baker Pegram,* of Dinwiddie
Co., who died 1822–3. Children : —

> 846, MARTHA PEGRAM, m. *Stephen Perkins*, of Louisa Co., d. s. p. 1839,
> leaving son who died, s. p. 847, WILLIAM HENRY, b. 1820.

284.

DR. AUSTIN WHARTON, of Cartersville, Cumberland Co., Va.,
was born in Albemarle Co., 1775 : educated at Dickinson College, Carlisle, Pa.: practiced medicine in Cartersville, from 1804 to 1834, when
he removed to Goochland Co., where he died. Married (1) LUCY
GOODE, daughter of John Goode, No. 109, born 1787, died 1818. Married (2) a sister of Hon. Edward Bates, of Missouri, Attorney General
of the United States. Children. (All by first wife): —

> 847½, CHARLOTTE WHARTON, d. unm. 848, THOMAS GOODE, d. yg.
> 849, ROBERT HENRY, b. 1811, d. 1857. 850, REV. CHARLES D.,
> Presbyterian clergyman, b. 1818, d. 1845. 851, RICHARD GOODE,
> b. 1815.

Dr. Austin Wharton was son of John Wharton, originally of Culpeper Co.,

---

*THE PEGRAM FAMILY.—This well-known Virginia family, according to Slaughter, originated with an
English civil engineer of the name who settled before the middle of the eighteenth century, in what is now
Dinwiddie Co., married a daughter of Col. Baker, and had five sons. Slaughter gives the names of three, and
a list of the descendants of Major General John Pegram, M. C., (son of Edward, the original settler), who
married Martha Ward Gregory. (See note on the Ward Family, p. 109.) Major Baker Pegram, the eldest
son of the original settler, was the father of the wife of No. 260. Some of the family lived near Amelia
C. H., and were related to the Prince Edward Goodes and the Hayes family.

Va., who died near Nashville, 1813; another son was Judge Jesse Wharton, of Nashville, another was William H. Wharton, a leader in the early political history of Texas, Senator of the Republic, and minister to the U. S.; still another John A. Wharton, was Adjutant General of the Texan Republic. (See H. A. Wise's *Seven Decades of the Union*, p. 147.)

285.

THOMAS TAURMAN, a farmer of Goochland Co., Va., married 1830, EMILY GOODE, daughter of John Goode, No. 109, p. 67. Children:—

852, JOHN G. TAURMAN, b. 1831, m. dau. of W. A. Deitrich; a farmer in Henrico Co., 1885. 853, HENRY E., Fine Creek, Powhatan Co., a farmer, m. Miss Bohannan, of King William Co. 854, THOMAS, farmer in Powhatan Co., m. (1) dau. of Samuel Taylor, of Powhatan; (2) dau. of John Woodfin. 855, WILLIAM, farmer, Henrico Co. 856, LUCY, m. *Mr. Bowles*, Lives near Ground-squirrel Meeting House, in Hanover Co.

287.

JOHN BENNET GOODE, of Mecklenburg Co., Va., son of Bennet Goode, No. 110, p. 67, was born about 1770. He was well educated, probably a non-graduate student of William and Mary College, and was a member of the Virginia House of Delegates. Married Miss Hendricks. Children;—

857, LUCY GOODE, m. *Richard Boyd*, of Mecklenberg Co. Daughter married *L. E. Finch*. 858, ELIZA, m. *W. H. E. Merrit*, a lawyer of Brunswick County. 859, two others, d. yg.

260-1.

REUBEN VAUGHAN, of Lunenberg Co., Va., married 1798, ALICE GOODE WATKINS, daughter of Samuel and *Elizabeth Goode* Watkins, No. 115½, who was born in Nottoway Co., Va., died June 9, 1885, at "Battersea," Marengo Co., Alabama. Children:—

860, EVELINA E. VAUGHAN, b. 1799, m. *Dr. Luke White*, of Petersburg, Va., living in Petersburg 1885, a widow. 861, EMILY GOODE, m. *Robert V. Montague*, lives 1885, in Marshall, Mo. Has a dau., *Mrs. Hardiman Cordell*, of Marshall. 862, MARTHA, m. *William A. Gasquet*, of New Orleans, children, 1. *Evelyn E. Gasquet*, m. John R. Marshall, of New York, has children, i. Mrs. William Kernochan, ii. Mrs. Louise Wysong. 2. *Louisa*, m. A. B. James, of New Orleans. 3, *Francis Jones*, of New Orleans, m. Louisa Lapeyre. 863, VIRGINIA, m. *Mr. Kidd*. 864, DR. SAMUEL WATKINS. 865, DR. ALFRED GOODE. 866, ALICE GOODE, b. 1825, m. *Henry Dugger*. 867, SUSAN, d. unm., 1845.

291.

WILLIAM GOODE POVALL, of Va., son of Charles and *Martha Goode* Povall, No. 115, p. 68, was born in Powhatan Co,, Va., 1778–80, died in Richmond 1851–2.   Married Rosina Moseby.   Both he and his wife are buried on the old plantation in Powhatan Co., now owned by Milton Atkinson :   many of the Povalls lie in this old burying ground but there are no stones to mark their names.   Children : —

> 871, MARY POVALL, d. unm.   872, EMILY, d. unm.   873, CHARLES BEN-
> NETT, d. unm.   874, SARAH, m. *Powhatan Selden*, of Richmond,
> Va.   875, LUCY, m. *Milton Noble*, of Amelia Co.   876, JOHN
> PETER, b. 1820, m. *Miss Wright* of Mississippi.   Removed to Co-
> lumbus, Miss., in 1844.   Has children.   877, CHARLES BENNETT.

William Goode Povall was a large operator in cotton at an early day. I find the following in the Richmond *Enquirer* of December 10, 1825 :

TO COTTON-GROWERS.

" Seeing that Richmond is likely to become an important cotton market, the subscriber has determined to offer his services to cotton-growers to sell that article on commission.   He can at all times be found at Shockoe warehouse.

BENJAMIN SHEPPARD.

Mr. Wm. G. Povall also announces to cotton-growers and cotton dealers that he has erected two cotton gins in the Boring-mill buildings, in rear of the Armory, and a cotton press at the same place, where he is prepared to pick bale cotton.   He is also " disposed to purchase about one hundred thousand pounds of seed cotton, for which the market price in cash will be given."

296.

WILLIAM CARRINGTON, of " Walnut Hill " Cumberland Co., Va., planter, was born Aug., 1774, died May 21, 1825.   Married (1) Jan. 31, 1799, Ann Hughes, dau. of Robert Hughes.   (2) Oct. 16, 1801, MARTHA POVALL, dau. of Charles and *Martha Goode* Povall, No. 115, p. 68, born in Powhatan Co., Va., Nov. 1, 1784.   Children : —

> 00, ROBERT HUGHES CARRINGTON, b. Sept. 7, 1799, d. unm. Feb.1, 1826.
> 878, JOSEPH POVALL CARRINGTON, b. 1802, d. 1805.   879, WILLIAM ED-
> WARD, b. Feb. 25, 1804, d. bef. 1883.   880, MARTHA ANN, b. Feb.
> 21, 1806, d. Apr. 29, 1865, m. *Codrington Carrington.* 881. HAR-
> RIET POVALL, b. June 8, 1808, d. Oct. 4, 1880, m. *Wm. H. Mayo.*
> 883, ELLEN SARAH THEODOSIA, b. Jan. 19, 1814, m. *Wm. Randolph
> Bradley.*   884, MARY ELIZA ANN, b. Feb. 22, 1817, d. Nov. 16,
> 1825.   885, LUCY VOLNEY GOODE, b. Feb. 12, 1819, d. Nov. 10,
> 1832, m. *Thos. Riddell Powell.*   886, CHARLES RICHARD, b. June
> 10, 1822, d. Jan 16, 1856.

EXCURSUS—THE CARRINGTON FAMILY.

The name Carrington, or Carington, occurs in Cheshire, Essex, Norfolk, Buckingham, Hertford, Leicester, and Yorkshires, England.   A barony was created in 1796, apparently in an Irish offshoot of the family.

Dr. Paul Carrington, b. 1600–20, a Royalist who fled from England during Cromwell's protectorate and settled in Barbados.   He was a neighbor and perhaps a companion in arms, of John Goode, of Whitby, who left England at the same time and for similar reasons. He married in Barbados, Heningham, dau. of Christopher Codrington, and had 11 children, (Nathaniel, Hannah, Codrington, Paul, William, George, Joseph, Edward, &c.) and had many descendants there in the last century, though the name is now extinct.

GEORGE CARRINGTON, was baptized in the Parish of St. Phillip, Barbados, 1711 and came to Virginia, about 1727, with Joseph Mayo, a Barbados merchant who settled at "Powhatan," nearly opposite "Whitby," and just below the present site of Richmond. He m. 1732, Ann Mayo, niece of his employer, whose store-keeper he was, removed to Willis Creek, Cumberland Co., and d. Feb. 7, 1785, leaving 11 children, from 8 of whom are descended all of the name and lineage of Carrington in America. Foote, Campbell and Meade have recorded briefly the family history, and Mr. Alex. Brown has published, (*Richmond Standard*, Feb. 26, and Mar. 5, 1881), a portion of his record, embracing 2,000 names in all, a considerable number of which occur also in the Mayo and Cabell pedigrees. Mr. Peyton R. Carrington has extensive MS. materials which he has generously allowed me to use in elaborating the GOODE section of the Carrington pedigree, embracing about 200 names. He has the family bible of George Carrington, the immigrant, with the entries of his children's births, in his own hand writing. George Carrington is No. 1 of Mr. Brown's record.

The most eminent of the family was JUDGE PAUL CARRINGTON, Sr., of "Mulberry Hill" on Staunton River, son of George, the immigrant, a prominent Judge and Revolutionary patriot, member of the Conventions, and of the Committee of Safety, and described in Grigsby's "Convention." He m. (1) Margaret, dau. of Col. Clement Read (see Read note). (2) Priscilla Simes. Three of his sons were Revolutionary officers; George, lieutenant in Lee's Legion, Judge Paul, Jr., who served at Guilford and Green Spring, and Col. Clement, wounded at Utah Springs, whose dau. Mary V., m. Hugh Blair Grigsby. Col. Henry was father of Eliza C., wife of Judge George Gilmer.

JOSEPH CARRINGTON, 5th son of GEORGE, m. Theodosia Mosby: (see Mosby note). Their son William, of "Walnut Hill," m. Martha Povall. (See Goode Genealogy for ancestry and posterity).

COL. EDWARD CARRINGTON, 8th son, an officer of the Revolution, Q. M. Gen. for the southern army under Greene, m. Eliza Ambler, dau. of Jacqueline Ambler, Treasurer of Va., and his wife Rebecca Burwell, and sister of the wife of Chief-Justice Marshall. No issue.

MARY CARRINGTON, dau. of George, m. Joseph Watkins. Her granddaughter, Ann, m. Maj. David Shields, whose son Thos. P. m. Martha C. Bradley, (dau. of No. 883, Goode Genealogy).

HANNAH, m. Col. Nicholas Cabell, an officer of the Revolution under Lafayette.

ANNE, m. Col. William Cabell, member of the Conventions and of the Committee of Safety.

295.

HON. SIDNEY MOORE GOODE, son of William Goode, No. 116, was born in Elbert Co., Georgia, Jan. 28, 1797, and died in Thibodaux, Louisiana, Nov. 3, 1846. Married Nov. 7, 1820, in Jackson, Clarke Co., Alabama, Louisiana Scudday, b. in Abbeville District, South Carolina, March 28, 1803, d. in Thibodaux, La., Sept. 19, 1883 : (dau. of John Scudday, b, in Louisa Co., Va., about 1770, and Eliz. Bickley, b. in Louisa Co., Va., about 1776.)   Issue :—

> 895, JOHN WILLIAM GOODE, b. Oct. 17, 1826. 896, MARTHA ANN, b. Feb. 13, 1829, m. *Rev. Daniel McNair.* 897, FLAVILLUS SIDNEY, b. Jan. 24, 1831, d. Dec. 1885.' 898, LOUISA CAROLINE, b. Jan. 25, 1833, d. 1863, in Rapides Parish, La., a refugee from the lines of the Northern army; m. *Rev. William McConnell,* who lives, 1884, at Craigville, Ont.: has child *Louisa Caroline,* b. 1863. 899, JAMES JEFFERSON, b. May 21, 1835, d. 1867. 900, REBECCA OVERTON, b. 1844, d. unm. 1853. 901, JOSEPH SCUDDAY, b. Sept. 2, 1837, d. 1884.

Sidney Moore Goode, when a boy, removed with his father to Clarke Co., Alabama.   Before he was of age he served on the Staff of General Andrew Jackson in the Florida war, and was present at the capture of Pensacola, but was invalided and at home at the time of the Battle of New Orleans.   He studied law in Clarke Co., and about 1827 removed to Marion, Perry Co., Ala., where he practiced his profession for some years.   Having inherited from his father and father-in-law a large number of negroes, he bought a tract of land in Kemper Co., Mississippi, where, from 1827 on, he was a successful cotton-planter.   Later he bought a sugar plantation in Lafourche Parish, Louisiana, upon which he lived until the time of his death.   His next neighbor was Bishop L. K. Polk, Lieut.-Gen., C. S. A.   While a citizen of Mississippi, he was, for a number of terms, member of the State Senate. The family mansion in Louisiana was burned about 1859, destroying all it contained, including the family bible, with its record of family history.

296.

JEFFERSON GOODE, of Alabama, son of William Goode, No. 116, was born in Georgia about 1800 and removed with his father to Alabama at an early age.   He died in Clarke Co., Ala., before 1850.   Children :—

> 902, ROBERT O. GOODE, a merchant in Camden, Ala., 1881. 903, JAMES JEFFERSON, b. about 1830.   Graduate of Univ. of Alabama, 1852. In 1870 a lawyer in Camden, Alabama. 904, REBECCA, m. *Mr. Bones* of Clarke or Wilcox Co., Alabama.

297.

CAPT. JAMES A. TAIT, of Wilcox Co., Alabama, only child of

Judge Charles Tait.* He was, says Garrett, in his *Public Men of Alabama*, "a gentleman of great substance in property and in moral worth." He married, 1810–20, CAROLINE GOODE, daughter of William Goode, No. 116, who died about 1870. Children : —

> 905, CHARLES W. TAIT, d. 1880. 906, FELIX, Camden, Ala., 1885. 907, ROBERT, planter, Black's Bluff, near Camden, Ala., 1885. 908, SARAH, m. *Dr. R. H. Erwin.* 909, MARTHA, m. *Franklin K. Beck*, a lawyer of Camden, Alabama. 910, REBECCA. 911, CAROLINE, m. (1) *Mr. Shropshire*, soldier, C. S. A., Ala. Inf., killed in battle. (2) *Mr. Delaney*, of Columbus, Texas, children 1. *Charles Delaney*, and others. 912, JAMES, planter, of Camden, Wilcox Co., Ala.

298.

BENJAMIN COLEMAN of Kemper Co., Mississippi, removed from Clarke Co., Alabama, where he married SARAH ANN GOODE, daughter of William Goode, No. 116, to Mississippi, where he became a wealthy planter. Issue : —

> 913, AUGUSTUS COLEMAN, living, 1884, near Memphis, Miss. A wealthy planter, unmarried. 914, SIDNEY, member of Mississippi Legislature. 915, AMANDA. 916, SARAH ANN, married.

299.

ISAAC W. NICHOLSON, of Kemper Co., Mississippi, removed thither from Clarke Co., Ala. A wealthy planter with extensive cotton lands and hundreds of slaves. Married, March, 1822, MARTHA JEFFERSON GOODE, dau. of William Goode, No. 116, born April 5, 1806, died Dec. 4, 1870. Children : —

> 917, THOMAS JEFFERSON NICHOLSON, b. 1823, d. 1853. Planter of Kemper Co., Miss. 918, CAROLINE, b. 1825, d. 1844. 919, FLAVILLUS GOODE, b. 1827, planter, of Shuqualak, Miss., soldier C. S. A., m. 1760, Josephine Wingate, children, 1. *Irene*, 2. *Wingate*, 3. *Henry*, 4. *Thomas.* 920, JAMES, d. y. 921, SARAH REBECCA, b. 1829, m. *Dr. P. H. Hamilton.* 922, MARTHA, m. REV. JOSIAH M. NICHOLSON, No. 927. 923, LOUISA A., b. 1840, d. 1880, m. *Dr. W. M. Mayes*, Ass't Surgeon, C. S. A., children, 1. Willie, 2. A son, b. 1880. 924, LUCY, b. 1847, m. *Wm. Ward*, soldier, C. S. A. A widow, 1885, no children.

---

*JUDGE CHARLES TAIT, says Brewer's *Alabama*, was a gentleman of very superior talents, and his scientific and literary acquirements made him one of the most interesting men of his day. He was born in Louisa Co., Va., 1767, and was a cousin to Henry Clay. While reading law in Baltimore, at the age of 19, he was thrown from a horse and his leg so injured as to necessitate amputation. A few years later he went to Georgia, became a successful lawyer, and was on the bench of the Supreme Court. He was also U. S. Senator 1809-19. While in Georgia occurred his duel with Judge Dooly, who refused to fight unless his leg was cased in a hollow tree to off-set Judge Tait's single leg. He removed in 1819 to Alabama where he was appointed Judge of the Federal district court. He resigned, 1826, and gave his attention to planting, and refused the office of Minister of England in 1828. He died in Wilcox Co., 1835. His first wife was a Baltimore lady, mother of No. 297; his second wife, Mrs. Griffin, sister of Judge Peter Williamson of Lowndes, Ala.

300.

THEOPHILUS NICHOLSON, of Kemper Co., Mississippi, removed from Clarke Co., Alabama. A wealthy cotton planter. Married RE-BECCA GOODE, daughter of No. 116. Children : —

> 925, LOUISA NICHOLSON. 926, MARTHA. 927, REV. JOSIAH M., a Baptist Clergyman, Bienville, Kemper Co., Miss., m. MARTHA ANN GOODE No. 922 : no children. Served through the war in 41st Regt. Mississippi Infantry, C. S. A.

301.

JOSEPH CABELL MEGGINSON, of " Clover Plains," near Greenway, in Buckingham Co., Va., was very near the age of his Aunt Elizabeth (Mrs. Lewis), who was named after his deceased mother, and they were nursed at the same time at the breast of his grandmother, Mary (Hopkins) Cabell. (Gen. B. W. S. Cabell's Memorandum.)

Elizabeth (Cabell) Megginson, his mother, died soon after giving birth to her only child, about the last of January, 1771. The following extract from Col. Wm. Cabell the elder's diary, is sent by Mr. Alexander Brown.

"January 31st, 1771, went to see my niece Betsy Megginson interred."

309:

SURGEON SAMUEL CABELL HORSLEY, U. S. N., son of Wm. and *Martha Megginson* Horsley, No. 116–5, was born 1779–85. Married Mary A. Denney, of Baltimore.

Samuel Cabell Horsley, was Surgeon in the Navy, and was in service during the war of 1812, in several Naval engagements. He was in Perry's flag-ship at the battle of Lake Erie, and when that was about to go down escaped with the Commodore and other officers, in an open boat to the nearest vessel of the American squadron. His share of prize money was $3,000. His portrait hangs in the Council Hall in Baltimore. He survived the war and died in the U. S., Service at Portsmouth, Va. (Note of Dr. W. A. Horsley, communicated by Alex. Brown, Esq.)

313.

THOMAS GOODE, of Raymond, Mississippi, son of Thomas Goode No. 117, was born 1800–1810. Married Miss Slocumb. Children : —

> 930, CHARLES SLOCUMB GOODE, b. 1803. Educated at the University of Mississippi, and Union University, Murfreesboro, Tennessee, receiving degree of A. B. from the latter in 1863. A soldier C. S. A. Living in New Orleans, 1880. 931, THOMAS, (?) a soldier, C. S. A. 932, MONROE, a member of the class of 1863, Brown University, Providence, returning South at the outbreak of the war. A soldier, C. S. A., probably killed in battle.

315.

COL. JOHN GOODE, of Washington Co., Va., son of William and

Marie Morrisette Goode, No. 119, p. 71., was born 1770–80 in Richmond, and removed at an early day to the Southwestern portion of the State, where he became a prominent citizen of Washington Co. Married (1) Ann C. Findlay, dau. of Connally Findlay of Abingdon, Va., who died 1831. (2) Mrs. Frances Watkins, dau. of John Cole of Chesterfield Co., Va. (3) Margaret Carter of Wythe Co., Va. Children (by first wife only) : —

> 933, ELIZABETH GOODE, b. Dec. 1, 1824, m. 1851, *M. H. Buchanan.* 934, RACHEL, b. Oct. 9, 1826, m. *B. K. Buchanan.* 935, ROBERT FINDLAY, b. June 29, 1828.

John Goode served in the Norfolk campaign of the war of 1812, in Captain Burford's Company of Virginia troops. He and his brother Robert, No. 317, inherited upon their father's death in 1821, 307 acres of land lying near the Midlothian coal mines in Chesterfield Co., probably a part of the old homestead, which they sold in 1822 to Bennet Goode, No. 318. John and Robert Goode were engaged to go to Washington County, in 1820, to prospect for coal for the Saltworks Company, and found small deposits in many places. John Goode was manager of the Saltworks in 1852. In middle life he was an officer of the State Militia. "The two brothers owned extensive tracts of land, and numerous slaves, brought from Chesterfield County. They were tall and considered very handsome—fit types of the Old Virginia Gentleman—freehearted and hospitable."

316.

WILLIAM GOODE, of Tennessee, son of No. 119, was born in Henrico Co., Va., 1770–80, and removed to Middle Tennessee, where he died. Children : —

> 936, JOHN WILLIAM GOODE, b. 1800-20, d. 1851-2. 937, MARY, m. (1) *John Childrey*, (2) *Mr. Johnson.*

318.

BENNET GOODE, of Chesterfield Co., Va., son of No. 119, was born 1770–80, died after 1829. Married Catherine Parsons. Children : —

> 937, JOHN GOODE. 938, ROBERT. 939, WILLIAM B. of Tunstalls, New Kent Co., Va., children, 1. *William N. Goode*, 2. *R. B.*, son *Joseph W.*, 4. *Thomas*, 5. *J. B.*, 6. *Sylvanus Lee*, 7. *Adalina*, 8. *Francis*, 9. *Catherine R.* 940, NANCY. 941, PATSY. 942, WINNIE. 943, SALLY. 944, POLLY. 945, BETSY.

320.

MR. MOORE, of Henrico Co., Va., married MARY GOODE, daughter of No. 119. Lived near Richmond. Children : —

> 946, MARY, m. *John Earnest*, children, (1) *John Henry Earnest*, of Washington Co., Va. 947-8, Sons, d. s. p.

321.

MR. JOHNSON, married ELIZABETH GOODE, daughter of No. 119, and removed to Lexington, Ky., where both died.   Children :—

> 948–1, EGBERT JOHNSON.   948–2, ELIZABETH.   948–3, AURELIUS, married in Kentucky, a soldier, C. S. A., killed at Chickamauga.

322.

RICHARD KENDALL WEISIGER,* of Manchester, Va., was born May 15, 1785, died Feb. 22, 1862.   Married Feb. 20, 1808, MARTHA GOODE, daughter of No. 119, born Aug. 20, 1788, died Sept. 17, 1853. Children :—

> 949, AMANDA FITZALLEN WEISIGER, b. Nov. 21, 1808, d. Feb. 17, 1861. 950, ROBERT DANIEL, b. March 19, 1810. 951, DAVID, b. Aug. 3, 1811. 952, POLLY GOODE, b. Nov. 16, 1812, d. Apr. 3, 1859, m. *Thomas Johnson,* of Richmond, Va., blacksmith, issue, 1. *Thomas Johnson,* a sailor, 2. *Wyndham,* Baltimore, 3. *Horace,* 4. *Kendall.* 5. *Julia,* m. Mr. Lipscomb, Tunstall's, Va., issue, 1. *Susan.* 953, RICHARD BEVERLY, b. Feb. 5, 1814, d. 1874 : a farmer, Baronsville, New Kent Co. 954, JOHN KENDALL, b. Oct. 4, 1816. 955, ADALINE SUSAN, b. Apr. 10, 1818, d. Apr. 3, 1859. 956, MARTHA F., b. Sept. 15, 1820, d. Sept., 1824. 957, DANIEL WASHINGTON, b. Feb. 14, 1823, d. Nov. 6, 1872. A soldier in the Mexican War, and C. S. A., m. M. J. Harriss, of Goochland Co., issue, 1. *John R.,* 2. *Arthur W.,* 3. *Ella N.,* m. Joseph A. Fowker, 4. *Adaline,* m. Chas. E. Hasker, d. Aug. 1885, 5. *Luther H.,* 6. *William D.,* 7. *Clifford L.* 958, DAVID KENDALL, b. June 14, 1825, d. Sept. 16, 1826. 959, MARGARET KENDALL, b. Dec. 16, 1826, d. Nov. 3, 1863, m. *Wesley Burnett,* of Tunstall's, New Kent Co., farmer, issue, 1. *Charles Burnett,* d., 2. *William,* farmer, New Kent Co., 3. *Emma Lipscomb.* 960, WILLIAM SAMUEL, b. Jan. 5, 1829, soldier, C. S. A., was in New Orleans, 1871.

323.

RENÉ CHASTAIN, of Chesterfield Co., Va., a descendant of the Huguenot family of Chastain† settled at Manakin Town, married about

---

*THE WEISIGER FAMILY.—SAMUEL WEISIGER, a native of Germany, was born as early as 1740–50, and settled in Chesterfield Co., Va , about the middle of the last century.   He always spoke English with difficulty.   He married, Nov. 16, 1769, Mary (Kendall) and from him, it is believed, are descended all of the name in Virginia, and the South.   His children were : 1. *Daniel Kendall Weisiger,* b. Dec. 3, 1770. 2. *John Kendall,* b. Dec. 27, 1771. 3. *Samuel,* b. Dec. 1, 1773. 4. *Daniel,* b. April 15, 1776. 5. *David,* b. Dec. 16, 1777, d. about 1825. 6. *Jacob Power,* b. Jan. 22, 1780. 7. *Washington,* b. Feb. 28, 1783 : the father of Dr. Wm. Weisiger of Manchester. 8. *Richard Kendall,* b. May 15, 1785, m. MARTHA GOODE, (see Goode Genealogy.) 9. *Jacob,* b. June 3, 1788. 10. *Eliz Kendall,* b. Apr. 22, 1792.
   David Weisiger, No. 5, was a captain in the war of 1812.   Married (1) Miss Branch, niece of Rebekah Hayes, (see Goode Genealogy, No. 171.) (2) Sally S. Gordon, of Powhatan, and had : i. Capt. Thos. Weisiger, sometime Commonwealth's Att'y of Amelia ; ii. Judge Samuel Weisiger, of Petersburg, b. 1823. Genl. D. A. Weisiger, C. S. A. was probably son of No. 6.

†JEAN CHASTAIN was the second Registrar of King William Parish, (Manakin Town). The patronym Chastain is perpetuated as a Christian name in many Virginia families.   R. A. BROCK.

1810, WINIFRED GOODE, daughter of No. 119, who died, a widow, at the home of No. 316, Nov. 18, 1828, aged 30. Children:—

961, JUDGE SAMUEL CHASTAIN, of Kentucky. 962, JOHN WILLIAM, moved to Kentucky.

323-1.

MR. COOK, of Richmond, Va., married SARAH GOODE, daughter of No. 119. Daughter:—

962-1, HIPAGEE COOK, m. Mr. ————, of Richmond.

323-2.

MR. BRANCH, of Petersburg, Va. (?), married MATILDA JONES, grand-daughter of No. 62. Son:—

962-2, PETER JONES BRANCH, of Petersburg, Va., m. Rachel Findlay, sister of No. 315 ; three of their children live in Abingdon, Va.

The Branch family are united to the Goodes by many intermarriages— see Appendix under No. 56.

324.

THOMAS GOODE, of Rutherford Co., N. C., farmer, son of No. 121, was born April 1, 1781, died Sept. 27, 1861. Married Sarah F. Elliot, of Mecklenburg Co., Va., born Jan. 6, 1793, died May 10, 1872. Children:—

963, BENJAMIN FRANKLIN GOODE, b. Oct. 26, living 1884, farmer and postmaster, Hull's X Roads, Lincoln Co., N. C., m. (1) Sarah Magness, (2) Eliza Hull, children, 1. *John Edward Goode*, b. 1828. 2. *Thomas J. G.*, soldier, C. S. A., in Arkansas Reg't, d. 1880. 3. *Sarah*. 4. *Martha*. 5. *Mary*. 6. *Maggie*, b. 1859. 7. *Laura*, b. 1862, and 7 others. 964, MARTIN ELLIOT, b. Mar. 23, 1810, d. 1858. 965, JOHN TURPIN, b. Apr. 12, 1811, a farmer of Cleveland Co., N. C., m. Barbara Warlick, children, 1. *Dr. N. A. Goode*, Waco, N. C. 2. *Thomas F.*, soldier, C. S. A. 3. *Julius*, soldier, C. S. A. 4. *David*, soldier, C. S. A., clergyman of the Methodist Church South. 5. *William*, soldier, C. S. A. 6. *Augustus*. 7. *Mary*. 8. *Sally*. 9. *Dicy*. 10. *Fanny*. 11. *Jimmy*.

326.

RICHARD GOODE of Ashville, Ala., son of No. 121, a planter, was born in Henrico Co., Va., 1783, removed to Alabama at an early day, and died at Ashville, 1855. Married 1802, Hettie Webb, of North Carolina. Children:—

966, NOAH GOODE, b. 1803, d. 1885, in St. Clare Co., Ala., had daughters. 967, MATILDA, b. 1809, living 1885 in Gillsville, Ga., m. *John Martin*, of Bellton, Ga., and had 17 children, including 9 sons who were soldiers in the Confederate army. 968, ROBERT, b. 1812, a soldier, C. S. A., lives 1885, at Augusta, Arkansas. 969, EDWARD, b. 1816. 970, MARY, b. 1819, m. *Mr. Blackwell*, of Delong, Ga.

971, ALFRED, b. 1821, lives at Springfield, Ala., a soldier, C. S. A.
972, MARTHA, b. 1825, m. *Mr. Thompson*, of Hill's Valley, Ala.
973, FRANCIS MARION, b. 1834.   974, JOHN, b. 1836.   A soldier,
44th N. C. Vols., C. S. A., d. Jan. 31, 1865, and buried in Holly-
wood Cemetery, Richmond, Section W., No. 282. 975, ELLEN, d.
1870–80, m. *Mr. Baugh.*   976, SALLY, d. æt. 35.

333.

NICHOLAS GOODE, of Elbert Co., Ga., son of No. 123, was born
1760–80, in North Carolina, or Virginia, and removed to Elbert Co ,
Ga., at a very early day.   Married in Virginia, Miss Key.   Children:—

977, JOHN GOODE. 978, JAMES T., blind, lives with 110. 979, THOMAS,
farmer, of Warlen, Texas, soldier, C. S. A., has dau. 1. *Elizabeth.*
880, JOSEPH, planter of Abafoil, Ala. 981, DAVID C., planter, of
Conyers, Ga., soldier, 1st Ga. Inf., C. S. A., children, 1. *J. M.
Barton Goode*, of Conyers, Ga., b. 1862, farmer and contributor
to the "Southern Cultivator." 2. *Joseph.* 3. *Tinie.* 4. *William.*

The experiences of the early settlers in Georgia are told in a most entertaining style by Judge George R. Gilmer in his "Georgians."

336.

JABEZ WATSON GOODE, of Oglethorpe Co., Ga., son of No 125,
was born 1780–1790, died 1840–50. A pioneer and planter. Children:—

982, WILLIAM MARION GOODE, b. 1849, lives at Mica, Pickens Co., Ga.
983, JAMES WATSON, music teacher, Mica, Ga. 984, JOSEPH T.,
b. Oct. 15, 1853. Merchant and Postmaster, Crackling, Ga., 1885,
m. Susan Emery ; children.

THE CULPEPER GOODES.

340.

DANIEL C. GOODE, of Marthasville (now Atlanta,) Ga., son of
No. 125, was born in Halifax Co., Va., 1762–70.   Removed at an early
day to Georgia, and settled where the city of Atlanta now stands.   Died
about 1840.   Children :—

985, DANIEL GOODE. 986, REUBEN JONES, b. 1800, d. 1879, in Texas,
removed in 1830 to Georgia : Children, 1. *George W. Goode*, b.
1833 in Ga., moved to Cincinnati, 1866, a confectioner, children,
2. *Dr. Reuben Jones Goode*, of Salado, Texas, and others.

987, BENJAMIN GOODE, who m. about 1832, Sarah Dawson, of Green
Co., Ga., is perhaps of this family.

341.

JOHN GOODE, of Norfolk, Va., son of No. 126, was born in Halifax Co., Va., 1760, died at Norfolk, 1804.   Son :—

988, DANIEL, b. 1780–1800.

342.

WILLIAM GOODE, of Carrolton, Illinois, son of William and *Mary (?) Glidwell* Goode, No. 126, p, 72, was born in Halifax Co., Va., 1775, died 1884.   Married Agnes Cole, daughter of Thomas Cole, a native of England, and a teacher in Halifax Co., Va., and his wife Nancy Glidwell, (cousin of wife of No. 126).   Children :—

989, MARY GOODE, b. 1805, m. *William Carlin.*   990, NANCY, b. in Halifax Co., Va., 1807, m. *Wm. Halbert*, a prominent farmer of Green Co., Illinois : descendants scattered and gone in 1881.   991, SUSAN, b. in Halifax Co., m. *Bird Woltrop*, farmer of Carrolton, Green Co., Ill., children.   992, MARTHA, b. in Kentucky, June 8, 1823, m. *Albert Halbert*, farmer of Green Co., Ill., children scattered and dead, 1881.   993, WILLIAM GOODE, b. in Lincoln Co., Ky., April 6, 1821, living 1881, in Neosho, Kansas.   994, PAMELIA, d. y.   995, ELIZABETH, d. y.

343.

WILLIAM GOODE, of Macoupin Co., Illinois, son of Campbell Goode, No. 127, was born in Virginia, 1770–90, died 1844.   Children :—

996, JOHN WESLEY GOODE, M. D., b. 1810, d. 1847.   997, JAMES, of Kirksville, Mo., d.   998, WILLIAM, of Kirksville, Mo., d.   999, ELIZABETH, m. *Tice Link*, of Kirksville, Mo., d.   1000, SARAH, m. *Mr. Smith.*

William Goode removed from Virginia to Kentucky, about 1880, and settled in Casey County.   He was one of the earliest Methodists in the State.   He was member of the Kentucky Legislature, 1815-16-19.   He moved to Ohio, and was member of the State Legislature from Green Co.   He subsequently lived in Missouri, and before 1831, had settled in Scottsville, Macoupin Co., Illinois.   He died in 1844, in Palmyra, Ill.

348.

MICAJAH GOODE, of Kentucky, son of Benjamin Goode, No. 128, was born in Amherst Co., Va., 1790.   Moved to Kentucky when a youth. Died 1866.   Children :—

1001, JOHN GOODE, of Taylorsville, Ill., b. 1822, children, 1. *Jasper Peyton Goode.* 2. *Mary Francis.* 3. *Susan.*   1002, DANIEL.   1003, WILLIAM.

DANIEL GOODE, lived 1880-85, at Danville, Ky.   He may have been No. 1002, or a descendant of 127, 128, 131, 131½, 137, 138, or 151.   So also, *John Goode*, of Gamaliel, Ky., *James C. Goode*, of Hustonville, Lincoln Co., ——. *Goode*, of Stanford, and *Lorenzo D.*, member of Kentucky House of Representatives, 1869–71, *J. C. Goode*, P: M., Eubank, Pulaski Co., Tenn., 1883, are doubtless descended.

350½.

C. B. GOODE, of Lauderdale Co., Ala., probably son of No. 128 or 131, was born 1790–1800, moved to Williamson Co., Tenn., and thence 1825, to Lauderdale Co., Ala. Son:—

> 1004, WILLIAM, of Lauderdale Co., Ala., has son, *Charles*, a planter of Rodgersville, Ala., 1885.

351.

GEORGE GOODE, of Rockbridge Co., Va., son of No. 129, was born in Botetourt Co., Va., 1770–80, married about 1800, Virginia Rodes, (daughter of Christopher Rodes of Rockbridge Co., and cousin of Gen. David Rodes, whose son Maj. Gen. Robert E. Rodes, C. S. A., born 1829, was killed at battle of Winchester, Sept. 19, 1884.) Children :—

> 1005, JOHN GOODE, of Abbott, Va., b. 1803. 1006, JAMES MADISON, "killed by a robber in Mississippi." 1007, WILLIAM L., went to Indiana. A. H. Goode, M. D., of Blennysport, Indiana, is perhaps his son.

351½.

MAJOR WILLIAM GOODE, of Akron, O., believed to have been a grandson of No. 40, but perhaps descended from No. 45 or 46, was born Jan 7, 1791. A soldier in the war of 1812, wounded at the battle of "North Fork." His descendants have his sword. Moved in 1820, from Campbell Co., Va., to the Western Reserve of Ohio Farmer and Surveyor. Married Mary Upshur of Norfolk, Va. Children :—

> 1009, JOSEPH GOODE, of Akron, O., children : 1. *John Goode*, Civil Engineer Northern P. R. R. 2. *William*, a farmer, Oakland, Cal. 3. *Joseph*, California. 1010, JAMES, b. 1818, d. May 10, 1818,·m. *Mary Campbell*, children : 1. *William Goode*, surveyor, Winona, Minn. 2. *John C.* 3. *Mary*. 1011, WILLIAM, JR., children : 1. *Joseph*, capitalist, Beaver Falls, Pa., m. Miss Germyn, has son William. 2. *Eliza*, Oakland, Cal. 3, *Edward*, sometime professor in Rensellaer Polytechnic Institute, Chief Engineer of Calumet and Hecla Mine. 4. *Samuel*, merchant in Calcutta, India.

352.

ALFRED GOODE, of Kentucky, son of No. 131, p. 72, was born in Virginia, 1796, died 1871. Removed to Kentucky at an early day, and was a soldier in the war of 1812, and also did some Indian fighting. Children :—

1012, JAMES T. GOODE, a soldier in the Union Army, Ky. Vols., and had a son, 1. *R. F. Goode*, a soldier U. S. A., now resident as U. S. Revenue official at Owensboro, Ky. 1013, E. R., soldier U. S. A. 1014, J. W., soldier, U. S. A. 1015, THOMAS J., soldier, U. S. A.

1016, D. B., 1017, RICHARD, and 1018, R. A. GOODE, of Kentucky, were all soldiers U. S. A., in the late war, some of them officers, and were grandsons of No. 352. 1019, EDWARD GOODE, "who went from the Chesapeake Bay to Missouri and thence to Arkansas," is possibly of this family.

353.

RICHARD GOODE, of Jefferson Co., Ky., son of Richard Goode, No. 131½, was born in Virginia or North Carolina, 1760–80. Died near Louisville, Ky., 1846–60. Children : —

> 1020, WILLIAM THOMAS GOODE. 1021, SIMON S. 1022. ROBERT HENRY. 1023, RICHARD, b. 1820–30, probably now living in Kentucky, a farmer. 1024, EDWARD, living in Kentucky, a farmer. 1025, MARY, d. unm. 1026, MARTHA, m. *Mr. Hartman*, probably living in Jefferson Co., Ky.

Richard Goode removed from North Carolina to Kentucky, with his father Col Richard Goode, 1800–1810. "He served in the war of 1812, under Col. Richard M. Johnson, and was present when Tecumseh fell by the hand of that Kentuckian at the battle of the River Thames. He also served one or two terms in the Legislature of Kentucky, and was the only Whig representative, ever sent by Henry Co. before the war." He lived near Newcastle, and late in life, in Jefferson Co., Ky., about 20 miles from Louisville, where he died.

354.

JOEL H. GOODE, of Huntsville, Ala., son of Richard Goode No. 131½, was born in Rockingham Co., N. C., 1760–80. Moved with his father to Kentucky, and subsequently became established in Huntsville, Ala. Children : —

> 1027, RICHARD NEWTON GOODE, b. 1812, d. Feb. 6, 1873. 1028, NOBLE M., b. 1814, d. 1872. 1029, BERTRAND, b. 1816, d. 1870–80, lived in eastern Texas, had 2 sons, one living in eastern Texas, 1885, and 2 daughters, dead. 1030, ROBERT, d. in eastern Texas. 1031, MARY JANE, m. 1846, *Josiah Frost.* 1032, SARAH, d. 1884, m. *William Sexton.* 1033, CYNTHIA, m. *Mr. Crawford*, of San Antonio, Texas.

358.

BENNETT GOODE, of Essex Co., Va. son of Willlam and *Polly Dennett* Goode, No 132, was born 1795, died 1840. A member of the State Guard at Richmond. Married Polly Rose. Children : —

1034, SILAS GOODE, d. s. p. 1840.   1035, WILLIAM S., of Richmond, m. Mildred Wayne of King and Queen Co., children , 1. *Chas. Samuel*, b. 1857.   2. *John Robert*, b. 1862.   3. *Willie Ann*, b. 1866, 4. *Sarah Virginia*, b. 1868.   5. *Mildred Diana*, b. 1871.   6. *Thomas Edwin*, b. 1873.   7. *Ida Lee*, b. 1876.   1036, JOHN, m. Peggy Brooks, of Essex Co., Va.   1037, RICHARD, Essex Co., Va.

SIXTEENTH GENERATION

We cannot pause to fill the gaps, for in this restless, roving, ever-moving, never-tiring population, they are as Uncle Toby said, " Here to-day and gone to-morrow." To-day they are whacking down primeval forest, living in log cabins with mud chimneys, imitating dirt-daubers; to-morrow in the city, rolling in carriages : then rushing onward for new lands, hunting for the place where the sun sets. The generations are scattered, and nature's marks lost and forgotten. They are driven from the old hives, and if new gums are not provided, will clean out hollow trees, and make new honey in the wild woods.—GEORGE WYTHE MUNFORD : *The Two Parsons.*

In a psychological point of view, it is perhaps questionable whether, from birth and genealogy, how closely scrutinized soever, much insight is to be gained. Nevertheless, as in every phenomenon, the beginning remains always the most notable moment.—THOMAS CARLISLE : *Sartor Resartus.*

THE PRINCE EDWARD GOODES.

368.

SAMUEL VENABLE GOODE, of Kentucky, son of John Collier and *Dorothea Venable* Goode, No. 137, p. 75, was born in North Carolina or Kentucky about 1795, died 1862. Married Elizabeth Ann Taylor. Children : —

> 1020, SAMUEL VENABLE GOODE, of Smith's Grove, Ky., a soldier in the 11th Ky. Inf., U. S. A., during the Rebellion, and in 1885, in U. S. Internal Revenue service, stationed at Riggs, Ky., children, 1. *Wm. Henry.* 2. *Lettie Eliz.*, 3. *Lela*, 4. *Belva.* 1021, WILLIAM A., of Bowling Green, Ky., children, 1. *Josephine Goode*, 2. *Margaret*, 3. *Ettie*, 4. *Samuel*, 5. *William.* 1022, HENRY A., of Smith's Grove, Ky., 1885, a soldier in the 11th Ky. Inf., U. S. A., during the Rebellion.

374.

ROBERT GOODE, of Green River Ky., was born about 1800, and inheirited the parental farm in Green River, referred to in the record of his father, p. 76. Children : —

> 1023, DAVID M. GOODE, of Kentucky, a soldier in the Rebellion in the 17th Kentucky Infantry, U. S. A.

THE FOLLOWING.are children of John H. and *Susannah Goode* Osborne, No. 139, p. 47.

> 376, REV. ROBERT MACKERNESS OSBORNE, a local preacher of the Methodist Episcopal Church.   377, THOMAS.   378, SALLY, m. REV. WILLIAM GOODE, of Tennessee.   379, FRANCIS, m. *Stith Farley*.   380, SUSAN, m. *Mr. Morris*.

395.

BENJAMIN M. GOODE, of Grayson Co., Texas, son of No. 151, was born in Trigg Co., Ky., 1800.   Removed to Texas 1853.   Children:—

> 1040, ELIJAH D. GOODE, of Pottsboro, Texas, 1885.   1041, JOHN, of Pottsboro, Texas, d. 1885: family living in Grayson Co., Texas.

408.

MR. DYSON, of Lynchburg, Va., descended from early German settlers in Virginia, married SARAH MACKERNESS TATE, dau. of Col. Edward, and *Lucy Barksdale* Tate, dau. of No. 157, p. 77.   Children:—

> 1042, CLAIBORNE DYSON, lived, 1885, near Parkersburg, W. Va.,   1043, WILLIAM, d. in Tennessee, 1840–50.   1044, PAULINE, m. *Thomas E. Hoy*, moved to Hayward Co., Tenn. and later to Austin, Texas: children, 1. *George Hoy*, d. 2. *Charles*, farmer in Texas. 3. *James*, Soldier C. S. A., killed at Vickburg, 4. *Mrs. N. P. Davidson* Wrightsboro, Texas. 5. *Mary*. 1045, GUSTAVUS, b. 1819.   1046, LUCY, m. *Mr. Ashe*, of Middle Tennessee, children, *Augusta Ashe*, m. and moved to Texas. 2. *Lucy S.* m..E. S. Wootten of Texas. 3. *Sarah*, m. Rev. Mr. Wootten of Texas.

410.

DAVID GAMBLE MURRELL, of Lynchburg, Va., was born 1793–7, died of heart disease 1840.   Married ALICE TATE, daughter of No· 157, born 1785, died Jan., 1880.   Children:—

> 1047, JOHN WILLIAM MURRELL, b. Feb. 12, 1822.   1048, EDWARD H. b. July, 31, 1825.

Mr. Murrell was a prominent citizen of Lynchburg, merchant, manufacturer and postmaster.   He was long a member of the City Council, and was associated with the Oteys, the Norvells, and others, in promoting the public interests of the city, and particularly in constructing the city water works, at the time of construction, the finest in America.

411.

CALVIN TATE, of New Orleans, son of Col. Edward Tate, No. 157, p. 78–B, was born near Lynchburg, about 1787, died about 1865. He was a wealthy merchant and prominent citizen.   He is not known to have married.

431.

DR. SAMUEL MACKERNESS GOODE, of Madison, Indiana, son of Philip and *Rebekah Hayes* Goode, No. 171, was born in Charlotte Co., Va., Sept. 2, 1795; died in Jefferson County, Ind., June 29, 1826; removed with his parents to Ohio, 1805; married, May 25, 1824, Mrs. Sarah G. Cravens (born Sarah Grover Paul), widow of Dr. Robert Cravens, of Madison, Indiana* Son:—

> 1051, SAMUEL MACKERNESS GOODE, b. Nov. 20, 1825.

The following reminiscences of Dr. Goode are furnished by his brother Francis C. Goode :—He attended Espey's Academy in Xenia, Ohio, 1813-14, studied medicine with Dr. Hunt, of Xenia, and subsequently attended medical lectures in Philadelphia, as a member of the institution presided over by Dr. James Rush. After receiving his degree he practiced in Springfield, Ohio, and in 1822 became established in Madison, Indiana, in partnership with Dr. Isaac T. Canby, father of Gen. E. R. S. Canby, U.S. A., and had just secured a fine practice at the time of his death, in 1826. An anecdote of one of his experiences in Madison will illustrate the manners of the times. No one was allowed at that time to practice medicine in Madison without a diploma from a medical school or a permit from the local medical association. Not having joined the association, Dr. Goode was cited before this body to give an account of himself. He presented his diploma, but not one of the members could read it, since it was in Latin, and furthermore not one of them possessed the like, so they were obliged to call in the principal of the Madison Academy, Beaumont Parks, who was not a friend of the local potentates, and who read the the translation with great gusto.

432.

JUDGE PATRICK GAINES GOODE, of Sidney, O., son of No. 171, was born in Charlotte Co., Va., May 10, 1798, died in Sidney, Shelby Co., O., Oct. 17, 1862. He was the namesake of his father's friend, Patrick Henry; by profession, a lawyer, and was member of Congress from Ohio, 1840-46. Married July 3, 1822, Mary Whiteman, daughter of Gen. Benjamin Whiteman, born at Yellow Springs, O., Nov. 19, 1803; died in Sidney, 1876. They had three children :—

> 1052, CATHARINE REBEKAH GOODE, b. Aug. 19, 1823, m. *William McCullough.* 1053, BENEDICT WHITMAN, b. April 27, 1826. 1054, MARIA LOUISA, b. July 21, 1838, d. Sept. 20, 1840.

The following autobiographical notes are from an old pocket-book, and in the handwriting of P. G. Goode :—" My father removed with his family to Ohio in

---

*THE PAUL FAMILY.—Col. John Paul of Madison, one of the pioneers of Indiana, had among others the following children :—1, Nancy Paul, m. Gov. Wm. Hendricks of Indiana, U. S. Senator, whose nephew, Hon. Thos. A. Hendricks was Vice-president of the United States ; 2, John Peter Paul of Madison, who m. Eliza Meek, sister of Fielding B. Meek, the paleontologist ; 3, Sarah Grover Paul, m. (1) Dr. Robert Cravens of Madison, (2) Dr. S. M. Goode ; her son, Judge John Robert Cravens was paymaster, U. S. A. and Lieutenant-governor of Indiana.

1805, when I was about seven years of age. At that time Ohio was just emerging from a wilderness. The rude forests had been broken, and only broken, when my parents settled upon their land in Warren County. In a few years my father had cleared up and improved a good farm. Though the dangers and hardships of the early pioneer had been removed, yet the privations still remained, and especially the want of schools. The refinements of polished scholarship could not so easily be obtained in Ohio at that day. . . . I went to school in winter and worked on the farm the rest of the year until I was sixteen years old, when my father sold his farm and moved to Xenia, in order to educate his family to better advantage. I was a student in the Xenia Academy two years, and having acquired a knowledge of Latin and a good beginning in Greek, I accepted a position as a teacher in a classical academy in Philadephia, where I remained four years, after which I studied law with Judge Joseph H. Crane, of Dayton, O., and Benj. Collett, Esq., of Xenia, and was admitted to the bar in 1821. I practiced in Madison, Ind.. 1822–28, and then settled at Sidney, Ohio."

After going to Philadelphia, he neglected, though he did not cast aside altogether, the early teachings of his pious parents. After he went to Sidney, he was awakened to a sense of religious duty, and (to resume the manuscript) he writes : "I sought protection and strength of Him who is omnipotent, and though in youth I was naturally of an ardent temperament, much inclined to the indulgence of pleasure, my mind by early parental example and instruction, was, when quite young, deeply impressed with the truths of revealed religion. . . . This sense of divine revelation was still upon me. My impression as to the divine origin of the Christian religion became so strong as to relieve me from all the embarassments which are so likely to perplex men of prejudice and short-sighted views. Whether engaged in my legal profession or in any of the various duties that have since devolved upon me, at the bar, on the bench in the State Legislature, in the House of Representatives in Congress, or in private life, it has been my effort to impress on those around me, in all suitable ways, the value of the revealed religion of the Bible, and proper views of the nature of religious obligation."

Speaking of the study of law he writes ; "With me it is the study of morals as well as business, both as a science and in practice admitting, in my view, of full and useful developements, fraught with results highly beneficial to society."

"Before 1833, I had built up a lucrative practice in Shelby and adjoining Counties. In the fall of 1833, I was elected to the State Legislature, and was re-elected in 1834. In 1835 I was duly and fairly elected to the Senate of the State, and secured a certificate of election, but in a contest (the *majority* of the Senate as returned differing from me in party politics) the seat was given to my opponent. . . . In 1836 I was elected a member of Congress, and was re-elected in 1838 and 1840. In the last elections, I became the candidate by the unanimous consent of the Whigs of the district, without a convention. I took my seat for the first time at the extra session of 1837, the first year of Van Buren's administration, and continued a member of the House till 1843.

"During this period important business came up for the action of Congress : the currency question with its subtreasury recommendation and the United States Bank. The tariff question in all its immensely important bearing on the interests of the country. The distribution of the proceeds of the sale of public lands among the states. On all these questions my vote stands recorded—against the sub-treasury, for the United States Bank, for the distribution of the sales of public lands among the States. I was actively in favor of the tariff, and uniformly gave my attention to the improvement of our harbors, rivers and lakes or their navigation.

After leaving Congress, he was elected Judge in the United States Circuit Court, and served in this capacity for a period of seven years. Subsequently he joined the Central Ohio Conference, and preached until near the close of his life, living at Sidney, and receiving ministerial appointments in that vicinity. He was a local preacher nearly all his life, occupying a pulpit almost every Sunday while in Washington. His sight was impaired in later life, through imprudence in observing an eclipse of the sun with unprotected eyes.

435.

REV. WILLIAM HENRY GOODE, D. D., son of No. 171, p. 79, was born in Warren Co., O., June 19, 1807, died in Richmond, Ind., Dec. 16, 1879. Married (1) April 30, 1829, Sarah Burfoot Pearson, dau. of Walton Pearson, of Louisville, Ky., (b. Aug. 31, 1809, d. Feb. 14, 1859) ; (2) Sept. 18, 1861, Matilda Hubbard. Children :—

    1055, WALTON PEARSON GOODE, b. Sept. 9, 1831, d. Sept. 1, 1867. 1056, PHILIP HAYES, b. Feb. 7, 1835, d. Sept. 27, 1877. 1057, MARTHA PAUL, b. Mar. 22, 1837, m. *John Elliott Raines.* 1058, CLARA MACK, b. Feb. 24, 1839, m. *John Wilson.* 1059, WILLIAM HENRY, born Sept. 15, 1841, d. 1060, SARAH FRANCIS, b. May 12, 1844, m. *John Singleton.* 1061, HARRIET MARY, b. Aug. 2, 1847, m. *George Crose.* 1062, ELLEN WILKINS, b. Dec. 6, 1849, m. *Daniel W. Humfreville, M. D.* 1063, ELIZABETH REBEKAH, b. June 30, 1852, m. *William Hendrickson.*

The following biographical sketch is abridged from the address read by Dr. Mendenhall at the funeral of Dr. Goode :

"He enjoyed rare educational advantages for that period in the instructions of Prof. James P. Espy, afterwards of national reputation, and generally known as the " Storm King," who was employed as a private tutor in the family for two years. He began the study of Latin at the age of seven, and that of Greek two years later. By the age of twelve he had taken a somewhat extensive course in the classics, and after two more devoted to mathematics, his school days were ended. After leaving school he carried on for several years a course of historical reading with his father. So rapid was his progress, and so mature his judgment, that he taught school in Old Town when only sixteen years of age. Soon after the death of his father he went to reside with his brother at Madison, Indiana, where he taught school, pursued his literary studies, and read law. He was admitted to the bar before he was twenty-one.

"When twenty years old, he was elected president of the Gallatin County Seminary, Port William, Kentucky, which position he occupied two years, after which engaged in farming near Madison, Ind., for seven or eight years.

"He joined the Methodist Church at the age of fourteen, was licensed to preach in 1835 ; ordained Deacon in 1838, and Elder in 1840.

"His first appointment was Lexington Circuit (1836). Elected principal of the New Albany Seminary, he served for two years in that position. He was the pioneer Methodist educator in Indiana.

"In 1839, he was appointed to Jeffersonville Station, and 1840–41, to Indianapolis Station, the most important charge in the State, 1842 Presiding Elder of the South Bend District, in 1842 transferred to Arkansas Conference, and appointed to the Charge of Fort Coffee Academy and Mission, an institution for the education of Choctaw Indians. He had been consulted concerning this appointment, which was to exert such a powerful influence on his future life, and it was accepted only after careful consideration of the many-sided aspects of the case, not the least consideration being the fact that he must leave a Christian civilization behind him, and remove his young family into a community of Indians, but a few degrees removed from savagery.

"The work prospered under his administration, and it was here that he formed that estimate of Indian character which made him a life-long friend of the Indian. In 1844, he formed the Indian Mission Conference.

"The demon of secession was already beginning to raise its head, and among the ever-memorable events in our national history, is the attempt by the Southern delegates to rend the Methodist Episcopal Church, in the General Conference which met in New York in 1844. This was followed by the Louisville Convention, consisting of delegates from the conferences south of Mason and Dixon's line, whose avowed purpose was to effect a separation from the North. Dr. Goode was a delegate to this Convention, but, foreseeing the result, declined to take his seat.

"When it became certain that secession would soon be accomplished, he obtained a transfer to the North Indiana Conference, not willing, even for a day, to become a member of a pro-slavery church.

"Attempts were made, especially by Bishop Soule, the head and front of the secession movement, to induce Dr. Goode to side with the South, with broad intimations that his personal interests should not suffer, but, however, no blandishments from men in high places could swerve him. He was classed with the conservatives of the church on the slavery question.

"The next eight years of his life (1845 to 1853) were spent as presiding elder of the Greencastle and Indianapolis districts.

"In 1853, he was appointed to Richmond Station, where his labors resulted in a great revival. But God had vaster field of sacrifice and activity for this man of apostolic zeal. The tide of emigration was beginning to overflow into the regions beyond the Mississippi and the Missouri. The bill erecting the territories of Kansas and Nebraska into States was passed, the Missouri Compromise repealed, and the conflict began which was to culminate in civil war.

"Until 1853, the church work in that vast territory was wholly unorganized. In their search for the right man for this immensely laborious work, requiring great clearness of judgment, great executive ability, great endurance, and a high degree of Christian heroism to endure the labor and exposure, our Episcopal Board was not long in fixing on William H. Goode. This involved another long removal with his family, and all the trials of pioneer life, but he did not confer with flesh and blood, and with military promptness he and his family were soon on their way to the far west.

"The impression that he was appointed at this time as a missionary to the Indians, is a mistaken one ; but in the explorations he made in that extended area, he exhibited a profound interest in the missions established among the several Indian tribes, and made many valuable recommendations to the missionary authorities of the church.

"His fields of labor included all the region between Texas on the South, and the extreme Territorial settlement in Nebraska on the North, and extended from the state lines on the East to the Rocky Mountains on the West. He exercised virtual Episcopal powers in arranging the work in that large field. Only two years after he reached Kansas, so rapidly had the church advanced, that the Kansas and Nebraska Conference was formed under the presidency of Dr. Goode (1856).

"In 1859, he made an exploring tour to the Rocky Mountains, and organized our mission work in that region. His appointments during that period were the following : 1854–55, Kansas and Nebraska Mission District ; '55, '56, '57, Nebraska District ; '58, Omaha District ; '59, Pike's Peak and Cherry Creek Mission (half year) and the remaining half in Oreapolis Station, rendered necessary by failing health; 1860, agent for literary institutions in Nebraska ; in the middle of the year transferred to Western Iowa Conference, and appointed to London District; 1861, Council Bluffs District : 1862, transferred to North Indiana Conference and appointed to Union Chapel, now Grace Church, Richmond. His appointments since that time have been as follows :

'63, '64, '65, Richmond District; '66, Centenary Agent for the conference; '67, '68, '69, Muncie District; '70, '71, '72. Anderson District; '73 to '76, Richmond District.

"We have now briefly outlined the labors of one of the very foremost men of Western Methodism, but the occasion and the subject demand something more, and we shall attempt a brief analysis of the character of the great man who has fallen.

" 1. Intellectually he possessed a very high order of endowment. His habits were those of a student. There was something in his presence, his manner, his style of expression, his bearing, which impressed all with whom he came in contact, that his was a mind of no common order. He would have shone with brilliancy in any profession. As a statesman he would have risen to a high place in the councils of the nation. He was for many years generally recognized as one of the principal ecclesiastical statesmen of the Methodist Church.

" 2. The deep religiousness of his character was conspicuously evident. There was no sanctimoniousness, and there was never any compromise of Christian or ministerial dignity. He was a gentleman of the old school, his father being a native of the Old Dominion. To those who had only a superficial acquaintance there was an apparent austerity, but no man had a kinder heart.

" 3. In the prime of his life he had great pulpit power. He was entirely free from anything of a sensational character, handling great themes in a manner becoming their greatness.

" 4. He filled the office of Presiding Elder during twenty-seven of the forty years of his active ministry. He was a born leader of men, and this office afforded an appropriate field for the exercise of his remarkable gifts.

" He was elected delegate to the General Conference by the North Indiana Conference in 1848, 1852, 1864, 1868 and 1872. In 1860 he was a delegate from the Kansas and Nebraska Conference. He was thus six times a member of the General Conference. In 1876, the time of his retirement, he declined an election.

" 5. The heroic element was a prominent trait in his character. His great soul was not content to enter into other men's labors. He delighted in pressing into the regions beyond. Despite the great self-denial he and his dear ones encountered, he often said to the writer hereof, that those were the days of his greatest enjoyment, when he was on the plains of Kansas, Nebraska and Colorado, preaching the Gospel and laying the foundations of the church in regions where are now three large States and many flourishing annual conferences.

" I cannot refrain from giving a summary of these useful services to the church, mainly in his own language :

"The country up the Red River was traversed to a point seven hundred miles from its mouth. The region upon the Arkansas was explored eight hundred miles up ; that upon the Missouri one thousand, while the tributaries, Kansas and Great Platte, have been followed, the one to the junction where it takes its name, and the other to its mountain sources. Nearly every military post has been visited and almost all the mission stations of every denomination. The lands of every tribe of Indians on the western frontier and many of the tribes beyond have borne the impress of my feet, and more or less intercourse has been had with them all. The white settlements have been explored in their infancy and watched in their progress, and an acquaintance has been formed with all the phases and circumstances of frontier life. In the course of these labors the valley of the Mississippi, from the States east, near or remote, to the Territories west, has been crossed twenty-three times, by different routes and modes of travel, besides the amount of traveling in the Territories themselves. The number of miles traveled over in the time is probably not less than sixty thousand, in about five thousand of which my family have participated in their necessary removals.

"The gospel, meanwhile, has been proclaimed to devout worshippers in the churches; to statesmen in legislative halls; to delegates in territorial conventions; to promiscuous crowds in court rooms and hotels; to soldiers in barracks, and to camps of armed men; to the thoughtless and dissipated in saloons; to emigrants in corall, and to miners upon the mountain sides; to savages around their council fires, and to slaves upon the cotton plantations in the South."

"6. It may seem like the statement of a mere truism, yet, knowing Dr. Goode as I have known him, I feel that it ought to be said that he was an eminent example of uncompromising integrity, even among men of high christian character.

"To illustrate this trait it may be stated that on his removal to a community after the assessor had finished his work, he of his own accord, when tax paying time arrived, listed his property (he was a man of considerable private resources), and paid his just dues to the state.

"7. It needs to be recorded that Dr. Goode was the steadfast friend of the Indian. With his wide experience with the Indian tribes, and his observations of the influence of Christianity upon them, whenever faithfully taught, he had a right to an opinion on this subject. I quote his well-matured convictions:—

"'The most interesting and important aspect of Christian missions among the Indian tribes remains: that which most thrills the Christian heart. It is the positive religious benefit conferred: the number of immortal souls purchased by the blood of the Redeemer, that have been converted and saved through Christian instrumentality: the thousands upon thousands that have landed safely, and the thousands more that are on the way. It is too late to doubt the reality and permanency of the work of grace upon the Indian's heart, or the adaptedness of the gospel to the Indian character. Just as well may the question be raised in reference to our own people or any other in christendom.'

"He bequeathed a considerable sum of money to the Missionary Society, to be devoted to work among the Indian tribes. He desired to leave this testimony in behalf of the humane treatment of the Indians, and their capability to take on a Christian civilization.

"8. Dr. Goode was entirely free from inordinate ambition. He was utterly incapable of resorting to any sort of scheming for place in the church. He steadily declined any position that would divert his attention from preaching the gospel, or that would assign to his labors in the pulpit a subordinate place. There was a time, when, if he had said the word, he would have been elected Agent of the Western Book Concern, an honor coveted by many eminent men in the church, but he declined because preaching is a secondary matter in that position. He was once the choice for the editorial chair of the *Western Christian Advocate*, but for the same reason declined the honor."

The following sketch of his wife's character and life, written by Dr. Goode himself, is quoted here as an illustration of pioneer life:

"SARAH BURFOOT GOODE, was born August 31, 1809, in Washington county, Virginia. She was the only surviving child of Walton Pearson, Esq., an early resident of Louisville, Kentucky. Her father had preceded his family to the west. They followed, making the trip over the mountains on horseback, Sarah an infant, being carried on the lap by her mother and grandfather.

"Mr. Pearson was a bold, generous, high-spirited Virginian. He was gay and fond of fashionable life. His little daughter was placed in a course of training suited to his views; and, even at that early age, was familiarized with the ball-room and other places of fashionable amusement. A relish for these scenes was contracted which remained and controlled her afterward till removed by the influence of Divine grace.

"At a camp meeting, held at the old Harrod's Creek camp-ground, at the age of about fifteen, she was converted, and united to the Methodist Episcopal Church.

" We were united in marriage in 1829, and for thirty years we journeyed together in a pathway, which, though strewed with many blessings, has, nevertheless, had its full share of the conflicts incident to mortality. Loving and ardently desiring domestic life, still, in the providence of God, we have been wanderers.

" While in Indiana, our fields of labor have successively embraced the center and the four extremes of the state ; and we always lived among our people. Twice, in the judgment of the appointing power, it has been thought proper for us to take a frontier position : at first with great reluctance ; but, upon the receipt of our appointment, yielding ourselves up to the work, upon our knees, in joint supplication. The region from the lakes almost to the Gulf, and from several states east of the Mississippi, to the extreme and beyond the extreme of white settlements west have been traversed, embracing an aggregate removal of some five thousand miles. Once, confined by illness to her state-room, during a long and wearisome trip, ending with the sinking of the steamer and all on board : life saved, in providence of God, by running the vessel into shoal water as she went down ; refuge sought and obtained for her and her little ones at the humble quarters of an overseer on a cotton plantation ; driven from this place, still sick, by Catholic influence, with no other refuge till God strangely sent it. Time after time she has seen her household goods under the hammer of the auctioneer ; and twice she has seen our effects sunk in the rivers of the west. Once, for the period of a month, she scarcely ever entered a human dwelling save our nightly-spread marquee. Once, unattended by any friend, she made her way with her little ones from Little Rock, Arkansas, three hundred miles up into the Indian country, whither I had necessarily preceded her, and to my great surprise and joy met me at the mission station. Living sometimes among the civilized and sometimes among savages ; sometimes in peaceful and refined society, and then amid scenes of bloodshed, and surrounded by menaces of personal assault and violence : myself often absent from one to three months at a time—amid all these scenes and with a constitution naturally feeble, she bore and reared a family of nine children.

Dr. Goode's book entitled *The Outposts of Zion*, published in Cincinnati, in 1863, gives the story of his work upon the frontier which is also frequently referred to in Dr. W. H. Benson's *Life Among the Choctaws*.

437.

FRANCIS COLLIER GOODE, of Washington City, son of Philip and *Rebekah Hayes* Goode, No. 171, grandson of Samuel and *Mary Collier** Goode, No. 76, was born in Waynesville, O., Aug. 28, 1811. A merchant in Ohio and Indiana until 1856. Married, May 7, 1850, (1) Sarah Woodruff Crane, of New Albany, Ind., daughter of Israel Cooper and *Hannah Lyon* Crane, born in Essex Co., N. J., Sept. 24, 1822, d. Oct. 18, 1852 : (2) May 28, 1855, Sally Ann Jackson, daughter of John T. and *Mary Ingraham* Jackson,† of La Grange,

---

*A notice of the Collier family is given in the Appendix.

†JOHN T. JACKSON, (b. 1770, d. 1854), was son of John Jackson of La Grange, a native of Long Island. He had a brother Samuel and a sister who m. Henry Van Benschoten of Duchess Co., N. Y., and had son Elias, of New York City, who m. Phebe Underhill, (issue, William H., of West Park, Ulster Co., N. Y., Augusta Kissam and John), and another son, father of Prof. James C. Van Benschoten of Wesleyan University, and Rev. Sanford V. B., of the New Jersey Conference of the Methodist Episcopal Church.

John T. Jackson had issue, i, John, ii, Phebe Eliza, m. David Lee, of Unadilla, N. Y., now of Orlando, Fla., iii, Sally Ann, m. Francis C. Goode.

GEORGE INGRAHAM, a native of Rhode Island, settled about the middle of the last century, in Amenia, Dutchess Co., N. Y., where he and his brother Samuel bought lands together. His descendants are num-

Dutchess Co., N. Y., born Feb. 23, 1823, died in Washington, Nov. 18, 1879.   Children :—

1064, GEORGE BROWN GOODE, b. Feb. 13, 1851.   1065, MARY REBEKAH, b. Feb. 13, 1856, d. July 8, 1857.

As has already been said, Philip Goode removed in 1841 from Waynesville to Xenia, for the purpose of giving his sons as liberal an education as could be obtained at that day in the West. The elder sons, Patrick, Mackerness and William, were all fitted for professional careers, and were eminent in their day and communities, in law, medicine, and the pulpit. The untimely death of his father prevented Francis from receiving the education which had been planned for him, and his elder brother, Mack, who became his guardian having died when he was fifteen, his school-days came to an end. He was offered a cadetship in the U.S. Military Academy at West Point, but the solicitude of his widowed mother prevented its acceptance, and a commercial career was the only one which remained open to him.

He was engaged in various business enterprises from 1827 to 1857; first, until 1835, in a country store in Liberty, Ind.; 1835-7, as commission merchant in Michigan City ; 1838-41, a member of the firm of Goode & Shotwell, drygoods merchants, New Albany ; 1845-6, in flour and grain business in Buffalo, N. Y., buying and shipping to New Orleans ; 1848-57, member of the firm of M. E. Reeves & Co., wholesale boot and shoe dealers, Cincinnati.

He was a clerk in the General Land Office, Washington, 1841-45, during his brother's term of service in Congress. Retiring from business in 1857, he lived in Amenia, N. Y. until 1866, then for four years in Middletown, Conn., and subsequently in Arlington, Fla., with occasional winters in the Bermudas, and sometimes in Tennessee, North Carolina, Virginia and Washington City.

He has never entered into public life, or accepted office of any kind. He was the first Secretary of the Congressional Temperance Society, which was organized during his residence in Washington, and was, for many years, President of the Board of Trustees of the Amenia Seminary. During his residence in Florida he has taken much interest in the efforts of the freedmen to attain to a position of self-support, and in the welfare of their village at " Lone

---

erous and have been prominent members of the Methodist Episcopal Church. He had seven children by his first wife (Miss Peck), and one by his second.

1. MARY BILLINGS, m. *John T. Jackson*, ch., i. *Mrs Goode*, ii. *Mrs. Lee*, (See Jackson note above).

2. A daughter, m. *Rev. Mr. Brown*, ch., i, *George Brown*, of Jackson, Mich., ii, *Prof. John Jackson*, of Syracuse Univ., iii. *Amanda B.* (Mrs. Elliot).

3. NANCY, m. *Daniel Lee*, of Dutchess Co., N. Y., ch., i, *Henry Lee*, of Wisconsin, ii, *David*, of Orlando, Fla., m. 1, Miss Rudd, (issue, a. Olivia, b. Bradley), m. 2, Phebe Jackson. iii, *Daniel* of Knoxville, Tenn. (issue, a, Ida, b, Emma, c, Grace). iv, *Nancy*, m. John Caulkins of Knoxville, Tenn. (issue, a, Will., prof. in E. Tenn. Wesl. Univ., b, Fanny, c, Douglass, d, Daniel, e, Henry, f, David). David Lee, of New York, merchant, brother of Daniel, just mentioned, had three daughters, who married respectively, Sir Charles Augustus Murray, the Baron Von Vechter, and the Prince de Noer. The Princess de Noer, after her husband's death, married Count Waldersee, second to Von Moltke in the command of the German army.

4. JANE, m. *Rev. Robert Seney*, of Brooklyn, N. Y. (a nephew of Albert Gallatin), children, 1, *Frances*, m. James Taft of New York, (issue, a, Rev. Marcus L., missionary to China, b. James H., Brooklyn, c, Rev. Wm. I., d, Charles) ; ii, *Jane*, m. Wm. M. Ingraham ; iii, *George*, banker of New York; iv, *Catherine* ; v, *Sarah L.*

5. GEORGE, of Amenia, N. Y., ch., i, *Samuel*, of Honeoye Falls, N. Y.; ii, *Dr. Timothy M.*, of Flatbush, N. Y.; iii, *Mary*, m. Bishop Gilbert Haven (issue, a, Rev. Wm. I., of Boston, b, Mary, m. Rev. W. P Thirkeld); iv, *Judge Richard*, m. Jane Dikeman, (issue, a, George, b. Fred. S., c, Jane); v, *William M.*, of Brooklyn, m. Jane Seney, (issue, a, Wm., b, Fanny, c, George); vi, *Sally*, m. D. G. Harriman, of New York ; vii, *Henry C. M.*, m. Winifred, dau. of Bishop E. G. Andrews ; viii, *Jane A.*

6. A daughter, m. *Mr. Rundall*, of Amenia, N. Y., many descendants.

7. LOUISA, m. *Jefferson Payne*, of Seneca Falls, N. Y., many descendants.

8. REBECCA, m. Crawford C. Smith of Brooklyn, (issue, a, Crawford, b, Anna, m. Ira Perego, c, Edward, d, Mary.

Star." He is a member of the Virginia Historical Society, in whose prosperity he maintains an active interest. His reminiscences of men and events would, if recorded, make a most entertaining volume.

The following estimate of his character is from the pen of a friend :—

"But for lack of professional education, the loss of which has been a perpetual sorrow, his friends have never doubted that Francis C. Goode would have attained an eminent position in life. A man of studious habits and keen observation, of great force of character, and possessing extraordinary powers of organization and administration ; his capabilities are properly appreciated only by his intimate friends. Few public men are better acquainted with the political history of the United States, and few naturalist more enthusiastic lovers of nature, or more familiar with the habit and appearance of plants.

"Although for thirty years in feeble health, he is now at the age of seventy-six, in full mental vigor, and as upright in carriage as when a young man. His face resembles so strongly that of Henry Clay, especially in its profile, that the resemblance is frequently remarked upon even by strangers. He inherited from his father the courtly bearing and cordial ways which was characteristic of the old-school Virginians, and few men have a larger number of devoted friends."

EXCURSUS.—SOME COLONIAL FAMILIES OF NEW JERSEY.

The following diagram shows the descent of the first wife of Francis C. Goode from seven of the families who were pioneers in the settlement of Northern New Jersey, and in that of Branford, Conn., in the case of the Cranes, Swaines and probably the Lyons. A brief review of the history of each is given below. Many of the facts in early history are derived from Stearn's *First Church in Newark*, Savage's *Dictionary* and Littell's *Passaic Genealogies*.

TABULAR DESCENT OF MRS. F. C. GOODE.

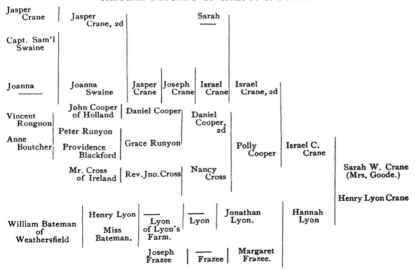

I, JASPER CRANE, THE PURITAN, AND HIS POSTERITY.

JASPER CRANE, probably a native of one of the western or southern counties of England, came to New England at a very early day, apparently within ten years of the first settlement. He is perhaps the Mr. Crane who is mentioned so frequently in the records of the proceeding of the Governor and Company of Massachusetts Bay, 1629-30, as one of the members of the Company (Young's Chronicles of Massachusetts.) He was born 1600-1605, died before Oct. 1, 1681. He removed from Massachusetts before 1639, and was one of the founders of the New Haven colony; the original constitution of the colony was drawn up by him, and his name heads the list of those who subscribed to it in 1639. He was a magistrate or "assistant" of the colony from 1640-1650; in 1663, a magistrate also in the Connecticut colony, and in 1665, after the union of the two colonies, received the same token of confidence under the new charter. In 1644, he had, with several others, removed to East Haven, where he built a house, and where many of his children were born. His wife was undoubtedly one of the Puritan maidens of Massachusetts Bay, but her name has not been handed down to us. In 1651, he removed to Branford, and in 1667, when the church at Branford, in pursuance of what was "probably the last attempt to realize the noble dreams of the old Puritan emigrant," removed in a body and founded the new colony of Newark, he, though an old man, with Robert Treat and Samuel Swaine, was a leader. "His name heads the list of subscribers to the Fundamental Agreement, and he figured largely in all the transactions of the town of Newark during the first fourteen years; its magistrate, the president of its town court, and chosen regularly, every year, for the first five or six years, as first on its list of deputies to the General Assembly." His associate in these offices of public trust, whose name always appeared second on the list, however, was Robert Treat, afterwards Governor of the colony of Connecticut, who was in the chair at Hartford when Sir Edmund Andros, attempting to seize the charter, it was carried out and hidden in a hollow tree, since called the Charter Oak. Jasper Crane was, says Stearns, "an active, energetic and, perhaps, restless man, who had aided in the commencement of two or three new settlements, and as early as 1651, had been prevented, by the 'injustice and violence of the Dutch,' from establishing yet another on the banks of the Delaware, whereby 'the Gospel, he said, 'might have been published to the natives and much good done, not only to the colonies at present, but to posterity.' The leaders in this enterprise were Jasper Crane and William Tuttle, and the settlement probably that contemplated near Cape May. Jasper Crane at this time petitioned the commissioners for relief, the Dutch having seized and fortified lands which he and associates had bought from the original proprietors of Delaware."*

Jasper Crane was a leader in the many contests which the Newark settlers had to carry on in defense of their rights against the Dutch in New York and the wavering representatives of the English crown. In 1669, July 28, says the Newark Records, "The town made choice of Mr. Crane and Mr. Treat to take the first opportunity to go over to York to advise with Col. Lovelace,

---

* TRUMBULL, ii, p. 197. MACWHORTER, Century Sermon, p. 8. HAZARD, State Papers, iii. STEARNS, First Church in Newark, p. 31.

concerning our standing, whether we are designed to be a part of the Duke of York's colony or no." (p. 19.)

He died 1880–81. "Jasper Crane, senior, shrewd, enterprising, ever active old Jasper," says Stevens, "on the first day of October, 1678, perceiving that he had made his last earthly settlement, and had but one remove more to be undertaken, thus declares his determination to address himself to his dying duties. 'I, Jasper Crane, dwelling within the province of New Jersey, belonging to the town of Newark—being aged and weak in body, yet well in understanding and memory—I do at this time think it my Christian duty to set my house in order, and I do dispose of all my worldly goods, as followeth :' "

He left children as follows :

2. HANNA, m. *Thomas Huntington*, b. 1636 (?), freeman of Connecticut, 1657, subscriber to the Fundamental Agreement, 1636, executor of Jasper Crane's estate, 1681.
3. JOHN, b. before 1660, subscriber to the Fundamental Agreement, d. about 1694.
4. DELIVERED, bapt. June 12, 1642, subscriber to the Fundamental Agreement, d. s. p., 1672.
5. MARY, bapt. Mar. 1, 1645.
6. MICAH, bapt. Nov. 3, 1647.
7. AZARIAH, b. 1647, d. 1730, m. Mary Treat, dau. of Gov. Robert Treat, of Connecticut. Littell erroneously makes Deacon Azariah Crane, son of No. 8. Issue, i. *Nathaniel*, ii. *Azariah*, iii. *John*, iv. *Robert*, v. *Mary* (*Baldwin*, vi. *Jane* (*Rule*). (See Stearn's, p. 76.)
8. JASPER, b. April 21, 1651, d. Mar. 16, 1712.

SECOND GENERATION.

8. JASPER CRANE, jr., of Newark, born in East Haven, Conn., April 21, 1651, died Mar. 16, 1712. Married Joanna, dau. of Capt. Samuel Swaine, b. 1651, d. Sept. 16, 1720. Children :—
9. JONATHAN CRANE, ESQ., m. Sarah, dau. of Governor Treat, of Connecticut. Stephen Crane, b. 1709, was probably his son, (See Littell, p. 107). Among his descendants were Gen. Wm. Crane, Col. Ichabod Crane, U. S. A., Judge Joseph H. Crane, of Dayton, O., Rev. J. T. Crane, D. D., Hon. Newton Crane, of St. Louis. Stephen Crane, his grandson, was killed by the British Troops, at the time of the engagement at Connecticut Farms.
10. JASPER CRANE, 3d.

Jasper Crane, 2d, was a representative of the town of Newark in the Legislature of New Jersey, in 1699, and indeed during the whole time of the Governorship of Lord Cornbury. He was a magistrate and held other offices of trust. In his house the Rev. Francis Makemie, one of the founders of the Presbyterian Church in America, held secret meetings, which were the subject of inquiry at the time of his trial for preaching without a license.*

Jasper Crane's epitaph, which the writer copied, in 1868, from a tombstone which was lying with hundreds of others in the graveyard opposite the First Church, which had been uprooted and broken by the vandalism of the Newark authorities, and which has doubtless long since been destroyed, was as follows :

---

*See Bowen's *Days of Makemie*.

```
┌─────────────────────────────────┐
│  Herᴱ Lyeth the Body of         │
│  Mᴿ· JASPER CRANE who           │
│  DEPARTED                       │
│  THIS LIFE MARCH THE            │
│  16ᵀᴴ ANNO 1712                 │
│  AGED 62 YEARS                  │
└─────────────────────────────────┘
```

THIRD GENERATION.

10. JASPER CRANE 3d, of Newark, N. J., was born as early as 1679. The name of his wife is not known, but she was no doubt the descendant of two or more of the "first settlers" of Newark, mentioned by Stearns. Children :—

  11. JOSEPH, b. about 1690.
  12. JONATHAN, m. Rachael ——, children, i. *Samuel*, b. 1712, d. 1746, ii. *Caleb*, iii. *Nehemiah*, iv. *Elihu*, v. *John Treat*, vi. *Margaret* (*Johnson*).
  13. ELIHU. Issue, i. *Lewis*. ii. *Christopher*, iii. *Charles*, iv. *Elihu*, v. *Isaac*, vi. *Hannah*, vii. *Phebe*.
  14. DAVID. Issue, i. *Jededia David*, ii. *Joseph*, iii. *Abigail* (*Johnson*), iv. *Phebe* (*Lawrence*), v. *Mary A.* (*Dorcas*), vi. *Sarah*.

FOURTH GENERATION.

11. JOSEPH CRANE, was a resident of Essex Co., N. J.   Children :—

  15. BENJAMIN.
  16. EZEKIEL.
  17. ISAAC.
  18. ISRAEL, b. 1711, d. 1785.
  19. JOSIAH.
  20. JOSEPH.
  21. ABIGAIL.
  22. JOANNA, b. 1720-25, m. *Samuel C* . d. 1752. Issue, i. *David*, ii. *Jonathan*, iii. *Stephen*, iv. *Samuel*. m, (2) *Joseph Camp*, issue, *Joanna*.

FIFTH GENERATION.

18. ISRAEL CRANE, of Newark, N. J., b. 1711, d. Mar. 27, 1785, and with his wife Sarah, (b. 1717, d. Aug. 14, 1785), is buried in the church-yard of the old First Church.   Issue :—

  23. PHEBE, b. Mar. 28, 1737.
  24. ABRAHAM, b. Jan. 10, 1739.
  25. SARAH, b. Feb. 28, 1741.
  26. RACHAEL, b. June 21, 1743, d. Feb. 21, 1826, converted under preaching of George Whitfield, at the age of 11, m. Capt. Nath. Camp, of the New Jersey Line in the Continental Army.   Issue, i. *Rachael* (*Beach*), ii. *Mrs. Tuttle*, iii. *Mary*, m. Cyrenus Beach, iv. *Abby*, m. Joseph Beach, v. *William*, vi. *Aaron*, et al.
  27. JONATHAN, b. July 20, 1745, m. Sarah ——, who d. Jan. 18, 1825.
  28. MARY, b. Jan. 26, 1747.
  29. RHODA, b. Apr. 24, 1750.
  30. ESTHER (WOODRUFF), b. 1751.
  31. LUCY, b. Nov. 20, 1753.
  32. ISRAEL, b. Oct. 18, 1755, d. Aug. 2, 1795.
  33. AARON, b. Mar. 26, 1759.
  34. ISRAEL CRANE 2d, b. Oct. 18, 1755, d. Aug. 2, 1795.
  35. AARON, b. Mar. 29, 1759.

SIXTH GENERATION.

33. ISRAEL CRANE 2d, of Newark, N. J., b. Oct. 18, 1755, d. Aug. 2, 1795, m. 1778, *Mary Cooper*, b. June 15, 1759, d. Feb. 25, 1831. (m. (2) Obadiah Meeker).   Issue :—

35. SALLY, b. Mar. 28, 1788, d. July 1. 1819, m. *Seth Woodruff*, moved to New Albany, Ind. Issue, i. *Israel Cooper Woodruff*, ii. *Mary (Tuley)*, iii. *William*, iv. *Phebe (Tuley)*, v. *Nancy (Walker)*, vi. *Israel*— all of New Albany, Ind.
36. WILLIAM, b. Aug. 26, 1780, b. June 15, 1799.
37. NANCY, b. Mar. 2, 1784, d. Sept. 1, 1854, m. *Nath. Johnson*, b. Sept. 2, 1779, d. Sept. 20, 1851. Issue, i.*Mary Crane Johnson*, m. Hon. Ira M. Harrison, (issue, James E., Anna Crane, Mary Thornton, Henry), ii. *John Cooper*, m. Hannah Magee, (issue, Walter Tufts, Florence Mary), iii, *Hannah Beech*, m. Ira M. Harrison.
38. ISRAEL COOPER, b. May 27, 1785, d. Jan. 30, 1845.

SEVENTH GENERATION.

38. ISRAEL COOPER CRANE, of New Albany, Indiana, born in Essex Co., N. J., May 27, 1785, d. in Indiana, Jan. 30, 1845, m. Dec. 31, 1812, Hannah Lyon, of Lyon's Farms, N. J., b. Dec. 25, 1794, d. in Cincinnati, Dec. 16, 1864. Children :—
39. MARY ANNE, b. 1815, d. y.
40. ISRAEL COOPER, b. 1861, d. 1840–50, from fever taken while pioneering on Salt River, Ky.
41. NANCY, b. Dec. 20, 1817.
42. SARAH WOODRUFF, b. Sept. 24, 1822, m. FRANCIS C. GOODE.
43. WILLIAM LYON.
44. HENRY LYON, of Cincinnati, O., m. Harriet Lupton, of Cincinnati, June, 1864. Children, i. *Ira Harrison*, b. May 1, 1865, ii. *William Henry*, b. Mar. 17, 1869, iii. *Helen*, b. Jan. 13, 1871, iv. *Robert Lupton*, b. May 14, 1872, v. *Walter Neave*, b. July 30, 1873, vi. *Edith*, b. Nov. 10, 1874.

11. CAPTAIN SAMUEL SWAINE AND HIS KINSFOLK.

WILLIAM SWAINE, born in England, 1585, came in the ship Elizabeth and Ann to Boston, 1635, admitted freeman in the General Court of Massachusetts, Mar. 3, 1636, and appointed one of the Commissioners to rule the new settlement of Connecticut, was a representative in the General Court of Mass., 1636, and in April held court in Connecticut. Settled at Wethersfield, and was Representative 1641-3, and Assistant 1644, in which year he removed to Branford where he probably died. He had issue :

1. CAPT. SAMUEL SWAINE, b. in England 1610-25, and one of the founders of the church and town of Branford, Conn., where he was Lieutenant and Representative, 1663. He removed to Newark, where, in 1673, Captain Treat having returned to Connecticut, he was promoted to the captaincy, or chief command of the forces of the colony ; he was constantly chosen for third man among the deputies, and as such served in the place of Jasper Crane, in the first General Assembly held in the Province of New Jersey. He was a millwright by trade, and his mill on "Mill Brook," was an important public institution, (See Stearns, p. 34). He married Johanna ———— who d. before Dec. 5, 1690. He died 1681-1682, with this testimony. "I, Samuel Swaine, being in perfect sense and memory, not knowing how long the Lord will continue the same mercy to me, being weak under His good hand of Providence, and willing to be at His dispose ; therefore, for life or death, do leave this as my last will and testament." (Newark Town Records, p. 87. Town Book, p. 35.) He left issue, i. *Joanna*. m. *Jasper Crane*, Jr., ii. *Elizabeth*, m. (1) Josiah Ward, (2) David Ogden, d. 1691, (Left issue, David Ogden, John, Col.

Josiah, b. 1680, d. 1763, Swaine, whose descendants are numerous in Newark and vicinity). Elizabeth Swaine, then a girl of nineteen, is said to have been "the first to land on the shore of Newark, having been merrily handed up the bank by her gallant lover, in his ambition to secure for her that mark of priority," iii. *Mary*, b. May 1, 1641. d. y., iv. *Phebe*, b. May 24, 1654, v. *Mary*, b. June 12, 1656, vi. *Christian*, b. Apr. 25, 1659, m. Nathaniel Ward, vii. *Sarah*, b. Oct. 7, 1661.

2. DANIEL, b. 1610–30, d. 1690–91 ; one of the founders of the church and town of Branford, Conn., where he died. Was Representative of Connecticut Legislature, 1673–7. Married, 1651, Dorcas, dau. of Robt. Rose, of Stratford. Savage gives list of nine children, all of whom died s. p. save i. *Deborah*, b. Apr. 24, 1654, m. Nov. 20, 1671, Peter Tyler, had issue, Peter, John, Deborah and Dorcas. ii. *Dorcas*, b. Dec. 2, 1657, m. (1) John Tainter, (2) Mr. Wheeler, (3) John Collins of Branford. iii. *John*, b. Dec. 20, 1660, d. 1654, leaving issue, Eunice and John.

3. MARY, b. in England, early a member of Roxbury church, and later a resident of New Haven, where she probably married.

4. A daughter, who was seized and carried off by a fierce Pequot chief at Wethersfield. Trumbull, in his "History of Connecticut," under the date of Oct., 30, 1639, remarks, " Nepaupuck, a famous Pequot captain, who had frequently stained his hands in English blood, was condemned by the General Court at Quinnipiac, for murder. It appeared that in the year 1637, he killed John Finch, of Weathersfield, and captivated one of Mr. Swaine's daughters. He had also assisted in killing the three men who were going down Connecticut river in a shallop. His head was cut off and set upon a pole in the market place." (Vol. 1, p. 115).

III. THE DESCENDANTS OF JOHN COOPER, FROM HOLLAND.

JOHN COOPER, was, it is supposed, a native of Holland : at all events he set sail from Holland for New York, in 1695, and died at sea, leaving an infant son :—

DANIEL COOPER, born at sea, May 1, 1695, d. May 2, 1795, aged one hundred. He lived first at Piscataway, but in Mar., 1732, moved to the Passaic Valley, and bought lot 32 of the Berkeley Tract. The first of his six wives, and the mother of his children, was *Grace Runyon*, b. Jan., 1706, d. Nov., 1755. He subs. m. (2) Jane Westbrook, (3) Grace Manning, d. Apr., 1777, (4) Mrs. Fanny Jones, d. Jan., 1787, (5) Barbara M. Gibbs, d. Dec., 1789, (6) Hannah, widow of Col. Ephraim Martin.   Children :—

I. CATHERINE COOPER, b. Jan., 1728, m. *Col. Cornelius Ludlow*, of Long Hill, had 7 children, including i. *John Ludlow*, m. his cousin Catherine, dau. of No. 2, was one of the first settlers in the vicinity of Cincinnati, O. (1790), and has numerous descendants in the west. ii. *Agnes*, m. *Judge Jonathan Pierson*, of Hamilton, O., a descendant of the Rev. Abraham Pierson, missionary to the Indians and minister of the Newark Colony. iii. *Patty*, m. *Mr. Remsen*, of Elizabethtown, N. J. iv. *Benjamin*, b. 1763, d. 1817, of Long Hill, Major General of New Jersey Militia, Judge of Morris Co. Court, member of General Assembly and Legislative council of N. J., m. Eleanor Harris. v.

Israel, m. Charlotte Chambers, of Chambersburg, Pa.; went to Cincinnati, and was one of the surveyors of the Symmes purchase, between the two Miamis, before 1800. His daughter, Sarah Bella, married (1) Hon. Japhtha D. Garrard, of Cincinnati, (2) Hon. John McLean,, Chief Justice of the United States, and had son Ludlow McLean. Another daughter m. Col. Ambrose Dudley, and his grand-daughter, *Sarah Bella Ludlow*, (dau. of James C., married Hon. Salmon P. Chase, Chief Justice, and Secretary of the U. S. Treasury ; and had dau.'Kate, who m. Gov. Wm. Sprague, of Rhode Island. Israel Ludlow's descendants in the west are numerous. vi. *Elizabeth* m. Col. Israel Day. vii. *William*, m. Betsy Haines, lived in Oxford, Ohio, and superintended the erection of the buildings of Miami University. Descendants numerous.

2. DANIEL, b. Jan. 14, 1729, d. May, 1787. Lived at Long Hill, N. J., on the five-hundred acre tract in the Passaic Valley, acquired by his father in 1732. Married (1) Miss Conover, had i. *Catherine*, m. John Ludlow, No. 3-i ; married (2) Nancy, dau. of Rev. Robert Cross, and had ii. *Lydia*, m. Samuel Annin, iii. *Polly*, m. ISRAEL CRANE, of Essex Co., N. J., iv. *Peter*, of Long Hill, m. Susan Boyle, has descendsnts. v. *William*, of Kentucky. vi. *Dr. John*, of Easton, Pa., d. 1855. vii. *Stephen*, m. dau. of Col. Israel Day. viii. *Ann*, m. Alex. Richards. ix. *Betsy*, m. Henry Freeman, of Elizabethtown, N. J. x. *Sally*, m. Capt. David Kirkpatrick, of Mine Brook, N. J. (for descendants, see Littell's Passaic Genealogies, p. 199.) xi. and xii. *Daniel* and *Joseph*, who went to Kentucky.

3. AGNES, b. May 15, 1732, m. *David Crane.*

4. PETER, b. Feb. 11, 1735, d. Oct., 1755.

5. JOHN, b. Aug. 20, 1738, d, March, 1778, m. *Lynche Boyle*, has descendants.

6. BENJAMIN, b. Dec. 13, 1741, d. Dec., 1794, descendants.

7. ROSANNA, b. Mar. 26, 1743.

8. GEORGE, b. Aug. 20, 1745, d. Sept. 20, 1801, m. *Margaret Lafferty*. His son, Daniel C., b. 1773, d. 1818, was one of the first settlers, and the principal proprietor of the town of Dayton, O., and his grandson George, was one of the earliest treasurers of the State of Michigan.

9. ANNE, b. Oct. 14, 1750, d. Feb. 5, 1795, m. *Jonas Carle*, of Long Island, and had numerous descendants.

IV. THE HUGUENOT FAMILY OF RUNYON.

THE first of the name came to America about 1700. He had at least three children :—

1. GRACE RUNYON, b. Jan., 1706, d. Nov., 1755, married DANIEL COOPER.

2. A daughter, m. Mr. Layton, and had i. *Capt. Peter Layton*, of Long Hill, N. J., d. unm. ii. *Providence*, m. Justice John Carle, of Long Hill, and had numerous descendants, mentioned in Littell, p. 201.

3. RICHARD, b. Apr. 14, 1719, m. Jane Van Court, and had numerous descendants, named in Littell, p. 364.

THE REVEREND MR. CROSS.

THE REV. JOHN CROSS, one of the early apostles of Presbyterianism in America, was probably from Ireland, though styled by Brownlee and Webster, "a

Scottish worthy." He was received into the Synod of New Jersey in 1732, and settled at a place called "Mountains," back of Newark. He was a friend and associate of Whitefield and a very successful revivalist, the story of whose work is referred to by various writers.* He was suspended in 1742, being charged with Antinomian principles. He seems to have been concerned in the great land riots in the Newark Mountains in 1747. Of his later life we have no record. He appears to have had at least two children :—

1. NANCY CROSS, who about 1758, m. DANIEL COOPER and had dau. *Polly*, who m. *Israel Crane.*

2. ROBERT whose son *Lafferty*, m. Mary Kirkpatrick, sister-in-law of Polly (Cooper) Crane, his cousin, and grandniece of Grace (Runyon) Cooper.

VI. THE LYONS OF LYON'S FARMS.

JONATHAN LYON, of Lyon's Farms, near Newark, N. J., was born June 28, 1765, d. Aug, 18. 1852. He is believed to have been grandson of Nathaniel or Eben-ezer Lyon, whose names are on the list of the Elizabethtown Associates in 1699, and great-grandson of Henry Lyon,† one of the earliest settlers of Newark and Elizabeth (See Stearns, p. 37.), who was town treasurer, 1668-9, and the person appointed by the church at that date, to keep an ordinary or public house "for the entertainment of travelers and strangers," He married 1791, Margaret Frazee, b. May 27, 1770, died May 9, 18—. Children:—

1. POLLY LYON, b. Aug. 1, 1792, m. Mar. 16, 1815, Lester Kennedy, of Lyons Farms, Children:— i. *Mary Eliza Kennedy*, m. Henry M. Mullison, (issue, Israel C., Harriet W., Tryphena J., Cassandra L.). ii. *John*, b. Aug. 8, 1819, New York city. iii. *Oliver*, went South and disappeared.

2. HANNAH, m. ISRAEL C. CRANE.

3. HENRY, b. Jan. 22, 1798, d. April 16, 1865, lived at Lyon's Farms, m. (1) Sarah Several. (b. 1799, d. 1823), (2) Hannah M'Crae, children, 1. *Jeannette Lyon*, m. Mr. Slate, sons, i. Henry Lyon Slate, ii. George J., d. y.

4. WILLIAM, b. Mar. 6, 1800, lives at Lyons Farms, married Thankful Rich, Children:— 1. *Margaret Ann Lyon*, m. Mr. Williamson, 2. *Jonathan*, of Newark. 3. *Thankful*, m. Mr. Stewart of Washington, Ind., 4. *Charles*, of Newark.

5 JABEZ, b. Apr. 30, 1802, d. June 26, 1866. Son, 1. *George Lyon*, Newark, N. J.

6. OLIVER, b. Dec. 30, 1806. Lived at Homer, N. Y. Children:— i. *Leander Lyon*, of Chicago, ii. *Alphonzo*, of Michigan, iii. *Appleton*, of Providence, R. I. iv. *Alpheus*, v. *Adelaide*, vi. *Alexander*.

7. PHEBE, b. Dec. 16, 1810, m. *John Baldwin*, of South Orange, N. J., Children :— i. *Marian A.*, m. Francis M. Blake, ii. *Anna*, iii. *Jeannette*, iv. *Justin*, v. *Henry E.*

8. MARGARET, m. Nov. 21, 1814, *Charles Guerin*, lives at Lyon's Farms. Children :— i. *Charles Guerin*, ii. *Newton.*

VII. THE FRAZEES OF ELIZABETHTOWN.

JOSEPH FRAZEE, one of the eighty Associates of Elizabethtown, who joined

---

*Edwards's *Thoughts on Revivals.* Fletcher's *History of Presbyterianism*, 1, p. 413.

†HENRY LYON, of Milford, 1646, was of Fairfield, 1652, m. only dau. of William Bateman, one of the early settlers of Concord, Mass., adm. freeman, 1641, and had bro. Thomas, of Concord, b. 1615, and d. in Fairfield, 1658, leaving son, Thomas, of Concord, and gr. ch. Joseph Middlebrook, of Fairfield, d. 1686.

together for the purpose of managing, settling, surveying, and disposing of the lands of the Elizabethtown grant, is believed to have been grandfather of MARGARET FRAZEE, who married NATHANIEL LYON. Joseph Frazee owned two one-hundred acre lots near Falls Mills in 1737. He had among other children,

1. CORNELIUS FRAZEE, m. Sarah Robins, perhaps the father of Margaret, who m. Jonathan Lyon.

2. JOHN, m. 1764, Hannah Willcockse. See Littell's "Passaic Genealogies," for fuller details.

438.

REV. SAMUEL TRUMBULL GILLET, D. D., son of Simeon and *Salome Smith Palmer* Gillet, was born in New York, 1809. Removed with his parents to Indiana, 1818. Appointed Midshipman, U. S. N., 1826; Passed Midshipman, 1852; Lieutenant, 1837. Chaplain, 1841; resigned, 1843. Member of Indiana Conference, Methodist Episcopal Church, 1837–1885. Married, Feb. 10, 1831, HARRIET ANN GOODE, daughter of No. 171, born in Warren Co., O., Aug. 24, 1813. Children :—

1066, PHILIP GOODE GILLETT, b. Mar. 24, 1833. 1067, FRANCIS TRUMBULL, b. Dec. 28, 1837, d. 1878. 1068, SIMEON PALMER, b. Nov. 2, 1840. 1069, OMER TOUSEY, b. June 28, 1848.

Dr. Gillet emigrated to Indiana with his father's family in 1818. They ascended the Wabash in a family flatboat, propelled by hand, and landed at old Fort Harrison, near the present site of Terre Haute. Appointed Midshipman in 1826, his first cruise was in the U. S. S. Lexington, in the Mediterranean. He passed his examination, graduating at the head of a class of sixty, Raphael Semmes, subsequently Captain of the Confederate cruiser Alabama, standing second, Admirals Dahlgren, Glisson, Rowan and Briggs, being also members. A second cruise in the Mediterranean, and a visit to the Holy Land, gave rise to religious impressions which changed the whole tenor of his life, and in 1837, being at that time a Lieutenant, he resigned his commission, and became a Methodist Minister, and for nearly fifty years has faithfully pursued his calling. In 1841, he was appointed Chaplain in the Navy, and was stationed at the Brooklyn Navy Yard for a few months, but soon resigned. In 1848, he was acting president of the Whitewater College, in 1841, declined the presidency of the Fort Wayne Female College to which he had been elected. Has several times been a delegate to the General Conference of the church.*

He is a man of deep learning, and refined traits, and his wife is one of the noblest of women.

Dr. Gillet is descended in the sixth degree from Jonathan Gillet who came to America in 1630, in the ship "Mary and John," and settled first at Dorchester, Mass., then at Windsor, Conn., where he died Aug. 23, 1677. He has published a "Genealogical Record of Simeon Gillet, Sr.," his great-grandfather, in broadside, lithographed, Indianapolis, 1876.

---

*For fuller biography, see Holliday's *Indiana Methodism*, 1873, pp. 343–50.

439.

JOHN WINGFIELD, of Amherst Co., Va., planter, married about 1810, MARY GOODE DAWSON, daughter of No. 172, p. 84. Children :—

> 1070, NELSON DAWSON WINGFIELD, Bedford Co., Va. 1071, LUCY GOODE, m. *William Bisbie*, of Lynchburg. 1073, JOHN, d. 1074, CHARLES C. 1075, ANN LEWIS, d. æt. 18. 1076, MATILDA D., m. *George D. Davis*, Clarksville, Mo. 1076, ELIZABETH, m. *C. D. Dawson*, Clarksville, Mo. 1078, ALMIRAH, m. *Chas. Rush*, Clarksville, Mo. 1079, SAMUEL H., Amherst Co., Va. 1080, SALLIE J., m. *Christopher Waddell*, Clarksville, Mo. 1081, MARY, m. *Steven Adams*, Clarksville, Mo. 1082, LEWIS M., Clarksville, Mo. 1083, FANNIE, d. y.

441.

SAMUEL GAINES DAWSON, M. D., of Lynchburg, Va., and Putman, Ohio, son of No. 172, was born in Amherst Co., Va., 1796, died 1835. A soldier in the war of 1812. Married, 1814, Maria Burwell, daughter of Nathaniel Burwell,* who was living, 1880, in Davenport, Iowa. Children :—

> 1084, FANNY DAWSON, d. y. 1085, MARTHA BURWELL, m. *Capt. David Munch*, of Lima, O., children. 1086, NELSON BURWELL, d. in Davenport, Iowa, before 1870. 1087, LUCY ANN, m. *Charles Armstrong*, of Iowa, children. 1088, MARY JANE, m. *Gilbert Irwin*, Rock Island, Ill., children. 1089, FANNIE, m. *Dr. Swan*, of Logansport, Ind. 1090, ROSALIE. 1091, EDWIN. 1092, REV. SAMUEL GAINES, b. 1830, d. 1875, m. Anna Maria Barker : lived in Toledo, O. 1093, THOMAS LEWIS. 1094, EDMONIA, m. *H. C. Hamilton*, Richwood, O.

In the war of 1812, Dr. Dawson went from Amherst Co., as surgeon's assistant under Dr. Austin, in Leftwich's Brigade, which was organized from Bedford Co. Dr. Austin died and Dr. Dawson was promoted to the position of Surgeon and served to the end of the war. He was mustered out of the service at Ellicott's Mills, Md. After the war he settled in Salem, Botetourt Co., as practicing physician. Here he lived two years, and here he married. About 1817, he removed to Lynchburg, where he formed a partnership with Mr. Jacob Haas, husband of his aunt, Susannah Goode, in publishing the "*Lynchburg Press.*" About 1820, he sold his share of the paper to John Hampden Pleasants, (subsequently killed in a duel), and returned to Salem to practice his profession. In 1831, he removed to Putnam, opposite Zanesville, O., where he died in 1835.

443.

CAPT. JAMES L LAMKIN, of Amherst Co., Va., died 1855, planter,

---

*THE parents of MARIA BURWELL DAWSON, were Nathaniel Burwell, son of Major Nathaniel Burwell, of "Vermont Place," and Lucy Carter, dau. of Charles Carter, of "Shirley"), and Martha Diggs, (daughter of Dudley Diggs, of "Little York," and Miss Armistead, and great-granddaughter of Sir Dudley Digges, of "Chilham," in Kent, England). See note on Burwell Family, *antea*, p. 63, *The Carter Tree*, Meade's *Old Churches and Families*, &c.

married ANN GOODE DAWSON, daughter of No. 127, p. 84, who was born about 1800, and died 1868. Children :—

    1095, FANNIE E. LAMKIN, b. 1855, m. *Jesse R. Adams*. 1096, JOHN M., b. 1827, d. in California, 1850, unm.; one of the "Argonauts of '49." 1097, ANNIE M., b. 1829, m., 1851, *Edmond C. Moore*, d. 1852. 1098, CAPT. JAMES N., b. 1831 ; unm. A contractor on public works, in partnership with his brother-in-law, Jesse R. Adams ; a soldier, C. S. A. 1099, DR. SAMUEL R., b. 1854, lived in Texas for many years; a successful medical practitioner ; d. 1875, at Cool Well, Amherst Co., a soldier, C. S. A., Surgeon in Moman's Battery.

448.

JOSEPH L. LYLE, of Waynesville, O., farmer, married, 1835, ELIZABETH PRIDE GOODE, daughter of No. 175, born Feb. 5, 1811, died July 1ŗ, 1841 Children :—

    1100, NARCISSA ANN LYLE, b. Aug. 28, 1846, m. S. G. GOODE, No. 485. 1101, WILLIAM GAINES, b. Aug. 5, 1838. 1102, JAMES GARLAND, d. yg.

450.

GIDEON JEWETT GOODE, of Jasper, Texas, farmer, son of No. 174, was born in Halifax Co , Va., Dec. 27, 1802, and emigrated with his parents to Texas, in 1835, stopping for a time near Nashville, Tenn. Living 1885. Married, 1823, Nancy Fulton, born in Virginia, July 15, 1802. Children :—

    1103, SAMUEL ROWLETT GOODE, b. Mar. 21, 1826, d. Nov. 19, 1873. 1104, FRANCIS ANN FLORIDA, b, Mar. 21, 1828, d. Sept. 4, 1862, m. *Jacob L. Holland*, of Jasper, Texas, children, 1. *Gideon Charles Holland*, 2. *Nancy Eliz.*, 3. *Alabama*, 4. *William*, 5. *Louisa*. 1105, MATHEW MACKERNESS, b. Sept. 10, 1831, d. Mar. 28, 1863. 1106, GAINES COLLIER, b. Oct 13. 1833, d. Jan, 27, 1865. 1107, GIDEON CARL, b. Dec. 25, 1840, d. Feb. 4, 1863. 1108, HANNIBAL FOWLER, b. Dec. 25, 1840, d. Mar. 4, 1863. 1109, SUSAN ELIZABETH, living 1885, in Jasper, m. (1) *Minor P. Good*, issue, 1. *Margaret Lydia Good*, 2. *Nancy Marrion*, 3. *Susan Eliz.*, m. (2) *A. A. Wood*, children. 4. *Eliz. Wood*, 5. *William Azariah*, 6, *Louisa*, 7. *Alice*.

451.

WILLIAM ROWLETT GOODE, of Jasper Co., Texas, farmer, son of No. 174, was born Feb. 6, 1805, living 1886. Married, June 1833, *Elouisa* ———, of Nashville, Tenn., who died August, 1853. Children, (all farmers) :—

    1110, MARTHA ANN FRANCIS GOODE, b. July 3, 1835, m., 1859, *John M. Durdin*, soldier, C. S. A., children, 1. *Elouisa Jane Durdin*, b. Dec. 13, 1855, 2. *Sarah Francis*, b. Dec. 5, 1856, 3, *William James*,

b. May 12, 1858, 4. *Mary Columbia*, b. Sept. 8, 1859, 5. *Nancy*, b. July 10, 1863, 6, *Hilliard*, b. Aug. 23, 1867, 7, *Inez*, b. Dec. 29, 1870, 8. *John Goode*, b. May 28, 1872.   1111, JOHN HENRY, b. Aug. 28, 1837, d. April, 1871.   A soldier, C. S. A.   1112, EMELINE CLEMENTINE, b. Mar. 13, 1840, d. Mar. 4, 1884, m. *Wesley Perkins*, soldier, C. S. A., Sept. 12, 1878, child, 1. *Francis Perkins*.   1113, WILLIAM THADDEUS, b. Mar. 14, 1842, d. April, 1863, while serving in the Confederate Army.   1114, JOSIAH WASHINGTON, b. April 14, 1844, m., 1871, Jane Parsons: a farmer, Tyler, Texas. 1115, SUSANNA AMANDA, b. Mar. 9, 1846, m. *James Wheat Parsons*, Feb. 23, 1873, children, 1. *Luella Parsons*, b. Apr. 24, 1874, 2. *Edmund Thurston*, b. Sept. 20, 1865.   1116, MARY JANE, b. May 30, 1848, d. April, 1867.   1117, SAMUEL LAFAYETTE, b. July 28, 1850, a farmer, Jasper Co., Texas, 1886, m. Dec. 15, 1875, *India Parsons*, children, 1. *Lawrence Edna Goode*, b. Nov. 8, 1876, 2. *William Oscar*, b. July 9, 1878, 3, *Mary Eliz.*, b. June 26, 1880, 4. *John Thaddeus*, b. Jan. 20, 1882, 5. *Montier Lafayette*, b. June 30, 1884. 1118, ELOUISA MELVINA, b. Nov. 20, 1852.

452.

MATHEW MACKERNESS GOODE, of Hunt Co., Texas, planter, son of No. 174, was born near Nashville, Tenn., about 1807, died in Hunt Co., Texas, 1863.   Son:—

1119, GIDEON GOODE, d. in Hunt Co., Texas.

468.

CHARLES NEAL WILKERSON, of Warren Co., O., was born near Fort Ancient, in Warren Co., Sept. 25, 1810, and died Sept. 14, 1881.   He married, April 16, 1834, MARTHA ANN GOODE, daughter of No. 176, p. 88; who was born, March 28, 1810, died Jan. 11, 1877. Children:—

1120, BURWELL GOODE WILKERSON, b. May 11, 1836.   1121, WILLIAM NEAL, b. Mar. 21, 1838.   1122, MARY ELIZABETH, b. June 18, 1840, m. *E. T. M. Williams*.   1123, GEORGE HENRY, b. Jan. 16, 1843. 1124, THOMAS SMITH, b. April 27, 1845.   1125, SAMUEL JAMES, b. May 14, 1847.   1126, CHARLES POAGUE, b. June 13, 1850.   1127, EDWARD, b. Nov. 1, 1853.

Mr. Wilkerson, was son of William Wilkerson, and his wife, Mary Neal, both natives of Loudoun Co., Va.   They were married in Kentucky, where their respective families had settled between 1790 and 1800.   They came to Ohio about 1803, and occupied the farm upon a portion of which Mr. Wilkinson lived until his death in 1881.

470.

THOMAS MILTON GOODE, of Carroll Co., Mo., son of No. 176, p. 88, was born Dec. 24, 1812, d. March 2, 1885.   Married (1), 1838,

Rebecca Kratz, (2) Oct. 12, 1841, Sarah Ann Chenowith, b. Sept. 3, 1818, died Dec. 7, 1878.   Children. (one by first marriage):—

1128, GEORGE WILLIAM GOODE, b. Jan. 27, 1839, d. Sept. 25, 1861. 1129, ANN ELIZABETH GOODE, b. Feb. 9, 1843, m. (1) *Wm. H. Corwin*, (2) *Martin Gons*. 1129½, JOSEPH CHENOWITH, b. Feb. 1844, d. Aug. 17, 1847. 1130, MILTON J., b. May 24, 1848; he removed with his father to Missouri, but disappeared, about 1870, and has never since been heard from. 1131, BURWELL, b. May 24, 1851. 1132, LAURA McCLELLAN, b. Oct. 5, 1853, m. *James W. Beaty*. 1133, MARY JANE, b. Nov. 5, 1856, m. *J. W. McLain*.

T. M. Goode lived, until 1861, upon the farm near Waynesville, which had formerly belonged to his father ; he then removed to Lebanon, O., and Oct. 5, 1865, to Carroll Co., Mo., where he carried on a farm, near Carrollton, until his death in 1885.

473

ROBERT DAVIS POAGUE, of " Woodlawn," near Spring Valley, O., son of Thomas Poague, was born in Green Co., O., Jan. 2, 1813, and died Aug. 10, 1859. Married Jan. 6, 1846, MARY ELIZABETH GOODE, daughter of No. 176, p. 88, born April 23, 1820.   Children :—

1134, MARGARETTA E. POAGUE, b. Mar. 31, 1847, d. Feb. 4, 1881, m. *Hon. Thomas J. Pringle*. 1135, WILLIAM T., b. July 31, 1849. 1136, JAMES B., b. May 9, 1852. 1137, MARY ELLEN, b. July 25, 1854, d. Jan. 11, 1857. 1138, CHARLES M., b. Aug. 25, 1859.

Mr. Poague was a farmer and stock-breeder in Ohio. He was greatly esteemed for his probity and energy, and was successful in his business undertakings, leaving at his death one of the largest landed estates in his county. After his death his wife carried on the business until her sons were grown. The Poagues have always been people of culture, and prominent in good works.

" Mrs. Mary E. Poague," writes a kinsman, " is a woman of remarkable qualities. Left as she was, when young, with a family of little children and a considerable estate, she has managed both admirably, and is held in highest regard throughout her connection and community. Her children are all substantial young men. All of the children own large and valuable farms, devised them by their father."

Thomas Poague, father of Robert Davis Poague, was a native of Virginia. He emigrated from the vicinity of Staunton in that State, to Ohio, in 1808, and at once settled upon lands the title to which has ever since remained in his family. He built his dwelling upon the site where the homestead of his descendants now stands. He married Dec. 19, 1809, Margaret, daughter of Robert and Sarah Boggs. of Fayette Co., Ky., and died in 1816. Upon the death of Thomas, his widow with her four children, moved to the home of her parents in Fayette County, Kentucky, where they continued until 1833, in which year they returned to their old home in Ohio. The two sons, Robert and William, with their own hands, cleared large tracts of their lands, then covered with dense forests.

The widow resided with her son Robert and his family until her death.

His brother William died at an early age, unmarried. Of his two sisters, the elder. Sarah, married Dr. Joshua Martin, an eminent physician of Xenia, O., and Margaretta, the younger, married Judge William Mills, of Yellow Springs, O.

474.

JUDGE JAMES SAMUEL GOODE, of Springfield, O., son of Burwell and *Elizabeth Smith* Goode, No. 176, p. 88, was born in Warren Co., O., Jan. 23, 1822. Married, Nov. 9, 1848, Mary Ann Cowan, daughter of William and *Rebecca Whitehill** Cowan, of Warren Co., O., who was born Aug. 19, 1825. Children :—

> 1139, JANE WHITEHILL GOODE, b. Mar. 21, 1850, d. July 23, 1851. 1140, ELIZABETH, b. Aug. 7, 1851, attended Vassar College, 1868–70. 1141, FRANK COWAN, b. Sept. 12, 1853. 1142, ALICE RODGERS, b. Sept. 16, 1855. 1143, MARY POAGUE, b. Aug. 18, 1860, m. *John B. Baskin.* 1144½, EDITH SMITH, b. July 28, 1864, d. Sept. 11, 1865, and JAMES BURWELL, b. July 28, 1864, d. April 26, 1867.

Judge Goode was graduated at Miami University, 1845 ; was admitted to the bar in 1848, and located at Springfield in the spring of that year, forming a partnership with Gen. Chas. Anthony, a prominent lawyer and politician of that time. Subsequently he was likewise associated in practice with the Hon. Samuel Shellabarger, M. C., now of Washington.

He was Mayor of the city of Springfield, 1854–56, Prosecuting-attorney of Clarke Co., 1857–68, and Judge of the Court of Common Pleas of the 2d Ohio judicial district, from 1875 to 1885. Since his retirement from the bench he has resumed, in a measure, the practice of his profession, as a member of the firm of Goode & Goode. He is president of the Mad River National Bank, of Springfield, and has filled many positions of private trust.

Concerning him a friend writes, " One of his most striking traits has been his industry and devotion to his work. He was a good lawyer and successful Judge—was twice elected to his position in the Court of Common Pleas. On his retirement from the bench, although there was no reason for further professional labor on his part, he would not consent to be idle, and entered into a partnership with his son. No man is more highly respected in this community than he."

EXCURSUS.—THE SMITH FAMILY OF POWHATAN CO., VIRGINIA.

Communicated by FRANK C. GOODE, Esq., of Springfield, O.

ELIZABETH SMITH, the wife of BURWELL GOODE, 176, was the daughter of Rev. James Smith, of Powhatan Co., Va. She was born in Powhatan Co., January 29, 1787, and is said to have been in her youth possessed of much beauty. She was noted for her energetic, business-like habits, of which the following

---

*For note on the Whitehill Family, see the following Excursus.

TESTIMONIAL of the Bar of Clark County, Ohio, to Judge James S. Goode, upon His Retirement from the Bench of the Court of Common Pleas in 1885.

THE members of the Bar of Clark County, upon the retirement of his Honor, JUDGE JAMES S. GOODE, from the bench at the close of an honorable service, desire to place upon public record an appropriate testimonial of their appreciation of his long, arduous and faithful labors ; to testify to the patient investigation and untiring industry which he brought to the discharge of his judicial duties and to recognize the learning, ability and integrity which marked his administration of justice.

JUDGE GOODE, in 1875, after an extensive practice of many years, accepted the position of Common Pleas Judge in the Second Judicial District, bringing with him settled habits of labor and research, an unusual familiarity with adjudged precedents, a skill and acumen developed by constant contests at *nisi prius*, and a judgment which was the growth of a ripe and varied experience. These elements, which had made the successful lawyer, were of admirable service to him as a Judge, in the rapid and proper disposition of our docket, obstructed by the lack of judicial facilities, and to this work he gave himself with great energy and ability.

At the close of his first term he was re-elected without opposition for a second term of five years, and now, upon his voluntary retirement from judicial honors to resume the practice of his profession, he carries with him the satisfaction that his judgments have been the result of careful investigation and an impartial application of legal principles, and if error have been committed the solace that infallibility has as yet found no place on earthly tribunals.

While maintaining the dignity of the judicial ermine, JUDGE GOODE's intercourse with the members of the bar, both on and off the bench, has been distinguished by a courtesy of manner which has gained him the good will of all. And the brethren of the district join with us in assuring him that as he leaves the court he carries with him the profound respect and kindliest feeling of those with whom he was associated during his ten years' service. And we trust that the active life which has been so well rounded by the period of judicial honors just closed may have in it yet many years of usefulness and the profession of the law long continue to have the benefit of his experience, his learning and his judgment.

We recommend the adoption of the following resolutions :

Resolved, That the chairman of this committee be instructed to present this testimonial to the Court of Common Pleas of Clark County at the first day of the next term thereof and request that the same be entered upon the journal of said Court.

OSCAR T. MARTIN,	
J. K. MOWER,	
S. A. BOWMAN,	Committee on Resolutions.
A. H. GILLETT,	
F. M. HAGAN,	

April 23, 1885.

circumstance, related by one of her brothers to his son, is an illustration. Upon her mother's plantation in Virginia was a "sugar camp," where, one Spring during a fine "run" of sap, Elizabeth remained with her brother during an entire week, without once going to the house, assisting in the making of the sugar. The water had to be boiled constantly, both day and night, and in performing this work the brother and sister alternated until the crop was saved.

She was a faithful member of her church, devoted to her family, exceedingly hospitable, and attached to all her kinsmen and friends; especially to such as were of the families of the early settlers of Ohio. She died Oct. 7, 1863, surviving her husband about 22 years. Her remains, as well as those of her husband, her parents, and many others of both families, rest in the beautiful cemetery at Corwin, within a short distance of her husband's home, the land being part of the original Goode farm.

That branch of the family or race of Smith to which Mrs. Goode belonged are the descendants of GEORGE SMITH, of Virginia, of whom little more is known than that as a young man he left his home in the extreme eastern part of the state, about the end of the seventeenth century, and moved westward, locating near to and east of the Blue Ridge : probably near the future home of his descendants in Powhatan and adjoining counties. The tradition is that he was a mighty hunter, his worldly possessions when he left home consisting of a buffalo robe, tomahawk, gun and knife. He became wealthy and left to his son large tracts of land on the James River, in Chesterfield and Powhatan Counties, about twenty miles above Richmond. This son was THOMAS SMITH, who lived and died upon these ancestral estates, parts of which including the old buildings, were, not many years ago, owned by some of his descendants:

Thomas Smith was able to leave each of his six children a fine farm and a considerable number of slaves. He and his family were originally members of the Church of England, but when Methodism was introduced into Virginia in 1772, they were among the first members of the new sect. (See note on the Hayes Family p. 83, and on Philip Goode, pp. 80–81, also note on p. 50). Two of his sons, however, became Baptist preachers. It is stated that Mr. Smith's home was the home of the early preachers, and that here was held the conference of 1780.*

He was married three times, and by each marriage had one son and one daughter. His first wife, a Miss Rapin, bore him George Rapin Smith, known in the family as "Millpond George," and Judith, who afterwards married a Mr. Guerrant, a son by a former marriage of the lady who became Mr. Smith's third wife. From George Rapin Smith was descended Gen. Geo. R. Smith, formerly of Kentucky, afterwards of Missouri, and founder of the City of Sedalia, where he died about 1879.

The second wife of Thomas Smith was a Miss Stovall, who became the

---

*This conference was held at the Huguenot settlement of Manakin Town. Hence it appears probable that the Smith homestead was there situate.   G. B. G.

mother of George Stovall Smith, and Elizabeth, who married Philip Gatch.* George Stovall Smith moved from Virginia about 1780, and settled in Jassamin County, Ky., in which state he has to-day a numerous posterity. One of his sons was probably John Steed Smith, M. C., b. 1792, d. 1854. From Mr. and Mrs. Gatch are descended a large family, residing mostly in southern Ohio, chiefly in Clermont County.

Thomas Smith's third marriage was with a Mrs. Guerrant, a widow, (her maiden name Margaret Trabue), of Huguenot descent, whose son was with Gen. Washington at Valley Forge. The children of this marriage were James Smith, the father of Mrs. Burwell Goode, and Martha who married Peter Sublett, and whose numerous descendants, of that name, reside in and near Richmond, Va.

JAMES SMITH, was born upon his father's plantation in Powhatan Co., Sept. 17, 1757. He and his brothers became preachers. He belonged originally to the Methodist Episcopal Church, but joined in a secession from that communion, which was headed by a Mr. O'Reilly, whose adherents were known as Republican Methodists. It is not believed that he ever had any definite pastoral charge.

He was a man of extreme conscientious scruples, and fervent piety. He became warmly opposed to the system of slavery, and convinced that the evils resulting from that institution threatened the safety of his state and the nation, and for many years prior to his removal from Virginia, seems to have been intent upon removing to a country where slavery did not exist.

Before his final removal from the state he made three trips to the west, the first in 1785, when he visited Kentucky, going by way of Cumberland Gap ; again, in 1795, he journeyed to that state going a part of the way by flatboat down the Kenawha and Ohio Rivers, and on this occasion extended his trip into Ohio, proceeding up the valley of the Great Miami, to Fort Hamilton, the site of the present city of the same name ; and in 1797, he undertook a third expedition, in the course of which he again visited the country now comprised in both these states, and this time traveling up the little Miami valley to the site of the Indian town of Chillicothe, near the present city of Xenia.

During each of these journeys he kept a journal, which document is still extant in the hands of one of his descendants.† The history of his travels and his reflections upon various topics as recorded in this book are of absorbing interest, and the work is of considerable literary merit. As might be supposed his several journeys, particularly the first, were attended with much hardship and some danger.

His experience of life in the wilderness, however, seemed only to stimulate his desire to escape with his family from the evil associations, as he deemed them, which were engendered by slavery.

Immediately on his return from the last of these trips he purchased a tract of land of about 2000 acres, lying on the Little Miami, at the mouth of Cæsar's

---

*Rev. Philip Gatch, known also as Judge Gatch, was born in Maryland, Mar. 2, 1751, entered the Methodist ministry, 1774, and labored with great zeal and success in the middle states and Virginia : removed in 1798, to a point near Cincinnati, where, after a long and useful life, he died Dec. 28, 1835.

†Judge J. M. Smith, of Lebanon, has the MS., and a copy is in the possession of the writer of this sketch.

Creek, and but a few miles distant from the land soon after to become the home of Philip Goode, and his brethren.   He settled his affairs in Virginia, emancipated all his slaves, and in 1798, he and his family bade final adieu to their old home, and in company with the family of their kinsman Gatch, started for the territory north-west of the Ohio.   After a journey of extreme difficulty they arrived at length, in the vicinity of Milford, Ohio, and took up the ir temporary abode upon a farm at Middletown Station, Hamilton County, until suitable arrangements could be made to occupy their own land.   Mr. Smith however, did not live to take possession of it, but died at Middletown Station, July 28, 1800.   A touching notice of his death and burial occurs in Chief-justice McLean's sketch of Rev. Philip Gatch.

At the time of their arrival in Ohio, the family consisted of two sons and six daughters; another son, George J. Smith, was born soon after their arrival at Middletown.

Upon the death of her husband the widow was left with nine children, the youngest a babe, and the oldest son but seventeen years old.   About Christmas of 1800, a log house having by this time been completed on their own land some forty miles further up the river, they moved thither and took up their abode.   Being almost the first settlers in that neighborhood, they experienced the privations of pioneer life in their extremest rigour, suffering inconveniences and hardships which none but a pioneer's widow and her fatherless children can know.

Here Mrs. Smith continued to reside until her death in 1825, and on this land several of the descendants still live.

FIRST GENERATION.

1. GEORGE SMITH, mentioned above as the progenitor of the family, born probably, 1660–1680.

SECOND GENERATION.

2. THOMAS SMITH, of Powhatan Co., son of the foregoing, born 1700–20. Children :—

    3. REV. GEORGE RAPIN SMITH.   4. JUDITH, m. *Mr. Guerrant.*   5. REV. GEORGE STOVALL, moved to Kentucky, about 1780.   6. ELIZABETH, m. *Philip Gatch.*   7. JAMES.   8. MARTHA, m. *Peter Sublett.*

THIRD GENERATION.

7. REV. JAMES SMITH, of Powhatan Co., b. Sept. 17, 1757, died July 28, 1800, m. Mar. 19, 1779, Elizabeth, dau. of John and *Sarah Watkins* Porter, b. Dec. 6, 1762.   Children :—

    8. SARAH SMITH, m. 1801, *Ichabod Halsey.*   9. THOMAS SMITH.   10. JOHN W.   11. ELIZABETH, m. *Burwell Goode.*   12. MAGDALEN, m. 1808, *Robert Sale.*   13. MARTHA, m. 1816, *William O'Neal.*   14. JUDITH, m. *Hiram Brown.*   15. CYNTHIA, b. Sept. 19, 1796, d. Aug. 24, 1818, unm.   16. GEORGE JAMES.

A grandson of No. 1, was probably Meriwether Smith, of Va., M. C. 1778-82, g. s. also of Francis Meriwether, emigrant from Wales to Va., was related to Philip Goode, No. 171, either through the Hayes or Collier families.   His son,

Gov. George W. Smith, was burned in the Richmond Theatre, 1811 ; another son, who m. a niece of President Monroe, lived on a farm in Ohio adjoining that first occupied by Goode brothers, Nos. 171–180, and his wife's sister, Lucy Monroe, taught the children of their families. They claimed relationship with the Goodes, and called Philip Goode, No. 171, cousin. There was probably another kinship through the Hayes family.

FOURTH GENERATION.

The names of the members of the fourth generation from George Smith, second from Rev. James Smith, and of their immediate decendants who reached majority are :—

8. SARAH SMITH, b. 1781, d. 1842, m. 1801, *Ichabod Halsey*. Children :—
> 17. JAMES S. HALSEY, for many years Probate Judge of Clark Co., O. 18. BENTON, and 19, MARTHA, m. *Isaac Jennings*, both of Plymouth, Ind. 20. MARY, m. *Gen. Charles Anthony*, a leading lawyer of the past generation, and 21, DANIEL, journalist, both of Springfield, O.

9. THOMAS SMITH, b. 1783, d. 1841, married *Mary Whitehill*, Feb. 6. 1817, (See Whitehill Genealogy, in next Excursus). Children ;—
> 22. JOSEPH W., and 23, JAMES GEORGE, both of Warren Co., O. 24. JOHN QUINCY, State Senator and Representative in Ohio legislature, 1860–3, member Congress, 1873–4, U. S. Commissioner Indian affairs, 1875–7, and Consul general of U. S. in Canada, 1878–82. He is also a distinguished writer and speaker upon political economy, being a radical advocate of free trade. 25. WILLIAM F. 26. MARY JANE, m. *Moses N. Collett*, of Warren Co., O., and 27. THOMAS E., of Paola, Kans.

10. JOHN W. SMITH, of Warren Co., O., born 1783, d. 1841. Children :—
> 28. JAMES. 29. GEORGE E., and 30, SARAH, m. *Isaac Rosebury*, all of Warren Co. 31. REBECCA, m. *William B. McClellan*, of Virginia. 32. CYRUS, and 33, JOSHUA, of Warren Co., the latter in 79th O. Regiment, who made the campaign of Atlanta and march to the sea, and 34, PHILIP, of Grinnell, Iowa.

11. ELIZABETH SMITH, the wife of BURWELL GOODE, (See Goode Genealogy, No. 176).

12. MAGDALEN SMITH, b. 1789, d. 1839, m. 1808, *Robert Sale*, of Warren Co. Children :—
> 35. JOHN, of Warren Co., Ind. 36. THOMAS, lawyer, of Paris, Ill. 37. GEORGE. 38. ELIZABETH. 39. CYNTHIA, m, *James Chenowith*, all of Warren Co., O. 40. CAROLINE, m. *Dakin Vanderbaugh*, of Virginia. 41. MINERVA, m. *William Smith*, of Indiana.

13. MARTHA SMITH, b. 1791, d. 1873, m. 1816, *William O'Neall*. Children, (all of Warren Co., O.):—
> 42. JAMES S., whose son, Joseph W. O'Neall, of Lebanon, is at present a Judge of the Court of Common Pleas. 43. J. KELDY, lawyer and prominent free mason. 44. ABIJAH P., and 45. GEORGE T.

14. JUDITH SMITH, b. 1794, d. 1858, m. *Hiram Brown,** of Indianapolis, Ind., in
1817. Children, (all of whom resided at Indianapolis except Mrs.
McKay):—
46. ELIZA, m. *J. C. Sohn.* 47. MINERVA, m. *Hon. Albert G. Porter*, Member of Congress, Comptroller of Treasury, Governor of Indiana,
etc. 48. MATILDA, m. *J. T. McKay*, of Lebanon, O. (See McKay
Excursus, on p. 92, No. 27). 49. MARTHA, m. *Samuel Dalzell.* 50.
IGNATIUS. 51. DR. H. C. BROWN. 52. JAMES. 53. MARY, m.
Mr. Jones.
16. HON. GEORGE J. SMITH, of Lebanon, O., b. 1799, d. 1878, an able and
distinguished lawyer and Judge. He read law with Thomas Corwin ;
was admitted to practice in 1820 ; was representative in general assembly, 1825-7 ; president Judge Com. Pleas Court, 1829-56 ; State Senator,
1836-40, serving as speaker in 1837 ; in 1850, was elected senatorial del-
gate to the convention which framed the present Constitution of Ohio.
rendering conspicuous service in that body ; and from 1859 to 1869,
served two additional terms as Judge. He was one of the most noted
and respected men in Ohio, and was particularly interested in all that
pertained to pioneer history. He married in 1822, *Hannah Whitehill*,
(see Whitehill Genealogy below). Children, (all of Lebanon):—
54. HON. JAMES M. SMITH, long honored as one of the ablest of living
Judges in Ohio ; from 1871 to 1885, Judge of the Common Pleas,
and at present Judge of the 1st (Cincinnati) Circuit Court. 55.
GEORGE W. 56. JOHN E., a prominent lawyer of southern Ohio.
57. HARRIET.
The facts embodied in this sketch were communicated by Judge J. M. Smith
and Hon. J. Q. Smith, of Ohio. A Smith Family Reunion was held Sept. 2,
1882, at the residence of G. T. O'Neall, Esq., near Waynesville, O., which was
attended by seventy-five of the descendants of Rev. James and Elizabeth
Smith. A notice of this meeting, together with the address of J. E. Smith,
Esq., may be found in the *Lebanon Gazette*, of Sept. 9, 1882.

EXCURSUS.—THE WHITEHILL FAMILY.

JAMES WHITEHILL, the ancestor of the American Whitehills, was of Scotch
descent, but whether born in Scotland, or in the north of Ireland, (whither
he or his parents had first emigrated,) or in the state of Pennsylvania is not
certainly known.
·One of his grandchildren was heard to say that she used to see, when a child,
in her grandfather's house in Pennsylvania, a painting of the arms of Lord
Stair, and was told that her family descended from the author of the Glencoe
massacre, or his father, the elder Dalrymple.
He was born in 1700, and married Miss Criswell, in 1728. Three of his five
sons were Members of Congress from Pennsylvania 1805-14, viz : JOHN, (b.
1720, d. 1815.), ROBERT (d. 1813), and JAMES, (d. 1822).

---

*Brother of HON. MILTON BROWN, M. C. from Tennessee, 1841-7, and member of the Confederate Con-
gress ; the author in 1845, of the resolution for incorporating Texas into the Union.

In McMaster's "History of the People of the United States," the name of Mr. Whitehill (one of the above), is frequently mentioned as a leader in the Pennsylvania legislature.

Robert was the great-grandfather of J. Q. A. Ward, the sculptor.

Joseph Whitehill, the tenth child and youngest son of James, (b. 1746). This son inherited or otherwise acquired the old family home and about four hundred acres of land : and also engaged in business as a merchant at Lancaster. He married in 1780, Mary Kenedy, dau. of Thomas Kenedy and *Rachel Clark*, born 1761.

Through the mismanagement of a business partner, Joseph Whitehill lost his property and land, and about 1800, moved to Botetourt Co., Va., where he lived upon a farm until his death in 1808. His widow died in 1810. The bodies of both lie in the old Presbyterian burying ground at Fincastle.

There were born to them ten children, three sons and seven daughters. The oldest son remained in Pennsylvania. The second son, Joseph, during the war of 1812, was a Lieutenant in a militia company raised in Botetourt Co., and during the.campaign at Norfolk, became Captain.

In 1815, the surviving members of the family moved to Ohio, settling in Warren Co. Beside Joseph there came his six sisters and one brother, the latter, however, dying in the first year after removal.

Two of these sisters, viz : Mary (b. Oct. 19, 1788), and Hannah (b. Nov. 28, 1790), married, respectively, Thomas Smith and Judge George James Smith, (see Smith Excursus, pp. 168–9).

Susannah (b. Oct. 29, 1792), m. 1817, John Tate, and left a large family who reside in Southern Ohio, excepting two sons, James S. and David Morris, prominent and successful grain merchants residing in New York and Chicago, respectively. Rachel married Dr. Morris, of Lebanon. Rebecca, b. in Lancaster Co., Pa,, Oct. 21, 1796, d. April 13, 1838, m. Nov. 9, 1824, William Cowan, a native of Pennsylvania, who died April 28, 1834, aged 34, and had a daughter Elizabeth, who married Judge James S. Goode, No. 474.

Neither Joseph Whitehill nor his sister Jane ever married. The former was twice elected Sheriff of Warren Co., and afterwards served four terms as representative in the state legislature. In 1834, he was elected Treasurer of State, an office he continued to hold through successive re-elections, for twelve years. Mr. Whitehill and his sister Jane moved to Columbus in 1834, and resided there, universally esteemed and respected, until the death of the former in 1861. Miss Whitehill, who was the eldest of the family coming to Ohio, and whom all the others regarded as a kind of second mother, was a woman of noble traits and great intelligence. She died in 1865, in Springfield.

477.

BURWELL SMITH GOODE, of Cincinnati, O., son of Burwell and *Elizabeth Smith* Goode, No. 176, p. 88, was born Aug. 9, 1830, and died Mar. 21, 1864. Married, June 29, 1852, Hannah Inghram Rinehart, daughter of Levi and Maria (McClellan) Rinehart, of Springfield, O., b. Jan. 28, 1831. Children:—

1145, EDWARD GOODE, b. July 17, 1813, d. Sept. 11, 1854. 1146, LEVI MONROE, b. Sept. 27, 1855. 1147, ELIZABETH, b. Dec. 11, 1857, d. Jan. 24, 1858,. 1148, HENRY WINSTON, b. May 4, 1859, d. Nov. 20, 1863, 1149, MARIA, b. Jan. 8, 1863, m. Oct. 2, 1883, *Benjamin Harrison*, of Indianapolis, great-grandson of President Harrison, (son of John C. S., son of Benjamin, son of William H. H.).

Burwell S. Goode was educated in the local schools of Warren Co., and in Springfield. After his marriage he settled in Indianapolis, and opened the first wholesale grocery store in that city, where he remained until 1858. He then transferred his business to Cincinnati, and continued it until his death in 1864.

In July, 1863, he enlisted with the local militia of that city, summoned to defend Cincinnati from the anticipated attack of John Morgan's command, during their celebrated raid through Ohio and Indiana. While in camp in the environs of the city he contracted the cold which ultimately resulted in pneumonia and caused his death.

Both parents of Mrs. Burwell S. Goode, Levi Rinehart and Maria McClellan, were natives of Waynesburgh, Green Co., Pa., where they were married about 1825. They came to Ohio in 1830, settling first at Steubenville, in 1834 moving to Cambridge, and in 1837 to Springfield, where most of their descendants still reside.

The father of Levi Rinehart, whose christian name is lost, was one of four brothers, who emigrated from western Germany to Waynesburgh, Pa., 1760–1770. The family name of *Hart* had been changed in Germany to designate that branch of the family dwelling upon the river Rhine.

The McClellans of were of Irish origin.

480.

SAMUEL GOODE HAAS, of Valparaiso, Ind., son of Jacob and *Susanna Goode* Haas, No. 179, p. 90, was born in Amherst Co., Va., 1821, died Nov. 14, 1859. A farmer and capitalist. Married, May 23, 1844, Sarah Heywood Everts, daughter of Dr. Sylvanus and Elizabeth (Heywood) Everts,* of La Porte Co., Ind. Children:—

1160, SUSAN ELIZABETH HAAS, b. May 23, 1845. m. *Rev. M. B. Lowrie.* 1161, JULIA, b. Mar. 11, 1849, m. *Sloan M. Emory.* 1162, FRANCIS GOODE, b. Mar. 8, 1858, d. 1873.

He graduated about 1840 at Hanover College, Madison, Ind., and was in after life chiefly engaged in the management of his large landed interests.

---

*THE EVERTS AND HEYWOOD FAMILIES.—Mrs. Haas is the sister of Dr. Orpheus M. Everts, Superintendent of the Cincinnati Sanitarium. Their grandparents were (1) *Ambrose Everts*, (born in Vermont, perhaps at Castleton, where his father, a native of England and a clergyman of the English church, was buried) who moved from Rutland, Vt. to Ohio, in 1795. (2) *Achsa Bingham*, his wife, born in Salisbury, Conn., and a descendant of Capt. Miles Standish, of the Plymouth Colony. (3) *Thomas Heywood*, born on the Kennebeck River, Me. and removed to Ohio, 1795, and (4) his wife *Sarah Copeland*, a native of Maine.

He was a man of medium height, with dark hair and eyes, nervous in disposition, and rather exclusive in his tastes and habits.

483.

JOSEPH SHAMBAUGH, of New Burlington, O.; farmer, married, 1851, ABIGAIL ANN GOODE, daughter of No. 180, p. 90, born Jan. 18, 1825, died June 5, 187. Mr. Shambaugh married (2) Miss Collett. Children, by first marriage : —

> 1163, FRANKLIN HENRY SHAMBAUGH, b. Oct. 9. 1852.   1164, WILLIAM GOODE, b. Sept. 14, 1856 ; merchant, Chicago.   1165, ELLEN MARGARET, b. Mar. 30, 1859, d. Aug. 26, 1865.   1166, MARY HARRIET, b. Feb. 8, 1862, d. Aug. 24, 1862.   1167, CHARLES LINCOLN, b. Nov. 4. 1863 ; attorney-at-law, Xenia, O.   1168, JOSEPH BURWELL, b. Nov. 13, 1869, d. Feb. 7, 1871.

485.

SAMUEL GAINES GOODE, of Xenia, O., son of No. 180, was born July 1, 1830. A farmer. Married, May 11, 1859, NARCISSA ANN LYLE, No 1100. Children : —

> 1169, JAMES MACKERNESS GOODE, b. Aug. 8, 1860, m. Orietta Bell, Apr. 26, 1885.   1170, ELIZABETH MARGARET, b. Aug. 17, 1862, d. Apr. 8, 1885.   1171, MARY ANN, b. Aug. 30, 1865.   1172, KATIE BELL, b. June 17, 1867.   1173, JOSEPH HENRY, b. Mar. 17, 1869, d. June 21, 1885.   1174, SAMUEL, b. Oct. 27, 1871.   1175, MOSES MCKAY, b. June 2d, 1873.   1176, LUELLA, b. May 26, 1875.

487.

DR. BURWELL PHILIP GOODE, of Cincinnati, O., son of No. 180, was born in Sidney, O., Feb. 25, 1833. Married, May 6, 1858, Ellen S. Smith, daughter of Norman Smith, of Hartford, Conn., born Feb. 8, 1837. Children : —

> 1177, SAMUEL BURWELL GOODE, b. Mar. 5, 1859.   1178, GEORGE HENRY, b. Feb. 14, 1861.   1179, LUCY MARGARET, b. May 27, 1853.   1180, MARY ELLEN, b. Aug. 1, 1867.   1181, EDWARD, b. Jan. 10, 1870. 1182, ALICE M., b. Sept. 17, 1872.   1182½, FLORENCE, b. Dec. 12, 1881.

Dr. Goode studied first at Ohio Wesleyan University, and graduated at Wesleyan University, Connecticut, 1856 : studied medicine and entered practice in Cincinnati, where he is one of the most successful physicians of the city. For a time he was Professor of Anatomy in the Miami Medical College.

His patients consider him the ideal physician. He is the kindest and merriest of men, and his skill in banishing physical ills is only one of the elements of his usefulness as a friend to the afflicted He is a member of the Methodist Episcopal Church, with which very many of this branch of the family are connected. The Rev. S. F. Upham, D. D., LL. D., President of the Drew Theological Seminary, Madison, N. J., married a sister of Mrs Goode.

491.

WILLIAM HENRY COLLIER GOODE, of Sidney, O., son of No. 180, was born Dec. 3, 1843, and was educated at Ohio Wesleyan University. Married, Sept. 8, 1875, Frances Mary Frazer, daughter of John Finley and *Caroline Cowan* Frazer, of Sidney, O. Children :—

> 1183, CAROLINE STIMMEL GOODE, b. Feb. 24, 1877. 1184, CHARLES HENRY, b. Nov. 8, 1879. 1185, FRANK FRAZER, b. Sept. 21, 1882. 1186, MARGARET MCKAY, b. July 4, 1885. 1186½, WILLIAM HORACE COLLIER, b. May 7, 1888.

Mr. Goode was for a time in the drug business in Springfield, O. He is now carrying on farming enterprises in the vicinity of Fargo, Dakota, and is engaged in the manufacture of road-scrapers at Sidney, being proprietor of the American Steel Scraper Co. He owns the estate which formerly belonged to Hon. P. G. Goode, No. 432. He is a capable and enterprising business-man. He is one of the most enthusiastic supporters of the Goode Genealogy, and has done much to secure its success. Shrewd, far-seeing, and enegetic, a public-spirited citizen and a leader in his community, without becoming a politician, strong and self-reliant, he is an excellent type of the sturdy manhood which is the best product of our new-world civilization.

492.

SMITH STIMMEL, of Fargo, Dakota, married, May 10, 1870, MARGARET NARCISSA GOODE, daughter of No. 180, born Nov. 14, 1846. Children :—

> 1187, WILLIAM GOODE STIMMEL, b. Nov. 26, 1871. 1188, ALICE GERTRUDE, b. Dec. 12, 1876. 1189, SMITH, b. Nov. 14, 1883.

Mrs. Stimmel was graduated in 1868 from the Wesleyan Female College, Delaware, O., with the degree of M. L. A. Mr. Stimmel was graduated from Ohio Wesleyan University, in 1869. After practicing law for several years in Cincinnati and Carthage, O., he removed in 1882, to Dakota, where he is resident at Fargo, as an attorney-at-law.

THE LUNENBURG GOODES.

500.

JUDGE THOMAS WHITFIELD GOODE, of Upson Co., Ga., son of John Goode, No. 181, was born in Sparta, Hancock Co., Ga., 1802; died in Thomaston, Nov. 30, 1859. Married, 1825-30, Amanda Virginia, daughter of Thomas and *Julia Rogers* Minor,* who died 1857. Children :—

> 1200, CHARLES THOMAS, b. 18-1, d. 1835. 1201, BENJAMIN WHITFIELD, b. 1849. 1202, JOHN. 1203, SIMEON ROGERS, b. 1845, d. 1878. 1204, JAMES, d. 1868-9. 1205, JULIA, m. *Col. G. P. Smoot.* 1206, MARY E., m *Henry C. Davis.*

---

* The Minors of Virginia deduce from one Doodas Minor, said to have been born in Holland, in 1644, and who was naturalized in Virginia, in 1673, where he married Miss Garret?, and had issue, four sons : William, Minor, Peter and Garret, progenitors of those of the name in Virginia, and in the Southern and Western States. R. A. BROCK

Judge Goode began the practice of law in 1823, and continued till a few months before his death. A man of fine mind and noble principles, stern and puritanical, though much less so in the later years of his life. White's "Historical Collections of Georgia," mentions John Goode, (No. 181), and T. W. Goode, (No. 500), as among the earliest settlers of Upson Co., Ga.

Thomas Minor, the father of Mrs. T. W. Goode, was a native of Virginia and a near relative of the Hon. John Minor Botts, connected with the Goodes by several intermarriages. "There is a romantic tradition in regard to his marriage," writes an Arkansas lady. "The legend runs that he, a wealthy Virginia gentleman, riding past the door of the log cabin in which her father lived, was smitten with love at sight of the coarsely-clad but beautiful maiden standing at the door. He swore a great oath that he would marry her if he could win her consent. This he finally gained, and having married and educated her, they lived long and happily together.

502.

BENJAMIN GOODE, of Coffee Co., Ala., son of No. 181, was born in Putman Co., Ga., 1804–8. Moved, while a boy, to Upson Co., and in 1854, to Ala., where he died. A farmer. Children :—

> 1207. WILLIAM GOODE, soldier, C. S. A., killed in battle. 1208, GEORGE, soldier, C. S. A., killed in battle.

503.

SANDERS SIMMS, of Meriwether Co., Ga., a planter, married SARAH GOODE, daughter of No. 181. Children :—

> 1209, JOHN SIMMS. 1210, BENJAMIN. 1211, JAMES. 1212, WILLIAM, a soldier, C. S. A., mortally wounded at the battle of Malvern Hill. 1213, FRANCES. 1214, JANE. 1215, SARAH. 1216-17, Two sons, d. y.

504.

WILLIAM SPIVEY, of Georgia. A planter. Married NANCY GOODE, daughter of No. 181. Children :—

> 1218, EDMUND W. SPIVEY, lawyer, died in Arkansas. 1219, DR. CHARLES a physician, living near Thomaston, Ga., 1885, married. 1220, JOHN GOODE, a lawyer and soldier, C. S. A., killed at battle of Bryant's Station, Ga., 1865. 1221, MARY EMILY, m. *Robert Richardson*, and lived and died where she was born, in Upson Co., Ga.

505.

MOSES JOHNSON, of Upson Co., Ga., was born in Columbia Co., Ga., 1811; died about 1845. Married MARY ELIZABETH GOODE, daughter of No. 181, born in Putnam Co., Ga. Children :—

> 1222, BENJAMIN WHITFIELD JOHNSON, b. July 23, 1835. 1223, JAMES GOODE, b. Nov. 2. 1837. 1224, ANNIE T.. born April, 1840, d. 1867.

David Johnson, a native of Wales, came to South Carolina in 1765, in his own vessel. His son Benjamin was born in South Carolina, 1770–90, his grandson Moses Johnson, (No. 505) in Georgia, 1811.

Mrs. Johnson married (2) Daniel R. Beall, of Upson Co., Ga., and has one son living by this marriage :—

> 1225, WILLIAM F. BEALL, b. 1844.

507.

MARCUS AURELIUS ANDREWS, of Taliaferro Co., son of John and *Ann Goode* Andrews, was born Oct. 9, 1790, died about 1832. Married Ann Connell. Children :—

> 1226, FRANCES ELIZABETH ANDREWS, m. *Joel M. Chivers*. 1227, SUSAN DARRACOTT, d. inf. 1228, JOHN WILLIAM, b. 1821, d. 1866. 1229, JAMES THOMAS, b. Jan. 31, 1830, m., has several children.

He was a planter, surveyor and school teacher, and a man of considerable literary attainments for those days, having written, it is said, some very creditable verses. His son writes : "He was from the time of the organization of the County of Taliaferro till his death, clerk of its Superior Court. As proof of his popularity, I have it from my honored friend and first guardian, the Hon. Alexander H. Stephens, that *his* father, being the opposing candidate to *mine* in the first election, was defeated by a considerable majority. Being a practical surveyor, he was employed to run the boundary lines of the county. His surviving friends all speak of him as a ripe scholar, kind and affectionate parent and polite and affable Christian gentleman.

"I have in my possession a manuscript, in his hand, of his Christian experiences, written in smooth, rhythmical verse, from which I find that at the age of eighteen he made a profession of religion, and united with the Baptist church, of which he continued a regular communicant up to the time of his death. Two of his songs occur in an old collection of Baptist hymns known as *Mercer's Cluster*.

"From the character of a small collection of hymns in his own handwriting found among his papers, I feel sure, had he not died at so early an age, he would have ranked high as a writer as well as an educator of youth."

510.

HON. GARNETT ANDREWS, of "Haywood," near Washington, Wilkes Co., Ga., son of John and *Ann Goode* Andrews, No. 182, was born Oct. 10, 1798, d. Aug. 14, 1873. Married April 10, 1828, Annulet Ball, daughter of Frederick and Eliza (Taxey) Ball, of Savannah, Ga. Children :—

> 1230, ANN CORINTHIA ANDREWS, b. Jan. 16, 1829, m. *Troup Butler*. 1231, JOHN FREDERICK, b. Nov. 12, 1830. 1232, JAMES GARNETT, b. 1832, d. 1834. 1233, HENRY FRANCIS, b. Nov. 20, 1834. 1234, GARNETT, b. May 15, 1837. 1235, ELIZA FRANCES, b. Aug. 10, 1840. 1236, WILLAMETTE, b. Aug. 3, 1845, m. *T. M. Green*. 1237, DANIEL MARSHALL, b. Oct. 24, 1853, unm., 1885. A civil engineer.

Judge Andrews was a prominent lawyer, and for nearly thirty years, from

1834 on, Judge of the Northern circuit in Georgia. In 1852 he was candidate for governor on the Know Nothing ticket. "During the war," writes his daughter, "he was an unflinching Union man ; not that his sympathies were with our enemies, but because he believed that the South would secure her rights better in the Union than out of it. His clear, logical, head foresaw consequences that more ardent and less thoughtful minds overlooked.

"He never doubted, from the first, that the South would be conquered : he saw that the odds against us were too great and that we must eventually succumb to the numbers and resources of the North. On the night when Georgia seceded, and all the town was running mad with bonfires and torchlight processions, he paced nervously up and down his room at home, and every now and then, when the sound of the shouting and bell ringing would penetrate there he would refer to Walpole and the Spanish war and say, almost with tears in his eyes : 'Poor fools! they may ring their bells now, but they will wring their hands,—yes and their hearts too,—before they are done with it.'

"As early as the first battle of Manassas, he used to say : 'It is not through Virginia that we were going to be conquered. There will come down an army through East Tennessee into Georgia, that will cut the Confederacy in two, and then we are ruined.' He talked of these matters only in the privacy of his family, for in those days it was almost as much as a man's life was worth to doubt the success of the Southern cause. When the war was over, he never used such influence as his Union record gave him for his own advantage, but employed it largely in protecting the lives and property of those whose opinions had differed from his own. His character was so universally honored and respected that even when party feeling was at the bitterest, such men as Toombs, Stephens, Hill, and other Southern leaders were on terms of warm personal friendship with him."

His writings have been mostly political, but he has also published "Reminiscences of an old Georgia Lawyer." (Atlanta, 1870).

The old Andrews homestead, "Haywood," a place noted for its beauty and its associations, is now the property of his son-in-law, Mr. Green.

Mrs. Andrews was daughter of Frederic Ball, b. in New Jersey, 1771, d. in Savannah, Aug. 10, 1820, m. Eliza Taxey (or Tarksey), of Georgia. He had eight children, *Tuscan Ball, Doric, Corinthia, Annulet* (Mrs. Andrews) *Lawrence, Frederic, Sarah,* and *Cornelius.* Being an architect, his four older children were given architectural names.

Francis Ball was son of Steven Ball, a surveyor and Revolutionary soldier, who m. Mary Rose of Springfield, N. J., and grandson of Ezekiel Ball, b. 1751–2, d. 1804, and Mary Jones, from Long Island. Ezekiel Ball built "Tuscan Hall," a quaint old mansion, still standing in the suburbs of Newark, N. J., the corner stone of which was laid in 1760. He was son of Thomas and Sarah (Davis) Ball, and grandson of Edward Ball, one of the founders of the Newark Colony, and an associate of Jasper Crane (see p. 162, preceding). There is a tradition that Edward Ball had a brother who settled in Virginia. This may have been the ancestor of the Balls of Virginia, one of whom was the mother of Washington.

512.

DR. ISAAC BOWEN, of Augusta Ga., a native of Rhode Island, married SARAH MARTHA ANDREWS, daughter of No. 182, who was born Feb. 23, 1803, died April 30, 1848. Children:—

1238, ELIZA ANDREWS BOWEN, b. 1828. 1239, A son, d. inf.

Mrs. Bowen, a highly accomplished woman, and like so many of her family, an accomplished botanist. She conducted for years a successful school for girls.

Dr. Bowen was a learned man and an eminent physician. He died of yellow fever in the epidemic of 1834, in consequence of his devotion to his profession and the cause of humanity.

513.

DR. WILLIS GREEN, of Chambers Co., Alabama, or Troup Co., Ga., married ELIZABETH ANDREWS, daughter of No. 182, p. 93. Children:—

1240, GEN. ALEXANDER A. GREEN, C. S. A., b. about 1840. 1241, DR. JOSEPH, of Rockmont, Polk Co., Ga., soldier, C. S. A. 1242, EZEKIEL, soldier, C. S. A., killed in battle. 1243, ANNA. 1244, EMILY. 1245, SARAH. 1246, A daughter, m. Mr. Holtzclaw, of Salem, Ala.

Dr. Willis Green, was undoubtedly a great-great grandson of Captain William Green, of the body-guard of King William III, who married Eleanor, sister of Sir William Duff. Their son, Robert Green, born about 1695, came to Virginia about 1712, and settled in Culpeper Co. Accounts of this family, which is also connected with the Goodes in the Maynard branch, occur in Slaughter's *St. Mark's Parish*, and in Paxton's *Marshall Genealogy*, p. 121.

516.

DR. DANIEL MARSHALL ANDREWS, of Wilkes Co., Ga., son of John and *Ann Goode* Andrews, No. 182, was born 1812–15, and died 1857, married May 3, 1849, Martha, daughter of Nicholas Wiley.

"He was a very accomplished physician and botanist, but a singularly unambitious man. When Robert Toombs and Alexander H. Stephens were sick at the National Capital, they always sent to Georgia for him. He was so much loved and honored by the people of Wilkes Co., that after his death they raised a handsome monument to his memory."

521.

WILLIAM SLATON, of Washington, Ga., planter, married FANNY GOODE, daughter of No. 183, who was born about 1797. Children.—

1249, SARAH ANN SLATON, b. Dec. 11, 1819, d. Feb. 16, 1880, m. *Grier Stephens*. 1250, MARY E., m. *Samuel E. Daniel*. 1251, JOHN DANIEL. 1252, ELONA, d. y. 1253, WILLIAM JASPER, d. May, 1864, a soldier, C. S. A. 1254, ALEXANDER AUGUSTUS, a soldier,

C. S. A.   1255, HENRY THOMAS, a soldier, C. S. A., in the Irwin Artillery, a crack company from Wilkes Co.   1256, CHARLES WESLEY, d. Oct. 12, 1846.   1257, FRANKLIN PIERCE.

William Slaton was a wealthy planter owning hundreds of slaves. His plantation fence stretched in an unbroken line for over five miles along one of the roads which leads to Washington, Ga.

524.

JOHN GOODE WRIGHT, of Philomath, Oglethorpe Co., Ga., son of No. 183, p. 94, was born Jan. 1. 1803.   Children:—

1258, CAPT. JAMES HULING WRIGHT, of Washington, Ga., b. 1832, a soldier, C. S. A., m. 1859, Cassandra J. Briscoe, issue, i. *Ernest, Wright*, b. 1861, ii. *Percy*, b. 1863, iii. *Anna*, b. 1865, m. E. T. Huntley, of Warrenton, Ga., iv. *James*, b. 1869, v. *May*, b. 1871, d. 1872, vi. *Carrie*, b. 1877.   1259, JOHN L., soldier, C. S. A., m., 1867, Celestia Bowden, issue, i. *Matthew C. Wright*, b. 1870, ii. *Fannie E.*, b. 1875.

A country farmer, who has always lived near the homestead of his grandparents.   In 1885, he removed to the vicinity of Greensboro, Green Co., Ga.

530.

JOHN VASON, of Morgan Co., Ga., planter, son of William and *Polly Goode* Vason, No. 187½, was born in Wilkes Co , Ga., 1781, died 1847.   Children:—

1260, DR. M. E. VASON, of Albany, Ga.   1261, DAVID A.   1262, MARCELLUS, m. and has descendants.   1263, WILLIAM.

THE BEDFORD GOODES.

534.

COL. EDMOND GOODE, C. S. A., son of John and *Ann Leftwich* Goode, No. 188, p. 95, was born in Bedford Co., Va., May 4, 1825. Graduated from the Virginia Military Institute, 1846. Died, Mar., 1862, from disease contracted while serving as Colonel of the 58th Virginia Infantry, C. S. A.   Married, 1850, Ann M. McGhee, of Bedford Co., Va.   Children :—

1264, LYNCH GOODE, b. 1851, d. 1860.   1265, ELIZABETH, b. Jan., 1852, m. *Louis Wroe*, planter, of Maryland.   1266, ROBERTA, b. 1854, d. Jan., 1881, m. *Jordan Moorman*, of Va.   1267, MARY, b. Feb., 1855, m. *A. N. Walker*, of Va.   1268, EDWARD, b. Oct., 1856, d. 1879. 1269, THOMAS, b. May, 1858, farmer, Bedford Co., Va.   1270, SUSAN, b. May, 1860.   1271, EDMONIA, b. 1862.

A full biography of Colonel Goode was printed in the *Memorial of the Virginia Military Institute*, an abridgment of which is here presented :

"He was educated at New London Academy, Bedford Co., an institution of high local reputation, and at the Virginia Military Institute, which he entered in 1843 as a state cadet, graduating in 1846, and serving during the last year as Captain of the cadet-corps. After teaching school for two years, he devoted himself to farming in his native county. In this avocation, so congenial to his tastes, as a modest, unobtrusive gentleman, he gained the respect and confidence of all who knew him.

"In the memorable Spring of 1861, when Virginia, threatened with invasion and the overthrow of all she held sacred, called upon her sons to come to her rescue, he responded with alacrity and zeal. He had no personal ambition to gratify, but he was a native-born Virginian; the blood of Revolutionary ancestors coursed through his veins; his grandfathers on both sides had fought in the ranks of the patriots in 1776, and his maternal great-grandfather (General Leftwich), had rendered distinguished service in 1812, as well as in 1776. He had been reared in the States-rights school, and had been taught that allegiance belonged first to the Commonwealth which gave him birth. He loved that Commonwealth for its historic glories and hallowed associations. His brother, as a member of the convention, had voted for the ordinance which dissolved Virginia from connection with the Federal Union. Prompted by the highest impulses, and feeling assured that every consideration of duty, honor and patriotism required him to take the step, he volunteered, with his four brothers, among the first of that noble band of citizen-soldiers which Bedford County sent to the field before the soil of the State had been touched by the foot of the invader, or the thunder of hostile guns was heard.

"He was appointed in May, 1861, adjutant of the 28th Virginia Infantry, and was ordered to Manassas Junction, and took part in the battle of Manassas, in July, 1861. In the Fall he was appointed Colonel of the 58th Virginia Regt., and ordered to the mountains of Virginia, west of Staunton, where he remained in camp through the subsequent winters, and where he contracted the disease which caused his death. After severe suffering in camp, he was removed to his home in Bedford Co., where he died, March, 1862,—a chivalrous gentleman and gallant soldier, of whom it is sufficient eulogy to say that he acted well his part as one of that noble army of martyrs who suffered and died in the cause of Southern independence."

536.

HON. JOHN GOODE, of Norfolk, Va., son of John and *Ann Leftwich* Goode, No. 188, p. 95, was born in Bedford Co., Va., May 27, 1829. Educated at New London Academy, and Emory and Henry College, where he was graduated, 1848. An eminent lawyer, who has held many public positions, and was appointed May, 1885, Solicitor-General of the United States. Married, July 10, 1885, Sallie Urquhart, daughter of Dr. Richard A., and Mary Norfleet Urquhart, of "Strawberry Plains," Isle of Wight Co., Va. Children:—

> 1272, MARY GOODE, b. May 11. 1856. 1273, RICHARD URQUHART, b. Dec. 8, 1858. 1274, JOHN BRECKENRIDGE, b. Aug. 18, 1864. 1275, ANNIE WALTON, b. May 5, 1869, d. Oct. 1872. 1276, JAMES URQUHART, b. June 2, 1873.

The Hon. John Goode is to day one of the most prominent among the public men of the South, not only by reason of his professional eminence and his capacity for administrative affairs, but because he is one of the few representatives of the old school of southern statesmen, whose influence was so potent in the national councils in the days when representative men were not replaced by ring-politicians. He was born and educated amidst the inspiring scenery of the Blue Ridge mountains. Having been unsuccessful in obtaining an appointment as state-student in the University of Virginia, he entered in 1844, Emory and Henry College, in Washington Co., where he graduated in 1848. During his academic career, his peculiar ability as a public speaker and debater became very manifest. Having read law for two years with Hon. J. W. Brockenbrough at Lexington, he was admitted to the bar in 1851, and began practice at Liberty, Va. When twenty-two years of age, he was elected to the Virginia House of Delegates, as a Democrat, over the head of a representative Whig, and as the representative of a county for many years decidedly anti-Democratic. He was a Presidential Elector on the Democratic ticket in 1852 and 1856, a member of the Virginia Convention of 1860, and an enthusiastic advocate of the Ordinance of Secession.

Volunteering at the outbreak of the war, he was assigned to duty on the staff of Gen. Jubal A. Early with the rank of Captain. His military career was brief, however, for on Feb. 22, 1862, he took his seat as a member of the Confederate Congress, and remained a member of that body until the close of the war.

Like other Virginians, he was obliged to begin life over again after the surrender of the southern armies, and believing that the eastern section of the state had better prospects for future prosperity, than his native county, he removed in the winter of 1865 to Norfolk, and the following year was again elected to the Virginia Legislature. From 1868 to 1880 he served as a member of the National Democratic Committee, and in 1874 and 1876 was a prominent candidate for the U. S. Senate, and came within a few votes of being nominated by the party caucus. In 1874, the Convention at Suffolk, nominated him for the 44th Congress, and although his competitor had, in the previous campaign, a majority of nearly 6,000, he was elected after a vigorous canvass, and received his credentials from the Governor of the State.* His claim to a seat in Congress was vigorously contested, ex-Governor Henry A. Wise serving as one of the counsel for his opponent, but although the Committee to whom the case was referred rendered an adverse report, Congress decided in his favor after a patient investigation. He was re-elected to the 45th and 46th Congresses, and was the Democratic candidate for a following session, but was defeated, owing to complications which had arisen in the State in regard to the settlement of its debt,—Mr. Goode having been very pronounced in his advocacy of full payment of all the just obligations of the Commonwealth.

As a member of the 46th Congress he was the author of the bill providing for the erection of a monument at Yorktown, and for the celebration of the surrender of Lord Cornwallis to the allied armies under Washington and La-

---

*Says Burton's *Norfolk.*—"November 3, 1874, occurred the most exciting election ever held in this Congressioral District. It was the day on which the Hon. John Goode, Jr., one of Virginia's noblest and most gifted sons, defeated the notorious Vermont carpet-bagger, James H. Platt, Jr., for Congress."

fayette. He was President of the Yorktown Centennial Association, and to his efforts much of the success of the celebration was due.

He served in congress for two terms as Chairman of the Committee on Education, and has been prominent in Virginia educational work, being a member of the Board of Visitors for the University of Virginia, William and Mary College, and the Virginia Agricultural and Mechanical College. He was a member of the National Democratic Convention in 1868 and 1872.

In 1884, he was Elector at Large on the Cleveland and Hendricks ticket in Virginia, and President of the Board of Electors. In May, 1885, he was appointed by President Cleveland, Solicitor General of the United States, the position next in dignity to that of a member of the Cabinet, and has several times served as acting Attorney-General.

"*Southern Opinion*" of Nov. 16, 1866, remarked :—

" Mr. Goode is a lawyer of methodical mind, that in its astuteness reminds us of Edmund Burke. He is emphatically an easy speaker, but, nevertheless the most effective of orators, by the very force and correctness of his opinion. Physically considered he is an ideal legislator, and though the least presumptuous, is the most prominent member of the Virginia House of Delegates."

EXCURSUS.—THE URQUHART FAMILY.

The Urquharts of Virginia, are descended from WILLIAM URQUHART, who settled in Southampton County sometime after the middle of the last century. His father, —— Urquhart, Esq., of Aberdeen, Scotland, a scion of the Urquhart clan, was probably one of the many Scotchmen loyal to the Stuarts, who, after the battle of Culloden, sought refuge in the American colonies : he was accompanied by three sons, one of whom settled in Montreal, acquired wealth and left a family of daughters. Another seems to be recordless, and the third, as has been stated, came to Virginia.

WILLIAM URQUHART had one son, John, educated at William and Mary College, and a member of the Virginia Convention, of 1829–30. The old homestead, "Oak Grove," in Southampton Co., was extended and improved by this son, who owned a line of packets, plying between Smithfield, Va., then an important port, and London. JOHN URQUHART, married Nancy Williamson. Her miniature, painted by Thomas Sully, shows her to have been a woman of unusual beauty, and it is traditionary that her name was a proverb in her neighborhood for lavish hospitality, as well as for the admirable manner in which she managed her department of her husband's then large estate. Although entertaining in the old time Virginia style, she gave to her servants the care and supervision of a conscientious Christian woman, and it was her pride that every article of clothing that they wore was manufactured under her supervision. The wool, cotton, flax, leather, etc., were grown on the plantation, and were there manufactured into garments for her dependents. Skilled weavers were brought from Scotland, and there are still in the family articles of table linen which were woven in her looms. The family has always been attached to the Episcopal church.

JOHN URQUHART had many sons, of whom six reached manhood, and who were men of high character and cultivated minds. They were 1. JOHN URQU-HART, d. unm., 2. JAMES, a wealthy planter: his home "Warrique," in Southampton County, now owned by his grandson, W. H. Urquhart, is one of the best preserved old estates in Virginia; 3. RICHARD ALEXANDER, (born 1823, died 1857), a physician, graduated at Jefferson Medical College : his daughter, Sally, m. JOHN GOODE, No. 536.   He was a wealthy planter and except as an act of charity he never practiced his profession, though deeply interested in its progress.   He was always to a certain extent a student, and a man of unusual grace and elegance.   He was noted for his philanthropic ideas, which were developed in the improvements of the dwellings and surroundings of the negroes who were by the providence of God placed under his care ; 4. CHARLES FOX, 5. ANSELM BAILY, 6. MURDOCK MIDDLETON, d. unm.   The younger sons were among the first students of the University of Virginia, since which time there have been few sessions of that school at which some of the name have not been students.

WILLIAM URQUHART, the emigrant-ancestor, was a man of education and taste, as may be judged from the choice books which were in his library, many of which still remain in the family.   He gave much attention to beautifying his home, especially to its grounds and gardens, and there are still standing at "Oak Grove" magnificent trees and shrubs planted by him.   Some of his descendants are now seeking their fortunes in other states, but most of them remain in Virginia.   Six generations are sleeping in the cemetry at " Oak Grove."

537.

WILLIAM GOODE, of Bedford Co., Va., son of No. 188, was born Jan. 21, 1831, died Apr. 14, 1866.

William Goode entered the Confederate army at the outbreak of the war. He saw much service in the south and west, and was captured at Pensacola and imprisoned at Mound City, where he contracted a disease from which he never recovered.

538.

WALTER IZARD, C. E., of South Carolina, (great-grandson of Ralph Izard, and great-nephew of Gen. George Izard, both prominent in Carolina colonial history), married SALLY GOODE, daughter of No. 188.   Children :—

1277, WALTER IZARD, M. D., physician in Liberty, Va., b. Oct., 1854, m. Annie Sale, of Liberty, Va., children. 1278, JOHN, b. Aug., 1856, a physician, living in Pocahontas, Va. 1279, LUCY, b. July, 1858, d. April, 1874. 1280, RALPH, b. March, 1860.

Concerning the history of the Izards, Dr. G. E. Manigault, of Charleston, writes : "There is no printed account of the family.   They were from Worcestershire, where they owned an estate called Beckley, which was afterwards sold.   One of the American descendants visited the old home in the middle of the last century, and saw in a small church near by many monuments to the memory of different members of the name. The founder of the South Carolina family came to America at the close of the 17th century.

" General George Izard who commanded the northern army on the Canada frontier during the summer and fall of 1814, was another son of the Hon. Ralph. His education had been entirely military after the age of 15, having been pursued at Marburg, in Hesse Cassel, and at Metz, in France, where he was allowed by the government to enter their school of engineering. He was perfectly competent to the command to which he was assigned, but was unable to accomplish anything on account of the small force at his disposal."

Mrs. Anne Izard Deas published in 1844, "Correspondence of Mr. Ralph Izard, of South Carolina, from the year 1774 to 1804, with a short memoir," which contains an excellent portrait. Several of the Izard heir-looms are illustrated in Mr. Edward Eggleston's papers on colonial history published in the "Century" Magazine.

Pedigree of Izard, of South Garolina, (Elder Branch).

541.

Dr. REGINALD HEBER GOODE, of Patrick Co., Va., son of No. 188, was born Feb. 2, 1838, graduated at the Richmond Medical College. A practicing physician. Married Fanny Scales, of Patrick Co., Va. Children :—

1281, FANNY SUE GOODE, b. 1873, d. 1880. 1282, MATTIE HEBER, b. Apr., 1879.

Dr. Goode entered the Confederate army as a trooper in the 2d Virginia Cavalry. In 1863, he was appointed Asst. Surgeon, C. S. A., and served in a North Carolina Regiment until the end of the war.

---

*THE NAME IZARD has been represented in Virginia from an early date. Rebecca Izard was granted 250 acres of land, Sept. 14, 1670, in behalf of her two daughters, Mary and Margaret, which land had been previously (Apr. 28, 1670) granted to Richard Izard (died), but had been escheated. (*Virginia Land Records*, book No. 6, p. 308.) Francis (*Index to Grants*), or Frances (*Records*) Izard, patented 1036 acres on the "Chickahominy Maine Swamp," in Henrico County, Apr. 21, 1681, (*Virginia Land Records*, book No. 7, p. 86.) The name Izard has been perpetuated as a christian name in the Bacon, Clopton, Whitlock and other well-known Virginia families. An instance is Judge William Izard Clopton, late Captain of Artillery, C. S. A., of Manchester, Va.   R. A. BROCK.

544.

GRANVILLE BRECKENRIDGE GOODE, of Bedford Co., Va., son of No. 188, was born May 17, 1843, and was killed in the battle of the Wilderness, May 6, 1864.

Breckenridge Goode enlisted in the Purcell Battery of Artillery,C. S. A., at the age of eighteen. He was in several engagements, and after the battle of Fredericksburg, where he displayed great coolness and courage, he was publicly complimented on the field by the commanding officer. He was killed in the battle of the Wilderness, and buried on the field.

THE EDGEFIELD GOODES.

546.

B. FRANK STALLWORTH, of Alabama, son of Nicholas Stallworth, was born Oct. 21, 1830, died June 27, 1854. Married, 1850, MARY ANN GOODE, daughter of No. 194, born June 24, 1833, died June 27, 1854. Son :—

> 1285, GARLAND GOODE STALLWORTH, b. Aug. 4, 1851.

Nicholas Stallworth was one of the earliest settlers in Conecuh Co., Ala., whither he removed from South Carolina, as early as 1822. He married Miss Adams, of South Carolina, and had sons, beside No. 546, Hon. James A. Stallworth, M. C., 1857–61, and Major Nicholas Stallworth, of Conecuh Co. See Brewer's "Alabama," p. 196.

547.

CAPTAIN GILES GOODE, C. S. A., son of Garland Goode, No. 194, p. 95, was born in Edgefield, S! C., June 24, 1833. At the beginning of the war he became Captain of the Monroe Guards, 5th Alabama Volunteers, a company which was fitted out chiefly at the expense of his father. He participated in the skirmish at Farr's X Roads, and the first battle of Bull Run, and died from exposure, in camp at Fairfax Station, Sept. 29, 1861, (Brewer's *Alabama*, p. 596.)

548.

BURTON GOODE, of Moss Point, Miss., son of No. 194, was born Sept. 1, 1841. Married, 1865, Bettie Davis, of Baldwin, Ala. Children ·—

> 1286, ANNIS STALLWORTH GOODE, b. 1867. 1287, MARY, b. 1869. 1288, MARTHA. 1289, CAROLINE. 1290, JOHN QUINTON. 1291, ELLEN, 1292, GILES. 1293, MACKERNESS. 1294–95, DUKE and GRACE, (twins). 1296, DAVID. 1297, BURNS. 1298, BURTON, b. 1885.

Burton Goode served through the war with the 5th Alabama regiment, from the engagements at Farr's X Roads, and the first Bull Run to the surrender at Appomattox, and was several times wounded. He is by profession a civil engineer, but has engaged in various occupations, among others that of steamboat captain.

549.

DR. PHILIP GOODE, of Colfax, La., son of No. 194, was born Aug. 11, 1842. He served through the war in the 15th Alabama Regt., C. S. A., stationed on the coast of Alabama. A graduate of the Mobile Medical College. Practicing his profession in Louisiana, 1886. Unmarried.

551.

DR. JOHN L. TALBERT, of Mobile, Ala., son of Gen. E. G. Talbert, of South Carolina, was born 1830–40, died about 1880. Married about 1868, ELLEN GOODE, daughter of No. 194, who lives, 1885, in Mobile. Children:—

> 1299, CORNELIA TALBERT, b. Dec. 18, 1869. 1300, FRANCES, b. Dec. 28, 1871. 1301, GARLAND, b. Jan. 21, 1879. 1302, SIDNEY, b. June 12, 1880.

Dr. Talbert was a graduate of the Mobile Medical College and a successful physician. He served through the war in an Alabama Cavalry regiment.

552.

DR. RHETT GOODE, of Mobile, Ala., son of No. 194, was born Dec. 5, 1852. Educated at Spring Hill College, and the Mobile Medical College, where he received the degree of M. D., 1870. He has been Demonstrator of Anatomy in the College of Alabama, and in 1885, was acting Professor of Anatomy and curator of the Museum. Dr. Goode is a prominent Surgeon in Mobile, member and councillor of the Medical Association of Alabama, and surgeon in the First Alabama Volunteer Infantry, member of the Manassas Club, and other local organizations. In the yellow fever epidemic of 1882, he served as physician to the "Can't-get-away Club," of which he is a member. He is a fine type of the vigor of the New South.

556–1.

JOHN GOODE, of Edgefield District, S. C., son of John Goode, No. 196, was born 1780–1810. He was a prosperous planter and died in early life. Children:—

> 1303, COL. SAMUEL FREEMAN GOODE. 1304, A Daughter, m. Dr. Mobley.

The record of John Goode, No. 196, was received too late for insertion in its proper place on page 96, and must be printed here.

196, JOHN GOODE, of Abbeville District, S. C., son of Samuel Goode, No. 81, born 1760–80, married Ann Freeman. Children :—

556–1, JOHN GOODE. 556–2, FREEMAN. 556–3, TALITHA, m. (1) *Coleman Watkins*, (2) *Col. Benjamin Sherrod.* 556–4, A Daughter, m. *Larkin Griffin.* 556–5, A Daughter, m. *Dionysius Oliver,* of Edgefield District, S. C. 556–6, ELIZABETH, m. *Mr. Burt,* of Edgefield Dist., S. C. 556–7, A Daughter, m. *Mr. Burt,* of Green Co., Ala. 556–8, FRANCES, m. *Mr. Brooks.* 556–9, LUCINDA, m. *Mr. McLemore,* of Edgefield, S. C. She moved to Alabama after her husband's death.

John Goode lived near old Cambridge, S. C. "Scarcely a vestige of this village now remains," writes Mr. C. F. Sherrod. "It is near ' Ninety-Six,' on the Greenville & Columbia R. R. John Goode's children were all thrifty and prosperous people, and had as high a sense of honor as any people I ever knew. The daughters were left widows with young families, whom they succeeded in bringing up and in most instances in accumulating wealth."

556-2.

COL. FREEMAN GOODE, of Lawrence Co., Ala., son of No. 196, was born about 1790, and died about 1870. A wealthy planter of high standing. At the age of sixty he married a young girl whose giddiness and improvidence reduced him to poverty. It is said that he died of a broken heart.

556-3-A.

COLEMAN WATKINS, of Georgia, son of William and *Susan Coleman* Watkins, married TALITHA Goode, daughter of No. 196. Children:—

> 1305, WILLIAM WILLIS WATKINS, of Texarkana, Texas. 1306, SAMUEL GOODE, Muldon, Miss.

556-3-B.

COL. BENJAMIN SHERROD, of "Cotton Garden" plantation, Lawrence Co., Ala., son of Isaac and *Mary Copeland* Sherrod, of North Carolina, was born in Halifax Co., N. C., 1776, died April 24, 1847. Was early left an orphan and was reared by his uncle, Mr. Ricks, of Halifax Co., N. C., and educated at William and Mary College, and the University of North Carolina. Married (1) about 1814, Eliza, daughter of Samuel Watkins, who died leaving three sons and a daughter. Married (2) 1818, TALITHA GOODE WATKINS, daughter of No. 196, b. Apr. 22, 1792, died May 14, 1873. Children (four by first marriage, three by second):—

> I. FELIX A. M. SHERROD, of Lawrence Co., Ala., married, Sarah A. Parish, issue, 1. *Benjamin Sherrod,* m. Daniela Jones, who after his death m. Hon. Joseph Wheeler, M. C., who was senior Cavalry general, C. S. A., 2. *Francis E.*, 3. *Mrs. Banks*, of Columbus, Miss. II. FREDERICK O. A., of Birmingham, had sons, 1. *J. Bolton Sherrod,*

of Montgomery, Ala., 2. *Benjamin*, of Birmingham, Ala., 3. F. O. A., of Birmingham, Ala. III. SAMUEL WATKINS, m. Frances Parish, sons, 1. *Henry Sherrod*, d. y., 2. *Walter*. IV. MARIE AN-TOINETTE.

1307, CHARLES FOX SHERROD, b. Nov. 3, 1827. 1308, SUSAN ADELAIDE, m. *Col. S. W. Shackelford*. 1309, Hon. WILLIAM CRAWFORD, b. Aug. 31, 1831.

Col. Sherrod served as a commissary of North Carolina troops, in the war of 1812, and about 1814, settled in Washington, Ga. After his second marriage, he removed to northern Alabama, to the county of Lawrence, then just opened, and at the time of his death, was described as one of the most prosperous and energetic men in the Valley of the Tennessee. Said the Nashville Christian Advocate :—"Methodical in his habits, industrious and enterprising, amassed a large estate. He contributed largely to building houses of public worship, and in sustaining the gospel. He was one of the first in this region to promote missionary operations among the colored population, and his humanity and unremitting attention to the temporal and moral wants of his numerous slaves entitled him justly to the appellation of philanthrophist."

He was President of the Tuscumbia and Decatur R.R. Company and to his energy was due the construction in 1832 of this line, the first laid in the South and the third in the United States—an enterprise in which the public had at that time little faith (See Brewer's "Alabama," p. 78-113.)

Mrs. Talitha Goode Sherrod died at the residence of her son-in-law Col Shackelford. She had long been a member of the Baptist Church.

556–5.

DIONYSIUS OLIVER, of Edgefield District, S. C., married a daughter of John Goode, No. 196, who died leaving and infant son :—

1316, LLEWELLYN OLIVER, who was brought up by Mrs. Sherrod, No. 554. He lived for a time in N. Alabama, and subsequently removed to S. Alabama, where he became a prosperous planter, and a man "highly esteemed by his neighbors as an exemplary Christian gentleman." Married. Children :— 1. *Dionysius Oliver*, 2. *Robert*, both living near Sherman, Sumpter Co., Ala., 3, *Carr*, dead.

556-6.

MR. BURT, of Edgefield District, S. C., married ELIZABETH GOODE, daughter of No. 196. He died, leaving a young family, and his widow removed with the children, to Franklin Co., Ala. Children :—

1317, BILLUPS BURT, lived and died near Kosciusko, Miss. 1318, FRANK, killed in the massacre by the Mexicans at Goliad. 1319, JAMES, a physician near Tuscumbia, Ala., m. a dau. of Isaac Winston. 1320, JOHN, lived near Kosciusko, Miss. 1321, Daughter, m. *James Payne*, issue, 1. *Philip Payne*, d. y., 2. *James Monroe*, lives Corinth, Miss., 3. *Sarah*, d. y. 1322, SUSAN, m. *William Willis Watkins*, No. 1305.

556–8.

MR. BROOKS, of Edgefield District, S. C., planter, married FRANCIS GOODE, doughter of No. 196, Died leaving a young family. Children : —

> 1323, MILTON BROOKS, moved to Texas at an early day. 1324, SMITH, moved to Texas, and was a member of Shackelford's "Red Rovers." 1325, WHITFIELD, massacred at Goliad. 1326, FRANCES. 1327, EMILY. 1328, ELIZABETH.

THE LUNENBURG GOODES.

557.

MAJOR HAMILTON GOODE, son of Samuel Watkins and *Eliza Hamilton* Goode, No. 197, p. 96, was born in Washington, Georgia, Jan. 1, 1801, died in Atlanta, 1867. Married 1841, Ann Eliza Hickey, daughter of Joshua* and *Molly Bunch* Hickey, who lives in Atlanta, 1886. Children : —

> 1331, EUGENIA HAMILTON GOODE, b. 1843, m. *Major Joseph H. Morgan.* 1332, MACKERNESS, b. 1848, d. 1853. 1833, CALLIE, b. May 13, 1856, m. *M. B. Torbett.*

Mr. Goode was prepared for college by the celebrated teacher Nathan S. S. Beeman, and was graduated at Middlebury College, Vermont, 1822. He was admitted to the bar, but never practiced law, being a man of private resources, but prepared many boys for college. He was a finished scholar, "could read his Bible in five languages, was one of the most lovable and elegant of men, polite and courtly, a second Chesterfield," In Jackson's Indian wars he served as a Major of Alabama volunteers. Aged and an invalid, suffering from paralysis at the time of the shelling of Atlanta by Gen. Sherman, in 1864, he was found in his bed covered with the lath and plaster scattered by the bursting of a shell in his house,—the shock producing paralysis. He was sent out of the city before it was burned but the family records were destroyed.

558.

DR. MACKARNESS GOODE, son of No. 197, was born in Washington, Ga., 1803, and died 1842. Married Martha Tucker, sister of the husband of No. 579. Children : —

> 1334, ELIZA HAMILTON GOODE, m. *Dr. J. R. Price*, of Macon, Ga. 1335, THOMAS SYDENHAM. 1336, MARTHA LYNN, m. *Mr. Jordan*, of Lee Co., Ga., has children.

He was a practicing physician in lower Georgia, especially in Stewart and Muscogee counties, a very devout man, a member of the Methodist Church. He and his wife died suddenly of a malarial epidemic disease.

---

*JOSHUA HICKEY, son of Cornelius Hickey, of Virginia, was one of the pioneers of Tennessee. His wife, Molly Bunch, was sister to Gen. Samuel Bunch, one of the heroes of the battle of New Orleans, in the war of 1812. He fought by Gen. Jackson's side and was the first man to spring over the breastwork of cotton bales.

560.

DR. SAMUEL WATKINS GOODE, of Stewart Co., Ga., son of No. 197, p. 96, was born in Washington, Ga., 1809, died June, 1860, in Stewart Co. Ga. Married 1840, Martha Eliza, daughter of James Kirkpatrick, of Alabama. Children : —

> 1337, ELIZA GOODE, b. 1843, m. *Dr. J. W. Mercer.* 1338, JAMES THOMAS. 1339, SAMUEL WATKINS, b. June, 1847. 1340, LAMIRA, m. *Dr. F. M. Bledsoe.* 1341, MACKERNESS. 1342, LIZZIE HELEN, m. *James H. Guerry.* 1343, EMILY, m. *Eugenius Dozier.* 1344, BEALL WATKINS, m. *Samuel Guerry.*

Dr. Watkins Goode was graduated at the University of Georgia, attended medical lectures in Augusta, New Orleans and New York, and practiced in Montgomery, Ala., and, 1850–1860, in Lumpkin, Stewart Co., Ga. He was a man of exceptionally polished manners, of decided literary taste, and a great student.

He avoided public life but was very active in the support of the schools and churches in the community in which he lived.

561.

REV. DAVID FINLEY, D. D., was born about 1810, near the "Old French Store," Washington, Ga. Married, 1836–40, EMILY WORSHAM GOODE, daughter of No. 197, p. 96, who was born 1811, d. Jan., 1873,—her husband dying in 1858. Children : —

> 1345, JOHN GOODE FINLEY. 1346, DAVID. 1347, THOMAS. 1348, MACKERNESS.

Dr. Finley was a Presbyterian clergyman, and a graduate of the University of Georgia, and was the bosom friend of William L. Yancey, leader of the Secession Party, and of Alexander H. Stephens, afterwards Vice-President of the Confederacy. The latter was a fellow student, Finley studying law, and Stephens theology, but tradition says that they agreed to exchange professions.

Sidney Herbert, writing from Atlanta, May, 1882, gave a very interesting reminiscence of Miss Emily Goode, in connection with the author of "Home Sweet Home," and M. B. Lamar, which I quote here almost at length.

"Payne drifted into Georgia during the troublous times which preceded the removal of the Cherokee Indians. His intimacy with the noted Chief, John Ross, resulted in his arrest. The State and National Governments were in conflict, and white men were prohibited visiting the tribes without permission of the State. Payne had failed to do this, and being a newspaper correspondent and a writer, his actions were considered suspicious. A thorough investigation, however, secured his release after a brief imprisonment.

"During his Southern tour he was a lion in society, and there are not a few old albums in Tennessee, Alabama, Georgia and Louisiana, in which he indited verses to some fair lady whom he met and admired. I have before me a once elaborate album, then the property of a charming young lady of Alabama.

" This album is now in the possession of a son of the lady, a daughter of Judge Samuel W. Goode, of Montgomery.   She married Rev. David Finley, D. D., an eminent Presbyterian divine.

"Miss Goode was a woman of rare loveliness, and had many admirers.   It was not strange, therefore, that when the brilliant author of "Home, Sweet Home," met her and was charmed by her beauty and accomplishments, there should have been equally brilliant rivals to challenge his knightly attentions and contest his advances. So, when he wrote the following flattering verse in Miss Goode's album, there was at hand a knightlier and equally brilliant Georgian match it with a verse as '*good*' if not '*better*' ":

> Lady ! your name, if understood,
> Explains your nature to a letter :
> And may you never change from *Goode*,
> Unless, if possible, to *better*.

Montgomery, Ala., July 21, 1835.   J. H. PAYNE.

" Mirabeau B. Lamar, was a journalist, a poet, and a gifted man. Coming across his verse in Miss Goode's album, penned the following sharp and personal reply :

> I am content with being *Goode*,
> To aim at *better* might be vain ;
> But if I do, 'tis understood,
> Whate'er the cause it is not *Payne*.

MIRABEAU B. LAMAR.

"Lamar knew, better than Payne, how to pay a delicate compliment to a beautiful woman.   He was indeed ' the warrior poet,' and we are told that ' the bravest are the tenderest.'   Surely no braver soldier ever penned a tenderer gem of poetry to a fair lady, than this to Miss Goode, from Lamar :

> The rose I saw upon thy breast,
> I deemed the happiest of its race ;
> In such a world of beauty blest,
> How could it wish a brighter place.
>
> But all its hues departed soon,
> Like fading clouds at closing day ;
> It could not brook superior bloom,
> And sank in envy's pale decay.

"What a different fate awaited these two men, both brilliant, witty, genial and poetic.   Payne, after many sad wanderings and misfortunes and few blessings and joys, died in a far-off land, ' an exile from home,' and desolate even to the last.   Lamar, brave, ambitious, impulsive, responded to the call of Texas, and the name of the heroic General Mirabeau B. Lamar, the President of the ' Lone Star Republic,' shines brightly to-day in the annals of her struggles, her victories, and her grand developments.   He drew his trusty sword for a struggling people and aided them to form a Republic of their own—now a part of our common country—of which he became the honored chief Magistrate. So long as the great State of Texas reveres the name of its gallant soldier-poet, Gen. Mirabeau B. Lamar shall live in history and in song."

564.

HINES HOLT GOODE, son of No. 197, p. 96, was born 1820–1826, graduated at Oglethorpe University, 1846, died 1872. He was a lawyer and a journalist—a brilliant man in his profession, and an accomplished musician. A soldier, member of a Texan cavalry company, C. S. A., in which he served for four years, having moved to Brazoria, Texas, in 1860. In 1867 he returned to Alabama. Married Bettie Hobdy, of Barbour Co., Ala., who lives 1885 at Union Springs, Ala. Children :—

    1349. ADDIE GOODE, b. after 1820. 1350. JAMES. 1351. ———

565.

JOSEPH BRYAN GOODE, son of No. 197, p. 96, lives in Montgomery, Ala., where he is a merchant. Married, 1866, Caledonia Edwards, Children:—

    1352, BRYAN GOODE, b. Dec. 1870. 1353, EDWARDS, b. Sept. 1873. 1354. DOUGLAS, b. Jan. 1375.

He was a member of Semple's Battery of artillery, C. S. A., in which he served until the fall of 1803, when he was recalled to fill a place in the Confederate Treasury. "He was a beautiful penman, and at the request of the Confederate Congress at Montgomery, in 1861; he engrossed upon parchment the original Ordinance of Secession, Constitution and By–laws, for which he received a vote of thanks." (Brewer's *Alabama*, p. 64.)

566.

JAMES M. MONTGOMERY, of Jacksonville, Ala., married 1853, MARTHA DOUGLASS GOODE, daughter of No. 197, p. 96, Children :—

    1355, ELLA STEELE MONTGOMERY, in *W. J. Smith*, St. Louis. 1356, JAMES, d. y.

"Mr. Montgomery," writes a friend, "was a dry-goods merchant of Montgomery, Ala., and at the breaking out of the Confederate war, was in so advanced a stage of consumption that he was not able to do active service, but did all he could in aiding to equip companies, by giving all the blankets, carpets, and all his personal property. He died in the early spring of 1863." Mrs. Montgomery is the owner of "Oakley," the family homestead, though, since 1884, a resident of St, Louis. She has contributed materially to the completion of this volume.

568.

JUDGE HENRY H. CUMMING, of Augusta, Ga., son of Thomas Cumming, a native of Frederick, Md., was born about 1800, and died in 1863. Married, 1824, JULIA ANN BRYAN, daughter of No. 198, p. 97. Children :—

    1357, ANNE MARIA CUMMING, m. *Rev. Charles H. Hall*, dead. 1358, ALFRED, 1359, JULIEN. 1360, THOMAS W., Augusta, Ga., 1885. 1361, EMILY HARFORD, m. *James H. Hammond*. 1362, JOSEPH BRYAN, b. 1836. 1363, HARFORD MONTGOMERY, Ass't. Surgeon

63d Georgia Regt., C. S. A., d. Oct. 17, 1872.   1364, MARIA BRYAN, m. *De Rosset Lamar*, d. July 20, 1873.

"Mrs. Cumming," writes one who knew her, " was a woman of brilliant power, highly educated and most beautiful."

THE CUMMING FAMILY came to Maryland soon after the settlement of the colony, and in the immediate service of Lord Baltimore. Col. William Cumming, U. S. A., of the war of 1812, was uncle to Judge Cumming.

569.

GEN. GOODE BRYAN, of Augusta, Ga., son of Joseph and *Ann Goode* Bryan, No. 198, p. 97, was born in Hancock Co., Ga., Aug. 31, 1811, and died Aug. 10, 1885. Married (1), July 1849, Francis Maria Myers, daughter of Mordecai and *Sarah Henrietta Cohen* Myers of Savannah, Ga., (sister of the wife of Barnet Phillips, of New York, novelist and essayist, long secretary of the American Fish-Cultural Association) born Jan. 28, 1822, died, Sept. 14, 1850.   Married (2), Anna E. Twiggs, of Augusta, Ga., daughter of Maj. Geo L. Twiggs, of Richmond Co., Ga , niece of Gen. D. E. Twiggs, C. S. A , who d. Sept. 13, 1884, and grand-daughter of Gen. John Twiggs, of the Continental Army.   Children :—

> 1365, GEORGE TWIGGS BRYAN, of Spartansburg, S. C.   1366, SARAH TWIGGS, m. *T. C. Walton*, of Shelbyville Texas, child, 1. *Goode Bryan Walton.*   1367, ANNA GOODE, d. Aug. 8, 1885, m. *Alexander H. Stuart*, of Providence, R. I., an actor of fine ability, being the chief support of Madame Janauschek.   1368, REBECA HOLT.

Goode Bryan was appointed a cadet in the U. S. Military Academy at West Point about 1830, graduated in 1834, was commissioned July 1, 1834, as Brevet 2d Lieutenant in the 5th Infantry, and resigned April 30, 1835.   He lived for many years in Tallapoosa, Ala. and in 1843 represented his county in the Alabama legislature.*   He served with distinction in the Mexican war as Major in Coffey's 1st Alabama Volunteers, was at Camargo, Tampico, Vera Cruz and Cerro Gordo, (See Brewer's *Alabama*, p. 588.) He was a member of the Georgia convention which passed the Ordinance of Secession, Jan. 16, 1861 : entered the Confederate service as Lieutenant Colonel in the 16th Georgia Infantry, commanded by Howell Cobb, was appointed Colonel, Feb. 15, 1862, and Brigadier General Aug. 29, 1863, resigning Aug. 29, 1863.   Among other engagements in which he led his command was the Seven Day's Battle before Richmond, July, 1862.   General Magruder in his report says : "Col. Goode Bryan, 16th Georgia, Cobb's Brigade, led his regiment gallantly into the thickest of the fight with the coolness and ability which characterized the well trained soldier."†   Col. Bryan's report of the engagement at Lee's Mill, siege of Yorktown, is in the War Record.‡

---

*Brewer's *Alabama*, p. 548.
†War Record, 1st series, XI, part 2, p. 672.
‡*Ibid.*, 1. XI, 1, p. 419.

572.

JUDGE THADDEUS GOODE HOLT, of Macon, Ga., son of Thaddeus and *Martha Goode* Holt, No. 199, p. 98, was born Sept. 20, 1793, and died May 8, 1873. Married, 1828, Nancy, daughter of John and Martha Flemming. Children:—

1369, HON. THADDEUS GOODE HOLT, Jr., b. Oct. 16, 1836. 1370, ALLEN F., m. *E. J. Monghon.* 1371, ELLEN, m. *D. E. Norris.* 1372, LEROY, d. aet. 23.

Judge Holt was educated at the University of Georgia, at Athens, and became a prominent lawyer. He was Solicitor-General of the southern circuit of Georgia, 1819–22, and Judge of the southern circuit, 1824–28.

Avery's *History of Georgia* mentions "a public meeting held in Macon, 1862, presided over by that noble gentleman, and distinguished ex-Judge Thaddeus G. Holt, to devise means to strengthen the army of the new nation."

573.

COL. PULASKI S. HOLT, of Macon, Ga., son of No. 199, was born, 1798, and lives, 1885, in Macon. Married Miss Grimes of Ga. Children, all dead, 1885, but two grandsons are living:—

1373, DAVIS HOLT. 1374, PULASKI.

Colonel Holt is a lawyer, and has for half a century been a leading citizen of Macon. His name appears in the history of many of the public movements during the war-period in Macon. In 1861, he was one of the committee appointed by the (National) Cotton Planter's Association, to organize a Confederate Cotton Planter's Association.

574.

DR. LEROY HOLT, of Columbus, Ga., son of No. 199, was born about 1802, and died 1861. Married Mary Chandler of Alabama. Children:—

1375, WILLIAM CHANDLER HOLT. 1376, THADDEUS GOODE, who lives, 1885, near Union Springs, Ala. 1377, ELIZABETH, m. *R. T. Butler.* 1378, MARTHA, unm., lives, 1885, in Alabama.

"A successful physician and eminent Christian, prominent in good works, and universally esteemed in Columbus, Ga."

575.

CICERO HOLT, of Athens Ga., son of No. 199, was born 1800, and died 1830. Married 1828, Emily, daughter of Asa and ——*Dougherty* Moore, of Athens. Children:—

1379, CICERO HOLT, M. D., of Athens, Ga., Surgeon, C. S. A., dead. 1380, CAROLINE, m. *Senator B. H. Hill.*

578.

SENATOR ALFRED IVERSON, of Macon, Ga., was born in Burke Co., Ga., Dec. 3, 1799, died in Macon, Mar. 4, 1873. Married, 1822,

CAROLINE HOLT, daughter of Thaddeus and *Martha Goode* Holt, No. 197. Died 1830. Children:—

   1381, ALFRED IVERSON.   1382, JULIA MARIA, m. *Rev. Isham Richardson Branham.*

Judge Iverson was graduated at the College of New Jersey, 1820, was admitted to the bar and soon attained distinction in his profession ; was three years member of the House in the State Legislature, and one year in the Senate. He was judge of the circuit of Ga. for seven years, and one of the electors at large on the presidential ticket, in 1844. He was Member of Congress, 1847–9, and U. S. Senator, 1855–61 : this position he resigned on the passage of the ordinance of secession, in 1861, which measure he ardently advocated. (See Biography by Hon. A. H. Stephens, in *Johnson's Cyclopædia*, p. 1345, in which the erroneous statement is made that he became a Brigadier General, C. S. A., a position which was held by his son of the same name.)

Senator Iverson's connection with the beginning of the late war is a matter of history. As a member of the Military Committee he startled that body by his boldness in seditious speech. · " We intend to go out of the Union." he said. " I speak what I believe, that before the 4th of March, five of the Southern States at least, will have declared their independence. ·   ·   · We intend to go out peaceably if we can ; forcibly if we must. I do not believe there is going to be war. · ·   We shall, in the next twelve months, have a Confederacy of the Southern States, and a government inaugurated and in successful operation, which in my opinion will be a government of the greatest prosperity and power that the world has ever seen. There will be no war in my opinion. · · · The fifteen Slave States, or the five now moving, banded together in one government, and united as they are soon to be, would defy the world in arms, much less the Northern States of this Confederacy. Fighting on our own soil, in defense of our own sacred rights and honor, we could not be conquered even by the combined forces of all the other States ; and sagacious and sensible men in the Northern States would understand that too well to make the effort. · · · I do not believe there will be any war ; but if war is to come, let it come. We will meet the Senator from New Hampshire, and all the myrmidons of Abolitionism and Black Republicanism everywhere upon our own soil, and in the language of a distinguished Senator from Ohio, 'will welcome you to hospitable graves.' " He was followed in the debate by Senators Jefferson Davis and Louis D. Wigfall, whose words were less fiery but not less positive. A few weeks later Mr. Iverson and his colleagues resigned and went South.

THE CHARLOTTE GOODES.

588.

SURGEON THOMAS CLAIBORNE GOODE, C. S. A., son of No. 206, p. 99, was born in Charlotte Co., Va., 1819, and was killed in the battle of the Wilderness, May 5–8, 1864. Married Mary Goode Read. Children :—

1390, ISAAC READ GOODE, b. Oct. 19, 1856. 1391, PANTHEA BURWELL, m. *R. B. Goode*, No. 1430. 1392, MARY BARKSDALE, unm. 1880. 1393, LUCY ARMISTEAD; m. *J. A. Coleman*, Norfolk, Va. 1394, SALLY BUGG, m. *C. A. Glascock*, of Halifax Co., Va. 1395, MATTIE DANIEL, unm. 1880. 1396, LIZZIE STITH, m. *W. D. Norvell*, of Charlotte Co., 1881. 1397, CLEMENT MELANCHTHON. m. Laura Moore, of North Carolina.

Mr. Goode was, at the outbreak of the war, practicing medicine in his native County. He was a surgeon in the Confederate army and was killed in battle. His wife, Mary Goode Read, was named for her aunt, Mary Burwell Goode, wife of No. 96. She was the daughter of Dr. Isaac Read, and his wife, Panthea, daughter of Armistead and *Lucy Crawley* Burwell, of "Woburn," and granddaughter of Col. Lewis and *Ann Spotswood* Burwell, of "Stoneland," whose eldest daughter married Col. Samuel Goode, No. 96. Dr. Isaac Read was son of the Rev. Clement Read, and Miss Edmunds,* and one of thirteen children. The grandfather of Rev. Clement Read was Col. Clement Read, [1707-1763], of "Bushy Forest," Charlotte Co., Governor of the Colony in 1749, who married Mary, daughter of William Hill, an officer in the Royal Navy. Col. Clement Read's daughter, Margaret, [1729-1766], married Judge Paul Carrington, Sr.; his son Col. Isaac Read, father of Rev. Clement Read, already referred to, was a Member of the House of Burgesses and an associate of Washington, Jefferson and Henry in their patriotic labors ; he was made colonel of a Virginia Regiment in the Continental army, and soon after dying, was buried with military honors in Philadelphia. His wife was Miss Embry, daughter of Henry Embry, of Lunenburg Co.

The Rev. Clement Read, his son, was doubtless the patentee of what was known as the Clement Read survey, in the northwestern territory, afterwards Ohio. This fine tract of land granted by Virginia to this descendant of a distinguished Revolutionary officer, was purchased in 1804, by Philip Goode, No. 171, and his brothers, and is still in part owned by descendants of the Goodes.

591-1.

GEORGE M. GOODE, of Virginia, son of William and *Mary Tabb* Goode, No. 207, p. 52, of Mecklenburg, was born about 1800. Son :—

1398, WILLIAM GREEN GOODE.

The name of William Goode of Mecklenburg Co., was omitted in the discussion of the fifteenth generation, but by the aid of our kinsman, Dr. Harriss, one group of his descendants have been restored to their proper place on the family tree. William Goode married Mary Tabb, daughter of Captain Tabb of Gloucester Co. The name Tabb has long been known in Virginia, and the family have intermarried with the Burwells, the Bouldins, the Taliaferros, the Wellfords, and other colonial stocks.

*Miss Edmunds was a descendant of Pocahontas. Thomas Eldridge, according to Mr. Brock, m. Martha Bolling (b. 1721, d. Oct. 23, 1749.) Their eldest son, Thomas, m H. E. Read, and *their* eldest dau., Sarah, m. Col. Thos. Edmunds.

591-2.

ADAM FINCH, of Mecklenburg Co., Va., son of Zachariah and
Mary A. Finch, was born June 23, 1800, died October 4, 1874. Married, Dec. 24, 1824, LUCY SWEPSON GOODE, daughter of William and
Mary Tabb Goode, No. 207, p. 52, who was born about 1800, and
died June 12, 1859. Children :—

> 1400, LANGSTON EASLEY FINCH, b. Oct. 28, 1825, m. dau. of No. 857.
> 1401, RICHARD HENRY, b. Apr. 24, 1827. 1402, WM. EDWARD, b.
> Dec. 21, 1828. 1403, JOHN BACON, b. Oct. 1, 1830. 1404, THOMAS
> ZACHARIAH, b. Aug. 29, 1833, d. yg. 1405, GEO. BEVERLY, b.
> Feb. 27, 1837. 1406, TYREE GOODE, b. Apr. 27, 1840. 1407, ADAM
> THOMAS, d. yg.

591-3.

JOHN P. KEEN, married MARIA GOODE, daughter of No. 207, p.
52. Children :—

> 1408, MARY KEEN, m. *John Pannill.* 1409, SALLIE, m. *Benjamin Morton.*

591-4.

EDWARD GOODE, son of No. 207, p. 52, was born about 1810,
and died unmarried.

591—5.

HENRY STOKES of Lunenburg Co., Va., married ELIZA GOODE,
daughter of No. 207, p. 52. Children live in Lunenburg Co.

591—6.

MR. FARRAR, married MARTHA GOODE, daughter of No. 207, p. 52,
who was born about 1812. Children :—

> 1420, MARY FARRAR, living, 1880, in West Virginia. 1421, ANNIE, living
> in West Virginia. 1422, MARIA, m. *Mr. Bacon,* of Mecklenburg
> Co., Va.

592.

EDWARD PARKS GOODE, son of Hillery and *Sarah Bacon*
Goode, No. 207, p. 99, was born in Charlotte Co., Va., 1807–11. He
was a student in Hampden Sidney College, 1823, and later a cadet,
1826, in Partridge's Military Academy, Middletown, Conn. For
many years he was a merchant in New York City, but returned South at
the outbreak of the war, and died in 1863, in Richmond. Married
Charlotte DeWolf, daughter of Gen. DeWolf, of New York, who in 1881.
was said to live in Patterson, N. J.

593.

MARSHALL L. HARRIS, of Charlotte Co., Va., married, 1824–34,
MARTHA ANN W. GOODE, born 1810-14, daughter of No. 208. Child :—

> 1428, ANN C. HARRIS, m. *William Leigh Watkins.*

594.

HILLERY MACKERNESS LANGSTON GOODE, of Charlotte Co., Va., son of No. 208, was born in Charlotte Co., Va., Oct. 16, 1815. A farmer. He served many terms as a Member of the Virginia House of Delegates. Married SALLY M. BOYD, daughter of Richard and *Lucy Goode* Boyd, No. 857. Children: —

> 1429, WILLIAM GOODE, Brownsville, Texas. 1430, RICHARD BENNET, m. *Panthea Burwell Goode*, No. 1391.

THE WEST CHESTERFIELD GOODES.

600.

COL. ROBERT GOODE, of Goode's Bridge, Chesterfield Co., Va., son of Major William, and *Phebe Bass* Goode, No. 210, p. 99, was born Sept. 21, 1789, died Dec. 31, 1840. Married (1) Jan. 30, 1817, Mary Hatfield, daughter of William and Rachel (Stokes) Loper,* of Barnwell District, S. C., who was born Sept. 1, 1801, and had 3 children. Married (2) Nov. 21, 1833, Martha, daughter of William Childrey, of Henrico Co., b. 1812, and had 3 children: —

> 1475, WILLIAM GOODE, b. 1818, d. y. 1476, LOUISA, b. Feb. 21, 1819, d. Jan. 1856, m. *Joseph R. Wooldridge.* 1477, ELIZA JANE, b. May 17, 1821, m. *Philip T. Southall, M. D.*
>
> 1478, ADELAIDE GOODE, b. Aug. 2, 1835, d. 1863, m. *Thomas Gresham*, who d. 1862, issue, 1. *Harry*, d. y. 1479, ROBERT WILLIAM, b. Aug. 4, 1837. 1480, JOHN CHESTERFIELD, b. Dec. 18, 1839.

Col. Robert Goode lived for many years in South Carolina, where he owned large cotton plantations, mills, gins, etc., but moved, later in life, to Virginia, where he devoted special attention to the rearing of blooded horses. He imported the celebrated stallion " Diomed, "and had a race course on his plantation.

In a MS. narrative of Isaac Jefferson, a former slave of Thomas Jefferson, taken down in Isaac's own words by Charles Campbell, the historian of Virginia, in 1847, it is stated that "Col. Goode, of Chesterfield, was a great racer, who used to visit Mr. Jefferson, at Monticello, and who owned a trainer named Pompey."

Col. Goode was a large man, tall and portly, weighing, it is said, over three hundred pounds.

604.

COL. JOHN B. GOODE, of Chesterfield Co., Va., son of No. 210, was born June 13. 1800, died October 5, 1843. Married Mrs. Harriet M (Bullington) Puryear. Children: —

> 1487, WILLIAM R. GOODE, b. Aug. 6, 1826, d. Mar. 1, 1843. 1488, RE-BECCA, b. July 31, 1848, d. Jan. 23, 1850. 1489, JOHN BULLINGTON,

---

*THE LOPER FAMILY was of Huguenot origin. The name was originally Lepere. The progenitor of the American Lopers is believed to have settled in Barnwell District, S. C.

b. Aug. 24, 1830, d. 1863.   1490, THADDEUS D., b. Dec. 13, 1832, d. 1861, unm.   1491, SAMANTHA O., b. Jan. 14, 1835.   1492, OCTAVIA, b. Nov. 3, 1840, m. *Edward A. Moseley*, of Powhatan Co., farmer.

Col. John B. Goode was a planter and stock-grower. He was devoted to dogs and blooded horses, and to fox-hunting in the old Virginia fashion.

607.

WILLIAM GOODE, of Chesterfield Co., Va., son of John and *Martha Walthall Cheatham* Goode, No. 211, was born April 20, 1797, died Nov, 1870. Married (1) Mary Moore, who died without issue. Married (2) Mary Randolph Porter, daughter of Peter and *Dorothy Randolph Woodson* Porter, of Powhatan Co. Children : —

> 1493, WILLIE GOODE, b. 1853, d. 1874, m. *Clifford Bargamin*, of Staunton, Va. 1494, MARVIN RANDOLPH, b. June 9, 1852 of Richmond, Va.

"William Goode was, in his day, Justice of the Peace, and High Sheriff of Chesterfield Co. A planter and schoolteacher, a most courteous and obliging officer, highly respected by all who knew him. He was portly and tall, six feet in height, and was considered one of the handsomest men in Virginia."

608.

WALTHALL CHEATHAM GOODE, of Mount Hermon, Chesterfield Co.,Va., son of No. 211, was born July, 1789, died June 16, 1870. Married (1) NANCY GOODE, No. 625, who died about 1825, leaving 2 children ; (2) about 1827, Margaret Anna Lewis, of Perth Amboy, N. J. Children : —

> 1495, WILLIAM WALTHALL GOODE, b. Oct. 31, 1821, d. July 3d, 1873. 1496, JOHN ROBERT, b. April, 1823, d. 1828.
>
> 1497, THOMAS BROWN GOODE, b. Oct. 10, 1828, a soldier, C. S. A., killed at Gettysburg, June, 1863. 1498, SAMUEL DORSET, b. Mar. 13, 1831. 1499, MARY SOPHIA, b. Mar. 16, 1834, m. *William H. Dillon.* 1500, HANNAH ARAMINTA, b. May 15, 1825, d. April 14, 1869, m. *James H. Huston.* of Swansonville, Va., farmer, daughter, 1, *Alice Huston*, m. Mr. Barbour. 1501, ANNA LEWIS, b. May 21, 1838. 1502, MARTHA WALTHALL, b. April 13. 1842. d. 1853.

Walthall C. Goode was a planter living in Chesterfield Co., until 1860, and subsequently in Pittsylvania Co. He was a man eminent in good works, and universally beloved, and his neighbors, we are told, considered him "the best man in the world."

609.

JOHN GOODE, of Chesterfield Co.,Va., son of No. 211,was born Oct. 1807, and died prior to 1870. Married about 1835, Lucy Bass. Children : —

> 1503, MARTHA ANN GOODE, d. 1863, m. *John Wm. Simms*, of Chesterfield Co., a soldier, C. S. A., in 6th Va. Inf. 1504, JOHN EDWARD,

soldier, C. S. A., killed at Petersburg. 1505, MARY WILLIAM, m. *Samuel D. Goode*, No. 1498. 1506, WILLIAM WALTHALL. 1507, LUCY J., m. *John W. Simms*, No. 1503. 1508, JAMES C. P. 1509, SEDDON. 1510, IDA, m. *Seddon Bass*, farmer, of Mount Hermon.

612.

WILLIAM MOODY, of Dinwiddie Co., Va., a farmer, married MEECAH PRIDE GOODE, daughter of No. 211, who was born Jan. 2, 1800, died Sept. 2, 1881. Children:—

> 1511, MARY MOODY, m. *William Robinson*. of Dinwiddie Co., Va. 1512, MARTHA, m. *Nelson Stowe*, of Dinwiddie Co., Va. 1513, WILLIAM, d. unm. 1514, SAMUEL, m. Miss Perkinson, of Dinwiddie. 1515, BENJAMIN, m. Miss Perkinson. 1516, REBECCA, m. *Alpheus Andrews*, of Dinwiddie Co., schoolteacher. 1517, LAVINIA, m. *James B. Perkinson*, of Petersburg, Va. 1518, ROBERT, soldier, C. S. A., died from wounds received in service. 1519, HESTER, m. *Zachariah Clark*, of Dinwiddie Co.

This record is to replace that of William Moody, upon page 100.

613.

SAMUEL PLEASANTS GOODE, of Skinquarter, Chesterfield Co., Va., farmer, son of No. 211, was born May 15, 1816, and died 1872. Married (1) Phebe Wilkinson, who died s. p.; (2) Martha Wilkinson, her half-sister. Children:—

> 1521, JOHN FLAVEL GOODE, b. 1860–65. 1522, MARTHA. 1523, CLARA.

615 and 619.

ALEXANDER SIMMS, of Skinquarter, Chesterfield Co., Va., married (1) MARTHA GOODE, No. 615, daughter of No. 212, born Dec. 1809, died young, leaving one child ; (2) SARAH GOODE, No. 619, sister of his first wife, born 1814, d. 1856. Children:—

> 1527, INDIANA GOODE SIMMS, d. y. 1528, FANNIE GOODE. 1529, SARAH LAVINIA, m. *Mathew W. Ford*, of Richmond, a soldier, C. S. A. 1530, INDIANA, d. unm. 1531, WILLIAM E. 1532, OPHELIA, m. CALEB GOODE, No. 663-3. 1533, CORNELIA, m. *Napoleon Crowder* of Powhatan Co. 1535, LUCIUS A., m. MARY HANNAH GOODE, dau. of No 1495. 1535½, EMMETT, d. unm. 1536, CLIFFORD, of Richmond, Va., m. (1) Miss Rudd,(2) Miss Priddy.

Mr. Simms was for many years public auctioneer of Richmond, and for his day and place, a man of wealth. He was also for a long time High Sheriff of Chesterfield County.

This record is to supplement that of Alexander Simms, upon page 100.

617.

WILLIAM HENRY BAGWELL, of Richmond, Va., a merchant, married, June 17, 1835, LAVINIA GOODE, daughter of John and *Martha*

Walthall Cheatham Goode, No. 211, who was born 1818, and died 1865.
Children : —

> 1537, JOHN GOODE BAGWELL, Louisiana, b. Nov. 1, 1838, d. 1876, m.
> Laura Knox, dau. of Judge Pritchard, of Harrisonburg, La., child,
> (daughter,) *Johnnie Bagwell.* 1538, WILLIAM H. H., b. Feb. 9,
> 1841. 1539, MARY LEIGH, m. R. W. GOODE, No. 1618. 1540,
> SARAH LAVINIA, m. *John W. Fisher.*

620.

ROBERT GOODE, of "Clover Hill," Chesterfield Co., Va., son of
No. 212, was born about 1790, and died 1852-3. A farmer. Married
Elizabeth Cheatham. Children : —

> 1541, ANN ELIZABETH GOODE, m. *William P. Cheatham.* 1542: MARIA
> JANE, m. *Mr. Redford of Richmond.* 1543, MARY EMELINE, m.
> *Samuel E. Osborne,* farmer, of Clover Hill, soldier, C. S. A., 8 child-
> ren. 1544, INDIANA, d. unm.

631.

CAPT. PASCHAL HICKMAN, U. S. A., of Franklin Co., Ky., was
son of the Rev. William and *Elizabeth Goode* Hickman. He was born
in Virginia, 1778-80, and when very young went to Kentucky with his
parents. He settled in Franklin Co., and in 1797 was registered at
Frankfort as a property owner. He was murdered by the Indians in
1813.

He served in most of the campaigns against the Indians, in which he was
distinguished for his efficiency and bravery. Collins, in his *Historical
Sketches of Kentucky,* writes: "In 1812 he was commissioned a captain, raised a
volunteer company and joined Colonel John Allen, who commanded the first
regiment of Kentucky rifleman, and served under General W. H. Harrison in
the northern campaigns. Part of the regiment was in the battle of Brownsburg,
Jan. 18, 1813. In the fatal battle of the River Raisin, Col. Allen's regiment
formed the left wing of the American army. Captain Hickman was severely
wounded, and like many kindred Kentucky spirits, was inhumanly tomahawk-
ed in cold blood by the Indians, in a house full of wounded, which was left
without a guard by the British soldiers, and which was burned while many of
them were alive." Hickman County, Kentucky, was named for him, and also
the county seat of Fulton Co., the name of which was changed from Mills
Point, by the Legislature in 1834.

632.

REV. WILLIAM HICKMAN, of Kentucky, was a Baptist preacher,
for many years pastor of South Benton Church He has, doubtless, many
descendants in the State.

633.

LIEUT. DAVID M. HICKMAN, of Kentucky, was an officer in Capt.

Garraud's troop of State Dragoons, in the war of 1812, and was wounded in the service. He probably left descendants.

638.

JOHN GOODE, of Richmond, Va., son of No. 217, was born 1794, died March, 1839, in Richmond. Married Catherine Moncrief Colburn, of Boston, widow of Walter Colburn, granddaughter of William McIntosh, of Boston, who died in 1866. Children : —

> 1600, JOSEPH OSCAR GOODE, b. May 3, 1831.

John Goode was, as a youth, a soldier in the war of 1812. He was a grocer in Richmond.

640.

JOSEPH GOODE, of Richmond, Va., son of No. 217, was born 1799, died Nov. 1851. Married (1) Eleanor Kirkpatrick Warrock, born Oct. 2, 1801, died Dec. 11, 1843, 7 children ; (2) Sept. 12, 1844, Eudora V. Jenks, who survived him and lives in Richmond, Va., 1886. Children : —

> 1602, ELIZABETH W. GOODE, b. May 2, 1824, d. May 21, 1828. 1603, ELEANOR KIRKPATRICK, b. April 11, 1826, d. June 2, 1828. 1604, JOSEPH, b. May 11, 1828, d. Oct. 14, 1828. 1605, JOHN, b. July 19, 1830, d. Nov. 18, 1833. 1606, JAMES EDWIN, b. Oct. 1, 1837, married EMMA GOODE, of Lynchburg. 1606½, ABNER, b. 1839, d. 1842. 1607, MARY VIRGINIA GOODE, m. *A. A. Scott*, druggist of Richmond. 1608, ELIZABETH JENKS, m. *William Gibbs*, of Manchester, Va. 1609, JAMES ELLA, m. *Chesley A. Jones*, of Manchester.

Mr. Goode was a leading and successful grocer in Richmond, and a communicant in the Monumental Church. His first wife was the daughter of John Warrock, referred to in Mordecai's "Richmond in Bygone Days," 1856, as the oldest citizen of Richmond, who was then living, at the age of 83, still handling the composing stick and publishing his almanac which had recorded half as many years as nimself. He died Nov. 7, 1858, aged 84 years. His daughter, Mrs. Goode, was a communicant in the Monumental Church, 1829. Her tomb is in the church yard of the old St. John's church. James E. Goode, No. 1606, has inherited his grandfather's profession, and still publishes the "Warrock Almanac."

641.

RICHARD GOODE, of Powhatan Co., Va., son of No. 217, p. 103, was born in Chesterfield Co., Feb. 23, 1802 ; moved 1849, to Powhatan Co.; died July 1, 1857. A farmer and merchant. Married, May 27, 1825, Mary Ann Paulina Gates, daughter of Alexander Gates, of Chesterfield Co., b. July 4, 1810, d. Oct. 18, 1867. Children : —

> 1611, MARTHA PAGE GOODE, b. Jan. 18, 1827, d. Dec. 5, 1867. 1612, BENJAMIN J., b. Sept. 11, 1829, d. July 5, 1830. 1613, BENJAMIN

ALEXANDER, b. Oct. 6, 1831, d. 1875, married *E. Reynolds.* 1614,
MARY EDWIN, b. April 5, 1833, married *H. W. Griffith.* 1615,
JOHN RICHARD, b. Dec. 25, 1836, married (1) Sarah E. Atkinson,
(2) Nannie Keezee. 1616, ELIZABETH OBEDIENCE b. Dec. 28,
1839, d. July, 1868, married *A. J. Simpson.* 1617, MARTHA PAGE,
b. Jan. 30, 1841, d. Nov. 10, 1841. 1618, RICHARD WATKINS,
Windsor, N. C., b. Oct. 17, 1842, married MARY ALICE BAGWELL,
No. 1416. 1619, EUDORA V., b. Feb. 2, 1845, d. Aug. 5, 1846.
1620, WILLIAM JOSEPH COX, Gilliamsville, Va., b. Sept. 17, 1847,
married Martha J. Johnson. JAMES ALBERT, b. Oct. 1, 1850, farmer in Cumberland, near Gilliamsville, Va., unmarried, 1880.

642.

REV. BENJAMIN E. GOODE, of Chesterfield Co., Va., son of No.
217, p. 103, was born 1804-10, d. 1865. A Baptist preacher. Married Ann Bass, Son :—

> 1622, REV. BENJAMIN E. GOODE, b. 1858, graduated at Hampden Sid-
> ney College, 1872. A Presbyterian preacher said to live, in 1880,
> near Nashville, Tenn.

658.

DANIEL BROWN GOODE, of Mt. Hermon, Chesterfield Co., Va.,
son of No. 219, was born about 1827, died about 1865. Married (1)
Mary Watkins, (2) Margaret Porter. Children :—

> 1681, SARAH A. GOODE, m. JOHN B. GOODE, No. 1489. 1682, DAVID
> MACK, m. JOSEPHINE GOODE, No. 1557. 1683, LEMUEL, d. 1880,
> m. Miss Duvall, of Powhatan Co., one child b. 1865-75. 1684,
> WATKINS, of Mt. Hermon, Chesterfield Co., Va., m. Miss Duvall,
> 1880. 1685, BENJ. GOODE, m. Miss Duvall, no children. 1686,
> ADDIE GOODE, m. *Joseph Worsham* no children.

Daniel Brown Goode, was sheriff of Chesterfield Co., and carried on a farm
near Mt. Hermon.

665.

COL. EDMUND J. GOODE, of Des Moines, Iowa, son of Rev.
Edmund Goode, No. 220, p. 105, was born in Chesterfield Co., Va.,
July 17, 1822. Married Sept. 6, 1854, Sarah D. daughter of Hon.
William A. Stone, of Rose Hill, Miss. Children :—

> 1695, LOWRY W. GOODE, b. April 14, 1857. 1696, FREDERICK D., b.
> Aug. 19, 1861. 1697, CLARENCE R., b. Jan. 31, 1864. 1698,
> FLORENCE ASHBY, b. Jan. 20, 1866, at New Orleans, educated at
> Lake Erie Seminary, Painesville, O. 1699, EDMUND J. Jr., b.
> July 27, 1868, d. Nov. 13, 1880.

Col. Goode was educated at Reedy Spring Academy, Va., read law with
David Edney and Chiswell Dabney, of Lynchburg. In 1847, he removed to

Monticello, Miss., where he entered upon the practice of his profession. In 1865, he removed to New Orleans, and in 1868, he transferred his home to Des Moines, Iowa. He served through the war as Colonel of the 7th Mississippi Infantry, C. S. A.

667 and 671.

REV. JOSEPH G. WOODFIN, of Virginia, a prominent Baptist clergyman, married (1) MARY GOODE, No. 667, (2) ORPHA GOODE, No. 671, (3) PHEBE GOODE, No. 606. Children :—

> 1700, EDMOND G. WOODFIN, soldier, Co. K, 6th Va. Inf., C. S. A. 1701, GEORGE, Soldier, Co. K, 6th Va. Inf., C. S. A. 1702, SAMUEL, killed in battle. 1703, WILLIAM, Soldier, Co. K, 6th Va. Inf., married MARGARET GOODE, No. 1693, (No. 663–4,). 1704, JAMES K., Soldier, Co. K, 6th Va. Inf. 1705, THOMAS. 1706–07, Others.

674½.

CHARLES LOVELACE, of Pleasant Hill, Dallas Co., Alabama, a native of Halifax Co., Va., married HARRIET BUTLER, daughter of No. 222, page 52, who died at Chatham, Va., 1853. Children :—

> 1735, JESSE BUTLER LOVELACE, of Marion, Perry Co., Ala., Soldier, C. S. A. 1736, JAMES ARCHER, of Danville, Va. 1737, CORDELIA ROYALL, m. *James R. Butler*, her cousin, now dead. She lives in Pleasant Hill, Ala. 1738, CHARLES W. 1739, MARGARET, 1740, BETTY.

THE HENRICO GOODES.

694.

JOHN GOODE, of Henrico Co, K., son of Samuel Goode, No. 229, was born, 1770–95. A farmer in the White Oak Swamp. Married Miss Garthwright. Children :—

> 1780, HON. GEORGE W. GOODE, b. 1814, d. Jan. 14, 1860. 1781, MARTHA, m. *Mr. Steen*, a native of England. Their daughter m. Mr. Savage, of Richmond.

John Goode was, in 1827, one of the Jury for trial of the Spanish pirates Caesares, Barbieto and Morando, concerned in the capture of the brig "Crawford," of Providence, R. I. (See *Richmond Standard*, Dec. 28, 1878).

THE WHITBY GOODES.

725.

SETH WARD, of Lynchburg, Va., son of Seth and *Martha Norvell* Ward, No. 233, p. 109, was born July 9, 1798, and died about 1830. Married Miss Hendrick. Children :—

> 1795. EDMUND WARD, b. about 1815. 1796, GEORGIANA, m. *Mr. Nelson*, of Northern Mississippi, an extensive planter on the Mississippi River.

727.

BENJAMIN WARD, of "The Cottage," Campbell Co.,Va., son of No.

223,was born Oct. 5, 1802, died 1840–50. A well-to-do planter. Married, 1829, Betsy White, (Aunt of Rev. A. White Pitzer, D. D., of Washington, D. C.), daughter of Col. Samuel White, of "Fort Lewis," Roanoke Co., Va., and his wife Fannie Penn, granddaughter of William Penn, the founder of the Pennsylvania Colony. Children, all dead but the youngest:—

> 1797, FANNY WARD. 1797⅓, PAULINA JANE. 1767⅔, SETH. 1798, MATILDA. 1798½, ALICE. 1799, JAMES PEGRAM, Soldier, C. S. A. In 1886, engaged in farming near Rome, Ga.

729.

REV. WILLIAM NORVELL WARD, of "Bladensfield," Richmond Co., Va., son of Seth and *Martha Norvell* Ward, No. 233, p. 109, grandson of Seth and *Mary Goode* Ward, was born in Lynchburg, Va., April 19, 1805, died Feb. 25, 1881. Married, August 9, 1836, Mary, daughter of Sampson and *Martha Jones* Blincoe, of Leesburg, Loudoun Co., Va., born Dec. 18, 1815. Children:—

> 1800, MARTHA WARD, b. June 8, 1837, m. *James Carey.* 1801, WILLIAM NORVELL, b. Mar. 3, 1839, d. Aug. 29, 1862. Soldier, C. S. A., killed in battle. 1802, MARY VIRGINIA, b. Dec. 24, 1840, m. *A. D. V. Burr.* 1803, EDMONIA KERR, b. Nov. 6, 1842, d. Dec. 8, 1882, m. *Dr. Pearson Chapman*, of Harford Co., Md. 1804, CHARLES BLINCOE, b. Feb. 14, 1845, d. June 9, 1863. Soldier, C. S. A., killed in battle. 1805, LUCY RANDOLPH. 1806, HENRY TAYLOE. 1807, ESTELLE. d. y. 1808, EVELYN DOUGLAS. 1809, FLORENCE LANDON. 1810, CHANNING MOORE. 1811, RANDOLPH GOODE.

Mr. Ward was appointed to the U. S. Military Academy, at West Point, at the age of twenty, and was a class-mate of Gen. Robert E. Lee, with whom, as well as with Jefferson Davis, who was in the class above him, he kept up a life-long friendship. During his cadetship he was much impressed by the preaching of Mr. Parks, who visited West Point, and in company with Leonidas K. Polk, afterwards Bishop of Louisiana, and Lieutenant-General, C. S. A., he left the Military Academy to enter the ministry of the Protestant Episcopal Church. He was graduated from the Theological Seminary of Virginia, at Alexandria, in 1834, and for nearly half a century lived the quiet self-sacrificing life of a country clergyman. He had invitations to city parishes, and to more influential positions in other states, but his love of country life led him to refuse the former, while his devotion to Virginia, forbade his removal to another state.

He was successively rector of parishes in Clarksburgh, and in Spottsylvania Co., and of Cople, Farnham and Lunenburg parishes in the Northern Neck of Virginia, and, in addition to his regular duties, devoted much time during the last four years of his life, to unremunerated missionary work in the region so greatly impoverished, and so nearly depopulated by war, in the neighborhood of the Wilderness battlefield, often traveling fifty miles in a week to visit churches which had no other provision for pastoral attention.

He owned a plantation, "Bladensfield," near Warsaw, Richmond Co., which was his home for many years before his death.

At the opening of the war, he yielded to the solicitations of Gen. Lee, and other friends, who knew that he had received a military education. He entered the Confederate Army, and was appointed by Gov. Letcher, Major in the 55th Virginia Infantry, in which capacity he served, and as commandant of Fort Lowery, near Tappahannock, until after two years he was forced by feeble health to resign.

After the death of two sons, a brother and many relatives near to him and dear, who were killed in battle, he became very much changed. "He was throughout the remainder of his life," writes a relative, " like one who walked in a dream; his mind was strong and vigorous, when any occasion roused him up, and it was said that one of his most powerful speeches was made in the last Convention before his death. Ordinarily, however, he looked as if he were living in the far away past."

He was a man of courtly manners and scholarly tastes—singularly unambitious and unobtrusive, and was greatly beloved by all who knew him.

Sampson Blincoe (b. 1779, d. 1826), father of Mrs. Ward, was the son of Thomas Blincoe, a native of Wales, (Brecknockshire?) and grandson of Sir Jeffrey Blincoe.

Martha Jones (b. 1782 d. 1824), his mother, was the daughter of William Jones, (b. about 1760), and Sarah Edwards. The latter was descended from the Edwards family of "Northumberland House" in Northumberland County, Va. John Edwards, who in 1653 received a grant of 1050 acres in Lancaster Co., and 300 in Northumberland,* and subsequently others in the same region, was her grandfather or great-grandfather. Her father, Mrs. Ward's grandfather, whose name has been lost sight of through the destruction of records was the heir to "Northumberland House," (long since in ruins), and from him it passed by sale to the Presleys and the Thorntons, when he married the wealthy Miss Smith, his cousin, and removed to Point Lookout, Maryland, where her family had long been established. He owned packets which plied between the Chesapeake Bay and London, and made investments in real estate in New York City, which, it is said, were leased for ninety-nine years and would have reverted, in 1879, to his heirs, but for the loss of their family records. His only son, John Swann Edwards, died unmarried. His nephew, Hon. Ninian Edwards, the first territorial governor of Illinois and U. S. Senator, b. in Northumberland Co. in 1779, was the father of Judge Ninian W. Edwards, whose wife was sister of the wife of President Abraham Lincoln.

The traditions of the Family, regarding their Jones ancestry, would indicate that they are descendants of Frederick, the elder of the two sons of Captain Roger Jones, a Cavalier, who came to Virginia in 1680, with Lord Culpeper, and commanded a sloop which was stationed in Chesapeake Bay for the suppression of piracy, and who, returning to London, died there about 1700.*

*Virginia Land Register, Vol. III, pp. 2, 45, Vol. IV, pp. 178, 194, 299, 489. For this reference and all others to this Register, I am indebted to the unweariable kindness of Mr. Brock.

This Frederick Jones,* who died in North Carolina in 1722, had a daughter Jane, who married Samuel Swann, and their daughter Jane, married her cousin Frederick Jones, and had an only son whose name was changed at the request of a wealthy and childless relative, (uncle, says the Ward tradition) to John Swann.   In some way, through an intermarriage with the Edwards family in all probability, the Swann name and wealth came into the possession of the great-grandparents of Mrs. William N. Ward.   I hope that with the assistance of Mr. L. H. Jones, of Winchester, Ky., who has prepared an elaborate history of the descendants of the descendants of Col. Thomas Jones, the younger son of Captain Roger Jones, this matter may be made somewhat more clear, and a fuller statement printed in the appendix to this book.   William Jones the grandfather of Mrs. Ward, was the grandson of one Jones who lived in North Carolina, married a Miss Orr (so says the Ward tradition), and had three sons who returned to Virginia.   One of these married Mrs. Martha (Gwyther) Burns, half-sister of Elizabeth Waughop, of St. Mary's County, Md.: his eldest son, Philip, died in the first year of the Revolutionary war, his second son, John Swann Jones, married Elizabeth Monroe, (aunt of President James Monroe); his fourth son, Roger Jones, a Tory, died single; his only daughter married Mr. Fields; his fifth son, William, was the grandfather of Mrs. Ward; his sixth, was Ap Catesby Jones; his seventh, has descendants now living in St. Mary's County, Maryland.

The tradition in the Ward family has it that one of their ancestors was the younger son of Robert Catesby, who, after the gunpowder plot, and the death of his father, was captured by emissaries of Packingham, and sent to Virginia, where he married the daughter of a Welsh planter named Jones, and assumed the family name.   Whether this be true or not, the Jones and Catesby families were associated intimately in early days, through the marriage of Col. Thomas Jones, younger son of Capt. Roger Jones already mentioned, to Elizabeth Cocke, niece of Mark Catesby, the English naturalist, who, during his scientific exploration of Virginia and the Carolinas, made his home with her and the other children of his sister, the wife of Dr. William Cocke, colonial secretary.   The name of Catesby in the younger branch of the Jones family is thus accounted for, but it is difficult to see how it crept into the elder branch, except through the influence of the tradition just referred to.

730.

FIELDING WILLIAMS, of Clarkesville, Tennessee, a native of Virginia, married LUCY E. WARD, daughter of No. 233, p. 109, who was born, May 12, 1805, and lives, 1886, in Clarkesville, Tenn. Son:—

1812, WALKER WILLIAMS, Ringgold, Tenn. A Soldier, C. S. A.

---

*THE arms, as described in a memorandum dated 1728, are, *Sable, a fesse, or, between three children's heads proper,* quartered with Hoskins, (Roger Jones's mother being heiress, as follows : *Party per pale azure and gules, a chevron, engrailed, or, between three lions rampant argent.* His wife's arms, those of Walker, of Mansfield, Nottinghamshire, were, *Argent, three annulets, between nine cinquefoils sable.*

The Jones crest was, *A child's head proper.*

These details are inserted for the purpose of calling attention to the fact that Mr. L. H. Jones, of Winchester, Ky., and Mr. Frank Binford, of Owensboro, Ky, are anxious to correspond with any one in England who is interested in either of the families concerned.

731.

MAJOR GEORGE EDWARD WARD, C. S. A., of Lamar, Barton Co., Missouri, son of No. 233, p. 109, was born in Lynchburg, Va., April 2, 1811, and died at Dover, Ark., Oct. 2, 1862, from the effect of wounds received at battle of Pea Ridge. Married at Harrodsburg, Ky., Dec. 10, 1833, Charity Green, who lives 1886, in Lamar, "a hearty, beautiful old lady of seventy-five years." Children:—

> 1813, JOSEPHINE WARD, b. Sept. 8, 1836, d. Dec. 29, 1860, m. *Judge J. C. Parry.* 1814, EDWARD GREENE, b. Feb. 28, 1839. 1815, THEO-DOSIA, b. Aug. 29, 1841, d. Aug. 8, 1873, m. (1) *Dr. Albert Smith,* soldier, C. S. A., killed in battle ; (2) *Hon. E. M. Hulett.* 1816, JAMES T., b. June 5, 1844. 1817, MARY, b, Nov. 8, 1846, m. *Robert J. Tucker.*

Major Ward, went from Virginia, to Kentucky, when a young man, and at the age of forty-one removed to Missouri, settling in what was then Jasper County,— a vast and beautiful prairie region with but few inhabitants. He was the founder of the town of Lamar, which he named for his dear friend Mirabeau B. Lamar, president of the Texas republic, and also of Barton County, named for David Barton.

He was a large and strikingly handsome man, six feet and one-quarter in height, with dark hair and rosy cheeks.

At the opening of the war, he with his sons, and his sons-in-law, joined with Shelby and Price, in their military operations. Their exploits are frequently referred by John N. Edwards, in his thrilling narrative of the war in the Southwest, entitled "Shelby and his men," and I am indebted to Major Edwards, now editor of the St. Joseph "Democrat," for placing me in communication with the surviving members of the family.

"The brave and devoted Major Ward, of Lamar, received his death wound," says Edwards, speaking of Pea Ridge, "and his gallant young son, James, although shot in the ankle, at Cassville, on the retreat, yet went again into the fight with his father and was wounded severely, the second time in the leg. Another son of the noble old veteran was struck down by his side with a painful wound, and the father and his two boy heroes were torn from the field, the one to die and the others to strike, afterwards, hard and heavy blows for the Confederacy.*

"They were from Barton Co., Mo., and their mother and sister suffered long and weary wants of shameful imprisonment in St. Louis, at the hands of men who had no heart to spare the helpless. The heroism of Missouri women, during the war, is a book of itself that abler hands than these will write.

"A beautiful and accomplished sister of the young soldiers, (James and Edward Ward,) Mrs. Theodosia Smith, was a heroine beyond comparison. Elegant, fascinating and diplomatic as Talleyrand, she made a dozen visits through the lines, braved many dangers with remarkable coolness, avoided

---

*Shelby, and His Men; or the War in the West. By John N. Edwards.

numerous grave dangers with great skill, and never failed once in the accomplishment of her mission, and in offering the most complete and valuable information.," (p. 411.)

Speaking of the campaigns around St. Louis, Edwards remarks, (p. 409.):

"There was scarcely a day of the time that Shelby's division operated, that he did not have his soldiers about the very headquarters of the Federals in St. Louis, and in the warriors camps and forts along the line he was watching. The adroit answer, the self-possession, the coolness and nerve necessary to a man who ventures into places where he may be certain that recognization would be death, and discovery might stare him in the face at any moment, require that address which few men possess and in which no soldier ever excelled those of Shelby's command. The hair breadth escapes and cunning exploits of such men as Brown Williams, Arthur McCoy, Newton, Hockinsmith, (finally taken in Clayton, post at Pine Bluff, Arkansas.,) · · · Sid. Martin, EDWARD WARD, or any one of a dozen I might name who were usually detailed for there meanness would fill a larger volume than this with truths that might appear stranger than fiction.

" Before leaving Pocahontas, General Price, had asked for a spy to go into St. Louis, and Shelby gave him private JAMES WARD, a brave and intellegent soldier of the advance under the wounded Thorp, and the daring Williams, and who was afterwards a Captain in the Old Brigade, in Slayback's Regiment, (and aid to Gen. Slayback, at the battle of West Point,) General Price, gave him his instructions minutely. He was to visit Gen. Rosecrans' headquarters in St. Louis, learn everything relating to troops and military movements possible, ascertain the sentiment and dispositions of the people toward a general uprising, and report at some point on the Missouri River. Ward started and gained Helena in safety. Leaving his arms and horse near the town, he entered that post afoot. He was quite young, almost a boy in fact, and was readily permitted to take passage on a steamboat as a fugitive from the conscript law. He went in this way as a cabin passenger, the ' higher civilization' folks from the North only discovering in him a specimen of the green Arkansas 'swamp-rat.' At St. Louis he reported directly to General Rosecrans, had several personal interviews with him, and from him and those around him got the very information he was sent to seek. He then asked permission to go to Iowa to attend school. This he was permitted to do. Taking the cars on the North Missouri Railroad he reached Chillicothe. From there he made his way to a camp of recruits, and with them rejoined the main force and reported to General Price at Waverly, having accomplished his hazardous undertaking exactly to the day and to the utmost satisfaction of his officers. This may seem a very simple thing, now, but in those days it was no child's play and the penalty of detection, especially if the papers he had on his person were found, would have been certain death. The military budget brought by young Ward was important, and known only to Gen. Price. This James Ward otherwise greatly distinguished himself, especially at the battle of Westport and in the defense of the arsenal at Tyler." (See Shelby and his men, p. 432).

"Edward Ward" says Edwards, "was another member of the advance who allowed no one to 'out-soldier 'him' as it was expressed in camp-phrase. Like his brother, James, he was frequently employed in secret missions within the enemy's lines." He was seriously wounded at New Iberia, early in the war ; was Lieutenant in McCoy's regiment and Captain in that commanded by Col. D. A. Williams. He was a young, beardless fellow, brave, and high spirited. See Appendix for additional notes.

732.

MATHEW M. KERR, of Clarksville, Tenn., a native of Scotland, married NANCY EDMONIA WARD, daughter of No. 233, p. 109, who was born June 24, 1813. Children :—

> 1816, WILLIAM KERR, of Henderson, Ky., d. 1876, m. ———, daughter, 1, *Mary Ward Kerr*. 1817, GEORGE MORRIS, accidentally shot on a hunting expedition, while in college at Lexington. 1818, LILY, m. *Michael Clarke*, of Clarksville, Tenn. 1818½, GRACE MORRIS. 1819, MARTHA, m. ——— *Anderson*, of Memphis, Tenn. 1820, VIRGINIA, m. *J. Louis Smith*, of Urbanna, Va., an extensive planter : no children. 1821, LUCY, a resident of Baltimore.

Mr. Kerr removed from Lynchburg to Tennessee about 1840. He was a wealthy planter and tobacco-farmer.

734.

SAMUEL GOODE WARD, of Texas, son of No. 234, was born Aug. 27, 1818. He was one of the companions of Houston in the struggle for the independence of Texas, in 1835–6, and probably participated in the later war between Mexico and the United States. He was an exceedingly handsome man ; six feet and a quarter in height, and well proportioned.

736.

STITH MAYNARD, of Richmond, Va., son of John and *Judith Stith* Maynard, was born in Halifax Co., Va., 1775–90, and died in Richmond, 1848. Married about 1810, LUCY E. A. HYLTON, daughter of Daniel L. and *Mary Ward* Hylton, No. 234, p. 110. Children :—

> 1822, LA FAYETTE MAYNARD, b. Feb., 1819, d. Dec. 29, 1876. 1823, ROBERT CLARK, d. 1844. 1824, GEORGE FLETCHER, b. 1829, d. May 10, 1879. 1825, MARY, m. *Gen. William Fisher*. 1826, LUCY ANN, m. *Henry Fisher*. 1827, HARRIET HYLTON, m. *Robert Mills*. 1828, HYLTON, d. s. p. 1833. 1829, JOHN CRINGAN.

Stith Maynard was a merchant in Lynchburg and Richmond, a man of noble character and excellent abilities.

EXCURSUS.—THE MAYNARD FAMILY.

TRADITIONS have it that the Virginia Maynards were of the lineage of Sir John Maynard, of England, Keeper of the Great Seal, &c.

The first of the name in Virginia is believed to have been LIEUTENANT GEORGE MAYNARD, famous in early Virginia history as the captor of "Blackbeard," the pirate.

"Governor Spotswood," writes Cooke, "was notified that the famous pirate, John Theach,* nicknamed 'Blackbeard,' was cruising in the waters of Virginia and the Carolinas, and he promptly sent two ships to attack and capture him. They found him in Pimlico Bay, (Nov. 21, 1718) and Lieut. Maynard, commanding the Virginians, boarded the pirate and a hand-to-hand fight followed. 'Blackbeard,' who is drawn in old pictures with a belt studded with pistols, made a hard fight. He was shot and fell dead when the crew surrendered; and the Virginians returned with the ghastly head of the buccaneer stuck on the bowsprit. Blackbeard's skull, fashioned into a drinking cup and rimmed with silver, is still preserved in Virginia." Benjamin Franklin, then an apprentice in a printing office, composed a ballad on the death of Theach, which was sung through the streets of Boston.

JOHN MAYNARD, presumably his grandson, a planter in Halifax Co., Va., b. 1740-60, d. 1814-16, m. *Judith Stith*, and had children :

1, STITH MAYNARD, (see Goode Genealogy, No. 736) 2, RICHARD. 3, EVAN·

4, FLEMING, emigrated from Halifax Co. to Vicksburg, Miss., 1830, m. *Christiana Carr*, and d. at Vicksburg, 1843. Children, 1, LUCINDA CARR, living , 1883, m. Mr. Pope, of De Soto Co., Miss., by whom (1) *Fleming E.*, M. D., of Honey Grove, Texas, living 1883 ; (2) *Caledonia*, m. Mr. James of De Soto Co., Miss. 2, EMELINE, d. 1869, m. *W. Horace Keyser*, of Boston, by whom, (1) *Osborne*, d. y., (2) *Alonzo*, d. 1878, m. Anna Beale, by whom, *Kate*, of Lexington, Miss.: m. (2) *Richard Munford Winn*, of Yazoo City, Miss, by whom, (a) *Richard*, (b) *Christiana*, m. H. T. Anderson, of Yazoo City, both living and having issue, two, d. y., and *Maggie Meacham*, (c) *James*, (d) *Luella W.*, living m. —— *Lewis*, of Yazoo City, by whom, *Robert Winn*, *Raymond Winn*, and *Lilian Maynard;* Emeline m. (3) *Osamus Winn*, by whom no issue.

5, PAMELIA, b. and d. at Randolph, Tipton Co., Tenn., m. *John Royall*, now deceased, by whom, 1, *Tecumseh*, who m. and had issue, *Robert*, of Nashville, Tenn., 2. *Lou.*, who m. *Joseph P. Royall*, her cousin, of Vicksburg, Miss., by whom *Imogen*, and two others.

6, JOHN, of Tazewell Co., N. C., 1820, where he married and died, leaving issue.

EXCURSUS.—THE STITH FAMILY.

THE STITHS were early seated in Virginia, and, although there are now but few bearing this surname, the prevalence of Stith as a Christian name indicates that the descendants in collateral lines are numerous.

---

*" BLACKBEARD'S NAME is variously rendered in the *Calendar of State Papers of Virginia*, and in the *Spotswood Letters*, Teach, Theach, Thatch, Thach and Tache. May not the name have been Tache'? I have heard the tradition that Blackbeard was engaged in the slave trade and largely supplied the planters of Virginia and North Carolina with slaves smuggled in without the payment of duty. This, perhaps, may explain the charge made by Gov. Spotswood, that Teach was protected in his lawless deeds by Gov. Charles Eden, of North Carolina.   R. A. BROCK.

See Paxton's *Marshall Family* (pp. 15-16) for curious legend concerning the relationship of Blackbeard to the Markham family and to Elizabeth Markham, grandmother of Chief Justice Marshall.

Col. John Stith, of Charles City Co., the first of the name in Virginia,was granted 500 acres of land in 1663. He revolted with Bacon in 1676, and was High Sheriff of his county in 1691. He had issue:

1, William Stith, of Charles City Co., who, in 1688, married Mary, daughter of William Randolph, of "Turkey Island." (see above page 115) Children : 1. Rev. William Stith, b. 1689, d. 1755, President of William and Mary College, and Historian of Virginia, who m. Judith Randolph, daughter of Thomas Randolph, of "Tuckahoe," and had, i. Elizabeth, ii. Judith. iii. Polly Stith, of Williamsburg, who d. s. p. 2. Capt. John Stith, of Charles City Co., who married Mary, daughter of Tarlton Fleming,* of "Rock Castle," and his wife, Mary Page, of "Rosewell," and had issue, i. *Judith Stith*, m. John Maynard, of Halifax Co., (see previous excursus, and Goode Genealogy. No. 735). 3. Mary Stith, who married *Rev. William Dawson*, of William and Mary. College, Commissary to the Bishop of London, &c., and had issue, i. A son, who m. Miss Johnson, of North Carolina, and had son *Hon. William Johnson Dawson, M. C.*, ii. *William*, member of the first House of Representatives in Virginia.

2, Drury Stith, who married Susannah, daughter of Launcelot Bathurst, who came to Virginia about 1670, and granddaughter of Sir Edward Bathurst of Lechdale, England, issue: 1. Drury Stith, of Brunswick Co. who m. Eliz. Buckner ; children 1. Griffin Stith of Northumberland Co., m. Mary Blakey 1743, and had a, *Catherine*, b, *Eliz. Buckner*, c, *John Buckner*, d, *Mary Blakey*, e, *Griffin*, f, *Drury*, g, *William*, h, *Susannah*, m. Christopher Johnson, i, *Lucy*, m. Mark M. Pringle, k, *Janet*. 2. Buckner Stith, of "Rocksbury," and others.

3, Anne Stith,who married, 1681, Robert Bolling, of "Kippax," or "Farmingdale," whose first wife was Jane Rolfe, granddaughter of Pocahontas. The descendants of the Bolling–Stith marriage are numerous. The first generation was as follows: 1, Robert Bolling, of Bollingbrook, b. 1682, d. 1749, m. 1706, Anne Cocke, and had nine children : one of his grandsons, Jack Bolling, m. Jinny Goode, (see Goode Genealogy, No. 65); 2, Stith Bolling, b. 1686 ; 3, Edward Bolling, b. 1687; 4, Anne Bolling, b. 1690, m. *Mr. Wynne* ; 5, Drury Bolling, of "Kippax," b. 1695, his only child, Frances, b. 1724, d, 1774, m. Theodrick Bland, and was granddaughter to John Randolph of "Roanoke," and the Tuckers, (see Goode Genealogy, pp. 55 and 114); 6, Thomas, b. 1697 ; 7, Agnes, 1700, m. *Capt. Richard Kennon*, (for descendants, see *Bristol Parish*, p. 182).

A record of the descendants of Robert Bolling, of Bollingbrook (3-1) is given

---

*The Flemings. The founder of the historic Fleming family of Scotland, is said to have come thither from Flanders, in the reign of David I, but the first of the name from whom descent can be traced was Sir David Fleming, who was made Sheriff of Dunbarton by Alexander III. Twelfth in descent from Sir David Fleming was Sir Thomas Fleming, second son of John 6th Lord Fleming, who was created Earl of Wigton by James I, in 1606. Sir Thomas Fleming married a Miss Tarleton, of an ancient English family (of which was also the truculent British Colonel Banastre Tarleton, of the American Revolution), and emigrated to Virginia about 1616, settling first at Jamestown and subsequently in New Kent. He had issue, three sons : 1, Tarleton, of "Rock Castle," who married a Miss Bates, of Williamsburg, from which family the Hon. Edward Bates, of Missouri was deduced ; 2. John ; 3. Charles. The Tarleton Fleming of the text, whose daughter Mary was the wife of Captain John Stith, was presumably the third son of Tarleton and ——(Bates) Fleming. The Flemings have intermarried with many of the most prominent families of Virginia. See article in Richmond *Standard*.   R. A. Brock.

in Slaughter's *Bristol Parish*, pp. 140–47. A full record of the descendants of the Bolling–Stith connection is much to be desired.

The arms of the Stith family are : *Argent, a chevron between three fleurs de lis, sable.*

738.

HENRY RANDOLPH, of "Warwick," Chesterfield Co., Va., son of No. 235, p. 111, was born at Warwick, about 1784, died Oct. 26, 1840, in Hanover Co.,Va. Married (1) Caroline Matilda Smith, dau. of Major Smith of Manchester, who died Sept. 25, 1808, no issue; (2) Eliza Griffin Norman, of a Henrico family, belonging to the Society of Friends, born 1785, died Oct. 7, 1825, 7 children. (3) Mrs. Perry, descendant of Thomas Tinsley,* planter, a native of Yorkshire England, Children : —

> 1830, HENRY SETH WARD RANDOLPH, b. July 15, 1810, d. July 26, 1874.
> 1831, BENJAMIN, d. y. 1832, JOSEPH WILLIAMSON, b. Aug. 19, 1815.
> 1833, WILLIAM. d. y. 1834, ELIZABETH ANNA, b. Feb. 21 1819, d.
> Nov. 2, 1885, m. *Rich. Channing Hall.* 1835, LUCY WARD, b. Feb. 14,
> 1821, d. in Henderson, Ky., Oct. 27, 1853, m. *Robert Saunders,*
> son, *James Randolph Saunders.* 1836, MARY GOODE, b. Nov.
> 13, 1823, m. *Wm. H. Hammond.* 1837, ANNA GRANTLAND, d. y.
> 1838, WILLIAM TINSLEY RANDOLPH.

Henry Randolph served in the war of 1812, as a subaltern in the Chesterfield Troop of Cavalry, and was with his troop through their dismal campaign about Norfolk, when half of its members died from exposure and camp fever. He was a tall, well-built, active man, always on horseback, who never was known to go through a gate, but always went over it. There are stories of his riding up the steps and through the broad hall of his country house. He was the owner of the celebrated " Broad Rock race-course " three miles from Richmond, in Chesterfield Co., and was passionately devoted to horse-flesh, whereby his ample paternal fortune was seriously impaired.

739.

GEORGE WASHINGTON THORNTON, of " Rumford," Stafford Co., Va., son of Maj. George and *Mary Alexander* Thornton, grandson of Col. William and ——— *Washington* Thornton, was born 1760–75, and died about 1815. Married, September 21, 1805, MARY RANDOLPH, daughter of Henry and *Lucy Ward* Randolph, No 235, p. 111, granddaughter of Seth and *Polly Goode* Ward, who was born at

---

*THE TINSLEY FAMILY. Thomas Tinsley, the ancestor of the prominent Tinsley family of Virginia, emigrated from Yorkshire in the latter part of the seventeenth century, and settled in Hanover Co., Va. He was an extensive planter ; shipped tobacco to England, and imported thence domestic luxuries and clothing. His will bears date Oct. 9, 1700. He mentions wife Elizabeth, and children, Thomas, John, Cornelius, Alice, Sicily and Anne. R. A. BROCK.
The Tinsleys frequently intermarried with the Goodes as will appear from the index.

"Warwick," May 25, 1785, died in Pensacola, Fla., Oct. 15, 1865.
Children:—

1839, HENRY RANDOLPH THORNTON, b. Feb. 23, 1807, d. Nov. 21, 1862.
1840, LUCY WARD, b. Mar. 21, 1811, d. July, 1840, m. *Richard Adams.* 1841, MARY GOODE, b. 1813, m. (1) *Lieut. Alex. C. Maury, U. S. N.,* (2) *Rev. J. Jackson Scott,* S. T. D., LL. D. 1842, SETH BRETT, b. May 25, 1815, killed in front of the city of Mexico, June 1847; Captain, 2d Dragoons, U. S. A.

George W. Thornton was second-cousin to General Washington. He was a wealthy planter in Stafford Co., and lived and died, at an early age, at "Rumford," a fine estate in Stafford Co., situated on the bank of the Rappahannock below Fredericksburg, which he inherited from his father and grandfather.

His mother, Mary Alexander, b. Nov. 26, 1756, was daughter of John and ·*Lucy Thornton* Alexander, granddaughter of Philip and *Lucy Hooe* Alexander, great-granddaughter of Philip and *Sarah Ashton* Alexander, great-great-granddaughter of John Alexander, (son of William Alexander, of Menstrie, Scotland, first Earl of Stirling), who came to Stafford Co., Va., in 1659, [see valuable papers by Alexander Brown and R. A. Brock, in *Richmond Standard*, Vol. III, Nos. 2, 6, 7, 36, 37, 44, 51; Vol. I, No. 39; Vol. II, Nos. 47, 49.] After her husband's death she married Gen. Thomas Posey, and removed to Kentucky. The following curious document tells the story of the death of Maj. Thornton, the father of the subject of this sketch:

CERTIFICATE OF MRS. MARY POSEY, relative to the death of Major George Thornton, late of the Virginia line of Continental Troops, and the supposed right of his heirs to pay from the Government of the United States.

State of Kentucky, Henderson County, Jan'y 30th, 1834.

I DO HEREBY CERTIFY that I was born, 26th day of Nov. in the year A. D. 1756, in Stafford County, Virginia, that my maiden name was Mary Alexander, that I was married to George Thornton on the 9th day of October, 1773, by the Rev. Wm. Stewart in Stafford County, St. Paul's Parish, Virginia, that my husband George Thornton was first a Militia Officer in the year ———: as such he was at the bombardment of Marlboro, the seat of Judge Mercer, on the Potomac, that again, being in the Legislature of Virginia, he was sent out against Lord Dunmore, that he returned home, and shortly afterwards, on the —— day of —— in the year ———, was commissioned a Major in the Virginia line on Continental Establishment, in the Revolutionary war that with this rank he fought under Gen'l Woodford at the battle of Governor's Island, mouth of the Piankatank, in the Chesapeake Bay; that afterwards he was marching with a detachment of his Regiment, when after a very hard day's march, he imprudently took a very large draught of very cold water, which was supposed to be the cause of his death, which occurred on the 30th day of April in the year 1781, on his way to Williamsburg.

That by my husband, Major George Thornton, I had two sons George W., and Reuben, and a daughter, Lucy Frances, that George W. and Reuben, though now dead, left children; that Lucy F., who is still living, married with

Capt. John Posey, by whom she has six children living ; that they are the only heirs of the late Major George Thornton.   That from laws of Congress, and the usage of the United States Government, I believe the above heirs are entitled to $—— from the Government.   That I nor they never received any part thereof in any way whatever.   I think it nothing but justice that they, the said heirs, should be paid.   That as afterwards, on the —— day of——, A. D. ——, I married Gen'l Thomas Posey, which act, although it may deprive me of any part or share of the sum due from the Government, I believe my children by my late husband, Maj. George Thornton, are justly entitled to it : and further believe the Government of the United States ought and will pay them."

EXCURSUS.—THE THORNTON FAMILY.

No adequate history of the Thornton family is, so far as I can learn, in existence, and this is much to be regrett.d since its members have been among the prominent citizens of Virginia.   The first of the name appears to have been Francis (?) Thornton, a native of Yorkshire, who came to Virginia at an early day and took up large tracts of land in the vicinity of the present location of Fredericksburg, and lived in the neighborhood of the "Falls Plantation."* Howison, in his *Fredericksburg, Past, Present and Future*, speaks of him at some length, [p. 28].   There are traditions of his valorous encounters with the Rappahannock Indians.   Howison relátes a curious story of a battle which he had with a large sturgeon, in which the sturdy Yorkshireman conquered by embracing the fish and carrying it by main strength out of its native element.   The original Thornton had apparently several sons, as follows :

I.   COL. FRANCIS THORNTON, of " Fall Hill," b. 1670-1700, m. Frances, dau. of Roger and *Mildred Washington* Gregory.   Issue :—

   1.   FRANCIS THORNTON, of " Fall Hill," m. 1759, Anne Thompson, b. 1744, and had,'1. *Mildred Washington*,† b. Dec. 20, 1761, m. *Col. Abraham Maury*, [see Goode Genealogy, below, No. 739-A.] 2. *Francis*, of " Fall Hill," b. 1760-70, m. Sally Innes, b. 1777, and had, i. Elizabeth Thornton, of Fredericksburg, b. 1792, m. John H. Fitzgerald,‡ ii. Rev. Frank, m. Jane Thornton, iii. Sally, m. Murray Forbes, of ·"Falmouth,"§ iv. Judge Henry Innes, b. 1797, d. 1867, a leading lawyer in Alabama and California, m. Lucy, sister of Gov. John J. Crittenden, son, Maj. Harry I. Thornton, 58th Ala. Inf., C. S. A.,‖ v. James Innes, b. 1801, planter, of Green Co., Ala., m. (1) Miss Glover, (2) Miss Smith, dau. m. John M. Gould,¶ vi. Robert Callaway, d. s. p., vii. Catherine, b. 1800,

---

*THE EARLIEST GRANTS I find of record to the name Thornton, in the *Virginia Land Register*, is to Wm. Thornton, 164 acres in Gloucester Co., Feb. 16, 1665-6, Book 5, p. 573.   William Thornton, jr., doubtless a son of the preceding, was granted 110 acres in Petsoe parish, Gloucester Co., April 26, 1704, Book 9, p. 589.   Anthony Thornton, of Stafford Co., and Francis Conway, 5,000 acres in St. Stephens parish, Spotsylvania Co., June 26, 1732, Book 74, p. 450, was a resident of Caroline Co.   R. A. BROCK.

†MILDRED, dau. of John or Francis Thornton, is said to have been the second of the four wives of Col. Samuel Washington, brother of the President, and to have had two sons,—Thornton, of Jefferson Co.,Va. b. about 1760, and Tristam, b. 1763.

‡Foote's *Sketches of Virginia*, II, p. 589.

§Slaughter's *St. Marks Parish*, p. 175.

‖Brewer's *Alabama*, p. 261.

¶Brewer's *Alabama*, p. 263.

d. 1826, m. 1822, Thomas Marshall, of "Happy Creek,"* near Winchester, the whole family dying from an epidemic within 20 hours, viii. Butler Brayne, d. s. p.†

2. MILDRED, m. *Col. Charles Washington*, brother of General Washington, the founder of Charlestown, W. Va. Children, 1. *Col. Augustus Washington*, b. 1763, m. Frances, dau. of Burwell Bassett, 2. *Capt. Samuel*, b. 1765, of Kanawha, W. Va., 3. *Frances*. b. 1872, m. *Col. Burgess Ball*, 4. *Mildred*, b. 1777, m. *Col. Thomas Hammond*.

3. ELIZABETH, m. (1), as 2d wife, *Dr. Thomas Walker*, (2) *Mr. Alcock*, of "Eldon," Albemarle Co., a British officer, who was a prisoner of war at Charlottesville, in the Revolution.

II. COL. JOHN THORNTON, married, 1700-20, Mildred Gregory, sister of his brother's wife. Issue :—

1. MILDRED THORNTON, who m. (1), 1738, *Nicholas Meriwether*, and had, 1. *Mildred Meriwether*, b. May 19, 1739, m. Col. William Syme ;‡ m. (2), 1741, Dr. Thomas Walker, of Castle Hill, and had 15 children. Their descendants are prominent in Virginia history and a full account of them is given by Dr. Slaughter, in his *Memoir of Joshua Fry*, p. 63, and by Dr. R. C. M. Page, in his *Page Family in Virginia*.

2. MARY, m. *Gen. William Woodford*, issue, i. *John Thornton Woodford*, of Kentucky, b. 1763, d. 1845, m. Lucy T. Taliaferro, ii, *William Catesby*, of White Hall, Caroline Co., b. 1768, d. 1820.§

III. REUBEN THORNTON, married Elizabeth Gregory. There is no record of his descendants, but to him, or to a brother, perhaps named George, belongs:–

1. CAPT. REUBEN THORNTON, who m. about 1810, Anna M. Washington, of Greenwood, b. 1788, dau. of Col. Samuel Washington, Issue, i, *Churchill Jones Thornton*, b. about 1812, ii, *Charles Augustus*, of Enfield, N. C.

IV. COL. WILLIAM THORNTON, of "Rumford," Stafford Co., married Miss Washington,‖ and had issue :—

1. DR. PHILIP· THORNTON. 2. GEORGE THORNTON, b. about 1750, [see Goode Genealogy, pages immediately preceeding.] 3. JOHN. 4. HOWARD. 5. STUART.

Lucy Thornton, who m., 1776, John Alexander, was perhaps a sister of Col. William Thornton.¶

V. COL. PRESLEY THORNTON,° of "Northumberland House," whose mother

---

*Paxton's *Marshall Family*, p. 138.

†*The Innes Family*, by Alexander Brown, Richmond *Standard*, III, 21.

‡A. B., in Richmond *Standard*, II, 40, says that this daughter was named *Sarah*, and that she married Col. *John* Syme, and gives the name of her children.

§For grandchildren, see note by L. H. Jones, in Richmond *Standard*, III, 22.

‖Wells, p. 173, says that Jane Washington, dau. of Augustine, m. Col. William Thornton, but since she was born about 1752, she cannot well have been this one.

¶Richmond *Standard*, III, 5.

°A legal advertisement in the Richmond *Enquirer* of March 27, 1812, gives the following as heirs of Col. Presley Thornton : His widow, Charlotte, of Great Britain ; Winifred Thornton, m. John Cocke ; Alice Thornton, m. —— Edmunds : Elizabeth Thornton, m. Wm. Fitzhugh ; Kitty Thornton, m. Joshua Tennison ; Jane Thornton, Lucy and Peter, Henry Ward Landon and Eliz'h Carter, his wife ; John Gordon and chil., Wm., Anne, Mary and Eliz'h ; James Moore and Sarah, his wife ; Dan'l, Thos. R., Anne and Mary Delancy ; William Lewis and Margaret, his wife ; Sharp D. Baldwin ; heirs of Sharp Delancy, of Philadelphia, dec'd ; Thos. Robinson, Josiah Lewis, John Tayloe, adm'r. of John Tayloe, dec'd ; Francis Thornton, William Hilson and Susan, his wife ; Presley Thornton, Virginia S. Thornton. William Presley was a burgess from Northumberland Co., 1663-6.   R. A. BROCK.

was doubtless a Presley, of the family to whom "Northumberland House"! passed from the Edwards family, [see Goode Genealogy, above, p. 205] was born 1710-20, d. 1769. He was a brother of Col. Francis Thornton, perhaps the No. I. of this Excursus. Married Charlotte Belson, an English lady, ward of Col. John Tayloe, of "Mount Airy," who returned to England at the outbreak of the Revolution, with her two sons, who became officers in the King's service with the understanding that they should never be required to fight against colonies. Children :—

1. PRESLEY THORNTON, served in the British army and was wounded at the siege of Gibraltar, returned to Virginia, 1783, and was admitted to citizenship on taking oath of allegiance. Married Elizabeth Thornton, dau. of Francis Thornton, of "Society Hill," King George Co., [who must have been grandson of the original Francis, and first cousin of Francis, of "Fall Hill."] Sold out his Northumberland estate about 1800, and removed to Genesee, N. Y., where he died 1807. He was Captain in the so-called "John Adams army," organized under the command of Washington, in 1798, for repelling an apprehended French invasion. (See complimentary letter to Washington, by Gen. C. C. Pinkney, in Spark's *Life of Washington*.) His son, Capt. Arthur W. Thornton, U. S. A., in the war of 1812, a gallant officer who died in service at Pensacola, about 1836. His daughter, Charlotte Belson, married Judge John Tayloe Lomax, of Fredericksburg, who, in 1858, contributed to DeBow's Review, [xxvi.,.p. 128], a brief account of the Lomax family, and of the Northumberland Thorntons, from which this notice is drawn, and whose son, *Presley Thornton Lomax*, of Keokuk, Iowa, m. Millie Henderson Wellford. (Standard, II, 29.)

2. JOHN TAYLOE THORNTON, served as midshipman in the British Navy, returned to Virginia and died, 1797, at "Kumerseley," Northumberland Co.

3. LIEUT-GEN. CHARLES WADE THORNTON, of the British Army, Equerry to the Duke of York, lost his arm in battle, perhaps in the West Indies, and said to have saved the life of the Duke of York, on the Walcheren expedition, to which was owing in part his popularity at court.

To this branch belongs, probably, JOHN THORNTON, who m. 1775-85, Catherine Yates, and had, i, William, killed in duel, 1804, ii, Mary Randolph, m. (1), Charles L. Carter, d. s. p. 1851, (2,) Dr. Robert Wellford, and had numerous descendants, who are enumerated in Richmond *Standard*, II, 29, (Mar. 20, 1880.)

———————— THORNTON, (grandson of Francis,) m. Elizabeth H., dau. of Richard and Eliz. Hartwell Cocke, of Curry Co., b. 1730-40, and had issue :—

1. NANCY THORNTON, m. ———— Branch, son, i, Henry F. Branch, d. 1815.

2. REBECCA. 3. FRANCIS, d. 1812. 4. LUCY. 5. ELIZABETH, m, (1), Mr. Wilkinson, issue, i, Cary Wilkinson ; (2), *Robert H. Taliaferro*, 4 children. (See Richmond *Standard*, II, 31.)

———————

739-A.

JAMES FRANCIS MAURY, of Jefferson Co., Missouri, son of Abraham and *Mildred Washington Thornton* Maury, was born in Madison Co., Va., Nov. 13, 1786, and died in Jefferson Co., Mo , Oct. 24, 1841. Married, Nov. 12, 1817, Mary Randolph, daughter of No. 235, (widow of George W. Thornton), who was born May 25, 1785, at "Warwick," died in Pensacola, Oct. 15, 1865. Children:—

1843, CAPT. THOMAS FRANCIS MAURY, C. S. A., b. Feb., 1819, d. in service, May 2, 1882. 1844, JAMES WOODVILLE, b. Jan. 4, 1821, d. y. 1845, JAMES WOODVILLE, b. Mar. 18, 1823. 1846, CATHERINE MILDRED, W., b. Aug. 11, 1825, d. y. 1847, AGNES GRAY, b. Nov. 26, 1828, d. y. 1848, GILBERT LAFAYETTE, b. Feb. 7, 1831.

Two of Mr. Maury's great-grandmothers were own cousins to General Washington. He lived for a time in Stafford and Spottsylvania Cos., Virginia. In 1836, he removed to Missouri and settled near St. Louis, where he was a successful planter. A man of enterprise and high integrity, he was greatly respected in the community in which he lived.

Col. Abraham Maury, of the Virginia line in the Revolutionary war, was son of Rev. James Maury, [b. 1717, d. 1769], rector of Fredericksville, and his wife, Mary Walker, (niece of Dr. Thomas Walker, the Kentucky explorer) and Mildred Thornton, referred to in previous Excursus, p. 215.

The grandparents of Col. Abraham Maury were Matthew Maury, Huguenot, a Refugee from Castel Mauron, Gascony, who came to Virginia in 1718, and Mary Ann Fontaine, of the illustrious Huguenot family of De la Fontaine, whose history is so well told in the *Memoirs of a Huguenot Family*, published in 1853, by Ann Maury. Mrs. Matthew Maury was great-granddaughter of John De la Fontaine, the martyr of 1563. There is in existence a lithographed *Chart of the Fontaine and Maury Families*, and in the 5th volume of the Collection of the Virginia Historical Society, Mr. Brock has published another of his valuable contributions to southern family history in the form of *A partial list of the descendants of John De la Fontaine*, pp. 119–150.

Many influential Americans are included in this list, among them the most distinguished Commodore Matthew Fontaine Maury, "the Philosopher of the Seas," [d. 1806, d. 1872], whose father, Richard Maury, was brother of Col. Abraham Maury, just referred to. Abraham Maury, uncle of Col. Abraham Maury, b. 1731, who married Susanna Poindexter, was the grandfather of Lieut. Alexander C. Maury, U. S. N., who married Mary Goode Thornton, now Mrs. Scott, No. 1841, of the Goode Pedigree.

The following transcript from the family bible of Col. Abraham Maury, kindly furnished by our kinsman James Woodville Maury, Esq., of Shuqualak, Miss., is printed in full, as a supplement to Mr. Brock's paper.

COL. ABRAHAM MAURY, son of Rev. James Maury, Rector of Fredericsville, Va.. was born April 28, 1858. Sponsors, Richard Beale and lady, Thomas Jefferson, and Mrs. Fannie Beale.

Mildred Washington Thornton, daughter of Francis Thornton and Anne, his wife, Dec. 20, 1751. Sponsors, Charles Washington and Wife.

COL. ABRAHAM and MILDRED WASHINGTON'S CHILDREN.

Mary Ann, 1st daughter	born	April 2, 1783.
Elizabeth B., 2d daughter	"	March 29, 1785.
James Francis, 1st son	"	Nov. 13, 1786.

Abraham, 3d son	born	May 5, 1788.
Butler, 3d son	"	April 15, 1790.
Willie Glassel, 3d daughter	"	April 2, 1792.
Catherine Matilda, 4th daughter	"	June 1, 1794.

MARRIAGES.

Col. Abraham Maury and Mildred Washington Thornton, daughter of Francis Thornton, of Fall Hill, near Fredericsburg, Va., were married June 13, 1782.

Thos. Walker Fry and Mary A., daughter of Col. Abraham and Mlldred W. Maury, were married May 20, 1805.

James Vass and Elizabeth B., daughter of Col. Abraham and Mildred W., were married Aug , 1816.

Butler, son of Col. Abraham and M. W., was married to Fannie B. Sawyer, May 15, 1817.

Abraham, son of Col. A. and M. W., was married to Nancy Bell, of Kentucky, June, 1818.

William A. Gregory and Willie Glassel, daughter of Col. A. and M. W., were married Dec. 5, 1818.

742.

JOSIAH BARTLETT ABBOTT, of "High Meadow," Henrico Co., a native of Connecticut, born Jan. 1, 1793, died Sept. 23, 1849, a lawyer and financier, married CATHERINE C. RANDOLPH, dau. of No. 235, who was born at Warwick, 1797, d. Dec. 12, 1852. Issue : —

> 1849, CAPT. WALTER RALEIGH ABBOTT, C. S. A., b. in Richmond, Apr. 19, 1838, killed in battle of Malvern Hill, June 13, 1862. 1850, VIRGINIA, m. *Claiborne Watkins.*

By a previous marriage with Miss Hening, Mr. Abbott had a daughter Eliza, who married William Lloyd; editor of the Richmond *Examiner*. He himself was for many years editor and owner of the Richmond *Whig* in company with John Hampden Pleasants. This partnership of "Pleasants and Abbott," was dissolved in 1846, by the issue of the duel between Mr. Pleasants and Thomas Ritchie, jr. Mr. Brock kindly supplies the following account of the affair :

The Richmond *Enquirer*, then edited by William F. and Thomas Ritchie, jr., sons of "the father of the Democratic Party," having published without comment a statement from its correspondent "Macon" at Washington, D. C., that John Hampden Pleasants, editor of the Richmond *Whig* proposed to establish in Richmond an abolition paper, he protested in the columns of the *Eveni g News and Star*, against the injurious and unjustifiable misrepresentation of himself. The editors of the *Enquirer* persisted in their disingenuous course. Finally there was a charge on their part of cowardice. Then Pleasants challenged the junior editor of the *Enquirer*, Thomas Ritchie, jr. The duel was fought on the south side of the James river, a little above Manchester, on the morning of Feb. 26, 1847. Pleasants was mortally wounded, dying on the 27th of February.

Public excitement incident upon the death of Pleasants was intense. It was felt that he had been goaded into the duel and that his death was encompassed to remove a powerful journalistic rival who was one of the most effective and influential champions of the whig party. Pleasants was a man of singular purity of life, and it was felt and believed that he had not justly incurred the enmity of anyone. Ritchie was arraigned for trial Mar. 25, 1846, and was acquitted. The attorney for the prosecution was Richard W. Flournoy, and the able council for the defense was Andrew Stevenson, Samuel Taylor, John W. Jones and William M. Overton. Richard Goode was one of the jurymen.

747.

ALEXANDER L. BOTTS, of New York, son of Benjamin and *Mary Minor* Botts, brother of Hon. John Minor Botts, and of Charles Botts, editor of the "Southern Planter," was born in Virginia about 1800. Married SARAH FRANCES RANDOLPH, daughter of No 235. Issue:—

> 1851, MARY BOTTS. 1852. LUCY. 1853, JANE, m. *Henry Chadwick*, of Brooklyn, N. Y. 1854, WILLIAM, d., married in New York, several children. 1855, THOMAS, m. Miss Hamilton, of New York, 2 children. 1856, ALEXANDER. 1857, JULIAN, m. in New York, children. 1858, RANDOLPH, m. in New York, children. 1859, STEVENS. 1860, VIRGINIA, m. *Beverly Botts*, son of Hon. John M. Botts, issue, 1, Beverly Botts, 2, Susan.

Mr. Botts, a lawyer, councellor of State, etc., removed to New York, where he became a contractor and a partner of the Stevens Brothers, of Hoboken, in their railroad and other commercial enterprises. He owned the Hoboken Race Course.

750.

BROCKENBROUGH STARKE MORRISON, of "Oak Hill," Powhatan Co., Va., subsequently of Chesterfield Co., d. Mar. 18, 1836, married, Feb. 27, 1816, MARY MOSBY GOODE, (dau. of Francis Goode, No. 239, p. 115), who was born Feb. 22, 1797, died Aug., 1821. Married (2), Oct. 18, 1826, *Mrs. Mary Garland Mosby* Royall, (widow of Joseph Archer Royall,) sister of Nos. 751 and 752, b. Dec. 15, 1789, d. July 18, 1864. Children:—

> 1861, FRANCIS GOODE MORRISON, b. Feb. 22, 1817. 1862, MARTHA HUGHES, b. May 10, 1820, living in Lynchburg, 1880. 1863, ANN, b. Jan. 24, 1819, d. 1853. 1864, JOHN, b. Jan. 24, 1821, d. 1868.

Mr. Morrison was a lineal descendant of Col. Francis Morrison, prominent in early Virginia history, member of the King's Council, etc., etc.

751.

EDWARD CARRINGTON MOSBY, of "Lethe," Powhatan Co., Va., son of Col. Wade Mosby, of "Woodland," Powhatan Co., Va., and

Susannah Trueheart,* of "Meadowbridge," born June 10, 1802, married
Aug. 18, 1825, SALLY BLAND GOODE, daughter of Francis Goode, No.
239, p. 115.   Children :—

> 1865, FRANCIS GOODE MOSBY, b. Aug. 6, d. Oct. 5, 1826.   1866, FOR-
> TUNATUS SYDNOR, b. Sept. 22, 1827, d. April 27, 1873.   1867,
> FRANCIS WADE, b. May 1, 1830.   1868, ROBERT GOODE, b. Mar.
> 1, 1822, d. July 21, 1833.   1869, EDWARD CARRINGTON, b. Jan. 15,
> 1834, d. April 5, 1873.   1870, PETER JEFFERSON ARCHER, b. Mar.
> 26, 1836, d. April 1, 1838.   1871, ROBERT GOODE, b. Feb. 21, 1838.
> 1872, WILLIAM WASHINGTON, b. Feb. 1, 1840, d. 1862.   1873, MAR-
> THA, b. April 7, 1842, "only breathed a few times, and was buried
> at ' Post Oak ' the next day."   1874, JOHN GARLAND, b. Dec. 27,
> d. Dec. 27, 1843.

Mr. Mosby was graduated at William and Mary College in 1811, and lived
at "Lethe " and "Inglewood," Powhatan Co., a prosperous planter.

Mrs. Sally Bland Goode Mosby with whom the author had the privilege of
talking in 1882, was at the age of eighty as sprightly as a girl, and contributed many valuable facts to this genealogy.

752.

WILLIAM WASHINGTON MOSBY, of "Comotomo," Powhatan
Co., Va., brother of E. C. Mosby, No. 726, was born June 20, 1800,
died 1873–75, married, Oct. 11, 1829, ELIZABETH HUGHES GOODE,
daughter of Francis Goode, No. 239, p. 115, born July 4, 1803, died
Dec. 7, 1839, at "Inglewood," and was buried at "Hughes' Creek."
·Children :—

> 1875, CHARLES LEWIS MOSBY, b. 1838, educated at Georgetown College.
> and in 1886, engaged in railroad enterprises in South Florida.
> 1876, ELIZABETH HUGHES, b. 1840, d. Aug. 17, 1773, m. *James
> Mitchel.*

EXCURSUS.—THE MOSBY FAMILY.

THE following facts regarding the Mosby family of Virginia, were in the
main derived from Mrs. Sally Bland Goode Mosby, of Powhatan Co., Miss.V.
Stuart Mosby, of Warrenton, Miss Elizabeth McLain, of Washington, and Mr.
Brock, as well as from Mr. Alexander Brown's note in the *Standard*, Vol. III,

---

*THE TRUEHEART FAMILY. The ancestor of the Truehearts, of Virgrnia, was AARON BARTHOLOMEW
TRUEHEART, who came from England, 1720–40, with his only son, Daniel, and settled at "Meadowbridge,"
Hanover Co. DANIEL TRUEHEART, m. Mary Garland, and had 7 children, as follows: 1, SUSANNAH,
b. Sept. 19, 1766, m. *Wade Mosby*, Mosby Pedigree, No. 15. 2, WILLIAM, who m. (1) Mary Tillman,
(2) Betsy Sydnor, (3) Nancy Mosby Shepparde 3, MARTHA, m. June 16, 1700, *Gervas Storrs*, of "Hunt-
sted Hall," Hanover, who m. (1) Susanna' Randolph Pleasants, and had dau., Louisa, who m. *Gen.
Littleberry H. Mosby*, Mosby Pedigree, No. 52. Another daughter apparently m. Wade Mosby, jr.,
No. 54. 4, BARTHOLOMEW, m. (1) Sally Seabrook, (2) Eliza Mosby, No. 31 of Mosby Pedigree; (3)
Marcia Burton. 5, LOUIS, d. unm.

FIRST GENERATION.

BENJAMIN MOSBY,* a native of Wales or England, came to Virginia at the end of the seventeenth or the beginning of the eighteenth century, and settled in New Kent County. He was a man of good education, but too poor to buy land, o he took up the business of making shoes. He became suitor for the hand of Mary, daughter of Benjamin Poindexter, a planter of New Kent County, and married her against the wishes of her family, who were wealthy and looked down upon him because of his trade. At the wedding dinner, says tradition, his father-in-law came behind him and touching him on the shoulder, said to him in the presence of the company, "Eat heartily, shoemaker, for it's all you'll ever get!" His wife never received a dower, but he accumulated a fine property before his death. They removed to Powhatan, at that time a part of Cumberland County, and lived and died at "Cumberland Old Court House." They had sons and daughters, but through lapse of time and imperfect record, history has been lost, and the connection of many descendants is unknown. They were probably the ancestors of all the Mosbys in the South, if not all in the United States. The names of the children, so far as known, were:

2, BENJAMIN MOSBY, 3, LITTLEBERRY, (the elder). 4, POINDEXTER. 5, POWHATAN. 6, THEODOSIA.

SECOND GENERATION.

2, BENJAMIN MOSBY, b. 1720–40, had children :—

7, THEODOSIA MOSBY, m. 1763, *Col. Joseph Carrington* : their son, *William Carrington*, m. Martha Povall, No. 296 of Goode Genealogy. (For posterity see Goode Genealogy, p. 128, et seq., and Richmond *Standard*, Feb. 26, and March 5, 1881.) 8. DANIEL.

3, LITTLEBERRY MOSBY, of Cumberland or Powhatan Co., m. (1) Eliz. Netherland, 8 children, Nos. 7–16, (2) Judith Michaux, 6 children, Nos. 17–22, (3) Martha (Scott) Thomas, sister of Gen. Chas. Scott, no issue.

9, BENJAMIN MOSBY, law student, drowned in the James River at "Mt. Pleasant." 10, JOHN, soldier of the Revolution, d. at Redstone, now Pittsburg, while emigrating to Kentucky. 11, LITTLEBERRY. 12, SALLY. 13, MARY, m. *Robert Hughes.* 14, BETSY, d. unm. 15, WADE. 16, RICHARD, m. Mary Vaughan, of Powhatan, d. s. p. 17, BETTY ANN. 18, MARTHA. 19, JUDITH. 20, BENJAMIN. 21, NARCISSA, m. *Benj. Binford*, of Buckingham Co. 22. JACOB MICHAUX.

4. POINDEXTER MOSBY, m. Mary Woodson.

THIRD GENERATION.

8, DANIEL MOSBY, had son :—

30, JOHN H. MOSBY.

---

*The only grants to the names Mosby and Poindexter recorded in the Virginia Land Registry, are as follows: Richard Mosby, Sept. 28, 1728, 400 acres in Henrico Co., on the south side of the James. Richard Mosby, Aug, 25, 1731, 400 acres in Goochland Co. John Poindexter, Sept. 27, 1729, 1,000 acres in Hanover Co. R. A. BROCK.

10, LITTLEBERRY MOSBY, a soldier of the Revolution, m. (1) Eliza, dau. of Gen. Charles Scott; (2) Mary Page Hoskins. Children :—
> 31, ELIZA SCOTT MOSBY, m. *Bartholomew Trueheart.* 32, EDWARD, m. Eliza Winston, of Louisa Co. 33, MARTHA FINNEY, m. *Merrill Booker,* of Cumberland Co. 34, SALLY, m. *Edward Munford,* of Powhatan. 35, MARY PAGE, d. unm. 36, LUCY ANN, m. *Mr. Freerson,* of Tenn. 37, ROBERT, m. Sally, dau. of J. Head Lynch. 38, ELBERT, m. Delilah Lipscomb, of Cumberland. 39, BENJAMIN CLINTON, m. Rachel Cardozo, of Powhatan. 40, DEWITT, m. a lady in Tennessee. 41, JOHN WADE, d. unm.

12, COL. WILLIAM CANNON, of "Mt. Ida," Buckingham Co., Va., m. SALLY MOSBY, children :—
> 42, BETSY CANNON, m. *Jordan Harris.* 43, MOLLY, m. *Gillis Lewis,* of "Manor Hill." 44, MARTHA. 45, SALLY, m. *Silas Flournoy.* 46, JOHN, d. unm.

13, ROBERT HUGHES, of Hughes' Creek, Powhatan Co., the third of the name, married MARY MOSBY, children :—
> 47, MARTHA HARTWELL HUGHES, m. FRANCIS GOODE, (No. 239, in Goode Genealogy). 48, ELIZABETH, d. unm. 49, ANN HARTWELL, m. *Wm. Carrington,* of Cumberland Co.

15, COL. WADE MOSBY, sr., of "Woodland," Powhatan Co., Va., b. about 1750, d. June 1, 1833, in Columbia, Tenn.; a soldier of the Revolution, who fought at the battle of Guilford, C. H., m. Susanna Trueheart, b. Sept. 19, 1766, d. Oct. 21, 1853, children :—
> 50, JOHN GARLAND MOSBY. 51, MARY GARLAND, b. Dec. 15, 1787, d. July 18, 1864, m. (1) *Joseph Archer Royall,* of Amelia Co., who d. 1810 ; (2) B. S. MORRISON, (see Goode Genealogy, No. 750), son, by first marriage, 1, *Joseph Wade Royall,* b. Nov. 22, 1809, d. Sept., 1865, 52, LITTLEBERRY HARDEMAN. 53, ELIZABETH TYRRELL. 54, WADE. 55, SUSAN MALVINA. 56, RICHARD HENRY, b. May 24, 1778, graduated, William and Mary College, 1818, d. in North Carolina, 1865, m., Feb., 1826, Mary Ann Little. 57, WILLIAM W., (No. 752, of the Goode Genealogy). 58, EDWARD C., (No. 751, of the Goode Genealogy). 59, CHARLES GERVAS, d. y. 60, CHARLES LEWIS. 61, BENJAMIN FRANKLIN, b. Dec. 24, 1805, d. 1871, at "Comotomo," unm.

17, BENJAMIN CARRINGTON, m. BETTY ANN MOSBY, children :—
> 62, BENJAMIN CARRINGTON, jr., d. unm. 63, LOUISA, m. *George Booker,* of Buckingham.

18, MARTHA MOSBY, m. (1) DANIEL SCOTT, son of Gen. Charles Scott, (2) ROBERT CARTER NICHOLAS, of "Seven Islands," Buckingham Co., children :—
> 64, JUDITH SCOTT, m. *Mr. Mosely,* of Buckingham Co. 65, JOHN NICHOLAS. 66, ROBERT CARTER. 67, GEORGE W., (for children, see *Carter Tree*). 68, LITTLEBERRY, d. y.

19, JOSIAH SMITH, of "Mt. Rose," Powhatan Co., m. JUDITH MOSBY, children :—

69, MARY SMITH. 70, WILLIAM, m. Susan Payne. 71, JOSIAH, m. Mary W. Dance, of Powhatan. 72, BENJAMIN, m. Miss Morrison. 73, EMILY, m. *Mr. Booker*, of Amelia Co. 74, JUDITH E., d. y. 75, ELIZA, d. unm,

20, BENJAMIN MOSBY, m, (1) Mary Crouch, of Goochland Co., (2) Mrs. Maria (Brown) Tinsley, of Richmond, child, (by first wife):—
76, JUDITH MICHAUX MOSBY, m. *George Flournoy.*

21, BENJAMIN BINFORD, of Buckingham Co., Va., m. NARCISSA MOSBY, child :—
77, JUDITH MOSBY BINFORD, m. *Mr. Allen.*

22, JACOB MICHAUX MOSBY, m. Judith Crump, of Powhatan Co., child :—
78, JACOB GOODRICH MOSBY, graduate of William and Mary College, 1808, m. Apphiah Woodson.

25, BENJAMIN MOSBY, (son of No. 2, 4, or 5), married Ann Povall, (see Goode Genealogy, p. 69), children :—
79, PETER WINSTON MOSBY. 80, ELIZABETH, m. *Mann S. Valentine.* 81, JOHN O. 82, ROBERT POVALL. 83, MARY ANN. 84, SARAH WINSTON. 85, BENJAMIN. 86, LUCY. 87, PATRICK HENRY. 88, WILLIAM H. 89, SUSANNA VIRGINIA.

26, HEZEKIAH MOSBY, son of No. 2, 4 or 5, m. Elizabeth Povall. (See Goode Genealogy, p. 69).

27, WILLIAM POVALL, married MARTHA MOSBY, daughter of No. 2, 4 or 5. (See Goode Genealogy, p. 69).

28, JOHN MOSBY, son of No. 2, 4 or 5, m. Eliza Winston. (See Slaughter's *Winston-Henry* Pedigree, and Goode Genealogy, p. 69). Children :—
100, JOHN A. MOSBY.

30, JOHN W. MOSBY, had children :—
101, ANNE MOSBY, m, *John Chilton.* 102, JOHN. 103, SARAH, m. *Harden Perkins,* issue, 1, *John Perkins,* 2, *Matilda,* m. C. Floyd. 104, ALFRED D.

FOURTH, FIFTH AND SIXTH GENERATIONS.

50, JOHN GARLAND MOSBY,* b. May 17, 1785, d. Dec. 26, 1857, graduate of William and Mary College, 1804, m. Feb. 14, 1810, Mary Webster Pleasants, (daughter of Robert and *Elizabeth Randolph* Pleasants of " Four Mile Creek " and " Curles,") "a very intelligent woman, who made graceful contributions in rhyme and prose to the local press," children :—
111, LOUISA MOSBY, d. 1863, m. *Rev. William McLain,†* children, 1, *William Mosby McLain,* 2, *Elizabeth,* 3, *Mary Webster,* 4, *Lewis Randolph,* 5, *John Speed.* 112, MARY RANDOLPH, m. *P. Moore,* d. Oct. 1, 1875, children, 1, *Mary Webster Moore,* 2, *Katherine,* 3, *Maggie,* 4, *John,* 5, *William,* 6, *Patrick Theodore.* 113, VIRGINIA, m. *Adair Pleasants,* children, 1, *Mary W. M. Pleasants,* 2, *Louisa M.,* 3, *Kate M.,*

---

*His descendants possess a portrait of him, drawn by St. Memin, and also the plate of an exquisite aquatint miniature by the same admirable artist.
†Rev. William McLain, D. D., was for a long period, Secretary and Treasurer of the American Colonization Society, faithfully performing his duties, even after he was confined to his bed by the disease which terminated his life. He was born Aug. 8, 1806, and died 1873,—the son of Joseph McLain, (b. 1775, d. 1834), and Betsy Runyon, (b. 1779, d. 1838), daughter of John Runyon, who was grandson of Peter Runyon, of New Jersey, referred to in this Genealogy, p. 157, and in the Appendix.

4, *Lydia*, 5, *Rosalie Harrison.* 114, LYDIA, m. *Matthew Pleasants*, children, 1, *Isabella A. Pleasants*, 2, *Virginia M,*, 3, *McLain*, 4, *Matthew.* 115, JULIET, d. 1813. 116, ELIZABETH, d. 1816. 117, SUSAN, d. 1826. 118, JOHN SPEED, d. 1833.

52, GEN. LITTLEBERRY HARDEMAN MOSBY, of Powhatan, b. Sept. 7, 1789, d. in Mississippi, May, 1848, graduate of William and Mary College, 1809, m. 1814, Louisa Pleasants Storrs, dau. of Gervas and *Susanna Randolph Pleasants* Storrs, of "Hunsted Hall," (see Trueheart note, p. 220). Children :—

 120, SARAH MOSBY, m. Oct. 27, 1817, *Edward Munford.* 121, SUSAN, m. *James McCutchen.* 122, CAROLINE, m. *Augustus McAllister.* 123, LINNÆUS SPEED, d. 1854. 124, JOHN SYDNOR, d. 1863. 125. 126, RICHARD N. 127, VIRGINIUS, d. 1860. 128, GERVAS STORRS, d. 1870, m. E. G. Burke, issue : 1, *John B. Mosby*, 2, *Littleberry*, 3, *Gervas.* 128½, JAMES WADE, d. 1864.

53, FORTUNATUS SYDNOR, of Lynchburg, probably son of Fortunatus Sydnor, clerk of Henrico Parish vestry, 1763–76. Married, Nov., 1814, ELIZABETH TYRRELL MOSBY, b. May 30, 1791, d. Nov. 15, 1815.

54, WADE MOSBY, jr., b. May, 30, 1793, d. in Bedford Co., 1872, m. (1) Mary Virginia Storrs, (2) Mary Ann Brown, (3) Mrs. Eliz. Tabb (Patterson) Yeatman, children :—

 129, JOHN SPEED MOSBY, d. 1819. 130, CHARLES HALL, d. 1824. 132, BETSY, d. 1876.

55, JOHN HENRY SPEED, of Mecklenburg Co., m. April 3, 1811, SUSAN MALVINA MOSBY, b. June 10, 1796, d. Aug., 1819, children :—

 132, ELIZA YEATMAN SPEED, d. Feb., 1863, m. *Commodore John Rudd,* *U. S. N.* 133, JOHN MOSBY, d. 1866.

60, CHARLES LEWIS MOSBY, b. Jan. 8, 1817, m. Mary Eliza, daughter of William and Judith Royall, of Lynchburg, and had 12 children :—

 134, WILLIAM ROYALL MOSBY, b. 1832. 135, LESLIE, b. 1839, d. 1863. 136–46, Others.

65, JOHN NICHOLAS, m. Anne Trent, of Buckingham, children. (See *Carter Tree*) :—

 147, BETTY NICHOLAS, m. *E. T. Page.* 148, NANNIE, m. *Thos. Jelles.* 149, NELLIE, m. *B. P. Ambler.* 150, JOHN S., m. Ellen Ambler, 151, WILLIAM T. 152, ROBERT CARTER, m. Mary Pleasants Carrington, (dau. of No. 886, Goode Genealogy).

66, ROBERT CARTER NICHOLAS, jr., m. Orilla Bigelow, of Vermont, children:—

 153, ROBERT C. NICHOLAS. 154, MARTHA, m. *Capt. D. U. Barziza*, of Texas. 155, HAMPDEN, m. W. S. Carrington, (dau. of No. 886, of the Goode Genealogy).

80, MANN S. VALENTINE, of Richmond, Va., a prominent merchant, married ELIZABETH MOSBY. Among his children are Edward Virginius Valentine, the Virginia sculptor, William Winston Valentine, artist and philologist, and M. S. Valentine, a leading citizen of Richmond. (For full record see Brock's Fontaine Pedigree, p. 142).

102, JOHN MOSBY, m. Virginia, danghter of Frederick Cabell, children:
166, ELLA FLOYD MOSBY, a writer of repute. 167, CARRINGTON, m.
Cora Clark, of Lynchburg.
104, ALFRED D. MOSBY, of Amherst Co., Va., m. Virginia McLaurine, dau. of
James, and granddaughter of Rev. Robert McLaurine, of the English
church, children :—
168, COL. JOHN S. MOSBY, commander of Partisan Rangers,*C. S. A., and
U. S. Consul at Hong Kong, m. Pauline, dau. of Hon. Beverly
Clark, of Kentucky, children, 1, *May*, m. Robert Campbell (g.-g.-
g.-son of Gov. Spotswood), of Warrenton, Va., children, a, Mosby,
b, Spotswood, 2, *Beverly*, 3, *John S., jr.*, 4, *V. Stuart*, 5, *Pauline*.
6, *Ada C.* 169, BLAKELY, 170, LUCY, m. *Charles W. Russell*, of
W. Va., children, a, Margaret, b, John. 171, WILLIAM H., m.
Lucy Booth, 6 children. 172, VICTORIA. 173, ELIZABETH. 174,
LELIA, m. *Charles W. Russell*, (2d wife). 175, ADA. 176, FLOR-
ENCE, a sister of charity.

754.

ROBERT GOODE SPOTSWOOD, of "The Wilderness," Orange
Co., Va., son of John and *Mary Goode* Spotswood, No. 241, p. 115, was
born Aug. 27, 1797, and died about 1838. Married, 1825, Betsy Hening. Children :—

1877, EDWARD TRAVIS SPOTSWOOD, M. D., b. 1826. 1878, JOHN BANKS,
b. 1828. 1879, RICHARD, b. 1830.

R. G. Spotswood was a young man of great promise. His wife was the daughter of William Waller Hening,† the author of the Virginia Statutes at Large,
"the most important work ever published upon the history of social affairs in
Virginia," who was born about 1750, and died March 31, 1828. Strangely
enough, the name of his father seems to have been forgotten, but his mother
was doubtless a Waller.

He married Agatha Banks (a near relation of Sir Joseph Banks, the English
explorer and naturalist, who accompanied Captain Cook, in his voyage around
the world), who had two brothers William and Henry, and whose mother was
a descendant of Robert Bruce. Their children were : 1, *Dr. William Hening*,
of Powhatan Co., who had Dr. William Hening, of Powhatan C. H., and six
other children. 2, *Anna Matilda Banks*, m. James Cabaniss, of Petersburg, a
soldier in the war of 1812, who has two living children, Dr. Thomas S. Cabaniss, Sup't of the Insane Hospital at Blackfoot, Idaho, and Julia, who m. (1) J.
D. Wilson, of Norfolk, who d. 1851, leaving 3 sons ; (2) Charles B. Hayden, of
Smithfield, who d. 1873, leaving a daughter, Eliza V. 3, *Maria W.*, d. unm.
4, *Elizabeth*, m. (1) Robert Goode Spotswood : (2) E. L. Schermerhorn. 5, *Rev.*

*See Major Scott's. "Partisan life with Col. John S. Mosby," New York, Harper Bros., 1867.
†"WILLIAM WALLER HENING," writes A. H. Hoyt, in his essay upon Early Printing in Virginia,
(New England Historic Genealogical Register 1872, p. 30), "is more generally known for his connection
with the Statutes at Large of Virginia, compiled and edited by him with great learning and ability. Mr.
Hening also published several law manuals and jointly with Mr. William Munford, several volumes of law
reports. We have not been able to ascertain anything definite in regard to his ancestors or early history,
and it would seem that his great services to his native state have not secured for his memory the notice
he deserved."

Edmond Waller, of the Episcopal church, for some years a missionary to Af-rica, d. in Philadelphia, 1884. 6, *Martha*, m. Mr. Swan, d. 1873. 7, *Virginia*, m. Mr. Abbott, d. in Williamsburg, 1830.

Mrs. Spotswood, who, after her husband's death, married Rev. E. L. Scher-merhorn, of New York, a Presbyterian clergyman, was a frequent contributor to the *Southern Literary Messenger*, *Knickerbocker Magazine*, and other literary periodicals. Among her best known verses are those entitled "The White Rose of Miami," "The Indian Chief," "The Polar Queen,""Lines on the Telegraph," and "Jephthah's Daughter." She died in Gosport, Indiana, in 1873.

Mrs. Schermerhorn was the author of the well known lines on "The Old Blandford Church," first published in the *Southern Literary Messenger*, and attri-buted to E. A. Poe and Tyrone Power. In Bishop Meade's private copy of "Old Churches and Families of Virginia," is a marginal note in his own hand writ-ing, stating that "these lines were written by a sister of Rev. Edmond Hening, missionary to Africa." Mrs. Hayden, her niece, writes :—

"There is no doubt in regard to her being the author of the lines on the walls of the old Blandford Church ; her sister, Mrs. Swan, saw her write them, and her daughter in a recent letter states that her mother told her she was standing by her side at the time when they were composed."

755.

JOHN ROWZIE SPOTSWOOD, of "Orange Grove," Spotsylvania Co., Va., son of No. 241, was born June 22, 1799. Married, 1826, Lelia Allison, daughter of Col. John Allison, of the Virginia line in the Revolutionary war, who died at Orange Grove, 1868, and his wife, Fan-ny Currie, of Williamsburg. Children :—

> 1880, WILLIAM CHURCHILL SPOTSWOOD, b. Feb. 24, 1831. 1881, MARY GOODE, b. Sept. 9, 1834, living, 1885. 1882, EDWIN ALLISON, b. Sept. 9, 1834, living, 1885, in Memphis. 1883, JOHN ROWZIE, b. Sept., 1832. 1884, ALEXANDER DANDRIDGE, b. Nov. 12, 1836. 1885, BEVERLY WELLFORD, b. 1842, d. 1845. 1886, FANNY CUR-RIE, b. May, 1839.

John Rowzie Spotswood is still hale and hearty, and is living, at the age of eighty-seven, upon the ancestral estate in Spotsylvania County. He was the owner of the "Spotswood Manuscripts," which were lent by him to Mr. Ban-croft, for use in the History of the United States, and which were subsequently lent to G. W. Featherstonehaugh, the geologist, who carried them to England, and from whose widow they were bought by the Virginia Historical Society, under whose auspices they have since been published, in the first and second volumes of new series of the Society's Collections.

"He was a very warm adherent of the Confederacy, and although too old to serve in the army during the late war, was taken prisoner twice by the Fed-erals, once at the battle of Chancellorsville, very near the rock where Stone-wall Jackson was wounded ; he was taken from there to Washington City, and lodged in Carroll Prison. On the route he was compelled, although about sixty-five years of age, to walk more than a hundred miles.

In speaking of his imprisonment, he says he could have borne the trials and hardships, with fortitude, but the anxiety for wife and daughters who were left without a protector, was very harassing. He had three sons in the southern army."

"Orange Grove," which was situated in the midst of the Wilderness battle-field, and may be seen indicated upon any of the military maps of that region, is one of the finest of old Virginia mansions.

756.

JOHN E. LEMOINE, of Petersburg, Va., was born in Alexandria, Va., July 31, 1838, died in Petersburg, Oct. 18, 1872, married, July 2, 1825, MARY BLAND SPOTSWOOD, daughter of John and *Mary Goode* Spotswood, No. 214, born at "Orange Grove," July 17, 1801, died Jan. 30, 1886, in St. Louis, Mo. Children:—

> 1887, EDWIN SPOTSWOOD LEMOINE, b. Aug. 27, 1826. 1888, MARY GOODE, b. Apr. 8, 1828, d, Jan. 7, 1853, m. *Robert. N. Nesbit.* 1889, PAUL ESTARE, b. Aug. 3, 1829. 1890, SPOTSWOOD, b. Oct. 31, 1841, d. June 6, 1842.

John E. Lemoine, of Petersburg, Virginia, was born at Alexandria, Va., July 31, 1798, and died in Petersburg, Oct. 18, 1872, aged 75 years, where he had long been the oldest merchant in the city, in business for himself 55 years. He died "in harness," attending, with the utmost vigor, clearness, and industry, to his affairs up to the last week of his life.

His father was M. Jean Marie Le Moine, a Parisian of good position, of a Catholic Loyalist family, whose displeasure he incurred by siding with the people, in the revolution which commenced with the "taking of the Bastile." He was the first to enter the Prison, and his son has a copy of the medal given him for gallant conduct on that occasion. He soon became disgusted with the "rule of the People," and deciding to emigrate to this country, joined a party who had bought Scioto lands in Ohio. On landing at New Castle, Delaware, in 1788, he proceeded to Philadelphia, and there found that he had been swindled by some land-sharks in Paris, and that his purchase was under

DIED.

In St. Louis, Missouri, at the residence of her son Dr. E. S. Lemoine, on the 30th January, 1886, in the 85th year of her age.

MRS. MARY BLAND SPOTSWOOD LEMOINE,

wife of the late John E. Lemoine, Esq,, of Petersburg, Virginia. Descended directly, through her father, from the Spotswoods and Dandridges, and through her mother, from the Goodes and Blands, illustrious names in the Colonial History of Virginia, all of them tracing their ancestry in unbroken lines to an early period of English history;—she held title to the character given to her by all who knew her, that of a true Christian

GENTLEWOMAN.

Cultured, refined, pure, upright, courteous and considerate of others' rights and feelings ; performing all the duties of life with admirable skill, patience and efficiency ; bearing its burdens and trials with Christian fortitude; endearing herself to all who came within her influence, and making her home a charmed spot to those who were privileged to dwell in it;—she died as she had lived in the blessed hope of immortality with the Savior, and has left to her loved ones the holiest and sweetest of memories,

Funeral Notice of Mrs. Lemoine.

water.* He left the colony (which afterwards founded the town of Gallipolis, Ohio), made his way to Alexandria, Virginia, where he married the daughter of M. John Estare, a merchant. After about ten years, he died in the island of St. Thomas, where he had been ordered for rapid consumption.

757.

RICHARD THORNTON SPOTSWOOD, of Richmond, Va , son of John and *Mary Goode* Spotswood, No. 241, p. 115, was born Nov, 7, 1803, and died in Petersburg, Va., 1863. Married, May 19, 1842, Martha F., daughter of John Shackleford, (for many years Commonwealth's Attorney of Culpeper Co., Va.), and his wife Lucy Tutt, daughter of Benjamin and *Elizabeth Pendleton* Tutt,† who was born in Culpeper, Va., 1817. Children:—

> 1889, LUCY SPOTSWOOD, b. July 25. 1843, d. 1868.   1890, SALLY BLAND,
> b. Dec. 11, 1847, m. in 1879, *William Randolph Smith*, of W. Va.
> 1891, MUSCOE LIVINGSTON, b. April 20, 1850.

Mr. Spotswood was for many years connected with the U. S. Post Office Department, in Washington, and at the outbreak of the war received an appointment in the General Post Office of the Confederacy in Richmond.

He was visiting his sister, Mrs, J. E. Lemoine, of Petersburg, Va., at the time of his death. He was buried in the old Blandford Cemetry, near Petersburg.

CONFEDERATE STATES OF AMERICA, POST OFFICE DEPARTMENT,
RICHMOND, VA., OCT. 6th, 1863.

At a meeting of the employees of the General Post Office Department called for the purpose of paying a fitting tribute of respect to the memory of their late associate, Richard T. Spotswood, Esq., on motion it was resolved that the Hon. John H. Reagan, act as chairman of the meeting, and Mr. J. Newton Lewis, as secretary. Judge T. P. A. Bibb addressed the meeting, and in conclusion offered the following preamble and resolutious :

Death claims his tribute alike from monarch's palace and the cabin of the cottager ; and it would seem, always demands those whom we most need and love. Again he has thrust his scythe into our ranks and stricken one whose loss cannot be well supplied.

Richard T. Spotswood departed this life in Petersburg, Va., on the 4th of October, 1863, full of years and honor.

Mr. Spotswood had been in the Post Office Department as a clerk under the U. S. Government and this together, for more than a quarter of a century. In service and in years he was a patriarch of our order.

A Virginian, he inherited those traits of generosity, manliness, and refinement which have made the character of the old Virginia gentleman famous the world over. Modest in his demeanor, combining affability with dignity, he com-

---

*For account of the sufferings of French colonists at this time, see McMaster's *History of the People of the United States*, II, p. 146, *et. seq.*
†For Pendleton Genealogy, see *St. Mark's Parish*, p, 155.

manded the love and respect of all with whom he associated. His heart was affectionate and pure, and his integrity strong and unbending, and at the day of resurrection, when the sea and earth shall give up their dead, there will not arise from the unseen and unfathomable depths, a purer spirit than that of our deceased friend.

Resolved : That we sincerely lament the death of our friend and colleague, and long cherish his memory—that we tender our condolence to his bereaved family, and commend them to God, the father of the fatherless, and the friend of the widow.

Resolved : That a copy of these preamble and resolutions be signed by the chairman, and transmitted to the family of the deceased.

Before putting the vote, the chairman rose and expressed in impressive language his deep sorrow at the death of Mr. Spotswood, and referred to the admirable character of the deceased.

The preamble and resolutions were then, on motion, unanimously adopted by the meeting.

JOHN H. REAGAN, Chairman.

761.

JAMES LYLE, 2d, of "Whitby," Chesterfield Co., Va., son of James and *Sally Bland Goode* Lyle, No. 242, p. 118, was born March 3, 1798, and died 1851. Married, 1820, Jane Le Vert Davidson, daughter of Robert and Anne Davidson (natives of Scotland.) Children :—

> 1893, JAMES DAVIDSON LYLE, b. 1821, d. 1862, unm. 1894, JANE LE VERT, d. y. 1805, JOHN TODD, b. 1828, d. 1886, unm. 1896, SARAH ANN, b. Oct. 30, 1824, d. Jan. 22, 1885, m. *P. D. McKinney.* 1897, HELEN BLAND, b. Jan. 27, 1827, m. *Col. S. Bassett French.*

James Lyle inherited "Whitby," the ancestral estate of the Goodes, and lived and died on the old plantation. He was a wealthy planter, a graduate of William and Mary College, class of 1817, highly cultured, well read, the owner of a valuable library. With the death of his son, John Todd Lyle, the name will become extinct.

Mrs. Lyle's home was at "Summer Hill," the plantation adjoining "Whitby," now owned by Col. F. G. Ruffin.

763.

COLIN CLARKE, of "Warner Hall," Gloucester Co., Va., son of Col. James Clarke, at "Keswick," Powhatan Co., was born Sept. 12, 1792 Married, April 16, 1818, MARY GOODE LYLE, daughter of James and *Sally Bland Goode* Lyle, No. 242, p. 118, born Oct. 25, 1792, died Dec. 22, 1884, at "Milford," South Carolina, the residence of her son-in-law, Governor Manning. Children :—

> 1898, JAMES LYLE CLARKE, b. Feb. 9, 1819, d. 1864. 1899, CASTILLION J., b. Sept. 26. 1820, d. inf. 1900, MARY ELLEN, b. Sept. 16, 1822, d. Dec. 1848, m. *Douglas T. Gordon.* 1901, POWHATAN, b. Dec. 8,

1824, d. unm.   1902, SALLY BLAND, b. Jan. 23, 1828, d. Dec. 31, 1884, m. *John L. Manning.*   1903, MAXWELL T., b. June 10, 1830. 1904, COLIN D., b. Mar. 22, 1832, d. Sept. 1862.   1905, JOHN LYLE, b. Dec. 16, 1833.   1906, POWHATAN, b. Sept. 16, 1836.

"Mr. Clarke was graduated at William and Mary College, 1811, and was for many years one of the board of visitors. He was a schoolmate of Gen. Winfield Scott, at the then famous school of James Ogilvie, afterward Lord Ogilvie, near Monticello, and spent much of his time with Mr. Jefferson, who was very fond of him, and from whom he had much prized letters. He was elected to the Virginia legislature at the age of twenty, and admitted as soon as he came of age. Lived in Richmond, practicing law for a time ; represented Powhatan County a second time in the legislature years after leaving the county. In 1834, he removed to Gloucester Co., where he lived until his death ; ' Warner Hall' is still owned by his son.

" The ancestor of the Clarke Family came from Surrey, England, 1710–30, and bought a large estate in Powhatan Co., a portion of which, ' Keswick,' is still in the family, and married M'lle Sallee, daughter of one of the Huguenot colonists of 1698. They had two sons ; Charles was one of the early settlers of Kentucky.

" James Clarke, the other son, served as a youth in the Revolutionary war, and commanded a regiment in the war of 1812, at the battle of Craney Island : one of his sons, Colin has already been mentioned : another, Major John Clarke, was owner of the Bellona Arsenal, and his granddaughter, widow of Senator Jackson Morton, of Fla., now owner of the ancestral estate of 'Keswick.' "

"My grandfather (Col. James Clarke), was a staunch republican," writes Prof. Powhatan Clarke. " My father told me when a boy, that on one occasion he asked his father what was the meaning of a picture which hung over the dining room chimney. He replied that it was a vestige of the ignorance and vanity of his ancestors, and threw it in the fire. It was his coat of arms. He described it to me, and it was the same as now borne by a family in England."*

Of Mrs. Mary Goode Clarke, the "Southern Churchman" remarked :

" None ever dispensed a more generous and graceful hospitality, and her society was not only the delight of persons of her own age, but she was the friend and confident of all the young people around her. She was a communicant of the Episcopal church, confirmed by Bishop Meade many years ago."

766.

ROBERT GOODE SAUNDERS, of Matthew's Co., Va., son of No. 242-A, was born Oct. 22, 1808, died 1865. Married Maria Louisa Manchester, of Rhode Island. Children :—

---

*The arms of Clarke, of " Dundon," Buckinghamshire, agree most closely with the tradition, viz : *Per chevron, azure and argent three eagles displayed, counterhanged: in chief a leopard's face, or*. The Clarkes of Norfolk, Oxford, Northampton, (Welton) and Warwick, had swans in their arms, but no animals heads. Col. Clarke went to England in the last century and obtained several thousand pounds as his share of the ancestral estate.

1907, CHARLES FREDERICK SAUNDERS, M. D., of Philadelphia, and others.

R. G. Saunders was with Houston in the Texan war of Independence, was imprisoned by Santa Anna, but released by interference of the U. S. Government. He was a highly educated man, a teacher, and "something of a poet."

772.

DR. RICHARD HERBERT TATUM, of Dayton, Va., son of No. 247, p. 120, was born at "Seven Oaks," 1821. Married, 1851, Lily, daughter of Charles and *Sarah Skelton* Selden, of Powhatan Co., Va. Children :—

1910, DR. RIVES TATUM, of Harrisburg, Va., b. 1853, grad. Richmond Medical College, 1876. 1911, PEEBLES, b. 1855. 1912, CONSTANCE, b. 1857, m. 1878, *James Hay*, of Madison C. H., Va., "a lawyer of great promise," children, 1, *James Hay*, 2, *William*. 1913, MARY GOODE, b. 1860, m. 1882, *Lucien B. Tatum*, of Richmond, Va. 1914, HERBERT, b. 1864. 1915, CHARLES HENRY, b. 1869, student in the University of Virginia.

Dr. Tatum was educated at William and Mary College, where he was graduated in 1841, and received his degree of M. D. from the University of Pennsylvania. He has been for fifty years a successful physician, practicing in the upper valley of Virginia, in the vicinity of Harrisonburg and Dayton. During the war he served as Surgeon, C. S. A., being at one time attached to the 18th Georgia Infantry.

780.

RUFUS K. HARRISON, of Essex Co., Va., son of William and *Louisa Alice Goode* Harrison of "Chester," Sussex Co., was born about 1730, and was appointed a cadet in the U. S. Military Academy at West Point, 1847.

N. B.—The names entered under numbers 773—6 inclulive, on page 120, should be cancelled.

784½.

ALICE HARRISON, daughter of No. 248, married Mr. Gregory, Daughter :—

1920, ALICE GOODE GREGORY, m. *Col. Burton Herbert.*

786.

WILLIAM HAMLIN HARRISS, son of James Belsches and Alice E. Harriss, was born at "Invermay," June 26, 1831. He was educated at Randolph Macon College, where he was graduated 1834, was a planter at the old homestead, and a Justice of the Peace for many years. He died unmarried, in Febuary, 1876.

787.

DR. SAMUEL GOODE HARRISS, of Boydton, Va., son of James

Belsches and *Alice Elizabeth Goode* Harriss, of " Invermay," Mecklenburg Co., Va., No. 250, p. 120, was born Dec. 1, 1833.   Married Mary
Alston, daughter of Dr. Alfred and *Frances Love* Plummer, of " Bellevue," Warren Co., N. C.   Children:—

> 2001, JAMES BELSCHES HARRISS, b. Dec. 25, 1868.   2002, MARY PLUM-
> MER, b. Jan. 22, 1861, m. *Rev. Oscar S. Bunting.* 2003, FRANCES
> LOVE, b. Sept. 22, 1863, m. *Benjamin Lee Partlow.* 2004, ALICE
> GOODE, b. July 17, 1867, unm. 2005, SAMUEL GOODE, b. July 28,
> 1872.

Dr. Harriss is a graduate of William and Mary College, from which institution he received the degree of M. A. in 1853, studied medicine at the University of Va., and received the degree of M. D. from Jefferson Medical College,
Philadelphia, 1855.   He is a leading physician in Mecklenburg Co., Va., having practiced in Boydton since 1855.

He has in his possession a beautiful miniature of his grandfather, Col. Samuel Goode, member of the Continental Congress, a copy of which appears in
this book through his courtesy. " He is an elegant old-time gentleman and
fond of his kin," writes a cousin.

" The first of the name of Harriss in Virginia, was William Harriss, a native of
Scotland, and a follower of the Stuarts, who came to Virginia with hundreds
of other cavaliers during the protectorate of Cromwell. His wife was Margaret Belsches, daughter of James Belsches, of " Inverness," who died about
1680."

William Harriss named his estate in Surry, on the James, "Broomfield." His
wife's brothers or cousins, who came to Virginia soon after her own arrival,
settled in Surry Co., and were ancestors of the families of the name who live
about Petersburg.   Descendants of William Harriss bear the names of Campbell, Jones, Eppes, Hamlin and Hardaway.   Articles in the possession of the
family bear the crest of Belsches of Scotland, as follows: *The trunk of an
oak tree, eradicated, with leaves sprouting out purpure,* and the motto, *Revirescit.*
The armor of Belsches are : *Or, three palets gules, a chief vaire.*

Hamlin Harriss, of " Turkey Island," Nottoway Co., was probably grand-
son of William Harriss, the first. He was born 1730–60, married his cousin,
Margaret Belsches.   Their daughter married Captain Roland Ward, of
Lynchburg, soldier of the war of 1812, nephew of No. 89 ; and their son, Cap-
tain James Belsches Harriss, of " Invermay," Mecklenburg Co., married Alice
Goode, No. 250, p. 120. " Invermay " or " Inverness " is a portion of " Whit-
by," on the Roanoke, (laid down on the large Virginia maps), named for
"Whitby on the James," by Col. Samuel Goode.

Maj. John Harriss, of " Norwood," Powhatan Co., Va., whose daughter,
Delia, married Blair Burwell, sr., of " Indian Camp," (see *Burwell Pedigree*),
and Thomas Harriss, of Powhatan, whose daughter, Alice, married Col. Francis Goode, No. 91, were near relatives of Hamlin Harriss.

Miss Plummer, who married Dr. Samuel Goode Harriss, was the daughter of
Dr. Alfred and Frances Love Plummer, of Warren Co., N. C.   Dr. Plummer

was son of Kemp Plummer, a distinguished resident of Warren Co., N. C., born in Virginia in 1769. (See Wheeler's *History of North Carolina*, II., p. 440, *Reminiscences of North Carolina*, p. 454). Mrs. Plummer was daughter of James W. Love, and his wife Pamelia Hendrick, whose first husband was John Bennet Goode, No. 287.*

789.

JAMES THOMAS HARRIS, of Montgomery, Ala., son of No. 250, was born Sept. 5, 1836, died in Montgomery, Nov. 18, 1884. He was educated at William and Mary College, and was by profession a civil engineer. After his removal to Alabama in 1855, he became concerned in railway enterprises, and had to do with nearly all the railroads in the State. He married, 1881, Sallie, daughter of Dr. Gilmer, of Montgomery. No children.

790.

CAPT. GEORGE T. BASKERVILLE, C. S. A., of "Mount Airy," Granville Co., N. C., son of Charles and *Lucy Goode* Baskerville, was born Nov. 1, 1830, and was killed at the battle of Gettysburg. He married his cousin, LUCY WALLER GOODE, No. 820, daughter of Hon. W. O. Goode, who died 1864. Children :—

> 2006, WILLIAM O. BASKERVILLE, b. July 25, 1854. 2007, C. THOMAS, b. Nov. 13, 1866. 2008, ALICE, b. Oct. 6, 1862, m. *Charles L. Finch.*

Captain Baskerville was graduated from the University of North Carolina in 1848, and settled in Granville Co., N. C., "where he was successful as a planter and prominent as a churchman." At the outbreak of the war he enlisted in the 13th North Carolina Regiment, C. S. A., and was appointed captain.

He was greatly respected for his piety and amiable character, and beloved and lamented by his whole community. He was buried on the field of Gettysburg, and the story of his death was brought home by a faithful old slave, who had been his body-servant. His wife died soon after, of a broken heart, it is said.

EXCURSUS.—THE BASKERVILLE FAMILY.

Communicated by COL. WILLIAM BASKERVILLE, of Mecklenburg Co., Va.

THE name Baskerville appeared in England at the time of the Norman Conquest. Sir Simon de Baskerville accompanied William the Conqueror to England. The name was originally called Basqueville. The most famous of the name is John Baskerville, of Birmingham, England, who had wonderful skill in penmanship, and made wonderful improvements in the art of printing.

----

*THE Hendrick family intermarried several times with the Goodes, see Nos. 287, 246, 818. BERNARD GOODE HENDRICK, of Columbus, Miss., son of BERNARD GOODE HENDRICK, is undoubtedly of the Goode lineage. A daughter of No. 47, is supposed to have married a Hendrick or Hendricks.

His editions of the classics, the Bible and Shakespeare, are now almost priceless. A near relative of John Baskerville, a merchant of Birmingham, named George Baskerville, who was the first one to come to Virginia, settled on James river and married Mary Minge. His son, George, owned estates in Nottoway and Mecklenburg Counties. He died and is buried in Mecklenburg.   William Baskerville, of Lombardy Grove, Mecklenburg Co., was grandson of the first members of the family in Virginia. He was a successful merchant and planter, and clerk of Mecklenburg Co. His brother, George, who married Martha Tabb, was clerk of the old District Court of Virginia. William Baskerville married Mary Eaton, daughter of Col. Charles Eaton, of Warren Co., North Carolina. He was in the revolutionary war, and died in 1814. From him and his brother, George, are descended many prominent families in Virginia, North Carolina, Tennessee and Mississippi.

Charles Baskerville, eldest son of the above, lived at Lombardy Grove ; he married first, Elizabeth Anne, daughter of Hon. Henry E. Coleman of Halifax Co.; second, Lucy, daughter of Hon. Samuel and Mary Burwell Goode, of Mecklenburg Co.

By the first marriage were, 1, Col. William Baskerville, of Mecklenburg Co., 2, H. E. C. Baskerville, Esq., of Richmond, Va., 3, Charles Baskerville, Esq., of Columbus, Miss., and 4, Mrs. A. V. Watkins, of Halifax Co. Of the second marriage, 1, Sarah Alice, 2, Samuel G., 3, Lucy G., died unmarried, 4, George Thomas, who was captain, C. S. A., and was killed at Gettysburg.

The coat of arms consists of a shield, surmounted by a wolf rampant, grasping a handful of arrows, below a scroll with the motto, "Spero ut fidelis." The name is often spelled without the final " e."

792.

JAMES W. BRAINE, of Mecklenburg Co., Va., married MARTHA W. BAPTIST, daughter of No. 253, p. 121, who was born in 1825. Children : —

> 2009, JAMES H. BRAINE, m. Miss Peters, of Helena, Ark., where he lives and is an extensive cotton planter. 2010, RICHARD H., d. y. 2011, EDWARD, d. y. 2012, MARY. 2013, PATTIE. 2014, ALICE. 2015, ADDISON.

Mr. Braine is prominent in Mecklenburg Co., as an educator and superintendent of public schools.

793.

SAMUEL GOODE BAPTIST, of Brooklyn, N. Y., son of No. 253, was born in 1823, died 1879. Married, 1849, Margaret Marion Mason, who lives, 1886, in Brooklyn.   Children : —

> 2016, SAMUEL GOODE BAPTIST, d. y, 2017, RICHARD H., d. y. 2018, MARGARET MARION, m. *Robert T. Currie*, children, 1, *Samuel Goode Currie*, 2, *Helen*, 3, *William*.

794.

RICHARD H. BAPTIST, of Petersburg, Va., son of No. 253, was born in 1830. Married Miss Butts. No children.

795.

THOMAS W. BAPTIST, son of R. W. and *Sally Goode* Baptist, No. 243, was born in 1727, died in 1881. Morried Miss Woltz, of North Carolina. Children:—

2019, ADA BAPTIST, b. 1876. 2020, SAMUEL GOODE, b. 1878. 2021, JAMES T., b. 1880.

796.

DR. JOHN GOODE BAPTIST, of Mecklenburg Co., Va., son of No. 253, was born in 1832. He is one of the principal physicians of his county, and unmarried.

797.

REV. EDWARD L. BAPTIST, of Boydton, Mecklenburg Co., Va., son of No. 253, was born in 1834. Married Emma Rolfe, of Meckburg Co. Children:—

2022, SALLIE GOODE BAPTIST, b. July 11, 1863, unm. 2023, EDWARD L., b. April 3, 1870. 2024, P. E., b. May 31, 1871. 2025, J. H., b. July 15, 1873. 2026, W. G., b. July 15, 1874. 2027, MARY A., b. Aug. 10, 1875.

Mr. Baptist was a soldier in the 3d Va. Cavalry, C. S. A., and is now a planter and a minister in the Baptist Church.

798.

SAMUEL GOODE JONES, of Sewanee, Tenn., son of Thomas W. and *Mary Armistead Goode* Jones, No. 254, was born Sept. 20, 1815. Married, (1), Nov. 1842, MARTHA W. GOODE, No. 758, and had eight children, (2), 1862, Aurie Elmore, of Sewanee, Tenn., and had seven children. Children:—

2030, COL. THOMAS GOODE JONES, b. Nov. 26, 1844. 2031, MARY V., b. April 6, 1847, m. *William Gesner*. 2032, SAM'L GOODE, jr., b. Oct. 2, 1849, d. May 16,1854. 2033, LUCY SPOTSWOOD, b. Aug. 3, 1851, m. Nov. 24, 1869, *F. H. Armstrong*, d. Feb. 1, 1879. 2034, EDWIN FRANCIS, b. Dec. 21, 1853. 3035, CARTER, b. March 19, 1855. 2036, MARTHA GOODE, b. Nov. 13, 1856, d. Feb. 8, 1859. 3037, CHARLES POLLARD, b. June 13, 1858, resides in Montgomery, Ala.

2038, ELMORE JONES, b. Sept. 19, 1864, d. Aug. 29, 1866. 2039, SAM'L GOODE, b. Nov. 19, 1855. 2040, JOSEPH BREVARD, b. Feb. 10, 1867. 2041, JACKSON SCOTT, b. July 14, 1868. 2042, GEORGE MASON, b. July 17, 1870. 2043, FRANKLIN ELMORE, b. July 18, 1872. 2044, CHARLES POLLARD, b. Dec. 18, 1873.

"Mr. Jones is a highly accomplished and intelligent man." writes a Florida correspondent. "He was for many years a civil engineer in Alabama, but is

now a resident of Tennessee." He was graduated at Williams College, Mass.
Thomas W. Jones, No. 254, was the son of John and *Lucy Binns Cargill* Jones, and great-grandson of "John Jones, Gentleman," of colonial days, who would appear from family tradition to have been a scion of the Jones family referred to on page 205, preceding.

799.

Dr. GEORGE MASON, of "Pleasant Shade," Greensville Co., Va. Married, March 2, 1836, Lucy B. Jones, daughter of Dr. Thomas W. and *Mary Armistead Goode* Jones, No. 554, p. 221, who was born March 26, 1801, died Sept., 1882. Children:—

> 2045, Edmunds Mason, M. D., b. Dec. 19, 1836. 2046, Thomas W., b. 1838, d. in Alabama before the war, a civil engineer. 2047, George, b. Sept. 17, 1840. 2048, Mary Goode, b. Jan. 7, 1844., unm. 2049, Fanny Young, b. Feb. 1846, d. Aug. 19, 1871. 2050, Rev. John Kercheval, b. Dec. 3, 1847. 2051, Emily, b. Feb., 1850, m. *W. H. Cole.* 2052, Robert, b. 1852, d. Sept., 1874. 2053, Samuel Goode, b. 1854, killed, 1884, by a falling tree. 2054, James, b. Dec., 1856. 2055, Nathaniel Y., b. June 15, 1860.

Dr. George Mason is a graduate of the Jefferson Medical College of Philadelphia.

The *propositus* of the Masons of Virginia was an English squire of Staffordshire, who flourished at the beginning of the seventeenth century. Two or three of his sons emigrated to Virginia about the middle of the century. William, who settled at or near the present site of Norfolk, was ancestor in the fourth degree, it is supposed, of Col. James Mason, an officer of the Revolution, who married Eliz. Harrison, of Sussex, and had sons (by her and another wife), 1. Rev. John Mason, one of the earliest Methodist preachers, 2, George, 3. Edmunds, who married Francis Young, and had issue, 1, Edmunds, (whose daughter, Emily, m. (1) Dr. Robt. Boykins, (2) Rev. Dr. Wingfield, of Portsmouth, Va.), 2, James, 3, Hon. John Young, b. 1799, d. 1859, U. S. Attorney General, Secretary of the Navy, and Minister to France, m. Mary A. Fort of Southampton, Va., 4, Robert, 5, William, 6, Eliza, m. James B. Mallory, of Brunswick Co., Va., 7, Peyton, 8, Anne, d. y., and 9, Dr. George, (No. 799 of the Goode pedigree).

An elder brother of William, Col. George Mason, born about 1600, was a member of the English parliament, and a Royalist officer, who, after the battle of Worcester, in 1651, escaped to Virginia, and in 1676, represented in assembly the County of Stafford, named in honor of his native shire, and was the ancestor of the Masons of "Gunston Hall," "Accokeek," "Doeg's Neck," and "Analostan, Id." One of his descendants married the daughter of Richard Goode, No. 62. Several of this family have been prominent in history, none more so than George Mason, author of the Virginia Declaration of Rights. It is very strange that the history of this family has never been elaborated. The best printed record of its members is that in Appleton's Cyclopedia; from this, in connection with that in Meade's "Old Churches and Families," a rather full deduction might be compiled.

800.

JOHN RAVENSCROFT JONES, of Lawrenceville, Brunswick Co., Va., son of No. 254, was born August 21, 1818. Married, December 11, 1839, Mary I., daughter of Col. William and Margaret W. Rice, of Brunswick Co., Va., who was born July 31, 1823. Children : —

> 2056, COL. WILLIAM RICE JONES, b. Nov. 21, 1840. 2057, THOMAS W., b. July 20, 1842. 2058, MARGARET W., b. April 27, 1844. 2059, MARY ARMISTEAD, b. Oct. 10, 1847, d. y. 2060, RAVENSCROFT, b. Nov. 10, 1849.

The following note is kindly given by Judge Buford, of Lawrenceville, Va.:

" Mr. J. Ravenscroft Jones was educated at Williams College, Massachusetts. He is a successful planter, and a man of the highest intelligence, with a mind well stored with accurate and valuable information on all subjects of general interest ; strong in his convictions of right, and bold and fearless in maintaining them, faithful and conscientious in the discharge of every duty, and withal possessed of a character above reproach. These qualities have won for him the respect and confidence of all who knew him, and have caused his selection to fill various positions of public trust. The duties of which he has invariably discharged in a manner that reflected the highest credit upon himself and to the entire satisfaction of the appointing power. The last of these positions held by him, was that of Superintendent of Public Free Schools for this county. If he were gone, there is not within the limits of this county one who could fill his place."

F. E. BUFORD.

803.

REV. EDWIN BURWELL JONES, M. D., of "Mill Site," Brunswick Co., Va., son of No. 254, was born Oct. 31, 1823. Married, Feb. 17, 1846, Cornelia Campbell, of Nottoway Co., Va., who died May, 1878. Children : —

> 2061, THOMAS W. JONES, of San Marino, Dinwiddie Co., Va., m. Mary Branch, children, 1, *Rebecca Pescud Jones*, 2, *Edwin Burwell*, 3, *Cornelia Campbell*. 2062, ARCHIBALD CAMPBELL, of Atlanta, Ga., m. Sue Gilmer, of Alabama, son, 1. *Edwin Burwell Jones*. 2063, EDWIN BURWELL, jr., m. Alice Pope, of Brunswick Co., Va. 2064, SALLIE E., m. *Richard Hardaway*, of Nottoway Co., Va. 2065, MARY Goode, m. *George Whitmore*, of San Marino, Va., children, 1, *Edwin Burwell Jones Whitmore*, 2, *George*, 3, *John Campbell*. 2066, CORNELIA CAMPBELL. 2067, MATTIE C. 2068, SAMUEL GOODE, of San Marino, Dinwiddie Co., m. Delia Pope, of Brunswick Co., son, 1, *Claiborne Turner Jones*. 2069, JOHN RAVENSCROFT, jr., Atlanta, Ga. 2070, LUCY BINNS, d. y.

" Dr. Jones has long been a physician, and is a clergyman in the Episcopal church, having charge of St. John's church in Lunenburg, and Sapony church in Dinwiddie Co. He is a man of very high character, and of great influence in his county, where he is greatly beloved by all. He was graduated at William and Mary College in 1842, and at some northern medical college."

804.

Col. THOMAS FRANCIS GOODE, of Boydton, Va., son of Dr. Thomas and *Mary Ann Knox* Goode, No. 255, p. 122, married, Nov. 27, 1860, Rosa Chambers, No. 838.   Children :—

2071, Edward Chambers Goode, b. Mar. 1, 1862. 2072, Kate Tucker, b. Nov. 22, 1863. 2073, Marion Knox, b. May 14, 1865, m. *Philip J. Briscoe.* 2074, Thomas Francis, b. May 27, 1869. 2075, St. John Chambers, b. July 28, 1879.

Col. Goode is a man of prominence in Virginia, and an acknowledged leader in the public enterprises of his section of the state.   He has frequently been a member of the Virginia House of Delegates, and was a delegate to the Virginia convention of 1861, and signer of the ordinance of secession.   He was candidate for Congress in 1859, in opposition to Gen. Roger A. Pryor, and was defeated by his opponent, who was elected as a successor to Hon. W. O. Goode, and who filled a seat until the opening of the war.

In the early part of the war he was an officer of cavalry under Gen. J. E. B. Stuart, and but for his resignation on account of feeble health, he would doubtless have attained a much higher rank than that of Colonel.

There are frequent allusions to his services in the volumes of war records already published.   In Gen. Magruder's report on the operations about Hampton, Aug. 9. 1861, reference is made to the able conduct of Capt. Goode, of the Mecklenburg Cavalry,* and in general order No. 89, Oct. 3, 1861, is a reference to Major Goode, of the 2d Cavalry.†

Gen. J. E. B. Stuart, in his report of a skirmish near Williamsburg, May 13, 1862, said : "Col. Goode's gallant conduct and the bravery of his men deserves the highest praise.   He captured the enemies flag and withdrew, bringing every wounded man in a very orderly manner,"‡ and in his report of the battle of Williamsburg, May 10, he mentions the unfaltering intrepidity of Col. Goode's regiment.§

Col. Goode was for many years the proprietor of the Buffalo Lithia Springs and under his management they have gained their present high reputation. These springs have recently been sold to a stock company, and the locality is advertised as "the Carlsbad of America."

He is a thoroughly representative man of his county and state, and the writer has often heard him referred to as one of the most able of living Virginians, who, if he had cared to do so, might have occupied a prominent position in public life.

805.

SAMUEL GOODE, of Middlebrook, Augusta Co., Va., son of No. 255, was born in 1827.   Married Mary Gatewood, daughter of Col. Samuel and Eugenia S. Massie, and granddaughter of Capt. Henry and

---

*War Records, Sec. I. Vol. II., p. 572.
†Ibid, p. 670.
‡Op. cit, Vol. XII., Part II., p. 444.
§Ibid, p. 572.

Susannah Preston Lewis Massie, of Nelson Co.   (See *Lewis Pedigree*, in Peyton's "History of Augusta Co., Va.")   Children:—

2076, MARY EUGENIA GOODE. 2077, NELLIE PLEASANTS. 2078, WILLIAM ALFRED. 2079, AURELIA. 2080, FLORINE.

A graduate of the Harvard Law School. Defective eyesight interfering with the practice of his profession, he has been connected with various summer watering places, and was for some time the manager of the Hot Springs and later of the Raleigh Springs, in Rockingham Co., Va.

807.

COL. GEORGE WILLIAM BRENT, of Alexandria, Va., son of George and *Elizabeth Parsons* Brent, was born August, 1821, and died 1872.   Married, about 1850, LUCY GOODE, daughter of No. 255, p. 122. Children:—

2081, THOMAS GOODE BRENT, b. Feb. 3, 1852. 2082, LUCY, m. (1) *William G. Howard*, (2) *Robert T. Thorp*, of Boydton, Va. 2083, SAMUEL G., b. June 28, 1855. 2084, MARY E., b. Sept. 2, 1857, m. *Charles A. Read*, of Atlanta, Ga. 2085, GEORGE G., b. Jan. 3, 1860. 2086, ALICE V., b. Nov. 8, 1863. 2087, CORNELIA W., b. Nov. 18, 1863. 2088, JESSIE INNIS, b. Jan. 15, 1870.

Hon. G. W. Brent was graduated at the University of Virginia in 1842. He practiced law at Warrenton, until 1852, and was for several terms a member of the Virginia Senate from Fauquier and Rappahannock Counties. From 1853 to 1861, he was a lawyer in Alexandria. He was member of the state constitutional convention of 1860–61, and a signer of the ordinance of secession. At the opening of the war he was appointed Major of Artillery, and subsequently was assigned to the 17th Va. Infantry.

In 1862 he was transferred to the Army of the West, and took part in the campaign under Beauregard, and subsequently became Adjutant-General and Chief of Staff to Gen. Braxton Bragg, commander of the Army of the West, and served in that capacity until the end of the war. After the surrender of Lee, he returned to Alexandria, and resumed the practice of his profession in partnership with C. W. Wattles. In 1870, he was seriously injured in the disaster at the Capitol in Richmond.

"His record" said the *Alexandria Gazette*, "shows him to have been prominent in the history of this State. As a lawyer he was learned, skilful, magnanimous and kind. As a soldier, brave and intrepid, he was, under the most trying circumstances, calm and collected—qualities which well fitted him for the prominent positions which he held. As a politician he recognized no servile dependency upon party, but was bold in the assertion of those principles which in the purity of his purpose he considered to be for the general good of his State and Country."

Col. Brent was descended from George Brent, who was land agent for Lord Fairfax and Lady Culpeper, about the year 1690. His kinsmen were prominent in the colonial history of Virginia and Maryland. A most interesting account of this family was printed in *De Bow's Review*, for May, 1859.

808.

WILLIAM PHILLIPS GARLAND, of Lynchburg, Va., son of the Hon. James and *Sarah J. Burch* Garland,* was born about 1835–40, and died 1863. He was a civil engineer. Married, Oct., 1860, at the residence of No. 798, in Montgomery, Ala., MARGARET KNOX GOODE, daughter of No. 255. Child :—

> 2089, WILLIE PHILLIPS GARLAND, b. Mar., 1863, and living, 1885, in Boydton, Va., with her aunts.

809.

WILLIAM G. FRIEND, of Drake's Branch, Charlotte Co., Va., married ELLEN GOODE, daughter of No. 255. He is a planter and a prominent member of the Presbyterian church in Charlotte. No children.

812.

DR. WILLIAM CRUMP, of Ivy Depot, Albemarle Co., Va., who died about 1869, married ALICE GOODE, daughter of No. 255, p. 122, who lives, 1886, in Staunton, Va. Children :—

> 2090, SALLIE CRUMP, m. *Rev. Mr. Goodwin*, now dead. 2091, ALICE.
> 2092, WILLIAM, of Texas. 2093, ELLEN. 2094, MARY.

813.

DR. M. M JORDAN, of Boydton, Va., was born in Isle of Wight Co., Va. Married (1) JULIET VIRGINIA GOODE, (No. 824), who died Nov., 1856, (2), Jan. 11, 1860, ELIZABETH B. GOODE, daughter of No. 256, p. 123. Children :—

> 2099, JENNIE JORDAN, b. Oct. 27, 1863. 2100, ALICE CORA, b. Sept. 8, 1865. 2101, ROBERT, b. June 22, 1872. 2102, BESSIE, b. Sept. 9, 1873, d. Aug. 1875. 2103, JOHN, b. Feb. 27, 1876. 2104, ROSE, b. Jan. 8, 1880.

Dr. Jordan is a graduate of Richmond Medical College, and of a similar institution in Baltimore.

817.

FRANCIS GOODE, of Winfield, Kansas, son of No. 256, died, 1885, in Kansas. He married Miss Hatcher. No children.

---

*THE GARLAND FAMILY. The Garlands of Virginia are descended from three brothers, Edward and John Garland and another, who emigrated from Wales, (to which kingdom the family removed from Sussex, England) to Virginia early in the 18th century. The elder brother settled in Richmond Co., and John and Edward in that part of New Kent Co., which now comprises Hanover Co. Edward Garland married Jane, daughter of Mr. Jennings, a large patentee of land, who died in 1719, and whose wife was a Cary. The name Garland is frequently used as a Christian name in the Goode family.

R. A. BROCK.

822.

COL. JOHN THOMAS GOODE, of "Sunnyside," Mecklenburg Co., Va., son of No. 271, was born 1835. Married (1) Dec. 9, 1857, Sarah Ravenscroft Buford, (2) Oct. 25, 1871, Carrie C. Sturdivant, of Mecklenburg Co., Va., (3) Bessie M. Morton, of Charlotte. Children : —

>2108, JULIET V. GOODE, b. 1858. 2109, MARY H., b. 1861. 2110, WILLIAM O., b. 1863. 2110½, LILA B., b. 1866.
>2111, BESSIE M. GOODE, b. 1878. 2112, JOHN T., b. 1879. 2113, MARGRET W., b. 1881. A2114, CARRIE STURDIVANT, b. 1882. 2115, 1884. 2115½, MORTON GRAHAM, b. 1886. SARAH BUFORD, b.

Col. Goode was graduated from the Va. Military Institute, and was appointed Second Lieutenant, 4th Cavalry, U. S. A., June 18, 1855, and 1st Lieutenant, June 10, 1857. At the outbreak of the war, he was with his company at Fort Floyd, near Salt Lake City. When he heard of the secession of Virginia, he resigned and went South. He was at once commissioned Major of artillery, and was in command of the Confederate batteries at Yorktown until its evacuation, and then of the artillery at Richmond. His command was assigned to infantry duty in the 34th Virginia Regiment, of which he was Colonel. He was in constant hard service until he received his parole at Appomattox C. H. In the last year of the war he commanded Wise's Brigade most of the time, and his commission as Brigadier-General was to have dated from the battle of Sailor's Creek, but for the end of the war a few days later.

Since the war he has been a planter in Mecklenburg Co., Va.

823.

HON. EDWARD BRANCH GOODE, of "Wheatlands," (Skipwith P. O.) Va., son of No. 271, was born 1843. Married Lucy, daughter of Joel and *Sallie Tarry* Watkins, of Granville, N. C. Children : —

>2116, GEORGE B., d. y. 2117, LUCY WATKINS. 2118, SARAH BELLE. 2119, HENRIETTA BOYD. 2120, EDWARD B. 2121, JOEL WATKINS. 2122, JULIET. 2123, MARY HAMILTON. 2124, WALLER MASSIE. 2125, WM. OSBORNE.

At the opening of the war he was a cadet in the Virginia Military Institute at Lexington. He entered the Confederate army, April 26, 1861, and served as drill-master in camp of instruction at Richmond, until July 4, when he was commissioned 2d Lieutenant, and assigned to duty as adjutant of Camp Lee. In October he became adjutant of the 56th Virginia Regt., serving with it in western Virginia and Kentucky. Invalided, 1862, with typhoid fever, at Russellville, Ky, he passed the "blockade," from Logan Co., Ky., to Chattanooga, on foot, Jan. 28 to July 4, 1862, and reached home after having been reported "dead." Adjutant 34th Virginia Infantry, 1862 to July 9, 1865, when he surrendered at Appomattox. He was twice wounded ; in the trenches in front of Petersburg, and at "Hatcher's Run." Since the war he has been planter and mill owner, in Mecklenburg Co., Va., and member of both houses of the Legislature.

825.

THOMAS H. BOYD, of Boydton, Va., a merchant, died in 1878. Married 1864, HENRIETTA WISE GOODE, daughter of No. 271, p. 123. Children : —

> 2120, JOHN B. BOYD, b. April 28, 1865. 2121, WILLIAM GOODE, b. Nov. 6, 1866. 2122, ALFRED W., b. Jan. 8, 1868. 2123, THOMAS H., b. Oct. 5, 1871.

THE BOYD FAMILY of Mecklenburg Co., from whom Boydton was named, are descended from Alexander Boyd, a young Edinburgh graduate, who came to this country early in the last century.

828.

WILLIAM H. PRYOR, son of No. 274, married about 1859, Margaret Walker, who was born about 1852, sister of Gen. Reuben Lindsay Walker, C. S. A., now of Texas. (see *Page Family*, p. 214.)

834.

DR. HARVIE LAIRD, married MARTHA CHAMBERS, daughter of No. 275, and not her sister JENNIE CHAMBERS, as is stated on page 124. Both are dead, leaving no children.

835.

DR. ALEXANDER LAIRD, married JENNIE CHAMBERS, (not MARTHA as stated on p. 124) daughter of No. 275. Son : —

> 2140, CHARLES LAIRD, m. Cora Holt, daughter of Dr. F. M. Holt, of Haut Rien, N. C.

839.

JUNIUS KEARNEY LONG, of Halifax Co., N. C., married ELIZABETH TUCKER, daughter of Hon. Thomas Goode Tucker, No. 256, died 1871. Children : —

> 2141, KATE TUDOR TUCKER LONG. 2142, EMILY A.

Junius K. Long was a planter's son, and is himself a planter. At the beginning of the war he was appointed Aide-de-Camp to Gov. Ellis, of N. C., after whose death he enlisted as a private in the service.

THE LONG FAMILY came from England to Maryland at an early day, and came then to Virginia. Col. Nicholas Long, Commissary-General of the North Carolina forts in the Continental Army, was a member of the General Assembly at Halifax, 1775, (see Wheeler's History), and a prominent citizen. His wife (Miss McKinney), and Mrs. Allen Jones (whose daughter m. Col. Long's son), are mentioned in Mrs. Ellet's " Women of the Revolution," as examples of " the patriotic zeal, noble spirit, and devotion to country, which gave tone to public sentiment in the days of '76." Of Mrs. Long, Wheeler says, " She was a woman of great energy of mind and body, and high mental endorsements. Her virtues and patriotism were the themes of the praise and admiration of the officers of the army of both parties." (North Carolina, p. 186.) Her grandson, Nicholas McKinney Long, was the father of the subject of this sketch.

840.

CAPT. THOMAS CAPEHART, of Kittrells, Granville Co., N. C., was born in Murfresboro, N. C., Aug., 1840, an officer in the Confederate Army, and since the war a planter, married AMELIA EPPES TUCKER, daughter of Thomas Goode Tucker, No. 256.   Children :—

2143, EMILY SOUTHALL CAPEHART, b. 1863. 2144, LUCY GOODE, b. 1865. 2145, KATE, b. 1867. 2146, TRISTAM. 2147, THOMAS TUCKER. 2148, CULLEN. 2149, JUNIUS LONG. 2150, ANTHONY ASHBURN. 2151, TUDOR STANLEY.

"Thomas Capehart's paternal ancestors, were the Byrds, of Virginia and the Ogilvies, of Scotland ; his maternal ancestors the Southalls, the Colemans, and the Gordons, of Virginia.   He was son of Tristram Capehart,* (b. 1796, d. 1859), and Emily Southall, (daughter of Daniel Southall); grandson of John Capehart, and Sophia Prajour (Razeur ?), of an old and extremely wealthy Huguenot family."   Thomas Capehart was educated at Chapel Hill College, N. C.; while an undergraduate he organized in this institution, the parent chapter of the "Chi Phi," fraternity, a Greek-letter literary society, which has numerous chapters in American colleges, and one in the University of Edinburg, Scotland.

At the age of 20 entered the Confederate Army as Lieutenant in the Edenton Co., commanded by Capt. James K. Marshall, grandson of the chief justice (afterwards Colonel, killed at Gettysburg).   This company, with one other, the Richmond Howitzers, fought the battle of Bethel, under command of Magruder.   After six months on the Peninsula, his terms of service expired.   He reorganized his company, providing them with uniforms at his own expense, the churches of his County furnishing the metal from which their guns were cast by giving their bells to be melted.   Served about Richmond, his company manning Battery No. 7, and other neighboring fortifications.   Served as member of General Court Martial under Judge Ould.   Subsequently appointed, by Gov. Vance, Captain of Cavalry, he served in skirmish duty along the Meherrin and Chowan Rivers until the close of the war.

842.

DR. JOHN H. TUCKER, of Henderson, N. C., son of No. 279, was born 1841.   Married, April, 1872, Willie Ruffin Hill, (daughter of Dr. John Hill, and grand daughter of Dr. John Hill, a wealthy and influential banker and planter of Wilmington, N. C.*)   Children :—

2152, WILLIAM TUCKER. 2153, A daughter.

---

*For biography of Tristram Capehart, see Wheeler's *Reminiscences of North Carolina*, p. 220.
*For an account of the Hill family of North Carolina, see Wheeler's *Reminiscences*, p. 303.

In 1861, Dr. Tucker left college and entered as a private in the "Dinwiddie Troop," 3d Virginia Regt., (Col. Thomas F. Goode), and was in the battles of Williamsburg, Seven Pines, &c. In 1812, on account of ill health, was transferred to hospital service in Chimborazo Hospital, Richmond. While here, under a permit from the War Department, was allowed to attend lectures at the Virginia Medical College, graduated 1864, and was assigned to duty as A. A. Surgeon in the hospital, soon after passed the examination for Ass't Surgeon, C. S. N., and ordered to the Steamer "Pedee," in South Carolina. When the coast was abandoned by the Confederate forces, he was assigned to the Naval Hospital on Drewry's Bluff, where he was in charge in 1865, and surrendered his sick and wounded to the U. S. naval forces. From 1865 to 1672, he was a physician and planter in Mississippi, and since that time has been a planter in North Carolina.

843.

DR. JOHN FEILD, of Hicksford, Greensville Co., Va., son of Dr. John and *Harriet Bolling* Feild, grandson of Alexander and *Susannah Bolling* Bolling (see Goode Genealogy, pp. 65, 211), was born about 1830, died 1873. Married MARIA TUCKER, daughter of No. 279, p. 226. Children:—

2136, EDWARD TUCKER FEILD. 2137, JOHN.

After his marriage he removed to Hicksford, Va., and was a successful physician there.

His widow returned to Brunswick County, and is living, 1886, with her brother, William C. Tucker, at her old home.

Dr. Feild was nephew of the wife of No. 101, and probably grandson of Theopilus and *Susan Thweat* Feild great grandson of Theopilus and —— *Taylor* Feild, and great-great-grandson of Theopilus Feild, the first of the name in Virginia, who came from England early in the 18th century, and was one of the founders of Blandford Church, in the chancel of which he was buried.*

844.

WILLIAM C. TUCKER, of San Marino, Dinwiddie Co., Va., son of No. 279, married, 1876, HELEN SCOTT, daughter of Dr. J. L. Scott, of Dinwiddie Co., Va., and Ellen Bolling, daughter of No. 258, p. 64, and cousin of Gen. Winfield Scott. Several children:—

2138, JOHN S. TUCKER, b. Nov., 1877. 2139, EDWARD BENNET, b. Oct., 1879. 2140, THOMAS GOODE, b. Aug., 1882. 2141, HELEN SCOTT, b. Aug., 1884.

THE POWHATAN GOODES.

847.

DR. WILLIAM HENRY GOODE, of Staunton, Va., son of No. 281, was born in Dinwiddie Co., Va., 1820. Graduated from Yale Medical

---

*See *Bristol Parish*, p. 173, for account of the Feild family.

College, 1842. Married, 1849, Elizabeth Morris, daughter of Owen C. Morris, of Goochland Co., Va. Children :—

> 2150, OWEN MORRIS GOODE, of Goochland, b. 1850 : in tobacco business. 2151, WILLIAM T., b. 1853, d. Dec., 1883, at Phoenixville, Pa., where he was engaged as engineer upon the Schuylkill tunnel. 2152, SUSAN PEGRAM, b. 1856, m. *H. C. Ball*, of Richmond, Va. 2153, ELIZABETH EMBRY, b. 1860, a teacher in Staunton, Va. 2154, JOHN VIVIAN, of Moberly, Mo., b. 1864, train-master of the Sedalia-Hannibal Division of the Missouri Pacific R. R. 2155, ROBERT E., b. 1868.

Dr. Goode was a wealthy planter before the war, owning "Shannon Hill," in Goochland Co. He was for many years connected with the Staunton Iron Works Company.

Dr. Goode was for five years a student of Prof. Draper at Hampden Sidney College and the University of New York, and was Assistant in Chemistry in the University of New York before and after he took his degree in Medicine at Yale Medical College. He writes, "I was connected in some way with nearly all the experiments and researches conducted by Dr. Draper while I was his assistant. At Hampden Sidney College, he discovered the principle of electrotyping, but turned it to no practical purpose. He took copies of some coins and medals, but nothing more. In New York he was the first to apply Daguerre's power of taking pictures by the sunlight on iodized plates, to taking pictures of the human face. My face was the first ever photographed by that process, for I sat for the pictures in the chapel of the University of New York within three days of the time Daguerre's pamphlet was received in New York. I was closely and intimately associated with Dr. Draper in his efforts to improve the camera and the process so that it could be used in taking pictures of men. Great advances were made in his laboratory, some by him and some by me. The camera now used in photography, is, I think, our joint production. The old iodine process was radically defective." (See contemporary files of *Silliman's Journal.*) He was also associated with Draper and Silliman in their first experiments in photography with the electric light.

849

DR. ROBERT HENRY WHARTON, of Richmond, Va., son of Dr. Austin and *Lucy Goode* Wharton, No. 284, was born in Cumberland Co., Va., 1811, died July 25, 1858. Married, Feb. 5, 1836, Lucy Hylton, daughter of William, and *Mehetable Hylton* Dabney. Children :—

> 2156, RICHARD GOODE WHARTON, Soldier, C. S. A. 2157, WILLIAM AUSTIN, b. 1844, a soldier, C. S. A., died July 6, 1863, from exposure in service. 2158, CHARLES DABNEY, b. 1846, a soldier, C. S. A., in Otey's Battery of Virginia Artillery ; died Nov. 24, 1863, of typhoid fever contracted in service. 2159, LUCY, m. *Joel McDowell Price*, of Danville, child, 1, *William Wharton Price*. 2160, JOEL HYLTON.

Educated at the Virginia Military Institute, Lexington, and Jefferson Medical College, Philadelphia, he was a successful physician in Hanover and Henrico Counties, Va.

851.

DR. RICHARD GOODE WHARTON, of Port Gibson, Miss., son of No. 284, was born in Cartersville, Va., Jan. 11, 1815. Married, 1845, Catharine Cronly of Port Gibson, daughter of Louis Cronly, Esq., a native of Ireland, who was born 1827, died 1867. Children : —

> 2161, CHARLES DABNEY WHARTON, b. July 1846, a merchant of Port Gibson, Miss., children, 1, *Charles R. Wharton*, 2, *Enfield*. 2162, HARRIET L., b. July 1848,, m. *Robert Hastings* of Port Gibson, who d. 1880, children. 1, *Richard Granberry Hastings*, b. 1875, 2, *Julia*, b. 1877, 3, *Roberta*, b. 1878. 2163, AUSTIN CRONLY, b. June, 1850, merchant, Port Gibson. 2164, CHARLOTTE, b. 1852. 2165, KATE, b. 1858, principal of Fayette Female Academy, Fayette, Miss. 2166, LUCY, b. 1860.

Dr. Wharton studied languages and mathematics at the University of Virginia, and received the degree of M. D. from the University of Pennsylvania, 1837. He began practice in King William Co., but soon removed to Grand Gulf, and in 1851, to Port Gibson, Miss. He has long been one of the principal physicians of eastern Mississippi, member of the State Medical Association, of which, in 1880, he was first vice-president, and has for many years been member of the State Board of Health. He has made a specialty of electro-therapeutics and diseases of the ear. His contributions to medical literature include among others, a paper on "The Congestive Fever of Mississippi," and another on "Malignant Epidemic Erysipelas" in the *American Journal of Medical Science*, others on "Opium Poisoning," and "Intestinal Obstruction relieved by Galvanism." in the *Philadelphia Medical Times*, and a paper on "Electro-Therapeutics," in the *Transactions of the State Medical Society of Mississippi*, 1876. (See sketch in Atkinson's *Biographical Dictionary of American Physicians and Surgeons*.)

857.

RICHARD BOYD, of "Bluestone," Mecklenburg Co., Va., married LUCY GOODE, daughter of No. 287. Children : —

> 2190, SALLIE M. BOYD, m. HILLARY M. L. GOODE, No. 594, p. 197. 2191, MARTHA, m L. E. FINCH, No. 1400, p. 196. 2192, PARMELIA, unm. 2193, ISABELLA, d. y. 2194, LUCY, d. y. 2195, JOHN G., m. Sallie Easley. 2196, ELIZA, m. *W. H. Humphries* of Clarkesville. 2197, JOSEPHINE, m. *Mr. Spencer*, d. in Texas. 2198, MARIA, m. *Benj. Roberts* of Charlotte Co. 2199, RICHARD, m. Pauline Rolfe. 2200, ROBERT, m. Miss Hatcher. 2201, MARY, unm. 2202, TABITHA, m. L. E. FINCH, No. 1400, (see above, No. 2191). 2203, PLENORA, m. *Mr. Orgain* of Brunswick. 2204-5, Others, d. y.

861.

ROBERT V. MONTAGUE, of Marengo Co., Ala., a native of Powhatan Co., Va., planter, died 1865, in Mobile. Married EMILY GARLAND VAUGHAN, daughter of No. 290–1, p. 127,* now, 1886, resident, a widow in Marshall, Saline Co., Mo. Children:—

> 2211, GEORGIANA A. MONTAGUE, d. about 1858. 2212, MICKLEBOROUGH L., d. about 1863. 2213, CESAR RODNEY, d. about 1870. 2214, EDWARD DESAIX, living in Marshall, Mo. 2215, REUBEN VAUGHAN. 2216, ROBERT G., d. about 1875. 2217, ALICE G. m. *Hardeman Cordell* of Marshall, Mo. 2218, HENRY CLAY, d. 1864.

" Mr. Montague being an old Whig-Union man, and taking no active part in the war, Mr. Lincoln appointed him in 1865, Collector of the Port of Mobile ; he had been a commission merchant in Mobile, had owned two cotton plantations in Marengo, and before the war had removed to Madison Parish, La. His planting interests there were destroyed by the invasions of both armies, including about 1000 bales of cotton which he had failed to sell. He intended to remove to Europe, and predicted the ruin of the South by war and secession. While Collector he aided his old friends."

862.

WILLIAM A. GASQUET, of New Orleans, La., married MARTHA JEFFERSON VAUGHAN, daughter of No. 290–1, p. 127, who died in Petersburg and is buried in Blandford Cemetery. Children:—

> 2219, FRANCIS JAMES GASQUET, m. Louise Lapeyre, dau. of Mr. Lapeyre of the old New Orleans firm of Pike, Lapeyre & Co., bankers, 2220, EVELYN, m. *John R. Marshall* of New York City, both dead, (daughters, 1, *Mrs. Louise Kernochan*, 2, *Mrs. Martha Wysong*, both living in New York City. 2221, LOUISA, m. *A. B. James*, of New Orleans, and living, a widow in New Orleans. 2222, VICTORIA V., m. *Philip De-la-Chaise*, of New Orleans, d. 1861.

863.

ALBERT J. KIDD, of Marengo Co., Ala., planter, married VIRGINIA VAUGHAN, daughter of No. 290–1, p. 127, who died, July, 1859. Children:—

> 2223, REUBEN VAUGHAN KIDD, soldier C. S. A., killed in battle. 2224, SUSAN A., m. *B. J. Duncan*, of Montgomery, Ala. 2225, VIRGINIA A., m. *Clarence Field*, of Montgomery, Ala.

864.

DR. SAMUEL WATKINS VAUGHAN, of Summerfield, Ala., son of No. 290–1, p. 127, was born in Mecklenburg Co., Va., 1800, died in Selma, Dec. 20, 1876. Married, (1) Martha Turner of Raleigh, N. C.,

---

*On page 127, 260–1 is a misprint for 290–1.

(2) Mrs. Jane (Alston) Jones, daughter of Judge Wm. Jeffreys Alston, of Marengo Co., Ala., born near Petersburg, Va., Dec. 31, 1800. Children, (eleven by first wife and two by second) :—

> 2226, EVELYN VAUGHAN, d. aged 18.   2227, SAMUEL WATKINS, Jr. 2228, REUBEN, d. in Louisiana. His son *James* lives with his mother Mrs. Kate Beasley. 2229, FREDERICK B. 2230, PAUL TURNER. 2231, HENRY WHITE, farmer, Dallas Co., Ala., un-married. A soldier C. S. A. 2232, SUSAN ALICE, m. *Rev. Robert Walker*, Fort Dodge, Iowa. 2233, VIRGINIA, m. *Dr. R. H. Hudson*, Summerfield, Dallas Co., Ala. 2234, DAVID ALFRED, of Selma, Ala., m. Susan Kennan. A soldier C. S. A. 2235, BETTIE, unm. 1886, Selma, Ala. 2236, GEORGE SEPTIMUS, unm., Selma, Alabama.

2237, WILLIAM WATKINS VAUGHAN. 2238, EVA MAY.

Dr. Samuel W. Vaughan studied medicine in Petersburg with Dr. Luke White, received his medical degree from one of the Philadelphia colleges, and spent several years in the hospitals in New York and Philadelphia. After practicing for some years in Denmark, Tenn., he was forced by ill health to abandon his profession and to engage in planting, first in Marengo Co., Ala., subsequently in Summerfield, and became very wealthy. A writer in the *Southern Argus* says :—

"In his long retirement from the practice of medicine, Dr. Vaughan lost none of his interest in that science. He kept abreast with all the discoveries. His ample library of well selected books was continuously enriched with the con-tributions of the best writers on medical science, and his cool and analytical mind, under the guidance of a large experience, was in constant meditation upon the truth of every new suggestion, and in testing the merits of accepted theories.

"His last act, in which he was arrested by the summons of death, was to min-ister to a friend who was brought to him sick. He stretched forth the hand of healing, but died before he could administer the balm. He had then been confined to his room during a long sickness, and, knowing his condition per-fectly, expected death every moment. Governed by the sense of duty which had regulated his whole life, he tried to relieve his friend from suffering, while death was present with himself. He died in his 76th year. His three score years had passed just at the time when his country was involved in its greatest trial. He was a patriot of the order that surrounded his cradle in the beginning of this century. So he laid his ample fortune on the altar of his country, and, following his sons to the field, bore the brunt of battle with the strength and heroism of a man in his prime. In one of the latest strug-gles of the war, he fought at Selma in a battalion of old men.

"Dr. Vaughan was a member of the Methodist church. His religious opin-ions were the considerate and resolute convictions of his judgment. He quietly conformed his conduct to his own views of duty, and by a golden example taught golden rules to others."

865.

DR. ALFRED GOODE VAUGHAN, of Demopolis, Ala., son of Reuben and *Alice Goode Watkins* Vaughan, No. 290–1, page 127, was born in Virginia about 1800. Married Mary O. Walton. Children :—

2238, MARY VAUGHAN, m. *J. S. Harwell* of Demopolis. 2239, HENRY CLAY, d. y. 2240, ADA B., m. *Hon. J. T. Jones, M. C.* 2241, SUSAN A., m. *Rev. H. A. M. Henderson*, of Jersey City, N. J. 2242, PLUTARCH. 2243, THEODOSIA B. 2244, TACITUS. 2245, ROBERT. 2246, IDA, m. *George Michael*, of Demopolis, 4 children. 2247, CECILIA, m. *J. Mastin*, of Woodford Co., Ky.

866.

HENRY DUGGER, of "The Canebrake," Marengo Co., Ala., was born in Brunswick Co., Va. He was a merchant in Petersburg till 1844, then removed to Alabama, where he died March 4, 1852. He married, 1832, ALICE GOODE VAUGHAN of "Battersea," near Petersburg, Va., daughter of No. 290–1, p. 127, who lives 1880, with her son Dr. H. C. Dugger, at Mistletoe Farm, Marengo Co., Ala. Children :—

2237, JOHN WATKINS DUGGER, d. 1855, in New Orleans. 2238, WILLIAM WAVERLY. 2239, REUBEN H. 2240, FREDERICK E., d. in battle. 2241, LUKE WHITE. 2242, ALICE VICTORIA, m. *Myron T. Sprague* of Mobile. 2243, HOBART C.

879.

WILLIAM EDWARD CARRINGTON, of Cumberland Co., Va., planter, son of No. 296, grandson of Charles and *Martha Goode* Povall, No. 115, born Feb. 25, 1804, died before 1883. Married, Nov. 16, 1831, Mary Gay Hatcher, daughter of Samuel Hatcher of Cumberland Co. Children :—

2300, ELIZABETH BOOKER CARRINGTON, born Oct. 14, 1832, m. July 28, 1852, *Bryant W. Rhodes*, (b. 1829,) of Perry Co., Ala., now of Grimes Co., Texas, farmer, issue : 1, *Samuel Edward Rhodes*, b. May 6, 1853, 2, *Oliver W.*, b. June 25, 1855, 3, *Alice*, b. Feb. 3, 1857, 4, *Efford B.*, Dec. 10, 1858, 5, *Willie*, 6, *Josephine*, b. June 10, 1866. 2301, EDWARD WILLIAM, b. Oct. 9, 1837. A soldier C. S. A., d. April 15, 2863, in hospital, Galveston, Texas. 2302, BERNARD, b. Sept. 16, 1839, d. Sept. 5, 1867, unm. A soldier C. S. A. 2303, THOMAS PRESTON, b. May 21, 1841, removed to Alabama and Texas before the war. 2304, ALICE, b. July 14, 1843, d. Sept. 19, 1865, m. Nov. 14, 1861, *Wm. H. Crawford* of Texas. Son :— 1, *Beverly Crawford*, d. y. 2305, SAMUEL HATCHER, b. April 22, 1847, d. 1873. 2306, WALTER H., b. Jan. 1 1849, d. Sept. 3, 1867, in Texas, 2307–8, Boy twins, not named, b. 1852, d. 1852, 2309, MARY LOUISA, b. June 29, 1853, d. Sept. 16, 1867.

880.

CODRINGTON CARRINGTON, of Cumberland Co., Va., farmer, son of Codrington Carrington, was born Oct. 23, 1801, d. Sept. 10,

1859, m. Aug. 11, 1832, MARTHA ANN CARRINGTON, daughter of No. 296, born Feb. 21, 1806, died April 29, 1865.   Children :—

> 2310, WILLIE ANN CARRINGTON, b. June 13, 1833, d. unm.   2311, ELLEN MARIA, b. Mar. 22, 1836, m. July 14, 1873, *Mr. Fox*, a farmer of Loudon Co., Va.   2312, MARTHA VIRGINIA, b. April 2, 1839, d. d. Feb. 13, 1833, m. *Dr. E. C. Mayo*, (No. 2318).   2313, ROBERT CODRINGTON, b. Sept. 6, 1842, farmer in Cumberland Co., Va., m. m. Sept. 5, 1866, Helen C. Walton, (dau. of Nath. and *Evelina Burton* Walton), children, *Martha Elvira Codrington*, b. Sept. 10, 1867, *et. al.*   2314, CORNELIA BOOKER, b. Feb. 1, 1845, m. Dec. 19, 1866, *T. B. S. Walton*, of Cumberland Co.   2315, WILLIAM A., b. Sept. 22, d. Sept. 25, 1843.

881.

WILLIAM H. MAYO, of "Boston Hill," Cumberland Co., a successful farmer, was born Sept. 21, 1798, d. Apr. 30, 1876.   Married, Oct. 8, 1823, HARRIET POVALL CARRINGTON, daughter of No. 296, born June 8, 1808, died Oct. 3, 1880.   Children :—

> 2316, HARRIET CARRINGTON MAYO, b. Nov. 14, 1824, m. *James M. Strange*.   2317, WILLIAM ROBERT, b. 1827, d. 1833.   2318, EDWARD CARRINGTON, b. May 23, 1830.   2319, JOSEPH HOWARD, b. Aug 13, 1832.   A private soldier, C. S. A., now a farmer, in Cumberland Co., unm.   2320, ELLEN MARIA, d. y.   2321, CATHERINE MARION, b. July 31, 1841, m. Dec. 16, 1857, *Gideon A. Strange*, (b. 1825,) a farmer in Fluvanna Co., private soldier C. S. A.   Issue : 1, *Harriet P. M.*, b. 1859, 2, *William*, 3, *Kate*, 4, *Marion*, 5, *A. T.*, 6, *Francis B.*   2322, GEORGE BOOKER, b. Nov. 28, 1844, d. June 5, 1873, m. Sept. 26, 1865, Louisa M. Harris, (dau. Peter F. Harris.)   A private C. S. A., "a better soldier never drew sword."   Issue : 1, *Ann Eliza Mayo*, b. 1866, and others.   2323, FRANCIS CODRINGTON, b. Nov. 12, 1847.   A soldier C. S. A., killed in battle.   2324, RICHARD LITTLEBERRY, d. y.

882.

COL. JOSEPH LITTLEBERRY CARRINGTON, of Richmond, Va., son of No. 296, was born Oct. 25, 1810.   Married, March 6, 1833 Adaline S. Jones, daughter of Powhatan Jones of Buckingham Co., Va. Children :—

> 2325, PEYTON RODES, b. Jan. 9, 1834.   2326, ELLA JOSEPHINE, b. June 29, 1836, m. *Gen. I. M. St. John, C. S. A.*   2327, SAMUEL JONES, b. May 9, 1838, d. Feb. 5, 1875.   2328, GILBERT MARION, b. Sept. 49, 1840, d. y.   2329, DELIA SCOTT, b. Oct. 10, 1842, m. *W. B. Bacon.*   2330, EDMONIA PRESTON, b. Sept. 20, 1844, d. y.   2331, MARTHA ELLEN, b. April 20, 1846, d. May 20, 1871, unm.   2332, NANNIE REED, b. June 24, 1849, m. *J. H. Blakemore.*   2333, WALTER BRUCE, d. y.   2334, WILLIAM ALLEN, d. y.   2335, WIL-

.LIAM ALLEN, b. Dec.25, 1856, d. Mar. 21, 1881, unm. 2336, ADA BOLEYNE, b. June 21, 1861, unm.

Col. Carrington is a veteran hotel manager, who has owned hotels in Cartersville, Farmville, Petersburg, and since 1863, in Richmond. He has long been the proprietor of the Exchange Hotel, the principal house in Richmond.

His name was accidentally omitted from the list of children of William Carrington, page 128.

883.

WILLIAM RANDOLPH BRADLEY, of Marshall Co., Miss., was born in Cumberland Co., Va., about 1820. Married, Dec. 19, 1829, ELLEN SARAH THEODOSIA CARRINGTON, daughter of No. 296, p. 128, b. Jan, 14, 1814. Removed to Mississippi in 1846, and lives near Holly Springs. Children :—

> 2337, MARTHA CARRINGTON BRADLEY, b. Dec. 15, 1830, d. Sept. 11, 1839, m. *Dr. Thos. P. Shields.* 2338, ROBERT EDWARD, b. Feb. 13, 1834. 2339, WILLIAM HENRY, b. 1836, d. y. 2340, RICHARD CARRINGTON, b. Feb. 6, 1838, m. Sept. 16, 1886, Sallie J. Gurley, (dau. of Rev. J. J. Gurley,) a soldier C. S. A.,, planter in Pickens Co., Ala., son, 1, *John Gurley Bankhead Bradley,* b. 1867. 2341, EMMA CABELL, b. Feb. 20, 1840, m. Mar. 19, 1858, *James Metcalfe,* of Ala. children. 1, *John Bell Metcalfe,* b. Aug. 27, 1860, 2, *James Kirkendoll,* b. 1862. 2342, VIRGINIA ELLEN, b. May 1, 1842, m. Dec. 23, 1859, *Wiley S. Metcalfe,* of Ala., children, 1, *Martha Elvira Metcalfe,* b. Nov. 25, 1860, 2. *Leander Raiborn,* 3, *Lee Henry,* 4, *Sarah Ann Elizabeth,* 5, *William,* 6, *Rosa Eleanor.* 2343, HENRY CLAY, b. May 6, 1835, d. July 2, 1864. 2343, BETTIE FRANKLIN, b. Apr. 23, 1847, m. Nov. 23, 1866, *Franklin J. Evans,*(or Irvin) of Alataug. 1, son. 2345, LUCY HARRIET, b. Jan. 1, 1853, d. y. 2346, THOMAS SHIELDS, b. May 18, 1852. 2347, WILLIE ANN, b. July 24, 1855.

885.

THOMAS RIDDELL POWELL, of Goochland Co., Va., a farmer, died 1877. Married, Nov. 22, 1837, LUCY VOLNEY GOODE CARRINGTON, dau. of No, 294, born Feb. 12, 1819, died Oct. 10, 1852. Children :—

> 2348, ELLEN WILLITT POWELL, b. Feb. 5, 1839, d. y. 2349, CHARLES HENRY, b. Jan. 21, 1843, private 3d Va. Cavalry C. S. A., merchant, and farmer, in Goochland Co. 2350, Infant, b. and d. 1845. 2351, MARY LUCY, b. Aug. 15, 1848, m. WILLIAM MAYO STRANGE, son of No..2016.

886.

CHARLES RICHARD CARRINGTON, of Cartersville, Cumberland Co., Va., son of No. 294, was born Jan. 10, 1822, died June 16, 1866. A merchant, lame and not in the war. Married Jan. 1, 1847, Jane

Randolph Pleasants, (born 1824, died 1868,) daughter of Isaac Pleasants, of Goochland.   Children : —

> 2352, WILLIE SUE CARRINGTON, b. Jan. 31, 1848, m. *Hampton B. Nicholas.* 2353, EMMA, b. Apr. 30, 1849, m. (1) *Mr. Nicholas*, d. (2) *Mr. Phillips.* 2354, NANNIE HARRISON, d. y.   2355, MARY PLEASANTS, b. May 12, 1853, m. Sept. 7, 1876, *Robert Carter Nicholas*, of New Canton Va., children.   2356, CHARLES RICHARD, b. Aug. 27, 1854, lives in Miss., unm.   2357, WILLIAM RANDOLPH, b. Feb. 25, 1856, lives south.   2358, ANN ELIZA, d. y.   2359, FRANCIS IRVING, b. 1860.

895.

JOHN WILLIAM GOODE, of Bellville, Texas, son of No. 295, p. 130, was born Oct. 17, 1826, in Marion, Perry Co., Alabama. He served through, the late war in Virginia, as a soldier in the Conconfederate Army, and has for several years, been practicing law in Bellville, Texas.   He married (1) Fanny Rowe, who bore him one son. (2) Callie Glenn, of Bellville.   Children : —

> 2370, SIDNEY GOODE, b. 1866.   2371, WILLIE, (dau.) b. 1872.   2372, FAY b. 1877,

896.

REV. DANIEL McNAIR, of Lafourche Parish, La., a Presbyterian clergyman, son of ——McNair, who came from Scotland to North Carolina about 1800, was born 1805.   Married July 3, 1843, MARTHA ANN GOODE, daughter of No. 295, born Feb. 13, 1829, living 1885, a widow in New Orleans.   Children : —

> 2373, LOULA McNAIR, b. 1850, d. 1882, m. *John B. Winder*, lawyer, of Terre Bonne Parish, La., children, 1. *Fay Winder*, b. 1877, 2. *Louise*, 2, *Sallie*.   2374, CAROLINE, b. 1858, m. *Henry Arthur*, of New Orleans.   2375, VINA, b. 1864.   2376, MAGGIE, b. 1866, m. *Nathaniel Perry*, of Terre Bonne Parish, who d. 1883, child 1. *John Perry*, b. 1882.

897.

HON. FLAVILLUS SIDNEY GOODE, of " Ridgeland," Terre Bonne Parish, La., son of No. 295, p. 130, was born Jan. 24, 1831, died 1886.   Married April 22, 1862, Sarah D. Perry, of Lafourche Parish, La., who died 1869.   Children : —

> 2377, BETTIE GOODE, b. 1864, m. *Van P. Winder*, lawyer, of Houma, La. 2348, CARRIE, b. 1866.   2379, LOULIE, b. 1868.

Judge Goode, was educated at Oakland College, and the University of North Carolina.   In 1852 he was admitted to the Bar, and settled at Houma La., when he practiced his profession and carried on a sugar plantation until the opening of the war.   In March, 1861, he entered the Confederate service as 1st Lieutenant in the Grivot Guards, of which company he soon became Captain, and which he commanded at Yorktown, and during the peninsular Campaign. In 1862, he was appointed Attorney-General of Louisiana, in which capacity he served until the end of the war. Subsequently, he retired to the quiet of professional practice in Terre Bonne Parish. From 1874 to 1878, he served in the State Senate, a position which he had previously held in 1857 and 1858. From 1879 to his death, he served as Judge of the 19th Judicial District of Louisiana. His plantation was eight miles from Houma, and he kept up also a town-house in New Orleans. He was for nearly thirty years prominent in Louisiana politics, and was a man of irreproachable public and private character.

899.

DR. JAMES JEFFERSON GOODE, of "Hope Farm," Terre Bonne Parish, La., son of No. 295, was born May 21, 1835, died March 22, 1867. Married, Oct. 4, 1865, Leonora H. Bisland, of "Mount Repose," near Natchez, Miss. Child :—

2378, SIDNEY GOODE, b. July 20, 1866.

Dr. Goode graduated at Oakland College, Miss., 1851, served through the war, as a soldier in the Confederate army in Virginia, and subsequently at Vicksburg, where he contracted a disease from exposure, which resulted in his death soon after the war, at Thibodaux, La.

901.

JOSEPH SCUDDAY GOODE, of Lafourche Parish, La., son of No. 295, was born Sept. 2, 1837, in Kemper Co., Miss., died Oct. 20, 1883. Married (1), Jan. 1, 1862, Fannie M. Holden, of Thibodaux, La., who died Nov. 28, 1865, leaving child: (2), Ellen Montgomery, of Fayette, Miss. Issue :—

2382, FRANK HOLDEN GOODE, b. 1870, d. 1878. 2383, FANNIE. 2384, PROSPER. 2385, NELLIE. 2386, EVELYN. 2387, JOSEPH. 2388, LEONORA.

He was graduated at Oakland College, Miss., 1851, and served through the late war 1861-63, in Virginia, as a soldier in the Confederate army. He was a successful lawyer, 1870–1883, in Lafourche Parish, La., and a very bright, enterprising man. He aided materially in the preparation of this Genealogy.

902.

ROBERT L. GOODE, of Camden, Wilcox Co., Ala., son of No. 296, was born about 1828, died in Miss., 1880. Married Viola Matthews, of Wilcox Co., Ala. Children :—

2389, WILLIAM GOODE, d. 2390, JAMES L., merchant, of Prairie Bluff, Wilcox Co., m. Miss Gaston. 2391, FLORENCE, m. *Leon Ratcliff*, of Wilcox Co., Ala.

903.

JAMES JEFFERSON GOODE, of Grove Hill, Clarke Co., Ala., was born about 1830, died 1879.   Married Caroline Williams, of Clarke Co., Ala.   Children : —

> 2392, LAURA GOODE, m. *Mortimer M. Barnwell*, of Sanford, Fla., an Englishman, issue, one daughter.   2393, ELLA.   2394, MARTHA.

J. J. Goode was graduated at the University of Alabama, in 1852, and practiced law in Clarke Co., Ala.   He was an officer in the Confederate army, and for some time a member of the Alabama Legislature.

904.

SAMUEL W. BONES, of Wilcox Co., Ala., planter, was born 1826–7, died about 1858, married REBECCA BELL GOODE, daughter of No. 296, who died 1851.   Children : —

> 2395, SARAH, m. *Joseph B. Dixon*, of London, Eng., and lives 1886, in Chattanooga, Tenn., children, 1, *Joseph B. Dixon*, 2, *Percy*, 3, *Arthur*, 4, *Anne*, 5, *Jessie*.   2396, REBECCA, m. *Mr. Snider*, of Texas.   2397, MARTHA, of Austin, Tex., unm.—"a lovely, industrious and self-reliant woman."

905.

HON. CHARLES W. TAIT, M. D., of Columbus, Texas, son of No. 297, was born June 4, 1815, died in Texas, Nov. 2, 1878.   Married Feb. 14, 1848, Louisa Williams.   Children : —

> 2400, CAROLINE TAIT, m. *Judge Wills Thompson*, of Columbus Texas., Speaker of the House of Representatives, and Lieut.-Gov. of the state; no children.   2401, MARTHA, b. 1859.   2402, GILMER, b. 1859.   2403, LOUISA.   2404, JANE, b. 1852.   2405, ROBERT, b. 1849.   2406, WILLIAM.   2407, ULTIMA, b. 1865, d. 1866.

Dr. Tait became a student in the University of Alabama at the time of its organization in 1832, and was graduated in 1835, afterwards receiving the degree of A. M.   He was appointed Assistant Surgeon, U. S. Navy, July 24, 1827, and Passed-Assistant-Surgeon March, 1843, resigning his commission Nov. 17, 1843.   He was concerned in a duel in youth, a circumstance which embittered his life, and interferred with the promise of a brilliant career.   He was for many years before his death in 1880, engaged in the practice of his profession in Columbus, Texas.   He was Surgeon of the 18th Reg't of Texas Cavalry, in the Mexican war, 1846.   He served several terms in the Legislature of Texas, and also as State Senator.   He was a Major in a Texas Regiment, C. S. A.

906.

HON. FELIX TAIT, of Camden, Wilcox Co., Ala., son of James and *Caroline Goode* Tait, No. 297, was born Nov. 13, 1822.   Married

Sept. 10, 1850, Narcissa Goree, daughter of John Rabb and Sarah E. Goree, of Perry Co., Ala. Children :—

2410, JOHN GOREE TAIT, b. June 24, 1851, d. Apr. 24, 1858. 2411, CAR-OLINE, b. Dec. 20, 1852, m. *Rev. Henry P. Moore.* 2412, ANNE, b. Apr. 18, 1854, m. *Wm. E. Moore,* of St. Johns, Hertford Co., N. C., a farmer, (boy soldier, C. S. A.), children, 1, *Helen Moore,* 2, *Alice Lisle,* 3, *Felix Tait.* 2413, SARAH KING, b. Nov. 6, 1855, d. Mar. 21, 1867. 2414, JAMES ASBURY, b. Feb. 28, 1857. 2415, CHARLES EDWIN, b. May 28, 1858, m. Adah L. Foster, son, *Fleet-wood F. Tait,* b. 1853. 2416, JULIA, b. Nov. 7, 1860, m. *S. W. Mc-Dowell,* of Camden, Ala., children, 1, *John McDowell,* 2, *Felix,* 3, *Wm. A.,* 4, *Edward L.* 2417, FELIX, b. Aug. 22, 1862. 2418, SALLIE, b. Jan. 18, 1865, now teaching school in Brooksville, Her-rando Co., Fla. 2419, ALBERT LUCAS, b. July, 9, 1867, d. near Palmetto, Manatee Co., Fla., Dec. 13, 1875. 2420, PORTER KING, b. Sept. 6, 1869, a student now in Marion, Perry Co., Ala., his home with his great uncle, Judge Porter King, of Marion, (a son of Gen. E. D. King.) 2421, ELEANOR ELIZABETH, b. Oct. 29. 1872.

Major Tait was graduated at the University of Alabama, in 1843. He served in the Mexican war as a member of the 1st Texas Cavalry, (Col. Jack Hays). He is an extensive cotton planter in Wilcox Co., Ala. In 1857–9, he was a member of the Alabama legislature, and 1875-7, in the State Senate. He served as Major in the 23d Alabama Infantry, (commanded by his brother-in law, Col. Beck), and participated in the operations of that regiment in Ken-tucky and Tennessee, and in the Campaigns of Vicksburg and Chicamauga.

907.

ROBERT TAIT, of Black's Bluff, Wilcox Co., Ala., a planter, son of No. 297, was born Dec. 12, 1824. Married Dec. 3, 1851, Mary Jane Erwin, daughter of Issac H. Erwin of Mobile. Children :—

2422, CHARLES TAIT, b. May 3, 1853, d. y. 2423, ERWIN, b. June 22, 1864, d. 1873. 2424, EMMA BOYD, b. July 20, 1855, d. 1864. 2425, ROBERT, b. Jan. 14, 1858. 2426, REBECCA, b. Nov. 4, 1859, d. y. 2427, SARAH, b. Feb. 8, 1861, d. 1876. 2428, MARY E., b. May 3, 1862, m. *W. R. K. Beck,* No, 2445. 2429. JAMES WOODS, b. June 1, 1863, d. Aug. 10, 1864. 2430, FRANK S., b. June 1, 1863, d. Mar. 11, 1865. 2431, ROSA, b. Sept. 7, 1867. 2432, HELEN, b. Mar. 29, 1869. 2433, ANNA, b. Feb. 28, 1872. 2434, GEORGE GILMAN, b. Jan. 23, 1874. 2435, SIDNEY GOODE. b. June 14, 1875. 2436, LOTTIE VASS, b. July 18, 1877.

908.

HON. ROBERT HUGH ERVIN, of Wilcox Co , Ala., son of Samuel Ervin, of South Carolina, who moved to Alabama in 1814, and his wife, the daughter of John Eades, are of the pioneer-settlers of Wilcox Co., was born at Coal Bluff, 1822, died Jan. 11, 1875, married Jan. 5, 1848, SARAH TAIT, daughter of No. 297, born Sept. 1, 1826.   Children :—

> 2437, ALBERT GOODE ERVIN, b. Sept. 20, 1848, m. Sept. 28, 1875, Eliz. Cumming, issue, 1, *Hugh Cumming Ervin*, 2, *Daniel*, 3, *Mary Ethel*, 4, *Gertrude Allan*.   2438, JENNIE FEE, b. Mar. 24, 1851. 2439, AURORA R., b. Mar. 18, 1853, m. Dec. 23, 1873, *Huriosco Austell*, issue, 1, *Maggie Austell*, 2, *Rob't Ervin*, 3, *Jennie Fee*, 4, *Huriosco*.   2440, CAROLINE, b. Nov. 23, 1854, m. Aug. 30, 1875, *Anderson Phillips*, issue, 1, *Anderson Phillips*, 2, *Adele*, 3, *Emma*. 2441, LEILA, b. Dec. 23, 1856, m. Dec. 12, 1883, *Arthur McDaniel*, issue, 1, *Blanche McDaniel*.   2442, MATTIE BECK, b. Dec. 3, 1858. 2443, SAMUEL JAMES, b. Nov. 27, 1860.   2444, ROBERT TAIT, b. May 25, 1863.

Dr. Ervin received the degree of M. D., from Transylvania University in 1845.   He was a member of the Alabama legislature, 1845-53, and of the State Senate in 1863.   In 1858-9, he was Grand Master of the Alabama Grand Lodge of Masons.

In 1861, he enlisted in a mounted company of Alabama volunteers, and participated in the battle of Shiloh.   After the close of the war he abandoned his planting interests and engaged in the commission business in Mobile, where he died in 1875.

Dr. Ervin is thus described : "a planter, stout and robust, with a brisk but kind deportment—a type of the Southern gentleman—of noble qualities of mind and heart, he sustained a high rank in public and social life."—(See Garrett's *Public Men of Alabama*, p. 731, and Brewer's *Alabama*, p. 500.)

909.

COL. FRANKLIN KING BECK, C. S. A. of Wilcox Co., Ala., son of Hon. John Beck, and his wife, (sister of Wm. R. King, Vice-President of the United States,) was born in Duplin Co., N. C., May 21, 1814.   Killed at battle of Resaca, Oct. 12, 1864.   Married, Dec. 18, 1845, MARTHA TAIT, dau. of James A. and *Caroline Goode Tait*, Children :—

> 2445, WILLIAM RUFUS KING BECK, b. 1849.   2446, JAMES TAIT, Lawyer of Camden Ala.   2447, MARY M. m. *E. N. Jones*, two sons and a daughter, living 1872, in Wilcox Co., Ala.

Col. Beck removed from North Carolina to Alabama with his parents in 1819.   He matriculated at the University of Alabama, and finished his education at Georgetown College, Washington, graduated at the Yale Law School, and settled in practice at Camden, Alabama.   In 1843, he was elected Solicitor of the Second Circuit of Alabama.   In 1843, he was in the Alabama legislature as a Union-Compromise man, and in 1855, as a Democrat, serving as Chairman of the Committee on Federal Relations, and was a member of the Constitutional

Convention of 1861, voting for secession. Garrett in his "Public Men of Alabama," p. 628, quotes from his speech denying the right of the government to coerce a seceding state, and urging Alabama to follow the lead of Virginia in her determination to resist invasions. He was elected Colonel of the 23d Regt. Alabama Infantry, at its organization in Montgomery Nov. 19, 1861, and led it in the Tennessee and Kentucky campaign of 1862, in the battles of Fort Gibson, and Chicasa Bayou, and Baker's Creek. The day after the latter battle, being left without orders at Big Black Bridge, Col. Beck held Grant's whole army in check twelve hours with his single regiment; and without severe loss. Returning into Vicksburg he shared in the siege, and surrendered with the city, was paroled, and soon exchanged, and joined the army of the Tennessee with his regiment in time to participate in the battle of Mission Ridge. His leg was fractured by a kick from a horse shortly after Vicksburg. At the battle of Resaca, while making a reconnoissance, a cannon ball struck the limb of a tree, glanced downward, passing through his legs, and killed his horse. He fel and expired in a few moments. His regiment under command of Col. Bibb was constantiy in front of Sherman from Resaca to Atlanta, and Jonestown, and fought at Columbia, Nashville, Branchville and Bentonville, and the 76 of the 1200 men on its rolls, who survived, surrendered at Salisbury in 1865.

"Col. Beck was a gentleman of fine character, a lawyer and advocate of established reputation, a wealthy planter, hospitable, talented, and popular," President of the Senate, and Vice-President of the United States, whose son, Capt. Wm R. King, m. E. H. Collier, (see Collier Excursus,) and also a daughter who m. Hon. John Beck.

His father, Hon. John Beck, member of the North Carolina House of Commons 1812-13, removed to Alabama about 1819, and was subsequently member of the Alabama General Assembly from Wilcox, 1823-24. He married Miss King and had two sons, Col. F. K. Beck, and Hon. Thos. K. Beck.

His grandfather, William King, a North Carolina planter, "a gentleman of fortune and character," of Irish descent, was one of the early citizens of North Carolina. He had sons William R., b. 1786. d. 1853, a Senator from Alabama,

910.

WILLIAM DOCK KING, of Bell's Landing, Monroe Co., Ala., son of General Edwin Davis King, died Nov. 20, 1866. Married Dec. 21, 1830, REBECCA SINGLETON TAIT, daughter of No. 297, p. 130. Children:—

2448, ANN ALSTON KING, b. Nov. 15, 1849, d. Apr. 24, 1880, m. *Francis S. Morrissett*, of Union, Perry Co., Ala., 3 children. 2449, EDWIN D., b. Dec. 5, 1851, of Bell's Landing Ala., unm. 2450, JAMES TAIT of Newberne, Hale Co., Ala., b. Nov. 2, 1853, m. Mary T. Scott, 2451, CAROLINE GOODE, b. Dec. 27, 1854, m. *Henry Hunter Lett*, of Bell's Landing, 6 childern. 2452, PAUL, of Dixon's Mill, Marrengo, Co., Ala., b. Mar. 16, 1856, m. Clementine DeLoach, 3 children. 2453, PHILIP WOODY, b. Aug. 24, 1857, d. y. 2454, ALABAMA, b. Jan. 23, 1860, d. 1886, m. *John W. Pharr*, of Lower Peach Tree,

Wilcox Co., Ala., son, 1, *John King Pharr*. 2455, ALEXANDER
CAMPBELL, b. Sept. 4, 1882, d. y.   2456, REBECCA, b. Jan. 12, 1864,
d. y.   2457, WILLIAM DOCK, b. Mar. 12, 1866.

911.

JOHN SHROPSHIRE, of Texas, a soldier C. S. A., killed in battle,
married CAROLINE TAIT, daughter of No. 297.   Child : —

> 2455, CHARLES TAIT SHROPSHIRE.

911-A.

COL. W. S. DELANEY, of Columbus, Colorado Co., Texas, married
MRS. CAROLINE TAIT DELANEY, daughter of No. 297.   Issue : —

> 2456, WILLIAM DELANEY.   2457, ERWIN.

912.

JAMES GOODE TAIT, of Camden, Wilcox Co , Alabama, son of
No. 297, was born July 4, 1853.   Married (1) Adele A. Barnes, (2)
Amelia Barnes.   Children : —

> 2458, MARY TAIT, b, Mar. 28, 1860.   2459, MARTHA, d. y.   2460. CARO-
> LINE, d. y.   2461, ROBERT, d. y.   2462, EDWARD BARNES, b. Feb.
> 27, 1868.   2463-64, ADELA and AUGUSTA, twins, d. y.   2465, GER-
> TRUDE, d. y.   2466, FELIX MILTON, b. Mar. 28, 1875.   2467, JAMES
> GOODE, b. Mar. 21, 1879.   2468, HELEN TAIT, b. 1884, d. y.   2469,
> ALBERT LUCAS, b. 1886.

913.

AUGUSTUS COLEMAN, of Memphis, Pickens Co., Alabama, was
a planter and merchant.   He married twice and left many children.   His
first wife Miss Windham, had three sons : —

> 2471, AUGUSTUS COLEMAN.   2472, OLIVER.   2473, JAMES.

914.

SYDNOR COLEMAN, of Memphis, Alabama, was a large planter.
He married Miss Hayes, who died.   Children.

915.

AMANDA COLEMAN, married (1) Mr. Dunn of Mobile, Alabama,
merchant.   He died 1856, and she married again and moved west.

921.

DR P. H. HAMILTON, of Shuqualak, Miss., a successful physician
in extensive practice, married 1845, SARAH REBECCA NICHOLSON, daughter of J. W. and *Martha Jefferson Goode* Nicholson, No. 300.   Served
throughout the war as Surgeon, C. S. A., in Georgia and Tennessee.
Children : —

> 2515, THOMAS HAMILTON, b. 1846, served 1862-5 in 1st Mississippi Cavalry,
> C. S. A.   2516, ISAAC.   2517, OSCAR.   2518, ERNEST.   2519, LULU.
> 2520, DELLA.

928-1

WILLIAM CABELL MEGGINSON, of Buckingham Co., Virginia, son of Joseph Cabell and *Sarah Bolling* Megginson, No. 301, pp. 70 and 132, was born April 17, 1794, died, Nov. 2, 1847. Married, Nov. 15, 1821, Amanda M., daughter of John T. Bocock of Buckingham, (now Appomatox Co.,) and sister to Hon. T. S. Bocock, who was born June 9, 1805. Children:—

2531, JOSEPH MEGGINSON, b. Nov. 15, 1822, d. 1838. 2532, JOHN, b. Sept. 9, 1824, d. Nov. 18, 1867, m. Sally Smith of Tennessee, children 1, *William*, 2, *Thomas*, 3, *Henry*. 2533, MARY, b. June 20, 1826, m. Dec. 8, 1850, *Capt. Jeter.* 2534, DAVIDSON, of Buckingham Co., children 1, *Caroline Davidson*, b. Sept. 28, 1852, 2, *Antonia*, b. 1856, 3, *Francis*, b. 1858, 4, *Virginia*, b. 1864. 2535, JUDITH, b. Nov. 19, 1828, single. 2536, SARAH, b. Feb. 4, 1831, m. Dec. 23, 1857, *Jessie Carter* of Appomattox, children, 1, *William Carter*, b. 1858, 2, *Charles*, b. 1860, 3, *Albion*, b. Oct. 1861. 2537, MARTHA, b. Jan. 18, 1834, m. May 1, 1866, MATTHEW FARRAR of Fluvanna Co., who d. Oct. 25, 1868, child, 1, *William Farrar*, b. Aug. 11, 1867. 2538, JANE, m. Dec. 24, 1867, *Peleg Bosworth*, of Amherst Co., Va., child, 1, *Amanda E. Bosworth.* 2539, MARIE, b. July 24, 1837, m. Nov. 28, 1867, *Thomas Farrar*, of Fluvauna Co. Va., child, 1, *Thomas Farrar.* 2540, WILLIAM, b. Oct. 28, 1840, m. Dec. 24, 1871, *Martha McCraw*, of Buckingham Co. 2541, POCAHONTAS, b. Aug. 29, 1842, m. (1) Nov. 14, 1865, *George Christian*, of Appomattox, who d. July 22, 1886, (2) Oct. 16, 1872, *Benjamin Farrar*, of Nashville, Tenn. 2542, FRANCIS, b. Dec. 6, 1844, m. Nov. 14, 1865, DR. WILLIAM N. HORSLEY, No. 929-15.

928-2.

WILLIAM BERKLEY, of Buckingham Co., Va., married Nov. 1820, ELIZABETH MEGGINSON, daughter of No. 301, born 1796. Child:—

2543, JOSEPH BERKLEY, m. ALMIRA V. MEGGINSON, No. 2556.

928–3.

ARCHIBALD BOLLING MEGGINSON, of Buckingham Co., Va., son of No. 301, p. 132, was born March 9, 1798, died Feb. 6, 1851. Married (1) Oct. 21, 1824, Ann R. daughter of Joseph White, of Nelson Co., born Aug. 1, 1807, died Oct. 8, 1829, had 3 children. Married (2) May 22, 1833, Elizabeth N., daughter of John Roberts, of Bent Creek, Appomattox Co., born Feb. 4, 1807, had eight children :—

2544, JANE C. MEGGINSON, b. Nov. 30, 1825, m. *James D. Campbell.* 2545, MARY A., b. May 28, 1827. 2546, ROBERT H., b. Aug. 8, 1829, d. Sept. 2, 1829. 2547, JOHN G., b. April 17, 1834. 2548, FANNY E., b. Feb. 26, 1838, d. Dec. 30, 1868. 2549, SARAH H., b. Oct. 10, 1838. 2550, BENJAMIN, b. July 24, 1840, d. Sept. 4,

1849. 2551, OLIVIA A., b. Dec. 17, 1841. 2552, LEWIS A., b. Dec. 22, 1843, m. Dec. 24, 1871, Ann D. Wright. 2553, JOSEPH C., b. June 16, 1846. 2554, ARCHIBALD B., b. April 21, 1849.

928-4

JOSEPH CABELL MEGGINSON, 2d, of Texas, son of No. 301, was born Feb. 11, 1800, died March 28, 1858. Married, Nov. 15, 1826, Almira, daughter of Capt. Joseph Montgomery, of Nelson Co., born Sept. 14, 1804, died April 13, 1831. Children :—

> 2555, SARAH J. E. MEGGINSON, b. Oct. 9, 1827, d. Aug. 1871, m. Sept. 13, 1845, *Hamilton L. Blair*, children, 1, *Catherine V.*, b, May 11, 1849, d. s. p. 2, *Mary E. L.*, b. June 11, 1853, 3, *Jessie B.*, 4, *Berkley.*, 5, *Henry*, 6, *Charles*, 7, *Roberta.* 2556, ALMIRA VIRGINIA, b. June 15, 1829, m. JOSEPH BERKLEY, No. 2543.

928-5.

SAMUEL B. MEGGINSON, of Buckingham Co., Va., son of No. 301, was born Jan. 14, 1802. Married June 10, 1828, Mary A., dauhgter of Christian Johnson, of Appomattox Co., born March 19, 8109. Children :—

> 2557, JOSEPH CABELL MEGGINSON, b. Aug. 14, 1829, m. 1, July 1, 1855. Eliza S. Alvis, b. Oct. 12, 1823, (2) Sally Spencer, children, 1, *William S.*, 2, *James B.*, and 2 others, also 4 by second marriage. 2558, SARAH J., b. Nov. 10, 1845, m. *Thomas Davidson*, 2 children. 2559, SAMUEL F., b. Dec. 11, 1850.

928-6

DR. NATHANIEL R. POWELL, of Nelson Co., Va., married JANE RANDOLPH MEGGINSON, daughter of No. 301, born 1804, died before 1835. Children :—

> 2561, SALLY POWELL, d. y., and one other.

928-7.

JOHN R. MEGGINSON, of Buckingham Co., Va., son of No. 301, was born May 1, 1806, died July 1875. Married Jan. 8, 1835, Mary R., daughter of William J. Dunn, of Appomattox Co. Children :—

> 2562, SARAH E. MEGGINSON, b. Feb. 9, 1836, d., m. Jan. 3, 1856, *James R. Phelps*, children, 1, *Ada B. Phelps*, b. 1857, 2, *Lee*, 3, *Alice*, 4, *Elizabeth.* 2563, ARCHIBALD B., b. Feb. 21, 1838, m. (1) Helen Brady, of Scottsville, who d. s. p. (2) Martha Howell, of Norfolk, children. 2564, JANE P., b. Mar. 7, 1840, m. *Peter N. Phelps*, of Appomattox, children, 1, *Walter S. Phelps*, b. 1858, 2, *Archibald*, 3, *John*, 4, *William*, 5, *Helen.*

DR. BENJAMIN CABELL MEGGINSON, of Nelson Co., Va., born July 31, 1809, living 1886. Married (1) May 25, 1837, Fanny, daughter of Capt. Alexander Blair, of Albemarle Co., who died 1879, leaving nine children. Married (2) 1880-81, Miss Hening. Children:—

2565, ALEXANDER MEGGINSON, b. June 14, 1844, d. Jan. 4, 1863. 2566, BENJAMIN H., b. Jan. 1, 1850, d. May 10, 1852. 2567, POCAHONTAS b. Sept. 7, 1842, d. Sept. 1864, m. July 10, 1862, *Dr. Wm. J. Hening*, of Powhatan, child, 1, *Benjamin C. Hening*, b. Sept. 15, 1863. 2568, SARAH L., b. Dec. 9, 1845, d. Aug. 8, 1870, m. Apr. 5, 1867, *Benjamin F. Farrar*, of Nashville Tenn., child, 1, *Laura Farrar*, b. June 14, 1869. 2569, ELLA O. C., b. Dec. 6, 1847, d. Jan. 7, 1863. 2570, ROBT. CRAIG, b. Feb. 7, 1852. 2571, WALTER B., b. Jan. 15, 1855. 2572, MARY FRANCIS., b. May 23, 1859. 2573, ELIZABETH J., b. Mar. 19, 1870.

929-1.

PAUL HORSLEY, of Nelson Co., Va., son of William Horsley, No. 303, p. 70, married Elizabeth Abbott, of Buckingham Co. Children:—

2574, LELIA HORSLEY. 2575, BENJAMIN. 2576, WILLIAM.

929-2.

WILLIS HARRIS, of Nelson Co., Va., married MARTHA HORSLEY daughter of No. 303. Children:—

2577, WILLIAM HORSLEY HARRIS. 2578, IDA.

929-3.

ELDRIDGE JEFFERSON, of Albemarle Co., Va., married MARY HORSLEY, daughter of No. 303. Child:—

2579, SARAH JEFFERSON.

929-6.

DABNEY P. GOOCH, of Amherst Co., Va., married EDNA PENDLETON, daughter of No. 304, p. 70. Child:—

2580, MARY GOOCH.

The children of Micajah and Mary Pendleton Horsley, omitted in their proper place in the fifteenth generation, (p. 132) were as follows: 929-4, MARTHA, 5, EDMUND, 6, EDNA, m. *D. P. Gooch*, 7, JOSEPH, 8, LETITIA, m. *H. M. Garland*, 9, ELIZABETH, m. *Thomas Emmet*, 10, ROBERT, m. Mary Talliaferro.

929-8.

HUDSON M. GARLAND, of Amherst Co., Va., married LETITIA PENDLETON, daughter of No. 304. Issue:—

2581, HENRIETTA GARLAND. 2582, BRECKENRIDGE.

929-9.

THOMAS EMMET, of Amherst Co., Va., married ELIZABETH PENDLETON, daughter of No. 304. Child:—

2583, PENDLETON EMMET.

929-10.

ROBERT PENDLETON, of Amherst Co., Va., son of No. 304, married Mary Talliaferro.   Child:—

2584, ROSE TALLIAFERRO PENDLETON.

929-11.

BENNET M. DEWITT, of Amherst Co., Va., editor, married JULIA HORSLEY, daughter of No. 307.   Children:—

2585, MARY ANNIE DEWITT. 2586, LOUIS J. 2587, BENNET. 2588, Dr. ROBERT HORSLEY, of Nelson Co., Va., who married Anna Hopkins, and had six children, whose names having been omitted in the proper place are given here, viz:—929-11, LAVINIA HORSLEY, m. *Dr. J. J. Twyman*, d. s. p. -12, JULIA, m. *Bennet M. DeWitt*, -13, *Rebecca*, -14, ROBERT H., -15, WILLIAM N. -16, ARCHIBALD.

929-15.

DR. WILLIAM N. HORSLEY, of Nelson Co., Va., son of No. 307, married Nov. 14, 1805, FRANCES MEGGINSON, daughter of No. 928-1, who was born Dec. 6, 1844.   Children:—

2620, WILLIAM HORSLEY, b. Aug. 7, 1866. 2621, ROLFE, b. Feb. 12, 1807. 2622, AMY, b. Oct. 10, 1871, d. June 6, 1874.

926-17.

WILLIAM HENRY HORSLEY, of Baltimore, son of Dr. Samuel Cabell and Mary Ann Denny Horsley, No. 309.

Dr. S. C. HORSLEY, No. 309, had three children, 929-17, WILLIAM HENRY HORSLEY, -18, SAMUEL C., -19, VIRGINIA, m. *Mr. Holland*, of Baltimore.

929-20.

DR. WILLIAM A. HORSLEY, of "Rock Cliff," Nelson Co., Va., son of No. 311, was born Sept. 6, 1815, and is living, 1886, married, 1845, Eliza G. Perkins, daughter of George Perkins of Cumberland Co.   Children:—

2630, ELIZA R. HORSLEY. 2631, JOHN DUNSCOMBE. 2632, MILDRED CABELL, m. *Mr. Easley*, of Halifax Co., children: 1, *Eliza Easley*, 2, *Charles*, 3, *Mildred Lee*, 4, *A. Horsley*, 5, *John O.* 2633, ANNA MARIA. 2634, CLARA LEE. 2635, MARY PERKINS. 2636, PHIL'A DUNSCOMBE.

The record of John Horsley, No. 311, having been omitted is here given. He married (1) Phil'a Hamilton Dunscombe and had one son, DR. WILLIAM A. HORSLEY, No. 929-20, married (2), Feb. 4, 1819, Mary Mildred Cabell, issue, 929-21, FREDERICK C., -22, EDMUND W., -23, NICHOLAS C., -24, ALICE W., m. Rev. *S. W. Watkins*, -25, PAULINA, -26, MARY ELIZABETH, -27, FRANCES MILDRED, m. *R. C. Anderson*, 28, JOHN, m. Rose, dau. of Dr. John M. Shelton, and has several children.

929-21.

DR. FREDERICK CABELL HORSLEY, of California, son of No. 311, was born Feb. 22, 1822, married, 1857, Dora Pleasants, of California. Children :—

2640, FREDERICK HORSLEY. 2641, MARY.

929-22.

EDMUND WINSTON HORSLEY, of Bedford Co., Va., son of No. 311, born 1824, married, 1857, Lucie G. Watkins, of Bedford Co., Va. Children :—

2645, MINNIE HORSLEY. 2646, EDMUND W. 2647, FANNIE OTEY.

929-23.

NICHOLAS CABELL HORSLEY, of Bedford Co., Va., son of No. 311, was born 1826. Married, 1852, Bettie Wilkes, of Bedford Co., Va. Children :—

2649, FREDERICK C. HORSLEY. 2650, BENJAMIN WILKES.

929-24.

REV. SAMUEL W. WATKINS, of Prince Edward, Co., Va., son of Henry E. and *Agnes W. Venable Watkins*, married, 1858, ALICE W. HORSLEY, daughter of No. 311. Child :—

2651, MILDRED C. WATKINS.

929-27.

ROBERT C. ANDERSON, JR. of Prince Edward Co., Va., married 1868, Francis Mildred Horsley, daughter of No. 311, born 1843, died 1882. Children :—

2652, MARY CABELL ANDERSON. 2653, FRANCIS POINDEXTER.

929-28.

JOHN HOLLOWAY MARSHALL, of Henderson, Ky., son of William and *Sarah Lyne Holloway* Marshall, and grandson of Col. William and *Lucy Goode* Marshall, No. 115¾ p. 44½, was born July 7, 1826, married Oct. 26, 1848, Martha E. Hopkins, born May 26, 1829. Children :—

2660, WILLIAM J. MARSHALL, b. Oct. 18, 1849. 2661, JOHN L., b. July 29, 1854, d. Feb. 18, 1855. 2662, LUCY GOODE, b. July 29, 1854, d. Feb. 24, 1855. 2663, JAMES B., b. Jan. 4, 1856. 2664, NANNIE MARIE, b. Sept. 22, 1858. 2665, JOHN H., b. Sept. 22, 1858. 2666, SAMUEL H., b. Nov. 28, 1863. 2667, LYNE HOLLOWAY, b. April 10, 1866. 2668, HARRY JOHNSON, b. May 6, 1870.

John H. Marshall and his brothers and sisters should have been catalogued with the fifteenth generation, but being contemporary with the sixteenth, and not having been discovered by me until the fifteenth was in type are

referred to here Mr. Marshall is described in. the matter relating to the
"Sullivant Memorial" as "a clever gentleman of integrity and good character." His mother was "the handsomest of the daughters of John Holloway, a
soldier of the Revolutionary war who married Anne, daughter of William and
Susanna Lyne Starling of Mecklenburg Co., Va.," and who removed to Henderson Ky., about the beginning of this century, and became a wealthy planter
and large slave holder. Their children are discussed at length in "the
Sullivant Memorial," a work full of interest to the student of American
history.

929-29.

WILLIAM J. MARSHALL, of Henderson, Ky., grandson of No.
115¾, p. 44½, was born Dec. 26, 1827. Married, Feb. 22, 1853,
Lucy F. Posey, daughter of William T. Posey. Children :—

> 2669, POSEY MARSHALL, b. Dec. 29, 1853, partner of his father. 2670,
> WILLIAM J., b. May 11, 1856. 2671, ELIZA DIXON, b. Dec. 14.
> 2672, STARLING, b. Dec. 9, 1859. 2673, THOMAS POSEY b., Aug.
> 1831, d. Aug. 14, 1865. 2674, ANNIE BEATTY, b. Nov. 22, 1864.
> 2675, GEORGE DIXON, b. April 10, 1866, d. July 15, 1866. 2676,
> HENRY DIXON, b. July 21, 1868. d. June 2, 1869. 2677, SARAH
> VIRGINIA, b. Dec. 12, 1869. 2678, STEWART OXLEY, b. Nov. 24.
> 1870. 2679, LEONARD LYNE, b. Jan. 11, 1874.

William J. Marshall, planter and banker, of Henderson, was in 1874, and
probaly still is an enterprising and successful business man with a high reputation for integrity and capacity, and an elder in the Presbyterian church. (see
the Presbyterian Cyclopedia for a biographical notice.)

His wife is great grand-daughter of Gen. Thomas Posey, an officer on the
staff of Washington during the Revolutionary war, U. S. Senator from Louisiana, and Governor of Indiana when that territory was organized into a state.

929-30.

JAMES BENNETT MARSHALL, grandson of No. 115¾, p. 44½,
was born July 1, 1832, married Oct. 22, 1867, Harriet E. Hickman, born
Aug. 9, 1845, died May 3, 1868. "A man of solid and reliable character."

929-31.

LEONARD H. LYNE, of Kentucky, born Jan. 6, 1826, married
Feb. 1, 1855, LUCY ANN MARSHALL, grand-daughter of No. 115¾, p.
44½, born May 5, 1836, died Dec. 6, 1860. Children :—

> 2682, SALLIE MARSHALL LYNE, b. July 15, 1856, died April 22, 1865.
> 2683, NANNIE MARSHALL, b. Feb. 6, 1859.

932½.

JOHN GOODE, of Prince Edward Co., Va., son of Joseph Goode,
and grandson of Richard Goode, No. 62, p. 44, should properly have
been discussed with the previous generation. For the following account

of the family I am indebted to the venerable Rev. Joseph Goode of Milo, Iowa, who at the age of eighty-eight writes an eight-page letter on the subject.   JOSEPH GOODE, whose brother William is referred to under No. 119, p. 71, was born about 1730.   He became impoverished by selling his plantation and taking as pay Continental paper money, just before it became worthless.   He moved from his home near Richmond to a small farm in the northern part of Buckingham, where he passed the remainder of his days in poverty, surrounded by a large family of children—chiefly girls.   He had a son Thomas, who was in all probability the man described under No. 117, page 70, also John the subject of this sketch, who was born 1760-70, and removed with his parents to Buckingham Co., and subsequently to Prince Edward, where he carried on the hatter's trade.   He married Miss Taggert, and had five daughters and three sons, two of whom grew to manhood.

He was a man of robust make, six feet high and weighed about 200 pounds, and was an invalid during his later years, although he attained nearly to the age of one hundred years.   Children :—

2684, PHILIP GOODE, b. Aug. 17, 1796.   2685. REV. JOSEPH, b. 1798.

THE MORRISETTE GOODES.

933.

MATHEW HAY BUCHANAN, of "Woodstock" Washington Co., Va., son of William and *Jean Keys* Buchanan, was born March 9, 1817. Married, Oct. 31, 1851, ELIZABETH GOODE, daughter of Col. John and *Ann C. Findlay* Goode, No. 315, p. 132.   Children :—

2701, BETTIE H. BUCHANAN.   2702, ROBERT GOODE.   2703, MARGARET K.   2704, THOMAS FINDLAY.   2705, RACHEL BUCHANAN.

M. H. Buchanan, was sheriff of Washington County for 16 years.   He bought his estate ("Woodstock") near Emory and Henry College in 1855, and has since been engaged in agriculture.

934.

BENJAMIN KEYES BUCHANAN, of "Keywood" near Saltville, Washington Co., Va., son of William and *Jean Keys* Buchanan was born, Oct. 31, 1815, married Nov. 22, 1843,   RACHEL GOODE, daughter of No. 315, born Oct. 9, 1826.   Children :—

2706, WILLIAM BUCHANAN, b. Feb. 15, 1846.   2707, JACK, b. July 14, 1848.   2708, THOMAS PRESTON, b. Apr. 3, 1854.   2709, JEAN KEYS, b. July 31, 1856.   2710, ALEXANDER FINDLAY, b. May 5, 1863.

Mr. Buchanan was born in Washington County.   He was connected with the salt works in Washington and Smythe Counties for many years.   He sold his interest there and bought his farm "Keywood," where he has resided and farmed for 26 years.

935.

ROBERT FINDLAY GOODE, of Bell Co., Texas, son of No. 315, was born in Washington Co., Va., June 29, 1828. Married, Feb. 12, 1857, Lula J. Morrison of Mississippi. Children : —

> 2711, ROBERT EDWARD GOODE, b. June 10, 1859, in Texas Co., Texas, m. EMMA BROOKS GOODE, No. 2820, child 1, *Marion Goode.* 2712, LULA PINKNEY, b. May 4, 1868, Guadalupe Co., Texas. 2713, JOHN CHESTERFIELD, b. Dec. 26, 1871, in Washington Co., Texas.

Mr. Goode removed to Texas in 1855. He was a soldier in Co. A., 22nd Texas Cavalry C. S. A., serving in the First Mississippi.

936.

JOHN WILLIAM GOODE, of Pulaski, Giles Co., Tenn., son of William Goode, No. 316, p. 133, was born 1800–20, in Tennessee and died, 1851–52. Married Pamelia Clack, 1820–40. Children : —

> 2714, WILLIAM SPENCER GOODE. 2715, SALLIE L. 2716, PATRICK, 2717, MARY.

937.

JOHN CHILDREY, of Matagorda Co., Texas, married in Tennessee about 1840, MARY GOODE, daughter of No. 316, p. 133, who after his death married MR. JOHNSON, of Monroe Co., Miss. Children : —

> 2718, JOHN WILLIAM CHILDREY, a soldier C. S. A., serving in Pyron's Regiment, stationed in New Mexico: living in 1885, in New Orleans La., m. Mary Brown, no children. 2719, GEORGE

THE NORTH CAROLINA GOODES.

969.

EDWARD GOODE, of Lakeland, Fla., was born in 1816, and spent the early years of his life in Hall Co., Ga. Children : —

> 2800, LELAND GOODE, m. *John Hake*, Bartow, Fla. 2801, WILLIAM E., b. 1850–60, educated in St. Johns College, Little Rock, Arkansas, 1872–3: lives in Lakeland, Florida, 1885, engaged in milling and hotel business. 2802, CAROLINE. 2803, JOSEPH, d. of consumption, 1870–80. 2804, THOMAS ALEXANDER, merchant, Bartow, Fla. 2805-8, 4 daughters, d. yg.

Mr. Goode was for a long time a resident of Jacksonville, Ala. He has been clerk of the courts in Alabama, and was a soldier, C. S. A. He is now engaged in real estate and other enterprises in Polk Co., Fla.

973.

CAPT. FRANCIS MARION GOODE, of Savannah, Indian Territory, son of No. 326, was born 1834 in Ashville, Alabama. He married 1860, ALICE E. ALLEN, Children : —

2820, EMMA BROOKS GOODE, b. 186J, m. 1880, ROBERT EDWARD GOODE, Galveston, Texas. 2821, JESSE H., b. 1863, of Savannah, I. T. 2822, ALICE E., b. 1867. 2823, LUCY M., b. 1869. 2824, LILY S., b. 1872.

He removed to Texas about 1865, settling at Sherman, Grayson Co., Texas, and subsequently removed to Savannah, Indian Territory. He was an officer in the Confederate Army, serving from 1862 to 1865, in the 44th Alabama Infantry, Anderson's Division, Longstreet's Corps, was in numerous battles, including the "Seven Day's fight before Richmond," "Frazier's Farm," and the "Second Battle of Manassas."

THE CULPEPER GOODES.

989.

WILLIAM CARLIN, of Carrollton, Illinois, was born in Missouri, 1804, died April 20, 1850. Married, Dec. 6, 1826, MARY GOODE, daughter of No. 342, born in Halifax Co., Va., July 3, 1805. Children :—

2901, THOMAS J. CARLIN, b. Dec. 13. 1827. 2902, WILLIAM P., b. Nov. 24, 1829. 2903, NANCY, b. April 11, 1832, m. *John Long.* 2904, ELIZABETH, b. June 27, 1834, m. *John Calvin Kelly.* 2905, GEORGE W., b. July 4, 1836, d. Oct. 5, 1870. 2906, EMILY, b. July 4, 1836, m. *Theophile Papin.* 2907, WALTER E., b. April 11, 1844. 2908, JULIA, b. Nov. 23, 1847, m. *J. Adair Hardin.*

The name Carlin was brought to America by two brothers who were with Emmett in the Irish rebellion of 1798, and who consequently were forced to leave Ireland. One of these brothers settled in the vicinity of Alexandria, Va., and had many descendants in Virginia and the South. Carlin's Springs, near Alexandria, perpetuates the name. The other brother, Thomas Carlin, found his way to Fredericktown, Mo., where he died in 1807, leaving two sons, Thomas and William. In 1819 the brother removed to Green Co., Illinois, where the elder laid out and named the town of Carrollton, and both of them died. Thomas Carlin was Captain of a company of Illinois volunteers, in the Black-Hawk war of 1832, and William Carlin was First Sergeant. Abraham Lincoln was a member of this or a sister company in the same campaign. After the conclusion of this campaign the elder brother became Register of Public Lands for Illinois, and in 1839, Governor of the State. William gave his attention to farming, and became also County Clerk, serving for many years in that capacity and also, during the latter years of his life, as Clerk of the Circuit Court. He was a man of capacity and influence. Like his brother, he was a strenuous adherent to the political tenets of Jefferson.

996.

DR. JOHN WESLEY GOODE, of Macoupin Co., Ill., son of No. 343, was born in Kentucky 1811, died 1847. Married Miss Bush, born in Jackson Co., Tenn., of parents who were natives of Tazewell Co., N. C.   Children :—

> 2920, REV. MARSHALL MONROE GOODE, b. Oct. 14, 1838.   2921, DARWIN LEDRAN, b. May 2, 1840, farmer and Postmaster at Stirrup Grove, Macoupin Co., Ill., 6 children, 1881.   2922, REV. GALEN MCGREGOR, b. July 4, 1842.   2923, MARTHA MARIA, b. June 25, 1844, m. *Rev. J. B. Conway.*

The following item was clipped from *The Reporter*, Verdes, Ill., April 1881 :— "Three brothers, Rev. Marshall Goode of Petersburg, Ill., Rev. Galen Goode of Harristown, and D. L. Goode from near Chapman's Point, were in Virden yesterday.   The two Revs. belong to the Christian denomination, and all three brothers stand not less than six feet in their stockings, and are fine specimens of physical manhood,"

1001.

JOHN GOODE, of Taylorsville, Ill., son of No. 348, was born 1822. Children :—

> 2924, JASPER PEYTON GOODE.   2925, MARY FRANCES.   2926, SUSAN.

THE RAPPAHANNOCK GOODES.

1004.

WILLIAM GOODE, of Lauderdale Co., Ala., son of Charles B. Goode, No. 350½ was born in Williamson Co., Tenn., Mar. 14, 1813, and died Sept 18, 1885.   He removed with his parents to Alabama, about 1827,   Children: —

> 2940, CHARLES GOODE, planter, of Rodgersville Ala,   2941, THOMAS, b. 1857.   2942, JESSE, b. Sept. 17, 1852.

1004-A.

HALBERT GOODE, of Limestone Co., Ala., a planter, son of No. 350½.

1004-B.

MILTON GOODE, of Limestone Co., Ala., son of No. 350½ died about 1874.   Several Children.

1004-C.

NATHAN GOODE, of Mississippi, son of No. 350½ was killed in the war.   A Soldier C. S. A.

1004-D.

CHARLES GOODE, of Union Co., Ala., son of No. 350½, removed from Alabama before the war.   He was murdered by Arkansas outlaws about 1883.

1004-E.

RICHARD GOODE, of Union Co., Arkansas, son of No. 350½, removed from Alabama before the war.   Died about 1883.

1004-F.

MARY GOODE, daughter of No. 350½, married MR. SHANNON, and removed from Alabama to Otto, Stone Co., Mo.

1004-G.

REBECCA GOODE, daughter of No. 350½, married MR. HUDSON, of Three Creeks, Union Co., Ark.

1004-H.

PEGGY GOODE, daughter of No. 350½, married JOHN HUDSON, of Three Creeks, Union Co., Ark.

1004-I.

JOSEPH GOODE, who lived before the war near Point Rock, Madison Co., Ala., was a half-brother of No. 350½.

1005.

JOHN GOODE, of Abbott, Rockingham Co., Va., son of No. 351, p. 138, was born 1803. Before the war a prosperous farmer, during the war a Union man, since the war, greatly impoverished, with unpaid claims against the Government. Children :—

> 2970, WILLIAM M. GOODE, of New Castle, Craig Co., Va. A soldier in 28th Va. Inf., C. S. A., and severely wounded at Gettysburg. 2971, JOHN P., of Salem, Va., (formerly of Harrisonburg). Soldier in 2nd Va. Inf., C. S. A. 2972, FERDINAND, of Salem, Va. 2973, JAMES L. Soldier C. S. A., killed. 2974, ALEXANDER C., d. bef. 1880. Soldier 22d Va. Inf., C. S. A. 2975, MARY C., m. *Dr. Thomas H. B. Dillard*, of Salem, Va. 2976, SALLIE A., m. *Rev. L. E. Busby*, Louisville, S. C. 2977, SALMA P.

THE RAPPAHANNOCK GOODES.

1020.

WILLIAM THOMAS GOODE, of Marionville, Lawrence Co., Mo., a merchant, son of No. 353, was born near New Castle, Henry Co., Ky., May 18, 1817, moved to Missouri, 1868. Married Nov. 14, 1848, Martitia Elizabeth Guthrie, born in Buckingham Co., Va., Aug. 23, 1822, died June 22, 1876. Son :—

> 3001, RICHARD L. GOODE, b. Feb, 4, 1855.

1021

COL. SIMON S. GOODE, of Decatur, Illinois, son of No. 353, p. 139, was born in Kentucky, 1820, killed at Mexico, Mo., 1865. Married Emma ———, who lives in St Louis, 1886. Children :—

> 3005, RICHARD GOODE, a graduate of the Louisville Law School, and a brilliant young lawyer who died an untimely death. 3006, LOLA W., a young lady of dramatic talent. 3007, MATTIE B. 3008, AUGUSTUS B. 3009, ALBERT L. 3010, CLARENCE S.

"Col. Goode, was a lawyer," writes R. L. Goode, "but led an adventurous life. He was brave and honorable, though choleric and turbulent. He went to California at an early day, I think in '49 or '50. On the trip across the plains he killed a man and at Salt Lake was tried and acquitted. From California he went to Australia and China, and was with Walker in Nicaragua. Afterwards he settled at Decatur, Ill., and resumed the practice of law. The war coming on, a regiment was raised in that town, and he was chosen its Colonel but his sympathies were thought by many to be with the Southern cause and on account of this suspicion of his loyalty, he was removed by Governor Yates from the command of his regiment, and U. S. Grant appointed in his place. On this trivial circumstance, we may fairly conclude, hinged the fortunes of the war, for though, I doubt not, our relative would have made a gallant and efficient officer, we can hardly expect that he would have been a Grant. He seems to have been very much chagrined at this treatment by Yates, for he took no further part in the war. He was killed in Mexico, Mo., in 1865."

1022.

Dr. ROBERT HENRY GOODE, of Washington, Mo., son of No. 353, was born in Kentucky, 1820–25. "He was a physician and a very fine surgeon. He died in 1879 of pulmonary disease." Child :—

> 3011, Daughter, b. 1865, living in 1881, in Washington, Mo., with her mother.

1027-1.

GEORGE GOODE, nephew of No. 353, went from Kentucky to Georgia to live.

1027.

RICHARD NEWTON GOODE, of Waco, Texas, Attorney-at-Law, was born in Alabama, 1812, moved to Texas, 1844, died in Waco, Texas, Feb. 6, 1873. Married, Elizabeth Virginia Mallory. Children :—

> 3030, RICHARD PAVIUS GOODE, b. 1845, soldier C. S. A., 15th Texas Reg't, farmer, Waco, Texas. 3031, JAMES WESLEY, b. 1849, farmer, Waco, Texas. 3032, ROBERT, b. June 5, 1851: graduated Waco University, admitted 1873, as attorney-at-law, Waco, Texas. 3033, URSULA CHASE, m. 1882, *B. C. DeBorde*, of Limestone Co., Texas. 3034, LULA BLANCHE, m. 1878, *Harry Hensley*, of Waco, Texas, has two children :—1, *Elizabeth Norna Hensley*, b. Aug. 30, 1880; 2, *Ernest*, b. May 1, 1882. 3035, JOHN, student Waco, Univ. 3036, OLIVIA, student, Waco Univ. 3037, IVANOWNA, student, Waco Univ.

1028.

NOBLE M. GOODE, of Texas, son of No 354, born 1814, d. 1872, had fourteen children :—

> 3038, JOHN GOODE, soldier C. S. A., Co. A, 15th Texas Reg't. 3039, JOSEPH. 3040, RICHARD. 3041, and others.

SEVENTEENTH GENERATION.

Like leaves on trees the race of man is found,
Now green in youth, now withering on the ground.
Another race the following spring supplies—
They fall successive, and successive rise.
So generations in their course decay
So flourish they, when those have passed away,

POPE'S HOMER : *Book VII.*

THE PRINCE EDWARD GOODES.

1024-(391.)

ROBERT SETH GOODE, of Cole Co., Mo., son of Thomas and Eliza Royall Jones, No. 150, p. 76, was born in Amelia Co., Va., 1820. Graduated Hampton-Sidney College, 1839, and removed with his father to Missouri the same year. He died in 1841. A young man of great promise. No. 1024, and his brother and sisters properly belong to the 16th generation.

1025-(392.)

WILLAM BURWELL SMITH, of Nottoway Co., Va., married MARY ELIZA GOODE, daughter of No. 150, who was born in Amelia Co., 1819, and died Aug. 12, 1845. Children :—

> 3092, OPHELIA KENNON SMITH, d. unm., 1846. 3093, WILLIAM BURWELL, d. unm., 1808. 3094, REBECCA BURWELL, m. *John S. Wiley.*

Mr. Smith was a scholar of fine attainments. He died in Nottoway Co., Va., of consumption, about 1848.

1024.

PETER SIDNEY SMITH, of Cole Co., Mo., son of Kennon Smith, born about 1810, died Aug., 1845, married 1840, LOUISA MARIA GOODE, daughter of No. 150, who was born March 31, 1822. Children :—

> 3095, MARY SIDNEY SMITH, b. Aug. 12, 1844, d. 1875, m. *B. H. Massey.*

1026-A.

GEN. JAMES L. MINOR, of "Braynefield," near Jefferson City, Mo., son of Garrit and *Eliza McWilliams* Minor, of Fredericksburg Va., was born June 9, 1813. Married (1) Mar. 27, 1844, SALLIE C. GOODE, daughter of No. 150, (2) LOUISA M. GOODE, daughter of No. 150, widow of P. Sidney Smith (1024), who died Apr. 17, 1886. Child (first marriage.) : —

3096, SALLIE GOODE MINOR, b. June 6, 1845, m. *Hamilton Gamble*, 1863.

The following sketch is abridged from one which is printed in the Missouri volume of the U. S. Biographical Directory, 1878 :—

James L. Minor, was born in the town of Fredericksburg, Va., June 9, 1813. His father was Garrit Minor, a lawyer of eminence, a participant in the war of 1812, for many years a delegate to the State Legislature from Spottsylvania County ; Mayor of the city of Fredericksburg, and one of the presidential electors of the State when Virginia, in 1824, voted for Gen. Jackson.   In 1803, he married Miss Eliza McWilliams, only daughter of Major Wm. McWilliams, who served during the War of the Revolution, as aid to Lord Sterling, and was greatly instrumental in detecting and defeating the conspiracy, headed by Conway, to supplant Gen. Washington, as commander-in-chief, and to substitute in his place Gen. Gates, then fresh from the laurels of Saratoga.

Young Minor was educated at the classical academy of his native town, and at the age of fifteen was elected as the assistant teacher of the classics.   He studied law with his brother, Gen. Wm. G. Minor in Caroline Co., Va., and finished his law course with Judge John. T. Lomax.   In 1835, Gen. Jackson offered him the post of U. S. District Attorney for the Southern district of Florida, at Key West, which he declined.

In May, 1835, he landed in St. Louis, and in June of that year commenced in Palmyra, the practice of law, which he prosecuted until the fall of 1838, when he was elected Secretary of the State Senate.   In February, 1839, he was nominated by Gov. Boggs, and confirmed by the Senate, as Secretary of State. This position he held continuously until April, 1845.   In April, 1839, he became Adjutant-General, and in 1842, Superintendent of Public Schools.

In 1845, Gen. Minor took leave of active public life, and devoted himself to the persuit of agriculture in the cultivation of a large farm of the alluvial lands of the Missouri river, and in the production of hemp and tobacco, found occupation congenial and profitable.   While a farmer he filled several important public trusts.   He was twice curator of the State University ; a manager of the first State Lunatic Asylum, and a member of the Board of public guardians.   He was also corresponding secretary of the State Agricultural Board, holding its fairs at Boonville, in which capacity, he labored by speech and pen to elevate the farmers as a class, to stimulate them to the necessity of a higher knowledge of the principles of their occupation, and to impress upon them its dignity and importance.   He was long secretary of the Lodge of Grangers in Cole County.

Gen. Minor took no part in the late Civil War, and has been uniformly a state-rights Democrat.   Since 1878, he has lived a retired life in the bosom of his family, in Jefferson City, Mo.

"In 1845," says *The Jefferson City Journal*, of Aug. 19, "Mrs. Minor connected herself with the Methodist church, South, and has ever since been a devout and active member of that organization.   Noted for her many Christian virtues, her devotion to her husband and family, her charities numerous and unobtrusive, for her kindness to the friendless and unprotected of her own sex, she has gone to her great reward."

1026-(392-3.)

THEODORE STANLEY, of Cole Co., Mo.,a native of Hartford, Conn., married, January, 1845, MARTHA M. GOODE, daughter of No. 150, born in Virginia, 1838. Children :—

> 3097-1, ELISHA STANLEY, b. 1847, m. Callie Abbott, child, *Lester Stanley*. 3097-2, THOMAS GOODE, d. 1883. 3097-3, THEODORE. 3097-4, ANTHONY DUMON, of Pleasant Hill, Mo., m. Alma Duer, children, 1 *Laura Stanley*, 2 *Pitkin*, 3 *Ada*. 3097-5, ADA, m. *Benj. Christopher*.

1027-(392-4.)

DAVID HUMPHREYS, of St. Louis, Mo., born in Leesburg, Va., a merchant, married FANNIE M. GOODE, daughter of No. 150. Children :—

> 3098-1, JANET HUMPHREYS, m. *C. A. Batterton*, of Alton, Ill., child, 1, *Fannie Batterton*. 3098-2, MATTIE STANLEY, 3098-3, LOUISE MINOR, single.

1030-1

MR. SHEPPERSON of "Cottage Home," Charlotte Co., Va., a planter and prominent citizen, married MARTHA DANIEL, daughter of Samuel and *Martha Friend* Daniel, No. 156-1, p. 77, who was born 1780-1820. Son :—

> 3100, JOHN SHEPPERSON, planter, of Charlotte Co., Va., m. Miss Burton of Petersburg,—several children.

1030-2.

SAMUEL DANIEL, of Charlotte Co., Va., planter, son of No. 156-1, was born 1780-1810, died about 1840. Married Mary Booker. Children :—

> 3101, EDWARD DANIEL. 3102, LOUISA, m. *Mr. Morton*, of Clarksville, Va. 3103, JENNIE FRIEND, m. *Mr. Catlett*, lawyer, of Staunton, Va. 3104, SUSAN, m. *David Eggleston*, lawyer of Charlotte C. H. 3105, LELIA. 3105-1, SAMUEL. 3105-2, ELIZABETH.

1030-3

HILARY RICHARDSON, of Charlotte Co., Va., planter. Married MARY DANIEL, daughter of No. 156-1. Children :—

> 3106, EDWARD RICHARDSON, d. y. 3107, BETTY, m. *Mr. Poe*, of North Carolina. 3108, MARTHA, m. *Rev. Patrick R. Low*, of North Carolina, a Presbyterian clergyman. 3109, REV. WILLIAM.

1030-4.

P. LIGON, of Prince Edward Co., Va., married LUCY DANIEL, daughter of No. 156-1. Daughter :—

3110, LUCY LIGON, m. *Frank Thornton*, of Appomattox, a merchant at Charlotte C. H., children.

1030-5.

JOHN W. DANIEL, of "Ingleside," Charlotte Co., Va., son of No. 156-1, was born 1821, died July 19, 1882. Married (1) Cornelia Worsham,* who had two children; (2) Charlotte Wharey, (daughter of Rev. Dr. Wharey, of Cumberland Co., sister of Rev. Thomas Wharey, D. D., of Texas, and Rev. James Wharey, of North Carolina,) who had four children.   Children :—

> 3111, ELLA DANIEL, b. 1858.   3112, SAMUEL PRIDE, b. 1862.   3113, WHAREY DANIEL.   3114, ANNIE GOODE.   3115-16, Others.

"Mr. Daniel," said a writer in the *Central Presbyterian*, "was one of the noble few whose sterling integrity gives tone to public morals.   For many years an elder in the village church at Charlotte C. H., afterward in the Drake's Branch church, he made an earnest effort to discharge in the best manner possible all the functions of his office.   *   *   *   Everybody had unbounded confidence in his changeless purpose to do what he deemed right   *   *   *   For the greater part of his life he was afflicted with imperfect vision.   The imperfection grew until he was almost blind.   He was successful as a farmer, with the assistance of an agent, cultivating a large plantation.   By using the eyes of others he also managed to keep up well in general literature, and on all subjects of general interest he had thoughts of his own worth hearing."

1030-6.

JOHN HUTCHINSON, of Charlotte Co., Va., a prosperous planter, married SUSAN DANIEL, daughter of No. 156-1.   Children :—

> 3117, MARTHA HUCHINSON, m. Rev. Mr. Miller, of South Carolina, a Presbyterian clergyman.   3118, LUCY.   3119, JOHN, of Charlotte Co., Va., a planter.

1031-7.

HENRY I. VENABLE, of Prince Edward Co., Va., a planter, married JULIA DANIEL, daughter of No. 156-2.   Children :—

> 3140, PITMAN VENABLE, soldier C. S. A., killed in battle.   3141, D., m. Miss Venable ; lives at Prospect, Prince Edward Co., 3142, LIZZIE.   3143-5, Others.

1031-5.

JOEL W. DANIEL, of Farmville, Prince Edward Co., Va., son of No. 156-2, a planter, married Elizabeth Dupuy, daughter of Joel Watkins Dupuy, M. D., of Prince Edward Co., Va., and his wife, Pauline Pocahontas Eldridge, of Brunswick Co., a descendant of the Indian Princess Pocahontas.

---

* Daughter of Branch Worsham, of Prince Edward C. H., now called Worsham in his honor ; clerk of Prince Edward County, and a man universally esteemed and beloved.

3150, SADIE DANIEL, m. and lives in Raleigh, N. C. 3151, JOEL DANIEL. 3152, LENA. 3153, ROBERT. 3154, LAVILLON.

1032-1.

JOHN DORAN HUNT, of Pittsylvania Co., Va., planter, married (1) MARTHA DANIEL, (2) SUSAN DANIEL, daughters of No. 156-3: each wife had two children:—

3160, MARTHA DANIEL HUNT, m. *Edward Coleman*, tobacco merchant of Danville, Va., several children. 3161, JOHN PRIDE, of Chatham, Va., merchant, m. Mattie, daughter of Judge William M. Treadway. 3162, ALICE. 3163, DORAN.

1033-7.

DR. HUMPHREY SINGLETON BELT, of Whitmell, Pittsylvania Co., Va., son of Dr. H. S. Belt, of Powhatan, a native of Maryland. Married, MARY A. DANIEL, daughter of No. 156-6. Children :—

3185, MARY D. BELT. 3186, WALTER GILMER. 3187, BENJAMIN LLOYD. 3188, HUMPHREY SINGLETON.

Dr. Belt was graduated from the law school of William and Mary, and in 1850, in medicine at the University of Virginia. He is one of the most influential citizens in his county, an accomplished public speaker, and a man of culture.

1033-9.

WILLIAM H. WARD, of Tazewell C. H., Va., son of William Ward of Wythe Co., died 1881. Married JENNIE C. DANIEL, daughter of Hezekiah Goode Daniel, No. 156-6, grand-daughter of William Pride and *Ann Goode* Daniel, No, 72, p. 49.

Mrs Jennie Daniel Ward, now a resident of Washington, is the only one of the Virginia third-cousins, save Dr. Murrell, whom the writer has been privileged to see.

1045.

COL. GUSTAVUS DYSON, U. S. A., son of No. 408, was born about 1819, and removed to Tennessee. He was Colonel of a Tennessee regiment in the Mexican war and was killed at the Battle of Chapultepec, aged twenty-five years.

1047.

JOHN WILLIAM MURRELL, of Bedford Co., Va., son of No. 410, was born Feb. 12, 1822. Married Mary Ann Hart, grand-daughter of Bishop Channing Moore. Children :—

3211, ALICE MURRELL, m. *J. B. Brockenbrough*. 3212, MARY, m. *Thomas Evans*. 3213, DAVID D. 3214, WILLIAM HART, of Perrowville, Bedford Co., Va., m. a lady of Mobile, two children. 3215, JOHN D. 3216, GEORGE EDWARD, a student in Washington and Lee University.

Before the war Mr. Murrell was a sugar planter in Louisiana.   He now lives about fifteen miles west of Lynchburg, where he is an extensive planter.   He is a man of culture and of high standing in his county.

1048.

DR. EDWARD H. MURRELL, of Lynchburg, Va., son of No. 410, was born July 31, 1825.   Married Oct. 9, 1849, Almira, daughter of Seth and Julia Halsey, of Lynchburg.   Daughter.

> 3217, JULIA ELIZABETH MURRELL, b. Oct. 22, 1850, m. *Senator John Warwick Daniel.*

Dr. Murrell was educated at Princeton College, and at the University of Pennsylvania, where he received the degree of M. D. in 1843.   He has been in the constant practice of his profession for more than forty years, and, though in his sixty-second year, is as vigorous as most men of forty.   Tall, portly, erect, active, and ruddy, he corresponds to the writer's ideal of his grandfather's grandfather's grandfather, the English ancestor who came to Virginia two-and-a-quarter centuries ago.   He is one of the most influential citizens of Lynchburg, and in winter is a resident of Washington.

1049-1.

THOMAS BARKSDALE COLLIER, of " Oak Hill," Haywood Co., Tenn., grandson of No. 159, was born in Mecklenburg Co., Va., Mar. 21, 1803, died, July 9, 1854.   Married, 1825, Catherine Page Nelson, daughter of Norborne Thomas and *Lucy Nelson* Nelson, of " Oak Hill," Mecklenburg Co. Va., born about 1805, died Oct. 6, 1863.   Children : —

> 3231, LUCY NELSON COLLIER, b. Aug 14, 1828, m. *John Carter Nelson.*
> 3232, SARAH CATHERINE, b. Oct. 27, 1830, d. Sept, 22, 1857, m.
> *Americus Hatchett.* 3233, MARY AGNES, b. Nov. 17, 1832 : " she
> is unmarried, and is one of the loveliest of women." 3234, CALVIN
> TATE, b. July 1, 1834, d. 1839.   3235, VIRGINIA, b. Mar. 14, 1836,
> d. Mar. 1852, in New Orleans.   3236, NORBORNE THOMAS, b. May
> 15, 1838, d. Aug. 1856.   3237, DABNEY CHARLES, b. April 21,
> 1840.   3238, ROBERT BARKSDALE, b. May 22, 1842, d. Oct. 19, 1857.
> 3239, SAMUEL, b. 1844, d. y.   3240, WILLIAM ARMSTEAD, b. Feb.
> 12, 1846.   3241, ROSA EVELYN, b. April 22, 1848, m. (1) *Dr. Jack
> Nelson Swayne*, (2) *Samuel W. Truss*, of Haywood Co., Tenn.
> children : 1 *Catherine Page Truss*, 2 *Lucy Armistead.* 3242, HENRY
> BARKSDALE, b. Dec. 15, 1879.

Mr. Collier removed when twenty-two years of age, and immediately after marriage, to Maury Co., Tenn., and in 1838, to Haywood Co., where he became an extensive and successful planter.   He was a man of culture, and his morality and integrity were of the highest.

Mrs. Collier was a woman of remarkable character.   " She was," writes her son, W. A. Collier, " one of the noblest, purest, and best of women.   I was only fifteen years old when the war began, and, like all Southern boys, wanted to go.   I begged her to permit it, and she finally said that she could not consent, but could not refuse when my country needed me.   She was an invalid and had about two hundred bales of cotton piled up on her place when our forces retreated from West Tennessee, and they would not burn it. She, with her forefather's patriotism, told them that, if they did not burn it, she would burn it herself, and was not satisfied until she had seen from her window that the whole was in flames."

THE NELSON FAMILY was very prominent in the history of old Virginia. Its *propositus* was Thomas Nelson, gentleman, founder of Yorktown, son of Hugh

and Sarah Nelson, of Penrith, Cumberland, England, (b. Feb. 22, 1677, d. Oct. 7, 1745,) who came to Virginia about the year 1700. A partial genealogy was printed by Mr. Brock in the Richmond *Standard*, Sept. 25, 1880, and a more extended memoir of the family in Dr. Page's "Page Family in Virginia," pp, 137-74.

Mrs. Collier's parents were both descendants in the third generation from Thomas Nelson, Secretary of Virginia, (b. 1726, d. 1782, youngest son of the immigrant), and Lucy Armistead, his wife,* her paternal grandfather was Col. William Nelson, of "The Dorrill," Hanover Co., an officer of the Revolution, who married Lucy Chiswell, daughter of Col. John Chiswell and Elizabeth, his wife, dau. of Counsellor William Randolph, of "Chatworth," and his wife,

ARMS OF THOMAS NELSON.
FROM HIS TOMB AT YORKTOWN.

Elizabeth, dau. of Peter Beverly, of Glo's-ter, and his wife, Eliza dau. of Robert Peyton, Esq., "of an ancient family in the County of Norfolk, England;† William Randolph being son of the original William Randolph, of Turkey Island."—(See above p. 113.) Her maternal grand parents were Maj. John Nelson, of " Oak Hill," Mecklenburg Co., and Nancy, daughter of John Carter,‡ of Williamsburg. Her mother, Lucy Nelson, was born, 1784, and married in 1801 her first cousin, Norborne Thomas Nelson, born 1776.

1049-2.

DABNEY CLAIBORNE COLLIER, of Haywood Co., Tenn., son of Captain Dabney, and *Sarah Barksdale* Collier, No. 159, was born March 24, 1807, died July 17, 1843. Married in Williamson Co., Tenn., Sept 28, 1836, Isabella White, only daughter of William and Eleanor White. Children :—

3243, ABNER COLLIER, b. Sept. 4, 1838, d. Sept. 14, 1838. 3244, ELEANOR, b. Oct. 8, 1839, d. Sept. 10, 1840. 3245, DABNEY WEST, b. Feb. 20, 1841. 3246, WILLIAM CLAIBORNE, b. Feb. 26, 1843, d. Jan. 6, 1844.

D. C. Collier was a native of Mecklenberg Co., Va. At the age of 22 he removed to Williamson Co., Tenn., where he married soon after. In Febru-

---

*For Armistead genealogy see *Standard* II, 38, 41, III. 38, and Slaughter's *St. Mark's Parish*, 185.

†For Peyton genealogy see Slaughter's " Bristol Parish," 63; Meade's " Old Churches," II, 466; Peyton's " History of Augusta Co., 320, and *Standard*, II, 7, III, 10.

‡For Carter genealogy see Maj. Carter's elaborate " Carter Tree ;" also, Slaughter's " St. Mark's," 131-166; Meade, II, 110-123; Campbell's History, 412; Dinwiddie Papers, I, 463; Page Family, 59, 74, 133, and *Standard*, II, 16, 42, III, 38, IV, 2.

ary 1837, he removed to Haywood Co., Tenn., where he died at the age cf 36. He was a planter and pioneer.

1049-3.

WILLIAM THOMPSON COLLIER, of Fayette Co., Tenn. Married 1831, his cousin, AGNES HOWARD COLLIER, daughter of No. 159, who was born in Mecklenburg Co., Va., Jan. 26, 1809, and died Aug. 22, 1833.   Children : —

> 3247, SARAH BARKSDALE COLLIER, b. 1833, d. y.   3248, WILLIAN DAB-NEY, b. June 24, 1835, d. 1874.   3249, MARY ISABELLA, b. Mar. 14, 1837, d 1870, m. *Peyton Skipwith.*

William T. Collier was married in Virginia, of which State he was a native, though at the time a resident of Boon Co., Ky.   From 1831 to 1836 he lived in Franklin Co., Tenn. and later in Fayette Co.   He was a planter and financier.

1050-1 (424.)

ARMISTEAD W. ADAMS, of Farmville, Prince Edward Co., Va. Married MARY STEGER, No. 424, daughter of No. 165, p. 79.

> 3250, THOMAS GOODE ADAMS, m. WILLIE PRIDE, No. 3261.

1050-2 (425.)

ANDERSON PRIDE, of Amelia Co., Va., planter, son of Gen. Thomas Pride. Married MARIA STEGER, No. 425, p. 79.

> 3251, THOMAS ANDERSON PRIDE, b. 1839, a soldier C. S. A., killed at Spottsylvania C. H.

1050-3 (426.)

JOHN THOMAS PRIDE, of Amelia Co., Va., son of Gen. Thomas Pride, married JULIA FRANKLIN STEGER, No. 426, p. 79.   Children : —

> 3252, BETTY PRIDE. 3253, THOMAS. 3254, BENNET. 3255, ALONZO GOODE. 3256, EMMA, m. *Philip S. Wood.* 3257, NANNIE CARY, 3258, JOHN WESLEY.

1050-4 (427.)

WADE STEGER, of Stony Point Mills, Amelia Co., Va. Married his cousin HARRIET STEGER, No. 427, p. 79.   Children : —

> 3259, LEROY STEGER. 3260, SALUDA. 3261, WILLIE, m. THOMAS GOODE ADAMS, No. 3252.

1050-5 (428.)

DAVID HENDRICK, of Cumberland C. H., Va., planter. Married ELIZA STEGER, No. 428, p. 79.*   Children : —

> 3262, GOODE HENDRICK. 3263, EMMA (*Woodson*) of Cumberland. 3264, CORDELIA (*Guthrie.*) 3265, JULIA (*Lambert*) of Arkansas.

1050-7 (430.)

MERRITT GOODE STEGER,† of Petersburg, Va., a wealthy tobacconist, died after 1857, unmarried.

---

*The entry on page 79, of *Garland Hendricks*, who married *Louisa Steger* is erroneous.
†Wrongly entered on page 79, as *Wade Steger.*

1050-8.

MACKERNESS STEGER, of Kentucky, son of No. 165, p. 79, has a large family.

1051.

DR. SAMUEL MACKERNESS GOODE, of Indianapolis, son of Dr. Samuel M. and *Sarah Grover Paul* Goode, No. 310, was born in Madison, Ind., Nov. 20, 1825, married Aug. 5, 1846, Eliza Eggleston, daughter of Judge Miles Cary Eggleston, one of the earliest and most prominent lawyers of Indiana. Children:—

> 3281, FRANCES ELIZA GOODE. 3282, SARAH PAUL. 3283, BLANCHE EGGLESTON, m. *Michael C. Garber.* 3284, HARRIET CARY. 3285, CORNELIA SUTHERLAND.

Dr. Goode was educated at Indiana Asbury University, studied law at Transylvania University, and practiced as attorney at Madison for some years. Relinquishing his profession, because of threatened failure of health, he engaged in the business of manufacturing iron. For many years he has been a successful dentist, first in Madison, subsequently in Indianapolis, whither he removed in 1873. From early manhood a member of the Presbyterian Church, he has been many years an elder in the same.

EXCURSUS.—THE EGGLESTON FAMILY.

The EGGLESTONS, long seated in Virginia, are believed to have been of Irish origin. The first of the name in the colony was Richard Eggleston, who came over in 1635 and settled on the "Eastern Shore." "Mr. Richard Eggleston," who, in 1656, participated in the disastrous fight against the Indians at the Falls of the James, was perhaps his son, while JOSEPH EGGLESTON of "Old Powhatan," was perhaps grandson of the first and son of the second. These probably constitute the first three generations.

FOURTH GENERATION.

4, JOSEPH EGGLESTON, son of Joseph, had issue :—
  5, WILLIAM; 6, JOSEPH; 7, JANE SEGAR.

FIFTH GENERATION.

5, WILLIAM EGGLESTON, of "Locust Grove," Amelia Co., born 1720–40, married Judith Cary (No. 56 of Cary list), issue: 10, EDWARD; 11, MATTHEW. 12, RICHARD. 13, WILLIAM CARY, d. unm. 14, JOSEPH, d. unm. 15, JUDITH CARY, m. *Joseph Eggleston*, No. 17, and died about 1857 at the age of 90. (See Meade's Old Churches.) 16, ANN, m. *William Hickman*, d. s. p.

6, JOSEPH EGGLESTON, of "Egglestetton," Amelia Co., m. Betsy Cary, No. 58 of the Cary Pedigree (not John), issue: 17, JOSEPH. 18, MARIA.

7, JANE SEGAR EGGLESTON, m. STEPHEN COCKE, issue: 19, JOSEPH EGGLESTON COCKE, m. Anne Mosby, d. s. p. (Goode Genealogy, p. 220.) 20, JAMES POWELL m. Caroline Lewis. 21, CHARLES, m. Sarah W.

Taylor. 22, JUDITH, m. *Peterfield Archer.* 23, MARY C., m. *Richard Archer.* 24, MARTHA. m. *W. T. Eggleston.* 25, NANCY, d. y. 26, JANE, SEGAR, m. *James Hobson.* 27, (son of 20 or 21.) CHASTAIN.

SIXTH GENERATION.

10, EDWARD EGGLESTON, of " Locust Grove," married Judith Booker, issue : 31, EDWARD. 32, ELIZABETH. 33, JOSEPH CARY. 34, MARY, m. *Chastain Cocke,* No. 27. (For issue see Brock's *Huguenot Immigration,* p. 198.)

11, MATTHEW EGGLESTON, of Amelia Co., married his cousin, a granddaughter of William Cary, No. 24, and had issue : 35, OVERTON. 36, MILES CARY. 37, HUGH (of New Orleans.) 38, CHARLES.

12, RICHARD EGGLESTON, m. (1) Nancy Hill, (2) Patsy Baugh. 39, JAMES, m. Emeline Bell. 40, ANN, m. *Richard Cunliff.* 41, JOSEPH E., m. Miss Carr. 42, WILLIAM CARY, m. Miss Jones. 43, HELEN, m. *Edward Eggleston.* 44, MARTHA, m. *Dr. Milbourne.*

17, HON. JOSEPH EGGLESTON, of "Egglestetton," Major in the Continental army under Light Horse Harry Lee, and member of Congress, 1798–1801, m. JUDITH CARY EGGLESTON, No. 15, issue : 50, EVERARD FRANCIS, b. 1798. 51, SALLIE MEADE, m. *Chastain Cocke,* No. 27.

SEVENTH GENERATION.

33, HON. JOSEPH CARY EGGLESTON, of Switzerland Co., Ind., an eminent lawyer and an early settler of Indiana, m. Mary Jane, daughter of Capt. George Craig.

75, EDWARD EGGLESTON, D. D., of "Owl's Nest," Lake George, N. Y., b. 1837, divine, historian and novelist, author of "The Circuit Rider," "The Hoosier Schoolmaster," and other studies of frontier life, nnexcelled as pictures of early days in the West, who is now engaged upon the history of the United States in the Colonial Period.

76, GEORGE CARY EGGLESTON, of New York, journalist and novelist.

36, JUDGE MILES CARY EGGLESTON, of Franklin and Jefferson Counties, Ind., was born in Virginia, read law in Richmond, and being oppressed by principle to slavery, removed at an early day to Indiana, where he was one of the most influential citizens in the early history of the State ; lawyer and circuit judge from 1827 to 1852, when he died. (See O. H. Smith's "Early Indiana Trials and Sketches.") Married Elizabeth Sutherland. Issue : 79, GUILFORD D. 80, ELIZA (Mrs. Goode.) 81, HENRY C.

50, EVERARD FRANCIS EGGLESTON, of "Egglestetton," b. 1798, d. 1857, m. Maria Judith Cocke. 82, JUDITH. 83, WILLIAM ARCHER, b. 1831, soldier C. S. A. 84, MARTHA JUDITH, m. 1860 *William Old, Jr.,* editor of the Richmond *Examiner,* Capt. C. S. A. 85, CHARLES, who has sons living.

" In later generations the Eggleston family," writes a friend, " has been noted for the number of magistrates and judges of ability produced by it. The

Egglestons have bore a very high reputation for integrity and a certain clear unpoetic intelligence. They were serious, stern, usually careful of their money, and hated ostentation and affectation with a sort of passion."

EXCURSUS.—THE CARY FAMILY.

THE CARYS, a family prominent in Virginia colonial history, are descended from the ancient Devonshire family of Cary, of which collateral branches have been conspicuous in England as Earls of Hunsdon, Monmouth and Dover, and Barons of Falkland. Branches are still seated at Tor Abbey and Follaton (See Burke's *Landed Gentry*.) The first of the name was Adam Carye, of Castle Carye in Devon, Esq., who lived about the thirteenth century, and who married Amy, dau. of Sir William Trewit, Kn't. The Devonshire Herald's Visitation of 1620 gives fourteen generations of his descendants. His grandson's grandson's grandson was Sir John Carye, Kn't., Chief Baron of the Exchequer in the reign of King Henry IV, who was banished into Ireland for political offenses. His son, Sir Robert Carye, was a favorite of King Henry V.

"In his time came out of Aragon a lusty gentleman into England, and challenged to do feites of arms with any English gentleman, without exception. This Robert Cary, hearing thereof, made suite forthwith to the Prince that he might answer the challenge.   *   *   *   At the time and day prefix'd both parties met and did perform sundrie feates of arms, but in the end this Robert gave the foils and overthrow to the Arragon Kt., disarmed and spoiled him, which his doinge so well pleased the Prince that he receyved him into great favour, caused him to be restored to the most part of his father's landes and willed him also for a perpetual memorie of his victorie that he should thenceforth give the same arms as did the Arragon Kt., which both he and all of his successors to this day enjoyed, which is *Argent, on bend sable three roses argent,* for before, they did bear, *Gules, chevron entre three swans argent. (Visitation of Devon,* 1620.)

The arms of the Carys of Bristol and of Virginia were identical with those of Sir Robert Cary of Devon, just referred to. There is a tradition in Virginia

that Sir Henry Cary, Knight, a Royalist leader, who went into exile after the defeat of Charles I, came to Virginia, and left posterity, and some of the descendants of Miles have claimed descent from him.

Descended from Adam Carye, perhaps in the tenth generation, was William Cary, b. about 1500, Mayor of Bristol 1546, d. 1572. His son Richard, merchant, of Bristol, (b. 1525, d. 1570,) had son William, (b. 1550 d. 1632,) who was Mayor of Bristol, 1611: his son James,

ARMS OF CARY. (b. 1600 d. 1681,) came to Charlestown, Mass., 1639 and was ancestor of the Carys of Massachusetts: Richard Cary, aide-de-camp to Gen. Washington, and Mrs. Agassiz were of this branch: another son, John, married Alice Hobson and was father of Col. Mylles Cary, *propositus* of the Carys of Virginia.

The accounts of the family published in Welles's "American Family Antiquity" and elsewhere, are very erroneous. Since several branches of the Goode connection interosculate with Cary, I have availed myself of an opportunity to examine the MS. notes of Mr. Guilford Eggleston, placed in my hands by his sister, Mrs. Goode, and shall present here, a statement of facts which can be substantiated by the records of Warwick Co., Virginia.

When Mr. Eggleston visited Warwick in September, 1851, he found at a place near the Warwick river, on a farm called Bensall's, then occupied by Mr. Lucas, a dilapidated tombstone in five fragments. Placing the pieces together and rubbing with soft bricks, it was found to bear a coat of arms and the following inscription :—

> HERE LYETH Yᴱ BODY OF MILES CARY, ESQ.
>
> ONLY SON OF JOHN CARY AND ALICE HIS WIFE
>
> DAUGHTER OF HENRY HOBSON OF Yᴱ CITY OF
>
> BRISTOL, ALDERMAN, HE WAS BORN IN Yᴱ SAID CITY.
>
> AND DEPARTED THIS LIFE Yᴱ 10ᵗʰ DAY OF JUNE, 1667.
>
> ABOUT THE FORTY-SEVENTH YEAR OF HIS AGE, LEAVING
>
> FOUR SONS AND THREE DAUGHTERS (VIZ.) THOMAS,
>
> ANN, HENRY, BRIDGETT, ELIZABETH,
>
> MILES AND WILLIAM.

The will of "Mylles Cary", (recorded in Book A, p. 448, June 21 1667,) corroborates the statements of the epitaph.

The coat of arms on the tomb of the original colonist is repeated upon articles handed down from early days, with the punning motto, *Sine Deo Careo.*

FIRST AMERICAN GENERATION IN VIRGINIA.

1, MILES CARY Esq., born 1620, died, 1667, came to Virginia 1640–46, and settled in Warwick Co., where he married Ann, (?) dau. of Thomas Taylor Hobson, one of the early settlers. He acquired and lived upon the estate known as "Magpy Swamps," obtained by his father-in-law, Capt. Dobson, which he devised to his eldest son Thomas. He mentioned in his will two houses in England, presumably in Bristol, one in Ballaum, the other in St. Nicholas St., to be sold for the benefit of his daughters. He owned nearly 2000 acres of land, well stocked, and numerous slaves, besides a store and a mill. Children, (born 1645–66) :—

2, THOMAS. 3, ANN. 4, HENRY. 5, BRIDGETT. 6, ELIZABETH. 7, MILES. 8, WILLIAM.

SECOND GENERATION.

2, THOMAS CARY, of "Magpie Swamp," who d. 1708, (Will in Book I, p. 23) was born after 1646, being under age at the time of his father's death. Married, perhaps, Mary Milnor. Issue :—

9, THOMAS. 10, JAMES. 11, MILNOR. 12, ELIZABETH.

4, HENRY CARY, of Warwick Co., born about 1650, died 1720, (Will in Book,

I, p. 199), inherited "The Forest." He was appointed to superintend the building of the College of William and Mary and the Capitol at Williamsburg. Issue:—

    13, HENRY. 14, MILES. 15, ANN (*Stukey.*) 16, ELIZ. (*Scarbrook.*) 17, JUDITH, m. *Mr. Barbour*, d. before 1720: sons, Thomas and William.

7, COL. MILES CARY, of Warwick, b. about 1665, d. 1709, (Will in Book E, pp. 348–369,) was, by his father's will, to be educated in England under the direction of Mr. Huele. He was Surveyor General of Va., 1692, and Clerk of Assembly. Married Mary, dau. of Col. William Wilson.* Issue:—

    18, WILSON. 19, MILES, d. s. p. 20, MARY, m. *Joseph Selden.* 21, ANNE, m. *Col. Whiting*, of Gloucester.

8, CAPT. WILLIAM CARY, of the Parish of Mulberry Island, County of Warwick, was born about 1657, d. 1713. (Will, 1711, Book E p. 570.) was to be educated in England under direction of William Beaty: inherited plantation up Warwick River, bought by his father from Capt. Thomas Flint, probably the "Skiff Creek" plantation upon which he lived. Member House of Burgesses, 1710. Married Martha Scarbrook (Scarborough.) Issue:— 22, HARWOOD, d. 1720. (Brock,) leaving eldest son William, who 1764 was authorized to sell Skiff Creek land and other lands and slaves, (*Va. Statutes*, VIII, 34.) 23, MILES, 24, WILLIAM, 25, MARTHA, m. 1697, *Edward Jacqueline.*

THIRD GENERATION.

9, THOMAS CARY. "The Elder," of Warwick, b. 1670–90, d. 1764, (Will. Book O, p. 488), leaving issue:— 26, THOMAS, probably he who d. 1790, (Book E, 1774) leaving i, *William* d. 1808 leaving son William, ii, *Miles*, iii Dau. m. *Edw. Curtis*, 27–28, DAUGHTERS, m. to *R.* and *G. Whitaker* (Numerous descendants named Bell, Branch, Gist Blair, Gratz and Langhorne. (See Standard, III, 9).

13, HENRY CARY, of "Rich Neck," b. 1670–1700, d. before 1761. Issue 29, ARCHIBALD, b. 1720, d. 1786. 30, JUDITH, m. *David Bell*, of Lynchburg [for *Marshall Family*, p. 297]. 31, MRS. SPEAR, said to live in Edinburgh, Scotland.

14, MILES CARY, of Warwick, d. 1924, [Book I, p. 313]. Issue:— 32, ANNE. 33, ELIZABETH, [m. Benjamin Watkins, of Chesterfield Co., and had numerous descendants, Benjamin Watkins Leigh, Conway Robinson, Finney, Royall, Sydner, Worsham, Leigh, Barksdale, Peary, Lockett, [see *Watkins Genealogy* pp. 46–50.] 34, BRIDGET. 35, DOROTHY. 36, MARTHA. 37, MILES. 38, THOMAS. 39, NATHANIEL. One of the daughters probably m. *John Collier,* of Brunswick Co. [see *Collier Excursus.*]

18, COL. WILSON CARY, of "Ceeley's" and "Great Neck," b. 1680–1700, educated at William and Mary and Cambridge England, County Lieutenant of Elizabeth City. Issue:— 40, WILSON MILES. 41, SARAH, m. *Geo. Wm. Fairfax.* 42, MARY, the first love of Washington, b. 1732–36, m. 1754, *Edward* AMBLER, ancestor of the Amblers of Virginia, who intermarried with the

---

*Brock says he m. (1) Mary, dau. of Thomas Milner, b. 1667, d. 1700, but the name of the eldest son indicates that his mother was a Wilson, while the name Milnor among children of No. 2 leads us to suppose that he may have m. Mary Milnor.

Burwells and Nortons, mentioned elsewhere in this book. (See *Marshall Family*, p. 43.) ANN, m. *Robert Carter Nicholas*, Treasurer of Va., and had distinguished descendants, Gov. Wilson Cary Nicholas, Judge Philip Norborne Nicholas, and others. (See also Nos. 2040, 2352, 2355, *Goode Genealogy*.) 44, ELIZABETH, m. *Bryan Fairfax*, Baron Fairfax, ancestor of the Virginia Fairfaxes.

21, MARY CARY, m. JOSEPH SELDEN,, had 45, JOSEPH whose son REV. MILES SELDEN, of Henrico Co., had a dau. *Rebecca*, m. *Thomas Watkins*, son of Benj. and Eliz. Cary Watkins, No. 33 and son *John A.*, student, Wm. and Mary Coll. 1822. 46, JOHN m. Grace Rosewell, and had son, REV. WILLIAM SELDEN of Norfolk and probably 46½, COL. CARY SELDEN who died before 1730, from whose daughter Mary are descended the Youngs and Purvances, and whose widow, Elizabeth, daughter of Col. Jennings, returned to England and was mother of Dr. Beilby Porteus, Bishop of London. A son or grandson was SAMUEL SELDEN, of "Selvington," Stafford, whose daughter, Anne Cary Selden, m. J. T. Brooke. Of this lineage is the wife of Dr. R. H. Tatum, No. 772, of the *Goode Genealogy*.

23 or 37, MAJOR MILES CARY, the elder, of York Co., d. 1766, Book O, p. 549,) married Ann, who d. 1768. Issue :—

    47, RICHARD, Judge of the Court of Appeals, grad. Wm. and Mary Coll., d. 1785, (Book F, p. 680,) leaving i, *Richard*, ii, *Miles*, iii, Daughters. 46, MILES. 48, ROBERT. 49, JOHN. 50, ANNE, m. *Mr. Thompkins*.

25, WILLIAM CARY, of Warwick, d. Apr. 3 1742, m. Judith Jones, (perhaps of Petersburg.) Issue :—

    51, MATTHEW JONES, unm. 52, MILES, d. unm. 53, JACQUELINE. 54, WILLIAM, of Yorktown, mayor 1789, d. 1805, m. (1) Miss Moody, (2) Sarah Dudley . Issue :— i, *Sally*, ii, *Miles*, iii, *Dau.*, m. Maj. William Dudley. 55, PATTY, m. *Wm. Goosley*, merchant of Yorktown, Issue :— *George*, student Wm. and Mary Coll., 1800, lived in the West Indies, ii, *William*, m. Miss. Harrison. 56, MARY d. unm. 57, JUDITH m. *William Eggleston*. 58, BETSY m. *John Eggleston*, dau. 1, *Maria Cary*. 59 NANCY.

25, EDWARD JACQUELINE, of Jamestown Va., who came to Va. from Kent, 1697, d. 1730, m. MARTHA CARY. Issue :—

    60, ELIZABETH, m. *Richard Ambler*, and had son *Edward*, who m. MARY CARY, No. 42. 61, MARY m. *John Smith*, of Westmoreland, had issue, 1 *Col.Edward*, 2 Gen. *John*.

FOURTH GENERATION.

29, COL. ARCHIBALD CARY CARY, of "Ampthill," Revolutionary patriot, married Mary Randolph, issue : 80, ANN, b. 1745, m. *Thomas Mann Randolph*. (See above page, p. 114.) 81, JANE, m. *Thomas Jefferson Randolph*. 82, SARAH, m. *Archibald Bolling*, (her daughter m. No. 301 of Goode Genealogy. See Bolling Excursus.) 83, ELIZABETH, m. *Joseph Kincaid*. 84, MARY, m. *Carter Page*, of "The Fork." (For issue see

Page Family p. 95).

40, WILSON MILES CARY, of Hampton, b. 1723, d. 1817, m. Sarah, dau. of Hon. John Blair. Issue: 85, SALLY, m. *Capt. Thomas Nelson*, of "Bear's Spring." (Issue, *Page Family*, pp. 169, 78.) 86, MRS. WILLIAM PEACHY. 87, MRS. FERD. FAIRFAX. 88, WILSON, b. 1770, m. Jean Carr, had issue: i, *Wilson Miles*. ii, *Mrs. Newsum*. iii, *Wilson Jefferson*, m. Virginia Randolph, ancestor of the Baltimore Carys, and the Carys of "Carysbrooke," best known of whom is Constance Cary (Mrs. Burton N. Harrison) and of Orlando Fairfax, whose biography, written by Dr. Slaughter, gives full information concerning this branch. (See also *Page Family* p. 239.)

57, JUDITH CARY, m. William Eggleston. (See Eggleston Excursus No. 50.)

1052.

WILLIAM McCULLOUGH, of Sidney, Shelby Co., O., nursery man, married Oct , 5, 1842, CATHERINE REBEKAH GOODE, daughter of Hon, P. G. Goode, No. 432, born in Madison. Ind., Aug. 19, 1823. Children :—

3286, SAMUEL GOODE McCULLOUGH, b. July 13, 1843. 2287. BENJAMIN WHITEMAN, b. April 20, 1845. 3288, WILLIAM, b. Aug. 10, 1847, d. Sept. 10, 1850. 3289, MARY HARRIET. b. April 25, 1850. d. y. 3290, FRANK GOODE, b. Oct. 25, 1851 ; in 1885 in railroad business in Dallas, Texas.

The McCulloughs moved from Pennsylvania to Ohio at an early day. Mr. McCullough was long a merchant in Sidney, and since 1880 has been proprietor of a nursery in the same town.

1053.

BENJAMIN WHITEMAN GOODE, of Sidney, O., born of No. 432, p. 143, was born April 27, 1826. Married (1) Jan. 16, 1882, Anna Schenck Evans, of Franklin, O., who d. July 12, 1864: (2) Mrs. Charlotte (Pettit) Brownell.

3291, EVANS GOODE, educated at Ohio Wesleyan University, and in 1886 a student of medicine.

B. W. Goode has been engaged in various business enterprises in Cincinnati, Fort Wayne, Toledo, and Sidney from 1850 to 1886. He was educated at Ohio Wesleyan University. He was for a time in the army, and his record is as follows : Sept. 21, 1861, commissioned 1st Lieutenant, 54th Ohio vols., and appointed Quartermaster. Jan., 1862, ordered to service in Sherman's Division at Paducah and Columbus, Ky., afterwards serving in the Tennessee war and in the operations which concluded in the battle of Shiloh. April 11, 1862, appointed Captain and Brigade Quartermaster, field Brigade 5th Division. Health failing, resigned Aug., 1862.

1055.

WALTON PEARSON GOODE, son of Rev. Dr. Goode, No. 435, p. 145, was born in Madison, Ind., Sept. 9, 1836. Died Sept. 1, 1867, in Logansport, Ind.   Married (1) Nov. 21, 1854, Ann Elizabeth, dau. of Judge Hall, of Hancock Co., Ind. (2), May 30, 1859, Lucy B. Beck, dau. of Samuel Beck, of Indianapolis, who lives, 1886, in Indianapolis.

> 3292, ALBERT HALL GOODE, b. Aug., 1860.   3293, HENRY WALTON, b. Sept. 26, 1862.

Walton Goode was educated at Indiana Asbury University and went to Kansas, where he participated in the early political struggles, and was secretary of one of the territorial conventions, his influence being thrown upon the side of anti-slavery.   For a time he was editor and publisher of the *Newcastle Courier*, and later a hardware merchant in Logansport, Ind.   Buried in Crown Hill Cemetery, Indianapolis.   " He was a man of genial manners, strict integrity and uncommon ability."—(*Indiana State Journal.*)

1056.

PHILIP HAYES GOODE, of Valiska, Iowa, son of No. 435, was born Feb. 7, 1835, d. Sept. 27, 1877,   Married Dec. 4, 1856, Margaret Frances Galleher, of Mills Co., Iowa.

> 3294, ANN JANET GOODE, b. Dec. 11, 1857.   3295, FRANCES GALLEHER, b. Jan. 24, 1859.   3296, SAMUEL RUSSEL, b. July 5, 1860.   3297, MARGARET BELKNAP, b. Jan. 4, 1869.

P. H. Goode began life as a saddler in Richmond, Ind., and subsequently studied law and became an attorney in Iowa.

" He entered the service in November, 1861, as 1st Lieutenant of Company F., 15th Regt., Iowa Infantry, and stayed in camp until spring, when the regiment was ordered into active service, arriving at Pittsburg Landing on the Saturday previous to the well-known engagement of 1862.   The regiment was ordered to an exposed situation, and the Captain having been disabled early in the fight, Lieut. Goode took command, and, though his sword hand was shattered by a ball. kept his men together and brought them off the field at the end of the day.   Confined in the hospital, he was unable to participate in the second day's fight.   He continued in command until after the evacuation of Corinth.   Disabled by disease and unable to obtain furlough, he was compelled to resign and seek his home.   After restoration to health, he re-entered the army and was appointed Captain of the 4th Iowa Battery of Artillery and was ordered to New Orleans, where he was stationed on garrison duty.   He was subsequently, and for several months after the close of the war, stationed at Thibodeaux, La., retaining his command, and at the same time acting as Judge Advocate in the military trials then in progress."

1057.

JOHN ELLIOTT RAINES, of Odell, Gage Co., Nebraska, farmer, married 1857, MARTHA PAUL GOODE, daughter of No. 435, born Mar. 22, 1837, educated at Worthington Seminary, Ohio.   Son :—

> 3298, WILLIAM ELLIOTT RAINES, b. Dec. 23, 1858, m. 1880, Alice Harter, of Gage Co., Neb.

1058.

JOHN WILSON, of Odell, Gage Co,, Nebraska, farmer, son of Judge Wilson, of Indiana, in 1853 accompanied the Rev. Dr. Goode to Kansas and settled in the "Wyandot Nation," where, in 1855, he married his daughter, CLARA MACK GOODE, who was born Feb. 24, 1839, and educated at the Worthington (Ohio) Seminary. From 1856–'80 they lived in Fremont Co., Ia., and in 1881 removed to Nebraska. Children:—

    3299, ANNA MARY WILSON, b. Nov. 2, 1856, m. 1879, *Frank Young*, of Fremont Co.,Ia., child, 1, *Ida Gertrude Young.* 3300, OSCAR GOODE, b. Aug. 23, 1858, m. 1880, Susan Harter. 3301, SARAH ALICE. b. Apr. 6, 1861, d. June 9, 1864. 3302, WILLIAM ALEXANDER, b. Aug. 16, 1863, d. June 9, 1864. 3303, KATE FLETCHER, b. Mar. 2, 1865. 3304, CARRIE ELLIOTT, b. Apr. 4 ,1867. 3335, HARRY HUTCHISON, b. Feb. 25, 1869. 3306, LUELLA MEAD, b. Mar. 22, 1871. 3307, EMMA GERTRUDE, b. May 21, 1873.

1059.

WILLIAM HENRY GOODE, Jr., of Glenwood, Iowa, a farmer, son of No. 435, was born in Indianapolis, Sept. 17, 1841, died May 29, 1870, married Mar. 15, 1886, Mary E. Hodges, of Mills Co., Iowa.

    3308, EMMA GOODE, b. Mar. 2, 1867.

"Industrious and energetic, he obtained, in the midst of the difficulties of a frontier rearing, with partial academic aid, an education which fitted him well for active usefulness in life. In 1861, when scarce grown to manhood, he was summoned to military duty by the report of an Indian aggression on the border. He entered the service at the age of twenty, in September, 1861, as private in Co. A., 4th Iowa Cavalry. His first winter was spent in camp in Iowa. In spring the regiment joined the command of Gen. Curtis in Arkansas, and participated in the summer campaign, waiting in Helena. In spring the regiment joined the command of Gen. Grant at Milliken's Bend, and later was under Sherman, watching movements of Johnston on Black River during the whole time of siege of Vicksburg, and engaged in almost continual skirmishes and one considerable engagement. Thence to Jackson, Miss., under Sherman. In a fight there. Then on raid to Memphis, destroying railroads, &c. Thence back to Black River, where they wintered. Then with Sherman on his raid to Meridian, Miss., following up the Rebel army and skirmishing all the way. After that (in April, 1864,) to Memphis, where he remained on detached duty till his discharge in December."

1060.

JOHN SINGLETON, of Odell, Gage Co., Nebraska, married 1882, in Charleston, Neb., SARAH FRANCIS GOODE, daughter of No. 434, who was born May 12, 1844, at Fort Coffee, Choctaw Nation, widow of James O. Smith, of Pottawattomie Co., Iowa. She was educated at Amenia Seminary, N. Y. Her children are:—

3304, HARRIE SMITH, b. 1853, d. 1874.   3305, MAGGIE, b. Jan. 12, 1884.
3306, FANNIE ELIZABETH SINGLETON, b. Aug. 21, 1868.   FRANK GOODE,
b. Sept. 17, 1872.   3308, JOHN WILLIAM, b. Jan. 4. 1874.

1061.

GEORGE W: CROSE, of Fremont Co., Iowa, farmer, married Jan.
4, 1872, HARRIET MARY GOODE, daughter of No. 485, who was born Aug.
2, 1847.

3309, CLARA BURFOOT CROSE, b. Dec. 27, 1872.   3310, ETHEL, b, Aug.
20, 1875.   3311, MINNIE ORPHA, b. July 29, 1877.   3312, WALTON
GOODE, b. Sept. 16, 1880.   3313. HARRY FULLER, b. April 6, 1883.

1062.

DR. DANIEL W. HUMFREVILLE, of Waterville, Marshall Co.,
Kansas, formerly a physician at Union City, Ind., married Dec. 31,
1867, ELLEN WILKINS GOODE, daughter of No. 455, p. 145.   Children :—

3320, WILLIAM GOODE HUMFREVILLE, b. Jan. 19, 1869.   3321, LOUIS, b.
Dec. 19, 1874.   3322, LILIAN, b. Feb. 21, 1881.

1063.

WILLIAM HENDRICKSON, of Sidney, Iowa, merchant and farmer,
married June 28, 1881, ELIZABETH REBEKAH GOODE, daughter of No.
435, p. 145, who was born June 30, 1852.   Children :—

3326, EDITH HENDRICKSON, b. Jan. 15, 1883.   3327, PAUL GOODE, b. Jan.
28, 1884.   3328, PETER DAY, b. July 2, 1885.

1064.

GEORGE BROWN GOODE, of Washington, son of Francis Collier
and *Sarah Woodruff Crane* Goode, No. 437, p. 149, was born, Feb. 13,
1851.   Married Nov. 29, 1877, Sarah Ford Judd, daughter of Orange
and *Sarah Lamson Ford* Judd, born in New York City, July 18, 1854.
Children :—

3330, MARGARET JUDD GOODE, b. March 23, 1879.   3331, KENNETH MAC-
KARNESS, b. Dec. 8, 1880.   3332, FRANCIS COLLIER, b. Oct. 5, 1884.
3333, PHILIP BURWELL, b. Dec. 6, 1886.

No. 1064, the author of this book, was born in New Albany, Indiana, passed
his early childhood in Cincinnati, Ohio, and his later childhood and early
youth near Amenia, N. Y. where he was prepared for college by private
tutors.   In 1866 he entered Wesleyan University, Middletown, Conn., was
graduated in 1870, and after a post-graduate course under Prof. Agassiz at
Cambridge, returned to take charge of the college museum, then being organized in the new Orange Judd Hall of Natural Sciences.   He retained relations with the college faculty until 1877, but in the meantime formed connections with the U. S. Fish Commission, in which he became a volunteer
assistant in 1872, the year after its organization, and with the Smithsonian In-

stitution, being appointed upon the museum staff in 1873, and upon the organization of the National Museum in 1881, became its Assistant Director. He was in charge of the natural history division of the display of the U. S. Government at the Philadelphia Exhibition, 1876, U. S. Commissioner to the Internationale Fischerei Ausstellung, Berlin, 1880, and the International Fisheries Exhibition, London, 1883, and member of the Government Executive Board for the New Orleans, Cincinnati and Louisville Expositions, 1884. In 1877 employed by the Department of State as statistical expert in connection with the Halifax Fisheries Commission, and 1879-80, in charge of the Fisheries Division of the Tenth Census. Author of various papers and pamphlets upon Ichthyology and fisheries, and of "A History of the Menhaden," "Game Fishes of the United States" and the articles "Pisciculture" and "Oyster Fisheries" in the Encyclopædia Britannica, also aided by associates, of "The Food Fishes and Fishery Industries of the United States," now being published. President of the Biological Society of Washington, 1885-6, member of various scientific societies, and corresponding member of the *Deutscher Fischerei Verein*, the National Fish Culture Society of Great Britain, and the Virginia Historical Society. [See *Alumni Record, Wesleyan Univ.*; *Encycl. Americana; Encycl. Britannica, Suppl*; *Johnson's Cyclopædia:* Portrait in *Century Magazine*, March, 1885.]

Mrs. Goode is only daughter of Orange Judd, the veteran agricultural editor, for so long a time identified with the *American Agriculturist* and the *Prairie Farmer*, "who is to agricultural journalism" says a recent writer, "what Horace Greeley was to that of politics."

EXCURSUS.—THE ANCESTRAL DERIVATIONS OF NOS. 3330-32.

"Every man is a bundle of his ancestors," said Emerson. For the future use of the four little bundles at this moment sheltered beneath his rooftree, the author has drawn up the accompanying scheme of their ancestral derivations.

Indications of the history of each of the ancestral lines are given below. Many of the families are discussed more fully, elsewhere in this volume.

GOODE. Samuel Goode was grandson of John Goode, of "Whitby," who came from Cornwall 1640-60, son of Samuel Goode and Martha, dau. or g-dau. of Philip (?) JONES, who came from Wales, 2650-60 ; his g.-m. was Martha or Francis MACKARNESS, daughter of William (?) Mackarness, of Barbados, who came, probably from Scotland to the West Indies, 1625-40.

BURWELL. The wife of Samuel Goode, grand-daughter of Maj. Lewis Burwell, of "Fairfield," descended from "the ancient family of the Burwells, of the county of Bedford and Northampton," b. 1626, came to Virginia, 1640, m. Lucy, dau. of Capt. Robert HIGGINSON, came from England, as it is supposed before 1622. Her mother was probably, Martha, dau. of John LEAR, Secretary of the Council of Virginia, came from England, 1620-40.

COLLIER. John Collier, an officer in Vernon's Carthagena Expedition, 1740-

42, son of John Collier (b. 1685,) and Miss GAINES, of a family early seated in King and Queen County, and believed to be descended from the Colliers of Staffordshire, whose ancestor, Robert Collier, came from France to England about 1460, and married Isabel, dau. and h. of Sir John Dodington of "Darliston."

MEREDITH.   The wife of John Collier, Miss Meredith, was of a Welsh family settled in Virginia as early as 1635.*

COOPER.   Polly Cooper, g.-grand-daughter of John Cooper, who sailed from Holland for New York, 1695.   Admixtures :— RUNYON or RONGNION, French, came to New Jersey before 1668.†. BOUTCHER, from Hartford, England, before 1668.   BLACKFORD, English, bef. 1704.   CROSS, Irish Presbyterian, came over before 1730.

HAYES.   Richard Hayes, of Amelia Co., b. 1710-20, perhaps g.-g.-son of Robert Hayes who came from England or Ireland before 1644.

LYON.‡   Nathaniel Lyon, of "Lyon's Farms," in fourth generation from Henry Lyon, early settler, 1646, of Connecticut, and one of the founders of Newark Colony.   Puritan and English.   Admixtures :—BATEMAN, English and Puritan, early settler, 1641, of Concord, Mass.

WRIGHT.   Rheuama Wright, descended in fifth generation from Deacon Samuel Wright, Puritan, native of England, came to Springfield, Mass., 1641.

DIKE.   Abigail Dike, descended from Richard Dike, Walter TYBBOT, Samuel DOLLIVER and Robert ELWELL, residents of Cape Ann and Marblehead, before 1600. Puritans, probably from the south of England.

JUDD.§   Timothy Judd, g.-grandson of Deacon Thomas Judd, born 1608, came

*MEREDITH is an old Virginia name, and in Wales the family, of which the Virginia branch is an off-shoot, claimes descent from EUNYDD GWERNGWY, a chieftain of North Wales and head of one of the fifteen tribes. Rowland Meredith of "Alington" who lived early in the fifteenth century, was one of the first to assume the name.
   Julian, Walter and *Philip Meredith* were in Virginia in 1635, and there were land-grants to *Thomas,* in New Kent Co., 1656, and to *John,* in Lancaster, 1652.
   Philip Meredith bought land in Northampton Co., after 1649, and, dying, left daughters, 1, Elizabeth, m. Paul Marsh. 2, Mary, m. Ralph Hinman. 3, Eleanor, m. George Drewit.
   George Meredith, b. 1640, d. 1734, his wife Alice —— and his son George, b. 1698. d. 1728, are buried in the colonial church-yard at West Point, Va., where the inscriptions on the tombs were seen some years ago by Dr. E. A. Dalrymple, and copies have been sent me by Mr. Brock.
   Descended from some of these, was, *Samuel Meredith,* sr. (b. 1680-1700, d. bef. 1762,) of the Parish of St. Paules and the County of Hanover, Va., whose widow, Margaret, m. 1762, Dr. William Cabell. Miss Meredith, who m. *John Collier,* is believed to have been his sister or niece.
   Samuel Meredith, sr., had issue, 1,Elisha, who son Elisha, b. Oct. 13, 1783, m. Sarah Bolling Cabell. 2, Col. Samuel, patriot and Revolutionary officer, m. Jane, sister of Patrick Henry, children, i, Samuel, m. Eliz. dau. of Col. Robt. Breckinridge. ii, Sarah, m. Col. Wm. Armistead. iii, Jane, m. Hon. David S. Garland, M. C., 1809-11. 3, Ruth, m. Col. Samuel Jordan, had issue, i, Margaret, m. Col. Wm. Cabell, sr., of "Union Hill." ii, Mary, m. Geddes Winston. iii, Caroline, m. Col. Hugh Rose. iv, Pauline, m. Col. John Cabell,—all having distinguished offspring, many of whom will be discussed by Mr. Alexander Brown in his Cabell History. 4, Daughter, m. Mr. Abney, (Paul or Abner.)

   †VINCENT RONGNION, of Poitiers, France, married in New Jersey, July 17, 1668, Ann dau. of John Boutch-er, of Hartford, England. (Licence granted by Gov. Philip Carteret, June 28, 1668, (see *XX. Car.,II.*) They had son Peter Rongnion, b. July 1, 1680, m. Oct. 4, 1704, Providence Blackford at Piscataway, N. J. Children :— John, b. Aug. 15, 1705. GRACE, b. Jan. 17, 1707, m. DANIEL COOPER. Joseph, b. Apl. 1, 1710. Rosanna, b. Nov. 16, 1712. Peter, b. July 25, 1715. Richard, b. Apl. 14, 1719. Providence, b. Apl. 10, 1723. Sarah, b. Dec. 12, 1725. Benjamin, b. Dec. 12, 1729. (Letter of *Hon. Theodore Runyon, LL.D.*)

   ‡See Welles's "American Family Antiquity" for a decidedly forced effort to connect the Lyons of Amer-ica, with an English family of Norman origin. The descent is in all probability veritable, but the con-junction is not happily made.

   §See Sylvester Judd's, "Judd Family," Northampton, Mass., 1856, 8o, pp. 112.

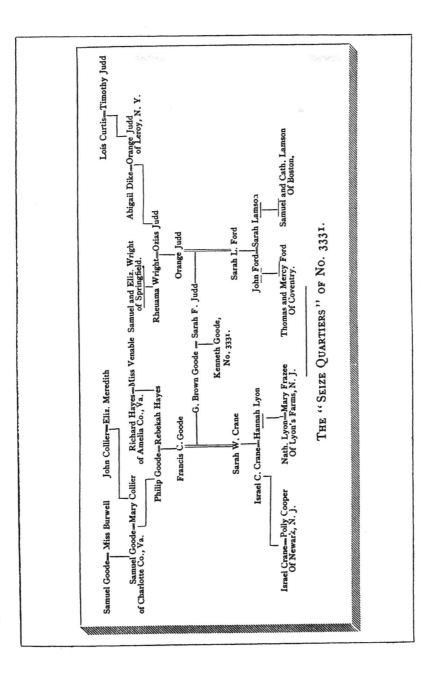

THE "SEIZE QUARTIERS" OF No. 3331.

to Cambridge, Mass., 1633-4, one of the founders of Connecticut. Admixtures :—LEWIS, came from England to Massachusetts, 1632. HOPKINS, believed to have come in the "Mayflower," 1620. DICKENS, came from England before 1700. CURTIS, came from England to Massachusetts and Connecticut, before 1658.

CRANE. Israel Crane, g.-g.-g.-grandson of Jasper Crane, Puritan, came to Mass., 1628-29, one of the founders of Connecticut and New Jersey. Admixtures :—SWAINE, English, Puritan, desc. from Capt. Samuel Swaine, b. 1585, came to Boston 1635, and one of the founders of Connecticut. Several of the pioneer families of the Newark Colony.

FRAZEE. Mary Frazee, probably grand-daughter of Joseph Frazee, early settler of Elizabethtown, N. J., 1730-40. Perhaps of Dutch origin, and from the New Netherland colony.

FORD. "Of an ancient race of substantial yeomanry in Warwickshire." Thomas Ford, sometime Alderman of Coventry, came to America from Coventry, about 1800.

LAMSON. English and Puritan : Probably in fifth generation, from Barnabas Lamson, settled in Cambridge prior to 1636. Some of the Lamsons claim descent from Miles Standish.

1066.

HON. PHILIP GOODE GILLETT, LL. D., of Jacksonville, Ill., son of Rev. Samuel Trumbull and *Harriet A. Goode* Gillett, No. 438, p. 159, was born in Madison, Ind., March, 24, 1833. Married, May 2, 1854, Ellen M. Phipps, daughter of Isaac N. and *Julia Cully* Phipps, of Indianapolis, born Sept, 22, 1834. Children :—

3335, HARRIET GILLETT, b. Feb. 13, 1855, m. *C. H. Cole, M. D.* 3336, CHARLES PHIPPS, b. May 30, 1857. 3337, ALMA, b. Feb. 23, 1862. 3338, SAMUEL TRUMBULL, b. July, 19, 1865, d. Nov. 12, 1876. 3339, FREDERICK PHILIP, b. May 6, 1870, a student in Illinois College. 3340, ELLEN, b. Dec. 28, 1875, d. July 4, 1876.

Dr. Gillett was graduated from Indiana Asbury (now De Pauw) University in 1852, and became an instructor in the Indiana Institution for the Education of the Deaf and Dumb. In April, 1856, he was appointed Principal of the Illinois Institution for the Education of the Deaf and Dumb. Upon his arrival at Jacksonville he found it disorganized, its faculty broken, and the entire fabric under a cloud of embarrassments. By skill and labor, he re-erected the institution, secured new and better buildings, established wholesome discipline, and adopted a course of study which was most adapted to the needs of the unfortunates for whose benefit the institution was intended. It has, under Dr. Gillett's management, become the largest of its kind in the world. The State grants it liberal support, and the last report of an examiniug committee of the Legislature was of the most favorable character, and flattering in its tribute to the talent and energy of its Superintendent, whose pen and voice have been directed towards arousing popular sympathy for the inmates of the institution.   He is recognized as one of the leading men in his profession and was chosen President of the Eleventh Convention of American Instructors of the Deaf and Dumb held in Berkeley, California, July, 1887, He was President of the International Sabbath-School Convention, which, in 1872, held its triennial meeting at Indianapolis, twice President of the State S. S. Convention, and, for fourteen years, a member of the International Committee, whose duty it is to designate a general course of study in the Sacred Scriptures.   In 1865, he succeeded in establishing, by legislative aid, an experimental school for the education of feeble-minded children, for the amelioration of whose condition, he was one of the first to move, and became its Superintendent, serving without compensation.   In 1871, his alma mater conferred on him the degree of LL. D.

1067.

PAYMASTER FRANCIS TRUMBULL GILLETT, U. S. N., son of No. 438, p. 159, was born in Manchester, Ind., Dec. 28, 1837, died in Rio de Janeiro, Feb. 15, 1878. Married Jan. 6, 1859, Mary Hester Conner,* daughter of Jefferson Conner, of New Albany, Ind., who died in Rio, Mar. 5, 1878.   Children :—

> 3341, ALICE LOUISE GILLETT, b. Nov. 1, 1859, m. *W. E. Barns.* 3342, FRANK GOODE, b. Mar. 12, 1862. 3343, JENNIE VAUGHAN, b. Sept. 7, 1864.

" Francis T. Gillett was educated at Indiana Asbury University. He entered the U. S. Naval service as Assistant Paymaster, Oct. 20, 1863, and was ordered to duty in the Mississippi Squadron under Admiral Porter, where he served until the close of the war of the rebellion, soon after which he was stationed at Jefferson Barracks, Missouri, in charge of naval stores. He was commissioned Passed Assistant Paymaster, July 23, 1866, and detached from Jefferson Barracks in 1867. Subsequently he was ordered to proceed by way of Panama, to the west coast of South America, and join the South Pacific Squadron, as Paymaster of the U. S. Steamer "Dacotah," where he served in 1868 and 1869. His vessel returning north, he was detached in Feb., 1870, and placed on waiting orders. He was next stationed at Mound City, Illinois, in charge of Government property, in 1871, 1872 and 1873. He was commissioned Paymaster Jan. 23, 1873, and detached that year from Mound City, it being discontinued as a Naval Station. In Dec., 1873, he was ordered to Key West, as Paymaster of the U. S. Steamer "Ticonderoga," from which he was detached in 1874, and again placed on " waiting orders." In April, 1875, he was ordered to San Francisco, to join the U. S. Steamer "Saranac," of the North Pacific Squadron, bound for Alaska. In June, that vessel, in endeavoring to pass through the Straits of Vancouver, ran on a rock and went down in sixty minutes ; the officers and crew escaped safe to shore, the Paymaster saving the ship's books and money. In Dec. 1875, he was ordered to Rio de Janeiro where he arrived

*The Conner Family moved from Virginia to Kentucky, at an early day.

in March, and relieved Paymaster Bacon, in charge of U. S. Naval Stores. On the 10th of Feb., 1878, he was seized with yellow fever, and died on the 15th. His wife contracted the same disease and died 18 days after her husband. Their remains are interred in the cemetery of that city, and a beautiful monument erected by the officers of the South Atlantic Squadron, marks the place of their burial.

1068.

SIMEON PALMER GILLETT, of Evansville, Ind., son of No. 438, p. 159, was born in Dearborn Co., Ind., Nov. 24, 1840. Married, Dec. 21, 1865, Anna Grace Lowry, of Evansville. Children :—

3345, Sarah Lowry Gillett, b. Feb. 28, d. July 25, 1867. 3346, William Lowry, b. Dec. 9, 1879.

Commander Gillett was educated at the U. S. Naval Academy at Annapolis, where he was appointed, Sept. 20, 1856, graduating in 1860, as No. 5, in a class numbering 83.

His first service was in the China squadron on the steamer "Dakotah," which was the first foreign vessel to penetrate to the interior of China, ascending the Yang-tse-Kiang. Returning in 1861, the "Dakotah" arrived at New York, in December, after an exciting cruise through the West Indies, after the privateer "Sumpter." In Jan., 1862, was ordered to Annapolis, in July commissioned Lieutenant, and after several applications for active duty, was ordered, in Jan. 1863, to the "State of Georgia" in the blockade of Wilmington, in August, to the "Glaucus," which after conveying President Murrillo to his seat of office in the United States of Columbia, joined the Wilmington blockading squadron, and was nearly destroyed by fire, the flames being extinguished after thirteen hours of hard work, and was sent to Philadelphia for repairs.

In June, 1864, was ordered to the "Sagamore," blockading Cedar Keys; in Sept. took north the prize steamer "Matagorda;" in Oct., to the "Canandaigua," blockading Beaufort and Charlestown, and in Dec., to the iron-clad "Sangamon," in the inner blockade of Charleston. He was present at the surrender of Charleston, Savannah and Wilmington, and then proceded to the James River, where he was employed until the fall of Richmond, in charge of boats dragging for torpedoes in the James, and went with the advance into Richmond.

In April, 1865, ordered to the staff of Admiral Radford, and in October, to the command of the flag and gunnery ship, "Santee," and to duty at the Naval Academy, as instructor in gunnery and infantry and artillery tactics, and was in command of the Battalion for two years.

In April, 1866, appointad Lieut.-Commander, he was attached to the "Idaho," as a member of the board to report upon the sea-going qualities of that great failure. In May, 1869, was assigned to the European squadron, as executive officer of the "Franklin." Returning to the United States in this ship he resigned his commission, Dec. 30, 1871.

For sixteen years he has been in the banking business in Evansville, Ind., and has long been President of the Citizens National Bank.

Mrs. Lowry's father, William J. Lowry, born in Baltimore, Oct., 1795, was the son of Irish parents, with whom in 1815, he went to Posey County, Ind., where he died Feb., 1873, having been during his long life one of the most prominent and influential citizens of that portion of the state, largely interested in lands, banks and mercantile enterprises. Her mother, Sarah Nettelton, born in New York, 1805, removed in 1817, with her father, to Posey Co., where the Netteltons have long been prominent people.

1069.

PROF. OMER TOUSEY GILLETT, M. D., of Iowa State University, son of No. 438, p. 159, was born June 28, 1848. Married Sept. 26, 1871, Mary A. Brokenshire, of Boston. Children:—

3347, PHILIP LORING GILLETT, b. Oct. 21, 1872. 3348, OMER RAND, b. Nov. 22, 1874. 3349, SUSY, b. Jan. 12, 1877. 3350, LEWIS GOODE, b. Aug. 13, 1878.

"During the latter part of the late war, Dr. Gillett served as a private in the 132d, Indiana Inf., U. S. A. In 1866, he was graduated from the State University of Indiana with the degree of A. B.

The winter of 1867–68, he spent in the Medical College at Ann Arbor, Mich., and the following winter at the College of Physicians and Surgeons, New York City, graduating therefrom March, 1860. Since then, his profession has received his entire attention, three years being spent in Chicago, and six in La Salle, Ill. In the spring of 1868, he moved to Iowa City, where he has since resided.

In the fall of 1868, he was appointed Assistant to the chair of Surgery, and in the summer following was elected Secretary of the Medical Faculty of the Iowa State University. Recently, his health failing, he has been living in Colorado.

1095.

JESSE R. ADAMS, of "Spring Garden," near Cool Well, Amherst Co., Va., was born in Halifax Co., Va., 1823, m. 1852, FANNIE E. LAMKIN, dau. of James L. and *Ann Goode Dawson* Lamkin, No. 443. Children:—

3371, ANNIE M. ADAMS, b. 1852, m. *Rev. William Franklin Kone*, of Baltimore, a Baptist clergyman, 1 child b. 1885. 3372, FLORENCE, b. 1856, m. 1887, Prof. *Wm. M. Baskerville*, of Vanderbilt Univ., Nashville, d. in Germany, 1878. issue, i, *John Adams Baskervile*, b. in Germany. 3373, FANNIE LAMKIN, b. 1864, m., 1885, *Robert Tait*, of Norfolk, Va. 3374, VIRGINIA LAMKIN, b. 1869, in 1884, a student at Hollins Institute, Virginia. 3375-6, 2 sons, d. y.

1101.

WILLIAM GAINES LYLE, of Waynesville, O., son of No. 448, p. 161, was born in Greene Co. O., Aug. 5, 1838. Married, April 5, 1868, Maria McKnight, (b. April 15, 1868.) Child:—

3380, ELIZABETH LYLE, b. Jan. 17, 1886.

1103.

SAMUEL ROWLETT GOODE, of Jasper Co., Texas, planter, son of No. 450, p. 161, was born Mar. 21, 1826, died Nov. 19, 1873. Married Eleanor Jones Scales, of Texas. Children:—

3400, NANCY EMILY GOODE, b. Mar. 7, 1853, m. 1876, *James Stewart*

Richardson, of Jasper Co., Texas. 3401, SARAH ELEANOR, b. Sept. 23, 1854, m. 1879, *W. T. Rigsby*, of Jasper Co., Texas. 3402, THOMAS FULTON, b. May, 1856. 3403, ANNETTE, b. April 17, 1858. 3404, GIDEON DANIEL, b. April 7, 1860. 3405, SAMUEL CARL, b. Mar. 1, 1862. 3406, FOWLER, b. July 4, 1864. 3407, MARY FRANCIS, b. Sept. 17, 1866. 3408, JENNIE, b. July 10, 1869. 3409, WILLIAM ELIAS, b. Dec. 11, 1872.

1105.

MATTHEW MACKERNESS GOODE, of Jasper, Texas, son of Gideon J. Goode, No. 450, was born in Tennessee, Sept. 10, 1831. A soldier, Gillespie's Reg't, Garland's Brigade, Texas Volunteers, C. S. A. Died, a prisoner of war, at Camp Butler, near Springfield, Illinois, March 28, 1863.

1106.

GAINES COLLIER GOODE, of Jasper, Texas, son of No. 450, was born in Tennessee, Oct. 13, 1833. A soldier in Winfield's Texas Legion, Ross's Brigade of Cavalry, C. S. A. Was discharged on account of sickness, Sept., 1863, and died from results of exposure in the service, June 17, 1863.

1107-8.

GIDEON CARL GOODE and HANNIBAL FOWLER GOODE, two sons of No. 450, were born in Jasper Co., Texas, Christmas, 1840. Were soldiers in Gillespie's Reg't, Texas Volunteers, C. S. A., and died prisoners of war, at Camp Butler, Illinois, the former, Feb. 4, the latter Mar. 4, 1863.

1111.

JOHN HENRY GOODE, of Jasper Co., Texas, son of No. 451, was born Aug. 28, 1837. He was a soldier, C. S. A., and died from the effects of exposure in service.

1113.

WILLIAM THADDEUS GOODE, of Jasper Co., Texas, son of No. 451, was born Mar. 14, 1842. A soldier, C. S. A., captured at the battle of Arkansas Post, and died in military prison, April 1863.

1120.

BURWELL GOODE WILKERSON, of Sedalia, Mo., son of Charles N., and *Martha Goode* Wilkerson, No. 468, p. 162, was born May 11, 1836. Married, Aug. 17, 1870, Sarah E. Doolittle, dau. of John T. and Ann M. Doolittle, of Painesville, O., and grand-daughter of Judge Joel Doolittle, of Vermont, born Nov. 2, 1846. Children : —

> 3440, FREDERICK D. WILKERSON, b. June 5, 1871. 3441, ELIZABETH GOODE, b. Sept. 26, 1872, d. June 24, 1877. 3442, GEORGE RAPPEEN, b. Nov. 20, 1873.

The following sketch is from the "United States Biographical Dictionary:" "Burwell Goode Wilkerson was graduated at Miami University, 1860, studied law at Wilmington, O., and was admitted to the bar at Columbus in 1862. He practiced in Wilmington, O., till 1867, when he moved to Sedalia, Mo., where he has since resided, engaged in the practice of his profession and is, in 1886, a member of the firm of Wilkerson and Montgomery, Attorneys-at-Law, 210 Ohio St.

He held the office of County Attorney, 1868-73, and City Attorney, 1869-70, and 1874-75.

In 1866, he became a Mason, and was a charter member of Granite Lodge, A. F. and A. M., organized in Sedalia, 1868, and master of the Lodge, 1872. He was High Priest of Sedalia Royal Arch Commandery in 1870, and in 1871-2, Eminent Commander of St. Omar Commandery, and in 1878, Grand Senior Warden of the Grand Commandery of the State. In politics he is a pronounced Republican.

He is of medium height, with a refined countenance, frank, honest, candid, upright, even his enemies being judges. He is a man of decided opinion, which on proper occasions he expresses boldly and fearlessly. As a lawyer, he stands high, and though not a fluent speaker, is well read and possessed of a clear, sound judgment.

Socially, he is affable, and a welcome companion, full of humor, kind and liberal, resolute and persevering."

1121.

WILLIAM NEAL WILKERSON, of Cowley County, Kansas, son of No. 468, was born in Warren Co., O., Mar. 21, 1838.

"In April, 1861, enlisted for three months in 12th reg't. O. V. I. Served 4 months, and was then discharged on account of sickness. In July, 1862, re-enlisted as private, Co. A., 79th O. V. I.: soon elected second Lieutenant of his company, promoted to first lieutenant, and in 1864, to Captain. In fall of 1862, served in Ky. and Tenn. in the campaign against Kirby Smith, and in the Atlanta campaign of 1864. Wounded in the battle of Resacca, May 15, 1864, rejoined the regiment in July and participated in the final engagements before Atlanta. Was with Sherman in the march to the sea, and at the battles of Bentonville and Averysboro, N. C., and was mustered out with his regiment at Washington, at the close of the War.

He is an extensive farmer and stock-grower. He moved to Cass Co., Mo. in 1866, where he resided until 1883, when he removed to Cowley Co., Kan., where he still lives. His post-office is Douglass, Butler Co., Kansas."

1122.

E. T. M. WILLIAMS, of Clarksville, Warren Co., O., a farmer, married April 15, 1868, MARY ELIZ. WILKERSON, daughter of No. 468, born June 18, 1840. Children:—

3443, MARTHA WILLIAMS, b. July 3, 1870, 3444, NELLIE, b. Feb. 27, 1875. 3445, ALICE, b. Mar. 16, 1878.

1123.

GEORGE HENRY WILKERSON, of Warren Co., O., son of No. 468, was born Jan. 16, 1843. Married Jan. 27, 1870, Mary Nancy, Harris, dau. of Samuel Harris, of Warren Co. Children:—

3446, THADDEUS WILKERSON, b. June 1, 1871. 3447, ROBERT, b. Feb. 20, 1874.

He enlisted, July 1872, in 79th O. V. I., U. S. A. Served with his regiment in Ky. and Tenn., until January, 1863, and was discharged for sickness. Re-enlisted May 1864, in 146th O. V. I., with which regiment he served in W. Va., as Lieut. in Co. H., for the term of its enlistment, 100 days. Resides in Warren Co., near Clarksville, engaged in farming.

1124.

THOMAS SMITH WILKERSON, of Warren Co., O., son of No. 468, was born April 27, 1845. Married, Dec. 30, 1884, Anna Austin, daughter of David Austin, of Clinton Co., O. Served 100 days from May, 1864, in the 146th regiment, O. V. I. A farmer, residing on his father's homestead, near Clarksville, O.

1125.

SAMUEL JAMES WILKERSON, of Springfield, O., son of No. 468, p. 162, was born May 14, 1847, moved to Clark Co., O., in 1878, and now resides, 1885, at Springfield, O., where he is engaged in business as a member of the Springfield Wheel Co. Married, Dec. 22, 1881, Emma McConkey, daughter of Alexander and Emma (Cartwell) McConkey, of Clark Co., b. Dec. 1, 1858. Children:—

3450, NELLIE CARTWELL WILKERSON, b. Dec. 13, 1882. 3451, CHARLES McCONKEY, b. Jan. 21, 1885.

1126.

CHARLES POAGUE WILKERSON, of Clarksville, O., son of No. 468, p. 162, was born, June 13, 1850. A farmer, residing upon a portion of his father's farm, near Clarksville. Married, Mar., 1877, Martha Jane Campbell, daughter of Artemas Campbell, of Warren Co.

3452, LUCY WILKERSON, b. Nov. 1, 1882, d. Sept. 6, 1883.

1127.

EDWARD WILKERSON, of Cowley Co., Kansas, son of No. 468, p. 162, was born Nov. 1, 1853. A farmer, residing upon his fathers farm until 1883, when he moved to Missouri. In 1884, with his brother, William Neal, removed to Cowley Co., Kan.

1128.

LIEUT. GEORGE WILLIAM GOODE, U. S. A., son of No. 470,

p. 162, was born in Warren Co. O., Jan. 27, 1839, died in the army Sept. 25, 1861.

He entered Ohio Wesleyan University, 1858, and had not finished his collegiate course at the outbreak of the war. In April, 1861, he left college and enlisted in Co. D, 12th Ohio Vol. Inf., was elected Lieutenant of his company, afterwards made First Lieutenant, and commissioned June 7, 1861. Proceded with his command to W. Va., took part in the engagement of Scary Creek, July 17, and was in other skirmishes, sickened of camp fever and died in hospital at or near Somerville, W. Va., Sept. 25, 1861.

George William Goode was a young man of highest character and great promise, was esteemed by his comrades, a brave, intelligent soldier, and his death, occuring so early in the war, created among them and his friends generally a profound and lasting impression.

1129.

WILLIAM H. CORWIN, of Warren Co , O., (cousin of Hon. Thomas Corwin, U S. Senator etc., and son of William Corwin,) was born Aug. 17, 1835, died Jan. 1, 1878. Married Dec. 17, 1863, ANN ELIZABETH GOODE, dau. of No. 470, born Feb. 9, 1843. Children :—

> 3455, NARCISSA CORWIN, b. July 25, 1865, d. Nov. 25, 1872. 3456, JENNIE, b. Feb. 8, 1873, d. Apr. 21, 1881.

1129-A.

MARTIN GONS, of Warren Co., O., (near Lebanon) a farmer, born Mar. 7, 1842, married Feb. 13, 1879, Mrs. ANN E. (GOODE) CORWIN, dau. of No. 470. Children :—

> 3457, JOHN QUINCY GONS, b. Nov. 14, 1879. 3458, FREDERICK, b. Jan. 2, 1882. 3459, EVA, b. Nov. 9, 1884.

1131.

BURWELL GOODE, of Carrollton, Mo., son of No. 470, a farmer, born in Warren Co., O., May 24, 1851. He lived with his father on farm in that Co., till 1861, in Lebanon to Oct. 1865, removed to Carroll Co., Mo., where he still resides near the town of Carrollton.

Married March 12, 1874, Ella Trotter, of Carroll Co., Mo., born Nov. 28, 1853. Children :—

> 3461, GEORGE WILLIAM GOODE, b. Dec. 16, 1874. 3462, ANNA MAUD, b. Nov. 14, 1879. 3463, BLANCHE, b. Apr. 5, 1881.

1132.

JAMES W. BEATY, of Rocky Ford, Bent Co., Colorado, (P. O., Catlin,) who was born April 6, 1843, married Jan. 27, 1872, LAURA McCLELLAN GOODE, dau. of No. 470, p. 162, born Oct. 5, 1853. Mr. Beaty is the owner of a very large cattle ranch in southern Colorado. Children :—

3465, ELLA BEATY, b. Dec. 29, 1873.   3466, WILLIAM CORWIN, b. Mar. 20, 1879.

1133.

J W. McCLAIN, of Catlin, Colorado, ranch owner.   Married Dec. 9, 1885, MARY JANE GOODE, daughter of No. 470.

1134.

HON. THOMAS J. PRINGLE, of Springfield, O., son of William D. Pringle, of Madison Co., O., was born in 1838.   Married, Oct. 26, 1870, MARGARETTA E. POAGUE, daughter of R. D.,and *Mary E. Goode* Poague, No. 473. p. 163, who was born, Mar. 31, 1847, died, Feb. 4, 1881. Children :—

3468, KATIE HALL PRINGLE, b. Nov. 3, 1871.   3469, ROBERT DAVIS, b. Oct. 2, 1875.   3470, MARY POAGUE, b. Nov. 26, 1877.

Mrs. Pringle was a student of Vassar College, 1865–66.   Mr. Pringle is a leading lawyer, was prosecuting attorney of Clark County, 1866 to 1873, and a member of the State Senate of Ohio, 1880 and 1881, an office to which he was re-elected in Oct., 1885, and which he now (1886) still holds.

1135.

WILLIAM THOMAS POAGUE, of Greene Co., O., son of No. 473, p. 161, was born July 31, 1846.   Married Oct. 23, 1884, Augusta Florence Steel, of Xenia, O., (born May 23, 1856,) dau.of Capt. David and Mary E. (Harbine) Steel.   Mrs. Poague's grandparents were 1. John Steel, 2. Mary Ankeney, 3. John Harbine, 4. Hetty Hess.   He resides in Greene Co., O., near Spring Valley, where he owns a farm. '' A gentleman of sterling character and worth,'' writes a neighbor.

1136.

JAMES BURWELL POAGUE, of Spring Valley, Greene Co., O., son of No. 473, a farmer, was born in Greene Co., O., May 9, 1852, married Jan. 25, 1882, Laura Flay Kelly, dau. of Ethan Kelley, (son of Moses and Abigail Kelly,) and Alcinda, dau. of Joshua and Allie Yeo, of Richmond, Ind.   Children :—

3471, ROBERT DAVIS POAGUE, b. June 18, 1883.   3472, HERBERT K., b. July 7, 1885.

1137.

CHARLES MARTIN POAGUE, of Spring Valley, O., son of No. 473, was born Aug. 23, 1856.   Married, July 11, 1883, Catherine Walker Smith, daughter of Dr. Walter and Cornelia (Buxton) Smith, of Mt. Vernon, Ohio.

He was graduated from Kenyon College, 1878, studied law in Cincinnati, in the office of Hon. Aaron F. Perry, was admitted to the bar, June 22,1880, and practiced his profession at Cincinnati until the summer of 1885, when he was compelled, by failure of health to break off, at least temporarily, from sedentary life. At present resides upon his farm in Greene Co., Ohio.

1141.

FRANK COWAN GOODE, of Springfield, O., son of James Samuel and *Mary Ann Cowan* Goode, No. 474, p. 164, was born in Springfield Sept. 12, 1853. Married Dec. 8, 1881, Jane McKnight,* daughter of Rev. W. J. McKnight, of New Brunswick, N. J. born Sept. 13, 1856. Child :—

3473, EDITH JEANNETTE GOODE, b. Nov. 13, 1882.

He was graduated at Yale College in 1873, admitted to the bar, 1876, and is in practice of his profession, as a partner with his father in the firm of Goode and Goode, Attorneys-at-Law. He is a member of the Virginia Historical Society, and an ardent student of historical matters. No one has done more than he to insure the publication of this volume.

1143.

JOHN BOYCE BASKIN, of Louisville Ky., was born at Camden, S. C., Dec. 28, 1854. Married May 23, 1883, MARY POAGUE GOODE, dau. of Judge James S. Goode, No. 470, who was born Aug. 18, 1860. Children :—

3474, BURWELL GOODE BASKIN, b. Sept. 2, 1884, d. Sept. 16, 1884.

Mrs. Baskin was educated at Mrs. Porter's Academy in Farmington, Conn., and in New York City.

Mr. Baskin graduated at University of Alabama, in 1876, soon after settled at Louisville, Ky., was admitted to the bar, and is now a prominent lawyer of that city.

He was at one time in partnership with Gen. Basil Duke, who during the war was a distinguished officer in the western armies of the Confederacy.

His parents were Andrew George Baskin, and Sarah Scotia (Bryce) Baskin, of Columbia, S. C., the former of whom was in early life clerk of the

---

* JANE McKNIGHT, wife of Frank Cowan Goode, is the daughter of Rev. William J. McKnight, D. D., pastor of 1st Presb. Ch. of New Brunswick, N. J., and Susan McConnell Hann. She was born, Sept. 13, 1856, at Danville Ky., while her father was professor in Centre College. Dr. McKnight was the grandson of James McKnight and Jane Reid, the former of whom was brought as a child, about 1763, from the vicinity of Belfast, Ireland, and settled first in Eastern Penn., but soon after moved to Steel Creek, Mecklenburg Co.,N. C. Many of their descendants are scattered through Western N. C., Eastern Tenn., and in Texas.

William J. McKnight was son of William Porter McKnight, son of the last named, and Jane Caroline Taylor of Mecklenburg Co., N. C. dau. cf John Taylor and —— Neely, also of North Carolina. John Taylor's father was a soldier in the Revolution, for whose head the British offered a reward of £40.

Susan McConnell Hann, mother of Mrs. Goode, was born in Danville Ky., her parents being Gelon Hann and Jane Wright. Gelon Hann was the son of John Hann and Jane Robertson, a sister of Judge George Robertson, on the Supreme bench of that state, and sister to the wife of Gov. Letcher ; still another sister was the wife of Samuel McKee. The three gentlemen last named, successively represented in Congress the same Congressional district. The Robertson family were of Virginia stock. (See remarks under James Robertson, No. 224½, p. 106.)

Mrs. McKnight's mother, Jane Wright, was the daughter of Alexander Wright (of Scotch Irish parentage) and Susan Boyle, who were married in Ky., Oct. 9, 1806. The latter was dau. of John Boyle and Jane Cowan. A cousin of Mrs McKnight, Rev. Gelon Rout, of Versailles, Ky., is married to Mary Young, great-grand-daughter of Cabell Breckenridge and niece of the late Gen. John C. Breckenridge.

Circuit Courts in Columbia, and a member of the state, and after the war was appointed Judge of the court in the provisional government. His paternal grandfather was Joseph Baskin, a native of England, who emigrated thence before the revolution, settling in Lancaster District, (now county) S. C., where he lived and died, a farmer.

His mother, Sarah Scotia Boyce, was the dau. of Peter Boyce, who came from Scotland about 1790, and was for many years, a merchant at Columbia, S. C., where he died. The wife of the last-named was Martha Smith, also a native of Scotland. Dr. Peter Boyce, Sup't of the Alabama State Insane Asylum at Tuscaloosa is Mr. Baskin's uncle.

1144.

LEVI MONROE GOODE, of Springfield, O., son of Burwell S. and *Hannah Rinehart* Goode, No. 477, p. 170, was born at Indianapolis, Sept. 27, 1885 : after the death of the father at Cincinnati, in 1864, he came with his family to Springfield, O., where he still resides ; being a member of the firm of lumber merchants, J. C. Hayward & Co., and President of the Springfield Fertilizer Company.

1145.

Mrs. SARAH LONG, of Lodi, Ill., Mrs. SUSAN WELCH, of Bloomington, Ill., and NATHAN, ANNIE, KATE, JACOB, HARVEY, ELLA, and JOSEPH SHOTWELL, supposed to be residents of Nebraska in 1886, are the children of ANN HAAS, No. 478, and her husband, EDEN SHOTWELL.

1160.

REV. MATHEW B. LOWRIE, of Galesburg, Ill., son of Rev. John M. Lowrie, D. D., of Fort Wayne, Ind., (born 1817, graduated Lafayette College, 1840,) and his wife, Hettie Dusenberry, was born in New Jersey, 1844. Married SUSAN E. HAAS, daughter of Samuel Goode Haas, No. 480, p. 171. Children :—

3476, WILLIAM LOWRIE, b. Oct. 18, 1871, d. y. 3477, ROBERT SAMUEL, b. Jan. 15, 1874. 3478, MARY ELIZABETH, b. Nov. 7, 1877.

Mr. Lowrie was graduated with honor from the College of New Jersey, 1863. He taught for a year in the Valparaiso Collegiate Institute. In 1865, he entered the Princeton Theological Seminary, and was graduated in 1868, and was ordained by the Troy Presbytery, and called to the South (now Woodside) Presbyterian Church, Troy. In 1871, he was pastor at Orange, Ill., and 1872, was called to the church at Galesburg.

"Mr. Lowrie," says the *Presbyterian Encyclopædia*, (p. 454,) "is an enthusiastic Hebrew scholar, and has been a successful teacher in the Morgan Park Summer School and of private classes. In 1883, he was chosen a trustee of Knox College. He is a scriptural preacher, a logical reasoner, conservative as a theologian, liberal as a neighbor and friend. He has been pastor of one of the strongest churches in Illinois for eleven years (1884) and is in the prime of bodily vigor and mental energy."

1161.

SLOAN M. EMERY, of Lake City, Minnesota, son of Phineas and *Delilah Keith* Emery, was born in Columbus, Texas, Sept. 23, 1848. Married, JULIA HAAS. Children :—

> 3479, HARVEY HAAS EMERY, b. Nov. 19, 1871.   3480, WILLIAM LEKOW, b. Oct. 31, 1874.

Mr. Emery lost both his parents in the yellow fever epidemic of 1848, when he was but six weeks old. He was educated at the Valparaiso Collegiate Institute. In 1871, he settled in Lake City. He was, for many years, President of the Lake City Bank. In 1883, he was a member of the Minnesota Legislature. He is extensively engaged in horticultural pursuits, and in the management of imported cattle.

1168½ (484.)

MOSES McKAY GOODE, of Fall River, Kansas, farmer, son of No. 180, p. 90, (omitted from sixteenth generation to which he rightly belongs) was born May 15, 1826. Married July 1, 1863, Maria Louisa Foster. Child (adopted.)

> 3481, STELLA MAY GOODE, b. April 4, 1875.

A dry goods merchant in early life, he went to California during the gold fever, crossing the plains in an ox wagon. On his return he engaged in stock raising near Sidney, O. He served in the Union Army during a part of the war.

1176½ (486.)

HON. C. W. WELLS, of Sidney, O., a civil engineer, he has held many offices of trust in Shelby Co., O., and also represented same County one term in the State Senate. Married MARY ELIZABETH GOODE, dau. of No. 180, born Feb. 21, 1828, died July 3, 1860, (omitted from 16th generation.) Son :—

> 3482, AZEL WILDER WELLS, b. June 29, 1860 : married Sept. 5, 1883, Ollie A. Hoover : lives near Sidney, O.

1177.

DR. SAMUEL BURWELL GOODE, of Elmwood Place, Hamilton Co., O., son of No. 487, p. 172, was born Mar. 5, 1859.

He was graduated from the Hughes High School, Cincinnati, 1879, and received the degree of M. D., from the Miami Medical College, 1885. He is now practising medicine.

THE LUNENBURG GOODES.

1200.

COL. CHARLES THOMAS GOODE, of Americus, Ga., son of No.

1178.

DR. GEORGE HENRY GOODE, of Cincinnati, O., son of No. 487, p. 172, was born Feb. 14, 1861.

He was graduated from the Woodward High School, Cincinnati, 1880, and from the Miami Medical College in 1883, and was Resident Physician in the West Pennsylvania Hospital at Pittsburg, Pa., in 1883 and 1884, and in 1885, went to Europe to continue his medical studies. Since March, 1887, he has been in practice at Cincinnati, devoting his time exclusively to the treatment of diseases of the eye and ear.

500, was born Oct. 26, 1835, died Jan. 15, 1875. Married, 1857, Cornelia, daughter of Gen. Eli and *Jane Love* Warner, who lives, 1885, in Hawkinsville, Ga. Children : —

> 3500, ELIA. VIRGINIA GOODE, b. in Thomaston, Ga., May 24, 1858, m. 1877, *E. T. Byington*, of Atlanta, one of the editors of the "Atlanta Journal." 3501, JANE LOVE, b. June 4, 1859, m. April 14, 1880, *Edward M. Brown*, of Eatonton, Ga. Children :— 1, *Charles Goode Brown*, b. June, 1881, d. June, 1881. 2, *Julia Maria*. 3, *Edward Martin*. 3502, CHARLES WHITFIELD, b. 1860, d. 1863. 3503, CORNELIA WARNER, b. 1804, d. 1866. 3504, LUCY LATHROP, b. Dec. 18, 1869 ; student, 1885, in the New England Conservatory of Music. 3505, ELI WARREN, b. Dec. 18, 1869. 3506, CHARLES JOSEPH, b. Dec. 15, 1870.

Col. Goode was graduated at the University of Georgia, 1853, read law and entered into practice, first at Thomaston in partnership with his father, Thomas W. Goode, and then at Perry, in partnership with Gen. Eli Warren. At the beginning of the war he entered the Confederate army as Captain of the "Houston Volunteers." He was wounded slightly at the battle of Chickamauga, and his horse killed under him. Three horses were shot under him during the war, but he had no wound except the one at Chickamauga. He was promoted to Major, 11th Georgia Infantry. He resigned from the 11th Ga., and raised a Co. of Partisan Rangers, and was made Major, 19th Ga. Cavalry. His Battalion was consolidated with an Alabama Co., and he appointed Col. of this regiment, called 10th Confederate Cavalry. After the close of the war he resumed his profession in Americus, Ga., and took an active part in public affairs. He was prominent in the struggle which led to the liberation of Georgia from the rule of "carpet-bagger" politicians.

He was a member of the committee appointed by a Georgia convention to draw up the petition to the President for the amnesty of disfranchised citizens of Georgia. (See above, under THADDEUS GOODE HOLT, p. 193.) In 1868, he was elector on the Seymour and Blair ticket, in 1872, a delegate to the Democratic convention which nominated Greeley for President. He was trustee of the University of Georgia, 1874. He was famous throughout the state as a public speaker, and known as the "silver tongued orator." His address at Mercer University, 1877, upon "The True Elements of Manhood," was highly lauded by the Georgia press.

1201.

DR. BENJAMIN WHITFIELD GOODE, of Hot Springs, Ark., son of No. 500, p. 173, was born in Thomaston, Ga., 1849. He served through the war as a soldier in the command of his brother, Col. Goode. He is a druggist at Hot Springs. Unmarried.

1202.

DR. JOHN GOODE, of Magnolia, Ark., son of No. 500, was born

in Georgia. A soldier in the Confederate Army, 1861–65. Practicing medicine, 1885, in Magnolia Ark. Married Lizzie Travers, of Thomaston, Ga. Children:—

> 3508, CHARLES WHITFIELD GOODE, of Magnolia, Ark., b. 1850, married.
> 3509, CORNELIA, married.

1203.

SIMEON ROGERS GOODE, of Hot Springs, Ark., son of No. 500, was born 1845, and was educated at Mt. Zion Institute. He was a soldier C. S. A., serving in his brother's regiment, and was taken prisoner at Shiloh. Admitted to the bar in Americus, 1866, he practiced law very successfully in Montezuma, until 1875, when he removed to Hot Springs, Arkansas, where he died, unmarried, Sept. 8, 1878.

1204.

JAMES GOODE, of Macon, Ga., son of No. 500, was born 1840–50, and was graduated at the Georgia State University. He was Quartermaster of the 19th Battalion of Georgia Cavalry, 1861–5, and, after the war, one of the editors of the "Macon Telegraph." He died, of consumption, about 1868. Married Celia Holcombe. Children:—

> 3511, JULIA GOODE, m. *Mr. Johnson.* 3512, WILLIAM, b. 1862, lives in Macon, 1885.

1205.

COL. G. P. SMOOTE, of Prescott, Ark., grandson of Dr. Charles and *Letty Tyler* Smoote, married, Mrs. JULIA (GOODE) MATTHEWS.

Col. Smoote served in the Confederate Army, removed from Tennessee to Arkansas, and for many years practiced law at Magnolia: in 1877 he removed to Prescott, Ark., where he is a member of the law firm of Smoote and Rae, no children.

1206.

HENRY C. DAVIS, of Hot Springs, Ark., married MARY E. GOODE, daughter of Thomas W. Goode, No. 500, p. 173, who died, Sept. 1882. Children:—

> 3513, ROBERT G. DAVIS. 3514, HELEN C. 3515, CHARLES. 3516, CARRIE.

1222.

COL. BENJAMIN WHITFIELD JOHNSON, of Camden, Ark., son of Moses and *Mary E. Goode* Johnson, No. 505, p. 174, was born near Thomaston, Upson Co., Ga., July 23, 1825. Married (1) 1856, Nannie H. Hawkins, dau. of John B. Hawkins, of Mt. Holley, Ark. who died Jan. 1878, (2) Sept. 1880, Lizzie J. Sherman, of Camden, Ark. Three children, who died young.

He was educated at Brownwood Institute, Ga., and graduated at the Law School of Louisville University, 1856. Joined the army 1861, as a private in the 15th Ark. Reg't, C. S. A., was made Adjutant and served in this capacity at Fort Henry and Donaldson, (See Reports of Col. Lee in Confederate Archives.)

Wounded and prisoner at Fort Donaldson, confined in Alton Penitentiary, Camp Chase, and Fort Warren. Exchanged 1862, rejoined his command and elected Col. of the 15th Arkansas. Again wounded and captured at Port Hudson, (See Report of Gen. Gardiner.) confined in the Parish Prison at New Orleans, and at Governor's Island, and Johnson's Island, where he remained until 1865, escaping in the spring by bribing the guards, but not in time to join his command before the close of the war. Twice recommended for promotion for gallantry.

Removed 1868, to Camden, Arkansas, and took up the practice of law, and is now a prominent member of the Arkansas bar of the firm of Barber and Johnson. From 1868 to 1874, being unwilling to practice in the court as then organized, was a farmer on the Ouachita River. In 1874, was elected to the Legislature and served as chairman of the Impeachment Committee and Military Committee in the sessions of that body known as the Baxter legislature, member of the Constitutional Convention of 1874. Resumed the practice of law and served as District Attorney of the 9th district, 1876–80. Attorney of the Texas and St. Louis R. R.

1223.

Hon. JAMES GOODE JOHNSON, of Texarkana, Ark., son of No. 505, p. 179, was born in Upson Co., Ga., Nov. 1837, and died 1879, Married (1) Hattie Culbertson (cousin of David B. Culbertson, M. C. of Texas,) and had 3 children. (2) Amanda Adair, of Salem, Ala., 1827. Children : —

> 3520, BENJAMIN W. JOHNSON. 3521, MAY C. 3522, FRANK. 3523, ANN TYLER.

Major Johnson at the beginning of the war went out as Captain in the 19th Arkansas Reg't, C. S. A. In 1862, he was appointed Quartermaster, and assigned to the 15th Arkansas Reg't commanded by his brother. In 1863, he became Brigade-Quartermaster under Gen. Dockery in the Trans-Mississippi Department, serving till the end of the war.

In 1874, he was elected a member of the Arkansas Senate, and served for four years. He died of consumption, in Texarkana, 1879.

1225.

WILLIAM F. BEALL, a lawyer, a resident of Thomaston, Ga., or Richmond, Va. "One of the best musicians in the South. He ran away from his father and joined the 2nd Georgia Reg't, C. S. A., at Pensacola, and soon organized the best band in the army. At the close of the war he was chief band-master of Cheatham's Corps."

1226.

JOEL M. CHIVERS, of Troup Co., Ga., married FRANCES ELIZA-
BETH ANDREWS, daughter of No. 507, p. 175. Children :—

> 3526, ANNA ELIZABETH CHIVERS, m. *Henry L. Hodges.* 3527, MARCUS
> ANDREWS, soldier, C. S. A., died in service at Richmond. 3528,
> HENRY THOMAS, soldier, C. S. A. 3529, JOEL M., soldier, C. S. A.
> 3530, EMILY, m. *Rufus Clark*, of Troup Co., Ga. 3531, JANE, m.
> *Ulysses Moseley*, of Peytonville, Arkansas. 3531½, CHARLES DAW-
> SON, soldier, C. S. A., died in service, Selma, Ala.

Mr. Chivers was descended from a Huguenot ancestry settled in South Carolina early in the last century. He was a wealthy planter in Troup Co., near
the Alabama line, and at times a resident of La Grange. A man of cultivation and influence.

1228.

JOHN WILLIAM ANDREWS, of Georgia, son of No. 507, was
born 1821, died 1866. Married Nov. 25, 1841, Martha E. Hilsman.
Children :—

> 3532, WILLIAM MARCUS ANDREWS, b. Aug. 28, 1842, m. 1865, Miranda
> Clay Hubert, 6 children, 1885. Served in the last year of the
> war in a company of cavalry, stationed at Macon, Ga., though
> only 17 years of age. 3533, LEONIDAS BENNETT, b. 1844, d. 1881.
> 3534, FANNY CHIVERS, b. 1846, d. 1879, m. 1865, *Dr. A. T. Rowe.*
> 3535, THOMAS ALEXANDER, b. Feb. 28, 1848, m. 1884, Lizzie Lane.
> 3536, CHARLES JASPER, b. Mar. 26, 1850. 3537, HARVEY HILSMAN,
> b. and d. 1851. 3538, WALTER STANLEY, b. 1855, d. 1861. 3539,
> JUDGE, b. 1858, d. y. 3540, MARSHALL ANDREWS, b. and d. 1859.
> 3541, ANNA MARIA, b. May 17, 1861, m. 1878, *Devany Lane*, 1 child :
> 1884, *Dr. S. A. Cooper*, of Powelton, Ga. 3542, JOHN W., b. 1863,
> d. 1866.

1229.

DR. JAMES THOMAS ANDREWS, of Sparta, Ga., son of No. 507,
was born, Jan. 3, 1830. Married, Nov. 17, 1852, Maggie Louisa Cul-
ver. Children :—

> 3543, MARCUS AURELIUS ANDREWS, b. Nov. 4, 1853, m. Jan. 20, 1876,
> *Mary Shields*, 4 children. 3544, ANNIE LAURIE, b. 1859, d. 1883, m.
> May 17, 1877, *J. D. Leonard*, 2 children. 3545, ROSA LOUISA, b.
> Feb. 11, 1860, m. Jan. 27, 1880, *W. D. Howell*, 2 children. 3546,
> MAGGIE MELVINA, b. Mar. 28, 1863, m. *L. A. Brake.* Mar. 5, 1881.
> 3547, THOMAS GARNETT, b. 1866, d. 1877. 3548, JOHN ELLINGTON,
> b. Sept. 15, 1871.

Dr. Andrews was, from 1880–1884, Clerk of the Supreme Court of Hancock
Co., and in 1885, is Chairman of the Board of Education and School Commission. He was a private, C. S. A., fought at Savannah in Taylor's Battalion, afterwards in the defence of Atlanta, in company commanded by the Hon. Linton
Stephens—but was generally on duty as surgeon.

1230.

CAPT. TROUP BUTLER, of Washington, Ga., married 1852, ANN CORINTHIA (Cora) ANDREWS, daughter of Hon. Garnett Andrews, No. 511, born Jan. 16, 1829. Children : —

    3549, THOMAS BUTLER, d. unm. 1878.   3550, JULIA, m. *William Henry Toombs.*

A wealthy planter before the war. Served through the war first as a Lieutenant in a volunteer Co., then as Captain in the Quartermaster's department.

1231.

MAJ. JOHN FREDERICK ANDREWS, of Washington, Ga., son of No. 511, p. 175, was born Nov. 12, 1830. A lawyer in successful practice. Unmarried.

Mr. Andrews served through the war, entering the service as a private in a Mississippi volunteer company, and at its close held the rank of Major in the Confederate Army. He was at Acquia Creek, Seven Days' Battle around Richmond, Malvern Hill, Cold Harbor, etc. At the close of the war he was superintendent of camps of instruction for conscripts.

1232.

DR. HENRY F. ANDREWS, of Washington, Ga., son of No. 511, was born Nov. 20, 1834. Married Cora Morgan, Nov. 20, 1860. Children : —

    3551, FREDERICK ANDREWS, b. 1861, d. y.   3552, MAUDE ANNULET b. Dec. 29, 1862.   3553, HENRY GARNETT, b. 1867, d. y.

Dr. Andrews served in the Confederate Army through the entire war, first as a member of the Irving artillery, a crack company from Washington : afterwards in the surgical department, with ranks of Captain and Major. He graduated at medical schools in Charleston and New York, and was for several years in Bellevue Hospital.

1234.

COL. GARNETT ANDREWS, of Chattanooga, Tenn., son of No. 511, was born, May 15, 1837. Married Aug. 23, 1867, Rosalie Champe Beirne, daughter of Colonel Andrew Beirne, of Monroe Co., W. Va. Children : —

    3554, ROSALIE CHAMPE ANDREWS, b. 1868, d. 1871.   3555, GARNETT, b. Sept. 15, 1870.   3556, GEORGE BEIRNE, b. 1873, d. 1874.   3557, CHAMPE SEABURY, b. May 13, 1876.   3558, ANDREW BEIRNE, b. July 10, 1878.   3559, ARNOLD ELZEY, b. 1880, d. 1881.   3560, OLIVER BURNSIDE, b. July 23, 1882.

Col. Andrews was educated at the Washington Male Academy and the University of Ga., and was admitted to the bar in 1857.

He was the first man in Wilkes Co., Ga.. to enter the Confederate army. and was made 2nd Lieut., 1st Reg't Georgia Regulars, Feb., 1861, serving at Savannah and Fort Pulaski. In June, 1861, was chosen by Gen. H. R. Jackson as Adj't-General and Chief of Staff.in the army of N. W. Virginia, to the command of which he succeeded at the death of Gen. Garnett, at Carrack's Ford. They met the retreating disorganized column of the army at Monterey, Highland Co., Va., where Mr. Andrews did the principal staff work of reorganization. Gen. Lee then took chief command, and after the action of Cheat Mouutain, Mr. Andrews was taken sick with camp fever and disabled for a year. In 1862, served in Cutts's Battalion of Ga. Artillery, in the valley of Va. In 1862, was made Captain and Ass't Adj't-General of Dayton's Brigade, Longstreet's Corps, and served with it at Fredericksburg. Later attached to staff of Gen. Arnold Elzey, comd'g dep't of Richmond. Here, among other things, he was charged with the organization of a corps of about 400 men, called "Local Defence Troops," composed of soldiers detailed about the city on special duty in the various government departments, offices, arsenals, etc. Gen. Custis Lee was placed in command, and on several critical occasions it was almost the only defensive force about the city. On the occasion of Dahlgren's raid, it repelled the enemies' column after it had penetrated to the third and last line of works in the very suburbs of the city. It also repelled Kilpatrick's raid. For his services in the organization of this force, Capt. Andrews was complimented in general orders, and promoted to Major and A. A. G. Served as Judge-advocate in the court-martial of Generals McLaws and Robinson, on charges preferred by Gen. Longstreet, involving the failure of his attack on Knoxville, 1863-4. Becoming tired of inactive life, resigned, in 1864 his commission as Assistant Adjutant-General, and at his own request was ordered to the 15th Georgia Reg't with his regular (Confederate) army rank of 2nd Lieutenant. Served through the campaigns and battles of "The Wilderness," "Spottsylvania," "South Anna River," "Second Cold Harbor," "Bermuda Hundred" and "Petersburg." While in the trenches at Petersburg, he was recalled to his former post and rank at Richmond, where he remained for some months.

For the remainder of his record, I quote his own words. "Our lines had now become frightfully thin, and among the last desperate efforts to recruit them, was the plan of soliciting voluntary enlistments of foreigners among the Federal prisoners. I was authorized to raise a battalion of six full companies of this material, with power to select my own officers from the army at large. I soon enlisted 1600 men at the prisons at Salisbury, N. C., and Florence, S. C., all without exception, foreigners, principally Irish, with some Germans, French and English. They were men who had enlisted in the U. S. army immediately on arrival in this country, and some of them could speak but little English. Out of the 1600, after several months careful study of them in camp under rigid drill and discipline, I cautiously selected 600 picked soldiers, got them thoroughly equipped and uniformed, and reported for duty in the latter part of 1864 or early in 1865. Was ordered to Charlotte, N. C., and promoted to be Lieutenant-Colonel. The War Department at first designated the corps as the "Second Foreign Legion," but soon afterwards changed the name to "8th Confederate Battalion of Infantry." But the public humor gave us the expressive appellation of "Galvanized Yankees."

"It was a very perilous venture. A regiment of like material conspired to mutiny at Savannah, and came very near succeeding : their plan including the capture and delivery to the enemy of their own officers. As this occurrence had now already taken place, we felt that in going into action we were exposed to double danger. But we had better fortune.

"In the night of April 11th, 1865, I was ordered by telegraph to report with the battalion at Salisbury, without delay, and to impress railway transportation if necessary beyond Salisbury. The wires had been cut, and though fearful of impending disaster, we were ignorant of Lee's surrender at Appomattox, on the 9th. I seized the first passing train, whose crew, including the engineer, at once deserted it, I manned it with another from our own ranks, and drew into Salisbury on one side, as Stoneman was entering it from the other.   We were immediately ordered into action, and straightway had all, and more, than we could do , for Stoneman had a magnificent division of cavalry and mounted infantry. The other confederate troops, few and hastily gathered, had been dispersed before we arrived, and I was entirely without support. But to my great relief I saw that our men were not only true, but some of them devoted ; for a sergeant, named Boothe, saved my life and was himself grievously wounded in the effort.   It soon became a hand-to-hand encounter, a few in the midst of many, we lost severely in killed and wounded, and I was sabered in the neck and shot through the right shoulder.   Was previously wounded slightly at Spottsylvania, and Cold Harbor.   We had to make the seemingly useless fight because I was ordered to hold Stoneman in check as long as I could, *at all hazards*, so that certain trains of valuable stores and treasure could be moved out, and to that extent we were successful."

Erwin Ledyard in the *Philadelphia Weekly Times*, June 16, 1883, wrote : " A remarkable feature of this engagement was the very effective fighting done by the battalion of ' Galvanized Yankees,' (who had been telegraphed for to Charlotte."   They stood up to their work like men, and only gave way when everpowered by numbers.   They were commanded by gallant and efficient officers, of whom several were severely wounded, including Col. Garnett Andrews commanding the battalion."

After the war Col. Andrews settled at Yazoo City, Miss., where he remained until 1882.   Served as a Representative in the Mississippi Legislature, 1880-81. Since 1882, he has been practicing law in Chattanooga.   He is the author of Andrews' " Digest of the Decisions of the Supreme Court of Mississippi," 1884.

1235.

ELIZA FRANCES ANDREWS, of Macon, Ga., daughter of Hon. Garnett Andrews, No. 511, was born Aug. 10, 1850.   Graduated at LaGrange Female College.   Miss Andrews is better known as a writer, under the names FANNY ANDREWS and ELZEY HAY.

Fanny Andrews is prominent among the literary women of America, and has published three novels : " A Family Secret," " A Mere Adventurer," and " Prince Hal," (Philadelphia, Lippincott & Co.)   Besides these works she has written a serial for the Detroit " Free Press," and been correspondent of the New York " World," the Augusta " Chronicle," and the Burlington " Hawkeye."   While doing all this writing, she has constantly been engaged in teaching, having been for eight years principal of a flourishing school for girls.   She is a lady of broad culture and besides speaking several languages, is an accomplished botanist.

Pleasants A. Stovall, writing under the heading " A Georgia Authoress " in the Augusta " Centennial Chronicle," remarks :

" A lady of rare talent and great modesty, it has been impossible for her friends to preserve records of some of her best productions.   *   *   * Gifted with creative fancy, and largely endowed with poetic power, she is a very industrious and practical person.   *   *   *   She is slender in figure and above the medium height.   Her face is fair, her hair dark, and her profile classical."

Several years ago she wrote a poem called the "Haunted House," which is fine enough to immortalize her.   Her first book was " A Family Secret," (1878) which created quite a sensation in the South. It was a charmingly told story, admirably descriptive of Southern life, with its vagaries, traditions and well-drawn provincialisms. The dialect and folk-lore of the Negro were estimable features of the work.

'A Mere Adventurer,' (1879) was a more ambitious and artistic work. It embodied a romance of exceptional power, and contained a convincing plea for more extended usefulness of woman.

To the mind of the writer "Prince Hal," (1882) about which little has been said, is the most interesting of her writings. It was a most unusual, even an extraordinary book.

I am permitted to copy from a private letter of Dr. A. G. Haygood the following comments upon "Prince Hal." "I have read the book, every word of it, with sustained interest to the last line. The characters are persons; I *know* them all. The author has been singularly felicitous where most writers have failed—in making a child grow up naturally, 'after its kind'—Hal in the last days is Hal of the first. So of the rest—Martha, Bulow, and that sweet, perfect flower, the doctor's good daughter, as strong-hearted as Joan Lowry, and sweet as little Nell. And the good parson is perfect.

"For the progress in the book, I thank the author. She tells of the good old days tenderly, eloquently, truly, but she knows it is 1882, and her readers know it."

"A Mere Adventurer," has been more warmly praised by the press than any other book from the pen of a southern woman. The "Chicago Times" contains this critique.

"There is so much force, naturalness and dash in this book that if the author does not keep on her guard she will one of these days startle us with the long expected and still dilitory 'Great American Novel.' The character painting is admirable. Mr. Thompson Henslow, the villian, is forcibly drawn and shows the touch of a master-hand."

"A Family Secret" will however be most entertaining to readers not of Georgia birth, and I predict that it will hold a prominent place among the standard works of the 'contemporary history' class. The scene is laid at the time of the close of the late rebellion; the plot is, I am told, practically the history of a gentleman still living in Georgia, and the scenes and characters are evidently studies from life. It is invaluable as a record of the days now gone by and which are about lost to memory, even to those who lived in their midst. "Prince Hal" also gives a most valuable record of Georgia plantation life before the war, and should stand in the book case by the side of Miss Kemble's "Georgia Plantation."

Of "A Family Secret," the New York "Graphic" remarks: "One of the best American novels that has been published since the war. The plot is originally and skilfully worked out. Curiosity is awakened at the very first page, and the interest is sustained without flagging to the end. The descriptive powers of the author are exceptionally fine," and the New York "World" says; "A Family Secret has the merit of giving good pictures of Southern Life."

Henry W. Grady in the Atlanta "Post Appeal" writes:—"Miss Andrew's book is the most powerful work I have seen from the hand of a southern writer in many years." The Philadelphia *Home Magazine* says : " The sharp insight into the ways of the world, and bits of wisdom scattered through its pages would do credit to Thackeray, while the fine expressions reminds us of George Eliot. As to the mere execution, it reminds us of a beautiful piece of embroidery, with every thread in its place and no ends left hanging."

1236.

THEODORE M. GREEN, of Washington, Ga., married June 1877, WILLAMETTE ANDREWS, dau. of No. 519. Child :—

3561, GARNETT ANDREWS GREEN, b. Apr. 5, 1885.

A wealthy and successful merchant, the owner of " Haywood," the Andrews homestead. Although a mere boy he saw active service in the latter part of the war as Lieutenant in a company of cadets.

1238.

ELIZA ANDREWS BOWEN, of Spring Hill, Tennessee, daughter of Dr. Isaac Bowen, No. 513, was born in 1828.

A successful teacher from 1868, to the present time in the Female Seminary, Washington, afterwards in the Girls' High School, City of Atlanta, in the Ala. State Normal, at Jacksonville, and in Beechcroft School, near Nashville, Tenn. For some years Atlanta correspondent of Boston *Journal of Education*, and a contributor to the *Popular Science Monthly*. Miss Bowen published, in 1886, a text-book on astronomy for the Appleton's educational series.

Of "Astronomical Studies," *Educational Notes*, says: "It is somewhat unique in form and character. Some of its distinguishing features are large quarto pages, admitting maps and views on a scale to give a better conception of the vast expanse of the celestial regions, directions for observing, in entertaining and instructive ways, the phenomena, position, and characteristics of the heavenly bodies. The author is an enthusiastic lover of the science, and her book will make enthusiastic pupils.

The Boston *Journal of Education* speaks of it in terms of high praise, and the book has been endorsed by such men as Stone, of the University of Va., Charbonnier, of the University of Ga., Broun, of the Alabama Polytechnic, Nichols, of the University of Kansas, Shoup, of the University of the South, Swift of the Rochester Observatory, and LeConte of California.

The book is to be translated into Chinese, and a considerable edition has been ordered for the use of schools in Japan.

1240.

GEN. ALEXANDER A. GREENE, C. S. A., of Chambers Co., Ga., son of No. 573, was born about 1844, killed in 1864, having just been commissioned Brigadier-General, one of the youngest in the Confederate service, at the age of 20 or 21.

Gen. Greene enlisted in the 37th. Alabama Infantry in the spring of 1862, under requisition of President Davis for 12,000 more Alabamians. His first battle was Iuka, where he was wounded : he participated in the battles of Corinth, Chicasa Bayou, Port Gibson, Baker's Creek, and was in the garrison of Vicksburg during the siege was captured with the fortress, and soon after exchanged. Fought at Lookout Mountain and Mexican Ridge, where he was again wounded, again at Mill Creek Gap, Resaca, Noonday Creek, and Kennesaw.

In the battles around Atlanta, where Col. Greene was in command of his regiment the colors of the 37th floated at the front, as the big list of casualties show. He led his regiment on the day of July 22, and fell dead with 40 out of his 300 men.

Out of 122,000 Alabamians in the Confederate army, one fourth filled soldiers graves.

1244.

AARON GRIER STEPHENS, of Taliaferro Co., Ga., planter, son of Andrew B. Stephens, and brother of Senator A. H. Stephens, of Ga., was born about 1810. Married, 1842, SARAH ANN SLATON, daughter of William and *Fanny Goode* Slaton, No. 521, p. 177, b. Dec. 11, 1819, d. Feb. 18, 1880. Child : —

   3565, ALEXANDER GRIER STEPHENS, b. 1843.

The founder of the Stephens Family of Georgia was Alexander Stephens, born about 1726, who in 1745 espoused the cause of Charles Edward, "the young Chevalier," and after his failure, sought refuge in America. His first shelter was among the Shawnee Indians. He served under Braddock, was present at his defeat, and fought in the Revolution, rising to the rank of Capt. In 1795 he removed to Wilkes Co., Ga., where he was the near neighbor of several of the Goodes, and where he died in 1813. By his wife Catherine, daughter of Andrew Baskins of Pennsylvania, who was discarded by her family on account of her marriage, he had many children, whom he took with him to Georgia, among these was Andrew Baskins Stephens, who was born in Pennsylvania, 1783, and died 1826. He married in 1707, Margaret, daughter of Aaron Grier, and sister of Robert Grier, the publisher of "Grier's Almanac," which year after year during the early part of the century hung beside the chimney-place in almost every house in the Southern States, and also of Gen. Aaron W. Grier, one of the heroes of the Creek Indian war of 1812. Their children were 1, Mary Stephens, 2, Aaron Grier, No. 1244, of the Goode Pedigree, 3, ALEXANDER HAMILTON STEPHENS, born Feb. 11, 1812, U. S. Senator and Vice-President of the Southern Confederacy. (See Life by Henry Cleveland, Phil'a, 1866, 8vo, pp. 1–833 with portrait.)

By a second marriage with Matilda S., daughter of Col. John Lindsay, a Wilkes county planter of Scotch-Irish descent, and commander of a Georgian Regiment in the Revolution, he had five children, three of whom reached maturity, viz : 4, John Lindsey, a prominent lawyer of Western Georgia, 5, Catherine B., 6, Linton b. July 1, 1823, d. July 14, 1872, graduated in 1843 from the Univ. of Georgia ; Associate Justice of the Georgia Supreme Court, Lieut.-Col. of the 16th Ga. Inf. (See Biographical Sketch by James R. Waddell, Atlanta, 1877, 8vo, pp. 1–434, with portrait.)

1250.

SAMUEL E. DANIEL, of Washington Co., Ga., a planter, descended from the Daniels of Virginia, and perhaps grandson of William Pride and *Ann Goode* Daniel, No. 72, p. 149, married MARY E. SLATON, daughter of No. 521, p. 177. Children :—

> 3567, AMAZIAH C. DANIEL, m. Eliz. Dillard, of Oglethorpe Co., Ga. 3568, JOHN GRIER, m. Emma Hilman, of McDuffey Co., Ga Farmer Washington, Ga., 1885. Issue, 1, *John F. Daniel*, 2, *Mary Curtis*, 3, *Emma F.*, 4, *Jennie Lee*. 3569, FRANCES STEPHENS, m. *Robert S. Dillard*, of Oglethorpe Co., Ga., Nov. 16, 1873. Issue, 1, *John T. Dillard*. 3570, SAMUEL ALEXANDER, m. Rebecca Bird, of Taliaferro Co., Ga. 3571, SARAH CORNELIA, m. *Julius Carleton*, of Union Point, Greene Co., Ga.,

Mr. Daniel, although above the age for military service, was for a time in the Confederate Army, going out with the Georgia militia to fight Sherman before Atlanta,

1257.

FRANKLIN PIERCE SLATON, of Washington Co., Ga., a planter, son of No 501, married (1) Cornelia J. Fouche, 4 children. (2) April 11, 1877, M. E. Victoria Armstrong. Children :—

> 3581, SARAH FRANCIS SLATON, b. 1856. 3582, WILLIAM HENRY, d. 3583, PAUL FRANKLIN. 3584, JOHN SIDNEY.
> 3585, WILLIAM ARMSTRONG SLATON, b. 1873. 3586, HENRY RALPH. 3587, CORINNE. 3588, ELOISE.

1261.

JUDGE DAVID A. VASON, of Albany, Ga., son of John Vason, No. 529, married (1) Mary Pope. (2) —— Pope. (3) Sarah Ficklen. Children :—

> 3595, WILLIAM VASON, m. *Jane Beasley*, has children, eldest, 1, *Sidney*. 3596, FRANCIS, m. *William Gilbert*, has several children. 3597, HENRY, unm., 1885. 3598, CAROLINE, unm. 3599, DOLLIE MAY, unm.

Judge Vason occupied the bench of one of the Superior Courts in Georgia for many years, is a trustee of the Georgia State University, a lawyer of distinction and a leading citizen of Albany, and his beautiful home in that city is noted for its hospitality.

1263.

COL. WILLIAM J. VASON, son of No. 530, p. 178, married Mrs. Clinton, of Augusta Ga. He was Colonel of the 10th Confederate Cavalry, as successor of Col. C. T. Goode, and was wounded at Bentonville. (Brewer's Alabama, p. 693.)

THE BEDFORD GOODES.

1265.

LOUIS WROE, of Hagerstown, Md., married LIZZIE GOODE, daughter of Col. Edmund Goode, No. 534. Children :—

3510, JOHN WROE, b. 1874. 3511, MARY.

1266.

JORDAN MOORMAN, of Florida, orange-culturist, married ROBERTA GOODE, daughter of No. 534, now dead. Child:—

3512, EDWARD MOORMAN, b. 1880.

1272.

WILLIAM THROCKMORTON BROOKE, C. E., of Norfolk, Va., son of James Vass, and *Mary Norris* Brooke, was born in Warrenton, Jan. 8, 1847. Married, Nov. 10, 1886, MARY GOODE, dau. of No. 536, p. 179.

Mr. Brooke is City Engineer of Norfolk. He served in the Confederate army and was educated at the University of Virginia. He was, 1870–74, in charge of construction of the "Church Hill Tunnel," of the C. & O. R. R., in Richmond. He was from 1879 to 1881, U. S. Vice-Consul and Deputy Consul at Hong Kong, during Col. Mosby's term as Consul General, and in 1881, engaged in construction of a portion of the C. & O. R. R., from Richmond to Newport News.

He is descended, in the sixth generation it is believed, from Col. Frances Brooke, of Essex Co., Va., Surveyor-General of Virginia under Spottswood, and one of the "Knights of the Golden Horseshoe."* The Brooke family has had many distinguished members, and it is to be hoped that Mr. R. N. Brooke of Warrenton, who has in his possession materials for a family tree, will soon prepare a history of the family for publication.

1273.

RICHARD URQUHART GOODE, C. E., of Washington, son of No. 536, was born at Liberty, Bedford Co., Virginia, Dec. 8, 1858. Educated at Hanover Academy and University of Virginia. A topographical engineer attached to the U. S. Engineer Corps in Virginia and North Carolina in 1878 and '79. A member of the Topographical Corps of the U. S. Geological Survey from 1879 to 1882. Resigned from the Geological Survey in 1882, and was connected with the Northern Trans-continental Survey during the two years of its existence. Re-appointed to the U. S. Geological Survey in 1884, and at present in charge of the Texas Division of Topography.

1274.

JOHN BRECKENRIDGE GOODE, of Washington, son of No. 536, was born August 18, 1854. Educated at Washington and Lee

---

*Edmund Brooke, of Georgetown, inherited the Golden Horseshoe from his ancestor, and it is doubtless to him that John Esten Cooke refers in his "Virginia."

University. Attached to the U. S. Coast Survey from 1882 to 1885. In 1886 a law clerk in the Department of Justice, and a student of the Columbia University.

THE EDGEFIELD GOODES.

1285.

GARLAND GOODE STALLWORTH, of Union Academy, Monroe Co., Ala., son of Benjemin F. and *Mary Ann Goode* Stallworth, No. 546, was born Aug. 4, 1851. Married Jan. 31, 1871, E. O. Bythewood. Children : —

3525, D. BYTHEWOOD STALLWORTH, b. Jan. 19, 1876, d. Aug. 11, 1878. 3526, MARY GOODE, b. Oct. 30, 1873. 3527, GENEVIEVE, b. July 19, 1878. 3528, ELIZA BYTHEWOOD, b. Mar. 30, 1881. 3529, SALLIE MARSHALL, b. Apr. 3, 1883. ANNIE OLIVIA, b. May 21, 1885.

Dr. Stallworth was educated at Spring Hill College, and is a dentist by profession.

1309.

COL. SAMUEL FREEMAN GOODE, of Minden, La., planter, lived until after the war at Edgefield C. H., S. C., where he was a man of prominence and an extensive planter. Children : —

3551, JOHN F. GOODE served with distinction in Hampton's Legion, C. S. A., lives in Memphis, Tenn. 3552, KATE, m. *Pierce M. Butler*.

1305.

WILLIAM WILLIS WATKINS, of Texarcana, Ark., planter, son of No. 556-3-A. married SUSAN BURT, dau. of No. 557. Children : —

3571, JOHN COLEMAN WATKINS. 3572, FRANK BURT. 3573, WILLIAM WILLIS. 3574, ADELAIDE, m. *Mr. Garber*, of Bibb Co., Ala. 3575, CAROLINE, m. *E. P. Shackleford*, of Courtland, Ala., bro. of No. 1314.

1307.

CHARLES FOX SHERROD, of Columbus, Miss., son of Benjamin and *Talitha Goode* Sherrod, No. 556-3-B, was born in Lawrence, Co., Ala., Nov. 3, 1827, Married 1851, Susan Billups, daughter of Col. S. C. Billups of Columbus, Miss. Children : —

3581, THOMAS BILLUPS SHERROD. 3582, CHARLES FOX. 3583, SARAH A. 3584, ELLA S. 3585, WILLIAM HENRY. 3586, LILY. 3587, ANTOINETTE. 3588, IRENE. 3589, LOLITA.

He attended school at home, conducted by a governess until 13 years old, then attended school at Courtland three years. Entered at LaGrange College, remained three years, then went to University of North Carolina : returning home commenced the study of medicine, but had to give it up to attend to the estate of his father, who had died a short time before, and has since been leading the life of an agriculturist. He has always been fond of country life Enlisted as a volunteer in 56th Regiment of Alabama Cavalry and served to the close of the war, when he surrendered by order of Gen. Johnston at Washington, Ga.

1314.

Col. S. W. SHACKLEFORD, of "Hard Bargain," Lawrence, Co., Alabama, (son of Col. Jack Shackleford,) a prosperous planter living near Courtland, Ala. Married Susan Adelaide Sherrod, dau. of No. 556–3–B. Children :—

> 3590, Maria Adelaide Shackleford. 3591. Jack.

Col. Shackleford was a son of Dr. Jack Shackleford who commanded "The Red Rovers," in the Texas Revolution, and who witnessed the massacre of his command at Goliad, was taken prisoner, and kept two years confined in the City of Mexico. Only three of fifty-two men in the company escaped. The Mexicans spared his life on account of his skill as a physician, and he made his escape by the assistance of a Mexican woman. Col. Shackleford's brother, W. J. Shackleford, was among the slain, as was also Whitfield Brooks, No. 1325.

1315.

Hon. WILLIAM CRAWFORD SHERROD, of "Locust Grove," Florence, Ala., was born Aug. 23, 1831. Married, Oct. 1856, Amanda, dau. of Col. Samuel D. Morgan, of Nashville, Tenn.* Children :—

> 3592, Charles M. Sherrod. 3593, William Crawford. 3594, St. Clair M. 3595, Lilian E. 3596, Benjamin. 3597, Lucile. 3598, Eugene.

Major Sherrod was educated at the University of North Carolina, devoted his attention to cotton planting. He was a member of the Alabama Legislature 1859–60 and in 1861 represented the Fifth District of Alabama in the Charleston Convention, which passed the ordinance of Secession, which however he did not favor. He served through the war as Commissary of Patterson's Brigade of Cavalry, C. S. A., with the rank of Major. In 1869, he was elected to Congress, serving until 1871, and was the only representative of his party in the 41st Congress who was born in the South.

Major Sherrod writes as follows, of his Congressional record :—

"My father lived ahead of his time. He was the originator and builder of the line of Railroad from Decatur to Tuscumbia around the Muscle Shoals, predicting at that early day that a Railroad would be built from the Mississippi River to the Atlantic Ocean, and that his line of Road would be a portion of the trunk line, all of which prophecy has been fulfilled. When I was elected to Congress I concluded I would take up his work where he left it off, and conceived the idea of connecting the oceans by railroad over the line built

---

* Col. Morgan was in early life a resident of Huntsville, Ala., but was for forty years or more one of the most prominent citizens of Nashville He was the Superintending Architect of the State Capitol building, which is his monument, his remains being interred within its walls.

by him, consequently I devoted the whole of my Congressional career to securing the passage of the Texas & Pacific R. R. bill, having the entire charge of that bill, the passage of which has done more to build up the Southern Country than any measure passed by Congress since the war."

1318.

B. FRANK BURT, son of *Elizabeth Goode* Burt, No. 557, was a soldier in the army of the Republic of Texas. He was a trooper in Dr. Jack Shackelford's famous company of "Red Rovers," and was in the command of Col. J. W. Fannin, who, after a hard-fought battle, surrendered to the Mexican forces under Gen. Urrea on the Goleta, in March, 1836, and were afterwards shot at Goliad, in violation of the terms of surrender, March 27, 1836,—385 officers and men in all. The spirit of the men and times is reflected by the following extract from verses, printed in the Houston *Telegraph*, 1842.

> Tell Mexico's degraded sons,
> Their bloody debt shall yet be paid,
> For Fannin and his martyred ones
> Due vengeance stands too long delayed,
> The blood-stained soil of Goliad,
> Still rises darkling on your sight,
> And shows the treacherous fate they had,
> Up ! men of Texas, for the fight.

> And think ye others will not lend
> In such a case, a helping hand?
> Will relatives forget the end
> Of those brave men, the Georgia band?
> Will Shackleford forget his boy,
> Will not Duvall come with delight,
> Lo ! thousands hail the shout with joy,
> Up ! men of Texas, to the fight.

1319.

Dr. JAMES G. BURT, son of Philip and *Elizabeth Goode* Burt, was a physician near Tusambia, Ala. Daughter:—

3599, MRS. GEORGE GARTH, Courtland, Ala.

1324.

Z. SMITH BROOKS, son of *Frances Goode* Brooks, No. 559, removed from South Carolina to Texas, in the days of the struggle of the Texans for independence. He with his cousin Frank Burt, and his brother Whitfield, was with Shackleford's "Red Rovers," and in the massacre at Goliad. When the prisoners were drawn up in line to be shot, he with a Kentuckian and Tennessean took his chances in running the gaunlet. They were shot at and separated, and the Mexicans following Brooks pressed him so closely that he threw his watch to them. They stopped to struggle for it, and he succeded in reaching the San Antonio river which he swam, and after hiding for several days, made his way to a place of safety. The experience of Mr. John C. Duvall, printed in Baker's *Texas Scrap-book* p. 365, under the title of" Adventures of a young Texan," is doubtless a fair counterpart of that of Brooks.

1325.

WHITFIELD BROOKS, son of *Frances Goode* Brooks, No. 557, was a trooper in Shackleford's Texan " Red Rovers," and was slaughtered by the Mexicans at Goliad.

THE LUNENBURG GOODES.

1331.

MAJ. JOSEPH HARRIS MORGAN, of Atlanta, Ga., son of John Morgan, of Poughkeepsie, N. Y., born Sept. 18, 1841, married, Jan. 1865, EUGENIA HAMILTON GOODE, daughter of Major Goode, No. 557, p. 188, who was born 1843. Children :—

> 3611, EUGENE HAMILTON MORGAN, b. Oct. 26, 1865. 3612, HARRY, b. Mar. 21, 1868. 3613, DONALD GOODE, b. Oct. 10. 1873.

Major Goode is a prominent business man of Atlanta : he served through the civil war, first in the "Georgia Hussars," Co. B, 2nd Battalion of Georgia Cavalry and subsequently as Inspector of Conscriptions for the District of Northern Georgia. He was the originator of the project for the erection of a monument to Senator B. H. Hill, and a prominent supporter of the enterprize. His wife was, during the war, Secretary of the Atlanta Hospital Association, was also the originator of "Memorial Day," in Atlanta, and Vice-President of the Confederate Memorial Association, under whose auspices, was erected in 1866, the Atlanta Soldiers' Monument.

1333.

MATTHEW BARROW TORBETT, of Atlanta, Ga., married 1881, CALLIE GOODE, dau. of Major Hamilton, and *Ann Eliza Hickey* Goode, No. 557, p. 188. Children :—

> 3615, ANNIE GOODE TORBETT, b. Jan. 12, 1882. 3616, CALLIE BARROW, b. Feb. 18, 1885.

Mr. Torbett is son of Granville C. Torbett, of Nashville, Tennessee, for thirty years President of the Bank of Tennessee and State Treasurer during the war. and his wife Martha Louise Barrow, of Dawson Co., Tennessee. He is one of the leading young citizens of Atlanta, and an officer of the Southern Agricultural Works Company.

1334.

DR. J. R. PRICE, of Macon, Ga., married ELIZA HAMILTON GOODE, daughter of No. 558, p. 188. Children :—

3620, JULIAN PRICE, graduated at Mercer University and New England Conservatory of Music, a merchant in Macon, Ga., and reported to be the best basso singer in Georgia. 3621, ALGERNON GOODE, graduated at Mercer University, 1879, a merchant in Macon, and a singer of fine local reputation. 3622, ROE, a student in Mercer University, and a pianist of local reputation.

1335.

THOMAS SYDENHAM GOODE, of Dover, Terrell Co., Ga., son of No. 558, p. 188, is a planter. Children :—

3623, MACKERNESS GOODE. 3624, ELIZA.

1337.

DR. J. W. MERCER, of Georgetown, Ga., planter and capitalist, married ELIZA GOODE, dau. of No. 560, p. 189, born 1843, who was educated at Georgetown Seminary Georgia. Son :—

3630, CHARLES GOODE MERCER, b. 1866, an undergraduate in Emory College, Oxford Ga.. 1885.

1338.

JAMES THOMAS GOODE, son of Dr. Samuel Watkins Goode, No. 560, p. 189, was born March, 1845, He served with the Quartermaster's Department in Gordon's Corps of the Army of Virginia. Is a lawyer in southwestern Georgia, and a man of brilliant capacity, though somewhat erratic. Married, 1872, Miss Georgia Berry, of Twiggs Co., Ga., who died, 1882. Son :—

3631, SAMUEL WATKINS GOODE, b. 1873.

1339.

SAMUEL WATKINS GOODE, of Atlanta, Ga., son of Dr. S. W. Goode, No. 500, p. 187, was born in Stewart Co., Ga., June 1847, as a boy served in the Confederate Army and was wounded. Married (1) Oct. 22, 1872, Miss Jennie W. Kendall, dau. of James T. Kendall, of Eufaula, Ala., (2) July 20, 1882, Miss Lizzie E. Stone, dau. of Edward Stone, of Woodford Co., Kentucky. Children :—

3632, MARY KENDALL GOODE, b. Aug. 16, 1873. 3633, MARTHA ELIZABETH, b. Jan. 20, 1875. 3634, ELLE, b. July 17, 1883.

A boy of fourteen at the opening of the war, his talent for music was called to account and he marched to Atlanta and Savannah as fifer in the first company, the "Stewart Grays," which was raised in southwest Georgia. He spent two years at "Waverly Hall," and the Georgia Military Institute, served in the trenches at the siege of Atlanta as a member of the Georgia Cadets and was shot through the shoulder at Boulevard Ridge. This closed his army career but he served the remainder of the war in the Engineer Dep't at Macon, seeing a little active service at the time of Stoneman's raid.

Graduated at the Albany Law School, 1871, and was admitted to the bar in New York, and in Albany to the U. S. Courts. Making a specialty of real estate law, he first practiced in Savannah, subsequently in Eufaula, La., 1872-80, then removed to Atlanta, where he is engaged in business as a banker and real estate agent, and is one of the representative business men of the most stirring cities in the South. The "Goode Syndicate" is only one of numerous enterprises by which he is helping to advance the interests of Atlanta.

1340.

DR. FRANCIS M. BLEDSO, of Georgetown, Ga., was born 1835–40. Graduated at the Jefferson Medical College, Philadelphia, 1859. Served in the Confederate Army, losing an arm. Mayor of Georgetown, 1883. Married LAMIRA GOODE, dau. of No. 560. 3 children.

1341.

MACKARNESS GOODE, of Lumpkin, Stewart Co., Ga., son of Dr. Samuel W. Goode, No. 483, p. oo, was born, 1879. A farmer, 1885. Married Miss Mary Humber, dau. of Charles C. Humber, Esq., member of the Georgia Legislature. 4 children.

1342.

JAMES H. GUERRY, of Dawson, Ga., son of Hon. Theodorus LeGrand Guerry, President, at one time of the Georgia Senate, and Col. of the 10th Ga. Inf., C. S. A., married LIZZIE HELEN GOODE, daughter of No. 560, p. 189, born about 1851–2, a graduate of Wesleyan Female College, Macon. Mr. Guerry is Solicitor-General of the Petaula Circuit, 1885, and resides at Dawson, Terrell Co., Ga. 5 sons.

3642, GOODE GUERRY. 3643, THEODORUS. 3644, FRANK, and others.

1343.

EUGNEIUS DOZIER, of Georgetown, Ga., son of Dr. S. P. Dozier, member of the Georgia Legislature, married EMILY GOODE, daughter of No. 560, b. about 1853, a graduate of Wesleyan Female College, Macon. Child:—

3648, BELLE DOZIER, b. 1884.

1344.

SAMUEL GUERRY, of Georgetown, Ga., farmer, married BEALL WATKINS GOODE, daughter of No. 560, graduate of Wesleyan Female College. Son:—

3650, JOHN GUERRY, b. 1881.

1345.

JOHN GOODE FINLEY, of Montgomery, Ala., son of No. 561, graduated at the University of Alabama, and served as Captain in the 23d Alabama Infantry, C. S. A., in Tennessee and Virginia. A lawyer in Montgomery, Ala., 1885. Married Miss Pierce. No children.

1346.

DAVID FINLEY, of Montgomery, Ala., son of No. 561, was graduated at the University of Alabama. A soldier C. S. A., serving with Semple's Battery in Virginia and Tennessee, at Murfreesboro, Chicamauga, Mission Ridge, and Resaca. Lives, 1885, in Montgomery, Ala. Unmarried.

1347.

THOMAS FINLEY, of Atlanta, Ga., son of No. 561, p. 189, served as Lieutenant of Engineers C. S. A., stationed at Mobile. Graduated at College of New Jersey, Princeton, 1869, with second honor. A lawyer in Atlanta, Ga. Married Miss Reynolds. Son :—

3657, THOMAS FINLEY, b. 1881.

1348.

MACKARNESS FINLEY, of St. Clair Co., Ala., son of No, 561, was born 1847-8, died 1872. Served in the war with the Cadets of the University of Alabama. Graduated from the University of Georgia, 1860. A lawyer in Athens, Ga., and, at the time of his death, District Attorney for St. Clair Co., Ala.

1357.

REV. CHARLES H. HALL, married, 1824, ANNE MARIA CUMMING, daughter of No. 566. Mr. Hall is rector of a Protestant Episcopal Church in Brooklyn, N. Y. His wife is dead. Son :—

3660, BRYAN HUGH HALL, b. Nov. 2, 1855.

1358.

GEN. ALFRED CUMMING, C. S. A., of Rome, Ga., son of H. H. Cumming, No. 566, grandson of Joseph and *Ann Goode* Bryan, was born in Augusta, Ga., Jan, 30, 1829. Married, 1861, Sarah Matilda Davis. Children :—

3661, JULIEN CUMMING. 3662, HENRY. 3663, CAROLINE.

A distinguished military officer. Graduated at U. S. Military Academy, West Point, 1849 ; 2nd Lieut. 8th Infantry, 1849 ; 2nd Lieut. 7th Infantry, 1850 ; 1st Lieut. 10th Infantry, 1855 ; Captain, 10th Infantry, 1856 : resigned, July 11, 1861. Entered the service of the Confederate States : Major of Infantry, 1861, Lieut.-Col. 10th Ga. Infantry, June, 1861, and Colonel, Sept., 1861. Brigadier-

General, Oct. 29, 1862, and assigned to a brigade in Stephenson's Division, Army of the West. He served through the war, was wounded at "Malvern Hill" and seriously wounded at "Sharpsburg," (Antietam): he did not fall at the battle of "Jonesboro," as is recorded in his biography in *Johnson's Cyclopædia*, though he received three wounds from the effects of the most serious of which he has never recovered.

1359.

JULIEN CUMMING, of Georgia, son of No. 566, described in Avery's "History of Georgia," as "the gifted Julien Cumming," was born 1830–40, was Adjutant of the 48th Georgia Infantry, C. S. A., was wounded and captured at the battle of Gettysburg, and died a prisoner of war at Johnson's Island, March 8, 1864. He was a candidate for presidential elector on the Douglass and Johnson ticket in 1860.

1360.

THOMAS W. CUMMING, of Augusta, Ga., son of No. 566, was Adjutant of the 16th Georgia Reg't, C. S. A. He was wounded at South Mountain in Sept., 1862, subsequently captured and for a great part of the war was in the hands of the enemy. He distinguished himself by leading the assault on Fort Sanders at Knoxville, November, 1863, and was the only member of the assaulting party that got into the fort, where he was disarmed and made prisoner.

1361.

JAMES HENRY HAMMOND, eldest son of Governor and Senator James Hamilton Hammond, of South Carolina,* married EMILY HARFORD CUMMING, daughter of No. 566. They live upon the old Hammond estate at Beach Island, South Carolina.

1362.

HON. JOSEPH BRYAN CUMMING, of Augusta, Ga., son of No. 566, was born in Augusta, Ga., Feb. 12, 1836.

He was graduated from the University of Georgia in 1854, with highest honors, studied three years in Europe and one year at the Harvard Law School, and was admitted to the bar in 1859. His subsequent military and public career is sketched as follows in a Legislative Manual published in 1878 :

"Early in 1861, he entered the services of the Southern Confederacy as a private in the 'Clinch Rifles,' Company A, 5th Georgia Reg., commanded by Col. John R. Jackson, and was first stationed at Pensacola.

"In September, 1861, he was made Lieutenant of Company I, from Columbus, in January, 1862, promoted to the Captaincy, and served in that rank as Assis-

---

*Son of PROF. ELISHA HAMMOND, of South Carolina College, native of Rochester, N. Y. : he was born Nov. 15, 1807, died Nov. 13, 1864, a prominent writer and statesman, the reputed author of the phrase, "Cotton is King." Biography in *Johnson's Cyclopædia*, II, p. 679.

tant Adjutant-General in Jackson's Brigade, at the battle of Shiloh, in the Kentucky campaign, and at the battle of Murfreesboro. In the latter battle he had his horse shot from under him, and was wounded in the battle of Shiloh. After the battle of Murfreesboro, he was ordered to report to Gen. Wm. H. T. Walter, and, being promoted to the rank of Major, he served in the Adjutant-General's Department of Walker's command until he was ordered to Atlanta in 1864, just in time to take part in the battle of the 22d of July.

"Major Cumming was in every battle of that army, from Shiloh until the surrender, excepting those only of Missionary Ridge and Jonesboro, and none received higher praise for gallantry. After the death of General Walker, Major Cumming was ordered to report to Gen. Hardee, on whose staff he served until ordered to report to Gen. Hood, who was then commanding the Army of Tennessee. He was with Hood in the Tennessee campaign, and was on his staff at the battles of Franklin and Nashville.

"Upon the removal of Hood and the reappointment of General Johnston to the command of the Army of Tennessee, Major Cumming was placed on Johnston's staff. Upon the reorganization of the Army in 1863, just before the surrender, he was appointed Colonel of a regiment, made up of Stephens's Brigade; but the army being on the eve of surrender, he did not take command but remained with Johnston until the disbanding of the army at Jonesboro, N. C.

"After his return home, Major Cumming returned to the practice of his profession. He is ranked among the ablest members of the Georgia bar, either in his knowledge of the principles of law, in his familiarity with the code of practice, or as a pleader before the bench or jury.

"In 1870, Major Cumming was elected from Richmond County to the Georgia House of Representatives and was chosen Speaker of the House, which position he held during the winter and summer seasons of 1872. He was not a candidate again for political office until his nomination in 1877 for the State Senate.

"Major Cumming is an effective public speaker, possessing an agreeable and finished style of oratory. He is one of the leading men in the upper House of the General Assembly, and his record in the past will fully warrant the prediction of more eminent public service in the future."

1364.

DeROSSET LAMAR, married MARIA BRYAN CUMMING, daughter of No. 566, who died July 20, 1873. Children:—

3665, HENRY CUMMING LAMAR. 3666, PAUL CAZENOVE. 3667, MARIA CUMMING.

There is some unexplained kinship between the Goodes and Lamars of Georgia. Mrs. Branham thinks that a daughter of John Goode, No. 83, married a Lamar and was probably ancestor of most of the Lamars in the State. John Lamar, of Macon, who was living about 1845, claimed to be a cousin of Thaddeus No. 199, or his children.

1369.

JUDGE THADDEUS GOODE HOLT, JR., of Macon, Ga., son of No. 572, was born 16th Oct., 1836 ; died Jan. 17, 1886. Married, June 30, 1858, Florine Russell, daughter of Benjamin and Louise Canthon Russell. Children : —

> 3691, RUSSELL HOLT, d. y., b. 10th Aug., 1859, lost on the "Alpena" in a storm on Lake Michigan, Oct. 16th, 1880. 3692, FLORINE, b. on the 15th June, 1862, d. 8th Oct., 1885. 3693, NANNIE, b. on 19th Sept., 1869.

Judge Holt was graduated with honor from Georgia University, 1855. He was Captain of Company F, Georgia Cavalry, and Major in the 10th Confederate Regiment, commanded by his kinsman, Col. C. T. Goode. He was the author of the address adopted by the Georgia Convention of 1865, asking the General Government for amnesty for the disfranchised citizens of Georgia.

He was Vice-President of the State Agricultural Society, and editor of the *Georgia Stock and Agricultural Journal*, established in 1885. The following which appeared in the paper for June, 1886, written by Robert E. Parke, of Holton, Ga. :

" The sudden death of Judge Holt was a surprise and shock, not only to the citizens of Macon and Bibb county, but to all Georgia, for he was well known and honored throughout the State. Judge Holt was a son of the distinguished and lamented Hon. Thaddeus Goode Holt, for so many years the Judge of Macon Superior Court. He was a graduate of the State University, and for years one of the Alumni Trustees. He was admitted to the Macon bar, but practiced only a few years, devoting himself, from preference, to agricultural pursuits, in which he had large interests in Bibb, Houston, Calhoun, and Dougherty counties.

" When the State of Georgia seceded from the Union, young Holt raised a company of cavalry, and served throughout the war in the Western army. During much of the war he, with his command, was on very hazardous duty connected with the headquarters of General W. H. T. Walker, General Leonidas Polk, and General Joseph Wheeler. Captain Holt was noted for his imperturbable coolness and courage in the hour of danger, his dash and intrepidity in battle, his gentleness and kindness to his men, and his reliability, faithfulness, and trustworthiness on all occasions, in camp or bivouac, on the march or on the field of battle. General Wheeler pronounced him one of the most graceful, gallant, and accomplished cavalry officers of the war.

" When the war closed, Captain Holt devoted himself to his planting interests and succeeded well, but some very unfortunate ventures in South Carolina railroad stocks and other risks resulted disastrously to him, and embarassed him financially. He was just emerging from his troubles when his lamented death occurred. He was the first President of the Bibb County Agricultural Society, and a regular member of the famous Holton Farmers' Club.

"Governor Colquitt appointed him Judge of the County Court of Bibb, in which capacity he served for eight years, and was noted for his clearness and quickness of perception, his suavity and dignity as presiding officer, and for the inflexible justice, tempered with mercy, of his decisions. Very many interested parties and attorneys preferred to abide his just and wise decisions rather than trust their causes to the verdict of juries.

"Judge Holt's influence in the city, county, and State affairs was potent, and always on the side of conservative progress. He was often made Chairman of county conventions, foreman of grand juries, chairman of county Democratic Executive Committee and delegate to the State conventions. He felt a deep interest in the State Agricultural Society, and has been a member of the Executive committee, treasurer, superintendent of State fairs, and at the time of his death vice-president from the Sixth Congressional District.

"Judge Holt was a fluent and forcible writer, a graceful and ornate speaker, a dignified, affable, and courteous gentleman, a warm-hearted, impulsive friend, an enterprising, patriotic, public-spirited citizen, and a very intelligent and useful member of society. As editor of this paper, he bade fair to wield a very important influence over the planting and stock interests of Georgia and the South, and his loss is an irreparable calamity."

1375.

WILLIAM CHANDLER HOLT, of Columbia, Ga., son of No. 574, was born about 1825. He was graduated from the University of Georgia in 1844, and served through the Mexican war as an officer of U. S. Volunteers. He died in 1849, of disease contracted in Mexico.

1377.

R. T. BUTLER, of Louisville, Ky., a prominent and successful educator. Many years Principal of the Louisville Boys High School. Married ELIZABETH HOLT, daughter of No. 574.

1380.

SENATOR BENJAMIN HARVEY HILL, of Atlanta, Ga., son of John and *Sarah Parham*, Hill was born in Jasper county, Ga., Sept. 14, 1823, died Aug. 16, 1882. Married No. 27, 1845, CAROLINE HOLT, dau. of Cicero Holt, No. 575, p. 193, g.-dau. of Thaddeus and *Martha Goode* Holt, No. 199, p. 98. Children : —

> 3701, MARY HENRIETTA HILL, b. Aug. 14, 1847, m. *Edgar Thompson.*
> 3702, BENJAMIN HARVEY, b. July 1, 1849. 3703, CHARLES DOUGHERTY, b. Nov. 3, 1852. 3704. EMMA LEILA, b. Dec. 2, 1859, m. *Dr. Robert Ridley.*

The career of Senator Hill, so closely identified with the history of the South, and especially that of the State of Georgia, has so often been printed that it needs not to be repeated here, except in outline :

He graduated at the University of Georgia in 1844 ; studied law and commenced practice at LaGrange. He was a member of the House in the State Legislature in 1851. As a member of the Georgia Convention in 1861, he advocated the Union until the ordinance of secession was adopted. He then made the cause of his State and of the Confederacy his own, was elected a delegate to Confederate Provisional Congress, and subsequently became a member of the Senate of the Confederate States. After the surrender in 1865, he was arrested by the Federal authorities and imprisoned in Fort Lafayette. He was twice elected to Congress as a member of the House, and in 1877 was elected to the Senate of the United States.

An admirable summary of his characteristics and his career is given by Vice-President Stephens in Johnson's Cyclopædia. His life was a series of brilliant successes. His death was a national calamity.

He was a patriot in days when patriotic statesmen were few, and as an orator, at a time when oratory is almost a lost art, Senator Hill has been very prominent.

When he took his seat in Congress in 1875, he at once went to the front, and stood at the head as the ablest representative the South had in the National Assembly. It was during his first term that the gladiatorial contest took place between him and Mr. Blaine, both recognized as opposition leaders, over the bill, introduced by Randall, to remove all political disabilities. It was a masterly debate, and one that thrilled the country from ocean to ocean. Mr. Hill crowned himself as the champion of the South. It was a battle of giants, with truth and justice on the side of the silver-tongued Hill. As a specimen of his eloquence on this occasion I give the following extract from the celebrated speech whose theme was " The South once more in the Union:"

" Oh, Mr. Speaker ! why cannot gentlemen on the other side rise to the height of this great argument of patriotism ? Is the bosom of this country always to be torn with this miserable sectional debate whenever a Presidential election is pending ? To that great debate of half a century before secession there was left no adjourned questions. The victory of the North was absolute, and God knows the submission of the South was complete. But, sir, we have recovered from the humiliation of defeat, and we come here among you and we ask you to give us the greetings accorded to brothers by brothers. We propose to join you in every patriotic aspiration that looks to the benefit, to the advancement, and to the honor of every part of our common country. Let us, gentlemen of all parties, in this centennial year, indeed have a jubilee of freedom. We divide with you the glories of the Revolution, and the succeeding years of our national life before that unhappy division—that four years' night of gloom and dispair—and so we shall divide with you all the glories of the future.

" Sir, my message is this : There is no Confederate in this House ; there are now no Confederates anywhere ; there are no Confederate schemes, ambitions, hopes, desires or purposes here. But the South is here, and here she intends to remain. Go on and pass your qualifying acts, trample upon the constitution you have sworn to support, abrogate the pledges of your fathers, incite rage upon our people, and multiply your infidelities until they shall be like the stars of heaven or the sands of the seashore, without number, but know this, for all your iniquities, the South will never again seek a remedy in the madness of another secession. We are here : we are in the house of our fathers, our brothers are our companions, and we are at home to stay, thank God "

Another of Senator Hill's most vividly eloquent addresses was delivered in Atlanta at the unfurling of the Stars and Stripes in front of the Kimball House, during the presence in that city of a large excursion of citizens of the Northwestern States, who had been invited to visit Georgia.

On May 1, 1886, a statue to his memory was unveiled in Atlanta in the presence of a vast gathering of people from all parts of the South.

Jefferson Davis was the guest of the city and of Mrs. Hill. The following account of his receptions upon this occasion is from the *Atlanta Journal* of May 1.

"When the carriage containing Mr. Davis reached the residence of Mrs. Hill the crowd sent up a deafening cheer. A number of gentlemen locked arms and held the crowd back from around the gate. Governor McDaniel, Mayor Hillyer, and Dr. Spalding arose and assisted Mr. Davis from the carriage, the crowd meantime shouting and cheering in a deafening roar. Along the graveled walk leading to the door stood fifty little girls, who threw flowers to the ground, each exclaiming anxiously :

" Please step on my flowers, sir, please step on mine ! "

The flowers that were stepped upon by the ex President were quickly caught up to be treasured as mementoes of the occasion.

One little girl when she saw Mr. Davis, and heard the shouts of the populace, burst into tears and exclaimed :

"Oh, dear me ; are they really going to hang Jeff Davis on a sour apple tree."

Mr. Davis walked to the door and was met by Mrs. Hill. They grasped hands cordially, and reverently kissed each other.

" Mrs. Hill led the ex-President into the parlor, and insisted that he should occupy the chair which her husband had last used before his death. Mr. Davis took the proffered seat and his eyes filled with tears. Tears also came to the eyes of Mrs. Hill. Both were deeply moved. Mr. Davis arose, and bowing low, kissed the hand of Mrs. Hill, and resumed his seat. Dr. Ridley, Mr. Charles Hill, Mr. Edgar Thompson, and others were present to receive Mr. Davis. Senator Hill's grandchildren were also present.

" In a moment or so after Mr. Davis' arrival the carriage occupied by Miss Davis reached the gate. All eyes were very naturally directed toward the lovely face of the ex-president's daughter. Mr. Ben. Hill, Jr., stepped from the carriage and assisted Miss Davis to alight. They walked to the house, followed by Major Livingston Mims and Mr. Brown, who had occupied the carriage with them. Miss Davis was, cordially received by the family.

" In ten minutes, Mr. Davis was escorted to his room on the second floor of the house. A large bay window overlooked the street. Outside the ex-president could hear the stamp of many feet and the shouts of the enthusiastic crowd. He was very much affected by the demonstration, and standing up in the middle of his room, exclaimed to Dr. Ridley and Mr. Ben. Hill :

"I never expected such a reception ! "

" He wanted to go down and address the people, but was forbidden to do so by Dr. Ridley, who had charge of the ex-president's health affairs for the time being. He was told that he needed rest for the ceremonies of to-day, that he had been through enough, and ought not to speak.

"After a short time the veterans marched down the street headed by a band, which on reaching the Hill residence struck up, ' Bonny Blue Flag,' and amid deafening cheers the old soldiers marched to the statue, counter marched and stopped in front of Mrs. Hill's. The cheering was continuous.

" What must I do ? " asked Mr. Davis.

" Keep quiet.' said the doctor."

" Then, Dr. Ridley added : ' You see, Mr. President, how these people love you."

"Mr. Davis decided that he should at least appear in the window. Mr. Ben. Hill raised a sash and the ex-president of the Confederacy looked down into the thousands of faces and bowed. Cheer after cheer rent the air. Soon Mr. Davis' lips began to move. He said :

"God bless you my countrymen ; God bless you ex-Confederate soldiers ; God bless your wives and your daughters, for what they have done in the past and for what they will do in the future."

"He then bowed several times, Mr. Hill pulled the sash down and the crowd cheered.

"There was the rattle of a drum corps, and the Means High School Cadets marched down, took position opposite Mrs. Hill's and fired a volley in honor of Mr. Davis.

"It was then five o'clock. The crowd waited around for a half hour or so, and then dispersed."

1381.

GEN. ALFRED IVERSON, C. S. A., of Kissimee, Fla., son of No. 578, was born in Clinton, Ga., 1829. Married (1) 1856, Harriet Holt Hutchins, daughter of Judge N. L. Hutchins, of Gwinnett Co., Ga., who died 1861, (2) Adela J. Branham, daughter of Dr. Joel Branham, of Atlanta, sister of No. 1382. Children :— (First marriage.)

3705, JULIA O. IVERSON, b. Sept. 1857, m. *R. T. Patton*, of Sanford, Fla.
3706, MARY C., b. Aug. 1859, m. *William B. Randolph*, of Florida.

Gen. Iverson began a course of study at Oglethorpe University, but left college at the age of seventeen, to join the Georgia Volunteer Battalion of Infantry, on its way to the Mexican war. He served as Lieutenant, and during one part of the war was in command of a company.

In 1852, was appointed by Jefferson Davis, Secretary of War, 1st Lieut. of 1st U. S. Cavalry, for services in the Mexican War. On the breaking out of the civil war, having resigned his commission, he was appointed Capt. in the regular Confederate Army. In 1861, was elected Col. of 20th N. C. Inf., and was promoted directly after the battle of Antietam to Brig.-Gen. Commanding Brigade of N. C. Infantry in D. H. Hill's division of Stonewall Jackson's Corps. In 1863, was ordered to Georgia to take command of Georgia Brigade of Cavalry, in the army of J. E. Johnston. In the battle of Sunshine Church near Clinton, Ga., commanded Stone brigades of Cavalry attacking the Cavalry Corps of Major-Gen. Stoneman, and after a fight lasting through the day, received the surrender of Gen. Stoneman and forces on the field. Was in front of Gen. Sherman, all the way through Georgia, in command of a division of Cavalry. At the conclusion of the war, he was in command of the post at Greensboro, N. C., and surrendered to Gen. Sherman.

In the official reports, especially those relating to the Gettysburg campaign, frequent reference to his gallant service may be found. After the war, settled in Macon, Ga., and from thence moved to Florida, where he is engaged in the peaceful occupation of orange culture.

1382.

PROF. ISHAM RICHARDSON BRANHAM, D. D., of Macon, Ga., son of Dr. Joel Branham, was born 1825. in Eatonton, Ga.

Married, 1867, JULIA MARIA IVERSON, daughter of No. 578.   Children : —

> 3707, EMILY COOPER BRANHAM, b. 1849, m. *Charles Lane.*   3708, CAROLINE HOLT, m. *Frank Means.* 3709, ALFRED IVERSON, b. 1885. 3710, ISHAM RICHARDSON, b. 1859, traveling for a Detroit mercantile house, 1886, m. Laura Adams, of Eatonton, Ga.   3711, ADELA m. *L. G. Walker.*   3712, ROBERT LEE, b. 1862, Conductor on the East Tennessee, Va., and Ga. R. R., unm.

Dr. Branham, a Baptist clergyman, was graduated at Emory College, 1847. He has been President of several female colleges in Tennessee, and a very successful teacher.   In 1872, the degree of D. D. was conferred on him by Union University.

Mrs. Branham thus speaks of her Goode ancestors, who were pioneers in Georgia, "The Goodes were more refined and literary and perhaps a little too proud and claimed to be ' F. F. V's,' but I believe not much can be said against them."

THE CHARLOTTE GOODES.

1384.

MACKERNESS HILLERY GOODE, of Pleasant Hill, Cass Co., Mo., son of John Goode, No. 205, p. 52, and his wife, Mary Jones, of Mecklenburg Co., and grandson of Mackerness Goode, No. 84, and Miss Mosely his wife, ought properly to have been discussed with the sixteenth generation, to which he belongs, but his existence and that of his brothers was not suspected when that chapter was printed.   He was born, 1812, in Charlotte Co., and removed with his parents in 1829 to Franklin Co., Mo.   Married (1) Paulina A. Brown, of Franklin Co., (parents from Charlotte Co., Va.), and had 3 sons ; (2) Harriet Powell, Nelson Co., Va., s. p.   (3) Harriet Ayres, of Mansfield, O., 3 children.   (4) Mrs. Mary A. Thruston, daughter of Josiah Walton, of Charlotte Co., Va., 4 children.

> 3725, JOHN GOODE, d. y.   3726, JOSEPH, d. at Gold Hill, Nevada, while mining.   3727, MACKERNESS, a soldier, C. S. A, who fell in the siege of Vicksburg.   3728, WILLIAM CLAY, soldier C. S. A., killed while with Marmaduke in the raid on Cape Girardeau.   3729, SCEPTER A., owner of a cattle ranche in Texas.   3730, SAMUEL O., farmer, of Index, Cass Co., Mo.   3731, THOMAS B., druggist, of Bunceton, Mo.   3732, JOSIAH WALTON, druggist, with his brother. 3733, SUSAN L., Pleasant Hill, 1886.   3734, IDA V., educated at Pilot Grove Inst., Cooper Co., Mo., lives in Pleasant Hill, 1886.

Mr. Goode, now 74 years of age, writes of his experiences since 1861.   " I have but little to tell.   I sent two sons to the service of the Confederacy, all that were old enough, and neither of them ever returned.   I entered the service at the beginning, and was at the battle of Wilson Creek, and at the storming of Lexington, Mo. I was detailed on special duty to take charge of military stores inside the Federal lines, and was caught with them, imprisoned for six months, court-martialed, released on a $5000 bond and limited to one county. I was finally forced to leave home, and went with my family to St. Louis, and remained till the close of the war. After the war ended, I was financially ruined. I never returned to my old home in Morgan Co., but came to Pleasant Hill, where I have educated my children in the public schools."

1385.

EDWARD JONES GOODE, of Franklin Co., Mo., brother of No. 1384, married Sarah North; they had a son and daughters, but all are dead.

1386.

MARY E. GOODE, sister of No. 1384, married (1) WILLIAM ROBERTS, of Franklin Co., Mo., (2) ASA BRECKENRIDGE, of St. Louis Co., Mo. Children, 3 sons and 3 daughters.

1387.

NATHANIEL MACON GOODE, son of John Goode, No. 205, p. 52, and his wife, Margaret Miller, of Charlotte Co., Va., grand-daughter of Col. Claiborne Barksdale. Emigrated to California.

1387–1.

JOHN GOODE, brother of 1384, married Miss Aligra, lived in Franklin Co., Mo.

1387–2.

LANGSTON T. GOODE, married Miss Billups, lived in Franklin Co., Mo.

1387–3 to 6.

FRANCES GOODE, married T. J. NORTH.

AGNES GOODE, married JOHN GREGORY.

VIRGINIA GOODE, married STEPHEN MAY.

MARGARET GOODE, married WILLIAM BILLUPS.

All these people lived at one time in Franklin Co., Mo., and their descendants are, no doubt, scattered over the entire western portion of the continent.

1388–1.

The descendants of JOHN McCUE, of Mecklenburg, Co., and SALLY GOODE, daughter of No. 84, p. 52.

1388–2.

The descendants of JAMES JONES, of Mecklenburg Co., Va., and MARY GOODE daughter of No. 84.

1388-3.

The descendants of ROBERTSON JONES, of Mecklenburg Co., Va., and ELIZABETH GOODE daughter of No. 84.

1390.

ISAAC READ GOODE, of Mossingford, Va., son of No. 588, p. 000, was born Oct. 19, 1853. Married Anna P. Adams, daughter of William Adams, of Pittsylvania, (family of Charlotte Co.)   Children :—

> 3771, MARTHA CLAIBORNE GOODE.   3772, THOMAS IRVIN.   3773, LANDON READ.

Mr. Z. R. Goode, is engaged in mercantile pursuits in Charlotte Co., Va., and is postmaster of the village of Mossingford.   He has aided materially in the preparation of this history.

1393.

JUNIUS A. COLEMAN, of Norfolk, Va., married LUCY ARMISTEAD GOODE, daughter of No. 588.   Children :—

> 3774, ANNA BOLEYN COLEMAN.   3775, LUCY GOODE.   3776, JUNIUS ARMISTEAD.

Mr. Coleman is clerk of the Corporation Court of Norfolk.

1394.

C. A. GLASCOCK, of Wolf Trap, Halifax Co., Va., farmer, married SALLIE B. GOODE, daughter of No. 588.   Children : —

> 3777, ESTELLE GOODE GLASCOCK.   3778, WILLIAM CLAIBORNE.

1397.

CLEMENT MELANCHTHON GOODE, of Readsville, N. C., merchant, married Laura Moore.

1397½.

THOMAS BROOKS, of Drake's Branch, Charlotte Co., married daughter of No. 590.

1400.

LANGSTON EASLEY FINCH, of Boydton, Mecklenburg Co., Va., son of Adam and Lucy Goode Finch, was born Oct. 28, 1825.   Married (1) 1847, MARTHA BOYD, daughter of Richard and *Lucy Goode* Boyd, No. 857 ; (2) TABITHA BOYD, daughter of same.   Children :—

> 3780, CHARLES L. FINCH, m. ALICE BASKERVILLE, No. 5008.   3781, PATTIE E., m. C. *Thomas Baskerville*, No. 2007.   3782, HUNTER WOODIS.   3783, PEARL.   3784, GEORGE.   3785, RUBY.   3786, GARNET.   3787, ADAM.   3788, MORTON EASLEY.   3789, JAMES LOVE.   3790, PANSY.

1401.

RICHARD HENRY FINCH, of Mecklenburg Co., Va., son of No. 000, was born April 24, 1827, married about 1858, Betty Burney, of North Carolina.   Children :—

3791, LUCY FINCH, m. 1885, *C. T. Ruckes*. 3792, MARY, m. 1861, *W. E. Moore*. 3793, HENRY. 3794, LENA. 3795, BETTIE.

1402.

WILLIAM E. FINCH, of Mecklenburg Co., Va., died unmarried.

1403.

JOHN B. FINCH, of Texas, married Mrs. Rodgers. One daughter.

1404.

GEORGE B. FINCH, of Boydton, Va., is a leading lawyer of Mecklenburg Co. Unmarried.

1405.

TYREE GOODE FINCH, of Mecklenburg Co. Va., born 1830-40, died July 4, 1884, married Miss Cunningham, of Mecklenburg Co., Va. Children : —

    3796, ADAM FINCH, b. 1874, others d. y.

1428.

WILLIAM LEIGH WATKINS, of Charlotte C. H., Virginia, married ANN C. HARRIS, daughter of Marshall L. and *Martha Ann W. Goode* Harris. Children : —

    3820, SALLIE WATKINS. 3821, JOSEPHINE. 3822, ANN. 3823, SYLVIA. 3824, JOEL. 3825, KATE.

1429.

WILLIAM EDWARD GOODE, son of H. M. L. Goode, No. 594, lives in Brownsville, Tenn.

1432.

HILLERY LANGSTON GOODE, son of No. 594, lives in Texas.

1433.

LUCY BOYD GOODE, daughter of No. 594, lives in Brownsville, Tenn.

1434.

SALLIE ISABELLA GOODE, daughter of No. 594, lives in Brownsville, Tenn.

1430.

RICHARD BENNETT GOODE, of Virginia, son of H. M. L. Goode, No. 594, married PANTHEA BURWELL GOODE, No. 1382. Children : —

    3827, WILLIAM CLAIBORNE GOODE. 3828, MAURY READ. 3829, ELLIA BOULDIN. 3830, PANTHEA BOYD. 3831, MINNIE M.

1431.

E. A. ROBERTS, of Richmond, Va., married MARTHA ANN GOODE, daughter of No. 594, p. 187. Children : —

3831, GEORGE J. ROBERTS, of Aurora, Ill. 3832, SALLIE GOODE. 3833, MARTHA FRIEND. 3834, HILLERY LANGSTON. 3835, EDMUND A.

THE CHESTERFIELD GOODES.

1476.

JOSEPH R. WOOLDRIDGE, of "Bleak House," Chesterfield Co., Va., a prosperous planter, descended from the old Virginia stock of Wooldridges, married Oct. 18, 1839, LOUISA GOODE, daughter of Col. Robert and *Mary Loper* Goode, who was born Feb. 21, 1819, died Jan. 1856. Children :—

> 3841, MARY ELIZA WOOLDRIDGE, b. July 29, 1840, d. Nov. 23, 1862. 3842, MARTHA WALKE, b. Jan. 18. 1842, d. y. 3843, ROBERT AR-MISTEAD, b. June 21, 1843. 3844, EMMA JANE, b. April 28, 1844, m. *Frank Anderson*, of Chesterfield Co., farmer, children ; 1, *Joseph Anderson;* 2, *William ;* 3, *Frank*. 3845, DANIEL SPENCER, b. Feb. 18, 1846. 3846, ANGELIA AUGUSTA, b. Oct. 23, 1848, m. *Oscar Webster*, of "Clover Hill," farmer, children: 1, *Royall Webster ;* 2, *Alma;* 3, *Louise;* 4, *Bettie*. 3847, SUSAN A., b. Nov. 10, 1850, d. Nov. 16, 1876, unm. 3848, JOHN WALKE, b. Oct. 10, 1852, d. Sept. 14, 1857, unm. 3849, BETTIE B., b. Oct. 6, 1854.

1477.

DR. PHILIP FRANCIS SOUTHALL, of "Woodstock," Amelia Co., Va., son of Dr. Philip Turner and *Frances Lockett** Southall, grandson of Maj. Stephen and *Martha Wood* Southall, great grandson of Col. Turner Southall, of Fairfield, Henrico Co., Va., was born April 6, 1822, at "Selma," Amelia Co., Va., the residence of his father, married Dec. 16, 1845, ELIZA JANE GOODE, daughter of No. 600, p. 197, who was born May 17, 1821. Children :—

> 3850, PHILIP TURNER SOUTHALL, d. y. 3851, DR. PHILIP TURNER, b. May 18, 1851. 3852, ROBERT GOODE, b. Dec. 26, 1852. 3853, STE-PHEN OSBORNE, b. May 1, 1855, d. Dec. 2, 1856. 3854, FRANCES TURNER, b. May 29, d. Jan. 26, 1856. 3855, FRANCIS, b. Nov. 29, 1856, d. April 24, 1857. 3856, REV. STEPHEN OSBORNE, b. May 15, 1858. 3857, MARY ELIZA, b. Nov. 10, 1860, confirmed by Bishop Whittle at Trinity Church, Chesterfield Co., March 19, 1876.

Dr. Southall (brother of Prof. S. O. Southall, of the University of Virginia, grandson of Col. Turner Southall, of Henrico Co., and great-grandson of Lucy, the sister of Patrick Henry,) is the principal physician in Amelia Co., and a communicant and vestryman of Trinity Parish, Chesterfield Co.

A genealogy of the Southall † family was published by Mr. R. A. Brock in

---

* Frances Lockett was daughter of Osborne Lockett and Agnes Scott, granddaughter of Stephen and *Mary Clay* Lockett, the latter a cousin of the Kentucky Statesman.
† ARMS OF SOUTHALL. Quarterly, gules and or ; on a bend argent a martlet, between two cinquefoils of the first. Crest, a rock, sable.

the *Richmond Standard*, Oct. 9, 1880. Dasey or Daisy Southall, ancestor of the family in Virginia, lived in Henrico Co. 1751–1755. Among his descendants are mentioned Col. James Southall, of the Revolutionary army ; Hon. Valentine W. Southall ; Richard Henry Southall ; Prof. S. O. Southall, LL.D., (brother of Philip Francis) of the University of Virginia ; Capt. Francis Winston Southall, (brother of Philip Francis) of Stuart's Cavalry, C. S. A. ; Capt. Valentine W. Southall, Stonewall's Brigade, C. S. A., killed at Gettysburg ; James Cocke Southall, LL. D., (cousin of Philip Francis) editor Central Presbyterian ; Col. Stephen Valentine Southall, Adjutant First Division, C. S. A.

A half sister of Dr. P. F. Southall, Lucy Henry Southall, married Richard Wood, and had son, Philip Southall Wood, Commonwealths Attorney of Amelia, who married Emma Pride, No. 326 of the Goode Pedigree, (p. 278.)

1479.

ROBERT WILLIAM GOODE, of Norfolk, Va., son of Col. Robert and *Martha Childrey* Goode, No. 600, p. 197, was born Aug. 4, 1857, married March 19, 1868, Lucy Evelyn, daughter of Samuel Gresham, of King and Queen Co., Va. Children : —

> 3859, LUCY ADELAIDE GOODE.   3860, WILLIAM, d. y.   3861, Gresham.
> 3862, MARTHA EVELYN.   3863, DOUGLAS.

R. W. Goode lived near Matoax, Amelia Co. until 1870, when he removed to Norfolk. He was a Confederate soldier, and served as Sergeant-of-Couriers on the staff of Gen. J. E. B. Stuart, by whom he was complimented for his bravery in official reports. (See *Southern Historical Society's Papers*.)

In the recently published "Memoirs of Robert E. Lee," by Gen. A. L. Long, there is related an incident on Robert Goode's career as a scout. In September, 1863, when Lee was facing Meade's army in Northern Virginia, and just before the battle of Bristoe Station, it happened that Stuart's division was cut off from the main army, and was in great danger :

"The position was a perilous one, as the coming of daylight would expose his battle force to capture or annihilation. * * * He sent one of his favorite scouts, Goode, to make his way on foot, directly through the enemies' columns, to General Lee, and give him his exact position, with the request that a heavy fire of artillery be opened in the Federal columns at a point near the village of Auburn, and thus facilitate the escape of his force, which he proposed to effect by simultaneously opening fire on them with his own guns, and then making a dash through, with a combined charge of cavalry and artillery. Meantime General Lee, who had camped near Warrenton for the night, hearing nothing from Stuart, became uneasy and remained awake until a late hour of the night, in order to make preparations and give the necessary orders for the early movement of his army. Goode made his way safely through the Federal columns and arrived at headquarters about one o'clock in the morning.

" General Lee, after listening by the camp-fire to Goode's account of Stuart's situation, returned to his tent. The scout, however, being very anxious in regard to General Stuart's danger, began, after the General retired, to explain more fully, with the map, to an aide-de-camp, the relative positions of Stuart's and the enemies' forces, and the exact point where the fire of our artillery would be most effective in promoting his safe retreat from his perilous environment.

"General Lee could hear from his tent something of this conversation, but caught from it only that Goode was talking of matters which scouts, as a rule, were permitted to tell only to the commanding general himself. So coming to the door, he called out with a stern voice that he did not wish his scouts to talk in camp. He spoke very angrily, and stepped back into his tent.

"The aide-de-camp went to the General's tent, and told him that the scout, who was devoted to Stuart, and naturally very anxious for his safety, was only endeavoring to mark accurately on the map the point at which the division of the artillery fire was to be made, and was by no means talking from the mere desire to talk.

"General Lee came out at once from his tent, commanded his orderly to have supper, with hot coffee, put on the table for Goode, made him sit in his own camp-chair at the table, stood at the fire near by, and performed all the duties of a hospitable host to the fine fellow. Few generals ever made such thorough amends to a private soldier for an injustice done him in anger." (Memoirs, p. 809.)

1480.

JOHN CHESTERFIELD GOODE, of Richmond, Va., son of No. 600, was born Dec. 18, 1839, married Blanche Beverly Gates, and has several children :—

A soldier, serving through the war in the First Virginia Cavalry, C. S. A. After the war a farmer in Chesterfield Co., more recently a farmer in Henrico, near Richmond, and engaged in real estate business in that city.

1487.

WILLIAM R. GOODE, son of No. 604, was born August 6, 1826, died a freshman in college, perhaps the University of Virginia, 1843 : a young man of brilliant promise.

1489.

JOHN BULLINGTON GOODE, of Powhatan Co., Va., son of No. 604, was born August 24, 1830, died 1873, married SARAH A. GOODE. Children :—

> 3867, JOHN GOODE, farmer, Powhatan Co. 3868, WILLIAM S., merchant, and sometime postmaster, Flat Rock, Va., m. and has children. 3869, L. CLIFFORD, conductor on Richmond & Danville R. R. 3870, HARVEY, d. y. 3871, ROBERT, farmer, Mt. Hermon, Va. 3872, HERSCHEL, b. about 1870. 3873, OCTAVIA.

He was a farmer and school teacher and influential citizen, and for a long time Sheriff of the county of Powhatan and moderator of the Middle District Baptist Association of Virginia.

1495.

WILLIAM WALTHALL GOODE, of "Seven Oaks," Chesterfield Co., Va., son of No. 608, was born Oct. 31, 1821, and died July 30, 1873, married Helen J. Bass. Children :— .

> 3880, MARY HANNAH GOODE, m. LUCIUS A. SIMMS. No. 1535. 3881, LILY, m. JOHN G. BASS, No. 614-3, child. 1, *Estelle Bass*. 3882, CHARLES.

William W. Goode owned "Seven Oaks," the plantation formerly the property of Col. Francis Goode, No. 91, directly opposite "Longwood," the estate of H. W. Tatum, No. 247, on the other side of the Appomattox. He was a farmer and schoolmaster.

1497.

THOMAS BROWN GOODE, of Chesterfield Co., Va., son of No. 608, was born Oct. 10, 1828. He was a farmer, and at the opening of the war enlisted in the 57th Virginia Infantry, C. S. A. He was killed at the battle of Gettysburg, June, 1863. The last time he was seen he was in the front of the line and within a few feet of the enemy's breastworks.

1498.

SAMUEL DORSET GOODE, of Salem, Roanoke Co., Va., son of No. 608, p. 198, was born March 13, 1831, married MARY W. GOODE, No. 1505. Children:—

> 3885, WALTHALL GOODE, b. 1857. 3886, CALLIE. 3887, JOHN. 3888, FANNIE, m. *George Reynolds*, 1 child. 3889, WILLIAM. 3890, LEWIS. 3891, ANNA MARY. 3892, SALLY. 3893, SAMUEL DORSET. 3884, THOMAS BARNARD.

S. D. Goode is a farmer, as are all his sons, most of whom in 1886 are living at the homestead.

1499.

WILLIAM H. DILLON, of Danville, Va., son of Henry Dillon, married MARY SOPHIA GOODE, daughter of No. 608. He was a school teacher. He was killed by a Union raiding party near Stanton River Bridge, 1864. His widow lives in Danville, and teaches school. Children:—

> 3895, ANNA KATE DILLON, m. *Edwin E. Carter*, of Danville, Va., children: 1, *Hughes Carter*; 2, *Stewart*. 3896, WILLIAM, d. y.

1501.

ANNA LEWIS GOODE, of Staunton, Va., daughter of No. 608, is one of the few members of the West Chesterfield branch, with whom the author of this book has had the pleasure of becoming personally acquainted. She has many of the characteristics of her fourth cousins of the Prince Edward branch. She has contributed extensively to the family record.

1504.

JOHN EDWARD GOODE, of Hallsboro, Chesterfield Co., Va., son of No. 609, was born about 1840. A soldier in Co. K, 6th Virginia Infantry, C. S. A., and killed in the trenches before Petersburg, 1862, married Miss Simms. Son:—

> 3897, ERNEST GOODE, farmer, Hallsboro, Va.

1506.

WILLIAM WALTHAL GOODE, of Chesterfield Co., Va., son of No. 609, was a soldier in the 38th Virginia Infantry, C. S. A., and was killed in the battle of Seven Pines, May, 1862.

1508.

JAMES K. P. GOODE, of Mt. Hermon, Chesterfield Co., Va., son of No. 609, married Mrs. Eugenia (Simms) Porter. Children:—

> 3947, THORNTON GOODE, b. Nov. 30, 1867. 3948, BERKELEY, b. April 21, 1869. 3949, VICTOR S., b. April 16, 1871. 3950, MAUDE O., b. Dec. 7, 1875.

He is a man of great popalarity in his community, and is usually the incumbent of some public office. In 1886, he was Sheriff of Chesterfield Co.

1509.

SEDDON GOODE, of Sussex Co., Va., son of No. 609, married Mrs. Porter, and had two or three children. He is the proprietor of a lumber mill.

1518.

ROBERT MOODY, of Dinwiddie Co., Va., son of No. 612, was a Confederate soldier, and died from wounds received in service.

1524.

WILLIAM ARCHER, of Powhatan Co., Va., son of William W. and *Rebekah Goode* Archer, No. 614, was a soldier, C. S. A., and died, 1863, in service.

1538.

WILLIAM HENRY HAWES BAGWELL, of Petersburg, Va., son of No. 617, p. 200, was born Feb. 9, 1841, married Sept. 27, 1866, ANN AUGUSTA GRESHAM, daughter of No. 606, p. 100. Children:—

> 3951, MARIA LAVINIA BAGWELL,. 3952, MARY ADELAIDE. 3953, WILLIAM H. H., JR. 3954, JOHN GOODE. 3955, AUGUSTA. 3956, THOMAS GRESHAM. 3957, WITHERS.

Mr. Bagwell served through the war, and was at its close Lieutenant in the 1st Virginia Infantry. He is now in the grocery and commission business in Petersburg, Va.

1540.

JOHN W. FISHER, of Petersburg, Va., married about 1873, SARAH LAVINIA BAGWELL, daughter of No. 617, p. 200. Children:—

> 3960, WILLIE AUGUSTA FISHER. 3961, NELLIE VIRGINIA. 3962, EDWIN BAGWELL. 3963, SARAH EMMA. 3964, JOHN GOODE. 3965, DAVID STEEL.

Mr. Fisher was a Confederate soldier, in the 4th Virginia Cavalry.

1545.

ROBERT GRESHAM, of Namozine District, (Church Roads P. O.) Dinwiddie Co., Va., son of Elijah and *Maria Goode* Gresham, No. 626, p. 101, was born 1826, married Mary Watkins, of Dinwiddie Co. Children :—

> 3966, ANNA GRESHAM, m. *Theodore Leonard*, of Sussex Co., Va., farmer, 4 children. 3967, SALLIE. 3968, SAMUEL, of Namozine, Dinwiddie Co., farmer, m. Miss Tucker, 1 child. 3969, WILLIAM, of Namozine, m. Miss Watkins, 2 children. 3970, FLORENCE, m. *Mr. Sutherland*, of Petersburg, farmer, 4 children.

Robert Gresham was a soldier, C. S. A., was captured at Five Forks, and a prisoner of war at Point Lookout, and was released several months after the close of the war. Since the war a farmer in Dinwiddie Co., Va.

1546.

EDWIN JAMES GRESHAM, of Washington, D. C., son of No. 626, was born July 5, 1831. Married (1) Josephine Lampkin, dau. of Richard and *Priscilla Pendleton* Lampkin, of King and Queen Co., 1 child. (2) Mary Meadow, dau. of John and *Sarah Haskins* Meadow, of Prince Edward Co., Va., 4 children. (3) Fannie Greenhow, dau. of Thomas Greenhow and *Mary Curtis* Williams, of Hanover Co., 5 children. Children :—

> 3973, CLARENCE GRESHAM, of Charlotte, N. C., proprietor of a hotel, m. Alice Kennedy, of Fairfax Co., 3 children. 3974, JOSEPHINE, m. *H. A. Robertson*, of Lynchburg, Va., merchant, 1 child. 3975, JOHN HOWARD, of Washington. 3976, SALLIE B. 3977 MARY PAGE, d. y. 3978, FANNIE WILLIAMS. 3979, BESSIE GREENHOW. 3980, EDWIN CURTIS. 3981, PAGE GREENHOW. 3982 ANNIE WHARTON.

Mr. Gresham was for many years a farmer in Henrico Co., Va. At the outbreak of the war enlisted in the 1st Va. Cavalry, served in the army of the Potomac and was discharged on account of ill health. From 1865–1875, in general railroad supply business in Richmond. Since 1875, in the insurance business, as general agent, N. W. Life Insurance Company, in Virginia, and 1885–1887, in same occupation in Washington.

He is a member of the Baptist Church, an active and enthusiastic supporter of its institutions, and a worker in the cause of temperence, which he has greatly advanced in various parts of Virginia by his public addresses.

1547.

WILLIAM GRESHAM, of Namozine, Dinwiddie Co., Va., son of No. 626, married Nannie Meadow, sister of his brother's wife. Children :—

> 3985, CHARLES IRVING GRESHAM. 5986, ELLA. 3987, FLOYD.

Mr. Gresham was a soldier in the 1st Virginia Cavalry, C, S. A., and served through the entire war, and was paroled at Appomattox C. H. He was taken prisoner in the Valley of Virginia, and was wounded at Harrison's Landing. Since the war a school teacher.

1600.

J. OSCAR GOODE, of Richmond, Va., son of No. 638, was born May 3, 1831. Engineer in the City Fire Department. Married, Dec. 28, 1853, Martha A., daughter of Joel and Mary Robinson, of Richmond. Children :—

    3990, AMASA S. GOODE, b. Nov. 18, 1854.   3991, ELLSLER T., b. Aug., 1861.

1606.

JAMES EDWIN GOODE, of Richmond, Va., son of Joseph and *Eleanor K. Warrock* Goode, No. 640, p. 201, was born Oct. 1, 1837. Married, Sept. 19, 1872, Emma Goode, of Lynchburg, Va. No children.

Mr. Coode is a leading printer in Richmond, the proprietor and publisher of the "Warrock-Richardson Almanac," established in 1815, by his maternal grandfather, John Warrock. For many years, the State Senate printer by election, and subsequently the public printer by contract.

1613.

BENJAMIN ALEXANDER GOODE, of Charlestown, W. Va., railroad contractor, son of No. 641, p. 201, was born Sept. 11, 1829, died 1875. Married, Ann E., daughter of James W. Reynolds, of Cumberland Co. Children :—

    4001, HENRY LESLIE GOODE, b. 1855, lives in Tennessee, and has children. 4002, ELIZABETH, b. 1867: 4003, JOHN RICHARD, b. 1870.

1614.

HIRAM WALLACE GRIFFITH, of Genito, Va., married 1856, MARY E. GOODE, daughter of No. 641, and had seven children. Mr. Griffith was a private in the 21st Virginia Infantry, C. S. A., and was wounded at Cedar Mountain.

1615.

JOHN RICHARD GOODE, of Richmond, Va., son of No. 641, was born Dec. 25, 1836. Married (1) Sarah E., dau. of Marlow W. Atkinson, of Powhatan Co., (2) Emily A., dau. of John Keezee, of Charlotte Co. Children :—

    4011, WYATT LEWIS GOODE, b. Dec. 18, 1866. 4012, RICHARD NEWTON, b. Aug. 5, 1866.
    4013, JOHN GOODE, b. May 16, 1875. 4014, MARY LOUISE, b, April 21, 1878.

J. R. Goode is a shoe merchant in Richmond. He was a private in the 4th Virginia Cavalry, C. S. A., and was shot through the lungs at "Front Royal."

1616.

ANDREW JACKSON SIMPSON, of Powhatan Co., Va., son of John Simpson, died, 1868. He had been a private in the 1st Virginia Cavalry, C. S. A. Married ELIZABETH O. GOODE, daughter of No. 641, born 1839, died July 1868. Son :—

> 4015, JOHN RICHARD SIMPSON, of Petersburg, Va., b. Sept. 16, 1866.

1618.

RICHARD WATKINS GOODE, of Windsor, Bertie Co., N. C., son of No., 641, was born Oct. 17, 1842. Married Jan. 9, 1866, MARY LEIGH BAGWELL, No. 1539. Children :—

> 4016, JULIAN R. GOODE, b. May 9, 1866. 4017, BAGWELL, b. July 21. 4018, MARY, b. Mar. 15, 1873.

R. W. Goode owns a farm and lumber mills. He was in the Confederate army, first in the 20th Va. Infantry, but his comrades having been for the most part killed and wounded, joined the 4th Va. Cavalry. He was wounded at Five Forks, April 5, 1865, taken prisoner at Rich Mountain, 1861, exchanged 1862, discharged 1865.

1620.

WILLIAM JOSEPH COX GOODE, of Gilliamsville, Va., son of No. 641, was born Sept. 17, 1847. Married, Nov. 28, 1870, Martha J. Johnson. Children :—

> 4019, MAUDE ALMA GOODE, b. May 2, 1872. 4020, MARTHA OLIVIA, b. Sept. 3, 1874. 4021, JOSEPH GATES, b. Sept. 27, 1876. 4022, CLARENCE LYNNE, b. Apr. 3, 1879, d. Oct. 22, 1879.

He was in the Confederate army, a member of the 2nd Va. Reserve. Lives at Gilliamsville, Va., where he is merchant, farmer, postmaster and magistrate.

1682.

CAPT. DAVID MACK. GOODE, of Genito, Va., son of No. 658, was born about 1840, died Aug 13, 1883. Married JOSEPHINE GOODE, daughter of No. 657, p. 105. Children :—

> 4101, DAVID MACK. GOODE. 4102, OSCAR. 4103, HORTENSE. 4104, AMBROSE. 4105, LOTTIE. 4106, GRACE. 4107, OVID.

He was a soldier, C. S. A., serving throughout the war, and when paroled at Appomattox was Captain of Co. K, 9th Virginia Infantry, Mahone's Brigade. On the occasion of his death, the Richmond *Dispatch*, (Aug. 15, 1883) said :

"One of the best and most useful citizens of Chesterfield county is dead. In the vigor of manhood, in the zenith of his popularity, and with a bright hope of immortality, he was taken from his family, from his friends, and from his country. No man was more beloved aud respected in the county of Chesterfield. His war record was worthy of the man. Leaving home as soon as the tocsin of war was sounded, he remained in the army until the surrender at

Appomattox, distinguished himself by a faithful and fearless discharge of duty. He was wounded two or three times while in the service, but considering his wounds only marks of honor, he returned to his command as soon as he was able to perform the duties of a soldier. He left the army with the rank of captain, and with the universal esteem of his comrades.

"Returning home at the close of the war, he found his property destroyed and his prospects of success dark indeed. With his natural hopefulness, and with a spirit dauntless and unsubdued, he beat his sword into a plowshare and his spear into a pruning-hook. Success crowned his unremitting labors and made his farm, which he found a wilderness, blossom as a rose. His fellow-citizens, desiring to honor such a man, elected him Supervisor of the County for four successive terms. As Chairman of the Board of Supervisors he reflected honor upon his county and protected the interest of her people. He was nominated as a candidate for the Legislature in 1881."

1691.

CYRUS GOODE, of Chesterfield Co., Va., son of Rev. Edmund Goode, No. 220, p. 105, was a soldier in Co. K, 6th Virginia Infantry, and was killed in the explosion of the Crater at Petersburg.

1700.

SAMUEL WOODFIN, of Chesterfield Co., Va., son of Rev. Joseph Woodfin, No. 599, was a soldier in Co. K, 6th Virginia Infantry, and was killed in the battle of Bristoe Station.

1695.

LOWRY W. GOODE, of Des Moines, Iowa, son of No. 665, p. 202, was born in Monticello, Miss., April 14, 1857, and removed with his parents to New Orleans in 1865, and to Des Moines in 1868. Married, May 29, 1879, Hattie S., daughter of John Newton, of Robinson, Ill., niece of Judge Curtis Bates, of Iowa. Children : —

> 4201, CURTIS BATES GOODE, b. May 13, 1880. 4202, EDMUND L., b. Nov. 13, 1881. 4203, ROGER N., b. July 7, 1885. 4204, KEITH L., b. Feb. 10, 1885.

Lowry W. Goode was the founder and is the proprietor and editor of the *Hawkeye Blade*, a Democratic state paper. A prominent journalist of Iowa. He was previously associated with his brother in the publication of the *Iowa State Leader*, and was a delegate to the National Democratic Convention at Chicago in 1884. He read law with his father, and graduated at the Albany Law School in 1878.

He is one of the most energetic of the citizens of Des Moines, the projector of Oakland, a suburb now rapidly advancing, and a leader in other real estate enterprises.

1696.

FREDERICK D. GOODE, of Bradford, Ark., son of No. 665, was born at Monticello, Miss., Aug. 19, 1861. Married, Sept., 1883, Mabel, daughter of N. E. Barber, of Des Moines, Iowa. Son :—

4205, FREDERICK D. GOODE, JR., b. Aug. 28, 1885.

F. D. Goode, now engaged in fruit-culture, was for a time city editor, and one of the proprietors of the *Iowa State Leader*, and the *Hawkeye Blade*, in Des Moines.

1697.

CLARENCE R. GOODE, of Des Moines, Iowa, son of No. 665, was born in Monticello, Miss., Jan. 31, 1864. He has been one of the editors of the *Iowa State Leader*, and business manager of the *Hawkeye Blade*.

1713-(668-6.)

RICHARD WILKERSON, of Virginia, son of William and *Elisheba Goode* Wilkerson, No. 668, was a soldier in Co. K, 6th Va. Inf., C. S. A., and was killed in battle.

1726-(672-l.)

EDWARD PHAUP, of Chesterfield Co., Va., son of John and *Emma Goode* Phaup, was a soldier in Co., K, 6th Va. Inf., C. S. A., and was killed in the Crater, at Petersburg.

1737.

CAPT. CHARLES W. LOVELACE, of Marion, Perry Co., Ala., son of No. 674½, p. 203, was an officer in the "Jeff Davis Battery," of Alabama Artillery, C. S. A.

THE HENRICO GOODES.

1764-(682-l.)

SYLVANUS GOODE, of Richmond, Va., son of William Goode, No 682, was a soldier in the Confederate Army and died in prison at Fort Delaware, in 1865.

1780.

JUDGE GEORGE W. GOODE, of St. Louis, Mo., son of No. 694, was born in Henrico Co., Va., 1814, died in St. Louis, June 14, 1860. Married Fannie, daughter of Judge Robert Wash, of St. Louis, Mo., descended from an old Virginia family who removed to Kentucky at an early day. Children :—

4225, JULIA WASH GOODE, b. 1850, m. *Sarpi Carr Cabanne.* 4226, ROBERT WASH, b. 1852. 4227, JOHN GRANVILLE, b. 1854, connected with St. Louis R. R. Co. 4228, GEORGE WILLIAM, b. 1856. 4229,

EDMUND CHRISTY, b. 1858, living in 1881, in San Antonio, Texas. 4230, FANNY LUCY, b. 1860.   4231, HOWARD MCNAIR, b. 1862.

Judge Goode was educated at William and Mary College, and removing to Missouri about 1850, became a prominent lawyer and politician, and a leading anti-Benton Democrat.   He retained his Virginia tastes, and his suburban home was a favorite meet for the fox hunters, and a centre of interest for lovers of good horse-flesh.   Goode Avenue in St. Louis was named in his honor.

THE WHITBY GOODES.

1795.

SETH EDMUND WARD, of Kansas City, Mo., son of No. 725, p. 203, was born in Campbell Co., Mo., Mar. 4, 1820.   Married, Feb. 9, 1860, Mary F. McCarty, daughter of John Harris, of Westport, Mo.   Children ;—

4291, JOHN EDMUND WARD, b. June 21, 1861.   4292, HUGH CAMPBELL, b. Mar. 10, 1863.   4293, MARY F., d. y.

The following sketch of Mr. Ward is from his biography in the U. S. Biographical Dictionary, Missouri Volume.

" Being deprived of educational advantages by the early death of his father, he went to Indiana, at the age of fourteen, and remained for a time under the charge of Jacob Haas, (See above No. 179, p. 90,) but soon began an independent career.   The year 1838 found him in Independence, Mo., where he joined the company of Capt. Lancaster P. Lupton, a fur trader, and shortly afterward entered service with the fur company of Thompson & Craig, and with them crossed the Rocky Mountains on a trading expedition—one of the earliest ventures in this direction.   Among his associates on this trip, was Kit Carson—the Nestor of the Rocky Mountains,—and his first horse was a gift from Carson, who had won it from an old mountaineer, on a wager that a green hand like Ward could not bring down a buffalo at first dash.   Ward accomplished the feat, though at cost of painful injuries to himself.   In 1839, he went with a party of trappers into the territory of the Navajo and Digger Indians, but the Indians shot many of their horses, and wounded one of the trappers, and the party returned on foot through the wilderness, bringing their companion on a litter to Taos, N. M.   For seven years he pursued his adventurous calling in various parts of the Southwest.   In 1845, he went with Bent and St. Vrain to Union fort in New Mexico (now Colorado,) and upon this trip was associated with Francis P. Blair, afterwards Senator, with whom he formed an enduring friendship.   In 1845, he had accumulated capital to the amount of $1000, with which he entered business for himself, as an Indian trader.   On one expedition, in 1848, he obtained 6000 buffalo robes.   After ten years profitable occupation in this business, he was appointed sutler in the U. S. Army at Fort Laramie, where he continued from 1856 to 1871.   During all these years his business was immense ; honesty and promptness in meeting all his paper had given him almost unlimited credit, and his increasing trade necessitated the building of large ware-houses for its accomodation."

" In 1873, he was elected President of the Mastin Bank, in Kansas City, a position which he still holds and in which he has been eminently successful. He is a member of the Baptist church, and of the Odd Fellows and Masonic orders.

" His home, near Kansas City, is described as beautiful and well appointed, standing in the midst of grounds four hundred and fifty acres in extent, such as might be found in the fertile blue-grass region of Kentucky, the green-sward dotted with trees and groves. He has been instrumental in introducing the short-horn breed of cattle into Western Missouri, and his herd is one of the finest in the state.

" Here he is spending his best days, surrounded with every luxury, blessed with an affectionate family, enjoying the confidence, the respect and the steadfast friendship of the many to whom his virtues, and his manliness have commended him." (p. 469.)

1796.

JOHN CALHOUN CLARK, of "York Place Plantation," Point Coupee Parish, La., a native of Massachusetts, married in Washington Co., Miss., about 1850, GEORGIANA WARD, dau. of No. 725. They lived for a time near Natchez, but in 1854, Mr. Clark removed to his plantation on Bayou Fordoche, six miles from Morganza, where he died. Mrs. Clark who died in 1861, is buried on the plantation of her second husband, Mr. McRae, in the Parish of Point Coupee, about twelve miles from the Mississippi river. Children :—

> 4295, ANNIE CLARK, d. y. 4296, MARY, b. April 17, 1852, m. *W. S. Winter*, of Greensville, Miss., (b. in Wilson Co., Tenn., Mar. 21, 1848.) children : i, *Newman Winter*, b. 1873, ii, *W. Neal*, b. 1880.

1796¼.

JUDGE NELSON, of Greensville, Washington Co., Miss., a planter, who died of yellow fever, 1878, married MARY CLARK, daughter of No. 725. No children.

1796½.

THOMAS L. AUSTIN, of Nebraska City, Neb., farmer, married, Feb. 26, 1846, MARTHA NORVELL WARD, of Bedford Co., Va., daughter of No. 725. Children :—(All born in Campbell Co., Va.)

> 4297, BETTIE ANN AUSTIN, b. 1847. 4298, SUSAN MELISSA. 4299, WILLIAM ALEXANDER. 4300, SALLIE BURGESS. 4301, MARY ELLA. 4302, MARTHA NORVELL. 4303, GEORGE EDMUND. 4304, LUCY WILLIAM. 4305, ROBERTA LEE.

1800.

JAMES CAREY, of Baltimore, Md., son of George and *Mary E. Gibson* Carey, of Baltimore, was born Oct. 2, 1832. Married, June 16, 1869, MARTHA WARD, daughter of Rev. William Norvell Ward, No. 729, p. 209. Children :—

4311, GEORGE CAREY, b. Mar. 23, 1870. 4312, ESTELLE WARD, b. Mar. 3, 1871.

Mr. Carey was educated in his native city, and was a banker until the beginning of the war. He was among the citizens of Baltimore who resisted the passage of Butler's troops through Baltimore, on the 19th of April, 1861, and on the same day, was arrested, ostensibly on the charge of wearing a tricolored cravat, indicative of southern sympathy. After a brief confinement in the Baltimore penitentiary, he was released and made his way through the lines in time to take part in the first battle of Bull Run. He served as a Lieutenant in the Signal Corps around Richmond, and later as Captain and Aide on the staff of Gen. Hood. Becoming dissatisfied with Hood's unprincipled career, he resigned with the intention of joining Mosby's Partisan Rangers, but was prevented by the close of the war. After the war he resumed his former occupation in Baltimore.

Mrs. Carey is an artist. In Jones's " Reminiscences of Gen. Robert E. Lee," is reprinted a letter from the Confederate chieftain, to Miss Martha Ward, thanking her for her picture of "Stratford," the Lee homestead, which she sent to him soon after the close of the war. (p. 364.)

1801.

CAPT. WILLIAM NORVELL WARD, C. S. A., son of No. 729, was born March 3, 1839. He entered the University of Virginia in 1857. At the beginning of the war, he enlisted in the 47th Virginia Infantry and served through the Peninsular Campaign in Gen. A. P. Hill's Division, receiving a mortal wound at the battle of Gaines's Mill, from the effects of which he died Aug. 29, 1862. " A splendid type of Southern manhood," talented, brave and gentle, he gave promise of a brilliant and useful career. See Johnson's " University Memorial," p. 755.

1802.

ALBERT DeVERE BURR, of Washington, son of DeVere and *Sarah Mac Daniel* Burr, was born June 20, 1847, died Oct. 26, 1883. Married, Dec. 5, 1872, MARY VIRGINIA WARD, daughter of No. 729. Children :—

> 4313, MARY WARD BURR, b. Aug. 27, 1873. 4314, ALBERT DeVERE, b. Sept. 1, 1875. 4315, WILLIAM NORVELL, b. Sept. 7, 1877. 4316, HENRY WARD, b. Jan. 11, 1880. 4317, FRANCIS WALKER, b. April 26, 1883.

Mr. Burr was educated at Georgetown College.

He was for a time Deputy Collector of Customs in Yorktown, Va., afterwards for many years a disbursing officer in the District government in Washington, and chief of the population division and Acting Chief Clerk of the Tenth Census. Although a young man, at the time of his death, he was a prominent citizen of the District of Columbia, trustee of the county schools and in many ways identified with the interests of the County of Washington.

1803.

DR. PEARSON CHAPMAN, of Perrymans, Harford Co., Md., son of Pearson and *Sigismunde Mary Alexander* Chapman,* of Glymont, was married, Nov. 20, 1876, EDMONIA KERR WARD, daughter of No. 729, born Feb. 14, 1845, died Dec. 8, 1882. Children:—

> 4318, NORVELL PEARSON CHAPMAN, b. May, 1878.   4319, CHARLES BLINCOE WARD, b. Sept. 2, 1880.

1804.

CHARLES BLINCOE WARD, of Richmond Co., Va., son of No. 729, was born Feb. 14, 1845. At the beginning of the war, just as he was entering the Virginia Military Institute, he was seized by the Federal troops and carried to Washington, where he was imprisoned. Although only seventeen years old his father entered his name on the roll of the 9th Virginia Cavalry, and he was exchanged and entered active service, and was killed at an engagement at Beverley's Ford, Culpeper Co., Va., June 9 1763, when only eighteen, having voluntarily left his position in charge of the horses of his company and gone into battle in the place of an elderly man in his company, whose life he felt could ill be spared by his family.

1806.

HENRY TAYLOE WARD, of "Bladensfield," Richmond Co., Va., son of No. 729, was educated at the Virginia Military Institute. A farmer. Unmarried.

1810.

CHANNING MOORE WARD, of Washington, D. C., son of No. 729, was born Aug. 15, 1857. He was educated at the Alexandria High School, and in 1878 and 1879, was with the U. S. Coast Survey, working on the North Carolina coast. In 1880, he entered the service of the Baltimore and Ohio Railroad, and in 1887 is Resident Engineer at Grafton, W. Va.

1811.

RANDOLPH GOODE WARD, of Uniontown, Pa., son of No. 729, was born May 24, 1860. Married, Nov. 21, 1882, Belle Manning Brown, daughter of William Warren and *Charlotte Hudson* Brown, of Portland, Me. Children:—

---

* For the lineage of Dr. Chapman, see Brock's genealogy of the Alexander Family, in the Richmond *Standard*, Vol. III, No. 35. His great grand-parents were Constance Alexander, descended from William, Earl of Stirling, and Nathaniel Chapman, of Charles Co., Md., a Captain in the army and a relative of Sir Walter Raleigh. His great-aunt, Louisa Chapman, married Samuel, brother of Gen. George Washington.

4320, CORNELIA CHANNING, b. Dec. 20, 1883. 4321, CHARLOTTE WARNER, b. July 14, 1885.

1813.

JUDGE JOSEPH C. PARRY, of Lamar, Mo., son of Thomas O. and Margaret Parry, of Canada West, married, Nov. 13, 1850, JOSEPHINE WARD, daughter of No. 731. Children:—

4322, GEORGE THOMAS PARRY, b. Jan. 13, 1857, m. Udella Avery, of Lamar, Mo.; he is now a rising young lawyer of Carthage, Mo. 4323, JOSEPHINE, b. Sept. 30, 1858, unm.

Mr. Parry was born at "Kennivere Castle," Anglesea, Wales, and removed with his parents to Dunville, Canada. When quite young he traveled through the South and in Louisiana he met and married Josephine Ward. He removed with his wife and her father's family to Missouri, where he became a farmer. After the war he served with much distinction as County Judge in 1867–8. He married a second time in 1862, Miss Nancy Oldham, and is now living a retired life in the suburbs of Lamar.

1814.

CAPT. EDWARD GREEN WARD, of Lamar, Barton Co., Mo., son of No. 731, was born Feb. 28, 1839. Married Jan. 31, 1869, Mary V., daughter of Dr. Johnson and Ann Eliza Logan, of Carlinsville, Ill. Children:—

4324, EDWARD L. WARD, b. July 1, 1870, 4325, ANNIE, b. April, 12, 1872. 4326, WILLIAM B., b. April 26, 1874. 4327, GEORGE E., b. July 19, 1877. 4328, WILLIAM, b. Oct. 6, 1880. 4329, JOHN, b. May 1, 1883.

Captain Ward served in command of a detached company of picked men, assigned to special duty under Gen. Price, until he surrendered himself and men at Shreveport. Some of his exploits, as described by Edwards, have already been referred to in the biographical notice of his father on page 207.

1815–A.

CAPT. ALBERT SMITH, C. S. A., of Springfield, Mo., son of Nicholas R. and Harriet Smith, was born in Springfield and was killed in battle at King's Mill, Ark., Jan., 1863, while serving as Captain of a company of cavalry. Married, May 10, 1858, THEODOSIA WARD, daughter of No. 731. Children:—

4331, GEORGE N. SMITH,. 4332, SUSAN; both died in infancy.

Mrs. Theodosia Smith, "elegant, fascinating, diplomatic as Talleyrand," had a history of her own in connection with the war in Missouri, which has already been referred to on a previous page. (p. 207, *supra*.) She was a very beautiful and accomplished woman.

1815-B.

HON. E. M. HULETT, of New York, son of Charles and Ann Elizabeth Hulett, was born in New York, April 30, 1839. Married, July 16, 1868, THEODOSIA WARD, widow of Dr. Albert Smith, who died Aug. 8, 1873. Children :—

> 4332, CHARLES E. HULETT, b. April 19, 1869. 4333, JOHN A., b. Oct., 1872, d. April 16, 1873.

1816.

CAPT. JAMES T. WARD, of Lamar, Barton Co., Mo., son of No. 731, was born June 5, 1844. He is living in Lamar, unmarried, 1886. His exploits as a soldier and scout have already been referred to. He entered the army at the age of seventeen, and was only twenty-one at its close, though Captain of a cavalry company. At the close of the war he was with Col. A. W. Slayback's Lancers, and went with him and other Missourians to Mexico, returning to St. Louis with Col. Slayback in 1866. He was one of the founders of the little city of "Carlotta," named for the Empress, and was present at the coronation of young Iturbide.

1817.

CAPT. ROBERT J. TUCKER, of Lamar, Barton Co., Mo., son of Seth Winn and Elizabeth Tucker, was born at Petersburg, Va., Sept. 17, 1841. Married, Nov. 22, 1866, MARY WARD, daughter of No. 731, who was born Nov. 8, 1846, in Many, Sabine Parish, Louisiana. Children :—

> 4334, MARY TUCKER, b. Jan. 27, 1869, d. Mar. 13, 1880. 4335, ROBERT WARD, b. Dec. 26, 1871, d. April 12, 1873. 4336, THEODOSIA, b. Feb. 28, 1874. 4337, PAUL H., b. Mar. 1, 1877. 4338, ROSE, b. Mar. 1, 1885.

Mrs. Tucker was confined with her mother in the Gratiot military prison at St. Louis, in Dec., 1864, and was afterwards banished by Gen. Rosecrans from his military department for communicating with her brother, who was accused of being a spy. Capt. Tucker commanded a company of Missouri Cavalry, and was paroled at Shreveport. He is now a lawyer of prominence in Barton county.

1818.

MICHAEL CLARKE, of Clarksville, Tenn., a farmer, married LILY KERR, daughter of No. 732. Children :—

> 4341, LUCY CLARKE. 4342, MICHAEL.

1819.

J. LOUIS SMITH, of Urbanna, Middlesex Co., Va., an extensive planter, married VIRGINIA KERR, daughter of No. 732. No children.

1822.

LaFAYETTE MAYNARD, of San Francisco, Cal., son of No. 736, p. 209, was born Feb., 1819, died Dec. 29, 1876. Married, June 24, 1844, Mary Eleanor Green, daughter of Gen. Duff Green,* of Washington. Children : —

4351, ELLEN HYLTON MAYNARD, b. Apr. 24, 1845. 4352, BENJAMIN GREEN, b. July 14, 1847. 4353, ROBERT PEACHY, b. July 24, 1849. 4354, CONSTANCE, b. Feb. 3, 1853, m. *H. S. Dixon.* 4355, LIZZIE, b. Dec. 10, 1854, m. *Lieut. Herbert Winslow, U. S. N.* 4356, SADIE, b. May 16, 1859. 4357, DUFF GREEN, b. Dec. 9, 1866 ; merchant in San Francisco. 4358, MARY, d. y.

The story of the life of LaFayette Maynard is full of interest. At the early age of fifteen years, having applied for admission to the Navy through the usual channels in vain, as he had neither interest or influence to assist him, he walked barefoot from Richmond to Washington, during a severe winter, sought and obtained a personal interview with President Jackson, told his story, and gained his object—an appointment as Midshipman. In those days there was no Naval school as now, and he, being desirous to obtain all possible nautical information before going into actual service, obtained permission to make a voyage aboard a merchantman, which he did, as a seaman before the mast. On returning and reporting for duty, he was appointed Midshipman, Feb. 4, 1832, and ordered, Aug. 20, to the sloop "Vandalia," W. H. Spencer, Commander, then lying at Norfolk, Va., under sailing orders for the West India Station. He was appointed Lieutenant, Oct. 19, 1843.

In 1836, he was a passenger on the "Atlantic," when she was wrecked on Fisher's Island, Conn., on the night of Nov. 27. By his personal efforts he saved about thirty passengers, and his gallantry was a matter of national renown. A sword was presented to him by the Richmond City Council ; a beautiful weapon, the blade of elaborately engraved steel, the hilt and scabbard, gilt, and of equally fine and elaborate workmanship. It was not ready for presentation until after his departure for Mexico ; in the following year, it was sent with the following letter, to his wife in Washington City.

RICHMOND, *January* 6, 1847.

MADAM :—
The resolution which I have the honor to hand you (enclosed) explains itself; and in presenting to you for your gallant husband, Lieut. May-

* MRS. MAYNARD was the daughter of Gen. Duff Green, of Washington City, and his wife Lucretia Matilda Edwards, daughter of Hon. Benjamin Edwards, M C., of Montgomery Co., Md., the patron of William Wirt. (For notice of the Edwards family see this volume, above, p. 205.) Through her father Mrs. Maynard was descended from the Washingtons, Randolphs, and Marshalls, he being son of William Green of Woodford Co., Ky., grandson of Duff Green, g-grandson of Robert Green, who with Sir Wm. Duff, Joist Hite and Robert McKay, was one of the first proprietors in the Shenandoah Valley. (See above p. 91, also Duff Green's "Facts and Suggestions," 1866, and genealogical notes in Richmond *Standard*, II, 46, III, 16, 18, 20, 52, and Slaughter's "St. Marks Parish," p. 138.) His mother was Lucy Ann, daughter of Markham and *Ann Bailey* Marshall of Westmoreland Co., Va., (see Paxton's "Marshall Family,") the latter granddaughter of Isham Randolph of "Dungeness." (See above, p. 114.) His grandmother was Anne Willis (see Slaughter's "Memoir of Col. Henry Fry,") daughter of Col. Henry Willis of Fredericksburg and Mildred Washington, aunt and godmother of Gen. George Washington, and also mother of the three sisters Gregory, who married the three brothers Thornton, referred to above, pp. 214–15.

nard, the sword which accompanies this, I perform a duty at once pleasing to myself and, I hope, gratifying to him.

I should however do injustice to my own feelings did I not add the tribute of my own admiration to that which the heroic self-devotion of Lieut. Maynard on the occasion referred to in the resolution, has elicited throughout our common country.

Belonging to the service which he does, all would expect of him, in the stern excitement of battle, deeds of valor and lofty daring, but actions such as this, emanating from a holy wish to save, not to destroy human life, and springing from motives so pure, and crowned under Providence with such happy results, entitle him to the gratitude of mankind, and the love of every philanthropic heart.

In the name, and on behalf, of the Council of the City of Richmond, I present to him the sword, which they have caused to be made for that purpose, and ask his acceptance of it, as commemorative of the exalted estimate in which his native city holds his generous and intrepid conduct, on the occasion referred to.

I have the honor to be, Madam,

Your obedient servant,

GUSTAVUS A. MYERS,

President of the Council.

RESOLUTION.

At a meeting of the Council of the City of Richmond, held on Monday, 11th of January, 1847, the following Preamble and Resolution were unanimously adopted:

The Council of the City of Richmond have regarded with high admiration the heroic valor and disinterested humanity displayed by their townsman, Lieut. Fayette Maynard, of the United States Navy, on the late melancholy occasion of the ship-wreck of the steamer *Atlantic*, in Long Island Sound, and being desirous that so noble an example of self-devotion, fortitude, and courage should be held up for imitation.

Resolved: That the President of the Council be, and he is hereby instructed, in the name, and on behalf of the City of Richmond, to present to Lieut. Maynard a sword, with appropriate devices and inscriptions as commemorative of the exalted estimate in which his native city holds his generous and intrepid conduct, on the occasion referred to.

A true copy from the Journal. WM. P. SHEPPARD, C. C. R.

In a letter dated February, 5th 1847, Camp Washington, near Vera Cruz, "on the eve of departure, in command of a naval battery, for the city of Orizaba," acknowledging the gift, Lieut. Maynard said:

"It is with feeling of no ordinary pleasure that I accept the sword thus presented to me. It was my good fortune, during that dreadful night, to have been instrumental in saving several passengers of that ill-fated vessel. I claim to myself no particular merit, as having but performed that duty which we all owe to each other: yet I feel happy that my efforts are appreciated by by citizens of my native place. * * * I shall ever retain the gift as a token of the generous impulses of the citizens of my native place : and although it will remind me of many melancholy scenes, I hope, if it is my lot to draw it in the service of my country, to prove to my friends that the sword presented to me for the rescue of my fellow men from a watery grave, can be of some service against her enemies.

He was especially kind to Dr. Armstrong, a prominent minister of the Presbyterian Church in Richmond, although unfortunately unsuccessful in his efforts to save his life. In evidence of their appreciation and gratitude to Lieut. M., some of the friends of Dr. Armstrong, presented him with a very handsome family Bible, and bearing on its cover complimentary inscriptions.

The following extract from the Richmond *Standard*, is one of many before me.

"Lieut. LaFayette Maynard, a man of whom we even now want words to speak in the manner in which his noble conduct deserves. Men talk of the press as a powerful engine, but it is weak   *   *   *   to do justice to such deeds as those of Maynard.   *   *   *   We glory in Virginia that she has produced such a son. We are proud of human nature that it is illustrated by such a character. It is not alone the courage of Maynard, splendid as it was, that it arouses such general admiration. It was the beautifully tempered union of valor and humanity which appeals so strongly to every heart.   *   *   *

"The calm judgment and consideration with which he arranged them [women, children and old men] in such a position as to make the best possible provision for their safety, his judicious advice,   *   *   *   these show the man of wisdom and of thought, as well as the fearless and whole-souled sailor. No hero ever surpassed his valor, no woman his gentleness and compassion.

"How shall we speak of that exalted self-devotion which prompted him to dash in the midst of the roaring surge, and   *   *   *   rescue at his own continued peril, twenty souls from an awful death? In the midst of these superhuman exertions he thinks of the fatigue and suffering of his comrade, who aided him in the noble work. He sends him to a neighboring house for shelter, and alone battles with the elements, never leaving the scene until his mission of mercy had been accomplished and the last vestige of the wreck had been swallowed by the remorseless waters. Can God forget such deeds? No never! Human applause may often awake no echo beyond the narrow circle of earth, but the thanksgiving of those whom Maynard saved, the blessings of wives and children whom he has rescued from widowhood and orphanage must rouse a response from Heaven."

Lieut. M. served with distinction throughout the Mexican war, becoming an officer of considerable note for his keen foresight and judgment in military matters, as also for gallantry and cool daring in action.

"It was this gallant officer," said the New London *News*, "who made the proposition for scaling the Castle of San Juan d'Ulloa.   *   *   *   He had permission to execute his bold enterprise, and set out from Washington to execute it on the 3d of March   *   *   *   But he was delayed too long in the consideration of his plan by the authorities at Washington. He arrived just in time to see the surrender of the Castle and City. That he would have accomplished all that he designed, no one who has noted his indomitable spirit can for a moment doubt.   *   *   *   His plan would have saved the awful effusion of blood that occurred in the City."

In 1849, he went to California on furlough, going around the Horn on the steamer "Senator" (She was afterwards run as a ferryboat on the Sacramento River, he being part proprietor.) In Jan., 1852, he was ordered to join the sloop "St. Mary," as Flag Lieut. of the Pacific Squadron, (Commodore Perry commanding,) then under sailing orders for Japan. But at this time he had become so thoroughly identified with the interests of San Francisco (then in its infancy) that he chose to resign his position in the Navy, which resignation was accepted, April, 1852. He was always interested in mining affairs, and made and lost several fortunes in such speculation. Though a most benevolent and public spirited man, who kept always the interests of the community at heart, he shunned publicity of every sort. He never sought office, but the office often unsuccessfully sought him. With "politics" so called he would have nothing to do, though a man of personally strong convictions on every subject.

He died, after years of wretched health, and a lingering illness, of paralysis of the brain; leaving his great estate (which included large tracts of land in the city of San Francisco) in so embarrassed a condition that nothing was saved, and his widow and children were left in poverty.

1823.

ROBERT CLARK MAYNARD, of Richmond, Va., son of No. 736, was born in Richmond; died 1884. Married Eveline Laness, of Norfolk, Va. Children :—

> 4359, FLORENCE MAYNARD, b. 1838, d. 1871. 4360, ALICE HYLTON, b. 1838, d. Mar. 16, 1874. 4361, NANCY ROBERTA, b. 1845, d. 1878, m. *Wm. Shelby Reed*, child : one son.

1824.

GEORGE FLETCHER MAYNARD, of San Francisco, Cal., son of No. 736, was born 1829; died May 10, 1879. Married Sarah, daughter of Col. Stafford Parker, of Richmond, Va. Children :—

> 4362, BLANCHE MAYNARD, b. 1854, m. *Hon. William M. Gwin, jr.* 4363, EVA. 4364, LENA. 4365, STAFFORD, d. y. 4366, SARAH.

Mr. Maynard was a man of high standing in San Francisco, and at the time of his death was Auditor of that city. His character was pure and beautiful. He served through the war in the Commissary Department of the Confederate army, at Richmond, with the rank of Major.

1825.

GEN. WILLIAM S. FISHER, of the Republic of Texas, was born in Virginia about 1810; went to Texas 1833; died 1845. Married MARY MAYNARD, daughter of No. 736. No children recorded.

He went to Texas before the Houston wars began. In 1835 he represented Gonzales Co. in the "General Assembly" at San Felipe, and was prominent in the struggle for independence. He commanded a company at the battle of San Jacinto when Santa Anna was captured; was promoted to Colonel, and appointed Secretary of War of the Texas Republic by Houston during his presidency. In 1843, as General of Texas troops, he commanded the "Mier Expedition," and after a battle of several hours, in which the Mexicans lost about 1,000 men, and the Texans, of whom 261 were engaged, 11 killed and 9 wounded, was captured, Feb. 11, and imprisoned in the Castle of Perote. A letter from Gen. Thomas J. Green, subsequently a prominent Confederate leader, who was Fisher's companion in captivity, is printed in Baker's "Texas Scrap Book," page 129. He speaks of their unhappy condition, confined in a filthy dungeon, loaded with chains, and tells the terrible story of the escape of the Mier prisoners at Salado, their recapture, and their subsequent decimation, after a selection by lottery.

1826.

HENRY FISHER, of Texas, a brother of No. 1825, an officer in the army of the Republic of Texas, married LUCY ANN MAYNARD, daughter of No. 736. Son:—

4367, WILLIAM HENRY FISHER, of San Francisco.

1827.

ROBERT MILLER, of Long Island, N. Y., son of Hugh Miller and Mary Clark, his wife of Kilmarnock, Ayrshire, Scotland, married April 2, 1844, HARRIET HYLTON MAYNARD, daughter of 736. Children:—

4370, MARY CASKILL MILLER, b. Dec. 28, 1884: m. Apr. 25, 1881, *Wm. M. Dodge*, official, N. Y. Elevated R. R.; child, 1, *Robert Miller*, b. Mar. 7, 1874. 4371, HYLTON MAYNARD, b. July 10, 1874, d. Feb. 16, 1864. 4372, ROBERT MILLER, b. Sept. 2, 1850, d. Apr. 5, 1857. 4373, ROBERTA MILLER, b. Dec. 7, 1858, d. Mar. 17, 1863. 4374, HARRIET MAYNARD, b. Aug. 28, 1860. 4375, WILLIAM HENDERSON, b. Oct. 14, 1864.

1829.

MAJ. JOHN CRINGAN MAYNARD, of San Francisco, Cal., son of No. 736, p. 209, was born in Richmond, July 26, 1837. Married (1) Samuella, daughter of Samuel and *Edith Lilly* Gwin, of Clinton, Miss., who was born July 29, 1837, died Dec. 9, 1862, leaving four children; (2) Oct. 5, 1863, Catharine, daughter of John and *Margaret Pickett* Heth, of Richmond. Children:—

4376, GWIN MAYNARD, b. Dec. 15, 1856, killed July 5, 1874. 4377, MARY, b. Nov. 8, 1885, *Henry Stanley Dexter*, of San Francisco. 4378. EDITH, d. y. 4379, HYLTON, d. y. 4380, ESTELLE MAYNARD, b. July 13, 1864. 4381, STITH, b. April 13, 1866. 4382, HETH, b. Oct. 28, 1867.

Mr. Maynard removed to California, where he was a farmer and an editor. He has been active in political affairs and a man of much influence. He served through the war in the Quartermaster's Department, C. S. A., with the rank of Major. He is now in the U. S. Sub-Treasury in San Francisco.

1830.

HENRY SETH WARD RANDOLPH, of "Mount Prospect," Henrico Co., Va., son of Henry and *Eliza Norman* Randolph, No. 738, p. 212 was born at "Warwick," July 15, 1810, died July 26, 1874. Married 1835, Deborah Perry,* daughter of Benjamin and Anna Perry, of

---

* MRS. DEBORAH PERRY RANDOLPH, was the daughter of Benjamin and Anna Perry, of Schaghticoke, (now Hart's Falls), New York. Her ancestors were among the first settlers of New England, John Perry, the first of the name in this country, living in Cambridge, Mass., in 1667. Mrs. Randolph's grandfather, also John Perry, great-grandson of the above, was born at Cambridge, Mass., 1754; after his marriage with Persis Mixer, 1775, removed to Rindge, N. H., where he died in 1834. From him descended a long line of sons and daughters distinguished for that stern uprightness and inflexibility of principle characteristic of the early Puritans. The annals of the Perry family record the names of several of its members who were ministers of the Gospel, lawyers, bankers, and also teachers of youth. The old homestead at Rindge, N. H., is still in the possession of the family, and occupied by Jason Bigelow Perry, a first cousin of Mrs. Randolph.

Schaghticoke, (now Hart's Falls,) Rensselaer Co., N. Y.   Children:—
    4383, ANNA LOUISE RANDOLPH, b. 1836, m. *Rev. William T. Price.* 4384,
    VIRGINIA, b. 1842, m. *James B. Mallory.* 4385, LUCY WARD, b.
    1847, m. *Rev. Robert H. Fleming.* 4386, JOSEPH, b. 1850, d. y·
    4387, HENRY, b. 1854.

Mr. Randolph early gave evidence of a taste for mechanics, and at the age
of fifteen was sent North to study machinery. He remained some years in
the State of New York, married there, and returned to Virginia in 1835. A
milling company, desirous of opening an enterprise near Houston, Texas, in
1837–'8, secured his services, and with his young wife and child, he set out for
that Republic. His health failing, after a year in Texas he returned to New
York, living in Brooklyn for eleven years, as superintendent of the large
machine works of H. W. Worthington. In 1854, he removed to a farm ("Mt·
Prospect ") near Richmond, Va., where he spent the remainder of his life, and·
where he is buried.

Mr. Randolph was of medium size, but handsome presence, possessing the
dark eyes almost peculiar to his line, but with a kindlier beam than the fierce
brilliancy which tells of the Indian blood. Although debarred the advantages
of a liberal education, by wide and varied reading, he had a well-stored mind,
naturally refined and vigorous, of an inventive bent. Several of his concep-
tions were highly commended, and encouraged both by his employer, Mr.
Worthington, and also by the Hon. John Y. Mason, when Secretary of the
Navy, but owing to a singular distrust in his own powers, Mr. Randolph never
brought any of his inventions to perfection.

1832.

JOSEPH WILLIAMSON RANDOLPH, of Richmond, Va., son of
No. 738, p. 212, was born at " Warwick," Aug. 19, 1815. Married Nov.
26, 1842, Honoria Mary Tucker,* daughter of Capt. John and *Susannah
Mary Ann Douglass* Tucker.   Children:—
    4388, JOSEPH TUCKER RANDOLPH, b. 1744; killed in battle Nov. 30,
    1864. 4389, NORMAN VINCENT, b. Nov. 2, 1846.

Mr. Randolph has been for nearly half a century the leading publisher of
Richmond, and from 1861 to 1865 more works were issued from his press than
perhaps all others in the Southern Confederacy. More recently, he has been
the senior member of the firm of J. W. Randolph & English, of which his only
son is also a member. He is an authority upon Virginia bibliography and

---

* DOUGLAS—TUCKER.—Charles Douglas, of Standes, Mt. Fitchett, Essex, England, b. Oct. 11, 1752,
at Sawbridgeworth, Herefordshire (son and heir of Capt. Charles Douglas, of the British Army, second
son of Col. Charles Douglas, of the "Old Buffs," killed at the battle of Carthagena, second cousin
and heir presumptive of James, Earl of Moreton), m. Jan. 23, 1783, at the Parish Church of N. Nobley,
in Gloucestershire, Susannah Randolph, sister of No. 235, Goode Genealogy.   Issue :—
    1. SUSANNAH MARY ANN DOUGLAS, b. at Curles Tract, James River, Va., May 1785, christened at
"Chester," Brett Randolph's seat, in Powhatan Co., m. in Alexandria, Va., June 2, 1808, Capt. John
Tucker, a native of Bermuda. Issue :—I. *Susan Jane Tucker*, b June 22, 1810, m. (1) Andrew McDon-
ald Jackson, Purser U. S. N.; (2) Henry Chandler Holt, Surgeon U. S. N. Lives at " Jackson Hill,"
Rock Creek, near Washington. II. *John Randolph Tucker*, b. Jan. 31, 1812, Lieut. U. S. N., Admiral
C. S. N., m. Virginia Webb; one of his sons, *Charles Douglas*, lost at sea in Confederate steamer "Juno,"
Mar., 1863. III. *Honoria Mary Tucker*, m. J. W. Randolph.
    2. HEATLY ARCHIBALD DOUGLAS, b. Dec. 25, 1786, at " Red Lodge," Amelia Co , Va.
    3. CHARLES BRETT and ARCHIBALD ABERDEEN DOUGLAS, twins, b. Dec. 31, 1789.

JOSEPH WILLIAMSON RANDOLPH.

No. 1832.

BY R. A. BROCK.

JOSEPH W. RANDOLPH, the oldest living bookseller and publisher of Richmond, was born at "Chester Lodge," Aug. 19, 1815. His parents were married in Philadelphia, Pa., April 20, 1809. His father died in Hanover County, Va., Oct. 26, 1840. His mother died Oct. 17th, 1825, in Rocky Ridge or Manchester, Va. His father was like many Virginians, of generous and impulsive nature, and in the heat of his enthusiasm his possessions melted away. His good and wise mother died when he was nine years old, and he fell to the care of his grandmother, Mrs. Lucy Ward Randolph, who moved to Richmond about 1815, and subsequently married Dr. Higginbotham.

Among the recollections of his boyhood, is a vivid one of the second visit to Richmond in 1824 of La Fayette, and joining in the procession in his honor. He was present when the generous patriot called on his grandmother, and saw him with customary gallantry, kiss her. In 1829, being in his 14th year, he entered the employment of John H. Nash, bookseller, thus beginning his life's connection with the material and intellectual interest of Richmond. His compensation for the first year was the meagre sum of fifty dollars, which was increased in the following year to one hundred and fifty. In 1831, Mr. Nash failed in business, and young Randolph was continued by the trustees of Mr. Nash in custody of stock, to sell it off by retail. At the final sale he purchased books and stationery to the amount of $200, and commenced business on his own account in a building on 12th street, opening in the same connection, a circulating library. In 1834, he bought out the stock of a bookseller in Norfolk, Va., and moved there, associating himself with his uncle, Josiah B. Abbott, (of the firm of Pleasant & Abbott, proprietors of the *Richmond Whig* newspaper) under the name of J. W. Randolph & Co. It was a small beginning, yet in three years the value of their stock had increased to $4,000.

In the panic of 1836-7, when specie payment was suspended, and there was a scarcity of silver for change, no notes being in circulation of less denomination than $5, the firm at the suggestion of Thomas Williamson, cashier of the Virginia Bank of Norfolk, issued notes as currency of the value from $12\frac{1}{2}$ cents to one dollar, to the amount of $4,000, which was circulated by the bank. These "shin-plasters" as they were termed, were redeemed by the issuers when presented in sums of five dollars and upwards. Mr. Abbott becoming seriously involved by a delusive investment in the stock of "The Virginia Gold Mining Company," his estate was sold to meet his losses. The business of J. W. Randolph & Co., was moved to Richmond, and Mr. Abbott took charge of the financial affairs of the firm, which in 1842, bought out the stock and good will of Richard D. Sanxey, bookseller and binder, and entered upon a career of increased prosperity, but Mr. Abbott, endorsing the notes of Thomas H. Drew, who failed, J. W. Randolph & Co., were left with a liability on their account of $17,000, which amount Mr. Randolph most honorably, on his own account, as the successor of his firm, undertook with the assets of Drew, to pay in four years. This, by strenuous efforts he accomplished, although the assets of Drew yielded but forty per cent. of the amount of his liabilities. Every creditor received the full amount of his claim with interest but *one*, James Dunlop, who, in attestation of the singular honesty of Mr. Randolph, refused to accept the interest, urging that the principal alone was more than double the amount the effects of Drew had yielded. After the liquidation of this debt, Mr. Abbott became again associated with Mr. Randolph until his death in 1849, from which time Mr. Randolph, continued the business alone in his own name with success and reputation until the disasterous fire incident upon the evacuation of Richmond, April 3rd, 1865, which destroyed his establishment, swept away the chief part of the available accumulation of his life—the earnings of the war were invested in Confederate bonds and other war securities. A small house near the city, and two other small places alone, remained, and to the farm he repaired, vainly attempting there to support his family.

The farm and other real estate was subsequently sold, and the proceeds of the sale devoted to the payment of Nothern creditors whom he had been debarred from paying during the continuance of the war.

In 1866, Mr. Randolph recommenced business on a borrowed capital of $100. only, associating with him Joseph J. English (who had learned the trade of book-binder, in his employ) under the firm name of J. W. Randolph & English. It may be of interest to note that the house occupied by them was the same in which Mr. Randolph had commenced business in 1832. A friendly editor said of Mr. Randolph's *post bellum* career that "when he commenced his business he could have taken his stock in a wheelbarrow, and that now it would take a steamboat to remove it." The present commodious establishment of the firm comprising the best appointed book-bindery, and the largest and most valuable stock of books in the southern states is located at Nos. 1302-4 East Main street. The firm of which Mr. Randolph has been the head, has ever been characterized by enterprise, fidelity and probity, and it is noteworthy that from the period of the embarrassment in 1842, he has conducted his business without giving negotiable notes of like obligations.

The publications issued by his house have been numerous and valuable, and have been effective in fostering the best interest of Virginia, and in contributing to her progress. Mr. Randolph was not in active service in the field during the war, but was a member of the ambulance Corps, a body of sterling citizens who preformed essential service in the care of the sick and wounded of the Confederate Army in the field, camp and hospital.

The following extract from the *Richmond Enquirer* of March 3rd, 1863, may be worthily cited here as exhibiting alike a characteristic trial of Mr. Randolph and his devotion to the Southern cause :—"A Stockholder of the Belvidere Manufacturing Company informs us that since the war began he had received dividends on $1,000 of shares amounting to $6,460. An amount which he considered if not extortionate, at least, improper, and he donated the *whole amount* to the army—This man was Mr. J. W. Randolph, of Richmond, Va."

An instance of the conscientiousness of Mr. Randolph may be given : In 1866, being summoned to serve as a Juror he was asked to take an oath to support the existing State government—that removed from Alexandria with J. H. Pierpont as Executive—and refused, regarding it as one of usurpation and was therefore fined for contempt of court. The *New York Herald* cited the action of Mr. Randolph as an evidence of the disloyalty of the people of Virginia. Mr. Randolph, himself, thus summarizes his life in a recent communication—"The world as a rule has treated me well, and will so treat others who try to do right. Every man, as long as he is able, is bound to do his part in the world, and it is better to wear out than to rust out. Being blessed with a good wife, a son who has nobly done, and is now doing his duty, and with cherished memory of another noble son who gave his life for a cause he thought just ; having a strong will and health, he hopes to go on and meet the end without fear."

history. The burning of Richmond at the close of the war frustrated his almost accomplished life-purpose, that of regaining possession of the ancestral estate, old "Warwick," on the James River.

His gentle, kindly face and pleasant ways have caused him to be universally beloved in the city of his residence.

1834.

RICHARD CHANNING HALL, of Richmond, Va., a merchant, son of Jacob and *Catherine Eliza Moore* Hall, and grandson of Bishop Richard Channing Moore, married ELIZABETH ANNA RANDOLPH, daughter of No. 738. Children:—

> 4390, CATHERINE ELIZA HALL, b. 1848, m. 1869 *George Brown*, of Southampton, England. Children, 1, *Elizabeth Brown*, b. 1868, d. y.; 2, *Kate Randolph*, b. 1879. 4391, MARY NORMAN, b. 1850, m. 1872, *Rufus Yarbrough*. 4392, LUCY, d. y. 4393, CHANNING, d. y. 4394, VIRGINIA DEAN, m. 1883, *James McCall Fox*, of Richmond. Children, 1, *Richard Fox*, b. 1886. 4395, FANNIE MACMURDO, m. 1886, *Walter Wren*.

1835.

ROBERT SAUNDERS, of Norfolk, Va., son of and probably nephew of No. 242–A, married LUCY WARD RANDOLPH, daughter of No. 738, who was born Feb. 16, 1821, died in Henderson, Ky., Oct. 27, 1853. Son:—

> 4396, JAMES RANDOLPH SAUNDERS, d. y.

Mr. Saunders died of yellow fever in Norfolk about 1859.

Of Mrs. Saunders a relative writes: "My aunt bore unmistakable signs in her beautiful dark eyes and other features of her Indian lineage, as did also my beloved aunt Lizzie, (Mrs. Hall,) lately deceased."

1836.

WILLIAM HENRY HAMMOND, of Petersburg, Va., merchant, son of Joel Hammond, of North Carolina, married MARY GOODE RANDOLPH, daughter of No. 738, born Nov. 15, 1823, living, a widow in Richmond, 1886. Children:—

> 4397, HENRY RANDOLPH HAMMOND, b. 1851, a merchant in Baltimore. 4398, LULA DOUGLASS, d. y.

1838.

CAPT. WILLIAM TINSLEY RANDOLPH, son of No. 748, was born about 1825. He was an officer of Crabb's ill-fated Sonora expedition, every member of which, except a drummer boy, was slaughtered in cold blood by the Mexicans about 1855.

1839.

HENRY RANDOLPH THORNTON, of Livingston, Sumter Co., Ala., son of George W. and *Mary Randolph* Thornton, No. 739, was born Feb. 23, 1807, died Nov. 21, 1862. Married (1) June 28, 1829, Maria Agnes Bradford, who had 3 children, (2) Sept. 7, 1848, Ellen, daughter of George Slaughter, and *Margaret Hansbrough* Thom, of Culpeper Co., Va., who is living (1886) in Birmingham, Ala. Children :—

> 4400, GEORGE THORNTON, b. 1880, d. 1880, m. 1860, Fannie Rew. Children 1, *Bradford Thornton.* 2, *Maria Agnes.* 3, *Kate Garrison.* 4, *Henry Williams.* 5, *Lillie.* 6, *Fannie.* 4401, ALEXANDER CUNNINGHAM. 4402, SAMUEL BRADFORD, d. y.
>
> 4403, REUBEN THOM THORNTON, of Birmingham, Ala. 4404, HORTENSE RANDOLPH, of St. Mary's Hall, Burlington, N. J. 4405, HENRY WARD, of Chicago, Ill. 4406, MARGARET VIRGINIA, m. *John S. Johnston.* children 1, *Reuben Thornton Johnston.* 2, *Emmie Holmes.* 3, *Ellen Thom.* 4407, LUCIE COBBS. 4408, SETH BRETT, d. y.

Mr. Thornton sold his ancestral estate of "Rumford" about 1833, and removed to Livingston, Ala., where he was one of the first settlers, at the time of the organization of the new county of Sumter. He was an extensive and wealthy planter and slaveholder. He lived an exemplary Christian life, and was a devoted member of the Episcopal Church. He is buried at Livingston by the side of his brother Capt. Thornton, whose remains were brought thither from Mexico.

1840.

RICHARD ADAMS, of Richmond, Va., son of Samuel Griffin Adams, (son of Col. Richard and Elizabeth Griffin Adams, and grandson of Ebenezer Adams, who came from England to New Kent Co., Va., early in the eighteenth century,) and his wife Catharine, daughter of Harry Innes, of Kentucky, was born Feb. 7, 1800, died June 11, 1851, married (1) MARY, daughter of Col. Miles Selden, jr.; 2, LUCY WARD THORNTON, daughter of No. 739, born March 21, 1811, died September 22, 1840. Children :—

> 4409, MARY ADAMS m. *Gen. George W. Randolph*, son of Gov. Thomas Mann Randolph, and grandson of Thomas Jefferson, b. 1801, d. Apr. 4, 1867, Brigadier-General C. S. A., and Secretary of War C. S. A.; later Confederate Agent in France. 4410, CATHERINE ADAMS. 4411, SAMUEL GOODE.

1841.

LIEUT. ALEXANDER CUNNINGHAM MAURY, U. S. N., son of Philip P. and *E. Cunningham* Maury, 9th son of Abraham and *Susanna*

Poindexter Maury, and cousin of Commodore Matthew Fontaine Maury, was born about 1806–'10. Appointed Midshipman U. S. N., Feb. 1, 1836 : Lieutenant, Mar. 8, 1837 ; married MARY GOODE THORNTON, daughter of No. 739. No children.

1841-A.

REV. JOHN JACKSON SCOTT, D. D., LL. D., of Pensacola, Fla., son of Joseph Adams Scott, a native of Scotland, and Mary McNish, a lady of Huguenot descent, married MARY GOODE (THORNTON) MAURY, daughter of No. 739, p. 212, who was born 1813. No children.

Dr. Scott is rector of Christ Church, Pensacola, and one of the leading Episcopal clergymen in the South.

His grand-father, Joseph Adams Scott, came to this country with his family and purchased an estate on Edisto Island, South Carolina, where he resided. He also purchased at the same time lands in St. Luke's Parish, in the district of Beaufort, S. C. His eldest son, Joseph Adams, was put in charge of the latter place, and married the only daughter of Mr. McNish, descended from a Huguenot family from St. Gaul, Switzerland. Among the refugees were the Zububuhlas, father and son, the former chaplain to the expedition that came to South Carolina under Sir Peter Percy, who founded a town bearing his name, and the latter was rector of Christ Church, Savannah, Ga., and chaplain to the British forces stationed there. Dr. Scott was given the name of his honored maternal ancestor, and has regretted since that his name was changed, having been taught to reverence the memory of the Zububuhlas and form himself as much as possible on their upright and holy example.

The Rev. Dr. Scott was born at " Rose Dew," St. Luke's Parish, on the banks of Thay river, the country residence of his parents. He was prepared for college chiefly by an Irish Priest, who was a graduate of Trinity College, Dublin. Subsequently, he was educated at William and Mary College, Va., and received his theological training at the Theological Seminary of Virginia, He was made a deacon by Bishop Thorne, of Virginia, and advanced to the priesthood by the Rt. Rev. Dr. Polk in Christ Church, New Orleans.

He has served as a missionary in Alabama and Florida and as Chaplain in the U. S. Army, but most of his life has been spent in the rectorship of Christ Church, Pensacola, Fla., where he still remains. While in the army he received the degree of D.D., from Columbia College, New York, and at a later period that of LL. D., from William and Mary College.

" Dr. Scott has never sought or desired anything more than a place to work, and where he might keep up his habits of study. Not having access to public libraries he has been compelled to purchase such books as he desired, and now has a large and most valuable library containing works on theology, science, literature, and languages. He has led a quiet life, devoted to his professional duties, his studies, and the charities that become his calling as a Christian Priest. He has led a life devoted to work, allowing but little time for travel and recreation. He has been prostrated by yellow fever, and served here through six epidemics of that fearful disease in attendance on the sick and dying, and inflexibly devoted to the duties of his sacred calling. The doctor has many warm friends who contribute to his social enjoyment and happiness. Among his friends may be numbered people of all forms of religious and political opinions. His former servants are still in attendance upon him, and serve him not only for liberal compensation, but for love. In this connection, it may not be out of place to mention a fact that speaks for itself as to the relation that existed between the doctor and his servants. When you enter his study you will see in a conspicuous place the picture of a venerable old man who was the husband of his nurse, and whom he considers as brave and good a man as he ever knew. This picture he had taken many years ago as a mark of respect and veneration for Abram Hardin, whom by this means he wishes to keep in remembrance to the latest period of his own life.

"As a missionary, Dr. Scott was successful. Immediately on his ordination to the deaconate, declining several invitations to large city parishes as assistant, he proceeded to Alabama, then under the jurisdiction of Bishop Polk, who placed him at Livingston, Ala. There he organized a parish and built a neat church; when it had grown strong enough to call a minister he left it and came to Florida, where he acted as general missionary in middle Florida before the diocese had a Bishop, he then accepted an invitation to this parish in 1848. In 1852-'53 he moved to Fort Barrancas and became Chaplain in the army, but moved back to Pensacola, where he has resided ever since. He organized the Parish of St. Mary's, Wilson, Fla., where for several years he held services during the week. He also organized the Parish of St. John's, Warrenton Navy Yard, giving it a third service every Sunday for many years. He succeeded in building a very neat, pretty church, all the appointments of which were attractive and convenient. In the bombardment from Fort Pickens, in 1861, it received the first shot, the steeple being the most prominent object in the town, and was burned. The church in this city suffered severely during the war. It has now been enlarged and renewed, and is a beautiful building, churchly in all its appointments. This and a successful parish school attests the wisdom and success of Dr. Scott."

1842.

CAPT. SETH BRETT THORNTON, 2d Dragoons, U. S. A., son of George W. Thornton, and Mary Randolph, No. 739, grand-daughter of Scott Ward and MARY GOODE, was born at "Rumford," Stafford Co., Va., May 28, 1815, and killed in front of the City of Mexico, Aug. 18, 1847.

This gallant young officer was intimately associated with some of the most stormy events in the Mexican war, and it was his hand which struck the first blow when, on the 23d of April, he and his dragoons were surrounded in the chapparal, by Mexicans.

Jenkins, in his "History of the War between the United States and Mexico," p. 88, says: "The fiery cross, borne by the swift-footed Walice, as the signal for the marshalling of the Scottish clans, did not arouse a deeper or more intense feeling of anxiety than the intelligence of the capture of Thornton and his command on the banks of the Brazos. With the rapidity of the electric fire it was communicated from one extremity of the city to the other. * * * Congress was in session when the information reached Washington. * * Two days were occupied in the deliberation and discussion of the subject, and on the 13th of May, an act was passed with great unanimity, declaring that a state of war existed ' by the act of the Republic of Mexico,' and authorizing the President to accept the services of fifty thousand volunteers. The sum of ten million dollars also was appropriated to carry on thé war."

Thornton was not only a dashing and brilliant officer, but a man whose pure and noble character caused his loss to be deeply mourned in the army and in his native State of Virginia.

The following sketch of his life was prepared, after earnest solicitation, by his sister, Mrs. Mary Goode Scott, of Pensacola.

He was born at "Rumford," on the banks of the Rappahannock, May 28, 1815, and was baptized by the Rev. James Woodville. His father, Major Thornton, of the Continental Army, had inherited "Rumford" from his father. To this ancestral home George Thornton brought his bride, and here he died, leaving four children to the care of his widow. Seth, the youngest, was the comfort and delight of his mother, to whom he ever rendered the most dutiful love and care. He seemed to have an inheritance of rare chivalry, as well as of personal comeliness. He was sent to a classical school in Fredericksburg, and in 1830, entered Kenyon College, Ohio, and in 1832, Trinity College, Conn. Pursuing his studies with great earnestness, at the end of two years his health so entirely failed that he was compelled to return home and give up books. His father sent him to Kentucky, to his father's relations, for rest and recreation. After two years, finding that he was not strong enough to pursue a course of professional study, he obtained a commission in the army, and Jan. 8, 1835, was appointed Second Lieutenant in the Second Dragoons and ordered to Florida, where he remained several years, seeing much hard service, and was made First Lieutenant Nov. 16, 1837, and Captain Feb. 1, 1841.

An incident occurred about this.time which illustrates his generous character. He was a passenger on the ill-fated steamer "Pulaski," which was burned at sea, between Savannah and New York, and was nearly the last to leave her. While others were anxious for their own lives he thought only of saving the helpless women and children. When all the passengers had been sent off in boats and on spars he threw off his boots and coat and sprang into the water. After aiding several persons to reach portions of the wreck as the steamer broke up, he found himself floating upon a portion of a state-room. After drifting for three days under the burning June sun, he rigged a rude rudder, and raising, for a sail, an old shawl which the waves had brought, he steered for the Carolina coast, where he was picked up by some fishermen, in a helpless condition, and nursed back to health in the home of Mr. Hall, a philanthropic banker, in Wilmington.

In the Florida war he passed through many extraordinary perils, and distinguished himself as a most gallant and active officer. Though ever in the front of danger, he was by no means physically a vigorous man, but of delicate constitution. His bold and manly heart made him always ready to dare any danger and assume the most trying positions which could be pointed out to him. I have several anecdotes of him, all showing the true and chivalrous spirit that governed all his life. While stationed at Fort Jessup a young lady visited that place, and, in the exuberance of her youth and gaiety, often subjected herself to unkind comment. On occasion of a dinner party among the officers, while giving toasts, this young lady's name was lightly given. Thornton rose to his feet and asked that it might not be drank, for he occasionally visited the lady, and could not listen to her name being lightly used. It had its effect, and the glasses were returned to the table untouched—all but one. Again, while walking in New Orleans arm-in-arm with a brother officer, a Creole gentleman met them, and, in passing, with his glove, offered an indignity to his friend. This was borne in silence, and when Capt. Thornton asked him what it meant, he replied: "That person has been trying for some days to provoke me to challenge him. He is the best swordsman in the city. Thornton, I have a wife and two little girls, and cannot afford to take the risk of depriving them of my life." Capt. Thornton made no reply, but, on returning to his hotel, sought a friend, by whom he sent a message to this gentleman, the purport of which was that, for reasons satisfactory to himself, Capt. —— chose not to take notice of the insult offered to him, but as he shared the insult by his position with Capt. ——, he demanded an apology, as he had not the reasons which governed his friend. This gentleman was so struck with the honor and delicacy of Capt. Thornton that he requested an interview and to be introduced to him. He made the apology, as desired, and an amicable adjustment followed.

In his manners he was strikingly gentle and courteous on all occasions. Family affections had a more than common hold on him, and seem to have been throughout his career the softening influence of his life. He had the advantage, while in college at Hartford, of being brought into contact and making friends with gentle Christian people, who exercised, by his warmth of affection and gratitude, a happy influence over him. Among others, he ever retained for Mrs. Sigourney, the poet, the liveliest admiration and affection for her kindness to him, only a youth at college.

He was cut off early in life, "and when no enemy was in sight his brave spirit was loosened from its natal tenement, and thus he fell with his face to the foe."

A brother officer, A. W. Hunter, wrote in 1846:

"For the last ten years I have been more intimately associated with Capt. Thornton than any officer of his regiment, and I can therefore speak with assurance of those sterling attributes which distinguished him alike as the soldier and gentleman. For five years we encountered alike the toils, privations and hardships of a warefare with the Seminole Indians, marched from Florida to the frontiers of Texas, and thence to Corpus Christi. Neither of us have been absent from duty connected with the war with Mexico since it commenced.

He struck the first blow and fell in the last attack upon the City of Mexico. Always held dear in the estimation of his friends, he wrung reluctant respect from his enemies, and found a solace for wrongs he could not avenge in death upon the battle-field."

Captain Thornton opened the Mexican war. The circumstances of the affair are told in the following words by the principal historian of this period :

"On the evening of the 23d of April, Gen. Taylor's spies reported that 2,500 Mexicans had crossed the Rio Grande above the American encampment and about 1,500 below, with the intention of surrounding his position and cutting off all communication with the depot at Point Isabel. Captain Ker was despatched on the following day with a squadron of dragoons, to reconnoitre the crossing near Burrita, and returned in a few hours, with the intelligence that the alarm was unfounded. At the same time another squadron, under Capt. Thornton, was sent to scour the country above. They proceeded up the river about twenty-six miles without discovering any signs of the enemy, although their inquiries on the way tended to show that they had crossed the river in strength. At this point the guide refused to go any further, alleging that the whole country was full of Mexicans. The orders of Capt. Thornton were to discover the position and force of the enemy, if they had passed the river, but to proceed with care and caution. He was entirely ignorant of the country, but perfectly fearless and somewhat impetuous. Having decided to go on without the guide, his advance guard was increased, and the party again moved forward. At a distance of about three miles further they discovered a plantation inclosed by a chapparal fence, except on the side facing the river, with a farm-house situated about two hundred yards from the entrance, which was narrow and secured by a pair of bars.

"Capt. Thornton halted the advance guard and went into the field ahead of his men to speak with some persons who appeared to be at work. Sufficient precautions had not been taken to guard against surprise,* and a signal to the guard was mistaken by the remainder of the force, all of whom entered the inclosure. In an instant the chapparal swarmed with Mexicans, who had completely surrounded them and apparently cut off every chance of escape. A body of cavalry also made their appearance and charged upon the little band, who met them gallantly and with success. A destructive fire was now poured upon them, which it was impossible to resist, and orders were given by Capt. Thornton to his men to cut their way through the enemy. With a single bound he cleared the fence, overturning a number of the Mexicans who endeavored to stop him, and darted ahead in the direction of Gen. Taylor's position... In leaping a precipice his horse fell with him, and he remained for some time insensible. When he recovered he again started for the camp, but was taken prisoner before he reached it. Meanwhile Capt. Hardee, who had succeeded to the command of the squadron, ordered his men to ford the river ; but the banks were found to be so boggy that this was impossible, and he then surrendered himself and men prisoners of war. In this affair the American loss was ten killed and about fifty taken prisoners. The Mexican force consisted of cavalry and infantry, over three hundred strong, commanded by Gen. Torrejon. Gen. Taylor forthwith communicated the particulars of the encounter to his Government."—*History of the War between the United States and Mexico*, by John S. Jenkins, pp. 86–88.

It was thought by the army that he had been killed, and I copy a few passages from the letters of officers written when it was known that he was alive :

---

* This is a misstatement. The Court decided that the destruction of Capt. Thornton's troop was not due to any want of precaution. See its Report.

(From Lieut. Don. Carlos Buell, afterward Major General.)

DEAR CAPTAIN :—

I am overjoyed to hear of your safety—I may call it your resurrection. May you soon be with us.

Yours truly,

BUELL.

(From Lieut. Alfred Pleasonton, afterward Major General.)

DRAGOON CAMP, 1846.

MY DEAREST THORNTON :—

I congratulate you on your miraculous escape. 'Tis worthy of your past career. My heart is too full to express all I feel in hearing of your life being safe. To us you have been dead two days, and your supposed melancholy end spread a gloom far and wide over our devoted army. Your conduct has been freely canvassed, and it has been as generously bestowed with praise and fame. Accept the warmest sympathies of my heart.

Ever yours,

PLEASONTON.

(From Gen. W. J. Worth, U. S. A.)

POINT ISABEL, *April* 12, 1846.

MY DEAR THORNTON:—

I have just learned that *en route* from the camp, God bless it, which I left with an aching heart, you gave your valued sabre to an unarmed, but gallant, naval officer, *en suite*. I believe I also comprehend the generous and noble sentiment which animated you. Will you accept and wear on hard service. that which I now unbuckle? It is plain and unpretending, as a service-sword should be, but of good metal and sharp as malignity, and will be found, like yourself, a friend in need and indeed, backed by a true heart and staunch arm like your own. The day may come when I shall ask you to accept and wear, for my sake, one more ornate.

Faithfully, your friend,

W. J. WORTH.

Capt. Thornton was kindly treated by his Mexican captors, was soon exchanged, and, after much effort, succeeded in having his conduct investigated by a court-martial. His vindication was complete, as is shown by the following letter from Gen. Worth:

(From Gen. W. J. Worth, U. S. A.)

CARMARGO, *Aug.* 4, 1846.

MY DEAR CAPTAIN :—

I sincerely rejoice at the handsome—nay, noble and generous—vindication Gen. Taylor has tendered in his admirable letters of the 18th ult. It does equal honor to you and to him.

Wishing you all honor and distinction,

I remain your sincere friend,

W. J. WORTH.

The defense of Capt. Thornton, presented by his friend, Lieut. Braxton Bragg, afterwards General, C. S. A., July 15, was a very strong paper, but is too long to be quoted here. In conclusion he said :

"Our little army was compelled, under its instructions, to keep up a peaceable attitude until the first blow should be given by them. It was my misfortune to receive that first blow upon my devoted head; but it had to be received, and why not by me? I contend, then, that the result of my expedition was not disastrous. Nearly half a squadron of dragoons were captured, I admit, but what signifies that, when compared with the immense advantages to a commanding General of knowing his real position—of being confident he no longer occupied debatable ground—of being certain the enemy are gaining his rear in force and determined to give him battle? If this was not important information, why the immediate requisition for heavy reinforcements? Why the redoubled activity in the completion of Fort Brown? Why the sudden and rapid move upon Point Isabel for ammunition and provisions?

"But for the loss of this squadron, gentlemen, for which I am called on to atone, the thanks of a grateful people might never have been tendered to the 'heroes of Palo Alto and Resaca de la Palma.' But, instead, the tears of destitute widows and the cries of helpless orphans might have been answered, as they have heretofore been, with cold indifference in the halls of our National Legislature. Rather than such should be the case I would willingly conceal in my breast again, however painful and difficult the task, the only bleeding heart, amidst the rejoicings of a victorious army."

A Virginia paper of the day contained the following lines, suggested by reading Captain Thornton's address to the court-martial:

> Thou soldier of the "bleeding heart,"
>   Columbia's daughters wept for thee;
> Thou coulds't not else have played thy part—
>   Let that suffice to comfort thee.
>
> Thy fault (if 'twas indeed a fault)
>   Was but the daring of the brave;
> Then sigh not at experience bought—
>   Forget the Bravo's sullen wave.
>
> Gird on thine armor once again;
>   Thy country's flag is waving o'er thee;
> Thy laurels yet are fresh and green,
>   And glory's pathway is before thee.
>
> —[MELANTHE.

Capt. Thornton was killed less than a year later, Aug. 18, 1847, by a cannon-shot fired from San Antonio, while he was reconnoitering that position.

"This gallant officer," wrote a contemporary historian, "met death with the same heroic resolution which he had uniformly displayed in all the events of his checkered career. The first to encounter the enemy in the present war, at Caracita, he was also the first of the many victims of this engagement (Contreras) who have sealed their devotion to their country with their lives."

His remains were cared for by Gen. Worth, and were, in March, 1848, laid in the family burying-ground at Livingston, Ala.

1843.

CAPT. THOMAS FRANCIS MAURY, C. S. A., of Kemper, Miss., son of No. 739, p. 212, was born Feb. 1819, died in the army May, 1862. Married May, 1847, Ann R., daughter of Richard Jenkins, of Virginia, who is living, 1887, in China Springs, McLennan Co., Texas. Children:—

4415, SETH THORNTON MAURY, b. Feb. 19. 1848. 4416, RICHARD RAN-
DOLPH, b. Feb., 1850. 4417, THOMAS F. and EDWARD KIMBROUGH,
b. May, 1851. 4418, JEANETTE WILLIAMS, b. Feb. 22, 1853, d. y.
4419, JOHN A., b. Dec., 1854. 4420, MARY LUCY, b. Feb. 23, 1856·
4421, JAMES WOODVILLE, b. May 6, 1858. 4422, BETTIE GREENE,
b. Oct. 9, 1860, d. y. 4423, FRANCIS ALEXANDER, b. May 5, 1862,
d. y.

Capt. Maury was a planter in Kemper Co., Miss. At the opening of the war
he enlisted in a Mississippi cavalry regiment, and died in service at Wahala
Station May, 1862.

1845.

JAMES WOODVILLE MAURY, of Shuqualak, Noxube Co., Miss.,
son of James Francis and *Mary Randolph* Maury, No. 739–A., p. 217,
was born in Stafford Co., Va., March 18, 1823. Married Feb. 22,
1848, Rachel Kittrell Harris, daughter of Richard and Elizabeth Harris,
of Pendleton District, South Carolina. Children : —

4425, RICHARD HARRIS MAURY, b. Dec. 6, 1848, d. Dec. 24, 1875. 4426,
JAMES FRANCIS, b. Mar. 22, 1850 : a planter in Shuqualak, Miss.,
m. Aug. 1, 1881. Willie Irene Allen. Children : 1, *Aline Maury*,
b. Feb. 1, 1883. 2, *Harris*, b. Mar. 3, 1885. 4427, EDWARD FON-
TAINE, b. May 27, 1852; m. Mary L. Shelton, of Virginia. Child-
ren : 1, *James Berkley Maury*, b. Mar. 11, 1878 ; 2, *Francis Lewis*;
b. Nov. 28, 1880 ; 3, *Richard Henry*, b. Dec. 23, 1882. 4428,
MATTHEW HENRY, b. April 16, 1854 ; m. Dec. 21, 1875, Mary J.
Galbraith, of Va. Children ; 1, *Richard Harris Maury*, b. Jan.
10, 1877 ; 2, *Kate Galbraight*, b. Sept. 3, 1879 ; 3, *Clara Kittrell*, b.
May 11, 1881 ; 4, *Henry Francis*, b. Sept. 23, 1883 ; 5, *Annie*, b.
April 23, 1884 ; 6, *Nellie*, b. Sept. 23, 1885, d. y.

Mr. Maury was educated in Fredericksburg, Va., and in Alabama. He is a
successful cotton planter in Kemper Co., Miss. During the war he was in
the Confedarate service in connection with the Mobile and Ohio Railroad.

1848

GILBERT LAFAYETTE MAURY, of Pushmataha, Ala., son of
No. 739–A, was born Feb. 7, 1831. Married Eliza Searsm, daughter
of James Scott, of Choctaw Co., Ala., b. Jan. 8, 1841. Children : —

4429, OSCAR FONTAINE MAURY, b. July 8, 1864. 4430, JAMES WOOD-
VILLE, b. Dec., 3, 1868. 4431, JULIA R., b. Aug. 31, 1870. 4432,
CHARLES D., b. July 4, 1872. 4433, DABNEY HERNDON, b. July 5,
1874. 4434, ERNEST CALEB, b. Jan. 22, 1880. 4435, b. Sept. 9,
1883.

Mr. Maury is a merchant and magistrate in Pushmataha. He served through
the war in the Trans-Mississippi Department of the Confederate Army.

1849.

CAPT. WALTER RALEIGH ABBOTT, C. S. A., of Lynchburg, Va., son of No. 742, p. 218, was born April 19, 1838 ; killed in battle June 13, 1862. Married Elizabeth Duval, of Richmond. Child:—

4436, WALTER RALEIGH ABBOTT, d. y.

Capt. Abbott was a banker in Lynchburg. At the outbreak of the war he was called to the command of the Lynchburg Artillery Company. On the morning of the battle of Gaines' Mill he was confined to his bed by illness, but rose and, putting on his uniform, rode out to his post, telling his family that he should never return. Early in the engagement a ball passed through the top of his cap, grazing his skin, and a few minutes later another struck just an inch below the first and ended his gallant career.

1850.

CLAIBORNE WATKINS, of Richmond, Va., son of Henry W. and Judith F. Watkins, g.-son of Henry W. and Nancy Montague Watkins, g.-grandson of John Watkins, married VIRGINIA ABBOTT, daughter of No. 742, who was born Mar. 30, 1855. Children:—

4437, WALTER ABBOTT WATKINS, b. Apr. 3, 1857. 4438, CHARLES HUNTER, b. Sept. 26, 1858. 4439, RANDOLPH, b. Aug. 30, 1860. 4440, CLAIBORNE, b. May 3, 1863. 4441, KATE WATKINS, b. June 16, 1866. 4442, HENRY, b. Apr. 22, 1869. 4443, VIRGINIA, b. June 6, 1870. 4444, ELIZABETH, b. Dec. 28, 1872. 4445, ADELAIDE, b. Apr. 22, 1875.

Mr. Watkins is senior member of the firm of Watkins, Cottrell & Co., wholesale dealers in hardware and cutlery, Richmond, and a substantial citizen of that town.

1853.

HENRY CHADWICK, of Brooklyn, N. Y., son of James Chadwick, of Manchester, England, married JANE BOTTS, daughter of Alexander Lithgow and *Susan Frances Randolph* Botts, daughter of No. 747, p. 219. Children:—

4461, RICHARD WESTLAKE CHADWICK, d. y. 4462, SUSAN MARY, b. July 5, 1851; m. *Thomas Slaight Eldridge.* 4463, ROSE VIRGINIA, d. y.

Mr. Chadwick is a brother of Edwin Chadwick, Esq., C. B., of London, well known as a sanitary and social reformer. Mr. Chadwick is an eminent authority on the American national game of base ball, and the author of several standard books on out-door sports, and he is on the editorial staff of the *Outing* Magazine, the New York *Clipper*, and the Brooklyn *Daily Eagle*. He edited John Minor Botts' work, "The Great Rebellion," published by Harper Brothers in 1866.

The following notice of Mr. Chadwick is taken from the *Philadelphia Times* of June, 1886:

Probably the best known of all men in any way connected with the game of base ball is Henry Chadwick, often referred to as the founder of the national game. Under his fostering care the game has grown from a crude sport to be the most popular pastime of the world, with a following counted by the millions. All the improvements made in the game in its early days were suggested by Mr. Chadwick. He was very justly referred to as the "authority," and the title still adheres to him. Mr. Chadwick, besides being the best known of all base-ball authors, has written a complete library of books referring to cricket and kindred sports. He has an imposing appearance, being over six feet in height, is heavily built, has an iron-gray beard, which adds a charm to his strong, ruddy face, and he has a pleasant, forcible way of expressing and explaining his ideas, which carries conviction with it.

Mr. Chadwick was born in England in 1824, and he is therefore in his sixty-second year. He is the son of Mr. James Chadwick, formerly editor of the *Western Times*, the principal West of England paper. He began his journalistic career in 1844, as contributor to the *Long Island Star*, of Brooklyn, but he did not adopt journalism as a profession until ten or twelve years later, when he became cricket reporter of the *New York Times*, in 1856. The same year he began writing for the *New York Clipper*, but was not regularly engaged on that journal until 1857. From 1856 to 1886 Mr. Chadwick was the leading reporter of base ball on the New York daily papers, he being the first to report the national game for the *New York Herald*, and he afterwards wrote up base ball for the *Times*, *Tribune*, *Sun*, *Daily News*, *Sunday Times*, *Sunday Dispatch*, and *Sunday Mercury*. All this time he was base-ball and cricket editor of the *New York Clipper*, and was on that paper from 1857 to 1867, when he gave up his position to take editorial charge of the *American Chronicle of Sports*. In 1868, however, he resumed his position on the *Clipper*, which he has since retained. In 1886 Mr. Chadwick concluded a period of thirty years of base-ball and cricket reporting on the New York dailies, and he permanently retired from that arena last winter, when he resigned all his positions on the dailies to accept a position on the editorial staff of *Outing*, a monthly magazine of sports, a position more congenial to his advancing years. In the '60s he took a position on the staff of the *Brooklyn Eagle*.

In "Chadwick's Game of Base Ball," published in 1868, Mr. Chadwick tells how he first became interested in the national game:

"It was in 1856," he says, "when, on returning from an early closing of a cricket match at Fox Hall, Hoboken, I chanced to go through the Elysian Fields during the progress of a base-ball match between the then noted Eagle and Gotham clubs. The game was being sharply played on both sides, and I watched it with deeper interest than any previous match of the kind I had seen. It was not long before I was struck with the idea that base ball was just the game for a national sport for Americans, and, reflecting on the subject on my return home, I came to the conclusion that from this game of ball a powerful lever might be made by means of which our people could be lifted into a position of more devotion to physical exercise and healthful out-door recreation than they had hitherto been noted for. From the period that I first became an ardent admirer of base ball I have devoted my efforts to the improvement of the game and to fostering it in every way I thought likely to promote the object I had in view, which was to build up a national field-game for Americans such as cricket was for England."

It would require pages to follow the progress of Mr. Chadwick from this period in the early history of base ball through that in which, as chairman of the committee on rules of the old National Association, he revised and improved the playing rules of the game, up to the time of the inauguration of the professional system of ball playing, when, after seeing the National League organized, he retired from further personal work in connection with association conventions, not, however, until he had seen the fruits of his early labors develop into a game fully established as the great popular field-sport of the country. Mr. Chadwick now devotes himself largely to the editing of books of instruction on the science of base-ball playing, striking examples of which are to be found in the series of base-ball books of the Spalding Library of Sports, published this season. Mr. Chadwick has been the unrelenting foe of all the abuses which have worked their way into the professional base-ball arena. He has no mercy for base-ball "crooks," no sympathy for drunken ball-tossers, and naturally is a strong opponent of that curse of all sports, pool gambling.

Mr. Chadwick has published the following books:

1884, Sports and Pastimes of American Boys, Routledge & Sons, publishers: 1885, Spalding Library of Athletic Sports, Spalding Bros., Chicago: 1860 to '78, Beadle's Dime Books of Base Ball, Cricket, Pedestrianism, Winter Sports, &c.: 1875, De Witt's Base-Ball Guide: also Cricket and Lacrosse, Chess, &c.: 1870, Chadwick's Base-Ball Manual, Churchill & Co., Boston: 1868, The American Game: How to Play It, Geo. Munro.

1855.

THOMAS LAWSON BOTTS, of New York City, son of No. 747, was born April 14, 1828 ; died June 5, 1854, a merchant. Married Catharine Martha Hamilton. Children : —

> 4449, ELLA FRANCES BOTTS, b. Oct. 29, 1852 ; m. *Henry Sickles*, Child : *William Sickles*. 4450, THOMAS, broker, New York City, b. July 19, 1854.

1857.

JULIAN BOTTS, of New York City, son of No. 747, an official of the Peoples' Insurance Company of New York, married Harriet Bishop. Children : —

> 4451, LYDIA FRANCES BOTTS, b. Jan. 2, 1859. 4452, CORA, b. 1865.

1859.

STEVENS KING BOTTS, of Brooklyn, N. Y., son of No. 747, married Mary Gaffney, a native of Ireland. Children : —

> 4457, VIRGINIA BROOKS BOTTS. 4458, HENRY CHADWICK. 4459, JOHN MINOR. 4460, KATE.

S. K. Botts, engaged in the insurance business up to 1861, entered the Ellsworth Zouave Regiment and fought at the first battle of Bull Run, where he was wounded in the face. He re-enlisted in the Tammany Regiment, N. Y. Vols., and was made Second Lieutenant, but resigned to accept a lieutenancy in Scott's Nine Hundred, a cavalry regiment, in which he served till the close of the war. He then secured an appointment in the Railway Postal Service, which he held till 1880, residing in Richmond ; since then a resident of Brooklyn, N. Y., and in the insurance business.

1858.

RANDOLPH BOTTS, of Albany, N. Y., son of No. 747, p. 219, married Cornelia Osborne, of Brooklyn. Children : —

4453, JOHN BOTTS. 4454, EMMA. 4455–6, Others d. y.

Mr. Botts was in business up to the outbreak of the war, when he enlisted in the Federal army and was made Assistant Quartermaster, with rank of Captain, and served through the war in that capacity, chiefly about Louisville and Catlettsburg, Ky., and afterwards with General Sherman during his march to the sea. Of late years he has been engaged with the Albany *Evening Journal.*

1854.

WILLIAM HENRY BOTTS, of Washington, D. C., son of No. 747, p. 216, was born Nov. 19, 1822 ; died in Washington, Sept., 1867. Married Evelina, daughter of John Ward Oddie, of New York, a native of England. Children :—

> 4464, ROSALIE BOTTS, b. 1845, m. *George W. Bates* ; children, 1, *Minnie Bates.* 2, *William.* 3, *Frederick.* 4, *Thomas.* 5, *Alison.* 4465, JOHN A., b. Oct., 1847, a clerk in War Dept., Washington, 1865–87, m. Julia Thompson ; children, 1, *Asbury H. Botts.* 2, *Adelaide.* 3, *Stella.* 4, *Julia May*, d. y. 5, *Frank.* 6, *Edna.* 7, *Henry.* 8, *Arthur.* 4466, EDWIN THORNE. 4467, BEVERLY RANDOLPH. 4468, ELIZABETH.

In business in New York until 1861, then Mr. Botts entered the service of the Quartermaster's Department, in which he remained until 1865. He then removed to Washington and practiced the profession of attorney until the time of his death.

1860.

BEVERLY BLAIR BOTTS, of Harrisonburg, Va., son of Hon. John Minor Botts, married VIRGINIA ANN BOTTS, daughter of No. 747, p. 219. Children:

> 4471, BEVERLY BOTTS, d. y. 4472, SUSAN, d. y.

Virginia Botts was a woman of remarkable beauty. Her husband was graduated at William and Mary College, 1848. During the latter part of the war he was connected with Quartermaster's Department in Washington. More recently he was Collector of Internal Revenue at Harrisonburg, Va. His second wife was Charlotte Lewis, daughter of Gen. Lewis and grand-daughter of Judge Lomax, of Va.

1861.

FRANCIS GOODE MORRISON, of Richmond, Va., son of No. 750, p. 219, was born Feb. 22, 1817, married Sept. 22, 1846, Martha A. White, of Isle of Wight Co., who died leaving one son, (2) Nov. 4, 1861, Mary C. Collins, of South Carolina.

> 4480, JAMES BROCKENBROUGH MORRISON, of Barberville, (Cabell C. H.) Cabell Co., W. Va. Children : 1, *Frank Morrison*, b. 1876, d. y. 2, *Ida*, b. 1850.
>
> 4481, MARY GOODE MORRISON, b. 1863. 4482, HELEN HUTCHINSON, b. 1864. 4483, WILLIAM ALONZO, b. 1867.

Mr. Morrison is Second Assistant in the Second Auditor's office, Richmond, and lives in Henrico Co., about four miles north of Richmond.

1864.

JOHN MORRISON, son of No. 750, p. 219, was born about 1823, and died about 1868. Married Caroline A. Wade, of Montgomery Co., Va. Children:—

> 4484, WADE BROCKENBROUGH MORRISON, of Round Rock, Williamson Co., Texas. 4485, MARY ELIZABETH, of Austin, Texas. 4486, SALLY, of Round Rock, Texas.

1866.

CAPT. FORTUNATUS SYDNOR MOSBY, son of Edward Carrington, and *Sally Bland Goode* Mosby, No. 751, p. 220, was born Sept. 22, 1827. He served through the war in the Confederate army, and subsequently went South and became Chief Engineer of the El Paso Railroad. Died, unmarried, at Columbus, Miss., April 27, 1873.

1867.

FRANCIS WADE MOSBY, of Columbus, Miss., son of No. 751, p. 220, was born May 1, 1830, at "Lethe," Powhatan Co., Va. married Sally Vick, daughter of Daniel and *Sarah Ewing Hill* Williams, of Columbus, Miss., formerly of Williamson Co., Tenn. Children :—

> 4487, SALLY BLAND GOODE MOSBY, b. July 8, 1861, d. Sept. 8, 1871. 4488, DANIEL WILLIAMS, b. May 21, 1863. 4489, FRANCIS WADE, b. Feb. 20, 1869. 4490, EDNA EWING, b. Jan. 16, 1875.

Francis Wade Mosby was educated in Powhatan, in the common schools of the county, moved to Richmond, Va., in 1848, and in 1856 removed to Columbus, Miss. At the outbreak of the war between the States enlisted in the 35th Regt. Miss. Volunteers, and was detailed to act in the Quartermaster's Department ; from 1862 to 1865 was traveling agent for the ordnance department of the Selma arsenal. Since the war he has been engaged in mercantile pursuits in Mississippi.

1869.

LIEUT. EDWARD CARRINGTON MOSBY, of Philadelphia, son of No. 751, p. 220, was born January 15, 1834. Married in DeKalb, Bowie Co., Texas, Mar. 7, 1858, Mrs. Mary Jane Crosby, born May 19, 1837, widow of William M. Crosby, of South Carolina, and dau. of William Lee, M. D., of Philadelphia. The widow and children lived in Philadelphia, 1882. Children :—

> 4491, SALLY BLAND GOODE MOSBY, b. Feb. 11, 1859, christened by Father Hennepin, of Nacogdoches. 4492, ELLEN THERESE, b.

June 12, 1861. 4493, JAMES EDWARD, b. April 13, 1866, at Sulphur Springs, Red River Co., Texas. 4494, MARY LEE, b. April 9, 1869. 4495, FRANCIS.

He went to Clarksville, Texas, 1855-7, and lived there until 1861, when he enlisted in a Texas regiment, C. S. A., fought at the battle of Shiloh, and was subsequently promoted to be Lieutenant of Engineers. After the war he became civil engineer for a railroad in Pennsylvania, and died in Philadelphia April 5, 1873.

1871.

MAJ. ROBERT GOODE MOSBY, of Richmond, Va., son of Edward C. and *Sally Bland Goode* Mosby was born at Jefferson, Powhatan Co., Va., Feb. 21, 1838. Married Nov. 25, 1862, Mary Gary, daughter of Dr. Geo. B. and *Emily P. Hodge* Hughes, of Prince Edward and Cumberland. Children :—

> 4496, WILLIAM WASHINGTON WADE MOSBY, b. 1866. 4497, CARRINGTON SYDNOR. 4498, EMILY JOHN. 4499, GEORGE HUGHES SPEED. 4500, MARTHA HUGHES. 4501, EDWARD FORTUNATUS. 4502, VIRGINIA BLAND.

Maj. Mosby was educated at Georgetown College. At the outbreak of the war he was clerk in the U. S. Navy, cruising in the Pacific in the "Lancaster," commanded by his kinsman, Commodore Rudd. He alone, of all on board, refused to take the oath of allegiance, and was put on shore at Chagres. Having made his way into the Confederate lines through New York city, through Ohio, Indiana and Illinois to Kentucky, he raised, in Powhatan Co., Company I, of the 59th Virginia Infantry, and subsequently was made Major in the 59th regiment of infantry of Brig. Gen. Wise's brigade, and was in the works at Petersburg at the explosion of "the crater," but marvelously escaped, and while leading a party sent to the rear of the Northern Army as it lay before Petersburg was captured with his command and imprisoned at Johnson's Island, where he remained till the close of the war.

1872.

WILLIAM WASHINGTON MOSBY, JR., son of No. 751, p. 220, was born Feb. 1, 1840. He was educated at Georgetown College. Just out of school, at the beginning of the war, he enlisted a few days after Virginia passed the ordnance of secession, in the "Powhatan Troop" of cavalry, C. S. A., and died at Hanover Academy Hospital June 6, 1862.

1876.

JAMES MITCHEL, of Powhatan Co., Va., married ELIZABETH HUGHES MOSBY, dau. of No. 752, p. 220, b. 1840, d. Aug. 17, 1873, at her father's plantation, "Comotomo," in Powhatan Co. Children :—

> 4504, JANE VERNER MITCHEL, b. Sept., 1872, d. Aug. 23, 1873.

James Mitchel was son of John Mitchel, the "Irish Patriot," graduate of Trinity College, Dublin, a political exile who came to this country in 1853, went back to Ireland in 1874, and was returned to Parliament from Tipperary, and died 1875. He had two sons killed in the Confederate army, and a daughter, Mary, who married, 1867, Roger Jones Page, of Louisville, Ky. (See "Page Family," p. 125.)

1877.

EDWARD TRAVIS SPOTSWOOD, M. D., of Perryville, Ind., son of No. 754, p. 225. Married Miss Schermerhorn, of New York. Children :—

4505, EDWIN SPOTSWOOD. 4506, MARY BLAND.

1880.

WILLIAM CHURCHILL SPOTSWOOD, of Williamsburg, Va., son of No. 755, was born about 1830. At the opening of the war he entered the army, and lost his reason through the hardship of soldier life. He died in 1870 in the Asylum at Williamsburg, of which he was librarian.

1881.

EDWIN ALLISON SPOTSWOOD, of Memphis, Tenn., son of No. 755, was born Sept. 9, 1834. Married (1) Mary Armour, (2) Mary Smith, of Hernando, Miss. Children :—

4507, EDWIN SPOTSWOOD, JR.

Mr. Spotswood was a soldier in the C. S. A., and served on the staff of Gen. Forrest, with the rank of Captain, and is now a successful merchant of Memphis.

1883.

JOHN ROWZIE SPOTSWOOD, son of No. 755, was born Sept. 13, 1832. A soldier C. S. A. While at home on furlough and sick with typhoid fever he was taken from his bed by a raiding party and sent to Fort Delaware. He contracted dysentery in prison from the bad water and poor food, was exchanged at City Point, and two weeks after died in Petersburg in spite of the best of care.

1884.

ALEXANDER DANDRIDGE SPOTSWOOD, of Orange Co., Va., son of No. 755, was born Nov. 12, 1836. Married Lucy Gordon. Children :—

4511, LELIA SPOTSWOOD. 4512, GORDON.

He served through the war, and surrendered at Appomattox. He is a farmer, and lives at the old home, "Orange Grove," Orange Co., Va.

1887.

DR. EDWIN SPOTSWOOD LEMOINE, of St. Louis, son of John E. Lemoine, No. 756, was born in Petersburg, Va., Aug. 27, 1826.

One of the leading physicians of St. Louis. Married May 7, 1857, Kate P. Rice, daughter of Rev. N. L. Rice, D. D., a distinguished divine of the Presbyterian church. Children : —

>   4515, LOUIS R. LEMOINE, of Philadelphia, Pa., m. Augusta Blair, of St. Louis. Daughter, 1, *Marie Louise Lemoine.* 4516, EDWIN SPOTS-WOOD. 4517, CATHARINE BLAND. 4518, JOHN BOTT. 4519, ADELE GOODE. 4520, MARY GOODE, d. y. 4521, EVA SPOTS-WOOD. 4522, GENEVIEVE.

1888.

ROBERT N. NESBET, of St. Louis, married April 12, 1849, MARY GOODE LEMOINE, daughter of No. 756, p. 227, was born in Petersburg, Va., April 8, 1828, died in St. Louis Jan. 7, 1853. Children : —

>   4523, JOHN LEMOINE NESBET, of New York, Secretary and Treasurer, Ontario and Western R. R. Co., m. Fanny Britton, of St. Louis. Children, 1, *Robert Nesbet;* 2, *Louise.*

1889.

PAUL ESTAN LEMOINE, of St. Louis, Mo., son of No. 756, is engaged in mercantile pursuits. He has rendered important aid in the preparation of this work, for which the writer returns grateful acknowl-edgements.

1893.

COL. MUSCOE LIVINGSTON SPOTSWOOD, of Richmond, Va., son of No. 757, was born at Culpeper, Va., April 20, 1850. He was educated at the Virginia Military Institute, where he graduated with distinction in 1872, then read law with Judge William Green, and is now practising his profession in Richmond. He is a prominent officer in the Virginia State Guard ; was in command of the Guard of the Commonwealth (Co. C, First Va. Inf.) at the Yorktown celebration, and of the Virginia troops at the funeral of Gen. Grant and the inaug-uration of President Cleveland. He is now Colonel of the First Reg-iment of Virginia Inf. He was elected to the Virginia Legislature in 1881. Col. Spotswood is unmarried.

1896.

PETER DUPUY McKINNEY, of Richmond, Va., son of William and *Martha Branch Dupuy* McKinney, was born June 6, 1815, died Aug. 6. 1875. Married SARAH ANN LYLE, daughter of No. 76., born Oct. 13, 1824, died Jan. 22, 1885. Children : —

>   4530, WILLIAM BARRETT McKINNEY, b. May 13, 1859. 4531, HELEN LE VERT, b. Feb. 28, 1858. 4532, LELIA BLAND, b. Sept. 20, 1861, d. July 4, 1862. 4533, CHARLES LYLE, b. Feb. 21, 1866.

Mr. McKinney was a commission merchant in Richmond for many years. A useful and highly respected citizen. Mr. Dupuy was descended in the fifteenth generation from Bartholomew Dupuy, the Huguenot, whose romantic story has already been referred to in these pages, and a list of whose descendants is given by Mr. Brock in the fifth volume of the Collections of the Virginia Historical Society. (See p. 159.)

1897.

Col. S. BASSETT FRENCH, of Manchester, Va., son of Rev. Dr. John and *Frances Moseley* French and a descendant of William Bassett, one of the corporators of William and Mary College, and of the Moseleys and Newtons of Norfolk, was born in the Borough of Norfolk, March 31, 1820. Married March, 5, 1846, HELEN BLAND LYLE, daughter of No. 761. Children :—

> 4534, JANE S. FRENCH, b. Jan. 3, 1847, d. Aug. 4, 1857. 4535, FANNY MOSELEY, b. Dec. 16, 1848. 4536, HELEN BLAND, b. Jan. 31, 1851, married *Robert Bolling Batte*. 4537, JOHN MARSDEN, b. Dec. 29, 1853, married Florence, daughter of Henry Holland, Oct. 7, 1884 ; one child. 1, *Lewis Marsden French*, b. Nov. 12, 1885. 4358, SALLIE BASSETT, b. Jan. 10, 1857, m. *George E. Gary*, of Manchester, Jan. 2, 1884. 4539, BASSETT CHARLES LEWIS, b. Aug. 18, 1858, m. a lady of Morganton, N. C.; child, 1, *Bassett French*. 4540, ANNIE COOPER, b. Aug. 30, 1860, m. *Robert Stanley Robertson*, of Manchester, Dec. 31, 1881, 2 children, 1, *Helen Lyle Robertson*, b. Oct. 23, 1883, 2, *Robert Stanley*, b. Dec. 8, 1885. 4541, JAMES LYLE, b. Oct. 13, 1862, d. Oct. 31, 1862. 4542, ROBERT LEE, b. Dec. 7, 1863. 4543. CARY BROADNAX, b. Dec. 9, 1867.

Col. French was educated at the classical school of George Halson, in Norfolk, Va., is alumnus of Hampden Sidney College, studied law with Robert Y. Conrad, of Winchester, Va.; licensed to practice law in 1840 ; removed to Chesterfield Co. in 1841 ; was attorney for Commonwealth in Circuit Court of Chesterfield for several years, and assistant clerk of House of Delegates of Virginia. Served through the war between the States as confidential Aide and secretary to Governors Letcher and Smith ; surrendered to Gen. Meade at Burkeville April 13, 1865 ; secretary to Lee Monument Association, and elected by unanimous vote of General Assembly, in 1880, corporation judge of city of Manchester.

Mrs. French and her sister and brothers inherited " Whitby," the homestead of the Goodes, which was owned originally by John Goode, the immigrant ancestor of all of the name in the South, and descended in regular succession without being once out of the possession of a descendant until it was sold in 1875 to A. D. Williams

1898.

DR. JAMES LYLE CLARKE, of Mariposa Co., Cal., son of Colin and *Mary Goode Lyle* Clarke, No. 763, p. 229, was born Feb. 9, 1819, in

Richmond, Va. Was Ass't Surgeon of Voltigeurs, U. S. A., appointed April 9, 1847, and served through the Mexican war. Went at an early day to California, and entered upon the practice of his profession in Mariposa Co., Cal., where he died in 1866. Unmarried.

1900.

DR. DOUGLAS H. GORDON, of Baltimore, Md., was born in Fredericksburg. A physician. Married July 8, 1845, MARY ELLEN CLARKE, daughter of No. 715. Daughter :—

> 4544, MARY ELLEN GORDON, m. *J. C. Wilson*, son, 1, *Gordon Wilson*, b. 1876.

1902.

Gov. JOHN L. MANNING, of Milford, Clarendon Co., S. C., was born in South Carolina about 1820, and was Governor of the State 1852. Subsequently, retired from public life and engaged in planting. Married, April 26, 1848, SALLY BLAND LYLE, daughter of No. 715, who was born Jan. 23, 1828, died December 31, 1884. Children:—

> 4545, ELLEN CLARKE MANNING, b. 1858.   4546, COLIN CLARKE, b. 1869.

The *Charleston Courier* of April 20, 1884, describing a wedding in Clarendon Co., S. C., remarks: "On Thursday Governor Manning opened his Milford' mansion. Whoever has visited this house knows that the antiquarian and the scholar, the artist and the architect can all find ample scope for enjoyment within its halls. There may be seen the halberd of the crusader and antique busts of Hercules and of Jupiter, of Scipio and of Cæsar. There also are portraits by Lely, vases, Japanese, American and Chinese, and bric-a-brac of all kinds. The architect can look upon doors of solid mahogany, both faces of which are of plate-glass mirrors imported from France, and running from floor to ceiling. * * * On Thursday last in this house was danced a remarkable measure. Four generations in one quadrille. At the head stood Mrs. Mary Goode Clarke, eighty-two years of age. Her partner was Gov. John L. Manning, himself no child, but whose brown eyes had lost no fire, and whose lofty form had not yet learned to stoop. Vis-a-vis to them was Mrs. Manning, daughter of Mrs. Clarke, a lady of noble mien—stately, handsome, dignified and portly, yet graceful. The ends of the set were occupied by Mrs. Gordon Wilson, granddaughter of Mrs. Clarke, and by her son, Master Gordon Wilson, a lad of eight years. Thus great-grandmother danced with great-grandson, and four generations walked the minuet together.

"Mrs. Mary Goode Clarke; who is she and what is her lineage? Richard Bland, the Cato of the American Revolution. From him on one side Mary Bland; from her Light Horse Harry and Robert E. Lee. On the other side Theo. Bland, with the blood of John Randolph, of Roanoke."

Gov. Manning is the grandson of Gov. Laurence Manning, one of the heroes of Eutaw Springs. He was a private in the "Palmetto Guards" at the opening of the war and the bombardment of Fort Sumter. For a graphic sketch of the times and people, see F. G. DeFontaine's sketch, "The First Day of Real War," in the *Southern Bivouac*, July, 1886.

1903.

CAPT. MAXWELL T. CLARKE, of Richmond, Va., was born in Richmond June 10, 1830. Married, June 2, 1857, Ellen Scott, daughter of No. 216. Children:—

> 4547, A son, died at age of 1 year. 4548, MARY GRACE CLARKE, b. March 20, 1862. 4549, SALLY BLAND, b. May 3, 1870. 4550, ELLEN SCOTT, b. May 3, 1870.

Educated at the University of Virginia. Studied law, and in 1857, entered a mercantile career.

In April, 1861, he enlisted in Co. F 1st Virginia Regiment, as a private. Was transferred to the Confederate navy, and after performing battery duty upon the Potomac was appointed Lieutenant Commander, and served upon the James River until the close of the war. Was engaged in the attack on Drewry's Bluff, as well as in thwarting the futile efforts of Gen. Butler to cut through Dutch Gap. Since the war has been in business in Richmond, a member of the firm of Scott & Clarke, "tobacco stemmers, rehandlers, and leaf-buyers, on commission." Vice-president of " F Company Association," organized, Oct. 19, 1876, by the survivors of the F Company of volunteers who served through the war. President of the City Council.

1904.

MAJ. COLIN D. CLARKE, C. S. A., son of Colin and *Mary Goode Lyle* Clarke, No. 763, p. 229, was born Mar. 22, 1832, died Sept., 1862. Married, Nov. 6, 1885, Betty Berkley, daughter of Rev. John Cooke, of Hanover Co., Va. Children:—

> 4553, MARY ELLEN CLARKE, d. y. 4554, ELLEN DOUGLAS. m. *John White*, of Austin, Tex., lawyer. 4555, ELIZABETH B. 4556, COLIN D., living in New York in 1885, an official of the Erie Railroad.

Major Clarke was a Quartermaster in the Confederate service, and died during the Peninsula campaign, from the effects of exposure while on duty. Mrs. Clarke lives in New York city.

1905.

COL. JOHN LYLE CLARKE, of Baltimore, Md., son of No. 763, was born Dec. 16, 1833. Married Nov. 12, 1856, Martha May Clarke, daughter of William H. and Eliza A. Clarke, of "Banister Lodge," Halifax Co., Va., whose mother was the daughter of Patrick Henry, eldest son of PATRICK HENRY the patriot. Mrs. Clarke died Dec. 29, 1866. Child :—

> 4557, MARY LYLE CLARKE.

J. Lyle Clarke was educated at the Rappahannock Military Academy, and in 1852, went to Baltimore, where he has since resided.

At the time of the secession of the South he was Captain of Co. A, "Independent Grays," of the 53d Reg't Maryland State Militia, and after the passage of the Federal troops through the city, on the 19th of April, 1861, he, with a large number of the men in his command, made their way to Richmond, via Harper's Ferry, when, May 24, 1861, they were mustered into the service as the "Maryland Guard of the Maryland Line, C. S. A.," which subsequently became Co. B of the 21st Virginia Regiment.

Mr. Clarke was soon promoted to be Major and Assistant Adjutant General on the staff of Maj. Gen. Loring, and Oct. 5, 1862, was commissioned as Lieutenant Colonel, and placed in command of the 30th Virginia Battalion of Sharpshooters, better known as " Clarke's Battalion." In July, 1864, he was disabled near Staunton, while with Early on his march into Maryland.

In 1879 a series of articles by S. Z. A(mmen) entitled "Doings of the Maryland Boys in Gray from '61 to '65," was published in the *Baltimore Telegram*, which consisted chiefly of personal reminiscences gathered from the words of Col. Clarke. I should be glad to quote them entire, but space will allow the introduction of only a few paragraphs.

When the Maryland Guard was first organized in Richmond, two Confederate battle-flags were sent to them by Baltimore ladies, who had made them; the second, which reached them in August, had an interesting history. While the ladies were engaged in making it, orders for the arrest of them engaged upon it were issued by the Federal officers in Baltimore. But neither the flag nor those making it could be found. It passed from house to house until completed, and Mr. John A. Robb tells the story that it was concealed by his wife at night under the table on which he played cards, and he had many a game over it without suspecting its existence. To be taken South it was put inside the cushion of a buggy that was going to Harper's Ferry. The buggy was captured, but the cushion was afterwards regained. It was finally brought through the lines by a lady who wore it as a bustle. The colors were of elaborate make, and displayed the coat of arms of the State of Maryland. Col. Clark still has both flags.

Col. Clarke's recollections of Jackson's Valley campaign are also very interesting:

In December, 1861, while in winter quarters in the cottages of the Bath Alum Springs, their brigade was ordered to join Stonewall Jackson at Winchester, and they were with him in the celebrated Valley campaign.

"The 1st of January, 1862, was a bright and beautiful day, and the troops began their march upon the Romney road in high spirits. No one knew where he was going, and the perplexity was increased when about ten miles out from Winchester Capt. Clarke's company was suddenly directed to 'take the right-hand road'—a narrow and obscure cross-road, which brought them out ultimately into the main road leading to Bath. Next day it snowed and became extremely cold. The remainder of the march of some fifty miles was through a rough mountainous country, amid rain, sleet, ice and snows often repeated. Many of the men were barefooted and badly clothed, so that their sufferings from the bitter cold and keen mountain winds and the frozen and broken roads were indescribable, far exceeding the pathetic traditions of Valley Forge."

The following is a history of "Clarke's Battalion:"

"In 1862, in order to have a suitable force to oppose the mountaineer riflemen serving with the Federals in Western Virginia, it was thought expedient to organize a battalion of sharpshooters, consisting of good shots picked from the entire division. The service demanded men of quick intelligence, vim and dash, and the Maryland boys impressed the General as having these qualities in an eminent degree. Maj. Clarke of Gen. Lowry's staff was promoted to Lieut.-Col., to raise, organize and command the battalion, (the 30th Va. Battalion of Sharpshooters, better known as 'Clarke's Battalion.') Suitable men were invited to volunteer, and four companies were speedily formed. Two others, composed of artillerymen who had lost their guns at Fort Donelson, were soon after added. Clarke's Battalion was organized at the Narrows of New River, Sept. 2, 1862, and attached to Wharton's Brigade.

"The Battalion served at Fayette C. H. and Charleston, then went to the salt works in Washington Co., Va., to protect them from a threatened raid, then to Carter's Station, Tenn., to protect the building of the Holston bridge, thence by forced march, by way of Staunton to re-enforce Lee in Maryland. The Battalion met him at Winchester returning from Gettysburg, and then went into winter quarters at Orange C. H., subsequently serving at 'Bull's Gap' with Longstreet. At the battle of 'New Market,' May 15, 1864, Col. Clarke within the space of two or three minutes lost forty-eight of his men. The Battalion also fought at 'Cold Harbor.'

"About the middle of July, being at that time in command of the brigade to which his battalion was attached, Col. Clarke was resting by the roadside near Staunton, under an oak tree, when a dead limb fell from the top, wounding him upon the head very severely and breaking and crushing his legs. The wounds were dangerous and exceedingly painful, and one of them has never entirely healed. It is hardly necessary to say that he was disabled for the rest of the war.   The command accompanied Early in his various subsequent fortunes and misfortunes till the close of the war."

1906.

Prof. POWHATAN CLARKE, of Baltimore, Md., son of Colin and *Mary Goode Lyle Clarke*, No. 763, p. 229, was born Sept. 19, 1836, at "Warner Hall," Gloucester Co.,Va.   Married, 1861, Louise F. Boyce.   Children:

> 4558, LIEUT. POWHATAN H. CLARKE, U. S. A., b. in Rapides, La., Oct. 9, 1862. 4559, HENRY BOYCE, b. Mar. 9, 1872, in 1886 at St. Mary's College. 4560, MARY ELIZABETH, b. May 7, 1876.

Prof. Clarke was educated at the University of Virginia, graduated at the University of New York in medicine, and studied two years in Paris. Was made Surgeon of Louisiana State University in Rapides, La., of which Gen. William T. Sherman was Superintendent, and was subsequent to the war made one of the Board of Visitors by the Governor.   He entered the Confederate Army as a private in the Crescent Regt.; was made Adjutant of 10th Mississippi Cav. at the battle of Shiloh ; passed examination as Captain of Ordnance in 1863, and was made Chief of Ordnance in Brig. Gen. C. J. Polignac's Brigade. Was made Lieut. Col. and Chief of Ordnance of District of West Louisiana and Arkansas by Lieut. Gen. S. B. Buckner, and surrendered at Natchitoches, La., in April, 1865. Removed to Baltimore, Md., in 1872, and was made Professor of Natural Sciences in Baltimore City College, which position he still holds.   He is Vice President of the Maryland Academy of Sciences.

Mrs. Clarke is the daughter of Thomas Henry Boyce, of Rapids Point, La., died 1873, U. S. District Judge for many years, and elected to U. S. Senate after late war, but refused his seat, and Irene Archinand, of an old Swiss family, whose great grandfather was commandant of Northwest Louisiana under Spanish rule.

1920.

COL. ARTHUR HERBERT, of Alexandria, Va., son of William and *Maria Dulany* Herbert, married ALICE GOODE GREGORY, daughter of William A. and *Maria Harrison* Gregory, granddaughter of William H. and *Louisa Goode* Harrison, No. 248, p. 120. Children :

> 4570, MAY GREGORY. 4571, ALICE. 4572, MARIANNE. 4573, FLORENCE. 4574, NORA.

Col. Herbert is a descendant of the Fairfax family of Belvoir, and great-great-grand son of the first William Fairfax of "Belvoir," President of the Council of Virginia, whose son, the Rev. Bryan Fairfax, succeeded to the title of Lord Fairfax, of Greenway Court, upon his death in 1781.* He was a gallant officer of the 17th Virginia Infantry, C. S. A., and since the war has been a banker in Alexandria. His home, "Muckross," occupies a commanding position on the heights back of Alexandria, about midway between "Arlington" and "Mount Vernon," the house being picturesquely placed within the earthworks of an old fortification.

1921.

WILLIAM GREGORY, of Petersburg, Va., is a planter, son of William Arthur and *Maria Harrison* Gregory, of "Linden," Prince George Co., Va., grandson of Elijah Gregory, of Petersburg.

The record on page 231 of this work is erroneous, and should be cancelled. The names of the children of No. 248, p. 120, having been omitted, for lack of information, on page 231, will be given below, although properly belonging in the sixteenth instead of the seventeenth generation.

1922 (777.)

SURG. RICHARD J. HARRISON, U. S. N., son of No. 248, p. 120, was born about 1810. He was appointed Assistant Surgeon in the U. S. Navy Sept. 1837, and died at Port Mahon in 1842, while on duty with the Mediterranean squadron.

The names of the children of Col. William Harrison, of "Chester," entered under Nos. 773-6, inclusive, on page 120, should be cancelled.

1923 (778.)

WILLIAM HARRISON, of "Chester," Sussex Co., Va., planter, son of Benjamin and —— *Trezevant* Harrison, married his first cousin, LUCY HARRISON, daughter of No. 248. Children :—

---

* THE FAIRFAX FAMILY has been more fully descended perhaps than any other in America save that of Washington. See Slaughter's "Life of Randolph Fairfax," p. 62–66; Browning's "Americans of Royal Descent," p. 27; Meade's "Old Churches and Families of Virginia," II, pp. 106, 281 ; "Dinwiddie Papers," I, pp. 19-20, and various magazine articles, catalogued in Poole's Index: also the British Peerages.

4575, TREZEVANT HARRISON, of North Carolina. 4576, RICHARD, of Austin, Texas, banker, 4577. WILLIAM, of Louisville, Ky. 4578, KATE.

It is to be regretted that the records of so large and prominent a family as that of Harrison of Virginia should have been allowed to become lost. The Harrisons of "Chester" in Sussex, are undoubtedly identical with those of "Berkeley" and "Brandon," and the relationship was recognized by members of the earlier generations.

Col. William H. Harrison, of "Chester," had brothers, Benjamin (father of No. 1923 and No. 1927) and John. Their father was William Harrison, son of William Harrison, who must have been born 1700 to 1730. In all probability this was the grandson of the Hon. Benjamin Harrison, of Surry, who was born in Southwick Parish, England, 1645, died 1712, and who was father of Benjamin Harrison, of "Berkeley,', and Nathaniel Harrison, of "Wakefield."

1925 (780.)

RUFUS K. HARRISON, of Stony Creek, Sussex Co., Va., son of William and *Louisa Alice Goode* Harrison, of "Chester," Sussex Co., was born about 1830. Married Henrietta Dillard, of Sussex Co. Children :—

4581, LAURA HARRISON. 4582, GEORGE. 4583, HENRIETTA.

R. K. Harrison was appointed a cadet in the U. S. Military Academy in 1846, but did not complete his course. He served through the war in Co. B, 7th Virginia Cavalry, C. S. A. He is now a farmer and Superintendent of Schools in his native county.

1927 (782.)

FRANK HARRISON, of "Crosses," Sussex Co., Va., a farmer, brother of No. 778, married VIRGINIA HARRISON, daughter of No. 248. Children :—

4584, JUNUS HARRISON. 4585, OTIS. 4586, WILLIAM.

1929 (784.)

THOMAS HARRISON, of Greenville Co., Va., farmer, married Mary Vaughan. Children:—

4587, SAMUEL HARRISON. 4588, FRANK. 4589, THOMAS.

1930.

DR. WESLEY HARRISON, of Texas, son of No. 248, p. 120, has a son :—

4590, CHESTER HARRISON and a daughter.

1931 (785.)

DR. WILLIAM OVERTON, of Stony Creek, Sussex Co., Va., married ALICE HARRISON, daughter of No. 184, p. 120. Daughter:—

4591, FANNY OVERTON.

2002.

REV. OSCAR S. BUNTING, of Harrisonburg, Va.. son of J. B. and *Mary Lindsay* Bunting, of Bristol, Tenn., married Nov., 1879, MARY HARRISS, daughter of Samuel Goode and *Mary A. Plummer* Harriss, No. 786, who was born Jan. 22, 1861. Children:

4600, MARY HARRIS BUNTING, b. 1880. 4601, OSCAR LINDSAY, b. 1883. 4602, PLUMMER GOODE, b. 1885.

Mr. Bunting is a graduate of Richmond College and the Theological Seminary of Virginia.

2003.

BENJAMIN LEE PARTLOW, of Lexington, Va., son of Milton Young and *Mary Eliza Lambert* Partlow, of Rappahannock Co., Va., married, Dec. 10, 1884, FRANCES LOVE HARRISON, daughter of No. 786.

Mr. Partlow was educated at St. John's Academy, in Alexandria, Va., where he attained the highest honor in his class. He was for some time an officer of the Baltimore and Ohio R. R., and is now a resident of Lexington, Va., in the employment of the Richmond and Alleghaney R. R.

2006.

DR. WILLIAM O. BASKERVILLE, of Oxford, N. C., son of GEORGE T. and LUCY GOODE BASKERVILLE, Nos. 790 and 820, pp. 233 and 123, was born July 25, 1854, married Oct. 9, 1878, Mattie, daughter of Henry Clay Watkins, of Richmond, Va. Children:—

4605, CORINNE BASKERVILLE, d. y. 4606, MATTIE.

Dr. Baskerville was graduated at the Virginia Military Institute and the Virginia Medical College, and has for some years been in practice in North Carolina.

2007.

C. THOMAS BASKERVILLE, of Boydton, Va., son of Nos. 790 and 820, was born Nov. 13, 1856. Married PATTIE E. FINCH, No. 378, daughter of L. E. FINCH, No. 1400, and MARTHA BOYD and LUCY GOODE, No. 857. Child:—

4608, LOUISE GORDON BASKERVILLE.

Mr. Baskerville was graduated from the Virginia Military Institute and the Law School of the University of Virginia. He was for a time partner of the Hon. John Goode in the practice of law, and is now postmaster at Boydton, Va., and editor and proprietor of the *Mecklenburg Democrat*. His daughter is, perhaps, more a representative of the Goode family than any one now living, since her four grand parents were all Goode descendants in different lines from the same ancestry.

2030.

HON. THOMAS GOODE JONES, of Montgomery, Ala., son of SAMUEL GOODE and *Martha W. Goode* Jones, No. 798, was born Nov. 26, 1846. Married Dec. 20, 1866, Gena C. Bird. Children:—

4651, MARSHAL BIRD JONES, b. Nov. 3, 1869. 4652, GENA MOORE, b. Nov. 26, 1871. 4653, MARTHA GOODE, b. Aug. 10, 1874. 4654, CARRIE BIRD, Aug. 25, 1876. 4655, GORDON HOUSTON, b. June 15, 1880. 4656, THOMAS GOODE, b. June 9, 1885.

Col. Jones was born in Macon, Ga., Nov. 26, 1844. In his infancy his parents removed to Montgomery, which has since been his home. At the outbreak of the war he was a cadet at the Virginia Military Institute, and was ordered, with other cadets, to Richmond to drill the volunteers there.

In 1862, he served in Jackson's celebrated valley campaign, and at its conclusion enlisted in the cavalry. Gen. Jackson, who, as a professor at the Institute, had known young Jones as a cadet, gave him a recommendation for appointment in the regular army. Upon this Gen. John B. Gordon appointed young Jones his Aide-de-Camp. He served on Gen. Gordon's staff during the remainder of the war, being twice promoted and several times wounded.

For "gallant conduct at Bristoe" he was commended in orders and personally thanked by Gen. Robert E. Lee. The same officer sent his thanks to the brave young Alabamian for his services at Hare's Hill, where, in the presence of Gen. Lee, young Jones volunteered to cross the space between the works of the two armies, which was plowed by a terrific fire of cannon and small arms, to bear Gordon's order for the withdrawal of his troops from the positions they had captured.

He was in the last action at Appomattox, and bore one of the flags of truce sent into the enemies lines just before the surrender. Gen. Gordon says of him:

"He was an invaluable officer, and young as he was, gave evidence of high military talent. He was assigned to my staff when a beardless boy, and was with me in whatever trials I experienced myself during the war. He never failed to discharge his duty, not only willingly, but gladly, whatever may be the promised cost. I may truthfully say, without one particular of exaggeration, that if the facts connected with his services in the Confederate army were written out it would furnish as thrilling a romance as one ever read."

At the close of the war he returned home and engaged in planting, and at the same time read law in the office of the late John A. Elmore, and afterwards under the direction of his near neighbor and friend, the late Chief Justice A. J. Walker. He was admitted to the bar in 1866.

His planting operations resulted disastrously. He surrendered everything to creditors, not even reserving a homestead, and devoted a large share of his professional earnings afterwards to paying these debts.

In 1868, he was one of the editors of the *Daily Picayune*, a Democratic paper published at Montgomery, and evinced much ability as a writer. In 1869, he was one of the Democratic nominees for aldermen of the city, but was defeated with the rest of the ticket.

His oration at Montgomery on Memorial Day, 1874, was a classical production full of thought and beauty, and at once brought him prominently before the country. The press throughout the Union published extensive extracts from it, pronouncing them high types of Southern oratory and feeling. The earnest and thoughtful words of the young Confederate, who would not wrong the cause by arguing its rights, and yet hoped that "something higher and nobler would rise from the graves of all our heroic dead than a sectional vendetta between the North and South," created a profound impression at the North; and were not the least among the happy causes which combined in 1874, to check the further tide of vindictiveness against the Southern people.

He was one of Gov. Houston's military staff in 1874, but resigned in 1876 to accept the Captaincy of the Montgomery Greys. He resigned the command of the Greys in 1880 to accept the colonelcy of the Second Regiment of State troops, which office he still holds. This regiment is one of the best in the country, and in morale, discipline and manly deportment is excelled by none. On several occasions portions of it have been ordered out under his command to suppress lawlessness, and each time peace was restored without bloodshed or bitterness. These triumphs of moral power, rather than that of mere physical force, were due not more to the splendid body of men under him than to the firm and humane hand which guided them.

He was put to a severe test at Birmingham, Ala., on his entrance with troops to restore order there on the night of Dec. 4, 1883. Of his conduct there the Governor in a general order, said :—

"Col. Jones, the commanding officer, was charged with a grave responsibility and a large discretion under circumstances of the greatest difficulty; and to his courage, temper, prudence and skill is mainly due the repression of a dangerous revolt against the laws and dignity of the State."

In 1875, when the affairs of the city of Montgomery were in a deplorable condition, and required almost Herculean efforts set matters to rights, he was one of the Democratic nominees for aldermen, and was elected. During four successive administrations he took a laborious and prominent part in shaping and executing the various measures and policies which aided in restoring its prosperity. The reports written by him on the numerous important matters arising during this period of the city's history, would make an ordinary printed volume, and added greatly to his reputation as a writer and thinker. While in the city council he published a paper on "Quarantine Law," which was extensively copied in medical and legal periodicals, and is now quoted an authority on such subjects. He resigned from the council after nine years' service.

In 1880, he resigned the office of reporter of the Supreme Court, which he had long filled with credit to himself, and satisfaction to bench and bar, to give his attention to the practice of his profession, in which he had gradually, but surely attained high rank.

In 1884, he was nominated and elected in a most flattering manner to a seat in the General Assembly. He took a prominent and useful part in the session of 1884–5, and soon became one of the acknowledged leaders of the House. His services were highly appreciated by his constituents, and he was renominated by a practically unanimous vote at the Democratic primaries and convention in the spring of 1886, and elected in August following. He was Speaker of the House Nov. 9, 1886.

Of irreproachable integrity and stainless character in all the relations of life; hospitable, generous and public spirited; tolerant of opposition, yet tenacious of his own convictions; of an open nature, pleasing address and great kindliness of heart, he has long enjoyed in full measure the confidence and good will of his fellow men.—*Montgomery Advertiser, Nov.* 9, 1886.

2031.

DR. WILLIAM GESNER, of Birmingham, Ala., son of Abraham Gesner, M. D., F. G. S., and a chemist by profession, married June 21, 1866, MARY VIRGINIA JONES, daughter of No. 798, born Sept. 20, 1815.

2034.

EDWIN FRANCIS JONES, of Montgomery, Ala., married April 18, 1820, *Bertha Stubbs*. A Civil Engineer. Educated at the Virginia Military Institute.   1 son :—

4657, SAMUEL BEYTOP JONES.

2045.

DR. EDMUNDS MASON, of Hicksford, Greenville Co., Va., son of No. 799, was born Dec. 19, 1836. Married Josephine Thibault, of Little Rock, Ark. Children:—

4671, GEORGE MASON. 4672, CECILE. 4673, LUCY BURNS.

Dr. Mason was graduated from William and Mary College 1851, and served through the war as Surgeon in Wise's Brigade, C. S. A., and is now a prominent physician at Hicksford, Va.

2047.

GEORGE MASON, son of No. 799, was born Sept. 17, 1840, was graduated from William and Mary College 1861, died Sept. 1881. He served through the war as a member of the 13th Va. Cav., C. S. A., and lost his leg in a battle below Petersburg. He married Cecile Thibault, of Little Rock, Ark., where she and his children live. Children:—

4674, GEORGE KEATS MASON. 4675, JOSEPHINE.

2050.

REV. JOHN KERCHEVAL MASON, of Fredericksburg, Va., son of Dr. George and *Lucy B. Jones* Mason, was born Dec. 3, 1847. Married Nov. 19, 1879, Claudia Hamilton Norton (daughter of Rev. George Hatley Norton, D.D., of Alexandria, and Nannie Burwell Marshall, and great granddaughter of Chief Justice John Marshall), who was born at "Leeds," Fauquier Co., Va., the residence of her grandfather, James Keith Marshall, June 29, 1856. Children:—

4676, HATLEY NORTON MASON, b. Charlotte, N. C., Sept. 5, 1880.
4677, LUCY JONES, b. Liberty, Bedford Co., Va., Feb. 28, 1882.
4678, CLAUDIA HAMILTON, b. Fredericksburg, May 5, 1884, d. Jan. 16, 1886.

Mr. Mason, who is rector of St. George's Church, Fredericksburg, is a graduate of Hampden Sidney College, class of 1870, and of the Theological Seminary of Virginia in 1876. He is one of the most prominent young clergymen of his church in the State of Virginia.

The Rev. George H. Norton, D. D., of Alexandria, father of Mrs. Mason, was son of George Hatley Norton, of Winchester, and Catherine, daughter of Philip and Catherine Clough Bush, of Winchester, great son of John Norton, of Yorktown, Va., who married daughter of Wilson Cary Nicholas, and great grandson of John Norton, a native of London, and *propositus* of the Norton family of Virginia. (See Paxton's *Marshall Family*, pp. 212 and 327.)

2041.

WILLIAM H. COLE, of Greensville Co., Va., son of John Cole, married EMILY ELIZABETH MASON, daughter of No. 799, who was born Feb. 25, 1850. Children:—

4681, JOHN COLE, b. May 2, 1869.   4682, FANNY MASON, b. July 3, 1871.
4683, WILLIAM HERBERT, b. Sept. 9, 1872.   4684, MARGARET
BUCHANAN, b. Aug. 10, 1875.   4685, MARY GOODE, b. Aug. 21,
1878.   4686, EMMA, b. Jan. 10, 1880.   4687, ANNIE HAWKINS, b.
July 9, 1881.   4688, RICHETTA, Jan. 9, 1884.

An acquaintance writes : "At the time of her marriage Mrs. Cole was one of
the most beautiful woman I ever saw, like her brothers and sisters, inheriting
beauty from both sides of the house."

2056.

COL. WILLIAM RICE JONES, of "Brunswick Springs," near
Lawrenceville, Va., son of No. 800, was born Nov. 21, 1840.   He was
educated at the U. S. Military Academy at West Point, having been
appointed as cadet in 1857, but not graduating on account of the opening of the war.   He offered his services to his native State, and served
through the war, first in Virginia and North Carolina, subsequently in
Texas, on the staff of Gen. J. B. Magruder.   He is a Civil Engineer.
Since the war he has been part of the time a resident of Texas.
Unmarried.

2060.

RAVENSCROFT JONES, "College Hall," Brunswick Co.. Va.,
near Lawrenceville, son of No. 800, was born Nov. 16, 1849.   A
planter.   Married Mary Lewis, daughter of Dr. Charles Stuart and
Elizabeth Washington Fitzhugh Lewis, of King George Co., Va.
Children : —

4690, MARY ARMISTEAD JONES, b. Mar. 13, 1878.   4691, CHARLES
STUART, b. Mar. 1, 1881.   4692, ELIZABETH LEWIS, b. Mar. 2,
1884.

2030.

EDWARD CHAMBERS GOODE, of Boydton, Va., son of No. 804,
was born March 1, 1862.   Married May 20, 1885, Belle, daughter of
William Moreton, of Clarkesville, Va.   He is at present a planter in
the County of Mecklenburg.

2032.

PHILIP J. BRISCOE, of Knoxville, Tenn., son of Philip and
Martha Briscoe, born Feb., 1865, married Nov. 4, 1885, MARION KNOX
GOODE, daughter of No. 804.

Mr. Briscoe is a native of Mississippi, but at present a resident of Knoxville,
Tenn., and a member of the banking firm of Briscoe & Swepson.

2081.

SAMUEL GORDON BRENT, of Alexandria, Va., son of Col.
George W. and *Lucy Goode* Brent, was born June 28, 1855.   A rising

young lawyer, identified with the interests of the ancient borough of Alexandria, and in March, 1887, was elected City Attorney.

2156.

DR. RICHARD GOODE WHARTON, of Ruffin, N. C., son of No. 833, was born in Richmond, Va., Feb. 3, 1842. Married 1872, Eliza Allen Courts, daughter of D. W. Courts. Children :—

4701, CHARLES ROBERT WHARTON, b. 1874. 4702, SARAH BROOKS. 4703, LUCY.

Dr. Wharton was graduated at the Virginia Military Academy Institute in 1861, and at the age of nineteen enlisted in the Confederate Army. He was engaged eight months in drilling infantry at Camp Lee and Richmond College. Served eight months as private in 1st Company, Richmond Howitzers, was then promoted to Adjutant and 1st Lieutenant, 56th Va. Regt., Garnett's, afterwards Hudson's Brigade, and served there to the close of the war. He was shot through the lungs, Aug. 25, 1884, in a charge near Petersburg, between the Appomattox and James Rivers.

2157.

WILLIAM AUSTIN WHARTON, a soldier C. S. A., son of No. 849, was born in 1844, died July 6, 1863, from exposure while on duty in the service.

2158.

CHARLES DABNEY WHARTON, a soldier C. S. A., in Otey's Battery, Virginia Artillery, son of No. 839, died Nov. 24, 1863, of typhoid fever contracted in service.

2195.

JOHN GOODE BOYD, married Sallie Early. Son and four daughters. One son and one daughter married.

2206 (858.)

EMBRY MERRITT, of Brunswick Co., Va., married ELIZABETH GOODE. Both lived to a good old age, and had six sons and six daughters. Children :—

4721, HOWELL MERRITT. 4722, BETTIE. 4723, LUCY, m. *Capt. William Benton*, Boydton, Va., they had sons who died in the war. 4724, ISABELLA, m. *George Rives*, child, 1, *Sophie Rives*, m. *Mr. Harding*, son of Gen. Harding of Tennessee, and had child, *Sophie Harding*. 4725, ROBERT. 4726, JENNIE.

2223.

CAPT. REUBEN VAUGHAN KIDD, C. S. A., son of No. 863, was born in Marengo Co., Ala., about 1840. He enlisted at the opening of the war in the 4th Alabama Inf., and served with honor at Manassas,

Seven Pines, Cold Harbor, Malvern Hill, Antietam, Fredericksburg, Suffolk and Gettysburg. He was killed in action at Chickamauga. His body was never recovered.

2227.

DR. SAMUEL WATKINS VAUGHAN, Jr., of Hot Springs, Ark., son of No. 864, was born in Marengo Co., Ala. Married Virginia Harrison, of Summerfield, Ala., and removed to Arkansas in 1858.

Dr. Vaughan was a Division Surgeon in the Confederate army. Like his father, he is a skilful and devoted member of his profession.

2229.

DR. FREDERICK VAUGHAN, of Dallas Co., Ala., served through the war as a soldier C. S. A. Married Annie Smith, of Summerfield, Ala. Children :—

> 4803, EVELYN, m. *Courtney Groves*, of Selma, Ala. 4804, ALICE, and
> 4805, FRANK, minors.

2230.

PAUL TURNER VAUGHAN, of Selma, Ala., son of No. 864, was born 1840. Married Anna Gholson, of Dallas Co., Ala. Children :—

> 4806, TURNER VAUGHAN. 4807, WATKINS. 4808, GRAHAM. 4809,
> BRESSIER. 4810, HENRY. 4811, EDITH. 4812, ETHEL.

P. T. Vaughan was Captain in the 4th Alabama Inf., C. S. A., and distinguished himself as a good officer at the first Manassas and in subsequent engagements. He is now a wealthy cotton broker in Selma, a member of the firm of J. C. Graham & Co.

2231.

HENRY WHITE VAUGHAN, of Summerfield, Ala., was born in 1846. died at Summerfield, Ala., Dec. 5, 1866, but left no family.

His educational advantages were interrupted by the war, but by thoughtful study since and much reading he had become a ripe scholar and a man of great general information.

Commencing after the war with nothing, he devoted himself to planting, at which he was more than ordinarily successful, having acquired a good estate, and having kept himself out of the hands of the money-lenders.

In all his relations to his fellow-man he was honorable, sincere and just. In all his business transactions he was the mirror of simple honesty and truth. As a neighbor he was considerate, kind and generous. His acts of charity were unostentatious, but they were many, and they linger in the hearts of those who were helped by his tender benevolence.—*Selma Times Argus*, Dec. 10, 1886.

2238.

ISHMAEL STERLING HARWELL, of Demopolis, Ala., married June 15, 1853, MARY EVELINA VAUGHAN, daughter of No. 865, p. 248. Children :—

4813, EVELINA HARWELL, b. April 5, 1854, or about 1864. 4814, MARY WALTON, b. March 7, 1856, d. Feb. 8, 1863. 4815, ALFRED VAUGHAN, b. May 14, 1859. 4816, SALLIE ALSTON, b. Jan. 26 1861.

2240.

HON. JAMES TAYLOR JONES, M. C., of Demopolis, Ala., was born in Richmond, Va., 1832. Married Mar. 12, 1862, ADA BYRNE VAUGHAN, dau. of Dr. Alfred Goode Vaughan, No. 865, born 1836, died 1873. Children:—

4817, PERCY WALTON JONES, b. Feb. 27, 1866. 4818, ADA THEODOSIA, d. y. 4819, CREED TAYLOR, d. y. 4820, MELANIE, b. Mar. 25, 1872.

Mr. Jones was graduated from Princeton College in 1852, and from the Law School of the University of Virginia in 1855. He was admitted to the bar in 1856, and has since practised the profession of law, except while in the public service. He was from 1861 to 1864 a member of the 4th Alabama Inf., C. S. A., first as a private, afterwards as an officer. A delegate to the Alabama Constitutional Convention in 1865; member of the State Senate in 1872-3, and Representative of the First District of Alabama in the 45th, 48th, 49th and 50th Session of the Federal Congress.

2241.

REV. HOWARD HENDERSON, D. D., of New York city, (223 E. 61st street), married in 1861, SUSAN VAUGHAN, daughter of No. 865, born 1840. Children :

4821, WILLIAM HENDERSON, d. y. 4822, WALTON. 4823, ADA, d. y. 4824, ALFRED. 4825, PRICE. 4826, CECILE. 4827, HOWARD.

2244.

TACITUS HENRY VAUGHAN, of Royal, Smith Co., Miss., son of No. 865, married in 1871 Nellie Sims. Children :

4828, WILLIAM VAUGHAN. 4829, CECILE. 4830, READER. 4831, EUGENIA. 4832-33, ADA and IDA, twins.

2245.

ROBERT VAUGHAN, of Georgetown, Williamson Co., Texas, was son of No. 865.

2246.

GEORGE J. MICHAEL, of Demopolis, Ala., married Dec. 3, 1871, IDA VAUGHAN, daughter of No. 865, born Dec. 23, 1847. Children:—

4834, ADA VAUGHAN MICHAEL, b. Sept. 13, 1873. 4835, MARY LOUISE, b. Oct. 5, 1875. 4836, GEORGE ALFRED, b. Feb. 24, 1819. 4837, GERTRUDE MASON, b. Jan. 10, 1881.

2247.

JOHN CALHOUN MASTIN, of Frankfort, Ky., married June 17, 1880, CECILE VAUGHAN, daughter of No. 865, born 1850. Child :—

4838, MARIE STANTON MASTIN, b. Oct. 19, 1881.

2258.

WILLIAM WAVERLY DUGGER, of Demopolis, Ala., son of No. 866, was born in 1836, at Petersburg, Va.; graduated at Madison College, Fayette Co., Pa., and attended the law school of the University of Virginia. Never married.

A lawyer in Demopolis, Ala. He enlisted April, 1861, and served through the war in Co. D, 11th Alabama Inf., C. S. A., participating in the battles of Seven Pines, Seven Days' Battle, Peninsula Campaign, Second Manassas, Antietam and Chancellorsville. He was then transferred to Selden's Battery, and served with it in Georgia and Tennessee until captured at Nashville, and imprisoned till July, 1865. "I returned home," he writes, in a private letter, "a poorer but wiser man, opened a law office in Demopolis, eschewed politics, seldom ever voting, avoiding office, attending no conventions, save those of the Episcopal Church, and attending faithfully to my profession. Now I have to regard my health and utilize a farm, and am considering the great question, What is the vast army of self-seeking legislators going to do to ascertain and accord to the colored race their true position, and to prevent the negroes from consuming our remaining substance? Whoever aids most in solving this principle will marry his name to an undying principle."

2259.

REUBEN H. DUGGER, M. D., of Gallien, Hale Co., Ala., son of No. 866, was born in Petersburg, Va., in 1839 or 1840. Received the degree of M. D. from the University of Pennsylvania, Philadelphia Medical College, in 1859. Married Margaret L., daughter of David Minge, of Virginia, then of Marengo, Ala. Children :—

4839, FREDERICK DUGGER. 4840, REUBEN. 4841, BENJAMIN. 4842, WAVERLY. 4843, LLEWELLYN.

2260.

SERGT. FREDERICK E. DUGGER, C. S. A., son of No. 866, was born about 1843.

He graduated at the University of Alabama, Tuscoloosa, in 1860. He was at the Theological Seminary, New York city, preparing for the ministry; returned home on account of the war, enlisted in Selden's Battery, and served at Resaca, Cassville, Kennesaw, New Hope and Peach Tree Creek. He lost his life in the last-mentioned engagement, July 20, 1864. He had charge of one of the guns, and was killed by a cannon ball while sighting his cannon, after he had nearly exhausted his ammunition. His body was recovered after the engagement by his brother, W. W. Dugger, who lay beside it until the firing had ceased.

2243.

LUKE WHITE DUGGER, of Petersburg, Va., son of No. 866, was born about 1843. He married Louisa Boisseau. Children :—

4844, ALICE DUGGER. 4845, LOUISA.

He was Lieutenant in Selden's Battery, C. S. A., and was present at all its engagements from Resaca until its capture under Hood at Nashville.

2244.

DR. HOBART COBBS DUGGER, of "Mistletoe Farm," near Van Dorn, Ala., son of No. 866, was born in 1848, in Marengo Co., Ala. Graduated at Alabama Medical College in 1880: now a physician and farmer.

2316.

JAMES M. STRANGE, of Fluvanna Co., Va., farmer, was born Aug. 6, 1818, married Sept. 28, 1842, HARRIET CARRINGTON MAYO, b. Nov. 14, 1824, dau. of No. 881. Children :—

4851, WILLIAM MAYO STRANGE, b. Aug. 5, 1844. A farmer ; private C. S. A., m. Dec. 16, 1861, MARY LUCY POWELL, No. 2039. 4852, HARRIET CARRINGTON, b. July 9, 1846, d.y. 4853, JAMES MAGRUDER, b. 1847; d. y. 4854, JOHN BOWIE, b. 1849, d. y. 4855, HARRIET CATHARINE, b. Jan. 24, 1852. 4856, SALLIE WILLIE, b. April 6, 1855. 4857, ANNIE EDMONIA, b. Dec. 28, 1858. 4858, JOSEPHINE EPPES, b. Nov. 29, 1861.

Mr. Strange has been several times a member of the Virginia Legislature and was a member of the Virginia Secession Convention of 1861.

2318.

DR. EDWARD CARRINGTON MAYO, of Cumberland Co.,Va., son of William H. and *Harriet P. C.* Mayo, No. 881, born May 23, 1830, married Nov. 20, 1856, MARTHA VIRGINIA CARRINGTON, dau. of No. 880, b. April 2, 1839. Children :—

4859, WILLIAM COVINGTON MAYO, b. Feb. 26, 1858; farmer Cumberland Co., Va. Unmarried. 4860, VIRGINIA E., b. Feb. 13, 1861. Widow. 4861, JOSEPH HOWARD, b. Oct. 25, 1862, died March 27, 1872. 4862, MARTHA, b. March 23, 1865. 4863, FRANCIS CARINGTON, b. March 23, 1867.

2323.

FRANCIS CODRINGTON CARRINGTON, son of No. 881, was born Nov. 12, 1847.

A soldier, C. S. A., killed at the battle of Five Forks, April 5, 1865.

2325.

PEYTON RODES CARRINGTON, of "Boston Hill," near Richmond, Va., son of Col. J. L. Carrington, No. 882, was born Jan.

9, 1834. Married Jan. 23, 1866, Sarah Jane, dau. of Col. George M. Carrington. Children :—

    4865, GEORGE MAYO, b. Dec. 1, 1866, d. y. 4866, SARAH JANE, b. 1868, d. y. 4867, PEYTON RODES, b. Feb. 19, 1871. 4868, MARGARET HERON, d. y. 4869, JOSEPH CODRINGTON.

Mr. Carrington is a dairy farmer near Richmond. He is an accomplished and industrious genealogist, and has made extensive researches into the history of the Carringtons, Mayos, and related families in Virginia and Barbadoes. He has aided me very materially in this work, particularly by searching the old records of Henrico Co.

He was a member of the 13th Va. Cav., C. S. A.; enlisted as a private, promoted to Orderly Sergeant ; was afterwards an officer of the Engineer Bureau in Richmond.

2326.

GEN. ISAAC MUNROE ST. JOHN, of Richmond and Louisville, was born in Augusta, Ga., Dec. 19, 1828, of Connecticut parents, died at the White Sulphur Springs, Va., April 7, 1880. Married Feb. 28, 1865, ELLA JOSEPHINE CARRINGTON, dau. of No. 882, born Jan. 29, 1836. Children :

    4881, ABBIE R. ST. JOHN, d. y. 4882, ELLA MUNROE, d. y. 4883, JOSEPHINE, b. Aug. 5, 1869, d. April, 1863. 4884, CAROLINE MUNROE, d. y. 4885, ROSALIE, b. Feb. 11, 1872. 4886, ABBIE R., b. Feb. 6, 1814.

Gen. St. John was a man of remarkable talents. A successful civil engineer before the war, he became an engineer officer in the Confederate service with the rank of colonel, and was in charge of the fortifications around Williamsburg. Later he was chief of the Bureau of Nitre and Mines and Commissary General, and under his administration Richmond was kept better provisioned than it was supposed possible. After the war he was city engineer of Louisville, Ky.; chief engineer of the Louisville and Cincinnati R. R.; of the Richmond and Danville R. R., and the Cincinnati and Ohio R. R. He died of overwork. He was author of a pamphlet ' Notes on the Coal Trade of the Chesapeake and Ohio R. R., in its bearing on the commercial interests of Richmond," in 1870, 8vo, p. 12.

2327.

SAMUEL JONES CARRINGTON, of Richmond Va., son of No. 882, was born May 9, 1838, d. Feb. 5, 1875. Married Susan E. Kelly, dau. of D. D. Kelly, of Boston, Mass. Children :—

    4887, MABEL CARRINGTON, b. Aug. 27, 1872. 4888, SAMUEL JONES, d. y.

Mr. Carrington was a hotel proprietor; during the war he was manager of the glass-works in Richmond, Va.

2329.

WILLIAM J. BACON, of St. Louis, Mo., a native of Trigg Co., Ky., married Nov. 13, 1867, DELIA SCOTT CARRINGTON, dau. of No. 882, born Oct. 10, 1842. Children :—

4889, DELIA CARRINGTON BACON, b. Oct. 4, 1868, d. y.   4890, JOSEPH
L. CARRINGTON, d. y.   4891, CARRINGTON.   4892, EDWARD.
4893, WILLIAM J., b. 1876.

Mr. Bacon was during the war a merchant in New York, and in 1885, in the
commission business in St. Louis.

2332.

JAMES H. BLAKEMAN, of Russelville, Ky., a native of Petersburg, Va., a merchant.   Served during the war on staff of Gen.
Magruder.   Married Mar. 12, 1867, NANNIE READ CARRINGTON, dau.
of No. 882.   Children :—

> 4895, GEORGE NEVILLE BLAKEMAN, b. Dec. 21, 1867.   4896, ADELINE,
> d. y.   4897, NANNIE READ.   4898, CLARENCE.

2337.

DR. THOMAS P. SHIELDS, of Cumberland Co., Va., living in
Ohio, 1885, married, June 3, 1859, MARTHA CARRINGTON BRADLEY,
dau. of No. 883, born Dec. 15, 1850, died Sept. 11, 1859.   Children :—

> 4899, CARY SHIELDS, b. Mar. 26, 1857, d. y.   4900, EMMA VIRGINIA, d. y.
> 4901, GAMBLE.   4902, MARTHA THOMASIA, b. Aug. 21, 1859.

Dr. Shields was a Surgeon in the Confederate service.

2338.

ROBERT EDWARD BRADLEY, of Marion Co., Ala., son of No.
883, was born Feb. 13, 1834.   A soldier C. S. A.   Married, Aug. 19,
1857, Mary Jane, daughter of William Brown.   Children :—

> 4903, MARTHA ELLEN, b. July 3, 1858.   4904, WILLIAM RICHARD.   4905,
> THOMAS VIRGINIUS.   4906, ROBERT FLEMING.   4907, NEWTONIA
> HENRIETTA, b. Sept. 29, 1867.

2343.

HENRY CLAY BRADLEY, of Alabama, son of William R. and
E. S. T. Carrington Bradley, No. 883, was born May 9, 1845.   Enlisted
in the Confederate service, and was killed in the battle of Atlanta, July
2, 1864.

2347.

HAMPTON B. NICHOLAS, of New Canton, Buckingham Co.,
Va., son of Robert Carter Nicholas, a lawyer, soldier C. S. A., mar-
ried April 21, 1869, WILLIE SUE CARRINGTON, daughter of No. 886.
Children :—

> 4919, ALICE RANDOLPH NICHOLAS, b. April 15, 1870.   4920, JAMES
> PLEASANTS.   4921, ROBERT CARTER.   4922, MARTHA BARZIZA.

2392.

REV. HENRY MOORE, of South Carolina, a Methodist minister,
graduate of the University of South Carolina, and chaplain of a South

Carolina Reg't C. S. A., married 1874, CAROLINE TAIT dau. of No. 906. Children :—

> 4951-2 JAMES and FELIX MOORE, b. Sept. 5, 1875. 4953, NARCISSA, b. Sept. 17, 1876. 4954, VICTOR I., b. May 23, 1882.

2440.

WILLIAM R. KING BECK, born 1849, died 1885, married Feb. 8, 1855, MARY E. TAIT, daughter of No. 907. Children :—

> 4971, FRANKLIN KING BECK, b. Dec. 3, 1883. 4972, WM. R. KING, b. July 27, 1885.

2442.

E. N. JONES, of Camden, Wilcox Co., Ala., a lawyer, married (1) Miss Blanchard, of Mississippi, who left him three sons ; (2) MARY BECK, daughter of No. 909. Children :—

> A, LIEUT. EDWARD N. JONES, U. S. A.; B, RICHARD; C, JOHN. 4991, KATE JONES. 4992, PAUL. 4993, MOLLY BECK.

2544.

JAMES D. CAMPBELL, of North Carolina, was born in Lexington, Va., about 1825, died Aug. 13, 1865. Married May 6, 1857, Jane C. Megginson, daughter of No. 928-3, born Nov. 30, 1825. Children :—

> 5001, ARCHIBALD CAMPBELL, who was in business in Wilmington in 1872. 5002, JAMES, d. y. 5003, MARY, m. 1871 *H. Garland Brown*, of Pulaski, Tenn, child, 1, Mary Virginia Brown. 5004, CLARA, m. *Everett Smith*, of Wayne Co., N. C., issue 1, *Bettie Smith*, d. y.; 2, *Archibald*, d. y.; 3, William ; 4, Julia.

2681.

JUDGE JOHN DUNSCOMBE HORSLEY, of Livingston, Nelson Co., Va., son of Dr. William A., and *Eliza Perkins* Horsley, No. 929-20, was born April 30, 1849. Married Mrs. Florence Tunstall (born Massie). Children :

> 5005, CATHARINE HORSLEY. 5006, BLAND.

Elected in 1886 Judge of the 5th Circuit of Virginia, which includes the counties of Nelson, Amherst, Appomattox, Campbell, Bedford, &c., and the city of Lynchburg, "a distinguished honor, especially for so young a man."

2686.

PHILIP GOODE, of Miami, Saline Co., Mo., son of No. 932½, was born Aug. 7, 1796, in Prince Edward Co., Va., and is living, at the age of 90, with his son-in-law, Judge Ferril. He married Miss Young, and removed about 1840 to Chariton Co., Mo. Children :—

> 5101, WILLIAM E. GOODE. 5102, MARY, m. Judge Ferrill. 5103, ELIZABETH, m. *Mr. Gilliam*, of Chariton Co., Mo. 5104, HARRIET, m. Mr. Bridges, of Saline Co., Mo.

2685.

REV. JOSEPH GOODE, of Milo, Mo., son of No. 932½, was born 1798. Married 1825, Miss Young, of Prince Edward Co., Va. Children:—

5105, W. P. GOODE, lives near Smith Centre, Smith Co., Kan. 5106, JOHN F., of Milo, Mo. 5107, H. H., of Milo, Mo. 5108, REBECAH, m. *John Smith*, hotel keeper, Milo, Mo. 5109, MARY BENSON, m. *T. Walton*, of Milo, Mo. 5110, LOCKEY W., m. *R. W. Kinzon*, of Milo, Mo.

Rev. Mr. Goode was a Methodist preacher, and was admitted to the Virginia Conference, and stationed at Swift Creek, Albermarle Co., in 1824-5. He removed to Ohio in 1836, and, soon after, to Missouri. He writes that he has never at any time, in the space of fifty years, since he left Virginia, lost any of his partialities for his native State. In early life he was "intimate with poverty." He continues: "The door to wealth has been open to me more than once, but this was never desired by me; nay, was feared by witnessing its effects on others, as well as viewing it from a gospel standpoint. Although now near the end of my eighty-eighth year, I regard it as my duty to eat bread by the sweat of my face. My children afford me great comfort; they are industrious and well settled, but too Southern in their views as well as proclivities to attain to eminence in the State in which we live. Neither sons or sons-in-laws, with one exception among the latter, bore arms in the war between the States."

2706.

WILLIAM BUCHANAN, of Washington Co., Va., son of No. 934, was born Feb. 15, 1846. Served in 1864-5 as a trooper in Co. D, First Virginia Cav., C. S. A., Married March 30, 1870, Mary P. Perkins. Children:—

5120, LIZZIE GOODE BUCHANAN, b. May 6, 1871. 5121, LOCKEY HENDERSON, b. June 11, 1872. 5122, BEN. KEYS, b. Nov. 18, 1873. 5123, GEORGE PALMER b. Jan. 2, 1876. 5124, RACHEL BRANCH, b. Feb. 18, 1878. 5125, DANIEL LITTELTON, b. April 9, 1880. 5126, JEAN, b. Dec. 13, 1881. 5127, WILLIAM GOODE, b. July 31, 1885.

2707.

JACK BUCHANAN, of Washington Co., Va., son of No. 934. Married Lizzie G. Perkins May 10, 1876. Children:—

5128, THOMAS PRESTON BUCHANAN, b. Sept. 1, 1878. 5129, WILLIAM PERKINS, b. March, 1881.

2708.

THOMAS PRESTON BUCHANAN, married Josephine B. Clarke Nov. 29, 1881. Children:—

5130, MARY ANNE BUCHANAN, b. Dec. 29, 1883.   5131, JACK GOODE, b. July 21, 1885.

2890(–985.)

DANIEL GOODE, son of No. 340, p. 136, lived in 1886 in Bell Co., Texas.

2891(–986.)

REUBEN JONES GOODE, of Bell Co., Texas, was born 1800, d. 1819, moved from Halifax Co., Va., to Georgia 1830, and later to Texas. Children :—

> 5200, GEORGE W. GOODE, of Cincinnati, Ohio, b. 1833. 5201, DR. REUBEN JONES, of Bell Co., Texas. 5202, JOHN, of Bell Co., Texas. 5203, DANIEL, of Bell Co., Texas. 5204, DR. WILLIAM, of Bell Co., Texas, 3 daughters. 5205, MARY, m. *Mr. McBurnett,* of Bell Co., Texas.

THE CULPEPER GOODES.

2901.

THOMAS J. CARLIN, of Carrollton, Ill., farmer, son of No. 989, was born Dec. 13, 1827.   From 1869–82 was Clerk of the Circuit Court of Carrollton.   Married 1850 Jenny Burney, of Delhi, Ill. Children :—

> 5250, LAURA CARLIN, b. 1851, m. *William Roberts,* of Carrollton. 5251, DOUGLAS FRENCH, b. 1853, of Cheyenne River Agency, Fort Bennet, Dak. 5252, LILY, b. 1856, m. *James Rives,* of Greenfield, Ill. 5253, EMILY, b. 1871. 5254, THOMAS, b. 1876. 5255, JANE, b. 1879.

2902.

GEN. WILLIAM PASSMORE CARLIN, U. S. A., son of William and *Mary Goode* Carlin, No. 989, p. 267, was born in Carrollton, Ill., Nov. 24, 1829.   Married July 10, 1869, Nettie Michael, daughter of John and *Clara Pinner* Michael, of Buffalo, N. Y.   Child :—

> 5256, WILLIAM EDWARD CARLIN, b. July 26, 1866.

Gen. Carlin was appointed a cadet in the U. S. Military Academy in 1846; he was graduated in 1850, and after a period of garrison duty was appointed March 3, 1855, First Lieutenant in the Sixth Infantry, and took part in Gen. Harney's Sioux expedition, and in 1857 commanded a company in Col. Sumner's expedition against the Sioux. In 1858 he participated in the quelling of the Mormon rebellion in Utah.   In 1858 he marched with his company from Utah to California, a distance of 2,400 miles, and was until 1860 on the Pacific Coast, stationed at the head of Russian River, at Fort Bragg and elsewhere, and was engaged in recruiting service in New York in 1860–61.   While stationed at Buffalo he drilled a volunteer company in which ex-President Fillmore and a future President, Grover Cleveland, were privates. In Aug. 1861, he was appointed Colonel of the 38th Illinois Volunteer Infantry, and went into the field at Frederickstown, Mo., where he defeated Gen. Jeff. Thompson in the engagement of Oct. 21.

He marched and fought his way to Goldsborough, N. C., April, 1865, serving under Buell, Rosecrans, Thomas, Sherman and Grant.

His last battle was at Bentonsville, N. C., March 19, 1865, where he was in command of the First Division of the 14th Army Corps (Sherman's), with rank of Brigadier and command of Major General.

His services during the war are referred to in all the histories, and especially in the Van Horne and Cists " History of the Army of the Cumberland." The official reports of Generals Mitchell, Jeff. C. Davis, A. M. McCook, Buell, Gilbert, Rosecrans, Thomas and Slocum and R. B. Mitchell, contain references to the gallant achievements of this eminent officer, as does also the report of the Committee on the Conduct of the War, Vol. 1, Supplement.

He was five times brevetted for gallant and meritorious service, as Lieutenant Colonel, Colonel, Brigadier General, Major General and Major General of Volunteers.

He took part in thirty fights and small affairs, and numerous skirmishes, and his principal battles were as follows :

> Frederickstown, Mo., Oct. 21, 1861.
> Perryville, Ky., Oct. 8, 1862. (Brig. Gen. of Vols.)
> Stone River, Dec. 31, 1862.
> Chickamauga, Sept. 19, 20, 1863.
> Chattanooga, Nov. 24, 26, 1863. (Lieut. Col. by brevet.)
> Sherman's Atlanta Campaign, May and June, 1864.
> Jonesboro, Sept. 1, 1864. (Col. by brevet.)
> Capture of Savannah, Dec. 21, 1864.
> Averysboro, N. C., March 16, 1865.
> Bentonville, N. C., March 19, 20, 1865. (Brig. Gen. by brevet, Major Gen. by brevet for services during the war.)

On the organization of the regular army in 1865 he resumed his position as Major of the 16th Infantry, and was stationed in Nashville, Tenn., as Assistant Commissioner of the Freedman's Bureau. In 1872 he became Lieutenant Colonel of the 17th Infantry, and in 1882 Colonel of the 4th Infantry. In 1886 he is the Commandant of Fort Omaha, Neb.

Gen. Carlin is the author of a valuable series of war sketches, printed in the *National Tribune* in 1865.

See Wilson's "Sketches of Illinois Officers." Chicago, 1863 : Appleton's "Cyclopædia of American Biography," 1 Vol., p. 527, and other works already cited.

2903.

JOHN LONG, of Carrollton, Ill., banker and capitalist. Married NANCY CARLIN, daughter of William and *Nancy Goode* Carlin, No. 989, born April 11, 1832. Children :—

5257, CHARLES LONG, of Topeka, Kan., b. 1856.   5258, NETTIE, b. 1866.
5259, ADA, b. 1869.   5260, JULIETTE.   5261, AUGUSTUS.

2904.

JOHN CALVIN KELLY, of Carrollton, Greene Co., Ill.   Married
ELIZABETH CARLIN, b. June 27, 1834.   Children ;—

5264, MARY, b. 1851, m. *John C. Woolford*, banker, died, has two sons.
5265, EUGENIA, b. 1853, m. *Mark Reed*, contractor, of Carrollton.
5266, LUTHER, b. 1855, farmer, Carrollton, m. Miss Clarke.   5267.
WILLIAM, b. 1857, a farmer in Carrollton.   5268, HENRY, b. 1864.
5269, EDWARD, b. 1867.   5270, JOSEPH, b. 1864.

2906.

THEOPHILE PAPIN, of St. Louis, Mo., a descendant of the
early French settlers at Kaskaskia, Ill., married EMILY CARLIN,
daughter of No. 989, b. July 4, 1856.   Children :—

5271, EDWARD N. PAPIN, b. 1869.   5272, LUCILE, b. 1872.

Mr. Papin is a prominent citizen of St. Louis, and extensively engaged in
the real estate business.   He has been U. S. Collector of Internal Revenue,
member of the City Council and Mayor of St. Louis.

2907.

WALTER E. CARLIN, of Carrollton, Ill., son of No. 989, was
born in Carrollton, Ill., April 11, 1844.   Married (1) Mary Cross, (2)
Mary Darneille.   Children :—

5273, EUGENIA CARLIN, b. 1869.   5274, ALMA, b. 1872.

Mr. Carlin has been a banker and member of the State Legislature.   He
was Democratic Candidate for State Auditor,   He is the highest official in
the Independent Order of Odd Fellows in the State of Illinois.

2908.

J. ADAIR HARDIN, of Shelbyville, Ky., a native of Missouri, a
Civil Engineer and railroad contractor, died Oct., 1883.   Married
JULIA CARLIN, daughter of No. 989, b. Nov. 23, 1847.   Children :—

5275, ADELE HARDIN, b. 1873.   5276, EMILY, b. 1877.

2920.

REV. MARSHALL MONROE GOODE, of St. Joseph, Mo., son of
John W. Goode, No. 996, p. 267, was born in Macoupin Co., Ill.,
Oct. 14, 1838.   Married (1) Miss Mary J. Russell May 20, 1860,
daughter of Henry G. and Eliza Russell, of Waverly, Morgan Co., Ill.,
born Oct. 9, 1840, died Dec. 17, 1877, at Petersburg, Ill.; (2) Nov.
5, 1885, Miss Florence A. Clark, daughter of John C. and Mary Noland
Clark, born in Nemaha Co., Neb., Dec. 10, 1860.   Children :—

5280, BERTIE F. GOODE, b. April 23, 1862.   5281, ETTIE M., b. March
2, 1867.

" Mr. Goode received a good English education in the public schools of
Macoupin Co., Ill.   He has ever been and is still a hard student in his own
library, which is quite extensive.   He was ordained as a minister of the
Christian Church Dec. 22, 1862. At present he is pastor of the Christian
Church in St. Joseph, Mo., a wealthy and influential congregation, having a
membership of more than five hundred.   He has been located with this
church more than six years."

2921.

DARWIN LEDRAN GOODE, born in Exeter, Ill., May 2, 1840,
farmer and postmaster at Stirrup Grove, Macoupin Co., Ill.   Married
Miss Margaret J. Moore, of Macoupin Co., Ill.   Children :—

> 5283, THOMAS A. GOODE.   5284, JOHN W.   5285, CLARA M.   5286,
> WILLIAM A.   5287, MARSHALL M.   5288, MARTHA M.   5289,
> LEANDER.   5290, NELLY.

2922.

REV. GALEN McGREGOR GOODE, of Normal, Ill., was born
July 4, 1842.   Married E. Nevins, of Macoupin Co., Ill.   Children :—

> 5291, CARRIE B. GOODE.   5292, JENNIE A.   5293, WALTER S.   5294,
> HARRY C.   5295, MARSHALL.   5296, ERRETT.   5297, LUCILE.

For the last three years Rev. G. M. Goode has been located at Normal,
Ill., as pastor of the Christian Church in that place.

2923.

REV. JOHN B. CORWINE, of New London, Mo., married Sept.,
1863, MARTHA MARIA GOODE, born June 25, 1845.   Children :—

> 5298, HARRY B. CORWINE.   5299, EDWIN L.   5300, J. ETHELBERT.
> 5301, ARTHUR L.   5302, J. HERBERT.   5303, HOMER D.   5304,
> JEWEL B.   5305, MARY.

J. B. Corwine is pastor of the Christian Church at New London, Mo.

THE RAPPAHANNOCK GOODES.

2940.

CHARLES GOODE, of Rodgersville, Ala., planter, son of William
and *Martha York* Goode. No. 1004, was born Nov. 28, 1849.   Married
April 29, 1869, Mary S. Fuqua.   Children :

> 5306, MARTHA E. GOODE, b. April 19, 1870.   5307, ARCHIBALD, b.
> May 20, 1872.   5308, THOMAS H., b. March 19, 1874.   5309, ROBERT
> EMMETT, b. Dec. 19, 1875.   5310, MARY S., b. Dec. 31, 1877.
> 5311, CHARLES ARDONIA, b. Nov. 17, 1880.   5312, EDNA EARL,
> b. Nov. 21, 1882.   5313, GROVER CLEVELAND, b. Nov. 4, 1884.

2942.

JESSE GOODE, of Greenville, Hunt Co., Texas, son of No. 1004, was born Sèpt. 17, 1852. Married Dec. 17, 1874, Mary E. Gray, of Limestone Co., Ala., born May 16, 1854. Children:—

> 5318, MINNIE BEATRICE GOODE, b. Nov. 16, 1875. 5319, PERCY ELMORE, b. Aug. 1, 1880. 5320, VIRGIL ARDONIA, b. July 27, 1882.

2943.

JOSEPH H. LENTZ, of Rodgersville, Ala., married Nov. 1, 1853, Mary Goode, daughter of No. 1004, born Oct. 12, 1836. Children:—

> 5321, WILLIAM H. LENTZ, b. Feb. 20, 1855. 5322, CHARLES T., b. Sept. 22, 1858. 5323, SARAH E., b. Dec. 10, 1860. 5324, JAMES A., b. July 19, 1863. 5325, MARTHA J., b. July 9, 1865. 5326, EDWARD J., b. July 7, 1867. 5327, MARY F., b. Oct. 25, 1869, d. July 2, 1871. 5328, SUSANNA J., b. Aug. 18, 1872. 5329, JOSEPH P., b. Sept. 21, 1877.

2944.

SIDNEY BROADWATER, of Alabama, born July 23, 1842, married July 31, 1865, REBECCA GOODE, born Mar. 23, 1838, daughter of No. 1004.

2945.

JAMES A. WILLBANKS, born Nov. 1, 1838, married ELIZABETH GOODE, born Aug. 3, 1840, daughter of No. 1004. Children:—

> 5330, WILLIAM H. WILLBANKS, b. Feb. 2, 1863. 5331, MARTHA A, b. Dec. 26, 1866. 5332, CHARLES T., b. April 27, 1869. 5334, JOHN W., b. Jan. 1, 1871. 5335, JOE ELLA, b. Dec. 1, 1874. 5336, JAMES E., b. April 21, 1879.

2946.

JAMES W. GOODE, of Rodgersville, Alabama, son of No. 1004, was born Jan. 13, 1843. Married Feb. 16, 1865, Harriet M. Holmes. Children:—

> 5337, C. RICHARD GOODE, b. Dec. 1, 1865. 5338, WILLIAM T., b. Nov. 19, 1867. 5339, J. WEAKLEY, b. Nov. 3, 1869. 5340, ROBERT LEE, b. Aug. 20, 1872. 5341, LOLA O., b. Nov. 11, 1874. 5342, JOSEPHINE E., b. July 10, 1877. 5343, JOHN OLIVER, b. Feb. 10, 1880. 5344, EDWARD F., b. Nov. 25, 1882, d. y.

2947.

THOMAS MILLER, of Rodgersville, Ala., born in Tennessee, 1832. Married May 17, 1876, SARAH GOODE, daughter of No. 1004, born Jan. 13, 1845. Children:—

5345, Dorcas Miller, b. Mar. 19, 1845. 5346, John, b. Oct. 14, 1876. 5347, Nellie, b. Sept. 4, 1878. 5348, Kate, b. Oct. 9, 1883.

2948.

PETER F. HAGOOD, of Alabama, born May 31, 1865, married Francis Goode, daughter of No. 1004, born May 7, 1847. Children :—

5349, Tiny Hagood, b. Mar. 7, 1847. 5350, William Willis, b. June 29, 1867. 5351, Sallie E., b. Nov. 24, 1868. 5352, Martha J., 5354, Samuel Josephus, b. Mar. 5, 1872. 5355, Laretta Ellen, b. Sept. 24, 1876.

2949.

EBENEZER LEE, of Harrisburg, Ark., married Narcissa Goode, daughter of No. 1004, born May 9, 1857.

2950.

JOSEPH GOODE, of Rodgersville, Ala., son of No. 1004, was born May 5, 1859. Married Nov. 9, 1882, Sarah Morrison, who was born Dec. 16, 1861. Children :

5356, Zethreus Knox Goode, b. Dec. 17, 1873. 5357, Elma Denver, b. June 24, 1885.

2973.

JAMES L. GOODE, of Abbot, Rockingham Co., Va., was a soldier in the 28th Virginia Inf., C. S. A., and was killed at Hatcher's Run, the last fight of the war.

3001.

RICHARD L. GOODE, of Springfield, Mo., son of William Thomas and M. E. Guthrie Goode, No. 1020, was born in Campbellsburg, Henry Co., Ky., Feb. 4, 1855. Married April 2, 1885, Estelle B. Maurer, of Fremont, Ohio. Child :—

5358, Grace Estelle Goode, b. Mar. 11, 1886.

Mr. Goode is a prominent lawyer of Springfield, a member of the firm of Goode & Cravens. He was educated at Jefferson College, Ky.; Harmonia College, Ky., and Drury College, Springfield, Mo., receiving the degree of A. B. from the latter in 1876, and A. M. in 1865. In 1876 he was Principal of the Springfield High School, and from 1877 to 1880, served as Superintendent of the City Schools of Springfield; admitted to the bar in 1879, and in the same year became a member of the firm with which he is still connected. In 1880 he was elected City Attorney of Springfield. Mr. Goode is a Democrat in politics, and non-sectarian in religion.

EIGHTEENTH GENERATION.

THE PRINCE EDWARD GOODES.

3080.

WILLIAM HENRY GOODE, of Riggs, Ky., son of Samuel Venable Goode, No. 1020, p. 141, is probably the oldest representative in the eighteenth generation of the oldest male line of descendants of John Goode, of "Whitby." The oldest male representative of the family at the time of the publication of this volume is, however, FRANCIS COLLIER GOODE, No. 439, a member of the sixteenth generation.

3094.

JOHN GOODE WILEY, of Jefferson City, Mo., son of Thomas and *Maria Jones* Wiley, of Amelia Co., Va., was born Feb. 1, 1833, and removed to Missouri in 1855, died March 29, 1887. Married June 9, 1856, *Rebecca Burwell Smith*, daughter of No. 892 (1025), p. 271, born in 1838. Children : —

> 5451, THOMAS GOODE WILEY, b. June 25, 1858, a civil engineer, now in lumbering business in Orlando, Fla. 5452, STANLEY, b. Aug. 12, 1860. 5453, WILLIAM GUY, b. Nov. 23, 1875. 5454, MINOR LENNOX, b. Sept. 8, 1878.

I am indebted to Gen. Minor for the following sketch: About the latter end of the last century there were born, in Amelia Co., Va., twin girls, one named Maria Jones and the other Eliza Royall Jones. In due time they married two young farmers of the neighborhood in no way connected, save in their occupation as tillers of the soil. Thomas Wiley, one of them, took for his wife Maria Jones, and Thomas Goode, his friend, took for his wife Eliza Royall

Jones, and the two families lived for many years on contiguous farms, with constant association and uninterrupted friendship. About the years 1832–33 a son, whom he called John Goode Wiley, the first name in honor of his brother, a distinguished politician of Virginia, and the other name, in *honorem amici*, Thomas Goode.

Actuated by a desire to improve his fortunes (almost an epidemic among Virginia farmers at that time), in 1840 Thomas Goode moved from Amelia Co., with his whole family, to Cole, the capital county in Missouri, where he settled, where he died in 1842–43.

In 1857 John Goode Wiley, then about 25 years of age, paid his relatives in Missouri a visit, and fell in love with his cousin, Rebecca Burwell Smith, then about 17 years of age, and, in the process of time (in the chronology of lovers not measured by any fixed dates) they were married, and with the exception of two years spent in Virginia and one in Florida, they have lived and are still living in this county and city.

John Goode Wiley was an enterprising farmer until the war deprived him of his slaves, and almost of his home. After peace was restored he returned to his old vocation of husbandry, but did not find it very remunerative. A few years ago he removed to Jefferson City in order to educate his boys, where he lived sustained by the rents of the farm and by such means of income as in the West fall to the lot of every man of culture.

3095.

BENJAMIN U. MASSEY, of Springfield, Mo., married April 17, 1869, MARY SIDNEY SMITH, daughter of No. 39?–?, who was born in Cole Co., Mo., Aug. 12, 1844. Children :—

5455, B. MINOR MASSEY, b. 1872. 5456, LAURA, b. 1845, d. y.

Mr. Massey is a lawyer of eminence in Springfield, Mo. He is descended from an old Maryland stook, long seated near Chester in that State.

3096.

COL. HAMILTON GAMBLE, of St. Louis, Mo., born Nov. 11, 1858, died April 11, 1877, in Salt Lake City. Married Dec. 23, 1863, SALLIE GOODE MINOR, dau. of Gen. James L. and *Sallie Goode* Minor, No. 392–4, born June 6, 1845. Children :—

5457, CAROLINE COALTER GAMBLE, Sept. 5, 1864. 5458, MARY MINOR, b. Dec. 27, 1865. 5459, FANNIE HUMPHREY, b. April 30, 1872.

Col. Gamble was the son of Hamilton Rowan Gamble, (born in 1798 and died in 1864,) son of Joseph Gamble, a native of Ireland, who came to Virginia in 1789 with his wife Annie, daughter of John Hamilton, of "The Strutts"). Judge of the Supreme Court and Governor of Missouri, and his mother was Miss Caroline Coalter, of South Carolina, whose two sisters were married to Senator William C. Preston, of that State, and Judge Edward Bates, of St. Louis. Col. Gamble was an eminent member of the bar.

3097–5.

BENJAMIN CHRISTOPHER, of Kansas City, Mo., a merchant in grain, married ADA STANLEY, daughter of No. 392–3. Children : —

    5465, STANLEY CHRISTOPHER. 5466, LEILIA. 5467, DINNON. 5468, CAMPBELL. 5469, JAMES KNIGHT.

3101.

EDWARD DANIEL, of Charlotte Co., Va., son of No. 1031–1. Married Jennie Hannah. Children : Several.

He is Clerk of the Court of Charlotte Co.

3109.

REV. WILLIAM RICHARDSON, of Troy, Ala., son of Hillery Goode and *Mary Daniel* Richardson, No. 1030–3, was born July 1, 1857, died March 1, 1887.

Mr. Richardson was a Presbyterian clergyman. Graduated from Hampden Sidney College and the Union Theological Seminary.

3111.

REV. SAMUEL M. SMITH, of Washington, N. C., son of Rev. Jacob Henry Smith, D. D., of Greenboro, N. C. A brilliant young Presbyterian clergyman. Married ELLA DANIEL, daughter of No. 1030–5. Child : —

    5491, REID SMITH.

3112.

JOHN DANIEL, of West Virginia, son of No. 1031–1, a lawyer, married and has several children.

3211.

MAJ. JOHN B. BROCKENBROUGH, of Portland, Or., son of Judge John White and *Mary C. Bowyer* Brockenbrough, of Lexington, grandson of Judge William Brockenbrough, of Richmond, and his wife, Miss White, great grandson of Dr. John and *Sarah Roan* Brockenbrough, of Tappahannock, great-great-grandson of Col. William Brockenbrough, immigrant, of Richmond Co., Va., and his wife, (Miss Fauntleroy), married Oct. 11, 1864, LUCY ALICE MURRELL, daughter of No. 1047. Children : —

    5501, ALICE BROCKENBROUGH, m. *Mr. Preston*, of Botetourt Co. 5502, JOHN W. 5503, WILLIAM M. 5504, EDWARD. 5505, ROBERT L. 5506, JAMES. 5507, MARION W.

Mr. Brockenbrough is Collector of Internal Revenue in Portland, Oreg.

3212.

HON. THOMAS DAVIS EVANS, of Lynchburg, Va., born July 18, 1849. Married, Sept. 6, 1876, MARY E. MURRELL, daughter of No. 1067, born Feb. 27, 1857. Children : —

5509, EDWARD STEPTOE. EVANS, b. May 24, 1879. 5510, THOMAS, b. Dec. 26, 1882. 5511, JULIA ANNE HART, b. July 11, 1886.

Mr. Evans was educated in Brooklyn, N. Y., and was for a time, a member of the firm of Joseph D. Evans & Co., tobacco-factors and commission merchants in New York city. He was subsequently engaged in farming near Liberty, Va. In 1883, he removed to Lynchburg, and became part owner of the Lynchburg *Advance*, and is President of the Advance Publishing Company. He is one of the leading citizens of Lynchburg.

3213.

DR. DAVID G. MURRELL, of Paducah, Ky., son of No. 1047, is a successful physician; sometime Professor in the Louisville Medical College. Married Miss Randolph.

3214.

WILLIAM HART MURRELL, of Coffee P. O., Bedford Co., Va., son of No. 1047, was born Sept. 14, 1857. Married Dec. 8, 1880, Mary Huntington, of Uniontown, Ala., born Aug. 4, 1856. Children : —

5512, ALFRED HUNTINGTON MURRELL, b. Sept. 14, 1881. 5513, CLIFFORD HUNTINGTON, b. May 22, 1884.

Mr. Murrell was valedictorian of his class in the Virginia Military Institute, and Lieutenant in the Cadet Corps. He was for several years a planter in Alabama.

3217.

SENATOR JOHN WARWICK DANIEL, of Lynchburg, Va., was born Sept. 5, 1842. Married, in 1869, JULIA ELIZABETH MURRELL, daughter of No. 1048-1, 276, born Oct. 22, 1850. Children :—

5525, JULIA ELIZABETH DANIEL, b. Nov., 1870. 5526, CAROLINE WARWICK, b. May, 25, 1873. 5527, JOHN WARWICK, b. Aug. 3, 1878 5528, EDWARD MORRELL, b. May 25, 1883. 5529, WILLIAM PATTON, b. Dec. 15, 1885.

" Senator Daniel," says a writer in *Harper's Weekly*, " is a native of Lynchburg, and forty-three years of age. His father, William Daniel, Jr., was at the breaking out of the war a Judge of the Court of Appeals of Virginia, and his grandfather had been a member of the same tribunal. When the war broke out young Daniel was a student at the University of Virginia, having been prepared for that institution in the schools of Lynchburg, and he joined one of the first companies formed at the University, and went to Manassas as a private, soon becoming Second Lieutenant 27th Va. Inf., Second Lieutenant 11th Inf., then First Lieutenant of the same regiment. Shortly after he obtained a place on the staff of Gen. Jubal A. Early, and was gradually promoted to the rank of Major, and made Adjutant of Early's division. In the battle of the Wilderness, in 1864, while heading a charge, he received a severe wound in his thigh, which was at first believed to be fatal. He still suffers from the wound at times, and is lame to a serious degree. At the close of the war he returned to the University, and after concluding his academic course, graduated from the law department with honor. He entered upon the practice of law in Lynchburg, and rapidly attained a high position at the bar, gaining considerable reputation as an eloquent and impassioned speaker. He was early chosen to the Legislature of Virginia. For four years prior to 1881 he was a member of the State Senate for Campbell County. In that year he was nominated for Governor by the debt-paying Democrats. On his defeat for that office he returned to his practice at Lynchburg, but has continued to take a prominent and active part in politics. He was elected to the Forty-ninth Congress from the Sixth District of Virginia, and he will soon take his seat in the Senate, his term expiring in 1893. He is a man of striking personal appearance, strongly resembling the distinguished tragedian Edwin Booth, has cultivated and scholarly tastes, and is well known not only as a graceful and effective public speaker, but as a clear and forcible writer. He is the author of ' Daniel on Negotiable Instruments,' ' Daniel on Attachments,' and other law books, and has delivered literary addresses on many occasions."

The eight great-grandparents of Senator Daniel were :

1, WILLIAM DANIEL (father of No. 72 of the Goode Genealogy), whose son (1.-A) Judge William Daniel, Sr., was father of 1.-AA, Judge William Daniel. The mother of No. 1, was Elizabeth Watkins.

2, PATTIE ALLEN, who married No. 1.

3, CORNELIUS BALDWIN, whose daughter, Mary Baldwin, married No. 1.-A.

4, MARY BRISCOE, wife of No. 3.

5, WILLIAM WARWICK, father of No. 5.-A. John M. Warwick, whose daughter, S. A. Warwick, married No. 1.-AA.

6, AMY BARKSDALE (sister of No. 73 of the Goode Pedigree), wife of No. 5.

7, WILLIAM NORVELL (father of the wife of 233 of the Goode Pedigree), whose daughter Caroline Norvell, married John M. Warwick, No. 5.-A.

8, MARTHA or CAROLINE (?) WYATT, wife of No. 7.

3237.

DABNEY CHARLES COLLIER, of Shelby Co., Tenn., (near Memphis,) son of Thomas Barksdale and *Catherine Page Nelson* Collier, No. 1049–1, p. 276, was born April 21, 1840. Married April 19, 1856, Catherine Eppes. Child :—

5531, CARRIE PAGE COLLIER, b. Jan. 21, 1876.

He lived in New Orleans from 1856 to 1860; they removed to Woodruff Co., Ark.; subsequently, in 1880, to Shelby Co., Tenn., where he still resides. He is a man of the highest integrity of character and a successful planter. He served through the war in Co. D, 10th Arkansas Inf., C. S. A.

3231.

JOHN CARTER NELSON, of Haywood Co., Tenn., a lawyer, nephew of 1049-1, son of Dr. Hugh (b. 1788) and *Polly Hunt* Nelson, of Columbus, Ky., (see " Page Family," p. 173) and grandson of Major John and *Nancy Carter* Nelson, of "Oak Hill," Mecklenburg Co., Va., was born about 1820, died 1866. Married LUCY NELSON COLLIER, daughter of No. 1049-1, p. 276. No children.

3232.

AMERICUS HATCHETT, of Memphis, Tenn. Married Jan. 14, 1856, SARAH CATHERINE COLLIER, daughter of No. 1049-1, who was born Oct. 27, 1830. Son :—

> 5540, THOMAS BROOKE HATCHETT, b. July 26, 1857, in 1886 a merchant in Memphis.

3240.

WILLIAM ARMISTEAD COLLIER, of Memphis, Tenn., son of No. 1049-1, was born in Haywood Co., Tenn., Feb. 12, 1846. Married Nov. 13, 1872, Alice Trezevant, eldest child of Nathaniel Mason Trezevant, of Memphis. Children :—

> 5542, WILLIAM ARMISTEAD COLLIER, JR., b. Jan. 5, 1876. 5543, ALICE CATHERINE, b. Jan. 5, 1876. 5544, THOMAS BARKSDALE, b. July 22, 1877.

"W. A Collier enlisted at the age of fifteen in Co. B of the famous 7th Tennessee Cav., C. S. A., which, under the command of Gen. N. B. Forrest, participated in all the battles of the West. He was a fine soldier, his associates say, and at the close of the war was still in his teens. Among his many daring exploits was to pass, on a long journey, disguised as a girl, through the enemies' lines, to visit his dying mother.

In 1869 he pursued a course of law studies at Cumberland University, and in the following year entered upon the practice of law in Memphis as a member of the firm of Smith & Collier; his partner being his father's friend and lawyer, Judge William Macon Smith. He is still a member of this firm, and is a prominent lawyer of Western Tennessee. He takes an active interest in the public matters of the State, and is a man of high standing and culture. In 1876 he was elected by the Democratic party a member of the State legislature to represent Shelby and Fayette counties, and served from 1877 to 1879. His engraved portrait is published in Lindsley's *History of Tennessee.*"

3242.

HENRY BARKSDALE COLLIER, of Shelby Co., Tenn., (near Memphis) son of No. 1049-1, p. 276, was born in Haywood Co., Tenn., Dec. 15, 1849. Married Oct. 18, 1877, Sallie Hine, of Athens, Ala. Children :—

5545, HENRY BROOKS COLLIER, b. June 29, 1880, d. June 22, 1883.
5546, JAMES DABNEY, b. April 8, 1884. 5547, KATE NELSON, b.
Sept. 23, 1885.

He lived in Haywood Co. until 1880, when he settled in Shelby Co., near
Memphis. He is a planter, and respected by all who know him.

3245.

DABNEY WEST COLLIER, of Haywood Co., Tenn., son of
Dabney C. and *Isabella White* Collier, was born Feb. 20, 1841.
Married, April 29, 1865, Pattie Elizabeth Maury, daughter of Dr.
William Henry and *Jane W. Worsham* Maury, of Somerville, Tenn.,
granddaughter of Abram P. (b. 1766) and *M. Worsham* Maury, great-
granddaughter of Abraham (b. 1731) and *Susanna Poindexter* Maury.
See Brock's *Fontaine Pedigree*, pp. 123, 134, 137, 138.) Children :—

5548, CARY COLLIER, b. Mar. 24, 1871, d. April 10, 1872. 5549, DABNEY
MAURY, b. May 4, 1873, d. Nov. 16, 1873.

"At the beginning of the war D. W. Collier was a resident of Memphis,
Tenn. He enlisted in April, 1861, as a private in the Bluff City Grays, afterwards Co. B of the 154th Regt. Confederate Volunteer Inf., and participated
in all the battles of the West. In 1863 this regiment was mounted and assigned to Gen. Forrest's command. After the battle of Chicamauga, while
leading his company in pursuit of the enemy, Lieut. Collier was wounded by
a shell which exploded in his horse and took off his leg. He was sent off the
field by Gen. Forrest in his ambulance, and his limb was amputated. After
an illness of several months he returned to his old home in Haywood Co. In
1865 he made his way through the Federal lines to New York city, where he
procured an artificial leg, and returned home, expecting to join his old command, but before he accomplished his object the Confederacy had ceased to
exist. He is a planter, and one of the truest, noblest and best of men."

3248.

WILLIAM DABNEY COLLIER, of Missouri, son of No. 1049–3, was
born June 24, 1835, d. 1876. He married in Missouri about 1865,
and had children :—

5550, AGNES COLLIER. 5551, SIDNEY. 5552, SARAH.

He removed to Missouri about 1858. During the war he served with distinction as a scout under Gen. J. B. Price.

3249.

PEYTON SKIPWITH, of Memphis, Tenn. Married, Mar. 24, 1859,
MARY ISABELLA COLLIER, daughter of No. 1049–3, who was born Mar.
15, 1857, d. 1870. Children :—

5553, WILLIAM GRAY SKIPWITH, b. Sept. 11, 1860. 5554, PEYTON, b.
Dec. 27, 1861. 5555, MARY ISABELLA, b. Nov. 20, 1864, d. y.
5556, VIRGINIA CARY, b. July 9, 1869.

3251.

THOMAS ANDERSON PRIDE, of Amelia Co., Va., son of No. 1050-2, enlisted in the Confederate army when barely of age, and was killed in the battle of Spottsylvania Court House, the Wilderness, May, 1864.

3256.

PHILIP SOUTHALL WOOD, of Amelia Co.. Va., son of William Richard and *Lucy Henry Southall* Wood, was born July 13, 1848, died July 24, 1884. He was a prominent lawyer, and was twice Commonwealth's Attorney of Amelia Co. Married, Feb. 16, 1876, EMMA PRIDE, daughter of No. 426, who was born Oct. 20, 1850. Children :—

> 5565, RICHARD HENRY WOOD, b. Dec. 20, 1875. 5566, JULIA PRIDE, b. Sept. 8, 1878. 5567, PHILIP SOUTHALL, b. June 2, 1880. 5568, LUCY HENRY, b. Nov. 24, 1883.

Mr. Wood's father was a lawyer of eminence, and his mother, now the wife of Mr. Henry Miller, of Richmond, is a lady of wide literary reputation in the South.

3283.

MICHAEL CHRISTIAN GARBER, of Madison, Ind., son of Col. M. C. and *Ellen Schell* Garber, of Madison, Ind., b. 1850, married Feb. 10, 1879, BLANCHE EGGLESTON GOODE, daughter of No. 1051. Children :—

> 5601, GUILFORD SCHELL GARBER, b. Oct. 27, 1875. 5602, HUGH GOODE, b. June 11, 1878. 5603, MICHAEL CHRISTIAN, b. June 14, 1880. 5604, SAMUEL MACKERNESS, b. Sept. 23, 1882.

"Mr. M. C. Garber is editor and part proprietor of the *Madison Courier*, one of the oldest and most influential papers in Southern Indiana. He is a graduate of Hanover College, 1872. As a boy he accompanied his father, Colonel Garber, in several campaigns of the Civil War, including Sherman's march to the sea. He is a skillful political speaker, and has been Secretary of the Republican Committee for six successive campaigns. He is President of the County Bible Society, and of the Sunday School Association, and Elder and Superintendent of the Sunday School in the Madison Presbyterian Church His portrait appeared in the Cincinnati *Illustrated Graphic News*, November, 1886. His lineage is as follows: 1, *Michael Garber* came from Holland to Pennsylvania in 1716–20; 2, *Michael Garber*, of Lancaster, Pa.; 3, *Michael Garber*, of Staunton Va., Major in the Revolution; 4, *Michael C. Garber*, a pioneer settler of Madison, Ind., Colonel U. S. A.; 5, *M. C. Garber*, No. 3283."

3286.

SAMUEL GOODE McCULLOUGH, of Toledo, Ohio, son of No. 1052, was born July 13, 1843. He is a journalist and President of the Toledo Bee Newspaper Company.

3287.

BENJAMIN W. McCULLOUGH, of Galveston, Texas, son of No. 1052. He is general passenger agent for 2,700 miles of the Gould System of Railroads.

3288.

FRANK GOODE McCULLOUGH, of Fort Worth, Texas, son of No. 1052 ; is engaged in railroad enterprises in Texas.

3335.

DR. CHARLES H. COLE, of Helena, Montana, son of Charles and *Louisa Wood* Cole, was born in Plainfield, Ill., April 5, 1853. Married June 22, 1881, HARRIET GILLETT, daughter of No. 1066. Child : —

5611, PHILIP G. COLE, b. Sept. 25, 1883.

Dr. Cole is a graduate of Lincoln University and the Miami Medical College. He practiced his profession for a time in Jacksonville, and has for some years lived in Helena, Montana. His reputation as a surgeon and physician extends throughout Central Montana. He is a bank director and an enterprising man of business.

3336.

CHARLES PHIPPS GILLETT, of Jacksonville, Ill., son of No. 1066, was born May 30, 1857.

He was educated at Illinois College. For several years he has been private secretary to his father, Dr. P. G. Gillett.

3337.

WILLIAM E. BARNS, of St. Louis, Mo., was born Aug. 29, 1853, in Vevay, Ind. Married Oct. 26, 1880, ALICE LOUISE GILLETT, daughter of No. 1067.

Mr. Barns was graduated in 1872 from Illinois Wesleyan University, Bloomington. He became, in 1873, editor of the Decatur *Republican*, and in 1879 New Orleans correspondent of the Chicago *Inter-Ocean*. From 1875 to 1883 he was associate editor of the *Central Christian Advocate*, and in 1883, upon the establishment of *The Age of Steel*, became its editor. Under the management of Mr. Barns this paper has become one of the most useful of its class. He has also been a leader in the discussion of certain phases of social and political economy; and his book entitled "The Problem of Labor" (New York: Harper & Bros., 1886), has been very favorably received by economists.

3371.

REV. WILLIAM FRANKLIN KONE, of Farmville, Va., is a Baptist clergyman. Married ANNIE M. ADAMS, daughter of Jesse R. and *Fannie E. Lamkin* Adams, No. 1095, p. 294. Child : —

5631, FANNIE ADAMS KONE, b. Jan. 8, 1885.

3372.

PROF. WILLIAM M. BASKERVILLE, of Vanderbilt University, Nashville, Tenn., married FLORENCE ADAMS, daughter of No. 1095. Child : —

5632, JOHN ADAMS BASKERVILLE.

3373.

ROBERT TAIT, of Norfolk, Va., married, 1885, FANNIE LAMKIN ADAMS, daughter of No. 1095. Child :—

5633, FLORENCE LE LESNE TAIT.

3379 (—1094½ Sixteenth Generation.)

REV. THOMAS A. WARE, of Charlottesville, Va., son of No. 442, p. 85, is a Methodist clergyman. He was born in Tennessee about 1826, and came in his youth to Virginia. Married Miss Pretloe, of Southampton, Va. Mr. Ware properly belongs with the seventeenth generation.

3482.

AZEL WILDER WELLS, of Sidney, Ohio, son of No. 1176½, p. 802, was born June 29, 1860. Married Ollie A. Hoover Sept. 5, 1883.

THE LUNENBURG GOODES.

3500.

E. T. BYINGTON, of Atlanta, Ga., editor of the Atlanta *Record*, married ELIA VIRGINIA GOODE, daughter of No. 1200.

3526.

HENRY L. HODGES, of Washington, D. C., son of Silas Wyllys and *Polly Gillet* Hodges, of Clarendon, Vt., married ANNA ELIZABETH CHIVERS, daughter of No. 1226. Children :—

5651, HELEN HODGES. 5652, FLETCHER. 5653, HARRY WYLLYS. 5654, MARY.

Mr. Hodges was from 1854 to 1863 Principal of the High School at La Grange, Ga., and has for many years been an official of the Department of Justice in Washington.

3527.

DR. MARCUS ANDREWS CHIVERS, of Texas (near Galveston), son of No. 1226, was a physician in Texas. At the outbreak of the war he enlisted in the First Texas Inf., C. S. A., and while serving as Acting Surgeon in the vicinity of Richmond, in 1861, he died. Married Sarah Clarke, of Antioch, Ga., (sister of 3530).

3528.

HENRY THOMAS CHIVERS, of West Point, Ga., son of No. 1226, died in 1883. Married Susan Reed. Children : —

   5655, LILLA CHIVERS.   5656, FANNIE.

Mr. Chivers was a soldier in the C. S. A. and a farmer.

3529.

JOEL M. CHIVERS, of Peytonsville, Ark., son of No. 1226. Married Caroline Neely, of Chambers Co., Ga., (sister of No. 3531. Children : —

   5657, ANNA CHIVERS. 5658, MARCUS. 5659, HELEN. 5660, FLETCHER.

Mr. Chivers was a soldier in the C. S. A., in Capt. Ferrell's Battalion of Artillery, and since the war has been a farmer in Arkansas.

3530.

RUFUS CLARKE, of Troup Co., Ga., a farmer, married EMILY CHEVERS, daughter of No. 1226. Children : —

   5661, JOEL M. CLARKE. 5662, FANNIE. 5663, MAMIE. 5664, WILLIAM.
     5665, FLETCHER.

3531.

ULYSSES MOSELY, of Peytonsville, Ark., a farmer, married ELIZA FRANCIS CHIVERS, daughter of No. 1226. Children : —

   5666, EMMA MOSELY.   5667, MARY ELOISE.   5668, FANNIE LOUISE.
    5669, STANTON ULYSSES.

3531½.

CHARLES DAWSON CHIVERS, of Troup Co., Ga., son of No. 1226, was born in 1846, and enlisted in the latter part of the war in Capt. Moses's company of infantry, C. S. A. He died in service at Selma, Ala., in 1865, in the nineteenth year of his age.

3552.

MAUDE ANNULET ANDREWS, of Washington, Ga., daughter of Dr. Henry F. and *Cora Morgan* Andrews, p. 307, great granddaughter of John and *Ann Goode* Andrews, was born in 1863. She is an accomplished writer of verse. Among her contributions to the press the author has seen several graceful efforts, among them " The Wind and the Lily," and " The Erudite Maid," printed in *Puck* March, 1887.

3550.

WILLIAM HENRY TOOMBS, of Washington, Ga , a lawyer, son of Gabriel Toombs, and nephew of Gen. Robert Toombs, married in 1875,

JULIA BUTLER, daughter of Troup and *Cora Andrews* Butler, No. 1230, p. 308. Children :—

> 5671, CORA BUTLER TOOMBS, b. Aug. 8, 1876. 5672, THOMAS BUTLER, b. Oct. 6, 1877. 5673, GABRIEL, b. Jan. 31, 1879. 5674, JULIA HARDEN, b. Sept. 14, 1880. 5675, LOUISE, b. Nov. 30, 1881.

3552. (Page 315.)

PIERCE M. BUTLER, of South Carolina, son of Col. Pierce M. Butler, (Governor of South Carolina and Colonel of the Palmetto Regt.; killed at the battle of Cherubusco), married KATE GOODE, daughter of No. 1309, p. 315. Children :—

> 5691, PIERCE MASON BUTLER, b. 1861. 5692, SAMUEL GOODE, b. 1867. 5693, JULIA D., b. 1868.

3659. (–1357.)

REV. CHARLES HENRY HALL, D. D., of Brooklyn, N. Y., was born in Augusta, Ga., November 7, 1820. Married (1) 1847, ANNIE MARIA CUMMING, daughter of No. 566, who died in 1855, (2) m. 1857, Elizabeth V. Ames, of Washington. Children :— (one by first wife, five by second.)

> 5694, BRYAN HUGH HALL, b. Nov. 2, 1855.

His preparatory studies were at Andover, Mass., from whence he proceeded to Yale College, where he was graduated in 1842. After a thorough course of reading in theology, including one year at the General Episcopal Theological Seminary, New York, he was, in 1844, ordained a deacon, and in the following year a priest of the Protestant Episcopal Church. His first settlement was at St. John's Church, Huntington, Long Island, where he remained two years. After this he was called to West Point, where he was married, in 1847, to Miss Annie Cumming, of Augusta Ga. Mr. Hall's next charge was at John's Island, S. C., where he was eight years pastor. His wife died there in 1855. In 1856 he received a call to the Church of the Epiphany, Washington, D. C. Dr. Hall has been rector of Holy Trinity, Brooklyn, since 1869. His church is a beautiful edifice, with about twelve hundred sittings, and one thousand communicants.

Previous to the war his church at Washington was made up about equally of northern and southern families. Mr. Jefferson Davis and his family had a pew in it. After the Confederate leader left the capital his pew was taken and occupied throughout the war by Edwin M. Stanton, Secretary of War. Epiphany Church was for a time used as a military hospital. During the years of civil conflict Dr. Hall's public teachings were exclusively religious and non-political. The services conducted by him were attended by many public men, both civilians and soldiers, and his influence was far-reaching. " Through the heat and fever of the war," says a writer of him, " he steered his pastoral bark safely through the smooth waters of a tranquil Christian faith. He believed firmly in the great doctrines of the nation, and that however dark appeared the national horizon, a morning of joy would at length break upon the night of heaviness, and the stormclouds of war and hatred would, in God's good time, pass away." Dr. Hall always has been a Democrat. He took a prominent part in the campaign of 1884, and was chairman of the great meeting in Brooklyn at which ex-Senator Thurman was the principal speaker.

His theological views are those of a devout thinker, loving his Church no less than his sympathies are broad and his recognition of Christian brotherhood in those who differ from him in denominational preference, ready and cheerful. In the great welcome to Dr. Talmage, after his return from Europe, in 1885, Dr. Hall and his friend, Mr. Beecher, were the principal speakers. He attended a meeting convened to honor the memory of the saintly Unitarian, Dr. Channing. In his own church he is at the head of the Standing Committee of his diocese. He received his degree of D. D. in 1860 from three colleges at the same time—Columbia College, New York; Hobart College, Geneva, and St. James College, Maryland. His principal published works are "Notes on the Gospel," "The Church in the Household," "The Valley of the Shadow," and a book of devotions for Holy Week. Dr. Hall preached a sermon of great power on the occasion of President Lincoln's death. In October of 1865, he published a discourse on "Conscience in its Relations to the Duties of the Citizens of the State." This was dedicated to Secretary Stanton. Many of his sermons have been published in the newspapers, and of his lectures and addresses, most notably perhaps is his lecture on Thomas Jefferson. Dr. Hall is a useful citizen, helpful in promoting the public good. As chaplain of the Twenty-third regiment, director of the Historical Society, and in numerous other ways, he shows a continuous interest in matters other than those ecclesiastical and religious.

In personal appearance Dr. Hall is of medium height, well proportioned, erect, and active. He gives an impression of character and power. His manners are courteous, self-possessed, and dignified.

Henry Ward Beecher, at whose obsequies he officiated, sketched his character on the occasion of a reception to Dr. Talmage upon his return from Europe: "We have present with us a distinguished citizen of Brooklyn—a man not born in the North, but connected in the North, without at the same time losing that generous and impulsive nature which belongs to the southern character; a good, sound man; one who in his own denomination stands second to none—an honest, fearless, upright, manly man, against whom men can lean as against a granite column, and woe be to the man on whom that column falls."—*Richmond Dispatch.*

3701.

BENJAMIN HARVEY HILL, of Atlanta, Ga., son of Hon. B. H. Hill and *Caroline Holt* Hill, No. 1380, p. 325, is a prominent young lawyer of Atlanta, Ga., appointed in 1885 U. S. District Attorney for the Northern District of Georgia. Married Mary Carter, of North Georgia, a niece of Senator A. H. Colquitt, an accomplished lady and a poet.

3702.

CHARLES D. HILL, of Atlanta, Ga., son of No. 1380, is a brilliant young lawyer: in 1885 he was Attorney-General of the city of Atlanta. Married Miss Hennie Hughes. Child :

5701, BENJAMIN HARVEY HILL, b. 1875.

3703.

EDGAR THOMPSON, of Atlanta, Ga., married HENRIETTA HILL, daughter of No. 1380. Children : —

5702, CAROLINE HILL. 5703, EDGAR.

3704.

DR. ROBERT RIDLEY, of Atlanta, Ga., a prominent physician, member of the Medical Association of Georgia, m. 1872, EMMA LELA HILL, daughter of No. 1380. Children : —

5704, JOHN RIDLEY, b. 1873. 5705, ROBERT. 5706, CAROLINE.

3707.

CHARLES LANE, of Macon, Ga., married EMILY COOPER BRANHAN, daughter of No. 1382. Two children.

Mr. Lane was educated at Mercer University, Oxford, Ga. He is Principal of the Alexander School of Macon, and a useful and popular citizen.

3708.

FRANK MEANS, of Butler, Ga., married CAROLINE HOLT BRANHAN, daughter of No. 1382. Four children.

Mr. Means was formerly principal of the York Valley Academy, and is now President of the Butler Female College.

3709.

ALFRED IVERSON BRANHAM, of Macon, Ga., son of No. 1382, was born in 1855. He was for a time a successful teacher in the Macon schools, and is now city editor of the Macon *Telegraph*. Married Lucy Tomes, of Eatonton, Ga. Two girls.

3711.

L. G. WALKER, of Chattanooga, Tenn., editor of the Chattanooga *Daily Times*, married ADELA J. BRANHAM, daughter of No. 1382, b. in 1861.

THE CHARLOTTE GOODES.

3731.

THOMAS B. GOODE, of Bunceton, Mo., druggist, son of No. 1389. Married. Has son : —

5721, MACKERNESS GOODE, and others.

3780.

C. L. FINCH, of Boydton, Va., son of L. E. Finch, No. 1400. Married S. ALICE BASKERVILLE, No. 2008. Children :—

> 5731, LELA GOODE FINCH. 5732, ELLIOTT. 5733, ALICE BASKERVILLE.

THE WEST CHESTERFIELD GOODES.

3841.

ROBERT ARMISTEAD WOOLDRIDGE, of Baltimore, Md., son of Joseph R. and *Mary Goode* Wooldridge, was born June 21, 1843. Married Grace Faris Jelke, dau. of Ferdinand Jelke,, of Cincinnati, Ohio, a native of Nordhausen, Germany, and Louisa Faris, his wife. Children :—

> 5751, LOUISE GRACE WOOLDRIDGE, b. Nov. 1, 1882, d. March 23, 1885. 5752, ISABEL JELKE, b. Dec. 17, 1884. 5753, GRACE LA PIERRE. b. Jan. 24, 1887.

Mr. Wooldridge was educated at Salem Academy, near Chesterfield C. H., and at the age of fifteen, family reverses preventing him from entering college, he went into a mercantile house in Richmond. At the outbreak of the war, and at the age of eighteen, he enlisted in the Confederate army, and served until Lee's surrender. His gallantry was rewarded by a complimentary furlough granted by Lee upon the recommendation of Gen. George H. Stuart. He was for a time a prisoner at Point Lookout.

At the close of the war and until 1867 he was in business in Richmond, except for a time when an official of the Holston Salt and Plaster Company at Saltville, Va. In 1876 he removed to Baltimore. Having, after twenty years of hard labor, overcome the misfortunes visited by the civil war upon himself and his family, he is now the head of the prosperous firm of R. A. Wooldridge & Co., importers, Baltimore.

Mr. Wooldridge is a member and trustee and steward in the Southern Methodist Church, and a prominent supporter of the Baltimore Young Men's Christian Association. He takes much interest in music, and was a sustaining member of the Oratorio Society in its days of weakness. He is interested also in art, and has a valuable collection of pictures, chiefly engravings and etchings. An engraving from a water-color sketch in his possession was presented by the Century Company in its series of war articles.

3843.

FRANK WILLIAM ANDERSON, of Chesterfield Co., Va., son of Dr. William M. and *Cicily F. Martin* Anderson, married Nov. 20, 1867, EMMA JANE WOOLDRIDGE, daughter of No. 1476, born April 28, 1845. Children :—

> 5761, JOSEPH ARMISTEAD ANDERSON, b. Jan. 16, 1867. 5762, WILLIAM

N. L., b. April 19, 1871, d. May 9, 1871. 5763, NANNIE MAY, b. May 6, 1872, d. Dec. 8, 1876. 5764, WILLIAM MATTHEW, b. Feb. 19, 1875. 5765, FRANK SPENCER, b. Nov. 28, 1879.

3846.

OSCAR THOMAS WEBSTER, of Clover Hill, Chesterfield Co., Va., farmer, son of Edward Thomas and *Rebecca Bowles* Webster, married, April 24, 1872, ANGELIA AUGUSTA WOOLDRIDGE, daughter of No. 1476, born Oct. 23, 1848. Children:—

> 5766, ROYALL THOMAS WEBSTER, b. Aug. 11, 1874. 5767, ALMA GRACE, b. Aug. 22, 1876. 5768, LOUISA GOODE, b. Nov. 17, 1880. 5769, BESSIE WOOLDRIDGE, b. Aug. 28, 1883.

3849.

JEREMIAH GALE JETER, of Carolina Co., Va., married Oct. 20, 1885, BETTIE BRANCH WOOLDRIDGE, daughter of No. 1476, born Oct. 6, 1844. Child:—

> 5770, ROBERT WOOLDRIDGE JETER, b. Jan. 9, 1887, d. Feb. 1, 1887.

3850.

DR. PHILIP TURNER SOUTHALL, of Amelia Co., Va., son of No. 1477, p. 333, was born May 18, 1851.

Dr. Southall was graduated in medicine at the University of Virginia in 1872, and at the Richmond Medical College in 1873. He is practicing his profession in Amelia Co.

3851.

ROBERT GOODE SOUTHALL, of Amelia Court House, Amelia Co., Va., son of No. 1477, p. 333, was born Dec. 26, 1852.

He was graduated in law, with the degree of B. L., at the University of Virginia in 1876, and is now Attorney for the Commonwealth in Amelia Co., Va., and is chairman of the County Democratic Committee. He was a delegate to the National Democratic Convention at Chicago in 1874.

3856.

STEPHEN OSBORNE SOUTHALL, of Chula, Amelia Co., Va., son of No. 1477, p. 333, was born May 15, 1858.

Mr. Southall was educated at Kemore School and the University of Virginia, and was for some time principal of the Public School of Amelia Co. He has for several years been a lay reader in the Protestant Episcopal church in Amelia Co., and is now a student in the Theological Seminary at Alexandria. Mr. Southall has been a diligent and voluminous contributor to this work.

THE HENRICO GOODES.

4225.

SARPI CARR CABANNÉ, of St. Louis, Mo., married in 1869 JULIA WASH GOODE, daughter of No. 1780. Children:—

5801, LUCIEN DUTIL CABANNÉ, b. 1870. 5802, FANNY GOODE. 5803, GRATIOT. 5804, SARPI CARR. 5805, GOODE. 5806, JULIA.

4226.

ROBERT WASH GOODE, of St. Louis, Mo., son of No. 1780, was born in 1852. He was graduated from William and Mary College in 1872. Attorney-at-law and politician in St. Louis. Captain in the Missouri Militia.

4228.

LIEUT. GEORGE WILLIAM GOODE, U. S. A., son of No. 1780, was born 1854. Graduated at U. S. Military Academy, West Point, 1880, and at present Lieutenant in the First Cavalry, stationed at Walla Walla, Oregon.

THE WHITBY GOODES.

4291.

JOHN EDMUND WARD, of Kansas City, Mo., son of Seth Edmund Ward, No. 1795, p. 343, was born June 21, 1861. Educated at William Jewell College. In business with his father in Kansas City. Married Nov. 10, 1886, Mary Octavia Jones, daughter of Major B. F. Jones, and *Mary Ann Nesbit* Jones, both descended from old Georgia families.

4292.

HUGH CAMPBELL WARD, of Kansas City, Mo., son of No. 1795, was born Mar. 10, 1863. Graduated from Harvard University in the class of 1886. A student of law in St. Louis since October 1886.

4352.

BENJAMIN GREEN MAYNARD, of San Francisco, Cal., son of No. 1822, p. 349, was born in Washington City, July 14, 1847. He was a soldier C. S. A., served with distinction in several battles, and is now in business in San Francisco.

4353.

HARRY ST. JOHN DIXON, of Fresno, Cal.. son of Judge Richard and *Julia R. Phillips* Dixon, of "Sycamores," Washington Co., Miss., was born in Jackson, Miss., Aug. 2, 1843. Married Feb. 14, 1874, CONSTANCE MAYNARD, daughter of No. 1822, p. 349, who was born in Washington City, Feb. 3, 1853. Children :—

> 5821, LAFAYETTE MAYNARD DIXON, b. Jan. 24, 1875. 5822, ROBERT LAWRENCE, b. Nov. 20, 1876, d. Jan. 6, 1877. 5823, REBEKAH PHILLIPS, b. Feb. 12, 1878. 5824, ELEANOR MAYNARD, b. Oct. 5, 1879. 5825, MILDRED WASHINGTON, b. Feb. 13, 1886.

Mr. Dixon was a student in the University of Virginia at the opening of the war, but left college to enlist in the Washington Cavalry, 28th Mississippi Regt. C. S. A., and served until the surrender, May 12, 1865. He then studied law in the University of Virginia, and in 1868, became a citizen of Fresno, Cal., where he is a leading member of his profession. From 1870 to 1874, he was County Clerk of Fresno County, California.

He is grandson of Capt. Henry St. John Dixon, an officer in the war of 1812, a leading lawyer of Abingdon, Va., a fellow-student of Henry Clay, who married Boadicea, daughter of Capt. Richard White, of Abingdon, who was with Campbell at King's Mountain, and Ella, his wife, daughter of Major Joseph Martin, of Washington Co., Va.

He is great grandson of Col. John Dixon, of "Liliput," who commanded a regiment in the Revolutionary War, and was publisher of the Virginia *Gazette* and printer to the State and Colony of Virginia; a descendant of the Dixon family of "Ramshawe," in Durham.*

4354.

ROBERT PEACHY MAYNARD, of Des Moines, Iowa, son of No. 1822, p. 349, was born in Washington City, July 24, 1849. Married, June 3, 1879, Hattie Lois Buell, daughter of David L. Buell, of Sherburne, N. Y., born Aug. 22, 1852. No children.

R. P. Maynard was educated at Yale College, lived in San Francisco, Cal., till 1880, followed his profession as a civil engineer till 1886, when he moved to Des Moines, where he is now engaged in the mortgage loan business, as secretary of the Lewis Investment Company.

4355.

LIEUT. HERBERT WINSLOW, U. S. N., son of Adm'l J. A. Winslow, who commanded the "Kearsarge" in the engagement with the "Alabama," was born in Massachusetts. He was appointed to the U. S. Naval Academy, 1865, graduated 1869, and appointed ensign, July 12, 1870, Master, April 1, 1872, Lieutenant, May 3, 1875, and in 1886, was ordered to the Washington Navy Yard. Married, June 26, 1876, LIZZIE MAYNARD, daughter of No. 1822. No children.

4356.

DUFF GREEN MAYNARD, of San Francisco, son of No. 1822, p. 349, was born in San Francisco, Dec. 9, 1866, and is now a resident of that city, engaged in business pursuits.

4359.

REV. W. B. HENLEY, of Amherst Co., Va., married FLORENCE MAYNARD, daughter of No. 1823, p. 352, who was born, 1838, died, Aug. 29, 1871. Daughter :—

5851, MABEL PARKER HENLEY, b. Oct. 18, 1869.

* Mr. Dixon has extensive MS. records of his family in England and America.

4362.

HON. WILLIAM McKENDRY GWIN, jr., of San Francisco, son of Senator William M. Gwin, and *Mary E. N. Bell* Gwin, a native of Kentucky, was born Feb. 24, 1843, in Vicksburg, Miss. Married, Nov. 28, 1871, BLANCHE MAYNARD, daughter of No. 1824. Children :—

> 5861, MARY BELL GWIN, b. July 27, 1876. 5862, WILLIAM McKENDRY, b. Jan. 19, 1879. 5863, RALPH, b. Mar. 8, 1881.

Mr. Gwin was a cadet at West Point, at the beginning of the war, and received also a part of his education at the University of Virginia. He served one year in a Mississippi cavalry regiment, C. S. A. He has been twice elected to the State Senate. He is by profession a miner, and has for twenty years been in charge of the Gwin Mine in Calaveras Co., Cal.

Senator Gwin, his father, was one of the earliest citizens of California, whither he went in 1848, and represented the state in the U. S. Senate, from 1850 to 1861. He was imprisoned by the Federal authorities, from 1861 to 1863, and in 1864-5 was engaged in an enterprise for the colonization of Sonora with people of southern birth.

4383.

REV. WILLIAM T. PRICE, of Marlins Bottom, Pocahontas Co., Va., son of James and *Margaret Poague* Price. Married, in 1865, ANNA LOUISE RANDOLPH, daughter of No. 1830, p. 353. Children :—

> 5871, WILLIAM RANDOLPH PRICE, b. 1866, d. y. 5872, JAMES WARD, b. 1868. 5873, ANDREW GATEWOOD, b. 1871. 5874, SUSAN ALEXANDER, b. 1873. 5875, NORMAN RANDOLPH, b. 1875. 5876, CALVIN WELLS. 5877, ANNA VIRGINIA, b. 1882.

Mr. Price is a Presbyterian clergyman; a graduate of Washington College, Lexington, Va., also of Union Theological Seminary, Prince Edward Co., Va. The first years of his ministry were spent in Bath and Highland Counties. In 1869 he removed to Rockingham Co., where for fifteen years he was pastor. In 1886 he removed on his farm in Pocahontas Co., W. Va.

Anna Louise Randolph was born in Manchester, near Richmond, July 15, 1837; spent some years under the tuition of her aunt, Miss Lucy Ward Randolph (Mrs. Robert Saunders), and Mrs. Mary Goode Jones, at West View Seminary, Brunswick Co., Va.. and at Homestead Seminary, Greensville Co., Va. After a thorough collegiate course, embracing Philosophy, the Greek, Latin and French languages, Miss Randolph was graduated at the age of sixteen from Prof. Abadee's Collegiate Institute, Brooklyn, N. Y. She then accepted the position of Assistant Principal at Homestead Seminary, Greensville Co., where for several years she successfully instructed large classes of girls—some older than herself—in music and the languages. This school, like many others in Virginia, was entirely broken up by the war. Previous to her marriage in 1865, to Rev. W. T. Price, of Pocahontas Co., W. Va., she contributed much both in prose and verse to some of the leading religious newspapers of the South. She is the author of "Singing Will," a little book published by the Presbyterian Committee of Publication in Richmond, Va., also "The Mother's Catechism," published by the same.

Mrs. Price is of a pronounced brunette type of beauty; her large, lustrous dark eyes and abundant black hair seem to speak of her well authenticated Indian lineage.

The following verses from her pen describe "Warwick," for several generations the home of her ancestors. It is almost equally applicable to "Whitby," the ancestral home of the Goodes, which was the adjoining plantation, next above on the James River, known to the Indians as the Powhatan:

"WARWICK."

Where Powhatan's broad stream flows by,
    And ancient trees their heads tower high,
There stands a chimney left alone,
    With glittering ivy overgrown.

In other years a home was seen
    Where now the ivy grows so green,
And there were smiles and voices of mirth
    Round this deserted, silent hearth.

Warwick ! how many hearts are stirred
    At mention of the household word ;
How many joys long buried rise
    As o'er the past fleet memory flies !

With vines a tree is still entwined
    Which oft my father's feet have climbed,
And close at hand a spot is found
    He claimed as his own cultured ground.

Still flows the river to the sea,
    And still towers high the ancient tree.
The spring is gushing o'er the stone,
    And murmurs in the same old tone.

These all remain to touch the heart,
    And bids its slumbering echoes start.
But naught speaks of the old hearthstone,
    As the ivied chimney which stands alone.

It tells how time has sped away,
    And brought a homestead to decay,
And so his hand has parted wide
    A group once sheltered side by side.

The ivy shines midst summer's glow,
    And peeps from out the winter's snow.
The graceful tendrils catch the breeze,
    And whisper to the neighboring trees.

Methinks they tell a tale of years
    Of household joys, and smiles, and tears;
And children of a stranger come
    To say "This was my father's home !"

                ANNA L. RANDOLPH PRICE.

4384.

JAMES B. MALLORY, of Brunswick Co., Va., son of William and Martha Mallory. Married June 20, 1859, VIRGINIA RANDOLPH, daughter of No. 1830. Children :—

5878, WILLIAM YOUNG MALLORY, b. Sept. 30, 1860. 5879, VIRGINIA PERRY, b. Feb. 16, 1863. 5880, JAMES BAUGH, b. Aug. 2, 1865. 5881, EDWIN MORRISON, b. Nov. 16, 1867. 5882, LOUISE RANDOLPH, b. March 2, 1870.

Mr. Mallory was a large cotton and tobacco planter in Brunswick Co., Va. He died very suddenly Dec. 4, 1874.

4385.

REV. ROBERT HANSON FLEMING, of Washington city, son of William Wier and *Margaret Lewis* Fleming, was born Oct. 12, 1846. Married June 24, 1875, LUCY WARD RANDOLPH, daughter of No. 1830, p. 353, who was born May 12, 1847. Children : —

5883, MARY RANDOLPH FLEMING, b. 1877.

Mr. Fleming was graduated with distinction from Washington and Lee University in 1871, and from Union Theological Seminary, Prince Edward Co., in 1874. He was a midshipman, C. S. N., and formed one of the escort of President Davis and the Confederate Treasury from Richmond to Georgia in the closing days of the civil war. On his mother's side he is a descendant from the Huguenot Lewis family, who are identified with the pioneer and Revolutionary history of Virginia.

He was from 1876 to 1886 a preacher of the Presbyterian church at Woodstock, Va., and in 1886 accepted the pastorate of Gurley Chapel, Le Droit Park, Washington, D. C.

The following notice of Mrs. Fleming is quoted from a Virginia paper :

"Lucy Randolph Fleming was born in Brooklyn, N. Y. Her primary education was begun under the unremitting and affectionate tuition of her eldest sister, Mrs. Anna Randolph Price, furthered by attendance at the school of an accomplished lady in Brooklyn. After her father's removal to Virginia, Miss Randolph spent several years at Homestead Seminary, Greensville Co., Va., until ill health interfered with her studies. In 1866 she entered a young ladies' school in Richmond, Va., conducted by Rev. P. B. Price, where she remained but a few months; afterwards studying at home under the direction of her sister. From a very early age Miss Randolph manifested a love for belles lettres, writing many little poems and essays, always speedily and carefully destroyed by the writer. Like Bridget Elia, she was tumbled early, by accident or design, into a spacious closet of good old English reading, without much selection or prohibition, and browsed at will upon that fair and wholesome pasturage.

"In 1875 she was united in marriage to Rev. Robert Hanson Fleming, a Minister of the Presbyterian Church. Since her marriage Mrs. Fleming has taken up literary work with more regularity, becoming a frequent contributor to several leading journals. She is much interested in wholesome literature for the young, and has recently written a little book for girls, entitled "Alice Withrow," which has been very well received.

The following notice is from the *Literary World*: "Alice Withrow, by Lucy Randolph Fleming. (T. Y. Crowell & Co.) Alice Withrow was a city girl, with brothers and a sister, all of whom had to stay at home one summer instead of going to the country, on account of their father's business reverses. This was a disappointment to them. How they took their disappointment, how they made the best of it, how Alice started out to be a Christian, and made a number of bad mistakes in finding the way, and how she contrived in the end to do good and learn her lessons and get into the light and peace of humility, dutifulness and submission—this is the story. It is a pretty story, well written, with some keen points and bright touches, and likely to interest girls and do good."

Her pen has also of late been busy in the interests of Foreign Missions in a series of tracts entitled, "Little Talks to Little Missionaries," and serial writing for "Children's Work for Children."

Mrs. Fleming's endowments of mind and heart are of a very superior order, and have been developed by a unique educational process, in which theory and experience have been wisely extended. Her intellectual powers are, therefore, equal to a discriminating and correct apprehension of the social and ethical questions peculiar to the times in which she lives. Her poems, essays and sketches have been read and admired by the readers of a large number of the prominent religious journals of the country, as well as by many of the literary periodicals also—*The Interior, The Christian Observer, The Household Christian Weekly, The American Agriculturist, ·The Womans Magazine, The Youths Companion, &c.* Like her kinswoman, Mrs. Mary Randolph, author of "The Virginia Housewife; or, Methodical Cook," Mrs. Fleming has a talent for what may be called domestic literature, and several prizes have been awarded her by domestic journals for articles on household topics.

4387.

HENRY RANDOLPH, of Richmond, Va., son of No. 1830, p. 353, was born in Brooklyn, N. Y., 1854. Married, 1877, Anna Slater, of Richmond. Children :—

5884, HENRY WARD RANDOLPH, b. 1878. 5885, RUTH SLATER.

4388.

CAPT. TUCKER ST. JOSEPH RANDOLPH, C. S. A., son of Joseph W. and *Honoria M. Tucker* Randolph, was born Sept. 19, 1843, and was killed in an engagement near Bethesda Church (Cold Harbor,) May 30, 1864. He was a young man of the finest promise, of brilliant mind and striking personal beauty. He enlisted in the Confederate army, April 21, 1861, as Corporal of "F Company" of Richmond Volunteers, a body of which he had been a member since 1860. He was soon promoted to be Sergeant, and was severely wounded at the battle of Kernstown, Mar. 23, 1862.   In May, 1862, he was appointed Aide upon the staff of Gen. John Pegram, serving as Inspector General for more than a year.   He was not twenty one years of age when he died on the battle-field.

4389.

NORMAN VINCENT RANDOLPH, of Richmond, Va., son of No. 1832, p. 354, was born Nov. 2, 1846.   Married, (1) April 16, 1873, Louisa Whelan Reed, daughter of William B. and *Louisa Whelan* Reed, who died Mar. 17, 1877, leaving two children ; (2) Janet Henderson, daughter of Richard A. and *Janet Cleiland Homer* Weaver, of Warrenton, Va., b. April 29, 1848.   Children :—

> 5886, CORNELIA WHELAN RANDOLPH, b. Mar. 24, 1874.   5887, NORA MARY, b. May 20, 1875, d. July 7, 1876.   5888, NORMAN VINCENT, b. Sept. 15, 1876.
>
> 5889, JOSEPH WILLIAMSON RANDOLPH, b. Dec. 14, 1881, d. Feb. 14, 1883. 5890, JANET CLEILAND, b. Nov. 15, 1884.   5891, META LEE, b. Sept. 10, 1886.

Enlisting in the 5th Virginia Cavalry at the age of fifteen, June, 1862, he was soon after transferred to the staff of Gen. Pegram, with the brevet rank of Captain, and served in the campaign of 1862–4.   In Nov., 1862, he joined Mosby's "Partisan Rangers" and served until paroled at Ashland, May 22.   After the surrender of Lee, he with a number of his comrades, refusing to surrender, were making their way to Johnson's command, but failed to reach him until he too, had capitulated.   After the war Mr. Randolph began an active business career and has for many years been one of the leading men of Richmond, a member of the publishing firm of J. W. Randolph and English, and proprietor of a paper factory, one of the largest in the world, employing five hundred operatives.   He was Commissioner for Virginia to the New Orleans Exhibition, and as a member of the Executive Committee of the Lee Camp Soldier's Home, has been the principal factor in the organization of that most worthy enterprize.   He is also a member of the Association of the Army of Northern Virginia, and Chief Ordinance Officer of the First Virginia Brigade, 1887, with rank of Major.

The following sketch of Lee Camp Home is from the pen of Mr. Cunningham, staff correspondent of the Nashville *American :*

" What a lovely place ! It is about two miles out of the city, in the suburbs, and comprises thirty-six acres.   The main building of the Home is a brick, originally two stories high, but which is now having the third story added. The gifts to the Home amounted to $47,500.   Hon. W. W. Corcoran gave $5,000, $1,850 of which was expended for a cottage.

"The Appleton's, of New York, gave $1,000, with which a cottage was built. The Stonewall ' cottage was a gift from Lewis Ginter, a successful cigarette maker of Richmond.   There are five cottages besides the mess hall, which is now being used for a chapel. The managers expect to build a chapel on the grounds ere long. They have in bank $7,480. There are eighty-seven inmates listed. Four have been buried from the Home. One hundred is all they will provide for at a time. About 75 per cent. of the occupants are Virginians. The State gives $10,000 a year for its maintenance, and occupants are received from any of the States except Louisiana, which State has the only other home of the kind. That State gives $5,000 a year to its Home, near New Orleans, which has twenty-two occupants. Where other States send to Richmond the management does not object to an appropriation of $120 a year, although as so many crippled and maimed dependents met with these misfortunes in Virginia none are refused while there is room, to the capacity designated.

"All honor to the management of this enterprise. I have known its workings from the first, and how zealously many good men have stood for the cause. Mention of a list is deserved, but in these extended notes I only use that of Mr. Norman Randolph, who has never flagged in his zeal, and but for whose courageous soul there never would have been established an institution where the most unfortunate of Confederates could feel that they really have a home."

4391.

ANDREW RUFUS YARBROUGH, of Richmond, Va., son of William James and Ophelia Yarbrough, of Richmond, Va., married Dec. 17, 1872, *Mary Norman Hall*, daughter of No. 1834. Children :—

> 5892, LILIAN MOORE HALL, b. Sept. 26, 1873. 5893, RUFUS NORMAN, b. June 25, 1882.

4411.

SAMUEL GOODE ADAMS, of Mobile, Ala., married Mary Campbell, of Mobile, Ala. Children :—

> 5901, LUCY THORNTON ADAMS. 5902, MARY TOULMIN, m. *Joseph Rich.* of Mobile, Ala.

4415.

SETH THORNTON MAURY, of Temple Junction, Bell Co., Texas, a merchant, son of No. 1843, was born Feb. 19, 1848, married Dec. 2, 1879, Kate Stevenson. Children :—

> 5911, LILLIAN MAURY, b. Sept. 6, 1883, d. June 1, 1884. 5912, ZAIDEE ELIZA, b. Dec. 10, 1886.

4416.

RICHARD RANDOLPH MAURY, of China Springs, McLennan Co., Texas, was born Feb., 1850. A farmer. Married, Jan. 1, 1880, Ida Clements. Children :—

> 5913, ANNIE LENA MAURY, b. Aug. 16, 1881. 5914, LOTTIE STEWART, b. May 29, 1883. 5915, THOMAS JOSEPH, b. Dec. 10, 1884.

4417.

THOMAS FONTAINE MAURY, of China Springs, Texas, a farmer, married Florence Heddin. Children :—

5916, CORA G. MAURY, b. July 29, 1884. 5917, MAGGIE FONTAINE, b. July 27, 1886.

4418.

EDMUND KIMBRO MAURY, of China Springs, Texas, a farmer, married Nannie Foster. Children :—

5918, CAROLINE ELIZABETH MAURY, b. Nov. 7, 1862. 5919, ANNIE RICHARD, b. April 19, 1885.

4420.

JAMES B. STEVENS, of Oenaville, Bell Co., Texas, a stock raiser, married MARY LUCY MAURY. Children :—

5920, WILLIAM HENRY STEVENS, b. Jan. 13, 1885, d. 1886. 5921, ANNIE GOODE, b. July 11, 1886.

4421.

JAMES WOODVILLE MAURY, of China Springs, Texas, is a farmer and stock raiser. Unmarried.

4450.

THOMAS BOTTS, of New York city, son of No. 1855, was born July 19, 1854. He is a broker.

EXCURSUS.—THE BOTTS FAMILY OF VIRGINIA.

The name Botts is perhaps identical with Butts and Butz, and of Dutch or German origin. It appears in the records of the Virginia Colony early in the eighteenth century.

Thomas Botts, who was granted by the Crown 1,398 acres of land in Henrico Co. Sept. 8, 1736,* was perhaps the ancestor of all of the name in Virginia.

FIRST GENERATION.

1, THOMAS BOTTS married, it is believed, Miss Jones or Miss Edwards. He was a "gentleman farmer" or "gentleman superintendent," and lived probably somewhere in the vicinity of Richmond. He had children :—

2, THOMAS BOTTS, b. 1750–70, emigrated to Kentucky. 3, MRS. NALLE, whose plantation was near Orange Court House. She had several children, one of whom, THOMAS B(OTTS) NALLE, b. 1810–18, was appointed Purser U. S. N. Oct. 17, 1839, resigned July 31, 1861. 4, BENJAMIN BOTTS.

SECOND GENERATION.

4, BENJAMIN BOTTS, of Richmond, Va., was educated in the law office of Gen. John Minor ; became an eminent lawyer and conspicuous in the trial of Aaron Burr for treason. Married Jane Tyler, of Dumfries, Va., with whom he perished at the burning of the Richmond Theatre in Dec. 26, 1811. A poem written at the time by Mrs. Page, of Williamsburg, tells the touching story of their death. Children :—

---

* Virginia Land Register, Book XIV, p. 140.

5, ALEXANDER LITHGOW BOTTS, b. May 20, 1799. 6, JOHN MINOR, b. Sept. 16, 1802. 7, THOMAS HUTCHINSON, b. 1804. 8, CHARLES TYLER.

THIRD, FOURTH AND FIFTH GENERATIONS.

5, ALEXANDER LITHGOW BOTTS, of New York city, born in Dumfries, Va., May 20, 1799. He was licensed to practice law at the age of 18, and in 1828, or before, was Counsellor of State. During a brief period of authority as Acting Governor of Virginia he freed all persons imprisoned for debt in the Richmond Penitentiary. In 1834 he removed to New York and engaged in commercial enterprises as a partner of the Stevens Brothers of Hoboken, at the same time practising as a criminal lawyer. He was devoted to out-door sports, and was owner of the Hoboken race course. He died in Washington in 1860, and is buried in the Congressional Cemetery, near his dear friend, John C. Calhoun. He married SUSAN FRANCES RANDOLPH, No. 747 of the GOODE PEDIGREE, which may be consulted for a record of his descendants.

6, JOHN MINOR BOTTS, of Culpeper Co., Va., was born in Dumfries Sept. 16, 1802, died Jan. 8, 1869. After practising law from 1820 to 1826 he became a gentleman farmer in Henrico Co., and from 1833 to 1839 served as a Whig in the Virginia legislature. In 1839 he was elected to Congress and served until 1849. He was a prominent member of the Whig and American parties, and in 1859 was proposed as candidate for the Presidency. He opposed secession, and lived during the war on his farm near Culpeper Court House. He was one of those who went bail for Jefferson Davis. In 1866 he printed his work, "The Great Rebellion, Its Secret History, Rise, Progress and Disastrous Failure."

He was for many years a patron of the turf, and bred "Johanna," "Revenue" and other horses of note. (See American Biographical Dictionary, 1887.) He married Mary Whiting, daughter of Archibald Blair. Children :

21, BENJAMIN BOTTS, d. y. 22, JOHN, d. y. 23, ARCHIBALD BLAIR, graduated U. S. Military Academy, West Point, appointed Second Lieutenant, 4th Artillery, July 1, 1846, died Jan. 1, 1847, in Texas, while on his way to join in the Mexican war. He is buried in Richmond, where there is a monument erected by his brother officers. 24, BEVERLY BLAIR, of Harrisonburg, Va., graduated at William and Mary College, 1848, married (1) MARY BOTTS, No. 1860, of the *Goode Pedigree*, and had two children. (See Goode Genealogy), m. (2) Charlotte, dau. of Gen. Samuel H. Lewis, of Rockingham Co., sister of Hon. L. L. Lewis. Five children. 25, MARY MINOR, m. *Capt. Walter Hoxie*, now dead, son of Gen. Thomas D. Hoxie, of Paterson, N. J. She lives in Harrisonburg. Two children. 26, ROSALIE S., m. *Judge Lunsford Lomax Lewis*, late U. S. Attorney for the Southern District of Virginia; was president of the State Court of Appeals, brother of Sir John Lewis and of the wife of No. 24, and a descendant in the sixth generation of John Lewis and his wife Margaret Lynn, daughter of the Laird of Loch Lynn, who settled in Augusta Co., Va., about 1727. (See Peyton's History of Augusta Co.) She died about 1810, leaving daughter and son. 27, ISABELLA McLAIN, m. *Daniel Sheffy Lewis*, (son of U. S. Senator John Francis Lewis), a lawyer, and editor of the *Spirit of the Valley* of Harrisonburg, Va. Five children.

7, THOMAS HUTCHINSON BOTTS, of Fredericksburg, Va., lawyer, born 1804, died 1854, married Ann Willis, (great niece of Gen. Washington, and sister of Catharine Willis, who married Prince Achille Murat, nephew of Napoleon 1.) son.

28, COL. LAWSON BOTTS, who was forced into the command of a regiment of Confederate soldiers against his will, and was killed at Bull Run, declaring himself a Unionist. T. H. Botts married (2) Mary Stone, of Fredericksburg, about 1829 ; both died before the war. Children :

29, WILLIAM, d. 30, BENJAMIN, of Galveston or Houston, Texas, a distinguished citizen. 31, HENRY, m. Miss Herndon, sister of the wife of the late President Arthur. 32, ALBERT. 33, MARY BERKLEY.

8, CHARLES TYLER BOTTS, of San Francisco, Cal., b. 1809, d. 1884, long editor of the *Southern Planter* of Richmond ; went to California in 1848, where he was prominent as lawyer, judge and journalist ; married Margaret Marshall, of Fredericksburg, Va. Children :

41, ELIZABETH, m. *Dr. Aylett*, of Virginia and Colorado, d., leaving two daughters. 42, CHARLES, killed in Nicaragua while a member of Walker's expedition. 43, BEN., killed in California while hunting the puma or mountain lion.

4462.

THOMAS SLAIGHT ELDREDGE, of Noyac, N. Y., married SUSAN MARY CHADWICK, daughter of No. 1853. Children :—

5951, JANE CHADWICK ELDREDGE. 5952, HENRY CHADWICK. 5953, AVICIA MORTIMER. 5954, LOUISE AYLMER. 5955, KATE HAMILTON and BESSIE TUCKER, twins.

4536.

ROBERT BOLLING BATTE, of Prince George Co., Va., married Dec. 17, 1873, HELEN BLAND FRENCH, daughter of No. 1897, born June 31, 1851. Children :—

5971, HENRY LARDNER, b. Sept. 14, 1874. 5972, S. BASSETT FRENCH, b. March 16, 1876. 5973, ROBERT BOLLING, b. Aug. 27, 1878. 5974, FRANCIS CARY, b. Oct. 1880, d. same year. 5975, HELEN BLAND, b. Dec. 31, 1881. 5976, MACON RANDOLPH, b. Dec. 2, 1885.

4458.

LIEUT. POWHATAN H. CLARKE, U. S. A., son of No. 1906, was born in Rapides, La., Oct. 9, 1862; was appointed to the Military Academy at West Point in 1880 and graduated in 1885, and was appointed Second Lieutenant in the 10th Cavalry, and stationed at Fort Grant, Ariz.

Lieut. Clarke was in command of Co. K, of the 10th Cavalry, in an engagement with the Apache Indians under Geronimo May 14, 1886, and was complimented in his commanding officer's report for his gallantry in this his first engagement.

The Baltimore *Sun* and the Richmond *State* quote the following account of the gallant act of Lieutenant Clarke :

"A correspondent writes to *Harper's Weekly* concerning an act of bravery which, he says, 'under any nation under the sun but the United States would be fitly rewarded.' He says : ' Troop K, of the United States 10th Cavalry, a regiment of colored men, but with white officers, while scouting in the Sierra Pinitas or Little Pine Mountains, in Sonora, Mexico, came upon a band of hostile Apaches, strongly posted upon an open plateau. In the resulting skirmish one man was killed and another seriously wounded. As Corporal Scott, the wounded man, fell to the ground, Lieut. Powhatan H. Clarke, the second in command, rushed forward through a heavy fire, took the corporal in his arms and carried him out of the line of battle to a place of comparative safety. Germany, France, England or any other foreign nation rewards its heroes with crosses, ribbons and stars, but our republic, in its Puritan simplicity, thinks an honorable mention in orders ample sufficient, and seldom grants that. I have not the slightest desire to see any order of nobility instituted in the United States, but so long as war lasts and brave deeds are told in song and story, so long will such decorations as are mentioned above improve the *morale* and increase the *esprit* of an army, whether that army belongs to a foreign power or our own republic.' This exploit of a Southern soldier risking his own life to save that of a colored comrade, apart from its merit as an act of bravery, is a conspicuous illustration of a phase of Southern character which some Northern people have not yet learned to appreciate."

5080.

WILLIAM E. GOODE, of Slater, Saline Co., Mo., son of No. 2684, is an extensive farmer. Children :—

> 6001, WILLIAM P. GOODE, of Johnson Co., Kan., an extensive farmer and stock breeder; has nine children, five of them boys. 6002, DR. GEORGE T. GOODE, of Johnson Co., Kan., a wealthy farmer; has three children.

5256.

WILLIAM EDWARD CARLIN, son of Gen. William P. Carlin, was born July 26, 1866. He is a student in the Rensselaer Polytechnic Institute, Troy, N. Y.

THE RAPPAHANNOCK GOODES.

Of this branch, perhaps, though possibly a son of No. 39 or No. 40, was —— GOODE, who died in Hillsboro, N. C., at an advanced age in 1784. His son, HENRY PENDLETON GOODE, was Captain of a company of Virginia troops in the Revolution, and serving under Washington, received medals for his gallantry ; he died in Knoxville. He had two sons, WILLIAM and JOHN PENDLETON (b. 1796, d. 1876), who went to Tennessee at an early day, and became printers. They came to Philadelphia, 1820–40. WILLIAM NEWBOLD GOODE, of Brooklyn, N. Y., is son of the latter.

Another family, perhaps of this branch, if not descended from Joseph Goode, No. 40, is represented by JOHN SWANZY GOODE, of Myrtle, Miss., son of THOMAS JEFFERSON GOODE, a native of Virginia, and grandson of JOSEPH GOODE, of Virginia, whose father was a soldier in the Revolution.

I am inclined to believe that certain of the Virginia family, settling on the Virginia peninsula, made their way to Maryland.– These people appear to have dropped the terminal " e," a thing not hard to do in those days. I reprint the following :

PROCEEDINGS OF MARYLAND COUNCIL OF SAFETY,
ANNAPOLIS, Tuesday, August 6, 1776.

Council met. Were present : The Hon. Daniel of St. Thomas Jenifer, Esq., Charles Carroll, Barrister, James Tilghman, Esq.

Commissions issued to the following officers of a company of militia, for the Flying Camp of Col. Charles Greenbury Griffith's Battalion :

Jacob Good, captain, dated July 4.
John B. Thompson, first lieutenant, dated July 15.
John Ghislen, second lieutenant, dated July 15.
John Smith, ensign, dated July 15.

Ordered. That Capt. Good's Company proceed directly up to the Bay to the Head of Elk, and thence to Philadelphia, to join the Flying Camp.

Ordered. That the Treasurer of the Western Shore pay to Capt. Jacob Good £75 on account of his company.

American Archives, v, 1348–9.

FREDERICKTOWN, July 21, 1776.

Gentlemen: Yesterday I received part of Capt. Good's company. Lieut. Ghislen now waits on you for commissions and orders. Capt. Good informed me that it will be out of his power to procure arms unless you will be pleased to furnish him with money, and then he can get both arms and blankets. I submit it to your consideration whether it would not be best. I believe Capt. Good to be a man of honor. I know him to be a man of property, and will, I dare say lay out the money to the advantage of the publick. * * *

I am, gentlemen, your most obedient servant,

B. JOHNSON.

To the Council of Safety of Maryland at Annapolis.

American Archives, i, 482.

APPENDIX I.

THE FAMILY IN ENGLAND,

WITH NOTICES OF AMERICAN OFFSHOOTS NOT OF THE WHITBY STOCK.

"This," he says with unction, "is Sir Solomon Sculpin, the founder of the family."
"Famous for what?" we ask respectfully.
"For founding the family."
"This," he says, pointing to a dame in hoops and diamond stomacher, "this is Lady Sheba Sculpin."
"Ah! yes. Famous for what?" we inquire.
"For being the wife of Sir Solomon."

Family Portraits.

The following pages contain a full discussion of a subject briefly reviewed in the early part of the book. When generations are referred to by number, the numeration is that already employed in the chapter entitled "Ten English Generations."

CORNWALL.

The Goodes, or Goods, of "Whitley" and "Whitston," were the ancestors of the Virginia Goodes. Robert God, as we have seen (*antea*, p. 3), lived 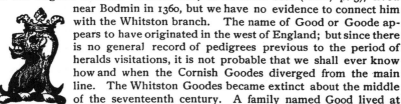 near Bodmin in 1360, but we have no evidence to connect him with the Whitston branch. The name of Good or Goode appears to have originated in the west of England; but since there is no general record of pedigrees previous to the period of heralds visitations, it is not probable that we shall ever know how and when the Cornish Goodes diverged from the main line. The Whitston Goodes became extinct about the middle of the seventeenth century. A family named Good lived at Polyphant, but its last representative, Thomas Good, coroner of Launceston, died in 1883. (See *Harleian MSS.*, 1079, folio 13 b.; 1493, folio 14 b.; 1162, folio 14 b.)

The following record of the will of Marmaduke Goode, obtained by Mr. Waters in the course of his investigations in behalf of the N. E. Historic Genealogical Society, is interesting to us because it makes mention of John Goode in Virginia. It is not certain, however, that this was John Goode of "Whitby," although the similarity of the names in this will to those of the children of John of "Whitby" is remarkable. It is curious, too, that Marmaduke Goode should have had two brothers named John, one in London and one in Virginia.

I place this with the Cornwall Goodes, because Marmaduke and his brothers were scattered through various countries, and seemed to have acquired the lands referred to in this will by purchase or lease, and not by inheritance. It is not impossible that Marmaduke and his brothers were grandsons of Richard Goode No. 12. At all events, the evidence that John Goode of "Whitby" is of the Cornish branch seems to me to be ample.

WILL OF MARMADUKE GOODE.

MARMADUKE GOODE, of Ufton, in Berkshire, clerk, 5 September, 1678, proved 20 February, 1678, by Samuel and Mary Goode. executors. To brother Samuel Goode all that messuage or tenement, with the appurtenances, lying in Sulhamsteed Abbots and South Bannister which I hold by lease from Francis Perkins, Esquire, to said Samuel to enjoy the same during his natural life ; and, after his death, I give the said messuage, &c., to my niece Mary Goode, the daughter of my brother John Goode, to enjoy for the remaining term of the said lease. To my brother John Goode, citizen of London, & to Susanna his now wife all my house, tenement, lands and hereditaments, &c., in Sylchester in the County of Southampton, which I purchased of John Carter of Sylchester, and after their decease, to my nephew Marmaduke Goode, son of the said John Goode, he to pay to his sisters, Elizabeth, Susanna and Anne, forty pounds apiece within twelve months after he shall be possessed of the said lands and premisses at Silchester. To my brother William Goode my messuages or tenements, &c., called or known by the name of the Heath lands or heath grounds, situated, lying & being in the several parishes of Ufton and Sulhamsteed, in the county of Berks, and which I lately purchased of Richard Wilder of Theale in the parish of Tylehurst, in the said County of Berks, innholder, during his natural life and afterwards to my nephew Robert Goode, son of the said William Goode and his heirs forever, he to pay to his two sisters, Elianor and Mary, forty pounds within twelve months, &c. To my sister Mary Haines and her two maiden daughters fifty pounds apiece within one year after my decease ; to my brother John Goode in Virginia ten pounds within twelve months after my decease, according to the appointment of my brother John Goode, citizen of London ; to my brother Thomas Goode, in Ireland, ten pounds. (in the same way); to my sister Ann Wickens of Upton ten pounds ; to my servant Alice Payce ten pounds ; to my servant Hugh Larkum five pounds. All the rest of the property to brother Samuel Goode and niece Mary Goode, daughter of my brother John Goode, who are appointed joint executors.

The witnesses were Samuel Brightwell and Robert King.

King, 17.

WORCESTERSHIRE AND OXFORDSHIRE.

The family was established in these countries as early as the sixteenth century, if not before. Nash, in his "History of Worcestershire," states that they possessed a considerable estate at "Redmarley D'Abitot."* Thomas Good, Esq., who died April 12, 1610, who probably belonged to the eighth generation of our numeration, is buried in the chancel of the church of Redmarley, and is supposed to have been a brother to Richard Good, mayor of Oxford. His son Henry must have been born in the latter part of the sixteenth century. "In the churchyard," writes Nash, "on the south, is a railed monument—a woman's—with this inscription: '*Qualis vitæ finis est*,' and underneath '*Ætatis suæ*, 45.' On the right a cross, graduated, with '*Mors Christi;*' on the other side '*Vita mihi*,' with arms as above." The inscription is "Anne, the wife of Henry Good, gent, who deceased the 11 Oct., 1630."

> HERE lieth buried under this stone
> A woman rare : few such or none ;
> Noble in blood, Virtue's true imitator
> In faith, in charity, in her Creator
> Pious, learned, wise, all do know,
> Humble to the meek, dauntless to the foe,
> Nor feared the death, but deemed her heart too stronge
> To keep from hearing Paridise so long.
> The last she said, the last she sung,
> Was sweet "*Te Deum*."

One of Henry's sons, "Thomas Good, armiger," was sheriff of Worcestershire in 1625 (9th Charles), and in 1632 paid compensation to the amount of £30 rather than take the order of knighthood. William Good, married in 1635, and Nicholas were other sons of Henry Good. Nicholas had a son Thomas, born in 1670 and married in 1696, the names of whose three children, Thomas, born in 1698; John, born in 1701, and Mary, born in 1705, are registered at the Heralds College in London. Capt. Good, R. N., the last of the name in possession of Redmarley, and who was murdered, was probably grandson of Thomas or John, just named, and in the fourteenth generation of our numeration.

The Goods of "Aston Court," in Worcestershire, claim descent from the Rev. Richard Good, Vicar of Neen Savage, who was closely related to the Goods of Oxford. Their lineage, as derived from family tradition and Guillim's "Heraldry," stands as follows. The generations are intended to correspond with those in the body of this work :

Eighth Generation.—(For first seven generations see above, pages 14 to 20.) RICHARD GOOD, of Allhallows Parish, alderman and twice mayor of Oxford, who died the 12th day of August, 1609, and was buried in Allhallows Church, was born 1630-60, and is supposed to have been brother or cousin of Thomas Good, of Redmarley, already mentioned.

Ninth Generation.—William Good, alderman of Oxford, and in 1634 one of the assistants to the recorder of Oxford.

* "Rydmarley D'Abitot," anciently called " Ridmerleya," was surnamed D'Abitot from Robert D'Abitot, steward of the household to William the Conqueror, and is in the southwest corner of Worcestershire, upon the river Leden. In 1782 the manor of " Redmarley " belonged to Edmund Lechmere.

Tenth Generation.—"Richard Good, chandler of Oxford," buried Nov. 21, 1673, married the daughter of Thomas Blagrove, of Oxon.

Eleventh Generation.—1, Thomas Good, A. M., D. D., &c., Fellow of Baliol College (b. 1609, d. 1680); 2, John Good, S. T. B. (b. 1621), and 3, Richard Good, Vicar of Neen Savage (b. 1605, d. 1709), who in 1660, with his wife Penelope, purchased "Boraston" in Worcestershire, and who, in 1672, bought "Aston Court."

Twelfth Generation.—Rev. Thomas Good (b. 1656), son and heir of the last, was rector of Aston, and is buried in the chancel of Aston Church, and Edward Good, of "Aston Court," his second son, married Miss Vernon, of "Shrawley." Samuel Good (d. 1756), third son, bought "Aston Court" of his brothers.

Thirteenth Generation.—Samuel Good, of "Aston Court," eldest son of the last, married Miss Bray, of "Burnhill."

Fourteenth Generation.—Thos. Good, of "Aston Court," married Miss Collins.

Fifteenth Generation.—Samuel Good married Sarah Wheeler of "The Moor." He was great grandfather of the Rev. Edward Good of "Forest Vicarage," Middleton, Teesdale, Darlington, who wrote as follows in 1881:

"My father took a good deal of interest in matters of pedigree, and had a family tree, now in the possession of my sister, Mrs. Santoni, in Rome. Our family belong to Worcestershire. We believe ourselves to be of the Redmarley Goods of Worcestershire. Nash, in his History of Worcestershire, says that this family is the same as that mentioned in Domesday Book. John Good, of Baliol College, and his brother Thomas, to whom my direct ancestor, the rector of Neen Savage, was brother, are said to have been of the same family as the Redmarley Goods and Thomas Good bore the Redmarley Good's arms. A corroborative evidence occurred in my grandfather's life time: An anonymous letter was received by him stating that on his looking after it, an estate near Oxfordshire might be had. Capt. Good, R. N., of Redmarley, was supposed to have died at sea, and his steward took possession of the estate. He had, however, been murdered by his steward, and his skeleton was discovered at Redmarley."

The Goods of Oxfordshire appear to be a numerous branch of the family, and were in all likelihood descended from Richard Good, the mayor of Oxford, and his kinsmen. John Goode, in 1449, gave bonds to the University of Oxford for repair of Coleshill Hall. In 1634 we find the name of William Good on the list of assistants to the recorder of the city of Oxford. Samuel Goode, born 1818, living in 1881, with his brother William and John upon a farm at Shotteswell, Oxfordshire, may possibly be in the ninth generation of descent. He writes that in "the register of deaths" he finds the names of 110 Goodes, the record extending so many years back that the record can with difficulty be read. It is difficult to surmise what register he refers to, but he states that his forefathers chiefly lived and died in Oxfordshire and Warwickshire.

William Good, M.R.C.V.S., London, writes that his family have resided since 1609 near Tenlinby in Worcestershire, and that he has in his possession a rapier worn by one of his ancestors on the occasion of a visit to his brother, while mayor of Oxford, an office to which he was twice elected. [Letter dated Ludford Lodge, Ludlow Salop, April 26, 1881.]

There seems to be no lack of evidence to prove that the Goods of Worcester and Oxfordshire are closely allied, and the similarity of personal names, as well as of arms, seem to indicate their close connection with the Cornish branch. Richard Good, of Whitby, Cornwall, and Richard Good, of Oxford, and Thomas, of Redmarley, were contemporaries, and in the eighth generation. The two latter may have been brothers, the first their cousins probably in the first and second degree.

It is, perhaps, worthy of remark that there is a parish called Wittley (Vecelage or Witlega) in Worcestershire, not far from Redmarley d'Abitot, and within whose limits is another manor similarly named, " Redmarley Adam and Oliver." It is hardly safe, however, to connect this Wittley with the Whitley in Cornwall, and draw conclusions as to the origin of the Cornwall branch, since Whitley is not an unusual name in other parts of England.

Two of the Oxford branch were men of note in their day, and I am sure that their biographies, as given in Wood's "Athenæ Oxonienses," a book relating to the graduates of Oxford University, will be of interest.

" Thomas Good, born in Shropshire in 1609; entered Balliol College, Oxford, in the latter end of 1624. He was made B. A. in 1628, and on the 24th of November he was admitted probationer fellow of that house. He ran through all the exercises of the college and university till he was admitted Bachelor of Divinity in 1639. Afterward, though he was absent in times of distraction, yet he kept his fellowship and submitted to the men of the interval. He was vicar of St. Alkmonds, Shrewsbury, in 1642–53. At length, having obtained a small cure at Coerley in his native county of Shropshire, he resigned his fellowship in 1658, and at the King's restoration was made Doctor of Divinity as a sufferer for the King's cause. About that time he was made one of the residentiaries of the Cathedral Church of Hereford and rector of Winslanston in his own county, and at length, on the death of Dr. Savage (1672), master of Balliol College. He was, in his younger years, accounted a brisk disputant, and when resident in his college a frequent preacher, yet always esteemed an honest and harmless Puritan. A noted author, Richard Baxter, of the Presbyterian persuasion, tells us* that he was one of the most peaceable, moderate and honest Conformists of his acquaintance, and subscribed the Worcestershire agreement for concord, and joined with the Presbyterians in their associations and meetings at Kederminster, and was the man that drew the catalogue of questions for their disputations at their meetings, and never talked to them of what he afterwards wrote in his book called *Dubitantius and Firmianus*, by which, when published, he lost his credit among them, and was lesser esteemed by Mr. Baxter, the pride and glory of that party. He hath written and published.

Dubitantius and Firmianus; or, certain dialogues concerning Atheism, Infidelity, Popery and other Heresies and Schisms, &c., Oxon., 1674, octavo.

A Brief English Tract of Logic, printed in 1677 in a little octavo of two sheets and a half. He had, as I have been informed, other things lying by him at his death, fit for the press, but of what subject they treated, or in whose hand they are gotten, I know not. He died at Hereford, April 9th, 1678, and was buried in the Cathedral Church there.—(*Athenæ Oxonienses, III.*, 1155.)

This is probably the Dr. Thomas Goode mentioned in the register of Burford, Shropshire as having officiated June 8, 1669, in the burial at Whitton of Robert Charlton.†

* Apology for the Non-Conformist Ministry.
† Genealogist II., 353.

It was this Thomas Good who bore arms as indicated above under No. 13, viz, *Gules, a cross, engrailed, charged with five ermine spots.*

"John Good," says Fasti Oxonienses, "fellow of Balliol College, was born in 1621. In 1659 it was allowed by the authorities that Henry Tozer, John Proctor, Richard Washington, of University College, and John Good, of New College, might have the liberty to be created D. D., but they refused for this year and the next."

He was made Bachelor of Divinity in 1661. He died early in the morning of Feb. 26, 1675, and was buried in the Balliol College chapel. There was an epitaph made for him, but not put over his grave, part of which runs thus:

"Hic jacet Johannus Good, S. T. B., Coll. Ball., XXX, plus minus annos socius meritissimus omnigena ornatus eruditione, neutiquam inflatus. Sic excultus ipse alios pariter excoluit sedulitate usus adeo indefessa, ut celibriori tutoris quam Johannus prænomen diu innotuerit, etc."

The following incident is related by Wood in his *Athenæ Oxonienses:*

"Mr. Grebby, chaplain of New College, Oxford, having always been dubious concerning the immortality of the soul, did, some years before his death, make a contract with two of his acquaintance of the same mind that he that died first of the three should make known to either of the other two his then state or being. Grebby, therefore, dying (1654) first, his resemblance shortly after appeared in the night time in the chamber of John Good, Batchelor of Divinity and fellow of Balliol College (commonly called Tutor Good), who was one of the other two who had made the contract, and opening his curtains said to him in a trembling and faint voice: '*Sors tua mortalis, non est mortale quod opto.*' Afterwards the resemblance vanished, and was, though much wished for again, seen no more. At the same time the other person, who was sometime chaplain of New College, but then living at his benefice near Oxon, had a dream that the said resemblance did appear to Good, and that the doubt seemed to be resolved, which I have heard him several times very confidently report; yet he being a reputed banterer, I could never believe him in that or anything else. 'Tis true that Good was a scholastical, retired and melancholy man, would sometimes tell these passages, but with great shiness, unless to his philosophical acquaintances, most of whom seemed to be well satisfied with, and some to believe them."

John Good, of New College, Oxford, was in 1547 a delegate of the University to confer with Parliament, and in 1642 a delegate of the University in connection with the Royalist movement among the students. He was evidently of the same politics as his cousins in Cornwall of the same generation.

WARWICKSHIRE.

Basil Goode, gent., of Stretton under Fosse, Warwick, lived 1550–1650, and bore arms of the Lincolnshire type, chevron gold and lions silver, but with the shield blue instead of red. His sole daughter and heir, Etheldreda, born 1599, married before 1633, John St. Nicholas, Esq., of St. Mary's, Lutterworth, Leicestershire, and died in 1654.*

---

*Nicholas' Leicestershire, VI., p. 266, pl. XXXVIII, fig. 29.

The following inscription is carved on a mural tablet in the chancel of the church of St. Mary's, and near it is an escutcheon with the arms of St. Nicholas,

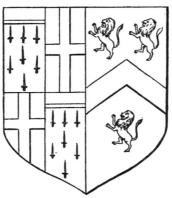

ARMS OF ST. NICHOLAS, QUARTERING APPULDERFIELD AND IMPALING GOODE.

quartering Appulderfield, impaling the arms of the Goode family as follows : *Azure, a chevron, or, between three lions rampant argent.*

IN the middest, betweene this and the opposite wall
Lieth interred the body of Etheldreda,
Wife of John St. Nicholas, Esq.,
Sole daughter and heire of Basil Goode,
Of Stretton under Fosse, in the County of Warwick, gent.,
Aged about 55 years,
Who departed this life the 9th of November, 1654.
And next to this wall lieth the body of
Vincent St. Nicholas, one of the sons
Of the said John by the said Etheldreda,
Aged 19 years, who departed this life
The 9th day of July, 1653.
Both rest in Hope.

LEICESTERSHIRE.

Rev. Henry Goode was a résident of Leicestershire in 1676. Penelope Goode, daughter of Rev. Mr. Goode, rector of Weldon, Northampton, married, about 1720, William Lee (born 1691, died 1759), mayor of Leicester.

Several of the name are mentioned in Nicholas' "Leicestershire," (1795, pp. 164, 173, 480, 546.) One Mr. Goode was owner of a stocking frame made by an ingenious mechanic, which was destroyed by a mob of stocking-makers of Leicester in 1773.

There are several Goodes living in this county in 1887, and about all are engaged in commercial pursuits. The unusual name of Goude occurs here.

SOMERSETSHIRE.

We find a record of one William Good, a Jesuit priest and educator, missionary to Ireland, Sweden and Poland, born 1527 in Somersetshire, Fellow of Christ's Church College Oxford, died in Naples in 1586. He was a contemporary of Richard Good, of Cornwall of William Good, of Oxford, and of the Worcester-Oxfordshire branch, and probably not remotely related. The story of his life is quaintly told by Wood in his *Athenæ Oxonienses.*

William Good, born in 1527 in the ancient town of Glastenbury, Somersetshire. He was there educated, and was admitted to Christ's Church College Oxford, Feb. 26, 1545, afterwards fellow, master of arts in 1552, and about that time humanity reader in said college. After Queen Mary came to the crown, being then a zealous Roman Catholic, he was promoted to an ecclesiastical benefice in his own country (sic), called Middle Chinnoke, and to a little prebendship in the church of Wells called Camba octava in Nov., 1556, besides the rectory of a school in that city. All which he keeping till Queen Elizabeth came to the crown, and for some time after he voluntarily left them and his native country for religion's sake, and retiring to Tournay in Flanders, entered himself there into the Society of Jesus in 1562. After he had served his probationship he went into Ireland with Father David, the titular archbishop of Armagh, who left no stone unturned there for the settling of that kingdom in the Catholic faith and obedience. Four years being spent in that country not without danger, he went to Lovain. In 1577 he was called to Rome to take upon him the profession of the four vows, which being done, he went into Sweden and Poland in the company of Anthony Possevein to settle certain affairs relating to the society.

Two years after that he returned to Rome and became confessor to the English College, then newly converted from an hospital dedicated to the Holy Trinity to a seminary for educating the youth of England that profess the Roman Catholic religion. " Vir fuit probatæ virtutis and doctrinæ (as says Peter Ribadaneira, one of his society), atque imprimis in historiis Sanctorum Angliæ optime versatus, quorum res gestas in templo collegu Anglicani coloribus exprimi, quæ subinde in aes incisæ prodierun, tacito ipsius tit. vel mun. inscriptæ."

He was the author of " *Ecclesiae Anglicanae Trophaea,*" Romæ 1584, folio. In the library of the English College at Rome there is also extant a manuscript digested according to the years of Christ and Kings of Britain, containing "*The Acts of the Saints of Britain.*" Which work is said there to have been composed and written by our author Good, who dying at Naples, 5 July, 1586, was buried in the College of Jesuits there, who have yet a great respect for his name, one or more of whom have promised me his epitaph if there be any, but no answer have I yet received.

                                        (*Athenæ Oxonienses,* 1, 516.)

Dr. Good, a Jesuit, is named in the Calendar of State Papers in 1594, probably this Father William Good, also spoken of as in correspondence with John Vincent in Brazil in 1593.[*]

Another member of the Church of Rome was Alexander Goode, the author of a work entitled "A Brief Account of the Mechalaristian Society Founded on the Island of St. Lazaro."—Venice, 1835.

A copy of this book, written in 1825, is in the New York State Library in Albany. The Mechalaristian Society was an Armenian Monastery.

BRENT GOOD, a native of Somersetshire, England, who died in Troy, N. Y., in 1837, was descended from the Goods of " Hutton Court," Weston Super Mare, Somersetshire, who came into possession of that manor in the last century by marriage with an heiress of the Brent family. Some of the

---

[*] Calendar State Papers, 1591–4, p. 353.

Brents came to Virginia and intermarried with descendants of the Cornwall Goodes, who settled in that colony. Brent Good, who died in Buffalo, N. Y., Oct. 26, 1839, was son of Brent Good already named, and upon his death the English estate was sold, and his children inherited the proceeds. Brent Good (until 1879 Brent S. H. Good), of New York city, one of his sons, married daughter of Henry J. Hoyt, of Norwalk, Conn. Issue: 1, Brent Barnes Good, d. y. 2, Henry Hoyt. 3, Kate Hamilton.

JAMES M. GOOD, of New York city, is another son of Brent Good, of Buffalo, N. Y.

LINCOLNSHIRE.

In the early part of the sixteenth century, and as late as 1591 we find records of a family of Goods at Girsby and Ownby, a few miles north of Lincoln. The two brothers whose names are first mentioned were, apparently, of our eighth generation. The arms as given in the Heralds Visitation are precisely the same as those of Surrey, while according to Burke they are more nearly identical with those of Thomas Good, of Oxford. The family appears to have become extinct in Lincolnshire at an early day. The pedigree stands thus :

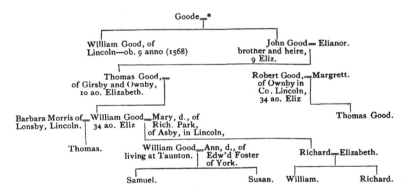

NOTTINGHAM.

Robert Good was, in 1566, assistant to the Rector of Newark.†
Thomas Good was, in 1626, Vicar of Lowdham, Gunthorpe.

DORSETSHIRE.

We find in Dorsetshire, in the sixteenth century, a family of Goods,

---

* Hart MS., 1190 (Vis., 1564), fo. 48 : 1550 (Vis., 1550–1564.) fo. 220, b.
† Visitation of Nottingham, p. 3.

with arms similar to those already described.　Their pedigree is as follows :

John Good of═╤═ *
Mayden Newton,
in Com. Dorsett,
b. 1500–1520

Robert Good, of═╤═Elinor d. of———Stitland [Stickland or Strickland] of Frome St. Quintin in
Mayden Newton, │ Com. Dorsett
b. 1550–60, d. 1628

John Goode, of═╤═Ann, da. of Thomas Savage, of Sidling, in Co m. Dorsett
Mayden Newton │

John Good, of═╤═Edith, d. . . . . Freake, of Chilthorne, in Com. Dorsett
Mayden Newton, │
in Com. Dorsett, ao.
1623, held in 1630 the
manor Axnoller,
Dorset.

John Good, sonne　　　Robert 2
　and heire, aet.　　　aet. 1
　5, 1623, d. 1680.

" Notton," wrote Hutchins, [History and Antiquities of Dorset, 1784, I, p. 519] speaking of the hamlet of that name, in the parish of Maiden Newton, Hundred of Tollerford, now a small hamlet and farm, half a mile south from Lower Crookston, on the same side of the river, is included in a tything of Maiden-Newton, but was a member of Crockway.　It formerly belonged to the Goods, but now to George Browne, Esq.　Robert Good, of Notton, is buried in the church of Maiden-Newton, on the south side of the chancel (an altar tomb, between those of Thomas Washburn and Roger Clavill.) He died March 4, 1628.　He was the father of eleven children.　The tomb was erected by his eldest son, John.

The burial of John Good, gent., is recorded in 1688 ; that of Frances, wife of Mr. John Good, in 1678.

Susanna Good, of Notton, married, 1719, John Sydenham, gent., of that same.　(Hutchins, Dorset, p. 528.)

The manor of " East Axnoller," in Dorsetshire, was held in 1630 by John Good, gent., from whom it passed to the family named Ridgway.　(Hutchins, i–i, p. 443.)

In 4 Eliz. (1565), Thomas Good was granted a pardon for acquiring the manor of Philipston, Philston, or Phipston, from Henry, Earl of Arundel, and John Lumley, Esq.　In the 37th year of Eliza. he had license to alienate it to ——— Baker.

Rev. Philip Henry Good, of Regents Villa, Milton, Portsmouth, is a descendant of this family.　He writes : " My father's ancestors were not royalists, they were Cromwellians, and are a Dorsetshire family.　They were yeomen, and had lived on one farm since Henry VIII's reign, (1509–1543).　But they have all died off since, I believe, my time." [Letter, May 25, 1881.]

* Harleian MSS., 1451, fo. 85, b. 1539, fo. 169; 1166, fo. 52.

Frances Good, daughter of John Good, of County Dorset, married 1620, John Hakewell, of Exeter. (See Tucket's Devonshire Pedigree.)

BUCKS, BERKS AND CAMBRIDGE.

[See Harleian MSS., 6774, p. 56.]

Simon Goode was Rector of Chenies Church at the time of his death in 1296. John Gole or Gode, M. P., from Agmondesbury, 1307, Robert Gode, of New Windsor, 1449, Richard Goode, of Windsor, 1500 and 1520, have been mentioned in the chapter on the family name.

In the records of the privy purse expenses of Henry VIII. is the following entry, June 18, 1530 : " To Good, of Windsor, for certain ground taken out of the King's farme, and yused to enlarge the little park of Windsor, 4*£*."*

The most eminent of the name in the county was Roger Goad, Sacritheológiæ Doctor, concerning whom Fuller, in his "Worthies of England," thus discourses :

" Roger Goad was born at Houton, in Buckinghamshire, and was admitted scholar in King's College, in Cambridge, in 1555. Leaving the college, he became a schoolmaster at Guilford, in Surry. But pity it is that a great candle should be burning in the kitchen, whilst light is lacking in the hall, and his public parts pent in so private a profession. He was made not to guide boys, but to govern men. Hence, by an unexpected election, he was surprised in-to the provostship of King's College, where he remained forty years. He was twice vice-chancellor of Cambridge ; a grave sage and learned man. He had many combats with the young boys in this college, because he loved their good better than they themselves. Very little there is of his in print, save what he did in conjunction with other doctors of the university. By his testament he gave the rectory of Milton to the·college, and dying on St. Mark's day, 1610, lieth buried in the vestry on the north side of the chapel." (Fuller, Worthies, p. 208.)

This Roger Goad was the first to break through the custom forbidding the marriage of heads of houses in the university in 1575. [Dyer, History of the University and College of Cambridge, 1814, I, p. 94.] He was, about 1580, the first chancellor of the church of Wells. He had a son Thomas, who also is described by Fuller :

" Thomas Goad, D. D., was son to Dr. Roger Goad, but whether born in the Provost lodgings, Cambridge, or at Milton, in this county, I am not fully informed. He was bred a Fellow under his father ; afterwards chaplain to Archbishop Abbot, rector of Hadley, in Suffolk, prebendary of Canterbury, &c.; a great and general scholar, exact critic, historian, poet (delighting in making verses till the day of his death), school-man, divine. He was sub-stituted by King James in the place of Dr. Hall, and sent over to the synod of Dort. He had a commanding presence, an uncontrollable spirit, impatient to be opposed, and loving to steer the discourse (being a good pilot to that purpose) of all the company he came contact with. Died about the year 1635." [Fuller, Worthies, I, p. 240.]

Another Thomas Goad, Esq., perhaps a grandson of Dr. Roger Goad, had a daughter Grace, who married, 1640–60, John Byng, of Grantchester, in Cambridge.

Thomas Goade, L.L. D., perhaps also of this connection, married, 1630–40,

---

* Letters and Papers of Henry VIII, v., p. 750.

Mary, daughter of Edmund Woodhall, Esq., of Little Munden, Herts. [Berry, County Genealogies, Herts, p. 32.]

Jane Goad, daughter and heiress of Dr. Thomas Goad, married John Thursby, of London, born 1635–55, son of Christopher Thursby, Esq., of Carter, Northampton. Their son, William Thursby, Esq., of Abington, was sheriff of Northamptonshire in 1724, died in 1730, and their daughter, Jane, married William Dixon, of "Ramshawe," great uncle of John Dixon, of, Williamsburg, Va. [Burke's Commoners, I, 1834, p. 319.] See GOODE PEDIGREE, No. 4354.

Other families of Goades and Goodes are recorded in Buckinghamshire in the seventeenth century. One of these, located at Wraysburg, has its pedigree printed in "Gyll's History of Wraysburg, pp. 247, 284." Thomas Goade, perhaps of our tenth generation, had two sons, William, baptized 1613, died 1658, and George, died 1684. The latter had nine children : Thomas, b. 1642 ; Susan, b. 1646 ; Sarah, b. 1649 ; Rebecca, Samuel, Elizabeth, b. 1658; Mary, b. 1661 ; Eliz, b. 1666, and Martha, b. 1667. The former had a son William, died 1671, whose son William Goade, M. D., died 1696, was a benefactor of Horton Church, concerning whom Lipscomb, in his "History of Buckinghamshire, VI, p. 514," discourses as follows :

In the churchyard at Horton, near Colnbrook, on a white stone opposite to the north side of the north wall of the isle, is the following inscription :

> Near ys place Lyes ye Body of
> William Goode, ye Father and William,
> his Son, both of Colebrooke.
> Physitians.
> And also Joseph and Sarah Fellowes, son and daughter of
> Geo. Fellowes, Surgeon, and Priscilla, his wife,
> And kinsman of ye late William Goode.

I have already suggested the probabilities that the Goodes of Buckingham and adjoining counties in the east of England are of this branch, the name having become modified by a natural euphonic change. The name Goade seems to have become less common about the end of the seventeenth century, and it is about this time that the name Goode became prevalent in this part of England.

One of the most prominent of the name was Rev. William Goode, M. A., born in the town of Buckingham in 1762; entered Magdalen College, Oxford, 1780 ; succeeded Romaine as Rector of St. Ann's Blackfriar's, London, 1795, died 1816. He published a work entitled, "Essays on all the Scriptural Names and Titles of Christ" in six volumes, of which an edition was printed in London in 1822 ; also, "A New Version of the Book of Psalms in Metre," and eight sermons separately printed.*

A memoir of this William Goode was written by Rev. William Goode, M. A., probably his son. The second edition, printed in London in 1828, had an appendix containing his select letters.†

---

* Darling, Encyclopedia Bibliographical
† Mr. —— Goode, undermaster at Eton, had a daughter who married Dr. William Battie, born 1704, died 1776, a poet and medical writer, educated at Eton and King's Colleges, Oxford, buried at Ham in Kingston ; another daughter married Mr. Harven, a brewer at Kingston.

Mr. C. H. Goode, of London, writes : " My father's family lived in Herefordshire and Worcestershire, and I believe they traced up to a certain Roger Goode, of Thornburg, who lived some three hundred years since." This family claims kinship with the Worcester-Oxfordshire family. The Mr. Good already referred to by the Rev. Edward Good as an authority upon the history of the Aston Court Goods, claimed Mr. C. H. Goode as a kinsman, thinking that the families were identical in their origin. " This seems borne out," writes the latter, " by the fact that my late father and some of the members of the Good family both thought they had some claim to a property of considerable importance in Oxfordshire, but neither has yet made good a claim to it."

Joseph Goode, of Hunderton, Hereford, died in April, 1881 ; he and his kindred were mostly shopkeepers and farmers ; and at one time were quite wealthy.

John Goode was incumbent of Collington Parish, Hereford, in 1667 ; Thomas Goode, D. D., a member of ecclasiastical jury at same place in same year.

Other worthies of Bucks, living in the same vicinity, and probably descendants of, or closely akin to, Dr. Roger Goad, are the following :

In 1623 Richard Goode gave to the town of Colnbrook, Buckinghamshire, three acres of land to be employed as follows : one acre yearly profit to be paid every year to the minister of the town on Good Friday in the chapel, and the yearly profits of the other two acres to be distributed on the said day and in the chapel to the poor and impotent people of the town forever. This, and another similar endowment amounted altogether to 101 pounds, 10 shillings a year is still distributed. [See Lipscomb's History of Bucks, 1847, IV., p. 432.]

Edward Goode, A. M., was licensed curate of Chilton, Bucks, Feb. 4, 1667-8. He was also curate of Long Crendon, and was indicted with others for making a forcible entry into Chilton Church during the dispute with Sir John Crokes, the patron.*

William Goode, b. in Bucks, 1762, died 1816, who entered at Magdalen Hall, Oxford, 1780, and became rector of St. Anns, Blackfriars, London, 1795, published "A New Version of the Book of Psalms," 1811, "Essays on the Scriptural Names and Titles of Christ, 1822, and a volume of Sermons." His son, W. Goode, perhaps the Rector of All Hallows, published a memoir of him.

SURREY AND MIDDLESEX.

Goods and Goodes were rather numerous in Surrey as well as in Bucks, on the opposite side of the Thames, as early as the middle of the sixteenth century.

John Good leased land at Kingston in 1550 (Manning, Surry I, p. 357), and John Good, of Thorp, was " husbandry protector " in 1592. In the Herald's

---

* Crokes' Genealogical History, p. 489. He was buried at Crendon, 1671. Lipscomb's History of Buckingham, 1847, 1, p. 141.

Visitation of 1620, 1669 [Harl. MMS., 4963, fo. 169b.] is the pedigree of a family of Goods of Malden, Surrey, as follows :

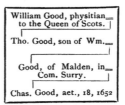

Lysons, in his "Environs of London," states that Lord Lumley gave lease of lands in Malden, Surrey, to William Good, physician to Mary Queen of Scots. This family used the arms described above under 3 and 9 (p. 9). There appears to have been another family with the same arms, owning land in Malden at the same time. James Good, of New College, Oxford, received the degree of M. A. in 1560, and later that of Doctor of Physick. He was one of the Fellows of the College of Physicians and Surgeons, and in 1573 was imprisoned for holding secret correspondence by letter with Mary Queen of Scots.*

"Goodus Medicinæ Doctor" is named by Camden in his "Annals of the Reign of Elizabeth" as one of the adherents of the Queen of Scots. I cannot learn which of the two men just referred to is meant in this allusion. They were probably, however, either brothers or cousins.

James Good, Doctor of Physic, seems to have lived in London, for the baptisms and births of various members of his family are recorded at the church of St. Dunstan's in the west. Francis, his son, was buried December 23, 1564, and Joan, his daughter, October 31, 1567, Mrs. Johanna (Joan), undoubtedly his wife, was buried May 3, 1589. There is no record of the baptism of his son John, but his grandson, John, son of John Good, gent, was baptised in this same place March 7, 1607. It is apparent that in the interval between 1567 and 1607 the family of James Good, M. D., had become landed proprietors, and in the Calendar of State Papers, 1623–5, p. 593, we learn how and when, for in 1622 John Good, of Surrey, is stated to have been engaged in a suit concerning the lease of Malden, Surrey, granted by Queen Elizabeth to Merton College, Oxford, for 5,000 years, subsequently given by her to the Earl of Arundel, who sold it to Joan, mother of John Good.

John Good, Esq., "Lord of the Manor of Malden," was in all probability the son of James and Joan Good, of St. Dunstan's Parish. He was born in 1567 or 1568, died in April, 1627, and is buried in St. John's Church, of Malden, where his monument of block marble is to be seen on the south side of the east window, bearing the following epitaph :

D. O. M. S et P. M. Clarissimi Viri Johannis Good, Arm. quondam D'ni hujus Manerii et Patronis hujus ecclesiae sub Collegio Mertoniensi in Acadèmia Oxon, qui vivus, corporis venustate morum suavitate vitæ probitate, linguæ fecundia, hospitalitate, cæterisque virtutibus enitunt. Hanc

* Fasti Oxonienses I, p. 158.

ecclesiam, penitus collapsam, ab imis fundamentis restituit. Post multa fortunæ discrimina hic in sedibus suis, placide in Domino obdonnavit tertio cal. Aprilis, anno salutis aeternae MDCXXVII, atatis sune LIX, cui conjux mœstissima hoc doloris suæ solatium Pietatis ergo consecravit.

Lyons states that the property of Malden held by John Goodue was alienated in 1583 from Merton College to the family of Goode.*

John Good, gent, as we have seen, had a son born about 1607, named John. It was doubtless his daughter and heir, Penelope, who married Sir Thomas Morley, and who, a widow in 1707, surrendered back to Merton College the land which had been in litigation for more than a century. He appears to have been regarded as a seditious character in 1625, for in that year a search was made for him in his home at Malden.†

Others of the name lived in Surrey. Sebastian Good was one of the Commissioners for the County of Surrey under Cromwell in 1649. Thomas Goode was a trustee of the Botanic Garden at Stockwell in 1800. John Good, master of Guilford School in 1580 and September 5, 1594, and is buried in Trinity Church, Guilford. John Goode, rector of St. Mary, Rotherhithe, 1655-75, died May 30, 1675.

John Good was rector of Shirmere, Middlesex, 1457.

Francis Good, son-in-law of Sir John Hart, was tried in 1591 for not delivering prisoners. [Calendar of State Papers, 1591-4, p. 84.] Another Francis Good, perhaps, married Hester, born 1570-90, daughter of William Cox and Alicia, daughter of Thomas Bromfield, gent, of London; her sister, Eliz. Cox, married William, Baron Compton, created Earl of Northampton in 1818.

Mr. Good is mentioned in the Calendar of State Papers as an attorney in the Star Chamber in 1590.

William Goode, a sword-cutter in New street, London, married in 1700, at Gray's Inn, Alice Blackbourne.

William Goode, B. P., published in London, in 1645, a sermon entitled, "The Discoverie of a Publique Spirit," and the following year a book of sermons.

William Goode, M. A., F. S. A., rector of All Hallows the Great and Less, London. Published "The Divine Rule of Faith and Practice" in 1842, and eight other theological works, 1834-1852.

Willoughby Good, Esq., is given by Burke as the representative in 1865 of the family of Sir Willoughby Hickman, created baronet in 1643; title expired in 1781.

Francis Goode has published several books in London, "The Better Covenant," "Watchwords of Gospel Truth," and various volumes of sermons, 1838-50

HAMPSHIRE.

Apparently closely connected with the Goods of Surrey, is the Hampshire branch, an acconnt of which is quoted below from Gregory's "Life of John Mason Good":

"They were highly respectable, and had for several generations before 1760

---

* Environs of London, I, p, 334.
† Calendar of State Papers, 1625-b, p. 168.

possessed property at Romsey in Hampshire and in the neighboring parish of Sockerley. The shalloon manufacture had for ages been carried on to a considerable extent at Romsey, and the family of the Goods long ranked among the most successful and opulent of the proprietary manufacturers.

"Inscriptions over the ashes of several of them, for two or three centuries back, may be seen in the aisles of the venerable Abbey Church, some with the cautious monumental description of 'gentleman and alderman of this town.' Richard Good was mayor in 1708. There are many Goods still in this county. The grandfather of John Mason Good, who was actively engaged in this manufacture, had three sons, William, Edward and Peter; of these the eldest devoted himself to the military profession, and died young; the second succeeded his father as shalloon manufacturer and possessed the family estates at Romsey and Lockerly; the third evincing early indications of piety, was devoted to the ministry of the gospel among the Independent or Congregational class of Dissenters. He attended the Congregational Academy at Ottery, St. Mary, in Devonshire. Was ordained pastor of an "independent church and congregation" at Epping, in Essex, in September 23, 1760, the Rev. John Mason delivering the charge. About a year after Mr. Good married Miss Sarah Peyto, daughter of Rev. Henry Peyto, of Great Coggeshall, Essex, and the favorite niece of Rev. John Mason, who died in 1766. She left three children: William Good, born Oct. 19, 1762; John Mason Good, born May 25, 1764; Peter Good, born Feb. 13, 1766."

Peter and William were living in 1829, one at Bath and the other in London.

William was at 15 articled to an attorney at Portsmouth; John Mason, at about the same age, to a surgeon-apothecary at Gosport; Peter was placed in a commercial house at Portsmouth.

John Mason Good's eldest daughter married Rev. Cornelius Neale, author of "Lyrical Dramas," &c., about 1816, and her son was the Rev. John Mason Neale, Warden of Sackville College, author of the English version of "Jerusalem the Golden," and many other famous Latin hymns. He has also written a "History of the Holy Eastern Church," "Mediæval Preachers and Mediæval Preaching," "Theodora Phranza, a Tale of the Fall of Constantinople," and other works; and has published a children's edition of the "Pilgrim's Progress."

Peter Good had two sons. William Good immigrated to America in 1822. The latter was graduated at Harvard Law School in 1856, was the author of "Good's Animalia," also printed a work on stenography and certain genealogical histories. He had a son, Peter, at one time a lawyer in New York.

NORFOLK.

Richard Gode, Good or Goode and Hugh Good were clergymen in Norfolk in 1396 to 1400, as we have seen. Alexander, son of John Goode, of Yaxley, was benefactor to the chapel or cell of St. Edmund the Martyr at Hoxney, Norfolk, in the thirteenth century. Mathew Good, gent, of Croxton, married in 1600–1620, Frances Woolmer, and left five children—Woolmer, Mathew, Thomas, Francis and Catherine. This is probably the Mathew Good, Esq., who, in 1829, controlled the leasing of Holebrook Hall, Aldeburgh, Norfolk. Goad, of Croxton, according to Burke, used the Good arms. Christopher Good, in 1647, bought the Manor of Abergavelly in the Bishopric of St. David's. Will. Goad or Good, S. T. B., was rector of the church of the Virgin Mary, Wexhall, in 1638, and George Goade, A. M., in 1646, of Coleshall Church.

The Croxton family seems to have become extinct, and the name is very rare in Norfolk.

Rev. William P. Goode, M. A., was rector of Earsham, Norfolk, in 1868.

SUFFOLK.

About 1350–1400, if the pedigrees of Sulyard and Tyrell in Berry's "County Genealogies" are trustworthy guides, there lived —— Goode, Esq., of Wilbye, Co., Suffolk, whose daughter, Joan, married about 1420 William Sulyard, Esq., of Eye, Suffolk. Sir John Sulyard, Knt., Justice of the King's Bench in 1485, was her grandson, Sir John Tyrell, Bart., 1809, her descendant in the eleventh generation. [Berry's County Genealogies, Essex, p. 64.] Sulyard quartered the arms of Goode, and, as has been already said, the earliest record of their use of arms by Goode is connected with this intermarriage. The family seems to have entirely disappeared from this county.

GLOUCESTER.

James Good, a native of this shire, (*Dimocki in Ayro, Gloucesteriense, natus*) is buried in the chancel of the church of West Drayton, and his memory is perpetuated by a curious old brass. He died Sept. 16, 1581.

Mary Goode, daughter of William Goode, Esq., of Newent, Gloucester, married about 1760, Rev. George Pollen, rector of Little Bookham. Among their children were Col. G. A. Pollen, M. P. for Leominster, drowned in the Baltic, Anna M., the wife of Maj. Gen. Coote Manningham, Col. of the 95th Regt. of Foot, and Henrietta, who married J. P. Boileau, Esq., and had Rev. G. P. Boileau, of the Manor House, Little Bookham, and John P. Boileau, who married Lady Catherine Elliott, daughter of the Earl of Minto. (See Burke's "Landed Gentry.")

OTHER COUNTIES.

"The Genealogist" gives the name of Anna Goode as marrying, in 1589, Francis Wakeman, of Eartham. (Vol. II., p. 252.)

Rev. Henry Goode was rector of Weldon in Northamptonshire.[*]

Rev. Robert Good was granted Dec. 1, 1533, the next presentation to the prebend of Bercleswyth or Berkswyth, in the Cathedral Church of Lichfield.[†]

William Goode was made constable of Watlingby, June, 1534.[‡]

Rev. Robert Good was rector of Holy Trinity, Colehaven, 1585–90, and vicar of Tolleshunt, Beckenham, 1590–1615. He died in 1615.

Rev. Henry Good, B. C. L., minister of Wimbourne Minster, Dorset, is of a Wiltshire family, descended in a line of only sons from the year 1599.

[*] Bridges & Whalley's Northamptonshire, ii, p. 356.
[†] History of Staffordshire, vi, p. 651.
[‡] Ibid, vii, p. 315.

Alexander Good married, about 1620, Olive, daughter of Henry Edmonds, gent, of New Sarum, County Wilts.

In addition to the record of the family in Warwickshire, p. 435, I have the following :

" Maria Good, daughter of Thomas Good de Com. Wigom., married, about 1600, Henry Mathew, Burswell, Warwick.*

One Goode, born 1710–1725, lived at Fenny Compton, Warwickshire. Most of his descendants live in Coventry ; his grandson, Edward Goode, was founder and first proprietor of the *Coventry Times.*

John Frederick Goode, of Birmingham, son of John Thomas Goode, of " The Moor " Church Lane, Handsworth (son of John Goode), has heard that his father's grandfather and greatgrandfather were natives of Dunchurch, a small village near Rugby, where, as at Coventry, there were others familiar of the same name. J. T. Goode said that the family was originally from Cornwall.

Sybill Good, Esq., of Birmingham, had a daughter Elizabeth, who married, 1658, Sampson Lloyd, Esq.

R. Good, gent, of Winsham, Somerset, had a daughter Dinah, who married 1815, J. F. Gwyn, Esq., of Ford Abbey, Devonshire.

Thomas Goode, a native of England, came to America 1820–30, and settled at Viroqua, Wis.; he had two brothers who came with him to America, one of whom, Richard, settled in Grant Co., Wis., and afterward went to Missouri, where one of his sons is a judge of some court. Thomas Goode had issue : 1, William H. Goode, b. 1823, lived in 1886 in Rose Creek, Minn.; has children : i, Mary A. Goode (Mrs. Russell), of Aspen, Pitkin Co., Col.; ii, John A., b. 1853, La Crosse, Wis.; iii, Horatio F., and iv, Ella A., of Rose Creek Minn. 2, John, of Newville, Wis., has son, b. 1871–3. 3, Mrs. Mary Marston, of Chicago, six children, one Cornelius, soldier U. S. A., killed in battle. 4, George, b. about 1845, lives in Iowa.

A family of Goodes of English origin lived in Sidney, Iowa, in 1885.

Perhaps of the same family is Alfred R. Goode, of Melbourne, Fla., whose father (name not given) came to Illinois in 1845 ; the son of Thomas, and grandson of Thomas Goode, both natives of Warwickshire.

ANGLO-SCOTCH GOODES.

Allusion has already been made to the Goodes of Paisley on page 19. A member of this family was Dr. William Good, a native of Paisley, Scotland, and a graduate of the Edinburgh Medical College, came to America in 1780–1800, and settled at Sharpsburg, Md., where he died in 1811. He had sons :

I, Josiah Good.

II, William, died in 1843, lived in Martinsburg, Va., and was member of the Virginia House of Delegates in 1829. A Mr. Good, perhaps his son, was a candidate for Congress about 1882.

III, John, b. 1776, d. 1844, lived in Ohio Co., Va., and was member of the Virginia legislature ; he had a son : 1, Moses Good, b. 1805, who had a son,

---

* Visitation of Warwickshire, p. 349.

Alexander C. Good, of Kirkwood, Mo., whose daughter Mary Lamar Good, married in 1882 Samuel Sloan, Esq., of Cumberland, Md.

A son or grandson, Lawrence W. Good, married in 1866, Columbia, daughter of Howell Lewis, and removed to Lewis, Henry Co., Mo., and had children: 1, Ida Good. 2, Archie L. 3, Henry C. 4, Lawrence B. (See Welles' "Washington Family," p. 237.)

Another of this family is believed to have been the Mr. Goode, of Virginia, who married Nancy, daughter of Zachariah Forrest, greatgrandfather of Rev. Douglas F. Forrest, D. D., of Cincinnati, and fifth in descent from Thomas Forrest, whose wife was the first gentlewoman who came to Virginia. Said Mr. Goode had issue: 1, Alexander Goode, of Kentucky. 2, Mary, married Joseph Avell. 3, Martha, married Rev. Mr. Douglas.

Here, perhaps, belong also those of the name who settled in New England in colonial days, and being Tories, sought refuge in the British Provinces at the time of the Revolution. David Good, b. 1747, removed to New Brunswick in 1783, and died at Kingsclear, York Co., N. B., in 1842, aged 95, leaving a widow and 111 descendants. Duncan S. Good, living at Kingsclear, 1869, claimed near kinship with Joseph Good, secretary to the Duke of Kent, father of Queen Victoria. George W. Goode, of Lowell, Mass., (son of George F., grandson of George of Frederickton) is a writer of novelettes and romances for the popular weeklies. His grandfather was lost at sea, and his father lived in his youth near Presque Isle, Me. Many of this family are mariners. (See Sabine's "American Loyalists.") Other New England Goods were John, a soldier in King Philip's war, 1675 (Savage's Gen. Dict.), Sarah, "an old woman who was bedrid," executed for witchcraft at Salem, July 19, 1692, (Hutchinson, li, 26) and Deborah arrested under charges of witchcraft (Savage). John Good was Chief Justice of Turks Island, W. I., 1789.

ANGLO-IRISH GOODS AND GOODES.

There are many of our name in the United States not of the Virginia English stock. Most of them are of Irish origin.* All the Irish Goods have

---

* Many people of German origin have modified their patronymics into Good and Goode. The most numerous group of these are descended from a family of brothers named Guth, who came from Zweibrucken, near Cologne, about 1763, and settled in Pennsylvania. In the course of five or six generations they have spread widely. Many of them are Lutheran clergymen. The village of Goode in Kansas was named from Adam Goode, b. in Cumberland Co., Pa., 1818, and who has many descendants in Phillips Co., Kan. John S. Good, of Camden, N. J.; Solon L. Goode, of Indianapolis; James L. Goode, of San Jose, Cal.; Jonathan Good, of Philadelphia, are of this family. Some emigrated at an early day to the valley of Virginia, where their descendants live in Rockingham, Page, Shenandoah, Craig, Patrick and Franklin counties. The commonest names are Jacob, David, Peter, George and John. Good's Mill, in Page Co., is named for John Good. Judge John J. Good, of Dallas, Texas, son of George, of Moscow, Ala, son of Jacob, of Woodstock, Va., is of the family, also Dr. R. H. Good, of Penns Store, Va David Goode, of Newfound, Va.; Jacob, Fountain, and David G., of Wadesborough, Va.; William, of Griffithsville; George W., of Concord, and Thomas M., of Iowa, and Dr. S. G. Goode, of Pemberton, Ohio; J. W. Good, of Springfield, Va.; William M., of Newcastle: Samuel, of Newmarket, and Samuel B., of Mt. Ciinton, Va.

Other Guths came later. Herman, of Sturgard, Prussia, had son Herman, of Schlochau, and grandson, Henry H. Good, of Denver, Col. Ludwig Guth, of Baden, settled in New Milford, Conn., 1856, and has sons Alexander L Good, of Boston, and George F., of New Milford. L. Guth, of New York, native of Prussia, is L. " Good " in the city directory.

A Swiss family named Gude came to Pennsylvania in the last century, and has multiplied: Dr. Samuel M. Good, of Leitersburg, Md., is one of the descendants. Two brothers, Anton and Bernard Gude, of Aschenbuttel, Frus ia, came to Richmond, Va., about 1840, have many descendants.

The name Gut also became Good. Adolf Good, of Galveston, is grandson of Max Gut, of Gailmgen, in Baden

The Russian name Goot becomes Good in the hands of the directory compilers. Julius Good, of San Antonio, Texas, is son of Baer Goot, of Poviainetz, Russia.

traditions of English origin.   In the will of Marmaduke Goode, made in 1678, there is reference to his brother, Thomas Goode in Ireland, (see p. 430) and we have record of one Good who went out to Ireland as a government official in 1750.   Most of the Anglo-Irish Goods seem to have come to America, though there are still many in the old country, particularly in County Cork. These trace their ancestry to a migration from England in Cromwell's time. One branch has long been established at Bandon, Co. Cork.   Robert Watson Goode, of Brooklyn; John C. Good, of Dayton, O.; Richard and John, of Bloomfield, Iowa, and others in Milwaukee, are of this line.   Timothy, of the parish of Desert, has descendants in Boston and Cambridge, sons of John, who came over in 1817, and others in Binghamton, Elmira, Cincinnati, Boston and New York descended from his son Timothy, who died in Ireland.   James Goode, of County Cork, had three sons who came to America in 1833 ; their children live in Boston, Troy, Philadelphia and Brooklyn.   Robert Goode, of Brylain, Cork, had son Robert in Orono and grandson, James A., in Bangor, Me.

Other Goodes live in County Galway.   Martin Goode came from Ballinasloe to New York in 1854.   William Francis Goode, born in Ballinasloe in 1810, grandson of an Englishman, came to America in 1834, settled in Baltimore, where he died in 1887 ; had a brother Patrick in Ireland, a brother Richard who came to America, another John, who died in Memphis, Tenn., and a nephew John, who lived in the South : W. F. Goode has a son William Richard Goode, of Baltimore, and a daughter Marie Virginia Goode, who married Fielding H. Lucas, of Baltimore.   Patrick and John, sons of John Goode, of Connaught, came to Baltimore in 1830 : Ignatius Goode, of Baltimore, is son of Patrick.

There are Goods at Swanlimbar, in County Cavan, some of whom no doubt have come to America.

Edward Good came from Ireland to Pennsylvania in 1750-90, and married Ellen Harris, of the Welch family who settled Harrisburg.   There are many descendants in Pennsylvania, Michigan, Missouri, Florida and Indiana.   Mrs. Rebecca Good Scofield, of Indianapolis, is his grandchild.

Patrick Goode came to New York in 1845.   His son Michael is city marshal of New York, and has a son John Goode, of New York.   Their traditions point to an English origin.

One Good moved to Ireland about 1750 as a government official.   His wife was Scotch, a near relative of Lord Lovet, who lost his head for attachment to the Stewarts.   He had one son who settled in Dublin, and had two sons. One of these has two sons still living, William J. Goode, of "Fingles House," Fingles Co., editor of the *Farmers' Gazette*, and Francis Goode, who moved to New York about 1852, and is a stationer.   A nephew of W. J. Goode is also in New York.   W. J. Goode has a son, surgeon in the Royal Navy, a graduate of Trinity College, Dublin.

APPENDIX II.

SOME ANCESTRAL FAMILIES.

" Most people know little about the genealogies of their maternal ancestors, and consequently hosts o f persons who are descended from the Plantagenets and earlier kings are unaware that such is the case. Those who are in a position to trace their female ancestry with any minuteness can usually derive themselves through females from one or more of the great historic families, and can consequently lay claim to numerous strains of royal blood."—The Athenæum.

In the following pages are noticed some of the families from whom John Goode, the ancestor of the Goodes of Virginia, is believed to have descended. To those who have read the quotation at the head of this chapter I need offer no apology for presenting some of the curious facts which have been noted down in examining manuscripts and old volumes of local history in the British Museum and elsewhere. It has been an amusement to the writer to trace out these pedigrees, and I have no doubt that they will afford like amusement to many of his kinsfolk.

PENKEVILL, OF "PENKEVILL" AND "ROSORROW."

An elaborate history of the Penkevills is presented by Sir John Maclean in the "History of the Rural Deanery of Trigg Minor," together with an extensive tabulated pedigree.

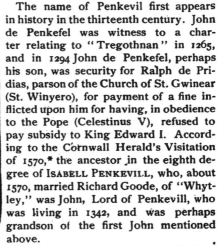

The name of Penkevil first appears in history in the thirteenth century. John de Penkefel was witness to a charter relating to "Tregothnan" in 1265, and in 1294 John de Penkefel, perhaps his son, was security for Ralph de Pridias, parson of the Church of St. Gwinear (St. Winyero), for payment of a fine inflicted upon him for having, in obedience to the Pope (Celestinus V), refused to pay subsidy to King Edward I. According to the Cornwall Herald's Visitation of 1570,* the ancestor in the eighth degree of ISABELL PENKEVILL, who, about 1570, married Richard Goode, of "Whytley," was John, Lord of Penkevill, who was living in 1342, and was perhaps grandson of the first John mentioned above.

The manor or barton of St. Michael Penkevil, is situated in Southern Cornwall, near Falmouth, and on the eastern bank of the River Fal, and was

---

* Herald's College, MSS. H. 16, fo. 117.

formerly contiguous to, and for many centuries has been a part of "Tregoth-nan," the estate of the Boscawen family, and now the seat of Viscount Falmouth.

The Penkevills obtained their family name from the manor which they held. "This ancient family," says Maclean, "is supposed to have derived its name from the Lordship of Penkevill in the Hundred of Pyder," and Davies Gilbert, in his "History of Cornwall,"* remarks :

"The Manor or Barton of Penkevil St. Michael, Co. Cornwall, belonged in the reign of Edward I to the family of De Wen, from whom Hals supposes it to have passed in marriage to the Penkevils ; it is, however, quite as proba-ble that the property remained in the same family, they assuming a new name from the place of their abode."

The collegiate church of St. Michael of Penkevil, was founded in 1319, and has since remained in existence, and has of late years become the family chapel of "Tregothnan." The writer visited it in 1883, and found that it had been "restored" in a manner to him most unsatisfactory, and was practically a new edifice. It was interesting, however, to see the monumental brass to the memory of John Trenowth, an ancestor of the Goodes, as well as of the Boscawens.

About the year 1330, or a little later, the family seems to have removed to the north of Cornwall, for the marriages were with families belonging in that region and the northwest of Devon, although more than two centuries later they seem to have held an estate called "Penkevill."

John Penkevill, son of John Penkevill the 3d, married in 1365, was Collector of Subsidies in 1384, and in 1387, in behalf of his wife, Alianora Penkevill, was "a party in a plea of novel dissezion " against William Lambron and others. His son John, who was living in 1408,† married Elizabeth, daughter and heir of Thomas Trevylles, and had two sons, John and Thomas. The elder married Alice ⸺, the heir of "Roisemyn" (Rosewyn ?), and his descendants "flourished here," (at Penkevill) says Hals, "in gentle degree, between the dignity of a justice of the peace and that of a Hundred Constable, until about the middle of Queen Elizabeth's Reigne."

RAYNWARD OF "PENMAYNE," IN CORNWALL.

Arms, (as quartered with Penkevill and Gilbert. Trigg Minor, iii, p. 72, Visitation of Devon, p. III.) Azure, guttee argent, a castle triple-towered : or azure, or sable, a castle with three battlements.

Isabell Raynward married, about 1557, John Penkevill, of Penkevill : her granddaughter, Isabell Penkevill, married Richard Goode, of Whitley.

"Among the most ancient of the families of the Parish of St. Minver," says Sir John Maclean, "is that of Raynward." Our earliest notice of the name is in 1283, when Ralph Reyn-

* Vol. III, p. 214.
† Assessor's Rolls, 9th Edward IV.

ward was party to a fine for effecting a settlement of the manors of Lanow-mure and Lanivet on Hugh de Moncton. In 1296 we find him as surety for David, vicar of Liskeard, and for Henry le Dennys for payment of the fines inflicted upon them for refusing, in obedience to the Pope, to pay the subsidies levied by the King [Edward]. * * * In 1306 we find him and his fellows (Reynward & Co., as we should now say) very large holders of tin, which was stamped at Bodmin and Lostwithiel. Richard Reynward was one of the assessors of subsidy for the Parish of St. Endellion in 1326, and Matthew Raynward was one of the valuers and venditors of the ninths and fifteenths in the Parish of St. Minver in 1340. In 1348 Jordan Reynward was one of the Burgesses returned to serve in Parliament for the Borough of Bodmin, on which occasion William and Richard Reynward were his manucaptors (or bondsmen). In 1337 John Reynward held a mill within the manor of Penmayne called Treswarlion, which he held also in 1345. In 1354 William Reynward was witness to a deed dated at Wynn, juxta Treglothian, and in 1361 to another dated at Trewythek. In 1423 William Reynward was a tenant of the manor of Trevisquite. In 1460 John Reynworth was *præpositus* of the Borough of Bissyny, and in 1469 we find reference to the manor of Penmayne, formerly held by Jordan Reynward. In 1504 John Reynward held a tenement in the manor of Penmayne. In 1506 John Reynward, Esquire, was witness to a charter dated at Kestel, in Egloshayle. In 1557 Sir Richard Reynward was instituted to the vicarage of St. Minver. About this time or a little later Isabell, daughter and coheir of John Reynward, married John Penkevill. The name, however, still lingered. Nov. 9, 1577, Thomas Raynward was buried at St. Minver, and in 1687 William Reynward levied a fine on John Billing, alias Trelawder, of three messuages, in Bosyerne, in Egloshayle. [Maclean's History of the Deanery of Trigg Minor, III, pp. 61–70.] Richard, William, John and Jordan Reynward, one of whom was no doubt the ancestor of Isabell, were contemporaries of Richard Goode. The name has long been extinct.

STRADLING, OF ST. DOMINICS, IN WALES, AND OF WILTSHIRE.

Arms. The accompanying sketch is from a MS. Cornwall Visitation. I have not found the blazoning. The cinquefoils are marked argent and the pales gules, or vice versa. John Raynward, father of Isabell Penkevill, *nee* Raynward, evidently married one of the daughters of Edmund Stradling, who married before 1497 Katharine, daughter of John Trenouth. The marriage of Joan Stradling to William Carnsew, of St. Kew, and of Johanna, her sister, to ———Kemeys, are matters of record, and the descendants of these marriages quarter the arms of Trenowth, Nanfant, Treiago and Chenduit, just as those of John Penkevill do. Maclean calls attention to the fact that if these families quartered Stradling, Penkevill is entitled to the same privilege, [Trigg Minor, p. 546.]*

*See Powell's History of Wales [Merthyr Tydvil, 1812], p. xli. Phillipps' Glamorganshire Pedigrees, p. 26. Aubrey's Topographical Collections, ed. Jackson, p. 217. Visitatio Comitatus Wiltoniæ, 1623. Collinson's Somerset, iii, p. 335.

TRENOWTH, OF "TRENOWETH," CORNWALL.

Arms.   Argent, on a fesse sable, three chevronels, palewise, the points to the dexter, argent.

John Trenowth, Esq., was grandfather of the wife of John Raynward, the grandmother of Isabell Goode, of Whitley.

The family of Trenowth, or Trenoweth, was of early Cornish origin.

The following pedigree, taken from an old visitation, begins with John Trenoweth, who lived in the time of King Edward I:

Johes de Trenoweth m. ———
Stephanus Trenowth, m. Johanna, filia Ric. de Trenance.
Michael de Trenowith m. Margarita, filia Butler.
Radus, b. before 1377, d. 1427, m. filia Rich. Bushell.
Johes, b. before 1403, d. 1444, m. Jana, filia 1. et coh. Steph. Treiago.
Radus, b. before 1377, d. 1427, m. Jana, fil, William Bassetf.
Katherine m. Edmund Stradling, whose daughter was mother of Isabell Goode.
Jones m. Johanna, filia, Jacobi Nanfan.
John, b. Sept. 8, 1426, d. Nov. 26, 1496, m. Honor, filia, William Tregarthen.

Ralph Trenowth, of the sixth generation, died in 1427, and his son John, b. bef. 1403, died in 1444.   One branch of the family remained at Trenoweth, and became extinct in the reign of Henry VIII.   Borlase, the Cornish naturalist appears to have descended from them : an heiress also married Boscawen, Another branch removed to Fentongollan in St. Michael Penkevil, acquiring this manor by marriage with Jane Treiago, and became extinct in 1497 with the death of John Trenowth (b. 1426), whose tomb, a fine monumental brass, is still to be seen in the Church of St. Michael Penkevil, on the floor of the south aisle.   The plate bears a fine effigy of John Trenoweth in military costume, and the following inscription in Gothic characters :

"HERE LYETH JOHN TRENOWYTH, SQUEYER, THE WHICH DEPARTYD THE XIIJ DAY OF MARCH, THE YEERE OF OURE LORD GOD MCCCCLXXXXVIJ, AND IN THE YERE OF KYNG HARRY, THE VIJ., THE XIIJ., ON WHOSE SOUL JHU HAVE MERCY.   AMEN.   IN DOMINE CONFIDO."

The four daughters of John Trenowth married as follows : 1, Margaret m. John Godolphin, of Godolphin, sheriff of Cornwall in 1503-4 ; Philippa m. John Carmynow, from whom is descended the present Lord Falmouth, owner of St. Michael Penkevil ; Matilda m. Thomas St. Aubyn, of Clowance ; Katherine m. Edmund Stradling, our ancestor.*

---

* Trenoweth signified in Cornish "the new town."   See the pretty little traditionary tale of "Nancy Trenoweth, the Fair Daughter of the Miller of Alsia" in Bothell's "Traditions of West Cornwall," p. 189 ; also, Dunkin's "Monumental Brasses of Cornwall," for a figure of the monument to John Trenowth.   Maclean's History of Trigg Minor, 1, p. 72.

TREGARTHIAN, OF GORRAN, CORNWALL.

Arms. Argent, a chevron between three escallop shells, sable. Honour, daughter of William Tregarthian, married John Trenowth, Esq., and was ancestor of Isabell Goode, of Whitley.

This ancient Cornish family became extinct about the middle of the fifteenth century by the marriage of Margaret, daughter and coheir of Thomas Tregarthian, to Sir John Chamand, of Launcells. [Harleian MSS., 1079, fo. 62.]

HENDOWER, OF COURT IN BRANNELL, CORNWALL.

Arms. Argent, a lion rampant, between an orle of escallop shells.

The Hendowers were of Welsh origin, and became established in Cornwall by a marriage with the heiress of Court. The heiress married Tregarthian and was thus ancestor of the Goodes of Whitley.

CORNWALL, OF COURT, IN CORNWALL.

Arms. Argent, a lion rampant gules, crowned or, within a border, sable, bezanty.

This family was descended from a son of Richard, King of the Romans [son of King John, created Earl of Cornwall in 1224], and Joan de Valletort. He was probably Edmund, Earl of Cornwall, whose seat was Launceston Castle. The elder branch of the family became extinct after a few descents, in the fourteenth century ; the heiress married Hendower, and through Tregarthian, Trenowth, Raynward and Penkevill was ancestor of the Goodes of Whitley.

NANFAN, OF TRETHEWELL, IN ST. EVAL, CORNWALL.

Arms. Sable, a chevron, ermine, between three wings displayed, argent.

Joan, daughter and heiress of James Nanfan, married about 1420-30 John Trenowth, whose granddaughter married Edmund Stradling, and was ancestor of the Goodes of Whitley.

This marriage marks the period of extinction of the family, which appears to have descended from crusader stock. In 1855 was exhibited at the Archeological Institute a certificate given by Sir Humphrey Nanfan, stating that being a captive among the Turks, money had been paid toward his redemption and for the purchase of a papal indulgence. " The seal bears an escutcheon, on which is a chevron, ensigned with a cross(?) between three human heads (heads of children—*enfants*) looking sinister, in heads of mail, or helmets. Of the legend the name Nanfan only remains."

Henry Nanfan was keeper of the fees in the Duchy of Cornwall in 1374. Maclean mentions others, probably ancestors of John Nanfan, sheriff of Cornwall. In 1450 the manor and town of Helston were granted to John Nanfan, Esq., who was descended from the families of Penneck and Lanyon.

TREJAGO, OF FENTONGOLLAN, IN CORNWALL.

Arms (ancient). Argent on a chevron, sable, between three balls, gules, five bezants. They afterwards bore, or, a chevron, between three cross crosslets, sable. The Trejago family, of Trejago, in Crantock, became extinct, says Lysons, in the reign of Edward IV. The Trejagos, of Fentongollan, seated there as early as Edward II (1308-27); were, according to Lysons, probably the same family. Fentongollan passed to the Trenowths by the marriage of Jane Treiago to John Trenowth, ancestor of the Goodes of Whitley. Fentongollan is now the property of the Boscawens, and a part of Lord Falmouth's estate, "Tregothnan." The descent of Treiago is given below under "Trewarthenick."

CHENDUIT, OF BODANNAN, IN ENDELLION, CORNWALL.

Arms. Gules, four lozenges, conformed in fesse, each charged with an escallop shell.

A family of considerable antiquity and distinction, says Lysons, which became extinct before the reign of Henry VI. The coheiress married Trejago, from whom descended the Goodes of Whitley and the Roscarrocks. The family was not, according to Maclean (I, p. 546), Cornish in origin, but appear to have emigrated to Cornwall in the reign of Henry III., 1266-73. Syman Chaine doit paid rates to King Stephen in Northamptonshire in 1140.

The following deduction, derived in its early stages from Maclean, is of interest as showing a long line of Saxon and Celtic ancestors, extending eighteen generations back of Richard Goode :

1. Simon Chaisnedoit, living 1140 in Northampton.
2. Ralph Chaisnedoit, m. Alice, d. before 1201.
3. Ralph Chendeduit d. 1229.
4. Ralph Cheyndut, living, Oxfordshire, 1229.
5. Ralph Cheyndut d. 1284.
6. Ralph Cheyndut, b. before 1263, living 1318.
7. John Cheyndut, b. before 1297, living 1318.
8. William Chendut lived 1347.
9. Joan Chenduit m. Stephen Trejago, knight, grandson of John Trevanion and great-grandson of Stephen Trewarthenick, knight.

10. Jane Trejago m. John Trenowth.
11. Ralph Trenowth, d. 1427, m. Jane Bassett.
12. John Trenowth, b. before 1403, d. 1444, m. Jane Nanfan.
13. John Trenowth, b. 1426, d. 1497, m. Honour Tregarthian.
14. Katherine Trenowth m. Edmund Stradling.
15. Isabell Stradling m. John Raynward.
16. Isabella Raynward m. John Penkevill.
17. Philip Penkevill m. Joan Trenance.
18. Isabell Penkevil m. Richard Goode of Whitley.

TREWARTHENICK, OR TRENNICK, OF TREWYTHENICK IN ST. CLEMENTS, CORNWALL.

Arms. Argent. A chevron and border, indented gules.

Very little is known, says Dunkin, of the family of Trewythynnyk, which is now extinct, who appear to have taken their name from a barton called Trethenak or Trewethenack, now Trennack, which descended to the Carminows through the Trenowths. Roger Trewythenick was one of the King's justices at an assize held at Penryn in 1402. Stephen Trewarthenick married, about 1300, Melior, daughter of Sir Osbert Taluerat, knight. Their son Stephen married Jane, daughter of Sir John Trevanion, knight, whose daughter and heir, Jane, married Sir John Trejago. Stephen Trejago, knight, their son, married Alice Chenduit, and had a daughter, Joan, who married John Trenowth, whose connection with the Goodes of Whitley has already been shown.

TREVANION, OF TREVANION, IN CARHAYES, CORNWALL.

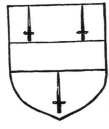

Arms. Argent, on a fesse azure, between two chevrons, gules, three escallop shells, or.

Sir John Trevanion was of Trevanion, in Carhayes, six generations before the reign of Edward IV. The name became extinct in the male line in 1767 by the death of William Trevannion, Esq., great grandfather of Lord Byron.

Stephen Trewarthenick married about 1330–60 Jane Trevanion; their descendant, twelve generations removed, was Isabel Goode of Whitley.

TRENANCE, OF TRENANCE IN WITHIEL, CORNWALL.

Arms. Sable, a fesse between three swords erect, argent.

Jane, daughter of Richard de Trenance, married in the fourteenth century Stephen Trenowth, and was ancestor of Penkevill and Goode. She was granddaughter of John Trevasgus, (Trevalscois.)

Trenance, or De Trenant, is an ancient Cornish family. The name of Luca de Trenance appears in an old document of 1306. In 1382 Richard Trenance granted to John Colyn his messuages in Peneton for twelve years.

Trenance of Trenance, in Withiel, afterwards of Lanhydrock, became extinct in the seventeenth century.—(Lysons.)

Withiel was near St. Minver, on the opposite side of the river.

TREGARRICK OF TREGARRICK, IN ROCHE, CORNWALL.

Arms. Argent, two chevrons paly, azure and or. "Tregarrick of Tregarrick in Roche; the heiress married Trenowth, whose heiress married Boscawen," says Lysons, probably erroneously.

Isabell, daughter and heir of David Tregarrack, married about the year 1500 John Penkevill, great grandfather of Isabell Penkevill, wife of Richard Goode. I have been able to learn almost nothing as yet of the family. Ricardo Tregerick, mentioned in a subsidy bill, anno. 1. Edward III., (1327) was perhaps great grandfather of David Tregarrack, mentioned above.

TREVILLA OF ETHY, IN ST. WINNOW, CORNWALL.

Arms. Argent, a chevron between three towers, triple turreted, sable.

This family, located at Ethy or Tethe, in St. Winnow, Cornwall, became extinct in the seventeenth century; one of the coheiresses married Arscott, represented now by the Molesworths. Thomas Trevilla, living about 1375, was ancestor in the fifth generation of Richard Goode of Whitley, his daughter Elizabeth having married John Penkevill. I find a memorandum to the effect that the manor of Trevilla and Tregarrick, descended to the family of Boscawen.

MOHUN OF POSTLINCH, IN ERRINGTON, DEVON.

Arms (as quartered with Upton), Or, a cross engrailed, sable.

Margaret Mohun, daughter of William Mohun, of Postlinch, described in Tuckett's "Devonshire Pedigrees," probably erroneously, as *Sir* William Mohun, married Thomas Penkevill, from whom, in the fourth generation, was descended Isabell Goode of Whitley. William Mohun married Mawde or Margaret, daughter of Robert Blerick, 1400–1450. Elizabeth, sister of Margaret, wife of Thomas Penkevil, married 1461, John Upton, to whom the estate of Postlinch descended.

William Mohun was undoubtedly a descendant in the third or fourth generation of John de Mohun, Baron of Dunster, b. 1268, d. 1330, and probably a son of one of the numerous sons of John, Lord Dunster, who died 1331—either Reginald, Pagan, Thomas, Patrick or Henry.

The Mohuns derived their surname from the village of Moyon near St. Lo, Normandy. William de Moyen was one of William the Conquerer's well rewarded companions, having been given the land upon which at present stands the Castle of Dunster, with other estates in Somerset, Wilts, Devon and Yorkshire. The title of Lord Mohun is now extinct, like almost all titles of that period ; the name, however, is not unusual, and in Cornwall, where many of the family are basket-makers, it has become corrupted to Moon. The following record is condensed from Burke's " Extinct Peerage," and is probably as reliable as most early pedigrees.*

1. Sir William de Mohun, companion of the Conquerer, had in his retinue at the battle of Senlac, 1066, forty-seven stout knights of name and note.

2. William, Lord of Dunster, who granted the Church of Whitford to the canons of Bridlington.

3. William de Mohun, who espoused the cause of Matilda of Anjou 1141–54, and fortifying his castle of Dunster, rebelled against King Stephen. With King David of Scotland he besieged Henry, Bishop of Winchester, in the castle at that place, and is said to have been created Earl of Dorset by Matilda. He founded the priory of Bruton in Somerset, and died before 1165.

4. William de Mohun died before 1202 ; had forty knights in his retinue ; married widow of Hugh Bigod, Earl of Norfolk.

5. Reginald de Mohun married, 1205, Alice, sister and coheir of William, Lord Briwere, with whom he acquired estates in Cornwall, Devon and Somerset. He died in 1213, leaving two sons, Reginald, his heir, and John, ancestor of the Mohuns of Ham Mohun.

6. Reginald de Mohun, who was, in 1242, chief justice of all the forests south of Trent, and later governor of Sanbeye Castle in Leicestershire. He died in 1250. He married Avise de Bohun, by whom he had a son.

7. John de Mohun, died in 1278, who married Joan, daughter of William de Terrers, Earl of Essex ; left a daughter Margaret, who married Sir John Cantalupe, and a son.

8. John de Mohun, born 1268, was distinguished in the wars of Gascony and Scotland, and a Baron in parliament in 1299–1330. He married Alinore Fitzpiers, and died in 1330.

9. John de Mohun died in 1331, married Auda, daughter of Pagan Tiptoft.

10. Reginald de Mohun, or one of his brothers, Thomas, Pagan, Patrick or Henry. From his brother Lawrence were descended the Mohuns of Tavistock. John, the eldest, left no male heirs in the third generation, and there are no Williams among his descendants as given by Tuckett.

11 or 12. William Mohun, of Postlinch, was son or grandson of one of the brothers named under the preceding number.

---

* See " Dunster and its Lords," by H. C. Maxwell Lyte, printed for private circulation.—*Athenæum*, 1882, p. 427.

BLERICK OF POSTLINCH, IN ERRINGTON, DEVON.

Arms (as quartered with Upton of Postlinch).   Sable, a fesse sable with borders, argent, between three bees, or.

Robert Blerick, or Bleryck, was ancestor in the fifth degree of Isabell Goode of Whytley, his daughter and heir Margaret having married William Mohun. He lived, 1400 to 1460, and married Joan Fleming, who appears to have been the heiress of Postlinch, in despite of the statement in one of the county histories that this manor was given by William de Ferrers to the name of Postlinch, and that it was held by Roger de Postlinch in the time of Edward I.   Maclean credits Penkevil with the right to quarter Postlinch (Polslithe) next after Mohun, but no such family is mentioned in the Devon visitation, and the family of Upton quarter Mohun, Blerick and Fleming, as should undoubtedly be done by the Penkevills, whose ancestor married the sister and coheiress of the Mohuns of Postlinch.

UPTON, [MOHUN, BLERICK, FLEMING.]

The estate passed to the family of Upton, and went in 1707, by marriage, to the family of Yonge.   It was variously known as Postlinch, Postlynch, Polslinch, Poslinche, Polyslinche, Puswithe and Polslithe, the last two, side by side, in the same MS.   Herald's Visitation.

John Upton was a descendant in the eighth generation of John Upton, of Upton, in Cornwall, who flourished 1130-50.

Robert Bleryck would seem to have had two daughters besides she who married William Mohun, namely, Joan married Richard Ryke, and Elizabeth married John Beckett.   (Visitation of Devon, 1564.)

FLEMINGE OF MENELEY, IN CORNWALL.

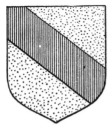

Arms, (as quartered by Upton).   Vair, a chief chequy, or and gules.

Joan Flemying, daughter and heir of John Fleming of Meneley or Bratton, in Cornwall, (see Tuckett's Devonshire Pedigrees, p. 201), married, 1420-40, Robert Bleryck, and was grandmother of the wife of Thomas Penkevill, ancestor of the Goode of Whitley.

The following deduction seems to be a safe one : (See Betham's, "Barony of Slane.")

1. Stephen Flandrensis, living at the time of the Norman Conquest, married the daughter and heir of Ercenbald, Lord of Bratton, in Devonshire.

2. Archibald Flandrensis, or le Fleming, succeeded his father and mother as heir of both, and was Lord of Bratton and Alverdescot, Devon.

3. Richard le Fleming attended Hugh de Lacey to Ireland, and got a grant of twenty knights' fees in Meath, afterwards called the Barony of Slane and Newcastle.

4. Richard le Fleming, 2d Baron of Slane.

5. Stephen le Fleming, 3d Baron, living in 1399.

6. Baldwin le Fleming, 4th Baron.

7. Richard le Fleming, 5th Baron, married Maria Martyn, daughter of Nicholas Martyn, daughter of Nicholas Martyn of Darlington, 1310.

8. Baldwyn le Fleming, 6th Baron, married Matilda, daughter of Sir Simon de Genevile, second son of Geffery de Genevile by Matilda, daughter of Gilbert de Lacey. (Walter de Lacey, Lord of Meath ; Sir Hugh de Lacey.)

9. Sir Simon le Fleming, knight, died 1370, married Cicely Champernon.

10. Sir Thomas le Fleming, born 1358, died 1434, married Elizabeth, daughter of Sir Robert Preston, Lord Kells and Gormanstone.

11. Sir Christopher Fleming, 4th Lord Fleming, died Nov. 30, 1448, married Leva or Levita Martyn, daughter of Martin Ferrers of Beere Ferrers.

12. John Flemyng, Esq., of Meneley, married Anne Rochfort.

13. Joan married Robert Blerick ; Amy, coheir, married John. Bellew ; Anna, coheir, married Walter Dillon, Esq., of Ireland ; Christopher Fleming, 5th Lord Fleming, brother of Joan, Amy and Anna, sat in Parliament in 1451, and died without children in 1458. On his death the peerage became in abeyance, and has since remained so. The descendants are numerous.*

FERRERS OF BEERE FERRERS, IN DEVON.

Arms. Or, on a bend sable, three horseshoes, argent.

"Beere Ferrers," says Pole, "takes his name of ye famyly of Ferrers th'ancient inhabitants, from whence all the Ferrers of Devon and Cornwall issued."

Ralph de Ferrarys was Lord of Beere in King Henry II's time ; Henry de Ferrarys, anno. vi of King Richard I.; Reginald de Ferrariis in the begynnynge of Kinge Henry ; Sir William de Ferrers, anno. 27, of King Henry III., which by Isota, his wief, had issue, Sir Roger de Ferrers, who died without issue, Sir Reginald de Ferrers and Sir Hugh de Ferrers of Churchton ; Sir Reginald Ferrers, of Beere, married Margaret, sister and one of the heirs of Sir Robert le Deneis, of Pancrasewike, by Matilda, his wife, had issue ; Sir John, which had issue ; Martyn Ferrers, the last of the name of Ferrers, Lord of Beere Ferrers, which had issue ; Joan, wife of Alexander, eldest daughter of Sir Richard Champernon, of Modbury ; Elizabeth, wife of Hugh Poyiugs Lo ; Sir John, of Bosnye, and Leva, wife of Sir Christofer Flemynge, Baron of Slane, in Ireland. (Pole's Devon, p. 336.)

*See Sir W. Betham's Memoir of the Family of Fleming of Slane, Co. Meath, Dublin, 1829.

VALLETORT OF HARBERTON.

Arms. Gules, three bends, argent, on a border, sable ten plates, or ; or, three bends gules within a border sable bezanty.

The Barony of Harberton, granted to the family of De Valletort in the time of King Henry I., became extinct about 1307. The name has become common in Vaulter. Thomas Champernon, father of Cicely, wife of Sir Simon Fleming, was son of Elizabeth de Valletort. The following line of descent is derived chiefly from Pole's Devon :

1. Reginald de Valletort, Lord of Harberton.

2. Roger de Valletort, living in 1108.

3. Raphe de Valletort, living in 1168, m. Joan, daughter of Reginald, Earl of Cornwall, and granddaughter of King Henry I.; also, apparently, ancestor of the Cornwall family of Cornwall.

4. Joel de Valletort, of Tawton, m. Emma, daughter of Sir Wm. Botreaux.

5. Sir Philip de Valletort, living in 1230.

6. Sir John de Valletort, living in 1250.

7. Hugh de Valletort m. Lucia, daughter of Adam le Brit.

8. Elizabeth de Valletort m. Sir Richard Champernon about 1300.

9. Thomas Champernon m. Elinor Rohant, daughter of Sir Roger Rohant.

10. Cicely Champernon m. Sir Simon le Fleming about 1350.

11. Sir Thomas le Fleming, b. 1358, d. 1434, m. Eliz., daughter of Sir Robert Preston.

12. Sir Christopher Fleming m. Leva Martyn.

13. John Fleming, Esq.. of Meneley, m. Ann Rochfort.

14. Joan Fleming m. Robert Blerick.

15. Maude Blerick m. William Mohun.

16. Margaret Mohun m. Thomas Penkevill.

17. John Penkevill m. Isabell Tregarrack.

18. John Penkevill m. Isabell Raynward.

19. Philip Penkevill m. Joan Trenance.

20. Isabell Penkevill m. Richard Goode of Whitley.

BOTTREAUX OF MOLLAND-BOTREAUX.

Arms. Argent, a griffin segreant, gules, bushed and legged, azure.

This ancient family resided at Molland-Botreaux, and at Botreaux Castle (now Boscastle), in Cornwall, from the time of Henry I, (1100–1135). William, Baron Bottreaux, was summoned to Parliament in 1637. The following deduction goes back to Richard Corbet, a contemporary of William the Conqueror :

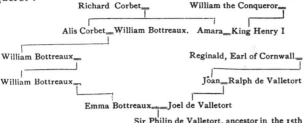

Richard Corbet___   William the Conqueror___

Alis Corbet___William Bottreaux.   Amara___King Henry I

William Bottreaux___   Reginald, Earl of Cornwall___

William Bottreaux___   Joan___Ralph de Valletort

Emma Bottreaux___Joel de Valletort

Sir Philip de Valletort, ancestor in the 15th degree of Mistress Isabel Goode of "Whitley."

DE BOHUN, EARLS OF HEREFORD.

Avis de Bohun, daughter of Henry de Bohun, first earl of Hereford, married Reginald de Mohun (see above, p. 457, No. 6), and was ancestor in the tenth degree of the Goodes of "Whitley." Her lineage, condensed from Burke, runs as follows :

1. Humphry de Bohun, kinsman and companion in arms of William the Conqueror, and known as "Humphrey with the Beard."

2. Humphrey de Bohun, surnamed the Great, who by command of King William Rufus married Maud, daughter of Edward le Saresbury (progenitor of the ancient Earl of Salsbury), by whom he acquired large estates in the County of Wilts," and had issue, a daughter Maud and his successor.

3. Humphrey de Bohun, who was steward and sewer of King Henry I. This feudal lord married Margery, daughter of Milo de Gloucester, Earl of Hereford, Lord High Constable of England, and sister and coheiress of Mabel, last Earl of Hereford.

At the instigation of the Earl of Hereford he espoused the cause of the Empress Maud and her son against King Stephen, and so faithfully maintained his allegiance that the Empress, by her especial charter, granted him the office of steward and sewer both in Normandy and England. He died April 6, 1187.

4. Humphry de Bohun, who died in 1182, was Earl of Hereford and Constable of England in right of his mother if the chronicles of Lanthony be correct. He married Margaret of Scotland, daughter of Henry Earl of Huntington, widow of Conan le Petit, Earl of Brittany and Richmond.

5. Henry de Bohun, who was created Earl of Hereford by King John April 28, 1199, died 1220. He took part with the Barons against King John, and had his lands sequestered, but they were returned at the signing of the Magna Charta at Runnimede, the Earl being one of the twenty-five Lords appointed then to inforce the observance of that celebrated charter. He was subsequently excommunicated by the Pope, and became a prisoner at the battle of Lincoln. He married Maud, daughter of Geoffrey Fitz-Piers, Earl of Essex, and eventually heiress of her brother William de Mandeville, Earl of Essex. He had daughter Margery, who married Waleran, Earl of Warwick, also—

6. Avise de Bohun, who married Reginald de Mohun.

This family name seems to have disappeared about 1400 after the death of Humphrey de Bohun, second Earl of Northampton, who was succeeded by his son-in-law, the Duke of Gloucester, who inherited the earldom of Northampton, which became extinct, and the Earl of Derby, who was created Duke of Hereford in 1397, prior to his ascending the thrown as King Henry IV.

The lineage that can only be traced among the descendants at the present day are the families of the Dukes of Stafford and Buckingham.

SOME ROYAL DEDUCTIONS.

"Nearly all of the great historic houses that were famous in the middle ages and were allied to royalty have died out in the male line," says a recent writer in the *Athenænum*, "but the Herald's Visitations having very fully recorded the alliances of their female descendants, a vast number of persons can be shown to descend from great families whose titles and surnames are extinct, but who boasted of royal descent, and many are descended from our early kings. The fact that in England there has never been the same rigid separation of classes which has prevailed upon the Continent has greatly facilitated the transmission of the blood of our Norman and Angevine kings, through the nobility and aristocracy to the masses."

It must not then be considered strange if at the close of this chapter it be shown that our emigrant ancestor could claim descent from some of the early kings of England. William the Conqueror, if he were now alive, might, like Abraham, number his seed like the stars in the Heaven. (Genesis xv., 5). His descendants, at the least calculation, number one hundred and fifty millicn. On the other hand, if we trace back our ancestry, twenty-seven generations, to the time of the Norman conquest, we find that, if no allowance is made for crossing of different lines of descent, each one of us had over seventy-five million of ancestors. This is of course absurd, and only shows us that we are lineal descendants of the majority, if not of all, of the Normans, Saxons and Celts in England in the eleventh century, and that if we wish to know the history of our forefathers we need only to study that of the English people.

At the same time, though few can trace back their ancestors in every line of descent more than three generations, it is interesting to know something of types picked out for us by accident among those who carried about in their bodies parts of own components five, ten or fifteen generations ago.

I do not hesitate, therefore, to print another series of deductions which I find in my genealogical portfolio.

This pedigree was prepared as a diversion one afternoon in the British Museum, when weary of long continued scanning of manuscript records, I resolved, in a somewhat venturesome mood, to follow Guillim and some of the other early pedigree-writers as far as they might lead into the arcana of family tradition. These lists of names, taken from old works on heraldry, are reproduced here rather as souvenirs of a "book-worm's enjoyment" in rummaging than with the intimation that they possess value as historical statements of fact. I may say, however, that the deduction in the Scotch line going back as it does seventy generations and twenty-two centuries, almost as many years before the English settled England, as have passed since the Norman occupation of the same region, appears to me to be a powerful aid to the imagination in the effort to appreciate certain kinds of historical facts. Unworthy of credence as it may be, it doubtless, like all traditionary history, contains here and there a kernel of truth, and like the other pedigrees here given, even if it be not exactly accurate, is unquestionably "something like the truth." I only regret that I could not have found the famous Scotch pedigree which was said to have been preserved by Noah among the ship's papers of the Ark. It could not be more than twice as long as this:

DESCENT FROM THE SCOTCH KINGS.*

1. Ferchar, or Ferodach, a prince of Scots in Ireland.
2. Fergus lived in 390 B. C.
3. Mamus, 261 B. C.
4. Domadil, 233 B. C.
5. Reuther, 187 B. C.
6. Josina, 134 B. C.
7. Fennan, 104 B. C.
8. Darstus, 95 B. C., m. a Briton.
9. (Dothan.)
10. (Gormac.)
11. (Europa m. Cadallanus.)
12. Corbred, A. D. 67.
13. Corbred II., or Galgacus, A.D. 106
14. (Daughter m. a nobleman.)
15. (Daughter.)
16. Etholdius, crowned, A. D. 192.
17. Etholdius II., A. D. 238.
18. Athurko, A. D. 250.
19. (Cormacus.)
20. Fincormachus, A. D. 357.
21. (Ethod.)
22. Erch, or Erth, m. Rocha, dau. of Roricus, Prince of Denmark.
23. Fergus II., crowned, A. D 420, m. dau. of Greme.
24. Dongard, A. D. 457.
25. Gonran or Goran, A. D. 535.
26. Aydan, A. D. 604.
27. Eugene IV., A. D. 622.
28. Donald, A. D. 650.
29. Malduin, A. D. 688.
30. Eugene V., A. D. 692.
31. (Findan.)
32. Eugene VII., A. D. 720, m. Spondana, dau. of Garnard, King of Picts.
33. Erhfin, A. D. 761.
34. Achains, A. D. 819, m. Fergiusiana, dau. of Hungust, King of Picts.
35. Alpin, A. D. 834.
36. Kenneth MacAlpin, first King of all Scotland.
37. Constantin II., A. D. 874.
38. Donald IV.
39. Malcolm I., A. D. 958.
40. Kenneth III., killed, A. D. 994.
41. Malcolm II., murdered 1033.
42. (Beatrix m. Albanact or Grimus, "Thane of the Scots Island.")
43. Duncan I., slaine by his cousin, Macbeth.
44. Malcolm Caenmohr, d. 1093, m. Margaret, dau. of Eadgar Aetheling.
45. David I., d. 1153.
46. Henry, Prince of Scotland, d. 1182.
47. David, Earl of Huntington, d. 1219.
48. Ada, m. Henry Hastings, Earl of Huntington.
49. "Margaret of Scotland" m. Humphrey de Bohun.
50. Henry de Bohun, Earl of Hereford.
51. Avise de Bohun, m. Reginald de Mohun, Earl of Dunster.
52. John de Mohun, Baron of Dunster, d. 1276.
53. John de Mohun, b. 1268, 1330.
54. John de Mohun d. 1331.
55. William Mohun—"Sir William Mohun."
56. Margaret Mohun m. Thomas Penkevil.
57. John Penkevill.
58. John Penkevill, of Penkevil, b. 1490, d. 1562.
59. Philip Penkevill and Rosorrow, d. 1562.
60. Isabell Penkevill m. Richard Goode of Whitby. (See page 20.)

*The names of those who did not actually occupy the throne are in parenthesis.

DESCENT FROM THE SAXON KINGS.

1. Cerdic, the Saxon, crowned at Westminster, A. D. 532, 3d king of England.
2. Cenric.
3-9.
9 or 10. Ecgberht, King of Essex, 802–837.
11. Æthelwulf, 837–858.
12. Ælfred the Great, 871–901.

13. Eadward the Elder, 901–925.
14. Eadmund the Elder, 940–946.
15. Eadgar the Peaceful, 959–975.
16. Æthelred the Unready, 979–1016.
17. Eadmund Ironside, d. 1017.
18. Edward, d. 1057.
19. Margaret, d. 1093, m. Malcolm I, King of Scots. No. 44 of preceding list.

DESCENT FROM THE DUKES OF THE NORMANS.

1. Rollo the Dane, 911–927.
2. William Longa-Spatha, 927–943.
3. Richard, Sans Peur, 933–996.
4. Richard the Good, 996–1026.
5. Robert the Magnificent, 1028–1035
7. King Henry I. of England, 1106–1135.
8. Matilda m. Geoffry, count of Anjou and Maine.
9. King Henry II., of England.
10. John of England, 1199–1204.
11. Richard, King of the Romans, Earl of Cornwall.
12-16. Cornwall of Court in Cornwall.

(Five generations.)
17-18. Hendower of "Court."
(Two generations.)
19. —— Tregarthian.
20. William Tregarthian.
21. Honour Tregarthian m. John Trenowth.
22. Katharine Trenowth m. Edmund Stradling.
23. —— Stradling m. John Raynward.
24. Isabell Raynward m. Philip Penkevill.
25. Isabell Penkevill m. Richard Goode, No. 60 of first list.

DESCENT FROM THE KINGS OF GERMANY AND FRANCE.

1. Pepin the Old, Mayor of Austrasia, d. 639.
2. Doda d. 640.
3. Pepin d'Heristal, d. 714.
4. Charles Martel, Duke of Franks d. 741.
5. Pepin the Stout, King of France, d. 768.
6. Charlemagne, d. 814.
7. Lewis le Debonaire.
8. Charles the Bold.
9. Baldwin Bras de Fer, 1st Count of Flanders, d. 880.
10. Baldwin the Bold, d. 918.
11. Arnolf the Great.
12. Baldwin, d. 962.
13. Arnolf, d. 988, m. Susanna, dau. of Berenger II., King of Italy.
14. Baldwin the Fan Beard, d. 1034.
15. Baldwin the Pious, d. 1067, m. Adela, dau. of Robert I., King of France, and granddaughter of Hugh Capet.

16. Matilda m. William the Conqueror.
17. King Henry I.
18. Reginald, Earl of Cornwall.
19. Joan m. Raphe de Valletort.
20. Sir Joel de Valletort.
21. Sir Philip de Valletort.
22. Sir John de Valletort.
23. Hugh de Valletort.
24. Eliz. m. Sir Richard Champernon.
25. Cicely m. Sir Simon le Fleming.
26. Sir Thomas le Fleming.
27. Sir Christopher le Fleming.
28. John Fleming.
29. Joan m. Robert Blerick.
30. Mawde m. William Mohun.
31. Margaret m. Thomas Penkevill. No. 58 of the first list.
32. John Penkevill.
33. John Penkevill.
34. Philip Penkevill.
35. Isabell Penkevill m. Richard Goode, No. 60 of first list.

DECENT FROM THE KINGS OF VIRGINIA.

"Whitby," was, as we have seen, in immediate proximity to one of the principal residences of Powhatan, and came into the possession of the Goodes, within forty years of his death, in 1618. Col. John Bolling, of "Cobbs," great-grandson of Pocahontas, was a contemporary and near neighbor of John Goode of "Whitby," and "Oropax," the burial place of Powhatan, was very close to "Winepeck," the plantation of Samuel Goode, No. 32, his eldest son. It is not strange, therefore, that the blood of the two families should have mingled in later generations, and I find that about 400 of the people named in this book may claim descent from "The Nonparella of Virginia." Judge Robertson recently published "Pocahontas and her Descendants" embraces only seven generations, and omits some of the lines of descent included in this book. The following "key" is intended to extend and amplify certain portions of Judge Robertson's tables :

POWHATAN or Wahunsonacook, "the mighty Weroance who ruled over Attanougkomouck or Virginia," b. 1530–60, d. 1618.

POCAHONTAS, "The Nonparella of Virginia," also known as Matoaca (White Feather) and "The Lady Rebekah," b. 1595, d. 1616, m. John Rolfe.

Lieut. Thomas Rolfe, b. 1615, m. Jane Poythress.

Jane Rolfe, b. 1656–55, d. 1676, m. Col. Robert Bolling, (1646–1709.)

Col. John Bolling, of "Cobbs," m. Mary Kennon.

1. Maj. John Bolling (1700–1757) m. Elizabeth Blair.

Thomas Bolling, of "Cobb," (1735–1804) m. Eliz. Gay. Five children. (See Bristol Parish.)

John, of "Chestnut Grove" (1737–1757) m. Martha Jefferson, niece of Martha Jefferson Goode, No. 59. 11 children.

Col. Robert, of "Chellowe," (1738–69) author of the "Bolling Memoirs," m. (1) Mary Burton, (2) Susan Watson. Six children. (See Bristol Parish, p. 142.)

Mary (b. 1744), m. Richard Bland, brother of Sally Bland Goode, No. 90.

Sarah (b. 1748), m. John Tazewell. Her granddaughter did not marry Hon. W. O. Goode, No. 241, as stated in "Pocahontas."

Archibald (b. 1750), 13 children, of whom no full record has been printed ; 4 are mentioned in "Pocahontas," one— Sarah Bolling, m. 1792, Joseph Cabell Megginson, No. 301 of the Goode Pedigree, and had 8 children, 21 grandchildren and at least 100 descendants in the eleventh generation, from Powhatan the names of about 50 being recorded in this volume, pp. 259–61 and 372.

Anne m. William Dandridge ; 10 children, 5 named in "Pocahontas."

2. Jane Bolling m. Col. Richard Randolph of "Curles," and had 7 children. (See Bristol Parish, p. 217. Goode Genealogy, p. 114. Page Family, p. 94), and at least 34 grand children: one son, Brett Randolph m. Mary Scott, and had son, Henry, who m. Lucy Ward, No. 235 of the Goode Genealogy, and had 11

children (p. 111), 31 grand children (pp. 212–19), 78 great-grand-children (pp. 353–68), and 79 great great-grandchildren (pp. 353–68, 418–26) in the twelfth generation from Powhatan. Brett had also daughter, Susan, who m. Dr. Douglas, and had daughter, who m. J. W. Randolph, No. 1632 of the Goode Pedigree, and had 2 sons and 6 grand children. William Beverly Randolph, of Florida, descended in the sixth genera-tion from Col. Richard, m. No. 3106, p. 328.

Richard m. Anne Meade had daughter, Jane, who m. Archi-bald Bolling, of Red Oak, and had daughter, who m. Joseph C. Megginson, No. 301. Goode Pedigree, already referred to. John m. Frances Bland, own cousin of Mrs. Sally Bland Goode, No. 90; had son, John Randolph, of Roanoke. Robertson says that Frances Bland was daughter of Richard Bland, which seems to be erroneous. (See Bland Papers.)

3. Mary Bolling m. Col. John Fleming ; 8 children ; fullest record in " Pocahontas."

4. Elizabeth Bolling m. Dr. William Gay ; 5 children and numer-ous descendants. Gideon A. Strange, No. 2321 of the Goode Pedigree, who had 6 children, recorded p. 250, was probably son of Mary B., grandson of William, greatgrandson of William and Elizabeth Bolling Gay.

5. Martha Bolling m. Thomas Eldredge. According to tradition of the descendants, not recognized by Robertson, m. in " Poca-hontas," they had a son Thomas, who m. H. E. Read, whose daughter Sarah m. Col. Thomas Edmunds, whose daughter m. Rev. Clement Read, and had 13 children. If this be correct, there is here a large additional group of Pocahontasites, including 8 children of Dr. Thomas Claiborne Goode, who m. Mary Goode Read, granddaughter of Rev. Clement Read (see No. 588, p. 194, and 8 grandchildren, p. 331). Another descendant not mentioned by Robertson was Pauline Pocahontas Eldridge (daughter of John ?), who m. Dr. Joel W. Watkins, and had 9 children, recorded by Brock (Dupuy Family, p. 157), one of whom m. Joel W. Daniel, 1031–5 of the Goode Genealogy, and has 5 children (p. 275.)

6. Anne Bolling, b. 1718, m. James Murray. (See Bristol Parish, p. 199). This daughter, Peggy, b. 1748, m. Thomas Gordon ; had daughter Peggy, m. William Knox ; had daughter, Mary Ann, who m. Dr. Thomas Goode, No. 255, and had 9 children (p. 122), and 23 grandchildren (pp. 538–40). Another descend-ant, Elizabeth Ann Coleman, was the first wife of Col. Charles Baskerville, No. 251 of the Goode Pedigree, and had 4 children, mentioned on p. 234.

APPENDIX III.

ADDENDA ET CORRIGENDA.

The only regret experienced by the author in connection with this chapter is that it is not longer, for he is quite well aware that many important facts have been omitted, and that many hundreds of the people who ought to have been mentioned are as yet undiscovered.

To those who feel that injustice has been done them in this book by misstatements or omissions, I frankly say that the fault is not always mine, but more frequently theirs or that of their friends. That venerable historian and genealogist, Dr. Philip Slaughter, well says :

"An author cannot spin genealogies out of his own brain, as the goddess sprung complete from the brain of Jupiter. He can only collate and digest materials gathered from various and often conflicting authorities. They then pass into the hands of copyists, and are thence committed to the tender mercies of that most formidable of all steam engines, the press. It will be a marvel if a family can make all these perilous passages without the loss of some members or suffering such dislocations and fractures that they often can hardly be recognized. If, therefore, one does not find himself married to his grandmother, he ought to be happy, instead of regarding himself as the victim of malice aforethought or culpable carelessness."

Owners of this volume are advised that the only way to make these changes of any value is to go through the book and mark the corrections with a pen.

Page 21.—For Jan. 19, 1667, read Jan. 9, 1607.
Page 23.—WHITSTONE, p. 231. This estate passed, 1840–50, from the hands of the I'Ans family to Henry Heitland, Esq., in 1865, to Joseph Spettigue, Esq., in 1880 to Edward Mucklow.
    Higher Whitley or Whetley belonged in 1880 to Mr. Baker ; Middle Whitley or Banbury, and Lower Whitley to the Duke of Bedford.
Page 27.—The change from " Whitley " to " Whitby " was accomplished just as that from " Inverness " to " Invermay " two generations later—possibly for euphony, say the family, but how or when they do not know, although the change has occurred within the last century. (See p. 232.)

No. 26, p. 27.—A tradition among the Goodes and Prides of Amelia Co. has it that John Goode and his wife were a runaway couple from England (John), and from Scotland (Martha Mackerness?), and that they were heirs to a large estate in the old country. (See possible confirmation of this in John Goode's conversation with Bacon, p. 30 c.)

John Goode, the immigrant, it now appears, had two sons by his first wife, Martha Mackerness. No. 32, Samuel, and No. 33, Robert, who inherited "Whitby." Tradition is rather explicit upon this point. Some of the descendants of Robert have traditions of the unkindness of John Goode's second or Dutch wife to her step-sons.

Page 30 A, line 2.—For 1869 read 1639.

Page 34.—Martha Jones, wife of Samuel Goode, was daughter of Samuel Jones, of Henrico Co., who, June 1716, gave 100 acres of land to his daughter and son-in-law. We know not whether it was he or his father who came from Wales.

Page 37, No. 33.—Robert Goode was son of John and *Martha Mackarness* Goode, not of Anne Bennet. He died in 1764, aged at least 75. No. 34.

Page 42, No. 88.—Elizabeth Goode m. Mr. Branch. The record of her descendants is lost, but she had a daughter who m. Edmund Goode, No. 79, and probably others. She was perhaps the sister of Thomas Branch, who m. Mary Eldridge. (See "Pocahontas," p. 34.) "Kingsland" was only a few miles from Whitby, perhaps in early days the adjoining plantation, and it is not strange that the families should have mingled, but it is a pity that the record of the Branches should have been lost. Mr. Brock tells me that the first of the name seems to have been Christopher Branch, of "Arrohattocks," planter, in 1634, who was living at Neck Land with his wife Mary and son Thomas, aged 9 months, and who probably died at "Kingsland" at an advanced age, 1681. He had son William and grandson John.

Nos. 39 and 40, p. 38.—Joseph and Thomas Goode's land in old Albemarle Co. was on "Great Bremore Creek," a tributary of James River, A. D. 1750.—*Alex. Brown.*

Page 42, No. 56.—Robert Goode died 1765, and his wife 1770.

No. 59, p. 43.—The Virginia Statutes, 1742, mention a ferry over the James River, from the land of Bennet Goode to that of Col. John Fleming in Goochland Co. (Henning, v. 100.)

No. 64, p. 45.—Daniel was apparently his name. Mr. Brown sends this extract from Col. William Cabell's diary, April 2, 1770: "Delivered Daniel Goode's £10 bill to S. Mitchell, which James Cooke judged to be a counterfeit."

Page 43, line 1.—Thomas Turpin, who m. Mary Jefferson, was brother of Mary Turpin, who married Robert Goode.

Page 43, No. 58 or 104.—Judge R. W. Hughes, of Norfolk, writes: "Thomas

Goode, Jr., of Chesterfield Co., Va., was one of the owners of the great horse "Diomede" in the early part of this century, in conjunction with Col. William Selden, of "Tree Hill," on the north side of the James, below Richmond."

Page 44.—Other children of No. 59 were 115½, ELIZABETH Goode, married *Samuel Watkins*, of Petersburg, Va., son of Samuel and Susan (Hancock) Watkins and brother of Henry Watkins, the stepfather of Henry Clay, the Kentucky Senator. Child: 290-1, *Alice Goode Watkins*, b. 1775-50, d. June 7, 1866, m. Reuben Vaughan, (p. 127;) 115 3-6, *Lucy Goode*, m. Col. William Marshall, of Mecklenburg Co., Va., son of William and *Ann McLeod* Marshall, of Caroline Co., grandson of William and Elizabeth William Marshall, of Mecklenburg Co., nephew of John and *Eliz. Markham* Marshall, whose descendants are enumerated in Paxton's "Marshall Family," brother of Sarah (Marshall) Anderson, from whom descended the Andersons of Virginia, had son *William Marshall*, b. 1796, d. 1835, who m. Sarah Lyne Holloway. Children:

929-28, *John Holloway Marshall*, p. 263. 929-29, *William J. Marshall*, p. 264. 929-30, *James Bennett Marshall*, p. 264. 929-31, *Lucy Ann Marshall*, m. L. H. Lyne, p. 264. (See also "Sullivant Memorial;" p. 93, p. 326, and Paxton's "Marshall Family," p. 11.)

Page 44, line 14.—For Flemming read Fleming.

Richard Goode, No. 62, was almost certainly son of Joseph Goode, No. 40, p. 34, and not of No. 39. He had additional children:

120-1, Daughter, m. *Mr. Mason*, near relative of Hon. John M. Mason. 120-2, Daughter, m. *Mr. Britain* (or Britton). 120-3, Daughter, m. *Mr. Jones*, of Petersburg; had daughter, No. 323-2, *Matilda Jones*, m. Mr. Branch, of Petersburg. (See p. 135.)

Page 44, No. 118.—See erratum for No 201, p. 50.

Page 45, No. 64.—Erase "John or"—the man's name was Daniel.

No. 66.—John Goode was born in 1750 in Henrico Co., died March 11, 1850, in Adair Co., Ky. He was possibly grandson of No. 52, p. 42, and not of the Rappahannock branch. He moved in 1794 to Lincoln Co., Ky., and in 1802-3 to Adair Co. He was drafted in 1779, and served at Cabin Point. In June, 1781, he joined Col. Taylor's regiment, and was stationed at the mouth of Rockfish Creek, on the James, to guard the ferry and the passage of provision wagons. After Cornwallis's surrender he was engaged in transporting by water to Richmond all provisions, arms and implements of war from the mouth of Rockfish Creek. Discharged Dec. 1781, and returned to his home in Buckingham Co. John Goode, perhaps his son, b. 1793, served in the war of 1812, was in the battle of New Orleans, and in May, 1871, was living at Monroe, Overton Co., Tenn.

Page 47, No. 141.—Mrs. Hatton left Virginia with her husband soon after their marriage.

Page 50, No. 77, Hunters of Georgia.—Margaret Hunter m., 1787, John Pope (b. 1749, d. 1802) and removed to Washington Co., Ga., in 1800.

Page 50 B.—GAINES was a name early known in Virginia, and its owners seem to have settled in New Kent, or one of the adjoining shores. Mary and Isabella Pendleton, of New Kent or Caroline Co., m. in 1720-40 two men named Gaines, probably brothers or cousins of Mrs. John Collier; Mrs. Isabella Gaines was grandmother of Gen. Edmund Pendleton Gaines, U. S. A. (*St. Mark's Parish*, p. 149.) Richard J. Gaines, of Charlotte Co., m. in 1820-30 Martha Venable, and had issue : i, Maj. Rich. V. Gaines, C. S. A. ii, Mary, m. Dr. Gaines, of Kentucky. iii, Elizabeth, m. Samuel Pryor, No. 827, of the Goode Pedigree. iv, William, m. Sarah G., daughter of Dr. William Fleming Gaines, of "Powhite," Hanover Co., whose mansion and the adjoining Gaines's Mill was the center of military operations in McClellan's siege of Richmond. v, Robert H. vi, Samuels vii, James. (For issue see *Standard*, II, 13-14.) Gaines Goode is a very common name in the Goode family.

Page 50, No. 201.—John Goode, probably 201, but possibly No. 118, p. 44, was born about 1780, and lived in Halifax Co. He enlisted June, 1814, in the Virginia militia, and died in service Aug., 27, 1814. His wife Elizabeth m. in 1833 Thomas Ivin, and was living, 1859, near Red Bank, Halifax Co.

Thomas Goode probably No. 203, but possibly No. 192, p. 95, was born in 1760, was a soldier in the Revolution, and was for a time in hospital at Trenton, N. J., though in active service at the siege of Yorktown and the surrender of Cornwallis Oct, 17, 1781. He married Sarah ——, b. 1762, living in 1824. He went to Jefferson Co., Ala , about 1827. Subsequently in 1828 to Tipton Co., Tenn., where his children lived. In 1835 he was at Covington, Tenn., a military pensioner, Edward Goode, Kentucky, was his son also ; Joseph Goode, of Jefferson Co., Ala., and perhaps also John Goode. For these three, in 1827, he relinquished all his property.

Page 50 F.—Edmund Goode, No. 79, died Oct. 15, 1812, his wife, Sarah Branch, whom he married in Bedford Co., Nov. 15, 1791, was born 1764, and was living in Bedford Co., in 1839, aged 84. He was a soldier in the Virginia Continental Line, serving in the South, and fought in the battles of Camden (probably the second battle, April 25, 1781), Guilford C. H., March 18, 1781, and at Eutaw Springs, April 18, 1781. He served under Gen. Greene, and was near Capt. Watts and Capt. Morgan when they were wounded at Eutaw Springs, and assisted in carrying them from the field; they were to have been cavalry officers under Col. William Washington, who was wounded also at Eutaw Springs.

No. 83.—Not only John Goode, No. 83, but several of his sons appear to have been engaged in the Revolutionary struggle. One son, perhaps Philip Goode, 201, was killed.

Page 51, No. 209.—Mackerness Goode died in Mecklenburg Co., March 25, 1849. He was a soldier in the war of 1812, in Capt. George Harman's company of Virginia militia. He married Mary Eliza Hayes, of Greensboro, May 25, 1822, who was living June, 1878, at Union Level.

Page 54.—Mary Goode Ward, No. 89, was born April 6, 1741, died 1799. She was "Polly Goode, the belle of James River," and was very lovely. Seth Ward lived at "Sheffield" in Chesterfield Co., and was the son of Seth Ward.

No. 90.—Col. Goode, in 1777, commanded a Virginia regiment stationed at Williamsburg and Hampton, as is shown by records of Pension Office. (See record of No. 210, p. 99.)

Page 55, footnote, No. vii.—I quote the following criticism, still maintaining that Sally Bland Goode, No. 751, who is my authority, was not likely to have made a mistake in the name of her own grandmother, since she was the acutest genealogist I have ever met. Mr. Alexander Brown writes:

"The Bland Genealogy says 'Richard, the eldest son, &c., * * and now lives at Jordan's, and has by his wife, &c.'—(See the extract sent you.) The entry was made in the lifetime of the said Richard, (there are later additions to it.) It seems to me evident that Anne Poythress was Richard Bland's wife from 4th March, 1729-30, to her death, 9th of April, 1758. Bland did not die until Oct., 1776; of course he may have married again."

The motto of the Blands was "*Sperate et vivite fortes.*"

Page 55, No. 240.—I extract from *The Visitor*, Richmond, May 12, 1810:
"Died, suddenly, on the 3d inst., at his place of residence, in Chesterfield Co., Mr. Theodrick Goode, youngest son of the late Col. Robert Goode, of Whitby."   R. A. B.

Page 58.—No. 91. was son of No. 56, not 51. His wife's father was Thomas Harris of "The Granyard." Statement as to daughter of No. 248 is erroneous.

Page 59.—No. 95 was probably the Thomas Goode who was sheriff of Chesterfield Co. in 1783. The Frances Goode who was deputy sheriff at about same time was probably No. 91.

Page 62.—Col. Samuel Goode called his place in Mecklenburg Co., "Whitby" after the old place on the James. This name still stands on the postal map of the United States. The portrait was not by Charles Wilson Peale; it is signed "I. P.:" perhaps John Paradise was the artist. His wife was a descendant of the Spotswoods.

Page 63, John Goode, No. 99 was a student in the University of North

Carolina, and in 1798 joined the Philanthropic Society of that Institution. "Twigg" appears to have been a familiar name, applied to him by his relatives aud friends, and not a real name.

The following pedigree shows the relationship between Lord Bacon, Nathaniel Bacon, acting governor of Virginia in 1688, Nathaniel Bacon, the rebel, and Mrs. Lewis Burwell. A. B.

Robert Bacon m. Isabella, daughter of John Cage
 i. Sir Nicholas Bacon m. Anne, daughter of Sir Anthony Cooke.
  i. Francis Bacon, Lord Verulam.
 ii. James Bacon, Esq., alderman of London, m. 2d, Margaret, and widow of Rich'd Gouldston, Wm. Rawlins,
  i. Sir James Bacon, (died 1618) m. Eliz. dau. of Francis and *Anne Drury* Bacon of Hessett
  i. Nathaniel Bacon, Esq., m Anne. dau. Sir Thomas Le Gross
   Thomas Bacon m. Elizabeth, dau. Sir Robert Brooke
    Nathaniel Bacon, "The Rebel," of Virginia
  ii. Rev. James Bacon m. Martha Honeywood
   i. Elizabeth Bacon m. Thomas Burrowes, of Bury St. Edmunds
   ii. Martha m. Mr. Smith, of Colchester
    Abygall Smith m. Major Lewis Burwell
   iii. Anne Bacon m. Mr. Wilkinson, of Burgate
   iv. Nathaniel Bacon, Esq., sometime acting Governor of Virginia, &c., m. Elizabeth Kingsmell ; d. s. p.

Page 64.—For Huiscull read *Heartwell*. Ellen Bolling, No. 258–2, m. Dr. J. L. Scott, of Dinwiddie, and her daughter, Ellen, m. William C. Tucker, No. 844, p. 244.

Page 64, footnote.

Page 65, line 3.—Maj. John Bolling d. April 20, 1729.

 Line 17.—Alex. Bolling m. *Susanna*, not Martha Bolling.

 Line 24.—Dr. John Feild's wife was *Harriet Bolling*.

Page 65, No. 272.—Agnes Eppes Goode (272) m. J. J. Williamson, of Dinwiddie Co., Va., and removed to Tennessee. They are both dead, but left 9 children, as follows :

 1. *Mary Ann* m. Mr. Murrell, of Macon, Tenn.; died, leaving 2 children, Junius and Herbert.

 2. *Harriet* m. Mr. Merriweather, of Madison Co., Tenn.; died, left Herbert, now in Europe.

 3. *Sally Tazewell* m. Joseph Granberry, of Macon, Tenn., where they live, and have two daughters unmarried.

 4. *Ella Bland*, unmarried.

 5. *John C.* m. Mary Moore, of Fayette Co., Tenn.

 6. *James J.*, unmarried.

 7. *Agnes* m. Dr. Julian Woodfork.

 8. *Henrietta Chambers*, unmarried.

 9. *Olin* m. Miss Smith, of Covington, Ky.

Elizabeth Goode (273) m. Thomas Baily, and moved to Tennessee ; both are dead, and left 2 sons, of whom I can learn nothing. This information was obtained of J. W. Williamson, who now lives in Boydton.

Page 67, No. 286.—Mr. Underwood's home was in "The Slashes" of Hanover Co.,—the house in which Henry Clay was born.

No. 110.—Isabella Lewis, wife of Bennet Goode, is said to have been a near relative of Gen. Washington.

Page 68, No. 116.—William Goode was a soldier of the Revolution, and at the age of 17 took part in the siege of Yorktown.

William Goode and Sarah James m. Sept. 17, 1789—their children were born as follows :

> 296, *James Jefferson Goode*, b. Sept. 17, 1789. 296½, *William Bennet*, b. Jan. 30, 1793. 297, *Elizabeth Caroline*, b. Nov. 15, 1794. 295, *Sidney* (Synor?) *Moore*, b. Jan. 26, 1797. 298, *Sarah Ann*, b. Feb. 27, 1799. 299, *Martha Jefferson*, b. April 15, 1806. 300, *Rebekah Singleton*, b. Nov. 13, 1803. 300½, *Plavellus Turpin*, b. Dec. 1, 1810.

Page 68, footnote.—Elizabeth Hooker, wife of Robin Povall, came to Virginia with John Minge. Robert Povall, Jr., and Elizabeth Povall entered in the Virginia Land Office as immigrants April 24, 1703. If the story of Elizabeth Hooker is true, this was probably the occasion of her return from England with her husband.

Page 70.—Thomas Goode, No. 117, is undoubtedly identical with No. 192, p. 51.

Page 70, No. 116-5.—The Horsley family probably is descended from Rowland Horsley, who, according to Brock, received a grant of 767 acres of land in New Kent Co., Va., March 1675-6.

Page 70, line 5.—After William Horsley insert "116-6, *Elizabeth*(?) *m. Francis Horsley.*(?)

Line 10.—Between "army" and in "August" insert *died*.

Line 12.—Erase children and insert "*only child.*"

Line 16.—"302, *Elizabeth*(?) *m. Francis Moseley.*(?)"

Line 2, notes.—Hon. John C. B., &c. Her sister Ann, &c.   A. B.

Page 71, No. 119.—William Goode was born 1722-26, his wife was born 1754, died 1821. He was probably not sheriff of Chesterfield. Mr. Brock tells me that the *Virginia Gazette* of Oct. 4, 1776, mentions William Goode living near Pocowhite Creek in Chesterfield Co.

No. 121.—Edward Goode spent part of his life in Georgia. He was a soldier of the Revolution, in the command of Gen. Lincoln, and it is believed participated in the attack on Savannah and the siege of Yorktown.

Page 72, No. 129.—Joseph Good, of Sprague, Mo., son of John Good, of Botetourt Co., is probably grandson of No. 129. Joseph Good had issue, Joseph of Sprague, Bates Co., Mo.; Thomas, Louisa, and Nancy (Mrs. Howard.)

Page 73, No. 355.—Robert Goode was born 1752, died in Mississippi in 1848. Add No. 356, Thomas Goode, a soldier of the Revolution, b. 1756, died in Tennessee or Mississippi after 1800.

> No. 357.—John, a soldier in the Revolution.

No. 13½.—Maj. Richard Goode was engaged in 1776 as captain of a company of North Carolina militia, in a campaign against the Scotch Tories, with whom a battle occurred at Moore's Creek Bridge Feb. 27, 1776. He was then with Gen. Rutherford's expedition against the Cherokees, destroying their town and crops ; he was adjutant of Col. William's regiment. In 1777 he was a captain of a company which went to South Carolina, and later appears to have been Gen. Rutherford's commissary. He was in the battles at Ramson's Mills, Guilford Court House, and Eutaw Springs. Before the Revolution he was sheriff of Stokes Co. He married, 1776, Rebecca, daughter of Benjamin Young, of Town Fork (Surrey), Stokes Co., N. C., who was born in 1767, and was living in 1839, a military pensioner in Henry Co., Ky.

Page 73.—Under children of 131½ insert 356½ *Charles B. Goode.* He is wrongly entered as 350½ on p. 138.

Insert No. 131¾.—Thomas Goode m. 1776 married in Surry Co., N. C., Nancy Beazley ; probably brother of 131½.

No. 131⅞.—Martha Goode, sister of No. 131¾, m. Mr. Blackburn ; lived in 1837 in Stokes, N. C.

Page 73, No. 132½.—James Markham appt'd May 20, 1776. Capt. in the Virginia navy of the Revolution ; received 6,591 acres of bounty land ; died prior to May 13, 1884 ; left issue : i, Elizabeth. ii, Minerva, m. —— Combs. iii, Anne M., m. George Goode. iv, James L. v, Mary Ann, m. William Barker. Thomas Markham was granted 600 acres in Henrico Co., July 11, 1636.

R. A. B.

Page 74, No. 136.—Ewing Goode died June, 1839, in Essex Co. He served in tne war of 1812 in the Virginia militia under Lieut. Col. Mitchell. He m. Feb. 16, 1816, Dorothy Patterson, of King and Queen Cos., b. 1797, living in 1879 at Miller's Farm, Essex Co., receiving a military pension.

Page 75.—Abraham Venable m. Mrs. John Nix. His son Joseph was ancestor, &c. I am sure this should be his " brother " Joseph. (See my note in the *Standard* for Dec. 25, 1880.) In the place of " on the Pamunky," read "on *the waters of* the Pamunky." These words in italics were in some way omitted. Abraham Venable quite certainly came to Virginia in 1692, and settled (exact date not known to me) on the waters of the Pamunky in the present County of Louisa. But the real point at issue is : Was Joseph, the immigrant to Maryland, a brother or a son to Abraham, the emmigrant to Virginia ? I am quite sure that the emigrants were *brothers*. A. B.

Page 76, before No. 147, insert 139.

John H. Osborne married Susannah Goode, daughter of No. 69, p. 47. Children : 376, *Rev. Robert Mackerness Osborne.* 377,

Thomas. 378, *Sally*, m. *William Goode.* 379, *Francis* m. *Stith Farley.* 380, *Samuel.* 381, *Susan*, m. *Mr. Morris.*

No. 381.—Mary E. A. Vaughan has a son, Richard V., living near Amelia Court House. A daughter of No. 147 m. Benjamin Vaughan, whose son William lives in Amelia Co.

Page 76.—The wife of No. 150 was Eliza. Royall Jones, No. 392, should be Mary Eliza, who m. W. B. Smith, and had daughter, Rebecca, who m. John Goode Wiley. (See p. 271.)

Dawson Family, p. 85.—Martin Dawson owned land in Amherst prior to 1751.

Page 85, No. 173.—James Goode was son of No. 76.

Page 91, No. 485.—Samuel James Goode married Narcissa Ann Lyle, No. 1100, daughter of 448 p. 101.

Page 91, 4th line from bottom.—For Joel McCloud read *Joel Cloud.*

Page 92, line 1.—For 1776 read 1766.

Line 5.—For below Harveysburg read *above.*

Line 19.—For 1796 read 1797 ; for *Oct.* 21, 1832 read *Oct.* 27, 1852.

Line 28.—After Sarah J. add *and Daniel.*

Line 34.—No. 25 died 1827, not 1826.

Line 40.—J. T. McKay m. *Matilda Brown.*

(See Smith Genealogy, p. 169.)

Page 93.—John Andrews, No. 182, was probably a descendant of Maj. William Andrews, of Accomac, a prominent colonist in 1630–70, who had son William, 1651, and perhaps son Robert. (See Neill's *Virginia Carolorum.*)

Page 95, No. 192.—(See No. 117, p. 70.)

Page 97, No. 198.—Joseph Bryan seems to have lived in Virginia in the latter part of the Revolution, and to have suffered persecution at the hands of the Tories. Mackerness Goode, afterwards his brother-in-law, is said by tradition to have saved him from death by cutting him down from a tree where he had been placed in ropes so that he would have to hang himself.

Page 98, No. 199.—Thaddeus Holt is spoken of in tradition as "the celebrated duellist of South Carolina."

No. 200.—Mackerness Goode was a soldier in the Revolution. He was born 1750–65, and died at the age of 86. He had issue as follows :

579, *Martha Goode* m. Daniel R. Tucker. Issue :

    1, *Robert Tucker*, d. 2, *Mackerness Tucker*, lived near Milledgeville, Ga. 3–6 others.

579 A, *James Goode.*

579 B, *Ninety* m. *Mr. Shepard.* Had issue :

    1, *Mary P. Shepard*, of La Grange, Ga.

Page 99, No. 210.—Major William Goode. In the summer of 1777 served for two months as a substitute for John Goode with Capt. Markam in a Virginia regiment commanded by Col. Robert

Goode, which marched across James River to Williamsburg, then to Hampton, and was stationed for a time at each place. In Oct., 1780, he volunteered for two months under Capt. Markham in the regiment of Col. James Monroe, in which Robert Goode was major, going to several places in the lower part of the State of Virginia. In July, 1781, he was a substitute for two months under Capt. Moody, who marched to the lower counties of Virginia, and were encamped sometime at Blackwater, near Hood's Fort. They were attacked in the night by the enemy, causing a retreat toward Richmond.

In April, 1781, he enlisted with Capt. Cheatham, in the command of Col. Gaskin, which ranged from place to place below Petersburg, Va., the British being present in the adjacent waters. The day after arriving at Petersburg the enemy landed at Hood's Fort, and a line of battle was formed on a hill ; when the enemy approached in sight the Americans took off their hats with huzzas, and when ordered to fire did so a few times, then retreated and scattered, Goode returning to Chesterfield Court House, up James River, then down to Richmond and Petersburg, with small field pieces, which were used in commanding the latter place. Soon after he was detailed with a party, under Col. Robert Goode, to Chesterfield County, where they were attacked by the British Col. Tarlton, who carried off fifty-four prisoners to Petersburg, the remainder of Col. Goode's force escaping to the army on the James River, which retreating, was pursued to Fauquier and Culpepper Counties. He was at the siege of Yorktown and surrender of Lord Cornwallis, Oct. 17, 1781.

579 C.—*Jesse Ellen Goode* m. *Mr. Whitaker*, of La Grange, Ga. Issue : 1, *Mackerness Whitaker*, a lawyer in the West. 2, *Mary.*

579 D.—*Samuel Gardner Goode*, of Alabama, b. 1801, d. 1849. Issue · 1, *Hugh Mackerness Goode*, of Arlington, Calhoun Co., Ga., a soldier C. S. A., m. daughter. i, Sarah Jane Goode, b. 1864. 2, *Mary T.,* m. Mr. Smyrl, of Texas. 3, *Elizabeth L.*, m. Mr. Hatcher, of Texas. 4, *Ninety T.*, m. Mr. Sellers, of Cottenwood, Ala. 5, *Martha A. M.*, m. Mr. Sikes, of Geneva, Ala. 6, *Matilda E. N.*, m. Ray, of Leesburg, Ala.

579 E.—*John Mackerness Goode*, of La Grange, Ga., m. Mary Stewart, of La Grange, and had 5 or 6 children : 1, Mary, m. James Rutledge, of La Grange. In this family are said to be old papers and a family bible record.

Page 95.—Maj. Garland Goode was an officer of volunteers in the Florida war with Gen. Andrew Jackson.

Page 97.—The family bible was not destroyed by soldiers, but accidently burned years before the war. For Medicus Jones read Medicus King.

Page 98, No. 569.—For George Goode Bryan read *Gen.* Goode Bryan.

No. 204.—Edward Goode died May, 1803. He did not marry Mrs. Woodson. (For correct record see under No. 84, p. 51.)

Page 101.—Cancel the Hickman record. Family tradition mislead me. Elder Hickman married (1) Miss Shackleford, of King and Queen Co.; (2), Elizabeth Abbott, of Kentucky. John Goode, No. 85, accompanied him in some of his early missionary expeditions to Kentucky. "Aunt Biddy Hickman" must have been his first wife and a relative of the wife of 85. (See U. S. Biographical Dictionary, Missouri volume, p. 487, for notice of descendants of William Hickman.)

Page 100.—Nora Perdue m. *John* Flournoy.

Page 105, line 24.—For No. 592–2 read No. 1683. (See p. 340.)

Page 105.—No. 220 died Jan. 29, 1841.

No. 233, p. 109.—Seth Ward died in Clarkesville, Tenn., April 16, 1845.

Rev. Jacob Ward was pastor of St. Peter's Church, New Kent Co., 1690–96.

Meade Family, p. 114.—"You have made a *terrible* mistake," writes Mr. Alex. Brown, " as Bishop Meade ; you make Col. R. K. Meade marry his own neice, Elizabeth Randolph, and have issue, the Bishop. This is a very serious error. Really Bishop Meade does not descend from the Randolphs at all. David Meade, 1690–1737, m. Susanna, daughter Sir Richard Everard. Anne, first child, m. Richard Randolph, Jr., who, according to your pedigree, had a daughter m. to Col. R. K. Meade. They had a daughter Elizabeth ; but she did not marry Col. R. K. Meade, who was her uncle. R. K. (4th child) m. first Elizabeth Randolph, sister (not daughter) to the above Richard Randolph, but left no living issue. R. K. (4th child) m. second Mary, daughter Benjamin and Bettie (Fitzhugh) Grymes, and widow of William Randolph, and left issue of several children, among whom Bishop William Meade. I know the above error is not yours ; because I have seen it before. I doubt if I know the real origin.

Page 114.—Mistake in Randolph pedigree, the wife of Gouverneur Morris was *Ann Cary* Randolph, and the wife of W. J. Cary was *Virginia* Randolph, both daughters of the *senior* Thomas Man Randolph. George Wythe Randolph was son of the *junior* Thomas M. Randolph.

Page 115, No. 8.—Mary Randolph m. *William*, not John Stith. (See p. 210.)

No. 750.—Mary M. Goode married (1), Joseph Archer Royall; (2), B. S. Morrison.

West, p. 118.—Concerning Unity West, Mr. Brown writes : "Why not say a descendant of Lord De la Warr. She descended from John West, it is true, a brother of one Lord De la Warr, but then he was the son of another Lord De la Warr. His grandmother, Katherine (Cary) Knollys, was a first cousin to Queen Elizabeth." (See Mag. Amer. Hist.)

Page 120, No. 247.—He inherited "Longwood," where he lived until 1877, the estate having passed from father to son for a century and a half, from the days of Josiah Tatum, who was the son of the English colonist, and who was born there in 1715. The line of descent is:

1, Josiah Tatum m. Sarah Brooke. 2, Lieut. Zachariah Tatum, of the Continental army, m. Miss Walker, of Amelia. 3, Henry Walker Tatum m. Mary Goode. 4, Richard H. Tatum, M. D. He was a magistrate of Chesterfield Co. under the old constitution, and was captain and surgeon C. S. A.

No. 1910 was born Jan. 25, 1853; 1911, March 12, 1855; 1912, March 6, 1857; 1913, Aug. 4, 1860; 1914, Oct. 25, 1864; 1915, Nov. 15, 1869. No. 1910 lives in Harrisonburg, Pa.

Cancel Nos. 773-776. These people never existed.

Page 120, No. 248.—COL. WILLIAM HARRISON, of Chester, Sussex Co., Va., son of William [1767-1822] and Mary Tatum [1752-89], Harrison, of Chester, was born Sept. 23, 1784, d. Aug. 30, 1840. He was married to Louisa Alice Goode [b. Jan. 1, 1793, d. March 16, 1843] by the Rev. Andrew Syme, of Petersburg, Aug. 10, 1813. Mary Tatum was daughter of Josiah and *Mary Brooke* Tatum. (See above under addendum to No. 247.) Children:

772 A, MOLLY ALICE, b. Aug. 17, 1814, d. Aug. 8, 1815. (1923) 778, LUCY ELIZABETH, b. Jan. 26, 1816, d. Nov. 24, 1848, m. *Dr. W. J. Harrison.* (1922) 777, RICHARD JAMES, b. Feb. 22, 1818, d. at Port Malcom Feb. 27, 1842. 783, WILLIAM FRANCIS, b. June 1, 1819, d. Aug. 30, 1866, 784, THOMAS ARCHER, b. July 15, 1820. 779, ANN MARIA, b. Feb. 5, 1822, d. Sept. 17, 1855, m. *William A. Gregory* Dec. 1, 1840. 781, JUNIUS, b. Jan. 23, 1824, d. July, 1846. (1927) 782, VIRGINIA, b. Aug. 13, 1825, d. Dec. 30, 1878, m. *Benj. Frahley Harrison* April 3, 1849. 780, RUFUS KING, b. Feb. 9, 1827. 773, JOHN, b. May 5, 1828, d. Aug. 9, 1834. 784 A, ANDREW, b. Nov. 25, 1829, d. Jan. 2, 1833. (1951) 785, LOUISA ALICE, b. Jan. 11, 1836, d. April 9, 1879, m. *Dr. William S. Overton.* 1930, JOHN WESTLY, b. June 22, 1838.

Page 121, bottom line.—For Suwannee read *Sewanee.*

Page 122.—For Suwannee read *Sewanee.*

No. 803 is *Edwin*, not *Edward* B. Jones.

No. 799 was born in 1816, No. 802 in 1822.

Page 123, No. 813.—*Dr. Mills M. Jordan*, not Mr. Morrison M. Jordan.

Page 123, line 14.—Erase "a major in the Virginia Line of the war of the Revolution." Sarah Maria was a daughter of Dr. Thomas Massie [b. about 1781-83, d. May 7, 1864] by his first wife, Miss Lucy Waller. Dr. Thomas was a son of Maj. Thomas Massie of the Revolution.   A. B.

After 819 erase "an officer, &c."

Page 124, No. 828.—Margaret Walker, b. about 1832, is sister of Gen. R.

Lindsay Walker, of Texas. (See " Page Family," p. 214.) All efforts to find whereabouts of William H. Pryor have been fruitless.

No. 834 m. Dr. Harvie Laird, No. 835 m. Dr. Alexander Laird. Charles m. Cora Holt, of Haut Rien.

Footnote.—" The Gaines Family." (See p. 290.)

Page 126.—No. 845 was b. in 1860, not in 1864. No. 846 surely did not die *sine prole*, since she left a son. No. 284 should be *Andrew* Wharton.

Page 127.—No. 287 married Pamelia Hendrick, a descendant of Judith Michaux.

No. 857 was " Lucie Ann Goode. No. 858 was " Eliza Willis Goode."

No. 260-1 should be 290-1.—Reuben Vaughan died in Marengo Co., Ala., Jan. 23, 1837. His wife died in 1866, not 1885. She was the 9th daughter of Samuel and Susannah Hancock Watkins.

No. 861 was Emily *Garland*, not Emily Goode Vaughan.

Page 127.—For 260-1 read 290-1. For more, " Louise Wysong " read "Martha Wysong." For " Francis Jones " read " Francis James Gasquet.

Page 128.—For 296 read 293. Insert "882, Joseph Littieberry Carrington."

Page 128.—Mr. Brown informs me that it is not definitely ascertained whether Henningham Codrington was daughter or neice of Christopher Codrington. She was either sister or first cousin to the celebrated Christopher Codrington of All Souls's, Oxford. The pedigree is as follows :

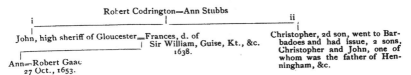

Robert Codrington=Ann Stubbs

i. John, high sheriff of Gloucester=Frances, d. of Sir William, Guise, Kt., &c. 1638.

Ann=Robert Gaac 27 Oct., 1653.

ii. Christopher, 2d son, went to Barbadoes and had issue, 2 sons, Christopher and John, one of whom was the father of Henningham, &c.

Pages 128, 129.—Where do you find that Dr. Paul Carrington, b. 1500-20, was a Royalist who fled from England, &c.? Dr. Paul Carrington's wife died in 1714; he died a few years earlier. One of their sons was born so late as 1714. In fact the Doctor was born about 1667, long after the death of Cromwell. Col. George Carrington is not the ancestor of all of the name and lineage of Carrington in America. There are two or more families of the name here. (See " Index to America Pedigrees, by Durrie.") Gen. Carrington, U. S. A., author of the " Battles of the Revolution," &c., I think, is of the N. E. family. Anne m. Col. William Cabell, Jr., [the son of Col. William Cabell, the elder, member of the conventions and of the committee of safety, &c.] an officer in the Revolution, &c. A. B.

Page 130.—James Jefferson Goode, No. 296, b. Oct. 29, 1790. No. 902 is Robert L. Goode.

Page 131, No. 297, m. *Elizabeth* Caroline Goode, b. Nov. 15, 1794.

No. 298.—S. A. Goode was b. Feb. 27, 1799. Benjamin Coleman died at Memphis, Ala.

No. 913 died in 1882 at Memphis, Ala., leaving a large family.

Page 132.—Thomas Goode, No. 213, is son of No. 80, and his sons should be enumerated among the *Edgefield Goodes* on p. 189. He is probably No. 192 and his children No. 545-1 and 545-2.

Page 132, No. 301.—Rebecca Goode, wife of No. 300, was b. Nov. 13, 1803. J. C. Megginson, m. about 1792, Sarah, daughter of Archibald Rolling, of "Red Oak," Buckingham Co.

Page 135, No. 326.—Richard Goode lived most of his life at Gillsville, Hall Co., Ga., though he died in Alabama.

Page 136, No. 971.—Alfred Goode lived in 1887 in Ashville, Ala.

No. 986.—Reuben Goode should have been mentioned on p. 267. He died in Bell Co., Texas, in 1879 or 1880. His children were : 2851, George W. Goode, of Cincinnati. 2852, Dr. Reuben J. Goode, of Salado, Texas. 2853, Dr. W. A. Goode, of Caldwell, Burleson Co., Texas, died in 1871, left daughter, Mrs. Delia Goode Willson, of Taylor, Williamson Co., Texas.

Page 136, No. 340, was son of No. 126, not of No. 125.

No. 987.—Benjamin Goode was doubtless the Benjamin Goode who settled in Grayson Co., Texas, and had son John Goode, of Sherman, and grandson James Goode, of Pottsborough, Texas.

Page 138.—In addition to those mentioned under No. 348 and No. 352, I find another Kentuckian, Timothy Goode, born about 1790, died at Rolling Fork, Mercer Co., Ky., March 18, 1750, a soldier of 1812, who served in Col. Davenport's regiment, and was near Col. R. M. Johnson when he killed Tecumseh. He married in 1809 Betsy Smith, of Mercer Co., who was living in 1873 near Mitchellsburg, Ky., aged 89 years.

Page 138.—C. B. Goode was son of No. 131½.

Page 139, No. 358.—For Bennett read Dennett Goode.

Page 139, after No. 354, add 356.—Robert Goode, of Mississipi, son of No. 131½, was born in Mecklenburg Co., Va., 1753, died in Mississippi in 1848. Son :

1033, WADSWORTH GOODE, Kempner, Lampasas Co., Texas, 1887.

Page 139, No. 353.—Richard Goode was born 1798, died Nov. 19, 1873, near Sheppardville, Bullitt Co., Ky. His second wife, whom he married in Indianapolis in 1864, was Louisa Robey, living in 1878, a military pensioner.

No. 356.—Thomas Goode, son of Major Richard Goode, No. 131½, p. 73, a soldier in the Revolution, was born about 1756, died in Tennessee or Mississippi after 1800. Probably married a Miss Hawkins in Virginia.

Page 142.—No. 1041 has son James Goode, of Pottsboro, Texas.

Page 143, line 13.—For Isaac read Israel.

No. 1053 is Benjamin Whiteman Goode.

Page 145, No. 1060.—Sarah Francis Goode.

    1033 A, JOHN HAWKINS GOODE, of Christian Co., Ky., b. 1796, d. 1840, a soldier in the war of 1812. Issue : *Robert Goode*, of St. Francis Co., Ark., d. in 1847, leaves son : i, Francis Goode. ii, *Jonathan Clark Goode*. iii, *John Hawkins Goode*, of Denton, Texas. 1033 B, JOSEPH. 1033 C, JEFFERSON. 1033 D, RICHARD.

Page 150, last line.—For Samuel Ingraham read Thomas.

    Footnote, eighth line.—For just mentioned read first mentioned.

    Line 27, Executive Temperance Society, not Congressional.

No. 357.—John Goode, a soldier in the Revolution. He and his brother Thomas were notorious for their fast running and general activity, being employed as scouts.

No. 357½.—Samuel Goode, son of 131½, living in 1837 in Henry Co., Ky.

Page 160, line 4.—For Bisbie read Bigbie.

Page 161.—For Jessie R. read Jessie E. Adams.

Page 165.—For notice of Gen. George Rappeen Smith see U. S. Biog. Dict. Missouri Vol., p. 130, (portrait.)

Page 160, par. 1.—John J. S. Smith, of Marion Co., Mo., born 1798, died 1852, married Mary S., daughter of James Lockett, and had fifteen children, one of whom, Rev. George William Smith, born 1837, was soldier C. S. A., and in 1885 pastor of the Baptist Church in Dover, Mo. (U. S. Biog. Dict., Missouri, Vol., p. 299.)

Page 161, No. 1095.—For Jesse R. read Jesse E. Adams.

Page 164, No. 1142.—Alice R. Goode, married in Springfield, Ohio, Oct. 5, 1887, Edward Benedict Cobb.

Page 167–8, No. 13.—In 1806, not 1816. She died Oct. 27, 1864, not 1873.

Page 169, No. 46.—For Sohn read Yohn.

Page 172.—No. 484 omitted. (See p. 302.)

Page 173, No. 491.—W. H. C. Goode was born Dec. 3, not Dec. 13, 1843.

No. 1200 was born in 1835.

Page 177.—No. 1252 was Elvira Slaton.

No. 549—Dr. Philip Goode is sheriff of Colfax, La.

Page 185, No. 552.—Dr. Rhett Goode was married Oct. 28, 1886, to Mabel Wylie Hutton, daughter of Dr. W. H. H. Hutton, of Mobile, Ala.

Page 186, No. 556–7.—Larkin Griffin lives in Edgefield, S. C.

No. 556–7.—Philip Burt, son of this daughter, was a wealthy banker of San Francisco, d. s. p. in 1884.

No. 556–9.—Mrs. McLemore has a daughter, Mrs. W. F. Sale, of Phillips Co., Ark.

Page 187, No. 556–6.—Philip Burt married Elizabeth Goode.

No. 1319 has a daughter, Mrs. George Garth, of Courtland, Ala.

Page 188, No. 556–8.—One daughter is Mr. Payne, of Corinth, Miss.

No. 1833 should be No. 1333.

Page 192, No. 1366.—Lives in Shelbyville, Tenn. Anna E. Twiggs was born Aug. 23, 1829. No. 1381 was born March 22, 1857. No. 1382, Sallie T. Bryan, April 11, 1859. No. 1383 was born Sept. 12, 1861. No. 1384 was born March 9, 1869.

Page 196.—No. 591-4 is Edward Tabb Goode.

Page 197, No. 594.—For Sally M. read Sally A. Boyd. The children of No. 594 are :

1429, WILLIAM GOODE, of Brownsville, Tenn. 1430, RICHARD BENNET. 1431, SALLY. 1432, LUCIE. 1433, HILLERY, of Branham', Texas. For Philip T. Southall read Philip F.

Page 199.—No. 1508 is J. K. P. Goode.

Page 201, No. 638.—John Goode was member of the common council of Richmond from Jefferson Ward in 1834 and later.

No. 639.—Edward Goode, in May, 1871, was residing in Ballard Co., Ky., aged 76 years. His wife was dead. He enlisted at Camp Bottom Bridge—probably in Chesterfield Co., Va.—to serve three months from Aug. 28, 1814, under Capt. Benjamin Goode, No. 217, in the regiment commanded by Col. Brown. His post office address is Milburn, Ballard Co., Ky., and his domicile is near that place.

No. 640 had 8 children. His first wife was born in 1800, not 1830, and was the daughter not of Joseph, but of John Warrock.

For " K " read Va.

Page 203.—The wife of No. 725 was Martha Hendrick ; she died at White Hall, Tenn., at the age of 72. No. 1796 married Judge Nelson. No. 1796½ was Martha Norvell Ward, who married Thomas L. Austin, another daughter.

Page 204.—In Leondas K. Polk erase the K.

Page 206, No. 730.—Fielding L. Williams died July 22, 1845, at Clermont, Carman Co., Tenn. He was junior warden of Trinity Church, Clarksville, and a man of the most exemplary character. (Biographical note in St. Louis "Missionary of the Cross," Aug. 9, 1845.)

Page 209, No. 1818.—Mrs. Clarke has two children : i, *Lucy;* ii, *Michael.*

No. 1827.—For Mills read *Miller.*

Page 211, line 4 from bottom.—For granddaughter read *grandmother.*

Col. Dudley Stith, of Brunswick Co., had daughter, Elizabeth, who married in 1770 Col. H. Fitzhugh.

Page 213.—Rogers, in his "House of Alexander," an exhaustive work in 2 volumes, says "John, the son of the first Earl of Stirling, died in 1641 ; that he never came to Virginia. John, of Virginia, died about 1677."

Page 214.—Anthony Thornton, Jr., of Caroline Co., is named in the *Virginia Gazette* March 23, 1778. Col. John T. Thornton, of Cooper Co., is referred to in the U. S. Biog. Dict., Missouri Vol., p. 25.

Page 215.—For Kumerseley read *Kinnerseley.*

Page 215.—The article signed "A. B. in Richmond *Standard* I, 40," was written by me ; *it is correct,* save the name *Sarah,* which should be *Mildred.* I suppose you must make an oversight in giving her husband's name as Col. *William* Syme. The correct name is certainly Col. *John* Syme, who was half brother to Patrick Henry. ALEXANDER BROWN.

Page 219.—For fuller record of No. 747, see p. 424. 1851 was Mary Page Botts, died young. 1854, William Henry. 1855, Thomas Lawson. 1859, Steven King. 1860, Virginia Ann. 1862, Beverly Blair Botts.

For Sarah F. Randolph read Susan.

Page 223, No. 50.—Mrs. J. G. Mosby was born in 1792, died in 1844. She published in 1840 "Pocahontas, a Legend with Historical and Traditional notes."

Page 231.—Cancel matter relating to 780 and 784½. The same persons are discussed on pp. 378 and 379.

No. 784½.—This entry should be cancelled, and the following substituted : William Arthur Gregory, of "Linden," near Petersburg, Prince George Co., Va., son of Elijah and Nancy Gregory, was born in 1811, died in 1877, married Maria Harrison ; had children :

1920, ALICE GOODE GREGORY, m. Col. Arthur Herbert. 1921, WILLIAM, b. 1849.

No. 787 was surgeon C. S. A.

Page 233.—No. 200 was born in 1856, not 1866.

No. 2008 married No. 3780.

Page 234.—Col. William Baskerville was graduated from William and Mary College in 1817.

For Braine read Brame.

Page 235, No. 797.—Rev. E. L. Baptist was graduated from William and Mary College in 1857.

Page 236.—For 554 or 221 read 254, p. 122. Dr. George Mason's plantation was "Homestead," where for many years was carried on a young ladies' seminary, where numerous scions of the Goode, Randolph, Mason, Jones, and related families were trained.

Page 239.—No. 2078 is in California. No. 2080½, Walter Goode, graduated in 1887 from Staunton Business College.

Page 241.—Transfer last line to make "Sarah Buford b." precede 1884.

Page 246, No. 857.—Mrs. Lucy Goode Boyd died in 1885. 2192 is Pamelia Goode Boyd, now of Chicago. 2195 is John Goode Boyd, who m. his cousin, Sally Easly.

Page 248.—No. 865 was born Nov. 2, 1801, died April 27, 1852 ; his wife was born Oct. 3, 1817. No. 2239 was born in 1838, died in 1862. No. 2240 was born Jan. 1, 1837 ; lived in 1887 in Demopolis, Ala. No. 2243 was born Nov. 24, 1840 ; lives in Demopolis.

Page 250.—The child of No. 2313 of course was named Carrington.

Page 257, line 21.—From the word " president to end of paragraph on line 24, should be transferred to follow line 31."

Page 258.—For Caroline Deláney read Caroline " Shropshire."

Page 260.—Dr. Megginson is No. 928–8.

Page 262, No. 929.—Bennett M. DeWitt was editor of the *Index*, a literary paper published in Richmond before the civil war, and one of the editors of the Richmond *Examiner*. He projected a history of the late war, and is said to have prepared the greater part of the work published by Edward A. Pollard under title of " The Lost Cause."

No. 2585.—The entry here is wrong. Dr. Robert Horsley was "father," not son, of 929–11, and his issue, 929–11–16, her brothers and sisters.

No. 929–20.—Phila H. Dunscombe, wife of No. 311, was perhaps the daughter of Mayor Andrew Dunscombe, native of New York, veteran of the Revolutionary war, who came to Richmond after the Revolution. R. A. B.

Page 266.—The military service of No. 935 was in the Trans-Mississippi Department, and not in the First Mississippi regiment.

Page 267, insert 988.—Daniel C. Goode, of John Goode, No. 341, p. 136, was a soldier of the war of 1812, was enlisted at Warren, Albemarle Co., Va., May, 1812, for five years in the Twentieth Regiment, and served as recruiting sergeant at Fredericksburg and Norfolk, where he died March 15, 1815. He married in 1811 Polly, daughter of William Griffin, of Rockingham Co., born in 1791 ; living in Lynchburg and applicant for a pension in 1853. Emma Goode, wife of No. 1606, possibly her grandchild.

Page 268, No. 1004.—William Goode married (1) Martha York, who died Nov., 1863 ; (2), March, 1864, O. S. McCartney, and had in all 17 children, 5 by the last wife. Children :

2940, CHARLES GOODE, b. Nov. 28, 1849. 2941, THOMAS, b. Nov. 22, 1850. 2942, JESSE, b. Sept. 17, 1852. 2943, Mary, b. Oct. 12, 1836, m. *J. H. Lentz.* 2944, REBECCA, b. March 23, 1838, m *S. Broadwater.* 2945, ELIZABETH, b. Aug. 3, 1840, m. *J. A. Willbanks.* 2946, JAMES W., b. Jan. 13, 1843. 2947, SARAH, b. Jan. 13, 1845, m. *T. Miller.* 2948, FRANCES, b. May 7, 1847, m. *P. F. Hagood.* 2949, NARCISSA, b. May 9, 1857, m. *E. Lee.* 2950, JOSEPH, b. May 5, 1854. 2951, ALBERT R. GOODE, b. Sept. 9, 1866, died young. 2952, EMMA P., b. Sept. 3, 1868. 2953, ROSANA M., b. Oct. 2, 1871. 2954, JOHN COLEMAN, b. Feb. 15, 1815.. 2955, LAURA E., b. Feb. 25, 1877.

Page 268, 1004 A.—Halbert or Holbert Goode, of Franklin, Co., Ala., had son :

2956, W. R. GOODE, of Round Rock, Texas, who has a daughter, E. Emma Goode, of St. Elmo, Texas.

Page 267.—No. 996 died Dec. 11, 1844, married Maria Bush.

Page 268, No. 2923.—For 1844 read 1845 ; for Conway read Corwine ; for Verdes read Verden.

Page 270, No. 3094.—For John S. Wiley read John Goode Wiley.

Page 275, No. 1044.—Thomas E. Hoy lived in Haywood Co., Tenn.: 1, *George*, d. y. 2, *Charles*, a farmer, living in Texas. 3, *James*, soldier C. S. A., killed at Vicksburg. 4, *Ottawaana*, m. Mr. Davidson, of Austin, Texas. 5, *Mary*.

No. 1046.—Mr. Ash had children : 1, *Lucy Stanton*, m. E. S. Wootton, of Texas. 2, *Sarah*, m. Rev. Mr. Wooton, of Texas.

Page 273, No. 1030-3.—Hillery Goode Richardson was son of John Richardson.

No. 3103 m. Richard H. Catlett, one of the leading citizens of Staunton.

Page 276.—No. 3242 was born in 1849.

Page 278, line 13.—Erase the words *and financier*.

Page 278, No. 1050-2.—Anderson Pride was brother of Gen. Pride.

Page 283, No. 7.—Col. Miles Cary died July 17, 1708. His first wife was Mary, daughter of Thomas and Mary Milnor, of Nausemaid Co., Va., born Aug. 6, 1667, died s. p., Oct. 27, 1700. R. A. B.

No. 18 died at Ceeleys, 1772.

Page 284.—Selden record erroneous. Mary Cary, No. 21, says Mr. Brock, married Joseph, daughter of Samuel and Rebecca (Yeo) Selden, of Elizabeth City Co., who died in 1727, leaving issue : CARY (No. 46½), SAMUEL and MILES. Cancel lines 7 to 17.

Page 284, No. 29.—Archibald Cary.

Page 293.—No. 1068 was born Nov. 2, not Nov. 24, 1840; his wife is Ann Grace, not Anna Grace. For Mrs. Lowry read Miss Lowry.

Page 294, No. 1095.—Jesse E. Adams, not Jesse R.

Page 304.—No. 1222 was born in 1835 ; erase " of the firm of Barber and Johnson."

Page 305.—No 1225 is William X. Beall.

Page 306, No. 1226.—was a member of the Georgia legislature in 1846–47.

Page 307.—No. 1231 is son of No. 511.

Page 308, line 3.—For troop read "troops ;" line 16, for defense read "defensive ;" line 21, erase the words "and Law ;" line 56, for passenger read "passing."

Page 309, No. 1235.—For Eliza Francis Andrews read " Eliza Frances Andrews. She is daughter of No. 511.

Page 318, No. 1331.—For Major Goode read " Major Morgan."

Page 319, No. 1338.—James Thomas Goode died Oct. 9, 1886.

Under children of No. 1339 read " No. 3635, Samuel W. Goode, Jr., born Aug. 10, died Sept. 9, 1886.

Page 320, No. 1343.—For Eugneius read " Eugenius."

Page 268.—Under No. 1004 A enter son : W. R. GOODE, of Round Rock, Texas, farmer, son of Halbert Goode, No. 1004 B, p. 268, has daughter, E. Emma Goode, of St. Elmo, Texas.

Page 321.—No. 1357 was married in 1867.

Page 331, under No. 3780.—Alice Baskerville, wife of C. L. Finch, is No. 2008, not No. 3081.

Page 333.—Frances Lockett was granddaughter of Stephen Lockett and Mary Clay, and cousin of Henry Clay.

No. 3841 was born July 29, 1840, died Nov. 23, 1862. No. 3842 was born Jan. 18, 1842. No. 3845 is Daniel Spencer. No. 3846 is Angelia. No. 3847 is Susan Alice, born Nov. 16, 1871. No. 3848 died Sept. 14, 1857.

Page 339.—The wife of No. 1606 is possibly grandchild of No. 129, p. 72.

Page 340, No. 4101.—D. M. Goode was appointed in May, 1887, at Otterdale, Chesterfield Co., Va.

Page 344, No. 1800.—A list of the descendants of James and Martha Ellicott Carey, of Baltimore Co., Md., in Thomas' Genealogy. Farm notes, p. 52. James Carey, No. 1800, was their grandson, and son of George and Mary Gibson Cary, also under Elliott, p. 69.

Page 349, line 26.—For 1836 read " 1846."

Page 372.—For Paul Estan Lemoine read " Paul Estare Lemoine."

Page 375.—Patrick Henry's oldest son by his second marriage.

Page 375.—For Berkley read " Berkeley."

Page 377, line 2.—For Lowry read " Loring."

Page 378.—William Herbert, who married Miss Dulany, was son of William Herbert, of Muckross, on the Lake of Killarney, in Ireland, who came to America, and was mayor of Alexandria and president of its bank, married a daughter of John and Sarah Fairfax, grandson of the fourth Baron Fairfax and sister-in-law of Lawrence Washington Carlisle, a sister of William Herbert, married John, ninth Lord Fairfax. Thomas Family, p. 87.

No. 1922.—Surgeon Richard James Harrison, born Feb. 22, 1818, died Feb. 27, 1842. Dr. William J. Harrison married Lucy Elizabeth Harrison Aug. 10, 1813.

Page 379.—No. 1925 was born Feb. 9, 1827. He married not Miss Dillard, but Mary Louisa Spencer.

No. 1927.—Benjamin Franklin Harrison.

No. 1929.—Thomas Archer Harrison lives at Poplar Mount, Va.

No. 1930.—Dr. John Westly Harrison, of Dripping Spring, Hayes Co., Texas, married Dora Hine, of Texas.

No. 1931.—Dr. William S. Overton was son of William S. Overton, grandson of Capt. Moses Overton, of Prince Edward Co., Va., an officer in the war of 1812. (Records of Overtons owned by Dr. Hillsman, of Amelia Co.) He married May 27, 1856, Louisa Alice Harrison, and had 7 children : 1, Louisa Elizabeth, died young. 2, Virginia Harrison, married John W. Cobb, of Bellfield, Greensville Co., and died March 22, 1886, leaving 2 children : William Overton and Alice Peeble Cobb. 3, Alice Goode, died young. 4, Fannie Westly. 5, Elizabeth Rudd, died young. 6, Grace, died yound. 7, William M., died young.

No. 4577 married Jennie Trezevant, of Memphis. (See errata for p. 405.)

Page 380.—No. 4605 was born Dec. 21, 1879, died Aug. 2, 1885.

 No. 4606, Mattie Watkins Baskerville, was born Aug. 8, 1883.

 No. 4859 is H. Carrington Mayo.

Page 383, No. 2041.—William Herbert Cole was son of John and Richetta Peter Cole, of Greensvile Co., Va. He served through the war as private in the Thirteenth Virginia Cavalry and as courier for Gen. Wise. He is a farmer, about one and a half miles from Petersburg, in Chesterfield Co., Va.

Page 389, No. 2323.—For Francis Codrington Carrington read "F. C. Mayo."

Page 390, No. 4869.—Joseph C. Carrington died young.

Page 392, No. 2686.—Philip Goode was a member of an independent company of cavalry in the war of 1812, and served on picket duty on Chesapeake Bay in 1814–15. He married, in 1819, Sarah P. Young.

Page 392.—For Livingston read "Lovingston."

Page 393.—For Milo, Mo., read "Miles, Iowa."

Page 394, No. 5251.—Douglass F. Carlin was married Aug. 26, 1887, at the Cheyenne Agency, Dakota, to Madien Duprest, the wealthiest Indian heiress on the Sioux reservation. Over one thousand Indians witnessed the ceremonies, and the festivities lasted three days.

Page 402, under No. 3211.—For Roan read "Roane."

Page 405.—The Trezevant family is derived from a Huguenot *immigré*, who came to South Carolina. His descendant, Dr. Trezevant, went to Virginia, and had three children, one a daughter, who married William Harrison, No. 1932 of the Goode Pedigree, page 378, are James, whose son Nathaniel Macon Trezevant, was father of Alice, wife of No. 3240; one John T., whose daughter Jennie married William Harrison, of Louisville, Ky., No. 4577, p. 379, of the Goode Pedigree.

Page 405.—No. 3231 was a planter. No. 3240, Mrs. Collier, was daughter of Nathaniel Macon (not Mason) Trezevant, and Amanda Avery, his wife. Mr. Collier is President of the *Memphis Appeal* Company, the *Appeal* being the largest and oldest newspaper in Tennessee. No. 5542 was born Jan. 25, 1874.

Page 409.—Rev. Thomas A. Ware was the editor of an edition of Tucker's "Partisan Leader."

Page 414, No. 5761.—Joseph Armistead Anderson died June 16, 1887. He was a young man of great promise. He graduated at the Richmond High School in 1886, and completed a course in the Richmond Business College just before his death, preparing to enter his uncle's office in Baltimore.

Page 419.—Warwick, Alexander & Co., merchants of Richmond, advertised in 1787 that they had laid off the town of New Glasgow, in

Chesterfield Co., south side of the James River, on the former site of the town of Orick or Warwick. May not Orick have been formerly the site of the Indian town, and the name Warwick subsequently adopted.   R. A. Brock.

Page 420, No. 4385.—Rev. R. H. Fleming, in Aug., 1887, accepted a call to the pastorate of the Presbyterian Church in Lynchburg.

Page 425.—Johanna should be " Gohanna." Botts was called in derision, in his earlier career, by his political opponents, by the name of his favorite stallion, Gohanna.   R. A. Brock.

L. L. Lewis is president of the Virginia Court of Appeals. His brother is *Senator* (not Sir) John F. Lewis.

Page 428.—Another of this branch was doubtless William Goode, who in Sept., 1833, was residing in Spartanburg District, S. C., and was 71 years old on the 4th of July previous. He enlisted in June, 1778, in Talbot Co., on the Eastern Shore of Maryland, for three years or during the war, with Capt. Handy, in the Fifth Maryland regiment, commanded by Col. Howard, who was in Gen. Smallwood's brigade, going to Valley Forge and joined the army June 19, which was leaving the camp to pursue the British, who had evacuated Philadelphia (June 18, 1778) to march across New Jersey to New Brunswick. Being overtaken at Monmouth, a battle took place June 28, 1778, but finally reached their destination, and the American army turned off across the Hudson to White Plains, at which place Goode remained sometime before going to West Point and into winter quarters at Bound Brook, N. J., and was there, or in vicinity, through 1779. In the spring of 1780 he went under Gen. Gates to the head of the Elk on Chesapeake Bay, and by water to Virginia, landing near Petersburg, from thence to Hillsboro', N. C. He was in the first battle at Camden, when Gen. Gates was defeated, Aug. 16, 1780, and detailed in charge of Lieut. Gibson of his company, who had been severely wounded and died while crossing Chesapeake Bay on his way home. Goode joined the army at Baltimore in the spring of 1781, and was ordered to Fort Henry for a time. He was engaged in the siege of Yorktown and present at the surrender of the army of Lord Cornwallis, Oct. 17, 1781. After that event he marched to Hillsboro', N. C., then to Camden, where he was discharged in Feb., 1782. In March, 1857, his daughter Diana was residing in Spartanburg, S. C., and stated that her father died in that district Jan. 16, 1852. (Records of U. S. Pension Office.)

Page 428.—Richard Charlett, in the Province of Maryland, in the County of Calvert, in Pawtuxen River, in Swanson's Creek, 28 August, 1686, proved 4 April, 1694. To cousin Hannah Kings £40; to cousin Richard Kings £10. All the rest to my brothers & sisters. Brother Richard Kings to be executor.

(Signed)   Richard Charlet.

Witnesses : Philip Rogerson, Thomas Vuett, Ann Rogerson, William Goode. Box 72.

This may have been the William Goode, aged 21, who sailed in the ship " Expedition " for Barbados Nov. 20, 1635, or one of the Rappahannock branch of the family.

Page 437.—For James M. Goode read "James W." James W. Good, uncle of Brent Goode, was for many years teller of the Peoples' Bank in New York, but returned to England many years ago. Brent Goode, of New York, has a silver tankard, being dated 1843, with coat of arms of the Goodes.

Page 435.—William Goode, of Christ Cnurch, Datchet, is lineally descended from Dr. Thomas Goode, D. D., master of Balliol College, Oxford, and used the arms referred to at the top of p. 435. He informs me that William and John Goode, fellows of the same college, were brothers of Thomas. William Good is grandson of Rev. Joseph Goode, of Balliol College, some time rector of End Lansbrook, Somersetshire. Dr. Thomas Goode is mentioned in Brown Will's "Survey of the Cathedral of Hereford."

Page 447, footnote.—Daniel Goode, of Greene Co., Tenn., born 1796–8, son of Jacob Goode, of Rockingham Co., Va., was a soldier in the war of 1812, in Col. Coleman's regiment. Moved to Tennessee in 1824 ; had brothers, John, of Washington Co., Va., born 1801, and Solomon, of Greene Co., Tenn., born 1803. Abram Goode, also a soldier of 1812, who served under Capt. Proctor and Capt. Slocum in the Chickahominy Swamp and about Fort Powhatan, was born 1800, died 1872, married in 1812 Mary Sullins, who died in 1813. Felix Goode, of Back Creek, Frederick Co., Va., born 1796; was also a soldier of 1812, Jacob Goode, of Page and Warren Co., Va., born 1788, died in 1863 in Greene Co., Mo.; was a soldier of 1812. His widow (born Catharine Burnes) lived in 1871 in Massanutten, Page Co., Va. Jacob Goode, of Franklin Co., Va., born 1795 ; was a soldier of 1812. Lewis Goode, of Grove Hill, Page Co., Va.; was a soldier of 1812. Samuel Goode, of Rockingham Co., a soldier of the war of 1812 ; removed to Ohio. His son Samuel lived in Lima, Ohio, 1882.

Page 95, No. 194.—Major Garland Goode d. Jan. 7, 1887. The Mobile papers speak of him as follows : Major Goode had been an invalid for many years, but at one time he was a power in this community. For many years he was the head of the cotton factorage firm of Garland, Goode & Co., was one of the company that built the Dog River Cotton Factory, was interested in various lumber mills and an enterprising citizen in those days when Mobile was the third exporting city in the Union. In politics Major Goode was a democrat of the old school. He espoused the cause of Stephen A. Douglas, and presided when that great statesman spoke in Mobile.

PRINCIPAL WORKS OF REFERENCE.

A.—John Smith's Works, edited by Arber.

B.—Brock's notes in "Collections of Hist. Society." MS., i–vi.

Boll.—"The Bolling Memoirs," edited by Wynne.

BP.—Slaughter's "Bristol Parish."

Br.—Browning's "Americans of Royal Descent."

C.—"The Carter Tree."

Cl.—Campbell's "History of Virginia."

DB.—De Bow's Review.

EC.—Wheeler's "Eminent North Carolinians."

F.—Slaughter's "Randolph Fairfax."

Foote.—Foote's "Sketches of Virginia."

Fry.—Slaughter's "Joshua Fry."

Goode.—Goode's "Virginia Cousins."

Gn.—Gilmer's "Georgians."

Gr.—Gregg's "Old Cheraws."

H.—Hardesty's Encyclopædia.

M.—Meade's "Old Churches and Families of Virginia."

Ml.—Paxton's "Marshall Family."

NC.—Wheeler's "History of North Carolina."

NGR.—New England Historic Genealogical Register.

OK.—Thomas's "History of Old Kent, Md."

P.—Page's "Page Family."

Pn.—Peyton's "History of Augusta Co., Va."

Po.—Robertson's "Pocahontas and Her Descendants."

S.—Richmond Standard, Vols. i–iv., edited by Brock.

SB.—Southern Bivouac.

SLM.—Southern Literary Messenger.

SM.—Slaughter's "St. Mark's Parish."

Sp.—Campbell's "Spotswood Papers."

Sull.—"The Sullivant Memorial."

TM.—Neill's "Terra Mariæ."

VC.—Neill's "Virginia Carolorum."

VL.—Neill's "Virginia Company of London."

VV.—Neill's "Virginia Vetusta."

W.—Watkins's "Watkins Genealogy."

Wash.—Welles's "Washington Family."

Wl.—Welles's "American Family Antiquity."

ALPHABETICAL INDEX,

WITH WHICH IS INCORPORATED A KEY TO SOUTHERN GENEALOGY, AND A
LIST OF VIRGINIA FAMILIES USING COATS OF ARMS
IN THE COLONIAL PERIOD.

" I for my part venerate the inventor of indexes, and I know not to whom to yield the preference, either to Hippocrates, who was the first great anatomiser of the human body, or to that unknown labourer in literature who first laid open the nerves and arteries of a book."—ISAAC DISRAELI.

The references in brackets following each surname are intended to serve as a key to all printed pedigrees of Southern families embracing three generations or more ; the abbreviations are explained upon the opposite page.

The figures in this index, unless preceded by the letter "p," refer to the entry numbers of the individual, and not to pages. If a given number is not found in its proper sequence at the head of an entry, it must be looked for in the record of the previous generation, under the secondary numbers, or those of the children of some person entered under a primary number. If you do not find the name you are looking for, look for that of his father, It has been found impracticable to index all names. " Ch." signifies *children.*

The list of families, about two hundred in all, claiming the right in colonial days to use arms, has been revised and extended by Mr. Brock.

A.

C.

F.

G.

H.

K.

L.

N.

O.

T.

W.

Y.

Z